Implications, Prospects, and Challenges in China's Global South Strategy

Enayatollah Yazdani
Sun Yat-sen University, China

IGI Global
Scientific Publishing
Publishing Tomorrow's Research Today

Vice President of Editorial	Melissa Wagner
Director of Acquisitions	Mikaela Felty
Director of Book Development	Jocelynn Hessler
Production Manager	Mike Brehm
Cover Design	Jose Rosado

Published in the United States of America by
IGI Global Scientific Publishing
701 East Chocolate Avenue
Hershey, PA, 17033, USA
Tel: 717-533-8845
Fax: 717-533-7115
Website: https://www.igi-global.com E-mail: cust@igi-global.com

Library of Congress Cataloging-in-Publication Data

Names: Yazdani, Enayatollah, 1965- editor
Title: Implications, prospects, and challenges in China's global South strategy / [edited by] Enayatollah Yazdani.
Description: Hershey, PA : IGI Global Scientific Publishing, [2025] | Includes bibliographical references and index. | Summary: "This book aims to address the role of China as a rising power in the global south"-- Provided by publisher.
Identifiers: LCCN 2025011206 (print) | LCCN 2025011207 (ebook) | ISBN 9798337309385 hardback | ISBN 9798337309392 paperback | ISBN 9798337309408 ebook
Subjects: LCSH: China--Foreign economic relations--Developing countries | Developing countries--Foreign economic relations--China | China--Foreign relations--Developing countries | Developing countries--Foreign relations--China
Classification: LCC HF1604.Z4 .D446675 2025 (print) | LCC HF1604.Z4 (ebook) | DDC 337.510172/4--dc23/eng/20250612
LC record available at https://lccn.loc.gov/2025011206
LC ebook record available at https://lccn.loc.gov/2025011207

British Cataloguing in Publication Data
A Cataloguing in Publication record for this book is available from the British Library.

Table of Contents

Detailed Table of Contents

In the post-Cold War era, China, as a new global power, is expanding its influence around the globe and regions through different strategies and means, including regional and global organizations. Accordingly, since the establishment of the Shanghai Cooperation Organization (SCO) in 2001, China, as one of the major founders of it, has tried to use the SCO as a platform for influence beyond its borders. This chapter aims to explore the influence and diplomacy that China is developing through the SCO in the Global South

The Belt and Road Initiative (BRI), which is an extensive transportation and infrastructure project, connecting Asia, Africa, and Europe is also seen as one of the important tools of South-South cooperation. Türkiye as one of the important members of the BRI has had several expectations, mainly improving Sino-Turkish relations through increasing Chinese investments in Türkiye and reducing the pressure of the trade deficit of Türkiye given to China. In addition, it was anticipated that the BRI would have improved trade and investment relations of Türkiye with the other members, so that the initiative would also play a role in Türkiye's rapprochement to the rising Global South. On the other hand, Chinese investments in Türkiye have been insufficient since its inclusion in the BRI in 2015, and the two countries would mutually put efforts to realize the potential benefits of the BRI.

Abstract Global events of recent years indicate that it is the turn of the developing world to take the lead in international relations (IR). China, which positions itself as the "largest developing country", and "member of the Global South", but at the same time "a responsible world power", cannot remain on the sidelines of this trend. The chapter states the reasons for the recent advancement of the developing world (RW) to the forefront of international life, which include the combined economic growth of the South, the increase in its political significance in the balance of power on the world stage, and the growth of the South's self-esteem. In addition, the author believes it is essential to determine the interpretation of the terms "Global South", "Third World", and "Developing World" to come closer to a better understanding of the essence of the excellent world phenomenon that these definitions denote.

The Southeast Asian region is one of the most important regions of the Belt and Road Initiative and the Maritime Silk Road. In the field of the Maritime Silk Road, measures such as the construction and equipping of ports, the construction of high-speed railways, the construction of equipped highways, and port industrial parks have been put on the agenda. Therefore, the question that arises is what are the most important measures taken by China in the form of the Belt and Road Initiative (the Belt and Road Initiative and the Digital Silk Road) in the Southeast Asia Region? Which countries in the region are the most important countries of the Belt and Road Initiative, which countries are the most important countries of the Digital Silk Road, and what measures has China taken in these countries?

Over the past decade, there have been various discussions about the past, present, and future of China-US relations. Since 2017, when the US National Security Strategy labeled China a strategic competitor, this term has consistently been used to describe Washington's relationship with Beijing. Examining US National Security Strategy documents over the past two decades reveals a shift in perspective from viewing China as a responsible actor to a serious and challenging competitor. Regarding the US approach to China's neighborhood policy, the main goal of the US Indo-Pacific Strategy is to provide strategic alternatives to weaken China's growing influence in its surrounding environment. The US believes that Beijing is striving to establish regional hegemony in the Indo-Pacific, control Taiwan, and dominate disputed areas in the East and South China Seas. Therefore, in recent years, the United States has expanded and strengthened its network of allies and strategic partnerships in the region to counter China's growing influence in the Indo-Pacific.

This chapter argues that China's engagement in mainland Southeast Asia illustrates a new mode of hegemony: one that substitutes formal empire with economic corridors and strategic interdependence. China's rise as a global power is reshaping the political economy of the Global South, and the Mekong region now stands as a revealing case of this transformation. Through the Belt and Road Initiative (BRI) and Lancang-Mekong Cooperation (LMC), Beijing has fused infrastructure, influence, and ideology into a model of state-led development that promises modernization, but at the cost of sovereignty. In the absence of robust institutional buffers, Chinese investments have embedded asymmetric relationships that erode state autonomy and fragment regional coherence in Mekong Region.

One of China's main foreign policy destinations is Central Asia, which is in the hinterland of Eurasia. The Belt and Road Initiative (BRI) has become the most significant tool for developing ties between China and the five Central Asian republics. The BRI's launch signaled the beginning of a new phase in China's foreign policy toward Central Asia and a new round of cooperation between China and the Central Asian republics. Since the BRI's implementation in 2013, China's foreign policy has made Central Asia a priority. The initiative's execution has boosted China's economic interests and influence in the Central Asian countries. Beijing's foreign policy encompasses its bilateral and multilateral interactions with the prominent Central Asian republics in the age of the multipolar world order, in which China is one of the major powers playing a prominent role. This chapter explores how China's BRI has changed China's influence and exchange connections with Central Asian nations, as well as how the BRI has operated in each of the region's countries

In this context, the aim of the study is to examine the role of the rising and expanding BRICS in shaping global financial norms and governance. The question "Does BRICS offer an alternative or a challenge to the leadership of Western institutions in the global financial system?" is the starting point of the study. It is aimed to understand the potential of the coordination provided by the members with their differences to act as a destabilizing force against the political and economic structure of the West. First, the BRICS establishment will be examined within the framework of its purpose and challenges. The second heading will reveal the economic and political capacity of BRICS. China's influence factor on BRICS will be explained under this heading. The last heading will discuss whether BRICS, through China, offers an alternative or a challenge to Western financial institutions and governance, in short, to the status quo. It will be understood that BRICS undoubtedly offers an alternative in the medium term; on this basis, it aims to challenge in the long term.

This chapter examines the health strategies of China and India in Africa, using the geo-health strategy framework to integrate health diplomacy with geopolitical and economic objectives. It analyzes how China's Health Silk Road and India's Maitri Initiative leverage health interventions to expand influence in the Global South. China's state-led approach prioritizes medical infrastructure, vaccine diplomacy, and Traditional Chinese Medicine (TCM), while India's market-driven model focuses on affordable pharmaceuticals, digital health, and medical tourism. Despite promoting South-South cooperation, both nations intertwine humanitarian efforts with economic gains and strategic competition. The chapter argues that health diplomacy serves not only humanitarian goals but also functions as a geopolitical tool for reshaping power dynamics and challenging Western dominance in African healthcare sectors.

The present study focuses on how China's Global South strategy impacts its globalization perspective, emphasizing this engagement's geopolitical, economic, and cultural dimensions. The research will explore how China attempts to reshape global governance structures and create a multipolar world order by focusing on initiatives such as the Belt and Road Initiative, the Global Security Initiative, and the Global Civilization Initiative. By analyzing these multifaceted approaches, the research seeks to understand China's role in reshaping global economic and political landscapes. This study adopted a mixed-methods approach. Qualitative data was gathered by analyzing Chinese government policy documents, academic literature, and media reports, while quantitative data on trade volumes and foreign direct investments (FDI) complemented the assessment. It aimed to build an understanding of China's Global South strategy in terms of how China's initiatives influence global trade patterns, investment flows, and economic alliances, affecting the broader international economic system.

In recent years, China has managed to establish itself as an important and influential player in the Persian Gulf. Despite the dominant role and actorness of the United States in the Persian Gulf over the past few decades, Beijing has succeeded in enhancing its relations with Persian Gulf countries within the framework of strategic hedging. China's desire to expand cooperation with Persian Gulf nations and strengthen its presence in the region has been met with a positive response from these countries. The Persian Gulf states, in turn, are keen to balance and diversify their foreign policies by strengthening their ties with China. This article, utilizing the concept of strategic hedging, examines the growing strategic cooperation between China and Persian Gulf countries in the economic, technological, and security domains. It also highlights that the United States, in an effort to maintain its position in the Persian Gulf, is attempting to prevent the expansion of these countries' cooperation with China, particularly in the fields of technology and armaments.

When the United States froze the reserves of the Russian Central Bank following Moscow's invasion of Ukraine in February 2022, it raised concerns in China. Previously, Washington had used the dollar as a weapon against countries such as Iran, Venezuela, and Cuba. This "weaponization" of the dollar and manipulation of it for domestic economic purposes by the US seems to have prompted China to reduce its vulnerability to it. There is ample data showing that China has taken several measures to mitigate the risks associated with the U.S. dollar. This chapter examines the various measures taken by China toward de-dollarization and internalization of the Yuan simultaneously and its prospects. The research is conducted in a descriptive-analytical manner, based on data from library and internet sources.

While China's economic influence in Africa has been widely studied, its security-related activities have received less scrutiny. This chapter positions China's security initiatives as a critical but underexplored dimension of its African policy. This chapter explores China's growing security engagement in Africa, framing it as an extension of its domestic principles of stability and strategic defense, symbolized metaphorically by the "Great Wall." It investigates how China's security policies in Africa align with its broader geopolitical and economic objectives. Through an analysis of military cooperation, peacekeeping missions, arms trade, and the establishment of overseas military bases, the chapter evaluates the implications of China's security engagement for Africa's governance, development, and global security dynamics. In doing so, the metaphor of the "Great Wall" is employed to symbolize China's efforts to project stability, safeguard its interests, and expand its strategic influence beyond its borders.

The concept of "Global South" has recently emerged as a symbol of unity, and geopolitical reality among postcolonial and developing nations. Following decolonization, these countries have sought to reclaim political and economic agency through movements such as the Non-Aligned Movement (NAM) and G77, consistently advocating for a more just international order. From the perspective of postcolonial studies, this research seeks to answer the following central questions: (1) How has the Global South deconstructed the Western liberal order in international relations? (2) What are the tangible manifestations of "agency" within this emerging order of the Global South? The findings suggest that over the past few decades, the Global South, led by countries like China and other emerging economies, has critically challenged the epistemological and ontological foundations of the liberal world order, which is Western, imperialist, and hierarchical, and has promoted its agency through South-South cooperation to escape from its inferiority/marginalized position in the international system.

China, a newly empowered state that aspires to regional and ultimately global hegemony, is interested in strengthening the extremely backward and underdeveloped Africa. We believe that the reason for this policy can be traced back to China's "grand strategy." To confirm this, the study aims to examine China-Africa relations in the context of the "Grand Strategy", analyze the reasons for China's interest in this region, and investigate how the Asian giant uses "soft power" on the African continent to achieve its goals. To this end, the study formulates the following research question: What role does Africa play in implementing the goals of China's fourth "Grand Strategy"? As a result of the study, we will try to show that China's interest in African states is related to the implementation of the goals of China's "Grand Strategy" (the fourth – the rising phase) and serves to increase the latter's political, economic, institutional, and cultural influence.

China's engagement with the Global South has emerged as a cornerstone of its foreign policy, reflecting a nuanced interplay between soft power and strategic influence. Through initiatives like the Belt and Road Initiative (BRI), foreign direct investments, and cultural diplomacy, China has positioned itself as a pivotal partner for developing nations in Asia, Africa, and Latin America. This chapter critically examines how China balances its economic, political, and cultural tools to advance its interests while promoting a narrative of mutual benefit. By offering a balanced critique of China's approach, this chapter contributes to a deeper understanding of the multifaceted and evolving nature of its Global South strategy. It underscores the need for a more inclusive and equitable partnership that aligns with the sustainable development goals and addresses the diverse needs of the Global South.

Preface

INTRODUCTION

China's Global South Strategy is a multifaceted approach to strengthen its relationships with developing countries in Asia, Africa, and Latin America. The Global South generally refers to the group of countries that are economically under-developed or in the process of development, often characterized by low to middle-income economies, compared to the more industrialized and wealthier countries of the Global North. The unfolding dynamics of China's engagement with the Global South have become a defining feature of 21st-century geopolitics, economics, and international development. This volume, *Implications, Prospects, and Challenges in China's Global South Strategy*, offers a timely and comprehensive exploration of how China's foreign policy—anchored in initiatives like the Belt and Road Initiative (BRI), the Health Silk Road, and the Global Security Initiative—is reshaping power relations, regional alliances, and global governance structures across Asia, Africa, and Latin America.

At the heart of China's Global South strategy is a complex interplay between economic ambition, strategic influence, and soft power diplomacy. The chapters in this book reflect a rich diversity of perspectives and regional contexts, brought together by scholars from China, Iran, India, Turkey, Thailand, Lebanon, Georgia, and South Africa. Their collective scholarship interrogates China's expanding reach—from the Mekong region and Central Asia to the Middle East, the Persian Gulf, and Africa—revealing a new mode of influence that blends infrastructure investment, political alignment, and cultural outreach.

Several chapters examine the dual nature of China's engagement, balancing promises of modernization and development with growing concerns over sovereignty, debt dependence, and asymmetrical relationships. Case studies on the Mekong region and Africa delve into the geopolitical implications of Chinese-led economic corridors and security cooperation. Other contributions investigate China's efforts to project power through multilateral platforms like the Shanghai Cooperation Organization (SCO) and the BRICS, as well as its strategic maneuvering in the Indo-Pacific and Persian Gulf.

Health diplomacy, an emerging pillar of China's soft power, is critically assessed alongside India's initiatives in Africa, providing insight into South-South cooperation that is both collaborative and competitive. Likewise, discussions on China's de-dollarization strategy and the internationalization of the yuan highlight Beijing's broader efforts to recalibrate the global financial order. The volume also provides a postcolonial critique of the current global system, positioning China not merely as a rising power but as a challenger to the Western-led liberal international order.

Throughout the book, a central theme emerges: China's Global South strategy is not monolithic but multi-layered, dynamic, and evolving. Whether viewed through the lens of economic infrastructure, strategic alliances, soft power, or financial reform, China's actions are reshaping international norms and institutions in ways that demand nuanced and critical analysis.

Chapter 1

China's use of the Shanghai Cooperation Organization (SCO) is analyzed as a key strategic platform to expand its influence in the Global South. The chapter details China's diplomatic engagement and regional leadership through the SCO, especially in post-Cold War geopolitical dynamics.

Chapter 2

This chapter explores Türkiye's involvement in the Belt and Road Initiative (BRI), assessing whether its primary motivation lies in improving trade relations with China or fostering broader integration with the Global South. It critiques the limited progress in Chinese investments and argues for mutual engagement to realize the potential of the BRI in Türkiye's economic and geopolitical agenda.

Chapter 3

This chapter highlights the increasing prominence of the Global South in international relations and China's positioning within it. It emphasizes the importance of clarifying the concepts of "Global South," "Third World," and "Developing World," while assessing China's dual identity as both a developing country and a global power.

Chapter 4

Focusing on Southeast Asia, this chapter details China's infrastructure and digital connectivity projects under the BRI and Digital Silk Road. It identifies key partner countries and projects, underscoring the region's strategic importance within China's Global South policy framework.

Chapter 5

The strategic rivalry between the United States and China in the Indo-Pacific is examined through the lens of U.S. counterbalancing strategies. The chapter discusses how the U.S. perceives and reacts to China's regional ambitions, particularly in terms of strategic partnerships and military presence.

Chapter 6

China's involvement in the Mekong region is portrayed as a new model of influence that merges infrastructure investment with strategic interdependence. The chapter critiques the asymmetrical nature of these engagements and their potential to compromise state sovereignty in the region.

Chapter 7

Central Asia's significance in China's BRI strategy is explored through an analysis of bilateral and multilateral relationships. The chapter outlines how the BRI has transformed China's foreign policy in the region, advancing its economic interests and geopolitical presence in a multipolar world.

Chapter 8

The BRICS coalition is analyzed as a challenge and potential alternative to Western-led financial systems. The chapter investigates China's leadership role within BRICS and the bloc's capacity to reshape global financial governance by promoting multipolarity.

Chapter 9

This chapter compares China's and India's health diplomacy strategies in Africa, examining how both nations intertwine humanitarian efforts with strategic and economic interests. It presents health diplomacy as a geopolitical tool in the broader competition for influence in the Global South.

Chapter 10

China's broader vision for partnerships with the Global South is assessed through a multidimensional framework involving economic, cultural, and geopolitical strategies. The study evaluates how initiatives like the BRI and the Global Civilization Initiative contribute to reshaping global governance and trade dynamics.

Chapter 11

Focusing on the Persian Gulf, this chapter explores the emerging strategic partnership between China and Gulf nations amid U.S. efforts to limit Chinese influence. It applies the concept of strategic hedging to explain the growing cooperation in economic, technological, and security fields.

Chapter 12

China's response to U.S. financial dominance is analyzed through its dual strategy of de-dollarization and promoting the yuan's internationalization. The chapter assesses the motivations, actions, and implications of this financial maneuver within the context of global economic security.

Chapter 13

This chapter explores China's evolving security presence in Africa, including military bases, peacekeeping, and arms trade. Using the metaphor of the "Great Wall," it frames China's security engagement as a projection of its domestic principles abroad, aiming to safeguard interests and expand influence.

Chapter 14

A postcolonial analysis of China's role in challenging the Western-led global order, this chapter emphasizes the Global South's growing agency. It highlights how countries like China are reshaping international norms through South-South cooperation and critiques of liberal internationalism.

Chapter 15

China's engagement in Africa is evaluated through the lens of its "Grand Strategy," linking development initiatives to long-term geopolitical ambitions. The chapter argues that Africa is integral to China's pursuit of global influence through soft power and strategic investments.

Chapter 16

The final chapter offers a comprehensive critique of China's Global South policy, emphasizing the balancing act between soft power and strategic interests. It calls for a more equitable and inclusive model of engagement that aligns with the sustainable development goals and addresses the diverse needs of partner countries.

This collection aims to contribute meaningfully to the academic and policy-oriented discourse on China's global strategy. It invites readers to grapple with the contradictions, aspirations, and consequences of Beijing's expanding footprint across the Global South. As China positions itself at the nexus of development, diplomacy, and global leadership, understanding its strategy's implications becomes necessary and imperative for scholars, policymakers, and global citizens alike. We hope this book will be a valuable resource for anybody looking to comprehend and capitalize on China's role in the Global South.

Any opinions, findings, and conclusions or recommendations expressed in the chapters are those of the authors and do not necessarily reflect the editor's views.

Enayatollah Yazdani
School of International Studies, Sun Yat-sen University, China & Department of Political Science, University of Isfahan, Iran

Chapter 1
China's Global South Policy Through the SCO

Enayatollah Yazdani
https://orcid.org/0000-0003-0462-6185
Sun Yat-sen University, China

ABSTRACT

In the post-Cold War era, China, as a new global power, is expanding its influence around the globe and regions through different strategies and means, including regional and global organizations. Accordingly, since the establishment of the Shanghai Cooperation Organization (SCO) in 2001, China, as one of the major founders of it, has tried to use the SCO as a platform for influence beyond its borders. This chapter aims to explore the influence and diplomacy that China is developing through the SCO in the Global South

INTRODUCTION

In the post-Cold War era, the world is facing a new emerging global order with the rise of multiple actors in the international arena. As a rising global power, China has significant leverage in international relations. In particular, during the last two decades, China has rapidly transformed its economy into a global leader in advanced technologies.

As a rising power and as one of the two principal founding members of the Shanghai Cooperation Organization (SCO), China has tried to use this regional organization, which has the potential to become an important politico-economic and security organization of the significant states located in the vast Eurasian landmass, for its global south strategy. For Beijing, the SCO represents a new and unique cooperation model, reflecting its vision of a multipolar world order.

DOI: 10.4018/979-8-3373-0938-5.ch001

China's approach to the Global South, especially through the lens of the SCO, is central to its foreign policy as it seeks to expand its influence in Asia, Central Asia, and beyond. The SCO is one of the key regional platforms through which China interacts with developing countries in the Global South, focusing on cooperation in areas such as security, trade, and cultural exchange.

China will likely continue to deepen its involvement in the SCO as part of its broader strategy for promoting a multipolar world. As part of its Global South policy, China aims to position the SCO as a counterbalance to Western influence, offering economic growth opportunities to developing countries while avoiding the "conditionalities" typically associated with the IMF or World Bank. The expansion of the SCO, with developing countries expressing interest in joining, could further bolster China's position as a major power in the Global South. By pushing for greater inclusivity and developing stronger regional partnerships, China can maintain its influence while ensuring that the SCO remains a key instrument in its broader foreign policy.

This chapter aims to answer this question: How has the Chinese government manipulated the SCO for its foreign policy and global and regional influence? To answer this question, the main discussion is about the SCO's capabilities and politico-economic potential. China has used this organization as a platform to expand its influence beyond its borders to the Global South.

China's Multilateralism Policy

Multilateralism is the embodiment of the democratization of international relations after the Second World War, the basis for the operation and development of multilateral mechanisms, an inevitable requirement for promoting global governance, and an effective way to maintain world peace and promote common development (Moreland, 2019). The basic principle of multilateralism is that all countries should handle international affairs through consultation and by the rules agreed upon by all, taking into account the legitimate interests and legitimate concerns of all countries. Accordingly, multilateral diplomacy refers to the interaction of several international relations actors in permanent or special global or regional international organizations, conferences and forums, which often appear in the diplomatic game of great powers in modern international relations, but the real attention is after the Second World War, marked by the establishment of the United Nations in 1945 and with the great expansion in the number of states (Srivastava,2014). In today's world, great powers are paying more attention to supporting and safeguarding their strategic interests through multilateral diplomacy.

There are four main reasons why major powers attach great importance to multilateral diplomacy: first, their comprehensive strength is strong, and their strategic interests will expand to a wider area; second, it is necessary to acquire the ability to operate peripheral and lead regional cooperation; third, it can propose and practice new cooperation concepts and initiatives to win wide recognition from the international community; the fourth is to seek international discourse and rule-making power, and be able to participate in the agenda of major global and regional issues(Mahbubani,2022, and Höne, 2020). Modern multilateral diplomacy begins with the co-founding of international organizations, especially the UN, the Council of Europe, the OSCE, and the European Union (EU).

In particular, in the post-Cold War era, the international pattern has undergone major changes, multilateral cooperation and regional cooperation in the context of globalization have become a new international trend, and various multilateral mechanisms, frameworks, diplomacy, and platforms have continued to emerge. Generally speaking, multilateral cooperation tends to form a relatively stable international pattern, which helps participants to accept unified rules of conduct and coordinate foreign policies, thereby enhancing the certainty of global and regional governance systems.

As for China at the beginning of the founding of New China, in foreign relations, it implemented a "one-sided" foreign policy towards the socialist camp headed by the Soviet Union, which was the basic stand of New China under the international political pattern of polar opposition between the East and the West at that time (Fairbank, 1969). Yet, soon China focused on getting rid of this transitional diplomacy, and the Chinese elite pursued a policy of cooperation with the world. Beijing advocated independent nonaligned diplomacy based on the Five Principles of Peaceful Coexistence, and actively participated in multipolar efforts to promote the world order through the Bandung Conference. After China resumed its lawful seat in the United Nations in 1971, it began multilateralism diplomacy with the United Nations as the stage, including the exposition of Chairman Mao Zedong's "three worlds" theory and the idea of changing the unequal international order at the sixth special session of the General Assembly in 1974 (Jiang, 2013, and Yee, 1983).

In the 1990s at the turn of the century, China's independent peace diplomacy underwent obvious adjustments and innovations in concepts, strategies, and policies. Under the concept of partnership diplomacy, China's multilateral diplomacy has become active. Accordingly, making and cultivating partnership relations with major global powers and important developing countries has been central to this approach (Papageorgiou and Cardoso, 2021). China's theory and practice of promoting multilateralism have been continuously enriched and improved, showing distinctive Chinese characteristics, injecting strong vitality into the development of multilateralism, strongly supporting the mainstream voice in the world that opposes unilateralism and adheres to multilateralism, and playing an essential role in promoting global governance and maintaining international order. The features of multilateralism with Chinese characteristics are mainly embodied in: morality first, faith and righteousness; consultation on an equal footing to convince people; harmony and difference; and openness.

Through multilateral diplomacy, China has disseminated Chinese ideas and demands on international relations, safeguarded the rights and interests of developing countries, and vigorously promoted the democratization of international relations. Through multilateral diplomacy, China has also vigorously promoted its own and regional economic development and maintained regional and global security and stability (Wuthnow and Diverse 2012). It can be said that China's multilateral diplomacy has made great achievements, even though Beijing's multilateral diplomacy has also faced some challenges

The game in today's world often escalates into a regional alliance-style game, such as Europe has the European Union, Southeast Asia has ASEAN, Arab nations have the Arab League, Africa has the African Union, etc. (Patrick, 2019). As a permanent member of the UN Security Council and the world's second-largest economy, China has actively put forward new concepts of cooperation and adhered to and safeguarded genuine multilateralism through regional organizations such as the SCO.

The establishment of the Shanghai Cooperation Organization in the post-Cold War Era

In the international context of the post-Cold War trend of peace, development, and cooperation, and the process of economic globalization, China-Russia-Central Asia relations have developed rapidly and healthily beyond differences in ideology and social system, and the common demand for national rejuvenation and economic development requires a stable surrounding environment. To meet the changes in the international and regional situation and to deepen cooperation among countries in the region, the Shanghai Cooperation Organization was established in June 2001 with the upgraded “Shanghai Five” mechanism, with security cooperation as the main axis.

Indeed, the establishment of the SCO was a response to the practical needs of regional countries for multilateral cooperation, while paying attention to and solving pressing regional economic and environmental problems. As Xi Jinping pointed out, “the SCO stands as a comprehensive regional cooperation organization that covers the largest area and population in the world. [It has] extensive cooperation relations with the United Nations and other international and regional organizations. With its ever-rising international influence, the SCO has become an important force for promoting global peace and development and upholding international justice and fairness"(Xi, 2018).

The multilateral cooperation of the SCO is comprehensive, sets cooperation goals in all aspects, and plays a unique role, which can be described as a model of a new regional cooperation mechanism in the age of globalization. Many political, historical, cultural, security, and economic factors led to the emergence of the Shanghai Cooperation Organization in the political space of Eurasia, the most significant of which are:

a- destruction of the bipolar system in international relations;
b- formation of a new world order as a result of the collapse of the Soviet Union and end of the Cold War
c- rise of new challenges and threats, among of which terrorism, extremism and separatism were the most dangerous phenomena;
d-realization of the principles of a just world order, dominated by the aspiration for joint development, taking into account the experience of relations that have developed among the countries of the region within the framework of the "Shanghai Five";
e- joint pursuit for new effective mechanisms that would enhance the regional integration of countries;
f- formation of a new model of cooperation in the region, where the priority areas are security, economic interaction, and cooperation in all areas (MFA, 2021).

The birth and development of the SCO has always been embedded in the process of adjusting the international pattern and the geopolitical and economic reorganization of the Eurasian region in the post-Cold War period, and the rapid changes in the external environment such as the collapse of the Soviet Union constitute a strong shaping effect on the predecessor of the Shanghai Cooperation Organization, the "Shanghai Five".

THE SCO'S DYNAMICS AND DEVELOPMENT

The SCO, on the one hand, can trace its origins to the rapprochement between China and Russia during the later years of the Cold War and continuing after the collapse of the Soviet Union in December 1991, in which resolving border demarcation issues played a considerable role. On the other hand, one can assume that the establishment of the Shanghai Cooperation Organization was the result of a profound adjustment of the system of international relations at the end of the 20th Century (Zhang, 2020, and Fremenko, 2019). With the collapse of the Soviet Union and the end of the Cold War, not only has the world not become safer, but new and unpredictable global threats and challenges have emerged. Yet, needless to mention that in the 21st century, global security cannot be guaranteed by one or a few states alone.

The key goals of the Shanghai Cooperation Organization are spelled out as follows:

> 1-Strengthening mutual trust and neighbourliness among the member states;
> 2-Promoting effective cooperation in economy, politics, trade, research, technology and culture, as well as in education, energy, transport, tourism, environmental protection, and other areas;
> 3-Making joint efforts to maintain and ensure peace, security and stability in the region; the SCO places a high premium on promoting and sustaining 'stability' in the region, and
> 4-Moving towards establishing a democratic, fair, and rational new international political and economic order (ASPIRE IAS, 2021).

In terms of institution-building, the SCO has established dozens of multi-level and multi-field meeting and consultation mechanisms, including meetings between heads of state, prime ministers, ministers, presidents of the Supreme Court and prosecutors general, and two permanent bodies: the Secretariat (Beijing) and the Regional Anti-Terrorist Structure (Tashkent, Uzbekistan). In regards with security, starting from solving the most pressing security problems of its member states, focusing on cracking down on the three evils, terrorism, separatism and extremism, and proceeding from the long-term interests of the region, the SCO has gradually "spilled over" its cooperation areas to the economic, trade, energy, cultural and other fields related to security cooperation, and established appropriate cooperation mechanisms and institutions to promote the expansion and deepening of regional cooperation (Garlick, 2025). Yet, the main tasks of the SCO at this stage are to combat terrorism, separatism, and extremism jointly, as well as transnational criminal activities such as drug trafficking, carry out information and intelligence exchange, and hold joint exercises (Pradt, 2020, a). In addition, the SCO also attaches great importance to the construction of emergency response mechanisms and pays attention to responding to new challenges such as network information security, global pandemic, and food security.

In regards with economic cooperation, the SCO has put forward the goal of trade and investment facilitation, and through the Multilateral Economic and Trade Cooperation Programme and its implementation plan, it focuses on promoting cooperation in the fields of transportation, energy, finance, customs, agriculture and border areas; at the same time, it pays attention to the combination of multilateral and bilateral to promote bilateral economic and trade cooperation among member countries(Dexue, 2021 and Pradt, 2020, b).

In terms of political cooperation, the main measures taken by the SCO are: issuing political statements and advancing legal development; mutual support in international affairs and domestic policies; actively participate in the peace and reconstruction process in Afghanistan; Expressing common positions on UN reform, arms control and other issues; contributing to the resolution of the political crisis in Kyrgyzstan; Sending observers to the general election of member states, etc. (Hao, 2021, a).

In terms of people-to-people cooperation, it is one of the troikas driving the development of the SCO. The areas of people-to-people cooperation of the SCO have gradually extended from science and technology, culture and education, to health, sports, tourism, environmental protection, women, youth, media, and poverty reduction, and the cooperation model has been expanded from government-led to public-private cooperation. Xue and Makengo, 2021). With the joint efforts of the member states, people-to-people exchanges and cooperation of the SCO have taken deep roots and flourished.

The SCO has established the largest number of meeting mechanisms in this area, carrying out flexible and diverse activities: launching a ministerial meeting mechanism in the field of educational cooperation, establishing SCO universities; youth and think tank exchanges; Exchanges and cooperation in culture, health, disaster reduction, science and technology, tourism, sports and media have been continuously expanded.

During the SCO's evolution, in addition to its 6 original members, other countries in the region, including India, Pakistan, and recently Iran, have attended this organization as official members. In addition, some other countries, such as Mongolia, Afghanistan, and Belarus, are observer members of the SCO (see Table 1).

Table 1. The SCO involved countries 1996-2001- October 2022(Shanghai Cooperation Organization, 2023)

Shanghai Five 1996-2001	SCO Members	SCO Observers	SCO Dialogue Partners
China	China	Mongolia	Turkey
Russia	Russia	Afghanistan	Azerbaijan
Kazakhstan	India	Belarus	Cambodia
Kyrgyzstan	Pakistan		Seri Lanka
Tajikistan	Uzbekistan		Nepal
	Kazakhstan		Armenia

continued on following page

Table 1. Continued

Shanghai Five 1996-2001	SCO Members	SCO Observers	SCO Dialogue Partners
	Kyrgyzstan		Saudi Arabia
	Tajikistan		Egypt
	Islamic Republic of Iran		Qatar
			Bahrain
			Kuwait
			The United Arab Emirates
			Maldives
			Myanmar

After Iran's accession in 2021, the area of the nine member countries reached 35.72 million square kilometres, 27% of the area of the globe; covering more than 60% of the Eurasian continent, and the nine member countries have a combined population of 3.3 billion, accounting for 42% of the global population. It can increase its power globally. Moreover, the presence of the four nuclear states, China, Russia, India, and Pakistan, in the SCO has given the organization nuclear power potential. It can increase its power globally. Now with the ninth member, the Shanghai Cooperation Organization may be regarded as a "Nuclear OPEC" consisting of the world's large oil and gas reserves (plus Russia and Turkmenistan) with a nuclear capability.

THE ROLE OF CHINA IN THE DEVELOPMENT OF THE SCO

During the last three decades, China's diplomacy has achieved a series of fruitful results in the bilateral field, and its role in the regional and international arenas has been increasingly appreciated. China has begun to actively work to maintain regional peace and stability, promote mutually beneficial cooperation among countries, and at the same time clarify its position on international affairs and hotspot issues and propose concrete solutions to problems, and the SCO has gradually become one of the most important regional cooperation platforms.

China is the birthplace of the SCO and has always regarded the SCO as a priority direction for Chinese diplomacy. Over the past 20 years of development, China has always attached great importance to SCO political cooperation, from advocating the "New Security Concept", "Shanghai Spirit" and "Harmonious Region" to proposing the building of an SCO community with a shared future (Wenting and Xiaoyi., 2022). From proposing to turn the "Shanghai Five" meeting mechanism into a cooperation mechanism, to actively promoting the institutionalization of the SCO; from advocating the formulation of a long-term treaty of good-neighborliness, friendship and cooperation among member states to actively promoting the implementation of the SCO's long-term development strategy, China has continuously contributed "Chinese wisdom" to the SCO political cooperation and provided "Chinese solutions", playing an important strategic leading role.

In fact, as the most economically powerful and populous country in the SCO, China undoubtedly plays a key role in this regional organization (Nawab, 2024). Regarding China's ineffective role in the Shanghai Cooperation Organization, the SCO Yellow Paper: SCO Development Report in 2016 stated that, as the world's second-largest economy, largest exporter of trade, and a founding member of the SCO, China should play a greater role within the SCO. Given China's status as a huge economy, its economic development will have strong spillover effects. The report added that it is undoubtedly a very necessary and realistic choice for China to accelerate the construction of the free trade area and establish closer and deeper economic ties among the SCO member states (The SCO Yellow Paper, 2016). Indeed, one can assume that from elaborating on China's visions on development, security, cooperation, civilization and global governance, to calling for the building of "a community of health," "a community of security," "a community of development" and "a community of cultural exchanges," the Chinese government has played an important role in the SCO's steady and long-term development (Xinhua, 2022).

To sum up, China has always played a pivotal role in the Shanghai Cooperation Organization, becoming the "twin engines" of the development with Russia, which is inseparable from the strategic partnership of coordination announced by China and Russia in 1996 and the deepening of good-neighbourly and friendly cooperation between China and Central Asian countries.

THE EFFECTIVENESS OF SCO AS A MEANS FOR CHINA'S GLOBAL SOUTH POLICY

Chinese foreign policy for the Eurasian region centres on regional stability and economic development, all to facilitate its 'peaceful rise' and 'harmonious world' hegemonic goals. China further holds multilateralism at the centre of this and the SCO due to the multilateral platform that China was pinnacle in establishing, thus giving China large amounts of influence over the organisation and making it a tool for China to meet its policy ends(Battams-Scott, 2019).

The SCO is of special significance to China's foreign policy and diplomacy. The most important goal of China's diplomacy in the new era is to build a community with a shared future for mankind and build a new type of international relations. Cooperation in the SCO is both multilateral and bilateral, China and Russia are a model of a new type of great power relationships, and China and the Central Asian republics are a model of equal cooperation between large and small countries. As a founding member of the SCO Chinese leaders summed up the practice of the "Shanghai Five" and put forward the "Shanghai Spirit" of "mutual trust, mutual benefit, equality, consultation, respect for diverse civilizations and seeking common development", which has become the norm and soul guiding the sustainable development of the Shanghai Cooperation Organization (Perskaya, et al., 2022).

Compared with other regional organizations, the establishment and development of the SCO have a series of special characteristics: first, it relies on the top-down political decisions of leaders to promote cooperation, and the summit and the resolutions adopted are of great significance to the development of the SCO. In June 2001, the first SCO summit was held in Shanghai, setting the tone for multilateral cooperation. Second, it has the foundation of cooperation during the "Shanghai Five" period, with the maintenance of stability and security in Central Asia as the key direction, and the "new security concept" explained by Chinese leaders on many international occasions is the prerequisite for cooperation. Third, the concept and principles of multilateral cooperation are clear, and the new regional cooperation model proposed by Chinese leaders, characterized by joint advocacy by large and small countries, security first, and mutually beneficial cooperation, has been widely recognized by member states (Serikkaliyeva, 2017).

In the past 20 years, the SCO has developed rapidly and made remarkable achievements, which are closely related to the role that has been played by China. In the face of the ever-changing international and regional order and situation, the multilateral cooperation promoted by China under the SCO framework fully takes into account the special conditions of the region and puts forward targeted cooperation proposals(Hao, 2021,b). In the initial stage of the SCO, on the one hand, China paid attention to the building of cooperation mechanisms and permanent institutions, and on the other hand, took the initiative to propose the main areas and basic directions of multilateral cooperation.

After the 2018 Qingdao Summit, the SCO entered a new stage of development, officially launching the "G8 Model" and inviting leaders of 10 international organizations to attend. In his speech at the 18th meeting of the Council of Heads of State of the SCO member states, Xi Jinping stressed the need to further carry forward the "Shanghai Spirit" under the new situation, advocate an innovative, coordinated, green, open and shared development concept, practice the common, comprehensive, cooperative and sustainable security concept, uphold the concept of open, integrated, mutually beneficial and win-win cooperation, establish a civilizational concept of equality, mutual learning, dialogue and inclusiveness, adhere to the global governance concept of consultation, joint construction and sharing, solve the problems of the times and resolve risks and challenges. He also proposed a series of new cooperation initiatives, such as member states working together to build a community with a shared future in the Shanghai Cooperation Organization (Xi, 2018).

As for Chinese characteristics for the development of the SCO, one can assume that, unlike other international organizations, the SCO upholds a distinctive concept of cooperation, many of which are China's diplomatic initiatives and closely related to China's role in international and regional affairs. From the “Shanghai Spirit” and the New Security Concept at the beginning of its founding, to the Qingdao Summit's proposal to enrich the “Shanghai Spirit” with a new connotation of the times, to the proposal to jointly build a community of interests and a community of common destiny, China has put forward a series of important cooperation concepts for the development of the SCO (Perskaya, et al., 2022). China's special role in the SCO has been praised by other member states, observer states and dialogue partners, and has been highly praised by the international community.

BELT AND ROAD INITIATIVE AND THE SCO

China has put forward several initiatives to promote security, political, economic and humanitarian cooperation in the SCO. One remarkable task of China role in the SCO is Chinese Belt and Road Initiative (BRI)(see map: 1). The BRI, which was proposed by Persident Xi Jinping in 2013, is a “multilateral proposal to upgrade infrastructure, improve China’s bilateral ties, and international institutions, as well as drive much needed global development” (Feldshuh, 2018). . The Belt and Road Initiative has won the appreciation and support of most SCO member states because the BRI is based on historical friendship, mutual respect, and mutually beneficial cooperation, and drives the common development of countries that carry forward traditional values.

The SCO is an important multilateral cooperation platform under the framework of the Belt and Road Initiative. The BRI is China's most important public good to the Global South, and almost all SCO member states and observer states are active participants in the construction of the BRI. The BRI has opened up a broader space for cooperation in the field of infrastructure, and connectivity is an important area of SCO cooperation. Nevertheless, connectivity is not only directly related to the effectiveness of economic and trade cooperation, but also provides a guarantee for smooth exchanges between people of all countries. In this sense, the Belt and Road Initiative would help promote the establishment and development of new bilateral and multilateral cooperation mechanisms in the field of transport and logistics, which is of great significance to SCO member states, especially Central Asian republics (Norov, 2019).

Under the implementation of the Belt and Road Initiative, the SCO has deepened economic cooperation, strengthened its role in ensuring regional security and stability, and gradually deepened people-to-people cooperation in the Global South. As an important platform for the Belt and Road Initiative, the SCO has played an important role and entered the legal process for the first time in terms of expansion (Lu, Huang and Lu, 2019). Both have entered a new era of development, providing each other with new development opportunities, giving play to their respective advantages and leveraging each other's strengths, and jointly building a community of shared destiny characterized by political mutual trust, lasting peace, mutual benefit and win-win results, and cultural tolerance.

Figure 1. Chinese Belt and Road Initiative Map (Bondevalue, 2018)

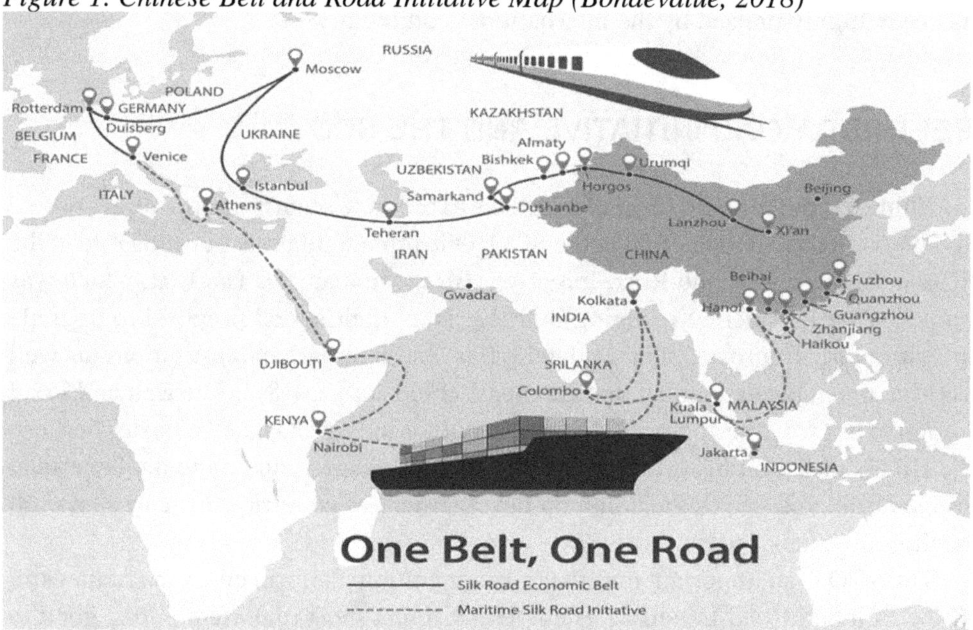

The six economic corridors of the Belt and Road cover almost all SCO member states and observer states, which can bring major opportunities for common development in the region(see Table 2). China has built an unprecedented multilateral diplomatic platform around the Belt and Road Initiative, and SCO member states are active participants in the two Belt and Road Forums for International Cooperation and multilateral exchange activities around policy coordination, infrastructure connectivity, unimpeded trade, financial integration, and people-to-people bonds. It should also be noted that while the joint construction of the "Belt and Road" has achieved many results in the SCO region, it has also encountered many complex problems, such as increasing geopolitical and security hotspot challenges.

Table 2. The Chinese BRI six Corridors (Belt and Road Initiative Website, February 2025)

No.	Corridor	Connection	Purpose	Countries
1	China, Central Asia, West Asia Economic Corridor	Rail	Trade and commercial	Kazakhstan, Kyrgyzstan, Tajikistan, Uzbekistan, Turkmenistan, Iran, and Turkey
2	China, Mongolia, Russia Economic Corridor	rail links and the steppe road—this will link with the land bridge	Trade and commercial	China, Mongolia and Russia
3	New Eurasia Land Bridge	Rail to Europe	Trade and commercial	Kazakhstan, Russia, Belarus, and Poland
4	China Indochina Peninsula Economic Corridor		Trade and commercial	Viet Nam, Thailand, Lao People's Democratic Republic, Cambodia, Myanmar, and Malaysia
5	China, Bangladesh, India, Myanmar Economic Corridor		commercial and security	China, Bangladesh, India,and Myanmar
6	China, Pakistan Economic Corridor	Water port	commercial and military	Links Kashgar city (free economic zone) in landlocked Xinjiang with the Pakistan port of Gwadar

The SCO covers the core areas along the Belt and Road Initiative, and the two have the conditions for coordinated development. The SCO has a relatively complete cooperation mechanism and cooperation achievements in the three major fields of security, economy and humanities, laying the foundation for the construction of the six corridors of the BRI.

THE ROLE OF SCO IN CHINA'S POLICY TOWARD THE GLOBAL SOUTH

In recent years, one of the most prominent features of Beijing's foreign policy behaviours has been its increasing activism in multilateral diplomacy. The Shanghai Cooperation Organization resulted in many of China's foreign policy ends being reached or at least having significant progress towards them. In particular, SCO is a reflection of current Chinese foreign policy orientation, which is based on the concept of China's 'peaceful rise' (*heping jueqi*) to great power status. China's role in the creation and evolution of the SCO is also one of the most significant foreign policy initiatives to emanate from that country in the last two decades. In essence, the SCO is becoming an instrument for the Chinese approach to international affairs, which currently involves a policy of accommodating Western interests in Asia while at the same time increasing Chinese influence in selected parts of Asia.

Moreover, another factor that pushed China to give the SCO the formal status of a regional organization was largely related to its security strategy. Since regional security was once at the forefront of the Chinese policy agenda, but through border forces reductions, focus on nonconventional threats such as terrorism, and the removal of external actors that may disrupt the political status quo, regional stability has improved(Battams-Scott, 2019). One major goal was to prevent Uyghur separatists from using Central Asian republics as a base for separatist activities in Xinjiang. The joint fight by SCO states against terrorism and threats to national sovereignty has won China assurances from Muslim Central Asian states that they will not assist their religious and ethnic brethren engaged in militant separatist activities in Xinjiang. Indeed, Islam is a salient characteristic of Xinjiang's eight-million-strong Turkic-speaking Uighur ethnic group, which constitutes around 45 percent of the region's population. Thus, Beijing's commitment to regional security through the SCO to fight separatism and terrorism is based not only on its fear of violent Islamic rebellion in Central Asia affecting the Uighurs, but also its concern for being branded an anti-Muslim country by Central Asian republics or Middle Eastern states if it suppresses major uprisings in Xinjiang.

In principle, China's regional foreign policy is based on four main pillars:

1- Expanding regional trade and economic relations.
2- Reducing distrust and concern in the regional security environment
3- Participate in regional organizations.
4- Expanding strategic cooperation and deepening bilateral relations with regional powers. Participate in regional organizations(HUI, 2019).

Based on these pillars, the Chinese government has been involved in the SCO very actively to achieve its objectives in the Global South:

A- INCREASING ROLE IN ASIA

For centuries, China has been the dominant power in Asia, and after significant economic growth in recent decades and its gradual transformation into a military and cultural power, has substantial capacity to play an important role in Asian affairs. On this basis, and in the current situation, China is seeking to expand its influence in the surrounding environment by playing a leading role and shaping the developments in this environment. China is trying to play this role in the form of multilateral mechanisms.

The Shanghai Cooperation Organization is a key symbol of China's efforts to play such a role, a multilateral mechanism that has long been an effective tool for achieving this goal. President Xi at the 20th meeting of the Council of Heads of State of the SCO on November 10, 2020, via video link, stated that true development is development for all and good development is sustainable. We should be guided by the vision of innovative, coordinated, green, open, and shared development and create more opportunities for practical cooperation to facilitate economic recovery and improve people's lives(Xi, 2020).

Generally, the expansion of influence and the role of leadership in the surrounding environment can be considered as China's long-term goal of shaping and strengthening the Shanghai Cooperation Organization. Indeed, China, like Russia, to some extent, considers the Central Asian region as part of its "backyard" or "sphere of influence" (Daily FT, 2017). However, one can assume that as Central Asia is Russia's traditional sphere of influence, Moscow does not like to share that influence with China.

B- STRENGTHENING STABILITY IN ASIA

Maintaining regional stability within Asia is undoubtedly a key priority of China. In the latest white paper, Chinese officials wrote that, "a prosperous and stable world would provide China with opportunities," underscoring the country's commitment to collective development among regional partners (White paper, 2019). Since 2001, the Shanghai Cooperation Organization has served as an intergovernmental body aimed at contributing to stability in Asia (Tzogopoulos, 2019). Indeed, creating Shanghai Cooperation Organization and strengthening it in two ways has helped to produce and maintain stability in China's security environment. One is that regional governments, especially in the Central Asian countries that have long-standing ethnic and religious ties to the people of Xinjiang, have warned against escalating the Xinjiang crisis. It is natural that if China can use this organization to consolidate the capacity of the countries in the region to deal with these three effective forces in the crisis of Xinjiang, which has deep international roots, it has taken steps to strengthen stability in its security environment. That is why stability in Central Asia is crucial to China in terms of its strategic position. Central Asia is part of China's security environment, and it is natural that dominating the region, especially by the United States, would be a long-term threat to the country.

C-COMBATING TERRORISM, EXTREMISM AND SEPARATISM

As mentioned, the SCO's prioritized purpose has been combating terrorism, separatism, and extremism ("three evils"). The SCO member founded the Regional Anti-Terrorist Structure (RATS) to fight against these threats, particularly terrorism. Since its founding RATS has played an important role for the SCO members to combat terrorism, separatism and extremism(Xinhua, 2019). In addition, under the framework of the SCO, China and other member states have signed the following documents to fight against terrorism, separatism and extremism: the Shanghai Convention on Combating Terrorism, Separatism and Extremism, Cooperation Between SCO Member States on Combating Terrorism, Separatism and Extremism, SCO Convention on Combating Terrorism, SCO Convention on Combating Extremism, SCO Cooperation Program on Fighting Terrorism, Separatism and Extremism for 2019-2021, and SCO Plan of Action for Cooperation with Afghanistan on fighting terrorism, drug trafficking and organized crimes.

On the other hand, according to the charter of the Shanghai Cooperation Organization, countering separatism, extremism, and terrorism as "three evils" is one of the main goals of this organization. In this regards, SCO Secretary General,Vladimir Norov, has proclaimed that: "three months prior to the tragic 9/11 events in New York [and Washington] in 2001, the Convention on Combating Terrorism, Separatism and Extremism was signed within the SCO, a document which served as evidence of the organisation's readiness to aggressively fight these "three maligned forces" (Norov, 2019). All three of these factors are contributing to the Xinjiang crisis. On the one hand, the rebels of Xinjiang are seeking independence from China. In addition, the Chinese government considers them extremist, and most importantly, the separatists of Xinjiang have links to insurgent forces in Afghanistan and Pakistan.

In particular, China has carried out a number of fruitful counterterrorism exchanges and cooperation with relevant countries through such bilateral and multilateral mechanisms as joint anti-terrorism exercises, joint border defence operations, and suppression of illegal cyberspace activities by terrorist, separatist and extremist forces, as well as security cooperation, intelligence exchange, and judicial cooperation during major international events. It has played an important role in maintaining international and regional security and stability)White Paper, 2019).

In the SCO summit on November 10, 2020 via video link president Xi expressed we should deepen solidarity and mutual trust, and resolve disputes and differences through dialogue and consultation, so as to cement the political foundation for SCO development. It is important that we forestall terrorist, separatist and extremist attempts to exploit the pandemic for disruption, curb the proliferation of drugs, crack down on internet-based propagation of extremist ideology, and strengthen SCO members' law-enforcement cooperation(Xi, 2020).

D-REGIONAL ENERGY ACCESS

Since the Industrial Revolution, fossil fuels have become the dominant energy source for most nations, particularly industrialized countries across the globe. China, as a rapidly developing economic country in recent years, has sharply increased its energy needs; this has made it the first largest consumer of oil in the world (see table 3). This growing energy requirements give Beijing a significant interest in getting access to the energy resources of Central Asia and the Caspian Basin as well (Liao, 2019; Huirong and Hongwei, 2012). As Table 3 shows, at present, China is the world's largest consumer of energy. Accordingly, Chinese majors like CNPC, Sinopec and CNOOC are highly interested in the Central Asian oil and gas deposits and they have contributed largely in the construction of gas and oil pipelines connecting Kazakhstan and Turkmenistan, which are today the biggest regional exporters of oil and natural gas respectively, to Chinese territory (Bolonina, 2019:6).

Table 3. The Top Oil Importing Countries (Workman, 2020)

Rank	Importer	Crude Oil Imports (US$)	%World Total
1	China	$238,707,061,000	22.6%
2	United States	$132,370,663,000	12.5%
3	India	$102,306,491,000	9.7%
4	Japan	$73,085,389,000	6.9%
5	South Korea	$70,193,489,000	6.6%
6	Netherlands	$46,414,486,000	4.4%
7	Germany	$40,737,628,000	3.9%
8	Spain	$30,499,660,000	2.9%
9	Italy	$29,615,998,000	2.8%
10	United Kingdom	$24,542,383,000	2.3%
11	France	$24,446,306,000	2.3%
12	Singapore	$24,224,539,000	2.3%
13	Thailand	$22,284,239,000	2.1%
14	Taiwan	$21,326,199,000	2%
15	Belgium	$18,784,563,000	1.8%

The Central Asian region contains significant oil and gas resources; therefore, as China attempts to secure and diversify its energy resources, Beijing is keenly interested in the region's energy. Central Asia's energy resources also benefit China's neighbourhood, such as Japan. This advantage is important because China has always been concerned about energy security, as it is largely maritime and controlled by the

United States Navy, and the United States can use this control as a lever in times of need, applying pressure on China. But Central Asia's oil and gas pipeline routes to China are by land and have little control. Therefore, China has quickly entered the energy market of this region and has been able to gain a significant share of it. Two main pipelines from Central Asia to China, the Central Asia-China gas pipeline and the Kazakhstan-China oil pipeline, are already in operation (see map 2). The Central Asia–China gas pipeline goes from Turkmenistan to Xinjiang in west of China. By connecting the Republic of Turkmenistan to China's domestic grid, this pipeline makes it possible to transport gas some 7000 km from Central Asia to Shanghai. According to the PetroChina West Pipeline Company,as of December 31, 2019, 294.6 billion cubic meters of natural gas had been imported via the China-Central Asia gas pipeline, benefiting over 500 million people in 27 provinces of China (Yamei, 2020). The Kazakhstan-China pipeline running 988 km from Atasu in Kazakhstan to Alashankou at the China's border, was completed at the end of 2005 and began operating in May 2006, with a total investment of USD 700 million(see map 2) (BBC Monitoring – Energy, 2006).

Figure 2. Central Asia oil and gas pipelines to China Map (Chen and Fazilov, 2018)

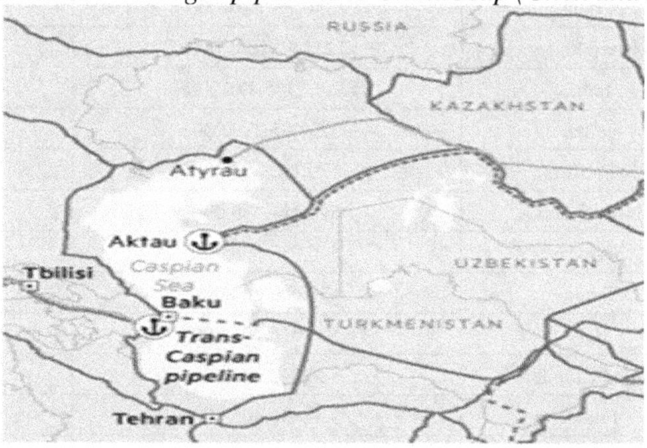

The Kazakhstan-China pipeline, which has a final capacity of 200,000 barrels of oil per day, is a symbol of China and Central Asia's energy cooperation. In addition, China reached an agreement with Turkmenistan on the gas pipeline in 2009, achieving an annual capacity of 30 billion cubic meters of Turkmen gas to China. Meanwhile, China has been negotiating with Kazakhstan to buy the country's gas through the construction of a new pipeline-as mentioned- that starts in Ishim, reaches Astana, and finally reaches Alashankou on the Chinese-Kazakh border. China National

Petroleum Corporation has also signed a USD 600 million contract to extract oil from 23 small oil fields with Uzbekistan, and hopes to acquire gas in these fields.

In addition to Central Asian countries, China has managed to reach important agreements with Russia, as its most important Western neighbour in the field of energy; Russia's strategic pipeline to the country is under discussion, and some have been implemented. The latest development in this area was the launch of the Russian-Chinese oil pipeline, which starts from the city of Skovorodino in the Amur region in the far east of Russia and reaches the city of Daqing in north-east of China, in early 2011. Construction of the 1,000-kilometer pipeline, 72 kilometres of which is inside Russian territory and 927 kilometres of which is in China's territory, began in 2010 and was completed quickly. According to the agreement between the two countries, 15 million tons of Russian oil will be transported to China annually through this pipeline between 2011 and 2030 (Simes, 2020).

E-FIGHTING AGAINST COVID-19

The outbreak of the novel coronavirus pneumonia in 2020 once again highlighted the importance of SCO health cooperation, and China has been the most active participant in this field of cooperation. In the age of the COVID-19 pandemic and its global impact, and based on the new circumstances, Beijing has tried to push the SCO to contribute to the prevention processes of coronavirus. In this regard, President Xi asserted that COVID-19 is still presenting an ongoing threat. Accordingly, has stepped up anti-epidemic cooperation and build a community of health for all SCO's nations. As President Xi believed, "to fight the virus that respects no borders, we must take up the most powerful weapon of solidarity and cooperation, and rise to the most imperative task of saving people's lives." President Xi emphasized that we should put the SCO's health cooperation mechanisms into full use and deepen exchanges and cooperation in epidemic monitoring, scientific research, and disease control and treatment. China proposes that hotline contacts be created between the SCO members' Centers for Disease Control (CDCs) for timely updates on cross-border transmission of communicable diseases. The unique value and important role of traditional medicine have been highlighted in the battle against COVID-19, and we should continue to hold the SCO Forum on Traditional Medicine to enhance exchanges and mutual learning in this field. He stressed that Vaccines play a vital role in defeating the virus. China has joined the COVAX facility and will actively consider the SCO countries' need for vaccines to help protect people's safety and health in our countries. President Xi said we can better coordinate the SCO's cooperation agenda with the necessity for a long-term fight against COVID-19, employ new working methods and flexible cooperation forms, and keep relevant mechanisms running effectively(Xi, 2020).

HOW DOES SCO MOVE AGAINST US GLOBAL HEGEMONY?

Generally, China's commitment to countering US influence within the region is both recurrent and thinly veiled. In 2015, CCP leaders wrote, "China]would]In … pursue an independent foreign policy of peace and a national defence policy that is defensive in nature, [and] oppose hegemonism and power politics in all forms"(Grace, 2016). In addition to China, Russia is also pursuing more or less the same policy to counter US global hegemony and indeed, the ongoing Russian war against Ukraine can be regarded as part of Moscow's anti-American hegemony stance. Accordingly, China and Russia, as two major powers of the Shanghai Cooperation Organization, have tried to use this organization as an important vehicle to prevent US global hegemony and influence.

In principle, Beijing's concern about American global hegemony and regional influence in particular back to the events of September 11, 2001, and the occupation of Afghanistan in 2002 at the end of the "war on terror". This has become a major concern for the Chinese government and has led Beijing to pursue more serious institutional cooperation with neighbouring countries in the framework of the Shanghai Cooperation Organization to balance Russia's growing influence with the United States. Of course, this does not mean that the interests of China and Russia are completely at odds with those of Washington in the region, but that the balance of the historical logic of relations between the great powers is balanced (Southerland, Green and, and Janik,2020, Rumer, 2006).

In fact, one can assume that China and Russia have used the SCO to counter American policies of economic penetration of the oil-rich Caspian Basin and to facilitate a global balance of power through a multi-polar order that would frustrate US global hegemonic goals.(Bhatty, 2000). It is believed that the SCO is becoming an anchor for stability in the Eurasian heartland and is mainly a response to the growing Western presence in the region. It is also believed that worries about the ability of the United States to project its power deep into the Eurasian heartland also helped to bring together Moscow and Beijing to move ahead with the transformation of the more informal Shanghai dialogue into an actual international organisation in 2001(Simha, 2015). America had maintained bases in Uzbekistan and Kyrgyzstan since late 2001, in support of the anti-terror operation launched in nearby Afghanistan after the events of September 11 in Washington and New York. In response to such military influence in the region, the 2005 summit produced one highly publicized communiqué. This SCO communiqué called for the United States to establish a timetable for the redeployment of its forces from Uzbekistan (Khanabad base) and Kyrgyzstan (Manas base). The SCO justification was reportedly based on the US-led anti-terrorism coalition's completion of the active military phase of operations in Afghanistan(Turner, 2005). Indeed, the 2005 declaration by the Shanghai Co-operation Organization for the US to vacate bases in Central Asia was a boost for Beijing and Moscow, both of whom have bristled at the growing influence of the US in the region (Goodenoug, 2005).

Nevertheless, the major anti-American stance of the SCO can be understood from the final declaration of the 2006 summit in Shanghai: "The SCO will make a constructive contribution to the establishment of a new global security architecture of mutual trust, mutual benefit, equality and mutual respect," the declaration asserted: "Threats and challenges can be effectively met only when there is broad cooperation among all countries and international organizations concerned. What specific means and mechanisms should be adopted to safeguard the security of the region is the right and responsibility of countries in the region." The statement went on to indicate that "Central Asian countries must choose development paths based on their needs and interests"."Diversity of civilization and the model of development must be respected and upheld. Differences in cultural traditions, political and social systems, values, and models of development formed in the course of history should not be taken as pretexts to interfere in other countries' internal affairs. "Model of social development should not be exported."(Weitz, 2006).

CONCLUSION

Since the 1978 reform and opening up policy, China has tried to participate actively in international organizations ranging from the UN and UN Security Council to the WTO, the World Bank, the ASEAN Regional Forum, and the SCO. However, the Shanghai Cooperation Organization is a notable departure from other aforementioned organizations. China, as one of the two major funding members of the SCO, has tried to play a more essential role in this regional organization. At the same time, Beijing has attempted to use this organization for its Global South policy.

The Shanghai Cooperation Organization is a regional cooperation mechanism that carries out its activities as an independent international actor with a legal basis and its own norms and norms of conduct. The SCO sets out a broad range of objectives and potential areas of cooperation, although it has mostly focused on fighting against terrorism, religious extremism, and ethnic separatism in the region.

The birth of the Shanghai Cooperation Organization is a landmark event in China's multilateral diplomacy. Unlike other international organizations, the SCO upholds a concept of cooperation that is mostly a diplomatic initiative put forward by China and is closely related to China's role in international and regional affairs. From the "Shanghai Spirit" and the New Security Concept at the beginning of its establishment, to the Qingdao Summit's proposal to enrich the "Shanghai Spirit" with the new connotation of the times, that is, the concept of development, security, cooperation, civilization and global governance, to the proposal to build a community with a shared future of the Shanghai Cooperation Organization, the development of the SCO has fully embodied "Chinese wisdom" and regional and global policy.

China's Global South policy through the Shanghai Cooperation Organization underscores its ambition to reshape the regional and global order by strengthening ties with developing nations. By providing economic opportunities, promoting security cooperation, and advocating for multilateralism, China aims to position itself as a leader for the Global South, offering an alternative to Western-dominated international institutions. However, challenges remain, including regional tensions, debt sustainability, and human rights concerns, which could shape the future trajectory of both China and the SCO.

REFERENCES

ASPIRE IAS. (2021, December 10). *SCO (Shanghai Cooperation Organization).* https://www.aspireias.com/studynotes/generatepdf/SCO-Shanghai-Cooperation-Organisation

Battams-Scott, G. (2019, February 26). How effective is the SCO as a tool for Chinese foreign policy? *E-International Relations.* https://www.e-ir.info/2019/02/26/how-effective-is-the-sco-as-a-tool-for-chinese-foreign-policy/

BBC Monitoring – Energy. (2006, June 21). Oil begins flowing through completed Kazakh-China pipeline. *BBC Monitoring – Energy.*

Belt and Road Initiative. (2025, February). *Belt and Road Initiative.* http://onebeltoneroad.com/en/

Bolonina, A. (2019). Security dimensions of China's presence in Central Asia. *Asian Focus*, (108), 6.

Bondevalue. (2018, March 5). "Belt and Road" bonds allowed to be issued via exchange. *Bondevalue.* https://bondevalue.com/news/belt-road-bonds-allowed-issued-via-exchanges/

Chen, X., & Fazilov, F. (2018, July). Re-centering Central Asia: China's "new great game" in the old Eurasian heartland. *Palgrave Communications*, *4*(1), 71. Advance online publication. DOI: 10.1057/s41599-018-0125-5

Cheng, J. Y. S. (2018). The Shanghai Co-operation Organisation: China's initiative in regional institutional building. In Cheng, J. Y. S. (Ed.), *Multilateral approach in China's foreign policy* (pp. 357–395). World Scientific. DOI: 10.1142/9789813221116_0008

Daily, F. T. (2017). China and Russia struggle to gain control over Central Asia. *Daily FT.* https://www.ft.lk/columns/China-and-Russiastruggle-to-gain-control-over-Central-Asia/4-64105517

Dexue, Y. (2021, May–June). Economic cooperation under the Shanghai Cooperation Organization: Achievements and prospects. *China Academic Journal Electronic Publishing House*, 94–122. https://rus.ecnu.edu.cn/u/5_2111/59269_1.pdf

Dickson, M. E. (2019). Great powers and the quest for hegemony in the contemporary international system. *Advances in Social Sciences Research Journal*, *6*(6), 168–176. DOI: 10.14738/assrj.66.6686

Efremenko, D. V. (2019). New stage in the development of the Shanghai Cooperation Organization. *China in World and Regional Politics: History and Modernity*, (25), 114–130.

Fairbank, J. K. (1969, April). China's foreign policy in historical perspective. *Foreign Affairs*, *47*(3), 449–463. DOI: 10.2307/20039389

Garlick, J. (2025, February 21). Beyond Central Asia: The ever-expanding influence of the Shanghai Cooperation Organization. *EuroHub 4Sino Policy Papers*. https://www.academia.edu/127817439/Beyond_Central_Asia_the_ever_expanding_influence_of_the_Shanghai_Cooperation_Organization

Grace, A. (2016). Quantifying China's influence on the Shanghai Cooperation Organization. *Cornell International Affairs Review*, *10*(1), 1–3. DOI: 10.37513/ciar.v10i1.484

Hao, D. (2021a). SCO political cooperation: Progress, challenges and future path. *International Studies*, (3), 47–66.

Hao, D. (2021b, July–August). 20 years of the SCO: Development, experience and future direction. *Contemporary International Relations, 31*(4).

Höne, K. E. (2020, October). The future of (multilateral) diplomacy? *DIPLO*. https://www.diplomacy.edu/futureofmultilateraldiplomacy2020

Hui, Z. (2019, August 16). The central pillars of China's diplomacy. *China Today*.

Huirong, Z., & Hongwei, W. (2012). China's energy policy towards the Caspian region: The case of Kazakhstan. *The Newsletter*, (62).

Jiang, A. (2013). Mao Zedong's "Three Worlds" theory: Political considerations and value for the times. *Social Sciences in China*, *34*(1), 35–57. DOI: 10.1080/02529203.2013.760715

Liao, J. X. (2019). China's energy diplomacy towards Central Asia and the implications on its "belt and road initiative.". *The Pacific Review*. Advance online publication. DOI: 10.1080/09512748.2019.1705882

Lu, N.-X., Huang, M.-F., & Lu, S.-B. (2019). How the Belt and Road Initiative can help strengthen the role of the SCO and deepen China's cooperation with Russia and the countries of Central Asia. *India Quarterly*, *75*(1), 56–68. DOI: 10.1177/0974928418821484

Mahbubani, K. (2022). *The Asian 21st century (China and Globalization)*. Springer. DOI: 10.1007/978-981-16-6811-1

MFA. (2021, June 29). 20 years of the Shanghai Cooperation Organisation (SCO): Cooperation for stability and prosperity. *MFA*. https://www.mfa.tj/en/paris/view/8131/20-years-of-the-shanghai-cooperation-organisation-sco-cooperation-for-stability-and-prosperity

Mikhaylenko, E., Ospanova, A., & Lagutina, M. (2022). The SCO and security cooperation. In Marochkin, S., & Bezborodov, Y. (Eds.), *The Shanghai Cooperation Organization: Exploring new horizons* (pp. xx–xx). Routledge. DOI: 10.4324/9781003170617-5

Moreland, W. (2019, September). The purpose of multilateralism: A framework for democracies in a geopolitically competitive world. *Foreign Policy, Brookings*. https://www.brookings.edu/wpcontent/uploads/2019/09/FP_20190923_purpose_of_multilateralism_moreland.pdf

Nawab, Q. (2024, July 3). China's role in shaping the future of the SCO. *China Focus*. http://www.cnfocus.com/china-s-role-in-shaping-the-future-of-the-sco

Norov, V. (2019, September 29). China has a creative and constructive role at the SCO. https://eng.sectsco.org/news/20190929/583793.html

Papageorgiou, M., & Cardoso, F. dos S. (2021). Chinese diplomacy, strategic partnerships and global economic supremacy. In Spigarelli, F., & McIntyre, J. R. (Eds.), *The new Chinese dream*. Palgrave Macmillan. DOI: 10.1007/978-3-030-69812-6_4

Patrick, S. M. (2019, December 16). The alliance for multilateralism makes sense. Can it make good? *World Politics Review*. https://www.worldpoliticsreview.com/articles/28414/the-alliancefor-multilateralism-makes-sense-can-it-make-good

Perskaya, V. V., Khairov, B. G., Revenko, N. S., & Khairova, S. M. (2022). Role of the People's Republic of China in the activities of the Shanghai Cooperation Organisation. *East Asia (Piscataway, N.J.)*, *39*(2), 149–160. DOI: 10.1007/s12140-021-09373-y PMID: 34493917

Pradt, T. (2020a). Security cooperation among SCO members. In *The prequel to China's new silk road* (pp. 87–99). Palgrave Macmillan. DOI: 10.1007/978-981-15-4708-9_7

Pradt, T. (2020b). Economic cooperation among SCO members. In *The prequel to China's new silk road* (pp. 71–85). Palgrave Macmillan. DOI: 10.1007/978-981-15-4708-9_6

Rumer, E. B. (2006, November). China, Russia and the balance of power in Central Asia. *Strategic Forum*, (223). https://www.files.ethz.ch/isn/46312/SF223.pdf

Serikkaliyeva, A. (2017, May–June). Does China seek the geopolitical agenda of the SCO? *Eurasian Research Institute e-Bulletin*, (118). https://www.eurasian-research.org/publication/does-china-seek-the-geopolitical-agenda-of-the-sco/

Shanghai Convention on Combating Terrorism. Separatism and Extremism. (2001, June 15). https://www.refworld.org/pdfid/49f5d9f92.pdf

Shanghai Cooperation Organization. (2020). https://eng.sectsco.org/

Shanghai Cooperation Organization. (2023). https://eng.sectsco.org/

Simes, D. (2020, May 27). Coronavirus gives Russia-China gas pipeline plan a burst of energy. *Nikkei Asian Review*.

Simha, R. K. (2015, July 24). SCO's next big challenge: Keeping the peace in Asia. *RBTH*. https://www.rbth.com/blogs/2015/07/24/scos_next_big_challenge_keeping_the_peace_in_asia_47985.html

Southerland, M., Green, W., & Janik, S. (2020, November 12). The Shanghai Cooperation Organization: A testbed for Chinese power projection. *U.S.-China Economic and Security Review Commission*. https://searchworks.stanford.edu/view/13860423

Srivastava, L. (2014). Strengthening multilateral diplomacy and sustainable development. *Conference Diplomacy, LI*(3). https://www.un.org/en/chronicle/article/strengthening-multilateral-diplomacy-and-sustainable-development

The SCO Yellow Paper. SCO Development Report. (2016). http://world.people.com.cn/n1/2016/0622/c1002-28469754.html

Turner, J. E. (2005, August). What is driving India's and Pakistan's interest in joining the Shanghai Cooperation Organization? *Strategic Insights, 4*(8). http://hdl.handle.net/10945/11450

Tzogopoulos, G. N. (2019, June 18). SCO and China: A new Asian regional order. *China.org.cn*. http://www.china.org.cn/opinion/2019-06/18/content_74896652.htm

Wang, Y. (2020, January 6). China-Central Asia gas pipeline transports 47.9 billion cubic meters in 2019. *XinhuaNet*. http://www.xinhuanet.com/english/2020-01/06/c_138682150.htm

Weitz, R. (2006, July 12). Reading the Shanghai SCO Summit. *The Central Asia-Caucasus Analyst*.

Wenting, X., & Xiaoyi, L. (2022, September 21). China to play important role in further development of SCO. *Global Times*. https://www.globaltimes.cn/page/202209/1275717.shtml

White Paper. (2019, March 19). The fight against terrorism and extremism and human rights protection in Xinjiang. *The State Council Information Office*. http://english.scio.gov.cn/2019-03/19/content_74585093_8.htm

Workman, D. (2020, April 23). Crude oil imports by country. *World's Top Exports*. https://www.worldstopexports.com/crude-oil-imports-by-country/

Wuthnow, J., Li, X., & Qi, L. (2012). Multilateralism: Four strategies in China's multilateral diplomacy. *Journal of Chinese Political Science*, *17*(3), 269–290. DOI: 10.1007/s11366-012-9202-6

Xi, J. (2018, June 8). Xi's memorable remarks on Shanghai Spirit, SCO cooperation. *Xinhua News*. http://www.xinhuanet.com/english/2018-06/08/c_137239146.htm

Xi, J. (2020, November 10). Xi Jinping's speech at 20th SCO summit. *CGTN*. https://news.cgtn.com/news/2020-11-10/Full-text-Xi-Jinping-s-speech-at-20th-SCO-summit-VjmMg1pMSA/index.html

Xinhua. (2019, December 13). SCO anti-cyber-terrorism drill held in China. *XinhuaNet*. http://www.xinhuanet.com/english/2019-12/12/c_138626263.htm

Xinhua. (2022, September 13). Xiplomacy: Xi's upcoming Central Asia trip to bolster SCO cooperation. *Xinhua*. https://english.news.cn/20220913/caa87b2b863143ce810c938819e90aca/c.html

Xue, Y., & Makengo, B. M. (2021, October). Twenty years of the Shanghai Cooperation Organization: Achievements, challenges and prospects. *Open Journal of Social Sciences*, *9*(10), 184–200. https://www.scirp.org/journal/paperinformation.aspx?paperid=112637#ref31. DOI: 10.4236/jss.2021.910014

Yee, H. S. (1983). The three world theory and post-Mao China's global strategy. *International Affairs*, *59*(2), 239–249. DOI: 10.2307/2619937

Zhang, Y. L. (2020). Shanghai Cooperation Organization: Exploring the way to get along in the new era. *World Knowledge, 72*(14).

Chapter 2
Türkiye and the Belt and Road Initiative:
Focusing on Trade Deficit Reduction With China or Integration With the Global South?

M. Nergis Ataçay
https://orcid.org/0000-0002-9723-0536
Kastamonu University, Turkey

ABSTRACT

The Belt and Road Initiative (BRI), which is an extensive transportation and infrastructure project, connecting Asia, Africa, and Europe is also seen as one of the important tools of South-South cooperation. Türkiye as one of the important members of the BRI has had several expectations, mainly improving Sino-Turkish relations through increasing Chinese investments in Türkiye and reducing the pressure of the trade deficit of Türkiye given to China. In addition, it was anticipated that the BRI would have improved trade and investment relations of Türkiye with the other members, so that the initiative would also play a role in Türkiye's rapprochement to the rising Global South. On the other hand, Chinese investments in Türkiye have been insufficient since its inclusion in the BRI in 2015, and the two countries would mutually put efforts to realize the potential benefits of the BRI.

DOI: 10.4018/979-8-3373-0938-5.ch002

INTRODUCTION

Alongside its objectives of fostering prosperity in developing countries and supporting global development, the Belt and Road Initiative (BRI) has been one of the most important instruments of South-South cooperation (SSC). Since its establishment, the number of BRI members has more than doubled. Such an expansion has certainly brought about an increase in the complexities and challenges that must be addressed for the initiative to bring about successful outcomes. Türkiye, which became a part of the BRI in 2015, has been viewed to be one of the important countries involved in the project.

The BRI marked the beginning of a new era in Sino-Turkish relations, which dated back to 1971. Bilateral relations between the two countries had developed through various phases beacuse of several causes and it is possible to argue that they had not reached their full potential. Specifically, economic relations have been dominated by Türkiye's trade deficit with China and the relatively low levels of Chinese investment, so that the BRI was perceived as a significant opportunity for Türkiye to address these issues. On the other side, Türkiye's geopolitical importance was considered to position it as one of the key players in the project. Consequently, it gains significance to understand the impacts of the BRI in Türkiye and its role within the project as more than a decade have passed since its announcement. The engagement of Türkiye to the BRI have played an important role not only in Sino-Turkish relations but also in Türkiye's apprach to the Global South, with which has not been historically close. Within this context, this chapter purposes to explore the critical question of whether the BRI, which has been one of the most important instruments of SSC, have played a role in increasing Chinese investments in Türkiye.

There is no clear consensus on which countries precisely constitute the Global South; however, it is evident that the region has gained considerable political and economic influence globally. SSC has been significant in increasing this influence. Post-development theory, which challenges the Western conception of development, also aligns with the rise of the Global South and the increasing relevance of SSC, as it contributes to the broader discourse surrounding the post-Western world. Western economic policies have historically been ill-suited to the different economic, social, political, and cultural contexts of non-Western countries. Türkiye, despite not being a former colony and maintaining historically close ties with the West, also exemplifies this mismatch. Therefore, Türkiye can be considered part of the Global South, as Western development models have failed to generate long-term economic progress, in addition to its efforts of approaching the Global South as a strategic complement to the West in its foreign policy. Such an approach could offer Türkiye a more advantageous role in the evolving post-Western global order, assigning more significance to the initiatives such as the BRI. In line with this perspective, the methodology of the study primarily involves a literature review, supplemented by a search of relevant newspaper sources. It is also crucial to highlight the lack of systematic data on Chinese investments in Türkiye, as this information is generally absent from both Turkish and Chinese official sources. The chapter has the contribution of presenting a discussion on Türkiye, having ties historically with the West and also improving the relations with the Global South, by overviewing the Turkish literature on the issue as well as the English references.

In order to achieve the purpose of the chapter, after the general features of the BRI and its relation with the SSC are overviewed briefly, it would be necessary for the reader to have an idea on the tendencies of the Turkish foreign policy for the period beginning since the early 2000s, giving also idea on Türkiye's attitude towards the Global South. The rest of the chapter is devoted to the discussion on the insufficiency of Chinese investments in Türkiye after its membership to the BRI. In addition to the other concluding remarks presented at the end, the chapter mainly concludes that China and Türkiye, two countries which have actually different priorities, others and the ones related to the Global South, would pay more attention to their bilateral relations. Specifically, the BRI would be one of the factors increasing the Chinese investments in Türkiye in the following years as expected since the beginning of its membership, bringing Türkiye closer to the Global South.

SSC, POST-WESTERN WORLD AND POST-DEVELOPMENT

SSC is defined as a multifaceted form of cooperation based on the sharing of knowledge, technology, experience, and resources among Global South countries. The discussions on the Global South had historically stemmed from the long-term divergence caused by the Industrial Revolution followed by the improvements in technology and communication in addition to the processes of colonialism and imperialism (Saad-filho, 2013: 582-583). Hence, Global South historically goes back to the conceptualization of "Third World", "largely equivalent to, but not identical with" (Dirlik, 2007: 12-13). The difference mainly stems from the fact that Global South left the post-colonial character behind and appears as a consequence of a period in which globalization has been in a crisis (Lopez, 2007 cited in Çelik, 2016:116). Hence, although South is seen as complementary to the concepts of Third World or developing countries, contrarily SSC brings about a relation among equals without a hierarchical order (Tekin and Dolu, 2020: 69). Consequently, "the categories of "North" and "South," "donors" and "recipients," and "developed" and "developing" countries are being blurred and challenged" (Bergamaschi et al., 2017, p. 3). Within this context, offering an alternative to hierarchical development models based on traditional North-South relations, SSC would be seen to be related to the post-development theory, particularly with the shared emphases such as equality, reciprocity, and local autonomy.

Post-development theory, developed by thinkers such as Gustavo Esteva, Arturo Escobar, Ashis Nandy, and Wolfgang Sachs since the 1990s, criticizes the Western-centered modernization approach by mainly treating "development" as a discourse. Development is a discourse having not only economic impact, but also a cultural and social construct through the coercive nature of Western development models as an ideological tool of transforming societies according to Western norms (Rist, 2019, p.125; Ziai, 2016, p. 94) and marginalizing local knowledge systems and community-based ways of life (Escobar, 2012, p.22, p.215). The theory also points out that many of these projects are rooted in a colonial historical context and often do not align with the characteristics of local populations (Escobar, 2012, p.22; Rist, 2019, p.131), relating the theory to the historical roots of the rise of the Global South and SSC.

Consequently, post-development theory rejects the singular understanding of development based on a linear progress of "economic growth, consumerism and commodification of nature, and so on" (Chuji, et. al, 2017, p.112). Post-development theory advocates that developing societies should formulate alternative development paths tailored to their own social, cultural, and economic contexts, without having to adopt the Western market developmentalism (Berthoud, 2019, p.92). Within this perspective, the questioning of the traditional global leadership role of the West and the growing influence of developing countries also forms the foundation of the concept of the post-Western world and the discussions on the multipolar world (Acharya, 2014, p.27; Stuenkel, 2016, p.109). Rejection of Western understanding of development by the post-development theory and the emphasis of the post-Western world approach on the end of Western hegemony in the global order complement each other in some aspects. Mainly, both of them criticize the dominant role of the West in development and global relations and point to the redistribution of global power. SSC would be seen as one of the important means to materialize this criticism.

SSC holds the potential to implement some of these alternatives at a practical level. On the other hand, some critics argue that SSC contrarily reproduces the neoliberal development practices, and thus falls short of achieving the radical breaks envisioned by post-development theory (Morvaridi & Huhhes, 2018, p.2). It is a discussion whether SSC is among equals based on mutal benefit, instead of donor-recipient relationship, since there could be some expectations in such relationships (Sidiropoulos, 2012, p.236). Therefore, it would be more accurate to view the relationship between SSC and post-development theory not as a directly overlapping equation, but as an intersection of paths that are sometimes parallel and at other times contradictory. For SSC to truly adopt a post-developmental aspect, it must be built within a framework that prioritizes not only technical and economic aspects but also social and cultural characteristics.

A BRIEF OVERVIEW OF THE BELT AND ROAD INITIATIVE

Over the past decade, extensive debate has revolved around China's precise objectives in launching a project as comprehensive and far-reaching as the the Belt and Road Initiative (BRI). The Chinese government has officially stated that the initiative aims to support developing countries and contribute to global development. From this perspective, the BRI has been characterized as a "global public good" and an "example of building a global community of shared future" (China Daily, 2023). Within this perspective, China's foreign direct investments, particularly in regions like Africa, exemplify a form of South-South economic integration, signaling a potential shift toward a new global political economy (Camba & Hung, 2018, p. 298), also playing an important role in increasing China's regional and global diplomatic influence (Pu, 2016, p. 115). The operation of the BRI has marked the expansion of Chinese investments beyond Central Asia and the Middle East, signifying the outward movement of Chinese capital, particularly through state-owned enterprises, to various parts of the world (Camba & Hung, 2018, p. 309).

It is not possible to overlook that the BRI is ultimately designed to serve for solving China's own economic problems (Tekdal, 2019, p. 137). The BRI is obviously significant for China's own economic development targets, particularly in ensuring energy security and promoting sustainable growth (Madani, 2021). This target gained further importance in 2014, when China's economy grew by only 7.4 percent, marking the lowest rate in the last 24 years. In addition, the BRI is viewed as a factor of continuation of China's integration into the global economy, a process that began at the beginning of the 1980s. The BRI has enhanced China's strategic maneuverability in the global economy and politics (Ergunsü, 2015). Specifically, the role of the BRI in strengthening China's position in SSC has been related to the US-China rivalry and the emergence of the post-Western World.

Despite its achievements after a decade of its announcement, the performance of the BRI has been subject to extensive debate, specifically concerning its sustainability and long-term impact. As the number of member countries has increased, the BRI has faced increasing complexities and challenges. In addition to pre-existing tensions between China and some of the member countries, bilateral issues also persist among these countries such as border problems, ethnic and religious diffrences, political disputes and competition, increasing the security concerns (Ergunsü, 2015; Akdağ, 2019, p. 80). Also, ensuring timely and accurate information sharing among all member countries of the BRI, especially transparency of China, has been viewed to be essential for the success of the initiative (Durdular, 2016, pp. 89-90). Most importantly, it should be noted that the member countries of the BRI differ significantly in terms geography, political systems, legal frameworks, levels of economic development and cultural charactersitics (Ergunsü, 2015). Türkiye, which has been one of the member countries of the BRI since 2015, shares to have some problems in its bilateral relations with China and needs to fulfill the policy obligations to realize the benefits of the project.

The Significance of the BRI in SSC

Global South, referred to a heregeneous group of 130 countries in different regions of Africa, Middle East, Asia, Oceania, Latin America and the Carebbean, represents 85 percent of the world's population and nearly 39 percent of global GDP under per capita criterion (Patrick & Huggins, 2023; Véron, 2023). Although there is not an agreement on which countries exactly form the Global South, its rise has been clearly observed as OECD (2010) explained by "shifting wealth". Brazil's President Luiz Inacio Lula da Silva, as Brazil took the Presidency of G20 in 2024 and expected to use this position to ensure that the Global South is more active in global decision making processes, emphasized that "There are those who question the concept of the Global South, saying that we are too diverse to fit together. But there are many more interests that unite us than differences that separate us." (Global-Is-Asian, 2024). Through the concept of "Three Worlds", Ikenberry (2024) emphasizes that the *global* West and the *global* East will be in competition to have the *global* South in their own side, which is weaker but full of capacities (Ikenberry, 2024, pp. 122, 131). In response to this, the Global South countries, emphasizing their distinctive charactersitics present a willingness to have strategic autonomy from both the West and the East and form "multiple alliances" (Kutlay, 2024, pp. 5-7).

Besides providing a picture of the multipolar world, the third summit of the BRI held on its tenth anniversary with 23 leaders and delegations from over 130 countries indicated, by especially the Western perspective, China's willingness to serve as the leader of the Global South (Arco Escriche & Burguete, 2023; The Economist, 2023). Within these discussions, post-Western global order will be formed by a new global political economy based on China's strategy which supports South-South economic integration (Camba & Hung, 2018, p. 298). The BRI has been one of the main tools supporting the development of the Global South and SSC (Zhou, 2024), enabling China to have the capacity to move strategically in the global political and economic order (Hussain et al., 2021). Within this perspective, SSC is viewed to reproduce neoliberal forms of global power relations. It is also mentioned that liberal democratic capitalism has been replaced by authoritarian state capitalism in this process (Öniş & Yalikun, 2021, p. 3) Such detection would be seen as a way to relate these discussions to the post-development theory, based on the supposition that Western capitalism has to change when faced to the distinctive charactersitics of Global South countries.

These discussions provide mainly two different approaches to the role of the BRI in SSC. According to the first approach, BRI is viewed to be consistent with the efforts of SSC, by strenthening infrastructure, increasing industrial productivity and innovation capacity of the member countries and improving trade and investment relations among them (Zhou & Haibing, 2019, pp. 11-12). Within this perspective, China represents an alternative model for the Global South countries and a cooperation *with Chinese charactersitics* (Sheng & Nascimento, 2021, pp. 5-6). AidData 2024 report analyzing Global South leasders'views indicates that 79 percent of leaders surveyed share the idea that China supports the development of their countries (Patterson, 2024). There is also a contrary approach which has mentioned that China has been criticized for 'neo-imperialism' by some of these countries (Zhao, 2024, p. 175). The main targets of the SSC would also be questioned in this context.

TURKISH FOREIGN POLICY AND THE GLOBAL SOUTH

Türkiye should also focus on its distinctive economic, political and social characteristics, instead of Western development prescriptions which has been a fact historically indicated. In other words, the need to listen post-development theorists is one of the most important common characteristics of Global South countries and Türkiye although it does not have a colonial past. On the other hand, the effort of Türkiye which has been historically closer to the West to integrate to Global South and SSC has been mainly based on its foreign policy.

With the Justice and Development Party (JDP) coming to power in Türkiye in 2002, there was also a shift in the Turkish foreign policy (Oran, 2013, p. 130). In this period in which the world became more multipolar, Türkiye has adopted a multi-dimensional foreign policy, shifting from a pro-Western policy to the emphasis on strategic autonomy, which is viewed to increase its bargaining power with the West (Oğuzlu, 2019, pp. 137-138). The power shift in Türkiye, occurred just after September 11 attacks, when the US hegemony began to fall and the Global South began to rise. For Türkiye, recording economic progress in this period, the perceptions of need for the US and the Russian threat since The Ottoman Empire disappeared and the focus was put on the Middle East (Oran, 2013:130-132). In this period, the European Union (EU) membership remaining on the agenda, regional and global integration, taking part in resolving the regional conflicts and to be among the top 10 economies in the world were among the main targets of Turkish foreign policy (Oran, 2013, p. 140). The global financial crisis of 2008 also played a role in the decline of the Western powers. In this process, Türkiye's relations with the US were deteriorating and the EU membership was less attractive. Consequently, Türkiye adopted a foreign policy based on strategic autonomy and strengthened its target of playing a leading role in the Middle East (Oğuzlu, 2019, pp. 133-134). On the other hand, in addition to many other regional developments, Arab Spring beginning in 2010 put pressure on Turkish foreign policy giving rise to a dilemma between *ethics versus self-interest*, which would be explained as staying in between the two coices of committing democratic principles and respecting independence of the states (Öniş, 2012, pp. 46, 60).

In this period, Türkiye's relations with China, Russia and other rising non-Western powers improved, especially relations with African countries developed. Such a change in Turkish foreign policy after 2007 was discussed within the context of the concepts of "axis shift" or "axis expansion", while it is possible to view the process as changing the methods and instruments of the policy without amending the target of making Türkiye more active regionally and globally (Kaya, 2015, pp. 79, 90; İstikbal et al. 2019, p. 59). "Zero problems with neighbours" marked the period as the policy principle of Ahmet Davutoğlu, served as the Minister of Foreign Affairs between 2009 and 2014 and still an important political figure in Turkish political life. This policy mainly represents minimizing problematic policy areas with neighbours and nearby geography and thus ensures stability and prevents chaos. As it is known, problems in the region have generally caused US intervention (Yalçın, 2011, pp. 47-48). Within this context, it is important to mention that the multi-dimensional foreign policy strategy of the Turkish government providing relative autonomy to Türkiye, did not exactly mean that the US impact totally disappeared (Uzgel, 2013, pp. 334-335) and it is also not possible to claim that the relations with the EU came to an end although they were not continuous and stable (Arat & Baykal, 2013, p. 398).

Figure 1. Total foreign direct investment in Türkiye (millions of US Dollars)

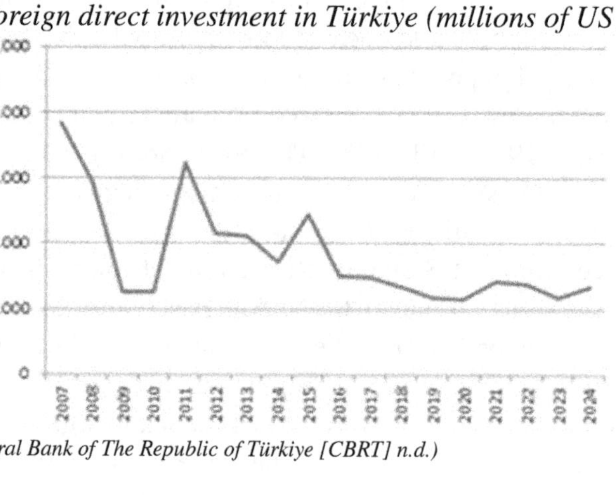

Source: (The Central Bank of The Republic of Türkiye [CBRT] n.d.)

As Donald Trump became the US President in 2017, who wanted to play an active role in Syria in contrast to the Obama administration, Turkish government was forced to make changes in its foreign policy (Oğuzlu, 2020, pp. 133-135). Moreover, Russian and Iranian involvement in Syria has decreased the role of Türkiye in the region. In addition to the historical disputes with the neighbours, these developments also indicated that Turkish foreign policy perception of "zero problems" would not be realized (Demir, 2024, p. 22). Instead, decreasing the number of enemies and increasing the number of friends turned out to be on the agenda. Under the impact of the coup attempt of 15 July, 2016, territorial integrity and social cohesion gained significance in addition to the regional developments (Oğuzlu, 2019, pp. 136-137).

Deteriorating relations with the US, mainly because Türkiye bought a S-400 missile defense system from Russia in 2017, financial fluctuations and decreasing foreign investment as indicated in Figure 1 put pressure on the Turkish economy. The reason for investor loss is seen as centralization of policy making process, specifically non-autonomous character of the Central Bank. Covid-19 pandemic and high depreciation of the Turkish Lira against the US Dollar deteriorated the economic conditions further, being another factor that China has gained more significance for Türkiye. In this process, Türkiye has become the second largest recipient of Asian Infrastructure Investment Bank (AIIB) loans, after India, with approximately 4.3 million US Dollars in terms of approved projects (Uluyol, 2024).

Under the impacts of the regime collapse in Syria and reelection of Trump as the US President at the end of 2024, Turkish government is expected to continue its multi-dimensional foreign policy. In this regard, it is expected that strategic autonomy will be on the agenda; however positioning between the US and China is obviously not easy under the existing regional and global conditions (Üngör, 2024). Within this context, it is also an important question whether Türkiye will be able to open a space for itself within the rising Global South.

Türkiye and the Global South

Türkiye, historically closer to the West unlike the other countries in the group, can be hardly viewed to be within the group of the Global South. As putting emphasis on strategic autonomy to have the ability to move freely under the unstable global and regional conditions, Türkiye has currently adopted a foreign policy increasing the relationship with the Global South. As a significant regional and global power, Türkiye which has also found itself in a 'hybrid'or 'in-between position' under the conditions of emerging post-liberal order and is forced to choose between the US or China, would have a good position within the Global South (Öniş & Yalikun, 2021, pp. 3-4).

Türkiye became a Dialogue Partner at the Summit of the Heads of the SCO held in Beijing on 6-7 June 2012. Within this context, MIKTA which was founded in 2013 as an informal consultation and coordination platform among Mexico, Indonesia, Republic of Korea, Türkiye and Australia would also be taken into consideration (Republic of Türkiye Ministry of Foreign Affairs n.d. a). Spreading over a wide geography, MIKTA has been an important formation with countires having differing levels of relations with the *North*, so that standing at different points between the *North* and the Global South (Cooper, 2015). Relations with Latin America also improved by increasing trade volume and official visits, while the number of embassies increased from 6 at the beginning of 2000s to 18 through the end of 2024 (Türkiye Cumhuriyeti Dışişleri Bakanlığı, 2025).

By joining the BRI in 2015, Türkiye was, first of all, willing to solve the standing economic problems with China (Özdaşlı, 2015, pp. 592-593). In addition to these, Türkiye would have the opportunity of having new export markets and moving the products from China to Türkiye in shorter periods of time (Karagöl, 2017, p. 5). In the same year, Türkiye became the member of the AIIB which has been seen as an alternative to the World Bank (WB) and in 2017, obtained sectoral dialogue partnership status in the Association of Southeast Asian Nations (ASEAN). Within this context, in 2019 "Asia Anew Initiative", prioritizing economic and trade cooperation with Asian partners, was announced by the Turkish Ministry of Foreign Affairs (Republic of Türkiye Ministry of Foreign Affairs n.d. b). Also, "Distant Countries Strategy" was announced by the Ministry of Commerce in 2022 with the target of increasing Turkish exports by 4 times to 18 countries which have average distance of 8500 kilometres, including a number of countries within the Global South (Ünal, 2023).

BRICS membership turned out to be on the Turkish agenda towards the end of 2024 after especially the attendance of Hakan Fidan, Turkish Minister of Foreign Affairs, to the Meeting of Foreign Ministers of BRICS member countries in Russia (BBC Türkçe, 2023). Türkiye has several reasons to be interested in BRICS. First of all, the Turkish government is in the idea that the global economic center has shifted to the East. Second, as also related to one of the issues dealt within this chapter, it is expected that closer relationships with BRICS would also increase Chinese investments in Türkiye. Third, improving the relations with African countries has gained significance by increasing trade volume, foreign direct investments and number of embassies of Türkiye since the beginning of the 2000s and also a military base is built in Somalia (Kutlay, 2024, pp. 9-10). The military base in Somalia, which was opened in 2017 and known as TÜRKSOM, is Türkiye's largest military base abroad (Aksoy, 2024). Fourth, BRICS is viewed to be an alternative to the International

Monetary Fund (IMF) and a way to avoid IMF's stand-by agreements by Türkiye (Üngör, 2024). Finally, but importantly, BRICS is not yet a structure that imposes responsibilities and has not established a common basis on the issues of economy, security and geopolitics. With this feature, BRICS obviously differs from the EU, although the Foreign Affairs Minister Fidan made a comparison by his statement that Türkiye would perhaphs not be in the search of BRICS membership, if it had obtained EU membership (BBC Türkçe, 2024).

At the end of the day, BRICS membership is a good way to take part in the Global South. By traditionally putting the emphasis on the notion that being a bridge between the East and the West has been an important part of Türkiye's foreign policy, which has generally significant repercussions over Turkish domestic politics, the Global South is viewed as a good complementary to the West although it is difficult to view as an alternative (Donelli & Gonzalez-Levaggi, 2016; Öniş & Yalikun, 2021, p. 10). The problems with the EU process and the tensions with the US especially regarding the Syria and most of the countries involved in the East Mediterrennian problem made Türkiye having a search for new alliances within the Global South (Kutlay, 2024, p. 10).

It is important to mention that there are also risks for Türkiye of getting closer to the Global South. Despite its increasing political and economic power, China is not very close to overcome the US hegemony both in economic and military terms, also meaning that post-Western world does not mean the disappearance of the West (Kutlay, 2024, p. 10). There is a kind of transition to the post-Western world; however it is not possible to claim that China or any other non-Western power has become the leader of the new order (Keyman, 2024, January 16). Countries within the Global South have recorded high economic growth; however they have different economic structures. China's export-oriented strategy, India's dominance on information and communication services sector, Brazil, Russia and South Africa's economies based on raw material exports make it difficult for them to take a common stance in some areas in addition to their different political structures (İstikbal et al. 2019, p. 59). Under these conditions, Türkiye has also competitors within this group such as India, Brazil, Suudi Arabia, South Africa and Vietnam (Keyman, 2024, Febuary 13). Besides, the regional and global problems of war, climate change, inequality, exclusion, high cost of living, poverty, culture wars, polarization and refugee flows increase the uncertainities in this process (Keyman, 2024, January 16; Keyman, 2024, May 7).

Moreover, the countries within the Global South, for instance BRICS members, are "middle income" countries with the problems mainly related to their social development indicators such as inequalities, and also lack of democratic institutions and rule of law (Kutlay, 2024, pp. 7-8, 10-11). It is difficult to claim that the countries within the Global South share a common political vision; rather it seems that each country has their own priorities. Economic targets would be seen to bring them together, however the economic institutionalization of the group is under question because of the noninstitutionalized structure of New Development Bank and lack of regulations regarding R5, which is seen as the common currency of BRICS (Boynukara, 2024). Approaching the Global South with some kinds of generalizations would be seen as repeating the fault of the US during the Cold War as treating all the Third World countries to have same charactersitics and interests. "Western-centrism" based on treating all of the other countries as having one characteristic of being non-Western, not only ignored the diffrences among these countries but also the significant interaction between them (Stuenkel, 2016, p.33), and also their own "development" strategies based on their different charactersitics in line with the post-develoment theory. Hence, Western polcymakers are warned against viewing Global South as a single entity and ignoring the countries which have been viewed as *pivotal (or swing)* states such as Brazil, India, Indonesia, South Africa and Türkiye (Patrick & Huggins, 2023).

Türkiye would also be careful about the noninstitutionalized structure of the BRICS and avoid talking too much and causing speculations on the membership (Boynukara, 2024), while one of these has emerged, regarding Türkiye's membership issue at the end of 2024. It is thought that India prevented Türkiye's membership to the BRICS because of the influence of the US. Hence, discussing the impact of Trump's reelection as the US president on Türkiye's policy preferences also gains significance. Trump may interpret Türkiye's interest in BRICS as a strategic move based on pragmatism rather than moving away from the West, which would give rise to mutually flexible relationship in this issue between Türkiye and the US (Aydın, 2024). On the other hand, President Trump immediately announced his policy of imposing high tariffs on China, demonstrating the economic, technological, military and political competition between the US and China. It is observed that President Donald Trump and the Turkish President Recep Tayyip Erdoğan had a good starting; however it is also pointed out that the Israeli-Palestinian conflict would seriously cause some problems (Yurdakul, 2025). Under the dynamic regional and global conditions, Türkiye should be realistic as a middle power, having less capacity of strategic autonomy when compared to the other countries adopting this strategy (Keyman, 2024, Febuary 13).

TÜRKIYE AND THE BRI

The Republic of Türkiye officially recognized the People's Republic of China in 1971. Initially, relations between the two countries remained distant under the conditions of the Cold War. As a consequence of significant economic liberalization policies implemented by both countries since the beginning of the 1980s, economic relations improved and high level visits began (Atlı & Ünay, 2014, p. 20). After the dissolution of the Soviet Union, Sino-Turkish relations improved in the second half of the 1990s. While China's economic power was rising, Türkiye was significant for its ties with the West. During this period, as indicated in Figure 2, Türkiye's trade deficit with China emerged as a major issue, growing rapidly in the following years and has still remained to be one of the key challenges in Sino-Turkish economic relations. Although there were also some political and diplomatic problems between Türkiye and China, relations have improved since the beginning of the 2000s, whereas it is difficult to claim that trade and investment relations reached the desired level (Ataçay, 2016, pp. 45-46). The strategic partnership agreement signed in 2010 between China and Türkiye represented a significant cornerstone of the bilateral relations (Atlı & Ünay, 2014, pp. 20-21).

Türkiye became a member country of the BRI by a memarondum of understanding signed during the G-20 summit held on 15-16 November 2015 in Antalya. The BRI, seen as the world's largest transportation and infrastructure project, has hold significant potential for Türkiye standing on the Middle Corridor. Among its most anticipated benefits, in addition to improving Sino-Turkish economic relations, was opening new markets to boost Türkiye's export potential. The project has promised to reduce the shipping time of goods between Türkiye and China from 30 days to 10 days. Similarly, goods shipped from Beijing to Istanbul, previously taking two months by sea, were predicted to arrive in less than two weeks. These improvements have underscored the significance of the BRI for Türkiye (Karagöl, 2017, p. 5). In addition to these, it has been expected that Türkiye would become a distribution center of energy corridors by the help of the BRI (Akdağ, 2019, p. 89; Koçakoğlu, 2021, pp. 764-765).

The BRI is also expected to attract foreign investments flowing to Türkiye from China and other member countries, while fostering a more balanced trade volume with China. Also, Türkiye has seen the BRI as a chance for gaining faster and more cost-effective access to Asian markets (Akdağ, 2019, p. 87). For Türkiye, the BRI would be primarily useful for approaching China while the initiative has also offerred Türkiye opportunities to enter new export markets and strengthen its role as a bridge between Europe and Asia. Also, it has been expected that infrastructure investments within Türkiye, driven by the BRI, would have increased (Özdaşlı, 2015, pp. 592–593). On the other side, Türkiye's geopolitical position, serving as a bridge, strengthens its strategic importance within the BRI. As the member of NATO and a candidate of EU, Türkiye has had a significant position in the competition between the West and China (Ülgen & Umarow, 2024). In addition, the East-West High-Speed Railway Line, linked with the Baku-Tbilisi-Kars Railway which was under-construction during that period, further reinforced Türkiye's role as a vital connection between the regions important for the BRI.

Figure 2. Sino-Turkish trade relations (millions of US Dollars)

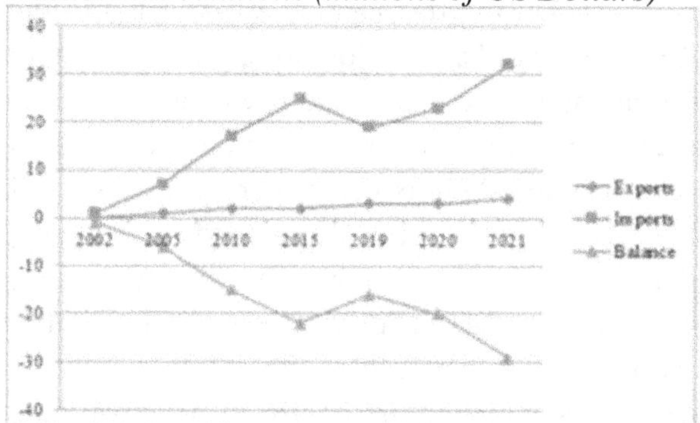

Source: (Turkish Statistical Institute [TÜİK]n. d.)

The fact that the BRI consensus agreement was signed under the conditions of some serious problems between Türkiye and China such as the Uyghur Turks issue, China's emphasis on terrorism and a cancelled agreement on a missile defense system, indicated the existence of important mutual expectations and the willingness of both countries to cooperate on carrying out the BRI at that time. In addition to the bilateral problems, Türkiye's geographically closeness to the Middle East which has been full of accelerating turmoil for some period of time, mainly Syrain civil war has also seen to stand as an obstacle against the good performance of Türkiye's integration to the BRI (Durdular, 2016, pp. 92-95). Under the impact of these problems, the membership agreement was followed by President Erdoğan's visit to China on July 2015, which was marked by especially significant tensions over the Uyghur Turks issue.

It is also important to mention that the BRI has represented both opportunities and challenges for Türkiye. While it was expected that the project would have increased Türkiye's strategic connectivity and economic potential, it also requires addressing key issues such as trade imbalances, regional political dynamics, and competitive disadvantages. Like other member countries, ensuring that Türkiye derives maximum benefit from the BRI will depend on its ability to navigate these challenges effectively. The Uyghur Turks issue continues to be a source of tension in Sino-Turkish relations. Additionally, NATO's reservations about closer Sino-Turkish ties present another problem (Ergunsü, 2015). As mentioned above, Türkiye's proximity to the unstable Middle East and its substantial trade deficit with China are further issues that complicate its participation in the initiative (Durdular, 2016, pp. 92–95). Moreover, the BRI has also posed potential risks for Türkiye despite its anticipated benefits. Within this perspective, one of the primary concerns has been the inability of Turkish goods to compete with Chinese products. In addition to this, it is pointed out that Türkiye's exclusion from certain BRI projects may lead to adverse effects, such as reduced competitiveness of critical economic assets, for instance there were fears that investment of Chinese firms in other Mediterennian ports would have decrease competitiveness of Mersin port, which is one of the biggest in Türkiye (Tekdal, 2019, pp. 131–133). Nail Olpak, who is Chairman of Turkish Foreign Economic Relations Board, highlighted some of the negative concerns regarding the BRI. He mainly pointed out that trade with China remains unfavorable for Türkiye; because Türkiye has experienced significant losses in its own access to the European markets, while Chinese goods reach these markets more quickly and efficiently by the help of the BRI (Yinanç, 2024).

Despite the challenges, the BRI is anticipated to provide long-term infrastructure financing and investment opportunities for Türkiye (Tekdal, 2019, pp. 132–133, 137), contributing to strengthen Sino-Turkish relations as well as Türkiye's ties with other members and its integration to the Global South. Considering both the benefits and the challenges, Türkiye has been in the hope of gaining from the BRI. Consequently, it would be critical to examine the impacts on Türkiye and the Turkish economy of the BRI membership. Specifically, the question whether BRI membership has caused China's investements in Türkiye to increase gains significance.

Chinese Investments in Türkiye since its BRI membership

Actually, several significant Chinese investments have taken place following Türkiye's inclusion in the BRI in 2015, while there are also some important examples before 2015 such as Ankara-İstanbul high speed train line which was completed in 2014 (Yılmaz, 2020, p. 5285). Also, Huawei, operating in Türkiye since 2002 has represented one of the most important Chinese investments in Türkiye, which played a significant role in the spread of 3G technology in Türkiye by a cooperation with the Turkish operators and built R&D centers in İstanbul in 2009 (Öztürk, 2012) and in Ankara by the end of 2022 (Aslanhan, 2022).

Beginning with the year of 2015, Cosco Pacific, a Chinese state-owned enterprise, acquired a 65 percent stake in Kumport Port, located in Istanbul's Avcılar district. At that time, Kumport was Türkiye's third-largest port, and the 940 million US Dollars deal represented the largest Chinese investment in Türkiye up to that point (Dünya Gazetesi, 2015). Additionally, in the same year the Industrial and Commercial Bank of China (ICBC), the world's largest bank by assets, purchased a 75.5 percent stake in a Turkish bank by the name of Tekstilbank, hence China entered also into the Turkish banking sector (NTV, 2015).

In 2017, ZTE, a partially state-owned Chinese telecommunications giant, acquired a 48.04 percent stake in Netaş, a Turkish information and communications technology company, for 101.3 million US Dollars (Sabah Gazetesi, 2017). In the following year, Alibaba Group acquired a 75 percent stake in Trendyol, a prominent Turkish e-commerce platform, for 728 million US Dollars. By 2021, Alibaba had increased its stake to 86.5 percent through additional capital infusions (Bloomberg HT, 2021, April 21).

In 2019, China Machinery Engineering Corporation (CMEC) initiated the construction of a boron carbide facility in Bandırma, Balıkesir, under the auspices of Eti Maden. The facility, completed in 2023 with an investment of 80 million US Dollars, and incorporated technology transfer from China (Eser, 2023). Also in the same year, a Chinese consortium attempted to acquire the majority shares of the Yavuz Sultan Selim Bridge and the North Marmara Highway, but the deal was eventually canceled (Bloomberg HT, 2021, August 2). Nevertheless, Chinese financial institutions and banks were among those financing the 1915 Çanakkale Bridge and Highway Project in 2018 (Topçu, 2018). In 2019, Turkish GAMA Holding signed a memorandum of understanding for the construction of Three-Deck Tube Tunnel Project in Istanbul with China State Construction Engineering Corporation Limited (CSCEC) and China Investment and Construction Group Holdings Limited (CICG) (GAMA Holding, 2019). Also, there has been a partnership between the state-owned China Electronics Technology Group (CETC) and Türkiye's Kalyon Group for the construction of a solar industrial park which would make a contribution to Türkiye's capacity of renewable energy. In addition to the other energy sectors, renewable energy have been one of the sectors significantly attratcting the attention of Chinese investors (Xiao, 2024). Between 2005 and 2020, Chinese energy investments in Türkiye reached 2.8 billion US Dollars, in which renawable energy has the share of 21.9 percent (Kaya & Arı, 2021:4).

In 2022, Shanghai Electric Power, another Chinese state-owned enterprise, completed the Hunutlu Thermal Power Plant in Adana's Yumurtalık district. The project, which began in September 2019, represented the largest direct Chinese investment in Türkiye to that date, with a cost of 1.7 billion US Dollars (Milliyet, 2022; Xin, 2023). More recently, on July 8, 2024, BYD, one of China's largest private companies and a leading electric vehicle manufacturer, signed an agreement to establish a facility in Türkiye. Scheduled to begin operations in 2026, the facility will have an annual production capacity of 150,000 vehicles and is expected to employ 5000 people (Euronews, 2024). While this investment is anticipated to bring benefits such as employment, technology transfer, and supply chain expansion, Professor Çağdaş Üngör has noted that its long-term success is uncertain due to the US-China technology rivalry and adds that competitiveness of Türkiye's domestic electric vehicle initiative, that is known as TOGG, may be risked by BYD's market presence (Hamsici, 2024). Türkiye's decision on June 2024 to impose an additional 40 percent tariff on imported Chinese vehicles was seen to be related to the protection of TOGG's competitiveness, whereas a new arrangement was set excluding the Chinese firms investing in Türkiye from this tariff (Toptaş, 2024). In addition to BYD, other leading automotive companies such as Chery, SAIC and Great Wall Motors have also searched to invest in Türkiye which is seen advantageous to reach European markets (Xiao, 2024). There are also future projects which attract Chinese investments such as Canal İstanbul Project, which has faced significant opposition in Türkiye (Öniş & Yalikun, 2021, p. 17).

Although the BRI has brought some notable Chinese investments to Türkiye, the scale of these investments remains relatively small. Consequently, it is questioned whether Türkiye have had significant economic gains in relation to its role in the BRI, specifically in terms of attracting substantial Chinese investments and addressing the trade imbalance with China. Figure 3 indicates that Chinese investments in Türkiye have increased between 2012 and 2015, to the peak of 451 million US Dollars, however decreased to the previous levels in the following 3-4 years. As also indicated by Gürel and Kozluca (2022), there has not been a steady increase in Chinese investments in Türkiye since it joined the BRI.

Figure 3. Flow of Chinese investments to Türkiye (millions of US Dollars)

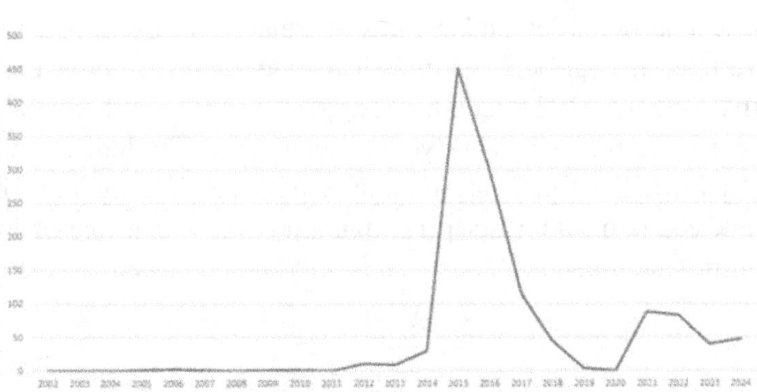

Source: (CBRT, n.d.)

On the other side, it is known that the BRI has led to significant infrastructure and energy investments across the Global South, including Asia, Africa, Latin America, and the Middle East. In Africa, BRI-related investments reached $29.2 billion in 2024, focusing mainly on mining and mineral extraction (Ecofin Agency, 2024). In Latin America, China invested $71 billion in Brazil alone between 2007–2023, while projects in Peru and Bolivia involve multibillion-dollar developments in ports and lithium extraction (RMC Global, 2023; Jütten, 2025). *China Statistical Yearbook 2024* indicates that China's outward foreign direct investment to Brazil, Mexico and Cayman Islands increased in 2023 when compared to 2022, whereas Türkiye does not even exist in the list. In Asia, China allocated $3.5 billion to green energy in 2023 and completed the $6 billion China-Laos railway, which played a significant role in strengthening regional logistics (Nedopil et al., 2023). Also, the Middle East has emerged as a leading recipient of Chinese BRI investments, totaling $39 billion in 2024 alone (Kader, 2025). As the Arab Investment and Export Credit Guarantee Corporation (Dhaman) points out, one third of foreign direct investments in the region is held by China (Bulard, 2025). According to the *China Belt and Road Initiative (BRI) Investment Report 2023,* Saudi Arabia took the lead in the area of infrastructure investments, followed by Sri Lanka. In other sectors, Indonesia ranked first with 7.3 billion US Dollars of Chinese investments, while Peru ranked third with 2.0 billion US Dollars (Nedopil Wang, 2024). It is expected that Chinese enterprises will invest over 8 billion US Dollars in the port of Khalifa in the United Arab Emirates (UAB), or the huge economic zone on the Suez canal in the following years (Bulard, 2025).

China Belt and Road Initiative (BRI) Investment Report 2023 also points out that Türkiye, along with 19 countries such as Kenya and Myanmar, experienced a 100 percent decline in project participation compared to 2022, indicating that these countries have to reevaluate their role and performance within the BRI. The decline in project participation underscores the relatively limited role that Türkiye has played in attracting significant Chinese investments and receiving expected economic benefits under the BRI (Nedopil Wang, 2024). On the other hand, relatively limited Chinese investments in Türkiye has been one of the indicators of the fact that China's BRI strategies vary significantly across regions, aligning with specific geopolitical and economic interests, prioritizing regions which are rich in resources and poor in infrastructure.

Figure 4. Total value of direct investments in Türkiye in the post-pandemic period (2022-2024) (million of US Dollars)

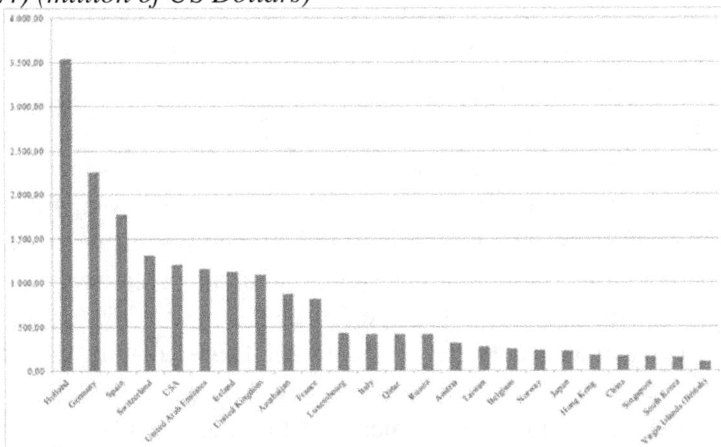

Source: (CBRT, n.d.)

Within this discussion, China's rank among the countries investing in Türkiye and Türkiye's rank among the countries where China invests also gain significance. According to Turkish Central Bank data, China's total investments in Türkiye between 2002 and 2024 ranked 23rd in the list of countries investing in Türkiye, falling behind, for instance Ireland and Lebonan. Although China's rank increased to 18 between the years of 2015 and 2024, there has not been a regular increasing trend (CBRT, n.d.) Figure 4 indicates that, between 2022 and 2024 that is called the post-pandemic period, China remained outside the list of 20 countries investing in Türkiye, with the rank of 21st just before Singapore, which has increased its investments in Türkiye in this period. Figure 4 also indicates the well-known fact that the European countries and the US has remained to be the most important investors in Türkiye. On the other hand, China has invested more in Iran, Israel and UAB (Öniş & Yalikun, 2021, pp. 6-7).

According to Ergenç and Göçer (2023), there have been external factors which have affected Türkiye's position in the BRI. Covid-19 pandemic and Ukraine war played a role of strengthening, whereas improving relations between China and the Gulf countries put a contrary pressure. In addition to the external factors, rising authoritarianism in Türkiye, specifically rising centralization and informal politics have played a role in the failure to attract enough Chinese investments under the discussions on "debt trap" without "political conditionality" related to the BRI (Ergenç & Göçer, 2023). Hence, Chinese globally competitive firms, which are mostly formed by large state-owned enterprises, act in line with the principles of global liberal economy in some cases. In addition, there are some sector specific barriers, such as Türkiye's preference to support its domestic solar panel production and the impact of the US-Türkiye relations on nuclear power plant project with China. In addition, Türkiye's willingness to increase Chinese coal-fired power plant investments, facing increasing opposition of the local communities and NGOs, also contradicts with national and international environment-friendly policies and regulations, even greening the BRI agenda (Kaya & Arı, 2021, p. 12).

The issue of China's relatively low level of investment in Türkiye, even within the framework of the BRI, becomes more pronounced when compared to China's investments in other countries. According to Gürel and Kozluca (2022), who also highlighted the lack of official and transparent data as a significant challenge in evaluating China's investments in Türkiye, Türkiye accounted for only 1.3 percent of China's total investments between 2013 and 2020 based on data from the American Enterprise Institute. According to this study, Türkiye ranked 23rd among 80 countries in receiving Chinese investments in this period. The same study also states that there were 1148 Chinese firms operating in Türkiye as of 2022, with a total estimated investment slightly exceeding 1 billion US Dollars, whereas Ülgen & Umarov (2024) mentions that the Chinese stock of foreign direct investment in Türkiye was about 9 billion US Dollars by the end of 2023, based on Turkish Ministry of Industry and Technology data. Such a difference in one year is one of the good examples indicating lack of sufficient data. Beyond the modest investment volume, it is worth noting that Turkish firms' expectations of benefiting from China's technical expertise, especially in the energy and telecommunications sectors, have largely remained unfulfilled (Gürel & Kozluca, 2022, pp. 807–811, 815-817).

CONCLUSION

Since Türkiye joined the BRI in 2015, which is one of the key instruments of SSC, it mainly expected that Chinese investments have increased and economic relations with the other member countries of the initiative have developed. SSC is often associated with post-Western world discussions, as it is expected to play an important role in the emergence of an alternative to the Western-centered global order. In this context, SSC efforts can also be linked to post-development theory, which emphasizes that countries should consider their own economic, political, social, and cultural characteristics and reject the Western-centered understanding of "development". In doing so, it becomes possible to criticize the Western-centered global system, which has been shaped by and continues to promote Western development paradigms.

Although Türkiye does not have a colonial past and has historically been closer to the West, it still shares the characteristic of being a non-Western country with other countries in the Global South. Turkish economic history demonstrates that Western development models and policies have not been suitable for Türkiye's distintive economic, political, social and cultural characteristics. On the other hand, it has been observed that Türkiye's engagement with the Global South is largely motivated by foreign policy considerations, as a complementary to the West, rather than an alternative. In terms of Türkiye's closer alignment with the Global South, fulfilling its expectations from the BRI, especially economic ones, is of great importance. However, Chinese investments in Türkiye since 2015 are generally considered insufficient and such an investment trajectory underscores the need for greater engagement and collaboration between Türkiye and China to better capitalize on the opportunities presented by the BRI. Such an effort would have a positive impact on Türkiye's relations with the Global South counties, which would be improved since they share the important feature of being non-Western.

The chapter has also the following concluding remarks regarding the causes and consequences of the insufficient levels of Chinese investment in Türkiye since its inclusion in the BRI:

- the West remains to be the main investor in Türkiye
- rising uncertainities in the Turkish economy stemming from the increasing authoritarianism and centralization of decision making would be the reason affecting the preferences of Chinese investors like the ones from other countries
- the important examples of Chinese investments are driven by mostly state-owned enterprises, supporting the discussions on globally rising state capitalism
- the sharp decline in project participation also signals the need for Türkiye to reassess its strategy for engaging with the BRI
- addressing data transparency would provide a clearer picture of the economic relationship between Türkiye and China, specifically the BRI

REFERENCES

Acharya, A. (2014). *The end of American world order*. Polity Press.

Akdağ, Z. (2019). Türkiye-Çin İlişkilerinde Kuşak ve Yol Girişimi'nin Önemi. *Birey Ve Toplum Sosyal Bilimler Dergisi, 9*(1), 65–96. DOI: 10.20493/birtop.558276

Aksoy, D. (2024, February 26). *TRT Haber, Somali'de Türkiye'nin yurt dışındaki en büyük üssü*. TRT Haber. https://www.trthaber.com/haber/dunya/trt-haber-somalide-turkiyenin-yurt-disindaki-en-buyuk-ussu-843529.html

Arat, T., & Baykal, S. (2013). AB'yle ilişkiler. In B. Oran (Ed.), *Türk dış politikası, kurtuluş savaşından bugüne olgular, belgeler, yorumlar* (pp. 337-400). İletişim Yayınları.

Arco Escriche, I., & Burguete, V. (2023). *Introduction: China's presence in the Global South*. CIDOB. https://www.cidob.org/en/publications/introduction-chinas-presence-global-south

Aslanhan, U. (2022, December 30). *Huawei Türkiye'nin yeni AR-GE merkezi Bakan Varank'ın katılımıyla açıldı*. Anadolu Agency. https://www.aa.com.tr/tr/bilim-teknoloji/huawei-turkiyenin-yeni-ar-ge-merkezi-bakan-varankin-katilimiyla-acildi/2776225

Ataçay, M. N. (2016). Türk-Çin ilişkileri: Türkiye-Rusya krizinin etkileri. *Ömer Halisdemir Üniversitesi İktisadi ve İdari Bilimler Fakültesi Dergisi, 9*(4), 37–56.

Atlı, A., & Ünay, S. (2014). *Küreselleşme sürecinde, Türkiye-Çin ekonomik ilişkileri. Siyaset, Ekonomi ve Toplum Araştırmaları Vakfı*. SETA.

Aydın, S. (2024, December 5). *Riskler ve fırsatlar: Trump'ın kazanması Türkiye açısından ne ifade ediyor?* Business Diplomacy. https://businessdiplomacy.net/tr/riskler-ve-firsatlar-trumpin-kazanmasi-turkiye-acisindan-ne-ifade-ediyor/

Bergamaschi, . (2017). Introduction: South–South cooperation beyond the myths—A critical analysis. In Bergamaschi, I., Moore, P., & Tickner, A. B. (Eds.), *South–South cooperation beyond the myths: Rising donors, new aid practices?* (pp. 1–25). Palgrave Macmillan. DOI: 10.1057/978-1-137-53969-4_1

Berthoud, G. (2012). Market. In Sachs, W. (Ed.), *The development dictionary: A guide to knowledge as power* (2nd ed., pp. 87–99). Zed Books.

Bloomberg, H. T. (2021, April 21). *Alibaba, Trendyol'a 350 milyon dolar yatırım yaptı*. Bloomberg HT. https://www.bloomberght.com/alibaba-trendyol-a-350-milyon-dolar-yatirim-yapti-2278870

Bloomberg, H. T. (2021, August 2). *3 köprünün Çinlilere satış görüşmesi durdu.* Bloomberg HT. https://www.bloomberght.com/3-koprunun-cinlilere-satis-gorusmesi-durdu-2285080

Boynukara, A. (2024, July 2). BRICS ve Türkiye. *Perspektif.* https://www.perspektif.online/brics-ve-turkiye

Bulard, M. (2025). Mart 17). *Behind China's breakthrough in the Middle-East. Orient (Paris), XXI,* •••. https://orientxxi.info/magazine/behind-china-s-breakthrough-in-the-middle-east,8096

Camba, A., & Hung, H. F. (2018). China, Africa, and global economic transformation. In C. Alden & D. Large (Ed.), *New directions in Africa–China studies* (pp. 318–331). Routledge.

CBRT. (n.d.). *Foreign direct investments in Türkiye by countries - stock (million USD) (annual).*CBRT. https://evds2.tcmb.gov.tr/index.php?/evds/serieMarket/collapse_36/5122/DataGroup/english/bie_odeayrsunum6/

Çelik, E. (2016). Güney Sosyolojisi'nin Yükselişi ve Türkiye'de Sosyoloji İçin İfade Edebileceği Anlamlar. *Mülkiye Dergisi, 40*(4), 113–148.

China Daily. (2023, September 27). *A global community of shared future: China's proposals and actions.* China Daily. https://global.chinadaily.com.cn/a/202309/27/WS65137a58a310d2dce4bb80af.html

Chuji, M.. (2019). Buen Vivir. In Kothari, A., Salleh, A., Escobar, A., Demaria, F., & Acosta, A. (Eds.), *Pluriverse: A post-development dictionary* (pp. 77–80). Tulika Books.

Cooper, A. F. (2015). MIKTA and the global projection of middle powers: Toward a summit of their own? *Global Summitry, 1*(1), 95–114. DOI: 10.1093/global/guv005

Demir, S. (2024). Türkiye's Century-Long Foreign Policy Experience: Key Take-aways. *Uluslararası Kriz Ve Siyaset Araştırmaları Dergisi, 8*(1), 13–28.

Dirlik, A. (2007). Global South: Predicament and promise. *Global Society, 1*(1), 12–23.

Donelli, F., & Gonzalez-Levaggi, A. (2016). Becoming a global actor: The Turkish agenda for the Global South. *SSRN, 1*(2), 93–115. DOI: 10.2139/ssrn.3462255

Dünya Gazetesi. (2015, September 17). *Kumport Limanı, Cosco Pacific'e satıldı.* Dünya Gazetesi. https://www.dunya.com/sirketler/kumport-limani-cosco-pacific039e-satildi-haberi-292370

Durdular, A. (2016). Çin'in "Kuşak-Yol" projesi ve Türkiye-Çin ilişkilerine etkisi. *Avrasya Etüdleri, 50*(2), 77–97.

Ecofin Agency. (2024, March 3). *China boosts investments in Africa to $29.2bn, up 34% in 2024.* Ecofin Agency. https://www.ecofinagency.com/finance/0303-46459-china-boosts-investments-in-africa-to-29-2bn-up-34-in-2024

Ergenç, C., & Göçer, D. (2023, May). *China's response to Turkey's volatile authoritarianism.* Carnegie Endowment for International Peace. https://carnegieendowment.org/research/2023/05/chinas-response-to-turkiyes-volatile-authoritarianism?lang=en

Ergunsü, U. (2015, June 10). *China's new Silk Road initiative attracts Turkey's attention.* Hürriyet Daily News. https://www.hurriyetdailynews.com/chinas-new-silk-road-initiative-attracts-turkeys-attention-78523

Escobar, A. (2012). *Encountering development: The making and unmaking of the Third World* (2nd ed.). Princeton University Press. DOI: 10.1515/9781400839926

Eser, E. (2023, March 20). *Bora böyle değer katacak.* Hürriyet. https://www.hurriyet.com.tr/ekonomi/bora-boyle-deger-katacak-42236993

Euronews. (2024, July 8). *Çinli elektrikli otomobil üreticisi BYD'den Türkiye'ye 1 milyar dolarlık yatırım.* Euronews. https://tr.euronews.com/business/2024/07/08/cinli-elektrikli-otomobil-ureticisi-bydden-turkiyeye-1-milyar-dolarlik-yatirim

Global, R. M. C. (2023). *Chinese Investment and Influence in Latin America and the Caribbean.* https://rmcglobal.com/chinese-investment-and-influence-in-latin-america-and-the-caribbean/

Global-Is-Asian Staff. (2024, April 24). *What does the rise of the Global South mean for the world?* Global-is-Asian. https://lkyspp.nus.edu.sg/gia/article/what-does-the-rise-of-the-global-south-mean-for-the-world

Gürel, B., & Kozluca, M. (2022). Chinese investment in Turkey: The Belt and Road Initiative, rising expectations and ground realities. *European Review (Chichester, England), 30*(6), 806–834. DOI: 10.1017/S1062798721000296

Hamsici, M. (2024, February 26). *Çin'in Türkiye'deki varlığı artıyor mu, Uygur meselesi gündemden düştü mü?* BBC Türkçe. https://www.bbc.com/turkce/articles/ce38wly3772o

Holding, G. A. M. A. (2019, August 5). *GAMA, Üç Katlı Büyük İstanbul Tüneli için Dünyanın En Büyük Firmalarından Çinli China Construction Third Engineering Bureau Co., Ltd ile Mutabakat Zaptı İmzaladı.* GAMA Holding. https://holding.gama.com.tr/tr/medya/haber/20013/

Hussain., ... (2021). Strategic implications of the Belt and Road Initiative. *Journal of Legal, Ethical and Regulatory Issues*, 27(1). https://www.abacademies.org/abstract/strategic-implications-of-the-belt-and-road-initiative-12801.html

Ikenberry, G. J. (2024). Three worlds: The West, East, and South and the competition to shape global order. *International Affairs, 100*(1), 121–141. DOI: 10.1093/ia/iiad284

İstikbal, . (2019). Dönüşen Dünya Düzeninde "Brics" Ve Türkiye'ye Etkisi. *Uluslararası Afro-Avrasya Araştırmaları Dergisi, 4*(7), 47–62.

Jütten, M. (2025). Expansion of BRICS: A quest for greater global influence? European Parliamentary Research Service. https://www.europarl.europa.eu/RegData/etudes/BRIE/2025/769504/EPRS_BRI%282025%29769504_EN.pdf

Kader, S. A. (2025, Şubat 28). *Middle East leads in China's Belt and Road Initiative with $39bln in investments*. Zawya. https://www.zawya.com/en/projects/construction/middle-east-leads-in-chinas-belt-and-road-initiative-with-39bln-in-investments-m7inkc16

Karagöl, E. T. (2017). Modern İpek Yolu Projesi. *Seta Perspektif*, 1-7. https://www.setav.org/assets/uploads/2017/05/174_Perspektif.pdf

Kaya, E. (2015). Dış Politika Değişimi: AKP Dönemi Türk Dış Politikası. *Karadeniz Sosyal Bilimler Dergisi, 7*(12), 72–92.

Kaya, M., & Arı, İ. (2021). Chinese Energy Investments in Turkey and Potential Investment Barriers. *Ulisa: Uluslararası Çalışmalar Dergisi, 5*(1), 1–19.

Keyman, F. (2024 January 16). *Batı sonrası dünya, stratejik otonomi ve Türk dış politikası*. Perspektif. https://www.perspektif.online/bati-sonrasi-dunya-stratejik-otonomi-ve-turk-dis-politikasi/

Keyman, F. (2024, Febuary 13). *Batı sonrası dünyada Türk dış politikası ve Türkiye meselesi*. Perspektif. https://www.perspektif.online/bati-sonrasi-dunyada-turk-dis-politikasi-ve-turkiye-meselesi

Keyman, F. (2024, May 7). *Batı-sonrası dünya, küresel Güney ve Türkiye: Nasıl bir stratejik otonomi?* Perspektif. https://www.perspektif.online/bati-sonrasi-dunya-kuresel-guney-ve-turkiye-nasil-bir-stratejik-otonomi/

Koçakoğlu, M. A. (2021). Belt And Road Initiative and Turkey China Relationships Through Soft Power Concept. *OPUS International Journal of Society Researches, 18*(39), 750–776. DOI: 10.26466/opus.831498

Kutlay, M. (2024). *21. yüzyılı kazanmak: Güç geçişleri döneminde küresel Güney ve Türkiye.* TÜSİAD Küresel Siyaset Forumu Makale Dizisi No. 7. https://tusiad.org/tr/yayinlar/raporlar/item/11667-tusi-ad-kuresel-siyaset-forumu-makale-dizisi-no-7-21-yuzyili-kazanmak-guc-gecisleri-doneminde-kuresel-guney-ve-turkiye

Madani, S. (2021). The BRI and its implications for China's energy security: The Four As Model Perspective. *International Journal of Energy Economics and Policy, 11*(4), 549–559. https://www.econjournals.com/index.php/ijeep/article/view/11221. DOI: 10.32479/ijeep.11221

Milliyet. (2022, December 29). *Hunutlu termik santrali açıldı.* Milliyet. https://www.milliyet.com.tr/ekonomi/milliyet-enerji/hunutlu-termik-santrali-acildi-6879815

Morvaridi, B., & Hughes, C. (2018). South-South cooperation and neoliberal hegemony in a post-aid world. *Development and Change, 49*(3), 867–892. DOI: 10.1111/dech.12405

Nedopil, C., ... (2023). China's investment in the Asia Pacific: 2023 report. Griffith Asia Institute. https://www.griffith.edu.au/__data/assets/pdf_file/0036/1932984/Nedopil_Zhang_Mi_China-Investment-in-the-Asia-Pacific_2023-Report.pdf

Nedopil Wang, C. (2024, February 5). *China Belt and Road Initiative (BRI) investment report 2023.* Green FDC. https://greenfdc.org/china-belt-and-road-initiative-bri-investment-report-2023/

NTV. (2015, May 25). *Tekstilbank artık resmen Çinli ICBC'nin Tekstilbank'ı satın alma işlemi tamamlandı.* NTV. https://www.ntv.com.tr/ekonomi/tekstilbank-artik-resmen-cinli,siJ49aFwUkiYo87vAbE0AQ

OECD. (2010). *Perspectives on global development 2010: Shifting wealth.* OECD. https://www.oecd.org/content/dam/oecd/en/publications/reports/2010/06/perspectives-on-global-development-2010_g1ghcb1a/9789264084728-en.pdf

Oğuzlu, H. T. (2019). Turkish foreign policy in a changing world order. All Azimuth: A Journal of Foreign Policy and Peace, 9(1), 127–139. https://doi.org/DOI: 10.20991/allazimuth.464076

Öniş, Z. (2012). Turkey and the Arab Spring: Between ethics and self-interest. *Insight Turkey, 14*(3), 45–63.

Öniş, Z., & Yalikun, M. (2021). Emerging partnership in a post-Western world? The political economy of China-Turkey relations. *Southeast European and Black Sea Studies, 21*(4), 507–529. DOI: 10.1080/14683857.2021.1981624

Oran, B. (2013). Dönemin dış politikası. In B. Oran (Ed.), *Türk dış politikası, kurtuluş savaşından bugüne olgular, belgeler, yorumlar* (Vol. 3, pp. 70-248, 2nd ed.). İletişim Yayınları.

Özdaşlı, E. (2015). Çin'in Yeni İpek Yolu Projesi ve Küresel Etkileri. *Turkish Studies, 10*(14), 579–596. DOI: 10.7827/TurkishStudies.8879

Öztürk, S. (2012, March 6). *Bu savaşta biz de varız.* Hürriyet. https://www.hurriyet.com.tr/teknoloji/bu-savasta-biz-de-variz-20060914

Patrick, S., & Huggins, A. (2023, August 15). *The term "Global South" is surging. It should be retired.* Carnegie Endowment for International Peace. Retrieved from https://carnegieendowment.org/posts/2023/08/the-term-global-south-is-surging-it-should-be-retired?lang=en

Patterson, S. (2024, March 26). *The BRI at 10: A report card from the Global South.* AidData. https://www.aiddata.org/blog/the-bri-at-10-a-report-card-from-the-global-south

Pu, X. (2016). One Belt, One Road: Visions and challenges of China's geoeconomic strategy. *Mainland China Studies, 59*(3), 111–132.

Republic of Türkiye Ministry of Foreign Affairs. (n.d. a). *MIKTA: A Partnership for Progress.*https://www.mfa.gov.tr/mikta-_meksika_-endonezya_-kore_-avustralya_.en.mfa

Republic of Türkiye Ministry of Foreign Affairs. (n.d. b). *Asia Anew Initiative.* https://www.mfa.gov.tr/asia-anew-initiative.en.mfa

Rist, G. (2019). *The history of development: From Western origins to global faith* (5th ed.). Zed Books.

Saad-Filho, A. (2013). The 'Rise of the South': Global Convergence at Last? *New Political Economy, 19*(4), 578–600. DOI: 10.1080/13563467.2013.829432

Sabah Gazetesi. (2017, August 3). *Çinli dev ZTE, NetAş'ın ortağı oldu.* Sabah Gazetesi. https://www.sabah.com.tr/ekonomi/2017/08/03/cinli-dev-zte-netasin-ortagi-oldu

Sheng, L., & Nascimento, D. F. (2021). The Belt and Road Initiative (BRI): The SSC (SSC) with Chinese Characteristics. In *The Belt and Road Initiative in South–South Cooperation*(pp. 1-44). Palgrave Macmillan, Singapore. https://doi.org/DOI: 10.1007/978-981-16-6357-4_1

Sidiropoulos, E. (2012). South Africa: Development, international cooperation and soft power. In S. Chaturvedi, T. Fues, & E. Sidiropoulos (Eds.), *Development cooperation and emerging powers: New partners or old patterns*? (pp. 216–242). Zed Books.

Stuenkel, O. (2016). *Post-Western world: How emerging powers are remaking global order*. Polity Press.

Tekdal, V. (2019). Çin'in Kuşak ve Yol Girişimi ve Türkiye. In Yağcı, M., & Bakır, C. (Eds.), *Çin bilmecesi: Çin'in ekonomik yükselişi, uluslararası ilişkilerde dönüşüm ve Türkiye* (pp. 125–142). Koç Üniversitesi Yayınları.

Tekin, S., & Dolu, M. T. (2020). Güney-Güney İşbirliğinin İdeolojik Temelleri: Bağlantısızlar Hareketi ve Küresel Güney. *Dicle Üniversitesi Sosyal Bilimler Enstitüsü Dergisi*, (24), 65–81.

The Economist. (2023, September 21). *China wants to be the leader of the Global South*. The Economist. https://www.economist.com/china/2023/09/21/china-wants-to-be-the-leader-of-the-global-south

Topçu, E. F. (2018, March 16). *1915 Çanakkale Köprüsü ve Otoyolu Projesi'ne 2,265 milyar Avro finansman*. Anadolu Agency. https://www.aa.com.tr/tr/isdunyasi/finans/1915-canakkale-koprusu-ve-otoyolu-projesine-2-265-milyar-avro-finansman/644036

Toptaş, M. C. (2024, July 25). *Çin menşeli otomobil ithalatında gümrük vergisi düzenlemesi*. Anadolu Ajansı. https://www.aa.com.tr/tr/ekonomi/cin-menseli-otomobil-ithalatinda-gumruk-vergisi-duzenlemesi/3266667

TÜİK. (n.d.). *Dış ticaret*. TÜİK. https://data.tuik.gov.tr/Kategori/GetKategori?p=Dis-Ticaret-104

Türkçe, B. B. C. (2023, June 10). *Rusya'da BRICS+ toplantısına katılan Fidan, Putin ile görüştü*. BBC Türkçe. https://www.bbc.com/turkce/articles/c511xq07kxyo

Türkçe, B. B. C. (2024, September 4). *Dışişleri Bakanı Fidan'dan BRICS üyeliği açıklaması: AB üyeliğimiz olsaydı belki de bu arayış içinde olmazdık*. BBC Türkçe. https://www.bbc.com/turkce/articles/cy54v7rxledo

Türkiye Cumhuriyeti Dışişleri Bakanlığı. (2025). Belirsizlikler çağında kararlı ve güçlü Türk dış politikası. https://www.mfa.gov.tr/site_media/html/belirsizlikler-caginda-kararli-ve-guclu-turk-dis-politikasi-2025-kitapcik.pdf

Ülgen, S., & Umarov, T. (2024, October 17). Transatlantic policies on China: Is there a role for Türkiye? Carnegie Endowment for International Peace. https://carnegieendowment.org/research/2024/10/transatlantic-policies-on-china-is-there-a-role-for-turkiye?lang=en

Uluyol, Y. (2024, March 20). Partnership with limits: China-Turkey relations in the late AKP era. Heinrich Böll Stiftung. https://tr.boell.org/en/2024/03/20/partnership-limits-china-turkey-relations-late-akp-era

Ünal, E. C. (2023, September 22). Uzak ülkeler stratejisi ile ihracatta sürdürülebilir artış sağlanıyor. Anadolu Agency. https://www.aa.com.tr/tr/ekonomi/uzak-ulkeler-stratejisi-ile-ihracatta-surdurulebilir-artis-saglaniyor-/2998528

Üngör, Ç. (2024, February 28). İki cihan arasında Türkiye: Jeopolitik açıdan Çin'in yükselişi ve Batı'nın cevabı. Heinrich Böll Stiftung. https://tr.boell.org/tr/2024/02/28/iki-cihan-arasinda-turkiye-jeopolitik-acidan-cinin-yukselisi-ve-batinin-cevabi

UNOSSC. (2022). *South-South cooperation in action.* United Nations Office for South-South Cooperation. https://www.unsouthsouth.org/about/about-south-south-cooperation/

Uzgel, İ. (2013). ABD ve NATO'yla ilişkiler. In B. Oran (Ed.), *Türk dış politikası, kurtuluş savaşından bugüne olgular, belgeler, yorumlar* (Vol. 3, pp. 249-336, 2nd ed.). İletişim Yayınları.

Véron, N. (2023, March 8). *How much of the Global South is on Ukraine's side?* Peterson Institute for International Economics. https://www.piie.com/blogs/realtime-economics/2023/much-global-south-ukraines-side

Xiao, E. (2024, October, 18). China-Turkey bilateral trade and investment profile. China Briefing. https://www.china-briefing.com/news/china-turkey-bilateral-trade-and-investment-profile/

Xin, Z. (2023, February 9). *No damage to China-operated power plant in Turkiye.* China Daily. https://www.chinadaily.com.cn/a/202302/09/WS63e4aee4a31057c47ebade71.html

Yalçın, H. B. (2011). Türkiye'nin 'Yeni' Dış Politika Eğilim ve Davranışları: Yapısal Realist Bir Okuma. *Bilgi Sosyal Bilimler Dergisi*, (2), 35–61.

Yılmaz, S. (2020). Bir Kuşak Bir Yol Projesinin Azerbaycan, Kazakistan ve Türkiye'ye Etkisi. *OPUS International Journal of Society Researches*, *16*(32), 5274–5301. DOI: 10.26466/opus.774914

Yinanç, B. (2024, September 16). *DEİK'ten BRICS yorumu ve Çin uyarısı: Kuşak Yol ne kadar lehimize?* T24. https://t24.com.tr/yazarlar/barcin-yinanc/deik-ten-brics-yorumu-ve-cin-uyarisi-kusak-yol-ne-kadar-lehimize,46376

Yurdakul, A. (2025, January 28). *Çin, NATO, AB: Trump'ın yeni döneminde ekonomi ve jeopolitik nasıl şekillenecek?* BBC Türkçe. https://www.bbc.com/turkce/articles/cgly18x18kyo

Zhao, M. (2024). The belt & road initiative and U.S.-China competition over the global South. *China Economic Journal, 17*(2), 166–181. DOI: 10.1080/17538963.2024.2344270

Zhou, G. (2024). Rise of the Global South and changes in contemporary international order. China International Strategy Review, 1-20. https://doi.org/DOI: 10.1007/s42533-024-00160-x

Zhou, T., & Haibing, Z. (2019). China's Belt and Road Initiative: An Opportunity to Re-energize SSC. *China Quarterly of International Strategic Studies, 4*(4), 1–18.

Ziai, A. (2016). *Development discourse and global history: From colonialism to the sustainable development goals* (1st ed.). Routledge.

Chapter 3
China – Global South: Current Evolution of Political and Economic Relations

Nika Chitadze
https://orcid.org/0000-0003-2806-6426
International Black Sea University, Georgia

ABSTRACT

Abstract Global events of recent years indicate that it is the turn of the developing world to take the lead in international relations (IR). China, which positions itself as the "largest developing country", and "member of the Global South", but at the same time "a responsible world power", cannot remain on the sidelines of this trend. The chapter states the reasons for the recent advancement of the developing world (RW) to the forefront of international life, which include the combined economic growth of the South, the increase in its political significance in the balance of power on the world stage, and the growth of the South's self-esteem. In addition, the author believes it is essential to determine the interpretation of the terms "Global South", "Third World", and "Developing World" to come closer to a better understanding of the essence of the excellent world phenomenon that these definitions denote.

INTRODUCTION

Transformations of world politics at the present stage are closely connected with transformations in the world economy, connected with dynamic processes, occurring, first of all, in trade and economics, transport and logistics, scientific and technological, and demographic spheres. Changes, occurring in the structure of international economic relations, are manifested in crisis processes in the world economy, changes in the ratio of potentials of developed and developing countries,

DOI: 10.4018/979-8-3373-0938-5.ch003

intensification of rivalry between transnational companies, as well as competitive interaction of industrial, financial and digital capitals, restructuring of transport and logistics trade routes. These processes influence foreign and domestic policies of international actors. In this regard, international researchers are increasingly turning to the study of significant economic factors, influencing the transformation of international relations and world politics at the present stage. An important theoretical and methodological basis of these studies is the geoeconomic approach.

This approach allows us to study current international processes taking into account the conjugation of such key areas for the global economy and world politics as space, territory, resources, energy, companies, production, capital, trade, finance, logistics, infrastructure, and security. The geoeconomic approach in international political studies is in demand when studying the influence of various spatial economic and political phenomena on the development of international relations, including international economic projects, economic initiatives, regional integration structures, and transregional economic and technological partnerships (Stoletov, 2024).

An important concept for the geoeconomic approach in modern international political studies is the concept of the "Global South". The key direction of such scientific developments is the problem of interaction between the countries of the Global South, as well as building relations between the states of the Global South and the Global North at a new historical stage. A significant area of research within the framework of the geoeconomic approach is the study of international relations in the context of the modernization transition of the states of the Global South, expanding the use of technologies of the Fourth Industrial Revolution.

In modern studies devoted to current issues of development of the Global South, priority attention is given to the Chinese factor, which at the turn of the mid-2000s began to occupy a fundamentally new position in the world economy and world politics. It seems possible to distinguish two possible approaches to interpreting China's interaction with the countries of the Global South in the economic sphere.

The first approach is based on China's official positioning of itself as the largest developing country that is part of the Global South and acts in its interests. This approach, promoted by the PRC at the diplomatic level, is reflected primarily in the works of Chinese researchers.

Within the framework of the second approach, prevailing among Western researchers, China is viewed as a great power with the potential to achieve global economic hegemony, competing with other centers of the world economy and striving in foreign economic policy and more broadly to maximize the promotion of its national interests (Stoletov, 2024).

Main aspects of the development Relations between the People`s Republic of China and Global South Countries

The PRC has demonstrated a high interest in cooperation with the Global South, once called the "Third World" and later matured into the "Developing World" (DW), ever since its proclamation in 1949. China's economic development has been taking place with the extensive use of the resource potential of that part of the Earth that is now preferably called the Global South. The political support of "friends from the developing world" since the restoration of China's rights in the UN continues to contribute to the ennobling of the country's international image and the strengthening of its global position. China's position as the world's second economy does not prevent it from calling itself a state of the Global South (Stoletov, 2024).

The PRC's self-identification as a developing country and skillful rhetoric on this matter have allowed it to establish a special tone in relations with the "southern" states. The main emphasis in propaganda aimed at the developing world is on stating the commonality of tasks facing China and other non-Western countries. The key one is the promotion of a new multipolar world order. During contacts between the top leaders of the countries of the South and China, the parties, as a rule, emphasize the commonality of positions on the rejection of "hegemonism", noting their commitment to multipolarity and democratization of international relations. It should be noted that for the developing world, China is an objective example of effective growth achieved in a historically short period - since the beginning of its economic reforms (late 1970s). And the Chinese case suggests that to develop dynamically, the South simply needs to know where to start. Namely, it needs to find a model of socio-economic development (MSED) that would not only hypothetically meet its desire for a better life, but also be based on its specific domestic and international realities. After all, it is precisely those countries that have acquired a "working" ISE adequate to their conditions, as well as effective political and economic levers for managing their national economy that are breaking into the ranks of countries with emerging economies (previously called newly industrialized countries). These levers should include the establishment of legal and tax regimes that are favorable to domestic accumulation and the attraction of foreign capital, measures to protect foreign investment and strictly control the use of earmarked funds, the implementation of rational financial, economic, and budgetary policies, structural reforms, the strengthening of state institutions, etc. On the issue of interpreting terms Let us begin with the fact that the world is an eternal "mosaic" of living standards. This mosaic is illustrated by the differences in the socio-economic development of the two main "poles" - the "golden billion" (the "developed world", the Global North) and the "third world", the "developing world", the "Global South". These differences are manifested not only in the economic gap between the two "poles", but also in the level of political stability, the presence of traditional and non-traditional threats, access to modern technologies, work, education, health care, etc. The term "Third World" in the Chinese interpretation appeared in the late 1960s and until the early

1970s denoted a group of "poor and developing countries" that were waging an increasing struggle with two "superpowers", which, according to the then Premier of the PRC Zhou Enlai, was the main feature of international politics (Chitadze, 2024). The harbinger of the Chinese version of the "Third World" concept was the theory of "people's war", outlined in the fall of 1965 in Lin Biao's article "Long Live the Victory of the People's War!" (Chitadze, 2011). The article described the international situation as the "encirclement of the world city" (imperialist states, which already included the USSR) by the "world village" (less developed, formerly colonial countries). The article called for the "world village" to unite against the "world city" and to carry out a "world revolution" to victory through a "people's war" (Chitadze, 2011). In his speech at a special session of the UN General Assembly on April 10, 1974, Deng Xiaoping clarified the balance of power, noting that "the United States and the Soviet Union constitute the First World. The developing countries in Asia, Africa, Latin America, and other regions constitute the Third World. The developed countries in between constitute the Second World" (Rondeli, 2003).

At that time, practical and research understanding of the realities of the "third world" took place in the context of the extreme ideological nation of international relations, which is why the "third world" became the designation of a group of countries that were not only economically less developed but also opposed to the world "hegemons". Later, in the 1980s, when the intensity of the global ideological struggle somewhat decreased, the "third world" received the designation "developing", in which the emphasis was placed on the desire for economic growth, and not on the political struggle. Nowadays, in scientific literature and the media, the term "developing world", according to our observations, is being supplanted by the definition of the "Global South" (UN, 2005). This is happening because the concept of the "developing world" has a persistent "material" coloring, denoting a set of less successful subjects of international economic relations. Now, the fact of precisely political disagreements in the dichotomous structure of international relations, associated with inequality and marginalization of the "southern" countries relative to the "northern" ones, is again becoming relevant. The idea of uniting developing countries based on an energetic rejection of Western dictates and their collective struggle for real participation in global decision-making processes is gaining primary importance. Thus, the developing world is being transformed into the Global South – an IR subject building up strategic "muscles" that neither developing countries nor the "Third World" had. However, the author considers it acceptable to use the term "developing world" where it is logically and stylistically appropriate. In Chinese political science, the concepts of "Global South" and "developing world" coexist, being equal in significance and breadth of use. It is noteworthy that a dual approach to the term "Global South" has been noticed in the Chinese academic community. In a political sense, Chinese scholars consider it a useful tool, but in an economic sense they believe that it would be more accurate to classify countries based on the size of their income (countries with either high, middle, or low income) (Chitadze, 2011). It seems that such an economically determined ranking conflicts with the position of Chinese official diplomacy, which emphasizes the geopolitical views of the states of the South. The term "Global South" itself is not perfect: it is controversial due to the uncertainty of its geographical boundaries (for example, the developing countries of Central Asia are located significantly to the north of developed Japan). The uneven political and economic dynamics of the states included in the Global South cast doubt on its interpretation as a single whole. However, in our opinion, a sign of its integrity should be sought more broadly: countries should be classified as Global South not so much by their level of "development", but by the degree of their readiness to build a new world order that rejects the international regime, based, as they believe, on Western "rules". The fates of the global North and South have always been inextricably linked according to the law of dialectics on the unity and struggle of opposites, and in its Chinese interpretation - the yin-yang construction. However, in recent years, unprecedented phenomena such as the migration and climate crisis, the growth of hot spots in the Republic of Moldova, and finally the COVID-19 pandemic have led to the consequences of political decisions taken almost single-handedly by the North having a disproportionate impact on the Global South (Nye, 2023). This in itself has led to a shift in the focus of global attention towards the aggravated problems of the South. A powerful trigger for the rise of the Global South to the forefront of the world has been the reluctance of most of its members to support the policy of "containing China". In total, many developing countries contribute to China's consolidation in the Global South. Thus, in 2021, China invested more in Latin America than in the United States, and about the same as in Europe. International experts believe that this happened because the United States and Europe themselves are closing themselves off to Chinese capital investment, fearing the growth of Chinese influence in their economic field. And because China has "very high savings rates," its investment in the Global South could resume growth in the coming years (IGI Global, 2022).

The Global South is boosting its "self-esteem". If earlier it saw the prerequisite for a more just world order in the expansion of cooperation along two lines – both "South-South" and "North-South", now it is inclined to see it in its own political and economic successes. This is understandable: the countries of the South provide more than 70% of the growth of the world economy, mainly due to the potential of China. It can be said that it was China, as well as India, that made the rise of the South a real phenomenon. The two countries doubled their per capita production in less than 20 years. If in 1950 the share of China, India, and Brazil was only 10% of the world production, while the share of the industrial leaders of the "North" exceeded half, today the South accounts for about 50% of the world GDP and about half of the total volume of international trade (Chitadze, 2024). In the 1970s and 1980s, The South's share in global trade flows did not exceed 20%, but now it is determined to be between 40 and 50% (Chitadze, 2024).

CHINA'S GEOECONOMIC STRATEGY IN THE CONTEXT OF THE "AWAKENING" OF THE GLOBAL SOUTH

"Awakening" of the Global South: Factors, Manifestations, and Risks

In this study, the "awakening" of the Global South refers to the growth of foreign economic and foreign policy activity of key developing countries that began in the late 2000s and early 2010s, aimed at strengthening their economic and political positions in the international system in the long term.

It is necessary to point out that China Announced the Establishment of a Global South Center to Support African Development. The center will develop strategies to promote progress in the continent's countries.

The head of the Development Research Center of the State Council of China Lu Hao said that the Chinese side intends to establish a Global South Center to stimulate interaction between northern and southern countries and promote the exchange of experience. This was reported by Fana Media Corporation (FMC), a partner of the BRICS TV network.

Lu Hao made the corresponding statement after a meeting with Ethiopian Finance Minister Ahmed Shide. During the talks, the president of the Development Research Center of the State Council of China also noted that at the third summit of the Forum on China-Africa Cooperation (FOCAC), Beijing supported dialogue between experts from think tanks to develop public policies in Africa.

Speaking about establishing the Global South Center, Lu Hao stressed that this institution will become a platform for expanding international ties and strengthening cooperation between developing countries. In addition, the center will develop political strategies aimed at supporting progress in African countries.

In turn, Ahmed Sheed pointed out the importance of creating this center for global development. He also noted that China's economic ties with Ethiopia and Africa as a whole contribute to the continent's growth (TV BRICS, 2025).

On March 7, 2025, at a press conference as part of the "two sessions", Member of the Politburo of the CPC Central Committee and Foreign Minister Wang Yi outlined China's position on cooperation with the Global South (Embassy of People`s Republic of China in Belarus, 2025).

In an era of great change, the rise of the Global South is one of the main megatrends of modern international relations and, perhaps, the most striking feature of our time. The countries of the Global South account for more than 40% of the world's GDP, they make up 4/5 of global growth and serve as one of the key factors in maintaining international peace, development, and improving global governance (Embassy of People`s Republic of China in Belarus, 2025). In the context of profound transformations unseen in a century, the balance of power in the world is undergoing historic changes in favor of the East and the South. How sustainably and successfully the world will develop will largely depend on the Global South.

The Global South must confidently strive forward. Since the beginning of this year, Indonesia has become a full member of BRICS, and 9 more partner countries have joined the association's family. Today, BRICS positions itself as a pillar of cooperation in the Global South and a driver of its growth. It is important to make "Greater BRICS" even more robust, thereby providing inexhaustible strength for the further development of the Global South. The Global South must act in solidarity. This year, the SCO summit will be held in China, and Brazil and South Africa will host the BRICS and G20 summits, respectively (Embassy of People`s Republic of China in Belarus, 2025). On the world stage, the countries of the Global South must act in solidarity, protect common interests, and tirelessly expand their representation and voice in global governance. The Global South must strive for development. Last November, President Xi Jinping announced China's 8 actions in the field of international development, which served as an additional impetus for the accelerated development of the Global South (Embassy of People`s Republic of China in Belarus, 2025). We must put development at the center of the global agenda, cultivate growth drivers, strengthen development potential, and move shoulder-to-shoulder along the path of modernization. China is naturally part of the Global South, where all countries are united not only by the common historical memory of the struggle against colonialism and hegemony but also by the same mission of national renaissance. No matter how the world changes, China will always care for the Global South, remain steadfast in it, and stand with other partners in opening a new chapter in the annals of the Global South.

We associate the beginning of the process of "awakening" of the Global South with the reaction of developing countries to the global financial and economic crisis of 2008, which called into question the leading role of developed countries in the global economy. Against the backdrop of the global financial crisis, China's position in the global economy has strengthened. It is significant that in January 2009, at a conference in Beijing dedicated to the 30th anniversary of the establishment of diplomatic relations between the United States and China, Zb., representing the American delegation, Brzezinski proposed joint leadership of the United States and China in the "Big Two" format (Junbo, 2009). At the same time, there was an intensification of interaction between China, India, Brazil, and Russia. In June 2009, the first BRICS summit was held in Yekaterinburg, and in December 2010, South Africa joined this international association (The BRICS Interstate Group, 2020).

At the turn of the 2000s and 2010s, there was an intensification of regional integration processes within the Association of Southeast Asian Nations (ASEAN), the Organization of Turkic States, and the Community of Latin American and Caribbean States, which unites the countries of the Global South, which are located in the Western Hemisphere.

In these conditions, the Belt and Road Initiative, announced in September 2013 by Chinese President Xi Jinping, has become an important component of the "awakening" of the Global South and, at the same time, has allowed many developing countries to rethink their role in regional and global economic processes in the medium and long term (Gong Jian, 2023).

At the present stage, the following seem to be among the significant factors stimulating the "awakening" of the Global South:

- increasing global economic turbulence, manifested in financial, economic, and energy crises;
- promoting the international energy transition agenda and reducing investment in hydrocarbon energy amid the growing energy needs of developing countries;
- increasing US-China strategic rivalry and economic "decoupling" between the US and China, escalating into a "US-China Cold War" (Brands, 2022);
- growing threat of technological neocolonialism;
- negative consequences of environmental and climatic processes, exacerbating socio-economic contradictions in many countries of the world;
- increasing global economic importance of Eurasia, caused by growing geo-economic and geopolitical competition in the sphere of transport, logistics, and trade routes, primarily in the Asia-Pacific and Indian Ocean regions;
- escalation of regional armed conflicts and growing global military-political tensions;
- difficult to predict risks of disruption of communication connectivity.

Considering global international trade as an environment that contributes to increasing the level of their well-being, the states of the Global South demonstrate an interest in developing the process of globalization and reducing the costs of "limited deglobalization". This attitude is manifested in the active participation of the states of the Global South in regional and transregional international associations and agreements on free trade zones, and international banks, as well as in the work of global forums. At the same time, the states of the Global South are increasingly focused on protecting their national interests, which is reflected in the diversification of foreign policy interactions and the formation of "flexible" international partnerships, including along the South-South line. Many states of the Global South are seeking to modernize their national economies without destroying the civilizational foundations of their countries.

China's Approach to the "Awakening" of the Global South

Chinese researchers Niu Haibin, Zhou Yuyuan, Lai Yuan, Li Yanliang, and Zhou Shengsheng, representing the Shanghai Institute of International Studies, in their work "The Rise of the Global South and the Role of China" link the increasing international significance of the Global South with the growing influence of developing countries on the world economy. The study notes that their contribution to global GDP has increased from 37% in the 1980s to 58.8% in 2023 (Niu Haibin, 2023). At the same time, the expected rates of economic growth of the countries of the Global South significantly exceed those of developed countries. The work indicates that the key incentive that prompted the countries of the Global South to sharply increase their international activity was the "imbalance in global governance" in the context of exacerbating global problems. The peculiarity of the current state of the Global South, according to Chinese researchers, is due to the increasing polycentricity of the global system.

The PRC views the strengthening of South-South cooperation as a necessary stage in the development of the Global South. An important place in this cooperation is given to China itself, its projects, and initiatives. In our opinion, China perceives the increasing role of the Global South in the world economy as the basis for the overdue transformation of globalization. China's positioning of itself as part of the Global South allows it to interpret its achievements as achievements of the Global South as a whole. At the same time, cooperation within the Global South with the active role of the PRC is viewed by the actors in this process from the position of more effective progress towards the implementation of the UN Sustainable Development Goals.

It seems that, as part of its geo-economic strategy, China is strengthening its focus on interaction with developing countries. This is evidenced by China's strategic documents on developing relations with the main regions of the Global South: China's Policy Towards Arab States (2016) (The State Council of the People's Republic of China, 2016), China's Policy Document on Latin America and the Caribbean (2016) (The State Council of the People's Republic of China, 2016), the White Paper "China and Africa in a New Era: Partnership of Equals" (2021) (The State Council of the People's Republic of China, 2021), "Vision for China-Africa Cooperation until 2035" (2021) (Secretariat of the Chinese Follow-up Committee of the Forum on China — Africa Cooperation, 2021), and the Xi'an Declaration (2023) (News Central Asia, 2023). It is important to emphasize that a number of these documents focus on the joint promotion of the Belt and Road initiative, as well as the alignment of this initiative with the national development strategies of China's partner countries. In addition, official documents emphasize China's desire to develop interaction with key integration associations of the Global South countries in a wide range of promising areas of economic and technological cooperation. Thus, China demonstrates interest in developing documents aimed at intensifying relations with developing countries in the long term.

It seems possible to consider the development of the Shanghai Cooperation Organization (SCO) and BRICS as an important component of China's geo-economic strategy to expand multilateral interaction with the countries of the Global South. In particular, China supports the expansion of these international associations.

At the same time, China actively supported the decision to include the African Union (AU) in the G20, adopted following the 18th G20 summit, held in September 2023 in New Delhi (China Daily, 2023). The synchronicity of the expansion of interaction between African countries and BRICS (African Business, 2024), as well as the enhancement of the international status of the African Union, which was manifested in the inclusion of the AU in the G20, is indicative.

Main Dimensions of China's Geoeconomic Strategy

Within the framework of China's geoeconomic strategy, it is possible to identify several dimensions: diplomatic, trade and economic, financial, energy, resource, transport and logistics, scientific and technological, and digital. These dimensions of China's geoeconomic strategy, in essence, correlate with its national security priorities.

Within the framework of the diplomatic dimension of the geoeconomic strategy, the People's Republic of China is increasingly active in the Near and Middle East. Thus, China and its strategic partner Pakistan are positioning the China-Pakistan Economic Corridor (CPEC) as an open and inclusive platform for mutually beneficial cooperation. It should be noted that back in the second half of the 2010s, Iran and Saudi Arabia received invitations from Pakistan to join CPEC (The Diplomat, 2019). Being interested in the development of CPEC, China seeks to align the economic interests of Pakistan, Iran, and Saudi Arabia.

On the diplomatic track of China's geoeconomic strategy, a significant event was the expansion of BRICS, as a result of which Egypt, Iran, the UAE, and Ethiopia officially joined BRICS on January 1, 2024 (El Dahan, 2024). The process of Saudi Arabia's integration into BRICS continues. It is assumed that the expansion of this international association will increase the authority of BRICS in the Global South, as well as intensify cooperation between BRICS member states in the financial sector. In particular, this concerns an increase in the assets of the New Development Bank, established by the BRICS countries in 2014 (The New Development Bank, 2024). In addition, it is envisaged that within the framework of the "expanded" BRICS, work will be intensified to create its international payment system. The political risks for the implementation of China's geoeconomic strategy in the countries of the Global South may be quite high. In the 2010s, The Arab Spring and its consequences, and the increased political and economic pressure from the United States and its allies on the Islamic Republic of Iran became a challenge for China. In the first half of the 2020s, a high level of instability manifested itself in the Sahel region, and in October 2023, there was a sharp aggravation of the Palestinian-Israeli conflict. The PRC reacts quite cautiously to political crises in various regions of the world. In particular, while opposing unconstitutional changes of power in African countries, the PRC does not seek to pedal its position on the domestic political situation in African states that have experienced military coups. In the trade and economic dimension of the geoeconomic strategy, it is significant to use mechanisms that allow China to increase bilateral trade with priority foreign partners located along the routes of the mega-project "Maritime Silk Road of the 21st Century". In particular, the United Arab Emirates (UAE) has a China-UAE Industrial Cooperation Demonstration Zone located at Khalifa Port in Abu Dhabi. In 2013, the Chinese company Shanghai Decent Investment Group Co. Ltd. and the Indonesian company Bintang Delapan Group signed an agreement to establish the China-Indonesian Economic and Trade Cooperation Zone Indonesia Morowali Industrial Park, which is engaged in the mining and processing of nickel, chromium, and iron ore. In February 2022, China and Pakistan signed a framework agreement on industrial cooperation in the context of the China-Pakistan Economic Corridor project (Pakistan Today, 2022), confirming the priority of developing 9 special economic zones of the CPEC in Pakistan. Special economic zones, which China began to create in the second half of the 2000s, play a significant role in China's trade and economic cooperation with African countries. The Arab Republic of Egypt and the Federal Democratic Republic of Ethiopia, as the largest economies in Africa, are the gateways to the African continent for China. To develop trade and economic cooperation with Egypt, China uses the China-Egypt Economic and Trade Cooperation Area, which was launched in 2008 and expanded in 2016 (Mo et al., 2023). At the same time, China is the largest foreign investor in the Suez Canal Economic Zone, established in 2015 (China Daily, 2017). China has been developing trade and economic cooperation with Ethiopia for a long time through special economic zones. In particular, in 2009, through the efforts of the two countries, the Eastern Industrial Zone was launched, which became the first in this African country (AidData, 2024). In August 2023, the Chinese company China Civil Engineering Construction Corporation signed an agreement on the joint development of the Gada Special Economic Zone in Ethiopia (Media and Communications Center, 2023). The creation of special economic zones in African countries contributes to the transformation of these countries into production centers of the African continent. By 2023, with the participation of the PRC, a total of 25 economic and trade cooperation zones were launched in Africa (Yankova, 2023). In terms of establishing free trade areas with ASEAN countries as part of the Global South, a significant step for China was the signing of the Regional Comprehensive Economic Partnership (RCEP) in November 2020, which entered into force on January 1, 2022 (Asian Development Bank, 2022).

Since 2004, China has been negotiating a free trade area with the Gulf Cooperation Council (GCC). By 2023, China and the GCC had reached an agreement on most issues related to trade in goods and had also begun negotiations on trade in services (The State Council of the People's Republic of China, 2023).

At the same time, prospects for liberalization of international trade in the Global South may be associated with the development of economic cooperation within the framework of the expanded BRICS and BRICS+ (Chitadze, 2024).

In the financial dimension of the geo-economic strategy, China has consistently pursued a policy of internationalizing the renminbi as a key currency for trade with countries in the Global South. In 2009, China first allowed trade payments to be settled in the renminbi (Nabar, 2024). In 2015, China launched the Cross-Border Interbank Payment System (CIPS) (SWIFT, 2024). In August 2015, the share of the renminbi in international payments made through the SWIFT system was 2.79%, which allowed the renminbi to overtake the Japanese yen for the first time in history (Sibos Issues, 2015). As of September 2023, the share of the renminbi in international payments made through the SWIFT system was already 5.8%, which allowed the renminbi to overtake the euro for the first time (SWIFT, 2023). It is significant that in March 2023, China and Brazil reached an agreement on yuan trade and also announced the establishment of a joint clearing house.

A way to internationalize the yuan is the conclusion in 2022 of an agreement initiated by the People's Bank of China to establish a yuan liquidity pool, in which, in particular, the Central Bank of Indonesia became a participant (Reuters, 2022).

In November 2023, the People's Bank of China and the Central Bank of the UAE extended the currency swap agreement worth US$4.89 billion for 5 years and also signed a memorandum of understanding to expand cooperation on the development of a digital currency. In addition, the Dubai Financial Market signed a memorandum of understanding with the Nasdaq Dubai International Exchange and the Shanghai Stock Exchange covering various areas of digital financial cooperation. In November 2023, the People's Bank of China and the National Bank of Saudi Arabia signed a US$6.98 billion currency swap agreement for 3 years, with the possibility of extension by mutual agreement (East Asia Forum, 2024).

China is seeking to expand the use of the yuan in commodity markets. In April 2015, the Qatar Central Bank and the Industrial and Commercial Bank of China announced the formal launch of a yuan clearinghouse for banks (Reuters, 2015). In 2018, China established the Shanghai International Energy Exchange, which is denominated in yuan, to trade commodities with suppliers from countries such as Iran. Significantly, in March 2023, China made its first-ever purchase of liquefied natural gas (LNG) from the UAE paid for in yuan (Global Times, 2023). Thus, the share of the yuan in international settlements is gradually increasing.

The volume of Chinese investment in the economies of the Global South participating in the Belt and Road Initiative may change over time, depending on the domestic political situation in these countries, as well as on the evolving international conditions. For example, from 2000 to 2021, the Islamic Republic of Pakistan was the largest recipient of Chinese investment (Dawn, 2023). Only from 2022 onwards, amid political instability in Pakistan, did Chinese investment in CPEC projects begin to decline. Under the 2021 Iran-China Strategic Agreement, China committed to invest US$400 billion in Iran's economy over 25 years in exchange for continued supplies of Iranian oil (Madanı, 2022). At the same time, China has been steadily increasing its investment in the Kingdom of Saudi Arabia. Following Chinese President Xi Jinping's visit to Saudi Arabia in December 2022, agreements were reached to sign investment agreements worth approximately US$50 billion (Asia House, 2023). Egypt is also a major recipient of Chinese investment, with much of Chinese finance going to the Egyptian industrial sector.

The goal-setting of the energy dimension of China's geoeconomic strategy has traditionally been associated with ensuring the diversification of energy supplies while simultaneously increasing its energy production capabilities. Given that Saudi Arabia and the UAE are among the main oil suppliers to China, the special importance of these countries for China should be taken into account. Since 2005, high-level meetings of the China-Organization of the Petroleum Exporting Countries (OPEC) energy dialogue have been held (OPEC, 2005). In March 2023, Saudi Arabia's Aramco and China's NORINCO Group signed an agreement to begin construction of a large integrated oil refining and petrochemical complex in northeast China (Azam, 2022). Iran is also a significant partner of China in the energy sector. Over the past decade, China has purchased 90% of Iran's oil exports (The Economist, 2024). The energy potential of the Islamic Republic of Iran is also important for China in terms of Iran's ability to ensure Pakistan's energy security.

The importance of African countries in the hydrocarbon sector for China is because these countries have a predominance of light oil, which is easier to extract and process compared to certain types of Middle Eastern oil, such as Oman and Upper Zakum (UAE). At the same time, China, promoting the "green" development agenda, is actively promoting the production of renewable energy in African countries, paying particular attention to sub-Saharan Africa. It is worth highlighting the participation of Chinese companies in the construction of the Grand Ethiopian Renaissance Dam in Ethiopia, the construction of hydroelectric power plants in Zambia, Uganda, and Nigeria, as well as the implementation of wind energy projects in countries such as Ethiopia, Djibouti, Kenya, Tanzania and South Africa (Stoletov, 2023). China is developing cooperation with Brazil in the development of oil and gas fields in that country. In particular, in 2023, the Chinese company China National Offshore Oil Corporation began oil production at the large Buzios field in Brazil (Belt and Road Portal, 2023). China's cooperation with Brazil in the hydrocarbon sector is very significant given that, according to the U.S. International Trade Administration, Brazil is capable of becoming the fifth-largest oil exporter in the world by 2030 (U.S. Department of Commerce, 2023).

Within the resource dimension of the geoeconomic strategy, China seeks to ensure the stability of its position in the ferrous metals market, as it is the world's largest producer and consumer of steel, as well as non-ferrous metals and rare earth elements, which it needs for the development of new materials, energy, computer, and military technologies. Brazil and South Africa are among the largest suppliers of iron ore to China, and the main suppliers of non-ferrous metal ores are countries such as Brazil, Guinea, Peru, Chile, South Africa, and Indonesia. Sub-Saharan African countries occupy a significant place in China's import of non-ferrous metals.

To ensure resource security, China is increasing its production of non-ferrous metals, improving the environmental friendliness of this industrial sector (Petushkova, 2022), and is also trying to gain access to the development of deposits of these resources abroad. In particular, China has invested US$30 billion in Indonesia's nickel supply chain as part of its Belt and Road Initiative (King & Wood Mallesons, 2023).

Lithium is of particular importance to China in the energy transition, with about 75% of the world's known reserves in South American countries, particularly the "lithium triangle" of Bolivia, Chile, and Argentina (World Finance, 2024). Brazil, Peru, and Mexico also have significant lithium reserves in Latin America. In 2023, Brazil, which has high-purity lithium ore reserves, began supplying so-called "green lithium" to China for the first time (International Energy Agency, 2023). China's interest in expanding lithium supplies from the Global South is because, by early 2024, about 55% of China's lithium raw materials continued to be imported from Australia (Hu W, 2024), which has a policy aimed at limiting Chinese investment in the development of its lithium deposits. China is implementing the transport and logistics part of its geo-economic strategy primarily through a system of economic corridors. Given that China continues to be heavily dependent on maritime logistics in international trade, the development of port infrastructure in the Indian Ocean region is of particular importance for the implementation of the mega-project "Maritime Silk Road of the 21st Century". In particular, the ports of Chittagong

(Bangladesh), Hambantota (Sri Lanka), Gwadar (Pakistan), Jask (Iran), and Djibouti (Djibouti) are of strategic importance for China. In addition, the Egyptian ports of Port Said and Ain Sokhna, located in the Suez Canal Economic Zone, are of great importance to China.

In developing cooperation with African countries in the transport and logistics sector, China takes into account the interest of large landlocked countries on this continent in gaining access to maritime logistics, which would help create new opportunities for international trade. The importance of Ethiopia in China's transport and logistics projects was demonstrated by the construction of the Addis Ababa-Djibouti railway, which was put into operation in January 2018 (Global Infrastructure Hub, 2020) and had a significant impact on the development of transport connectivity in East Africa.

In terms of logistics development in Africa, the Sahara-Sahel region, located at the intersection of the East-West and North-South corridors and connecting such strategic waters as the Mediterranean Sea, the Gulf of Guinea, the Atlantic Ocean, and the Gulf of Aden, is of strategic importance for China (Rajosefa, 2023).

Within the transport and logistics dimension of China's geo-economic strategy, the states of the Near and Middle East, which are the "gateways" to Europe, are of particular importance. China takes into account that the states of this region are in competitive relations about the transport and logistics sector, and seeks to strengthen cooperation with these countries, relying on various routes of the Belt and Road initiative. Thus, the development of cooperation between the People's Republic of China and the Republic of Turkey within the framework of the conjugation of the Belt and Road and Middle Corridor initiatives is largely determined by the prospects for unlocking the transport and logistics potential of the countries of Central Asia and the South Caucasus (Chang, 2024). To solve this problem, China uses the Shanghai Cooperation Organization. It is significant that at the 2022 SCO summit held in Samarkand (Uzbekistan), an agreement was signed between China, Kyrgyzstan, and Uzbekistan on cooperation in the construction of a railway between these countries. It is assumed that the new railway route will become the southern branch of the Eurasian continental bridge and will open access to the markets of Southeast, and West Asia and the Middle East.

In the context of intensifying contradictions with the countries of the "collective West", the scientific and technological dimension of China's geo-economic strategy concerning the countries of the Global South is being updated, within the framework of which the emphasis is placed on the key areas of scientific and technological development identified in the 14th Five-Year Plan for National Economic and Social Development and long-term goals until 2035. These areas include a new generation of artificial intelligence; quantum technologies; integrated circuits; brain research; genetics and biotechnology; clinical medicine and healthcare; research into deep space, the deep structure of the Earth, the deep sea, the Arctic, and Antarctica (Zhong, 2021).

To expand scientific and technological cooperation with countries participating in the Belt and Road Initiative, the International Association of Scientific Organizations of the Belt and Road Initiative (ANSO, 2024) was established in China in November 2018. It comprises 36 academic institutions (ANSO, 2019), and by 2024, its membership has increased to 78 organizations (ANSO, 2024).

Saudi Arabia and the UAE are significant partners for China in the fields of AI, semiconductors, and supercomputers. King Abdullah University of Science and Technology has collaborated with the Chinese University of Hong Kong and the Shenzhen Big Data Research Institute to build an Arabic-language AI system. This collaboration has resulted in the launch of the AceGPT AI system (Pessarlay, 2023). China is developing cooperation with Iran in the field of nanotechnology. In 2015, the first branch of the Iran Nanotech China Center was launched in Suzhou, China, and in 2018, the second branch of this structure was opened in Guangzhou, China (Tehran Times, 2018).

A priority for China is the development of scientific and technological cooperation with partner countries in the BRICS format. In September 2023, the first BRICS Symposium on Neuroscience was held in Shanghai (Neuroscience Bulletin. 2023). At the BRICS Summit in Johannesburg in 2023, Chinese President Xi Jinping announced his intention to form a research group on artificial intelligence in BRICS member countries (GIP Digital Watch, 2023). In addition, at this summit, China's plans to create a new-era science and technology incubator for BRICS countries were announced (GIP Digital Watch, 2023).

As part of the digital dimension of its geo-economic strategy, China is stepping up efforts to develop the global Internet infrastructure, forming its digital connectivity with the countries of the Global South. In November 2018, the South Atlantic International Submarine Fiber-Optic Cable (SAIL) was put into operation, linking Kribi (Cameroon) and Fortaleza (Brazil), with the Chinese company China Unicom taking part in its construction (AidData, 2024). The Chinese side has implemented a project to build the Pakistan and East Africa Connecting Europe (PEACE) submarine fiber-optic cable system, connecting countries in Asia, Africa, and Europe (Stoletov, 2022). In 2022, the Pakistan-Egypt-Kenya and Egypt-France segments were built within the PEACE system. Ethiopia and Djibouti are also connected to the PEACE system. Chinese technology

Companies China Telecommunications Corporation, China Mobile Limited, and China United Network Communications Group Co. Ltd. are implementing a project to build the Europe-Middle East-Asia (EMA) submarine internet cable linking Hong Kong (China), Singapore, Pakistan, Saudi Arabia, Egypt and France, which is scheduled for completion by the end of 2025 (Brock, 2024).

China has been developing cooperation with Turkey in the field of mobile communications technologies for a long time. Significantly, the Chinese company Huawei has been operating in Turkey since 2002, and since 2010, a Huawei research and development center has been operating in Turkey (Technology Marketing Corporation, 2010). In 2022, Huawei and the Turkish company Türk Telekom signed a memorandum of understanding on cooperation in the development of a 5G technical standard for broadband cellular networks in Turkey (Huawei, 2021). In 2023, Huawei launched its first localized cloud service in Turkey (Huawei, 2023). In the same year, Huawei opened a cloud data center in Riyadh, Saudi Arabia (Swinhoe, 2023). In the Global South countries under consideration, Huawei has cloud data centers in Johannesburg (South Africa), Sao Paulo (Brazil), and Indonesia (Swinhoe, 2022).

In the context of restrictions on free trade in high-tech markets promoted by the countries of the "collective West", China supports maintaining open trade in the field of semiconductor technologies, which are extremely important for it. To address this issue, in 2022, the International Trade Center for Electronic Components and Integrated Circuits (ITC) was established in Shenzhen, China (Kaur, 2023), designed to promote the development of trade in semiconductors and microchips between Chinese and foreign companies.

CONCLUSION

The so-called global "rise" of China is a recent historical process that has had a noticeable impact, on the one hand, on various regions of the world and their economies, politics, and societies, and the other hand, on the global order and the world economic system in general. 1 China's emergence as a global power can be explained by the unprecedented growth of its economy, both quantitatively and qualitatively. If in 1978, at the beginning of market reforms, the nominal gross domestic product (GDP) of the People's Republic of China was 149.54 billion US dollars, according to 2022 data it is 17.96 trillion US dollars. From 1990 to 2022, China's GDP grew 30-fold, from US$1.11 trillion to US$30.33 trillion in terms of purchasing power parity (PPP) (Kartvelishvili, 2024). China is now the world's largest economy by GDP (PPP) and the world's second-largest by nominal GDP. 2 Meanwhile, between 1960 and 2022, China's population grew from 667 million to 1.41 billion, and more than 800 million people were lifted out of poverty (Kartvelishvili, 2024). 3 This large-scale quantitative transformation of China's economy and society has been accompanied by a qualitative increase in its global economic influence, especially since the 2010s. In the 21st century, China has transformed from a capital-deficient and capital-importing country into a capital-exporting economy. Of particular interest in this process are developing countries, where China is particularly active. This primarily refers to the global South.

From its turn, the "awakening" of the Global South is a process of awareness by key developing countries of their increasing importance in world politics, accompanied by an increase in their international activity and an increase in economic opportunities. This process began in the late 2000s and early 2010s, developed throughout the 2010s, and intensified in the first half of the 2020s. The "awakening" of the Global South is characterized by the formation of new institutions of regional and transregional international economic and political interaction, which are designed to help developing countries adapt to fundamental economic, technological, and demographic changes that are causing the restructuring of the existing model of globalization and the formation of a new world order. China, considering itself an important part of the Global South, promotes an inclusive approach to South-South cooperation, which is manifested in the logic of the SCO and BRICS development that it supports. China's geoeconomic strategy, implemented in the context of the "awakening" of the Global South, is characterized by a high level of complexity. The logic of China's consistent implementation of its strategy shows that the PRC, by forming new global supply chains, seeks to change international economic processes from within. By developing relations with a wide range of key states in the Global South, China is trying to form a global communications system in such a way that it is at the center of the main trade routes, providing it with strong ties with various regions of the world. Extensive ties with the global economy are necessary for China to ensure sustainable opportunities for export and import, and access to resources, capital, and technology.

China's geoeconomic strategy is implemented through parallel cooperation formats, implemented both on a bilateral and multilateral basis. The PRC is paying increasing attention to the countries of the Near and Middle East, the African continent, as well as Latin America and the Caribbean.

In the context of implementing this strategy, China is observing the growth of the ambitions of key states in the Global South and the processes of self-organization taking place in the Global South. The countries of the Global South see China as a source of economic development, an alternative to Western countries, and at the same time, by developing cooperation with China, they are inclined to contribute to the formation of a situation in which the states of the Global North would be more interested in them and are ready to take into account their point of view and interests. The prospects for the transformation of globalization will be determined by further steps in the implementation of China's geoeconomic strategy, as well as the development characteristics of key states of the Global South.

REFERENCES

African Business. (2024). BRICS Expansion Offers Opportunity to Boost African Trade, Say Experts. Retrieved from: https://african.business/2024/06/trade-investment/ BRICS-expansion-offers-opportunity-to-boost-African-trade-say-experts

AidData. (2024). Project ID: 1347. Retrieved from: https://china. aiddata.org/projects/1347/

AidData. (2024). Project ID: 58439. Retrieved from: https://china. aiddata.org/projects/58439/

ANSO. (2019). ANSO Update. No. 1. Retrieved from: http://www.anso.org.cn/publications/update/201904/P020190429632242183804.pdf

ANSO. (2024). ANSO Members. Retrieved from: http://www.anso. org.cn/membersNetworks/members/

ANSO. (2024). The History of ANSO. Retrieved from: http://www.anso. Org.cn/about/history/

Asia House. (2023). Saudi — China Relations Deepen: The Implications for Global Trade, Business and Geopolitics. Retrieved from: https://asiahouse.org/research_posts/middle-east-pivot-to-Asia-update-saudi-china-relations-deepen/

Asian Development Bank. (2022). The Regional Comprehensive Economic Partnership Agreement: A New Paradigm in Asian Development Bank Cooperation? Retrieved from: https://www.adb.org/sites/default/files/publication/ 792516/rcep-agreement-new-paradigm-asian-cooperation.pdf

Azam, A. (2022). China Can Play Important Role in Saudi Arabia's Economic Diversification. China Daily. Retrieved from: https://global.chinadaily.com.cn/a/202203/22/WS62398eaba310fd2b29e52938.html

Belt and Road Portal. (2023). Chinese Firm Puts Project in Buzios Oilfield into Production in Brazil. Retrieved from: https://eng.yidaiyilu.gov.cn/p/321571.html

Chang, F. K. (2024). Central Asia's Middle Corridor Expansion: Opportunity for China and Iran. Foreign Policy Research Institute. Retrieved from: https://www.fpri.org/article/2024/01/central-asias-middle-corridor-expansion-opportunity-for-china-and-iran/

Chitadze, N. (2011). *Geopolitics*. Universal.

Chitadze, N. (2024). World Politics. International Black Sea University East Asia: Facts and Analytics 2024. China – Global South: Current Evolution of Relations. Retrieved from: https://lk.iccaras.ru/assets/components/dsgfileupload/files/6330f762.pdf

Daily, C. (2017). China Now Biggest Investor in Suez. Retrieved from: https://www.chinadaily.com.cn/ business/2017-03/23/content_28648386.htm

Daily, C. (2023). Xi Says China Supports African Union's G20 Membership. Retrieved from: https://www.chinadailyhk.com/hk/article/347410

Digital Watch, G. I. P. (2023). BRICS Announces Formation of AI Study Group. Retrieved from: https://dig.watch/updates/brics-members-announce-formation-of-ai-study-group

Embassy of People's Republic of China in Belarus. (2025). Wang Yi: The rise of the Global South is one of the main megatrends of modern international relations. Retrieved from: http://by.china-embassy.gov.cn/rus/zgyw/202503/t20250307_11570140.htm

Global, I. G. I. (2022). World Politics and Challenges for International Security. Information Science Reference. Pennsylvania, USA International Energy Agency, 2023. Latin America Energy Outlook. P. 126. Retrieved from: https://www.oecd.org/content/dam/oecd/en/publications/reports/2023/11/latin-america-energy-outlook-2023_d1e97165/fd3a6daa-en.pdf

Global Infrastructure Hub. (2020). Addis Ababa — Djibouti Railway. Retrieved from: https://www.gihub.org/connectivity-across-borders/case-studies/addis-ababa-djibouti-railway/

Global Times. (2023). China's First Cross-Border LNG Shipment, Settled in Yuan, Completes Offloading. Retrieved from: https://www.globaltimes.cn/page/202305/1290796.shtml

Hu, W. (2024). China — Australia Efforts Needed to Stabilize Lithium Sector Amid US 'Decoupling'. Global Times. Retrieved from: https://www.globaltimes.cn/page/202401/1306370.shtml

Issues, S. (2015). Stay Calm: Internationalise the RMB. P. 1. Retrieved from: https://www.sibos.com/ sites/default/files/2019-01/Sibos Issues_Thursday_Preview_2015.pdf

Junbo, J. (2009). China Says 'No Thanks' to G-2 // Asia Times Online. Retrieved from: https://web.archive.org/web/20090531065554/http://www.atimes.com/atimes/China/KE29Ad01.html

Kartvelishvili, G. (2024). "Global China" and its impact on Georgia's 2022-2030 Development Strategy. Retrieved from: https://dspace.tsu.ge/server/api/core/bitstreams/7e2dddbc-834d-4663-a8da-2e013e50bca7/content

Kaur, D. (2023). China: Shenzhen Has a New Trading Exchange for Semiconductors. Here's What It Does // Tech Wire Asia. Retrieved from: https://techwireasia.com/ 2023/01/china-Shenzhen-has-a-new-trading-exchange-for-semiconductors-here's-what-it-does/

Nabar, M. (2024). Tovar C. E. Renminbi Internationalization // International Monetary Fund. P. 252. Retrieved from: https://www.elibrary.imf.org/downloadpdf/book/9781513539942/ch09.xml

News Central Asia. (2023). Xi'an Declaration of the China — Central Asia Summit. Retrieved from: https://www.newscentralasia.net/2023/05/20/xian-declaration-of-the-china-central-asia-summit/

Nye, J. S., Jr. (2023). What Is the Global South? Project Syndicate. Retrieved from: https://www.project-syndicate.org/commentary/global-south-is-a-misleading-term-by-joseph-s-nye-2023-11

Organization of the Petroleum Exporting Countries. (2005). Joint Statement of the 1st China — OPEC Energy Dialogue. Retrieved from: https://www.opec.org/opec_web/en/press_room/1040.htm

Pessarlay, W. (2023). Saudi Arabia Enters AI Race with AceGPT Launch // CoinGeek. Retrieved from: https://coingeek.com/saudi-arabia-enters-ai-race-with-acegpt-launch/

Rajosefa, L. (2023). The Future of Strategic Competition in the Sahel Region: Placing Partnership First. FAOA Journal of International Affairs. Retrieved from: https://faoajournal.substack.com/p/the-future-of-strategic-competition

Secretariat of the Chinese Follow-up Committee of the Forum on China — Africa Cooperation. (2021). China — Africa Cooperation Vision 2035. Retrieved from: http://www.focac.org/eng/zywx_1/zywj/ 202201/t20220124_10632442.htm

Stoletov, O. (2024). China's Geoeconomic Strategy in the Context of the "Awakening" of the Global South. Retrieved from: https://journals.rudn.ru/international-relations/article/view/41021/ru_RU

SWIFT. (2023). RMB Tracker. Retrieved from: https://www.swift.com/swift-resource/252125/download

Swinhoe, D. (2022). Huawei to Launch Indonesian Cloud Region Later This Year // DCD. Retrieved from: https://www.datacenterdynamics.com/en/news/huawei-to-launch-indonesian-cloud-region-later-this-year/

Swinhoe, D. (2023). Huawei Launches Saudi Cloud Region in Riyadh // DCD. Retrieved from: https://www.datacenterdynamics.com/en/news/huawei-launches-saudi-cloud-region-in-riyadh/

Technology Marketing Corporation. (2010). Huawei Opens Research, and Development Center in Turkey. Retrieved from: https://www.tmcnet.com/usubmit/2010/02/27/4646214.htm

Tehran Times. (2018). Second Iran Nanotech China Center Opens in Guangzhou. Retrieved from: https://www.tehrantimes.com/news/425286/Second-Iran-Nanotech-China-Center-opens-in-Guangzhou

The BRICS Interstate Group. 2020. Russian BRICS Chairmanship (2020). Retrieved from: https://eng.brics-russia2020.ru/ russia_in_brics/20191226/1444/The-BRICS-interstate-association.html

The New Development Bank. (2024). History of the Bank. Retrieved from: https://www.ndb.int/about-ndb/history/

The State Council of the People's Republic of China. (2016). China's Arab Policy Paper. Retrieved from: https://english.www.gov.cn/archive/publications/2016/01/13/content_281475271412746.htm

The State Council of the People's Republic of China. (2016). China's Policy Paper on Latin America and the Caribbean. Retrieved from: https://english. www.gov.cn/archive/white_paper/2016/11/24/content_281475499069158.htm

The State Council of the People's Republic of China. (2021). China and Africa in the New Era: A Partnership of Equals. Retrieved from: https://english.www. gov.cn/archive/whitepaper/202111/26/content_WS61a07968c6d0df57f98e5990.htm

The State Council of the People's Republic of China. (2023). China, GCC Member Economies Keen to Step Up Free Trade Talks. Retrieved from: ttps://english.www.gov.cn/news/202310/26/content_WS6539fb2fc6d0868f4e8e0b03.html

Today, P. (2022). Pakistan, China Sign Framework Agreement on Industrial Cooperation. Retrieved from: https://profit.pakistantoday.com.pk/2022/02/ 04/Pakistan-china-sign-framework-agreement-on-industrial-cooperation/

TV BRICS. (2025). China Announces Global South Center to Support Africa's Development. Retrieved from: https://tvbrics.com/news/kitay-anonsiroval-sozdanie-tsentra-globalnogo-yuga-dlya-podderzhki-razvitiya-afriki/

UN. (2005). *Basic Facts about the United Nations*. UN Department of Public Information.

US Department of Commerce. (2023). Brazil — Country Commercial Guide // International Trade Administration. Retrieved from: https://www.trade.gov/country-commercial-guides/brazil-oil-and-gas

World Finance. (2024). Who Will Win the Lithium Race? Retrieved from: https://www.worldfinance.com/markets/who-will-win-the-lithium-race

KEY TERM AND DEFINITIONS

China: Officially the People's Republic of China (PRC), is a country in East Asia. With a population exceeding 1.4 billion, it is the second-most populous country after India, representing 17.4% of the world population. China spans the equivalent of five time zones and borders fourteen countries by land across an area of nearly 9.6 million square kilometers (3,700,000 sq mi), making it the second-largest country by land area.

Developing countries: Refer to nations characterized by a low standard of living, poor infrastructure, and a lack of industrialization. They are also known as less-developed countries, Third World countries, or non industrialized countries.

Global North: Does not refer to a geographic region in any traditional sense but rather to the relative power and wealth of countries in distinct parts of the world. The Global North encompasses the rich and powerful regions such as North America, Europe, and Australia.

Global South: According to UN Trade and Development (UNCTAD), the Global South broadly comprises Africa, Latin America and the Caribbean, Asia (excluding Israel, Japan, and South Korea), and Oceania (excluding Australia and New Zealand).

The Belt and Road Initiative (BRI or B&R): Known in China as the One Belt One Road and sometimes referred to as the New Silk Road, is a global infrastructure development strategy adopted by the government of the People's Republic of China in 2013 to invest in more than 150 countries and international organizations. The BRI is composed of six urban development land corridors linked by road, rail, energy, and digital infrastructure and the Maritime Silk Road linked by the development of ports.

Chapter 4
China and Global South:
BRI in Southeast Asia

Bahareh Sazmand
https://orcid.org/0000-0003-4838-8430
University of Tehran, Iran

ABSTRACT

The Southeast Asian region is one of the most important regions of the Belt and Road Initiative and the Maritime Silk Road. In the field of the Maritime Silk Road, measures such as the construction and equipping of ports, the construction of high-speed railways, the construction of equipped highways, and port industrial parks have been put on the agenda. Therefore, the question that arises is what are the most important measures taken by China in the form of the Belt and Road Initiative (the Belt and Road Initiative and the Digital Silk Road) in the Southeast Asia Region? Which countries in the region are the most important countries of the Belt and Road Initiative, which countries are the most important countries of the Digital Silk Road, and what measures has China taken in these countries?

INTRODUCTION

In the last two decades, the number of developing countries and emerging markets has increased, and a trend towards fragmentation and fragmentation of global economic governance has emerged. This framework has become increasingly complex, with an increasing number of intergovernmental cooperation groups emerging, each of which encompasses a set of behaviors and practices that may sometimes conflict with each other: cooperation versus competition, and convergence versus fragmentation. Thus, with the emergence of a new set of emerging powers and extensive initiatives to promote transregional cooperation since the early 2010s, a

DOI: 10.4018/979-8-3373-0938-5.ch004

complex nature of global governance has emerged. Thus, according to the Global South approach, a pluralism of the concept of global order is envisaged, which is present in the policies, traditions, and practices of many countries in the Global South. Emerging powers have long stressed the need for pluralism and recognition of differences and diversity, and have sometimes been dissatisfied with the homogenizing processes of globalization. The complaint and dissatisfaction of emerging powers and developing countries with globalization is that in the globalization space, the benefits are unevenly distributed, highly selective, and unequally applied and that Western-style globalization has ignored the countries and societies of the developing and emerging world and presents Western narratives of how globalization should develop. Therefore, a new pluralism must return to the international political space, and according to this pluralism, more complex mechanisms and institutions for global governance should be formed. Accordingly, diverse social patterns are formed that are not necessarily the same as the pattern originating in the West. In this pluralist perspective, liberal narratives of progress and modernization are being challenged both from within the emerging Western world and from the emerging non-Western world.

This major shift in the international structure has been termed the "rise of the South" and refers to a political phenomenon that has affected the global balance of power. It has been driven largely by China and India – supported by Brazil, South Africa, Mexico, and Indonesia. These countries have acted in different ways, demanding a stronger voice in international forums on different issues and pushing for specific reforms in some institutions of global governance, especially those controlled by Western powers – for example, those created by the Bretton Woods agreement. Overall, these emerging powers prefer to expand cooperation among themselves without the mediation of traditional powers and actors. This has led to the creation of various regional groupings such as IBSA, MINT, G20, and BRICS. Previously accustomed to "obeying" and following existing norms and institutions, they are now aware of their ability to do things differently. Some analysts claim that we have now entered a new phase in the global arena called the "post-American world order", while others prefer to call it "post-Western" or posit a new Cold War between China and the United States.

Therefore, a new world order has been formed with the emergence of the global South, and on this basis, the pattern of easternization of power and the role of Eastern actors (states, organizations, and institutions) can be explained. In this new framework of governance, a kind of regional inter-civilizational pluralism is formed, and it challenges the purely Western materialistic perspective. In this easternized pattern of power, the structure of the international system requires a careful review. Of course, this pattern involves cooperation with other countries to review the global order. We can call this pattern of power easternization the pattern of "cooperative change." This pattern of power easternization in the international system shows that Eastern powers such as China, Russia, India, and other BRICS countries are reluctant to participate in all aspects of the liberal global order. But at the same time, they all seek to play a more active role in global power arrangements and the international system and resist the wholesale acceptance of Western-dominated international norms.

One aspect of the Easternization of power is the formation of the Global South. Although, the history of the Global South goes back several decades. The Asia-Africa Conference in Bandung, Indonesia, in 1955 marked the first meeting of the Global South. The conference participants focused on issues such as colonialism, the desire to confront Western dominance and intervention, as well as maintaining non-alignment and racial discrimination. It was at this conference that China and India first began to compete for leadership of the Global South.

Despite becoming the world's two largest economies and emerging powers, China and India continue to classify themselves as members of the Global South. China has positioned itself as an alternative to the United States by investing heavily in developing countries and building infrastructure through the Belt and Road Initiative (BRI).

Since the announcement of the Belt and Road Initiative by Xi Jinping in 2013, 150 countries have joined the Belt and Road Initiative based on the signing of memorandums of understanding, 10 of which are located in Southeast Asia. The Southeast Asian region is one of the most important regions of the Belt and Road Initiative and the Maritime Silk Road. In the field of the Maritime Silk Road, measures such as the construction and equipping of ports, the construction of high-speed railways, the construction of equipped highways, and port industrial parks have been put on the agenda. By providing loans and setting up special cooperation funds, as well as working with multilateral development institutions, including the Asian Development Bank and the Asian Infrastructure Investment Bank, China is stepping up efforts to help regional countries improve their infrastructure and logistics and transportation efficiency. Chinese enterprises have provided large-scale overseas operations and investments, becoming important players in improving infrastructure in Southeast Asia. The China-Laos Railway, Indonesia's Jakarta-Bandung High-Speed Railway, Cambodia's Sihanoukville Port Upgrade, and the Phnom Penh-Sihanoukville Expressway Project are some large-scale infrastructure projects financed and built by China under the BRI in the region. The construction of these infrastructure projects is of great significance in terms of strengthening connectivity between countries in the region and improving the socio-economic situation and local people's livelihoods. Beijing is very keen to see the decline of American hegemony and dominance in the Southeast Asia through its push for the BRI.

In the field of the Digital Silk Road, Chinese companies are bringing more benefits to the countries of the region by establishing training centers and research and development programs to strengthen cooperation between scientists and engineers of these countries and their Chinese counterparts and the transfer of technical knowledge in fields such as smart cities, artificial intelligence, and robotics, the use of clean energy, etc.

The ASEAN is accelerating its internal economic integration and building a unified regional market to achieve the free flow of goods, services, people, investment and technology. These efforts will inevitably bring new business opportunities for Chinese companies and increase direct investment in ASEAN. Many Chinese enterprises, such as Huawei, ZTE, TCL, Midea, and BYD, have already set up factories and regional headquarters in Southeast Asia. Improvements in interregional connectivity infrastructure, as well as reductions in non-tariff barriers brought about by the implementation of the Regional Comprehensive Partnership (RCEP) from January 2022, and additional measures to enhance trade and investment facilitation will encourage Chinese companies to further expand their direct investment in Southeast Asian countries

BRI implementation in the region remains on track, despite the impacts generated by changes in the regional and geopolitical environment. Among the 358 BRI projects launched in Southeast Asia between 2013 and 2021, 210 (58.6%) have already been completed. Another 90 projects are currently under construction, while 54 projects are in the planning stage. In contrast, only four (around 1%) of the projects have been cancelled or terminated. The two countries hosting the most BRI projects are Indonesia and Cambodia, with 63 and 47 projects, respectively. The BRI is expected to have a long-term impact on infrastructure development, industrialisation and economic growth in Southeast Asia .Setting aside for the moment the geostrategic and geoeconomic considerations behind China's push for the initiative, there is evidence of the pervasiveness of economic benefits derived from the BRI by the ASEAN countries. ASEAN is the key region for China's outbound investment under the BRI umbrella. According to the "China Global Investment Tracker" statistics, the accumulated value of Chinese investments and contracts in the ASEAN under the BRI umbrella rose to US$125.26 billion between 2013 and 2022, accounting for 34% of China's investments and contracts under the BRI during the same period. Singapore, Indonesia and Malaysia were the three top recipients of Chinese investment in ASEAN countries, with US$32.57 billion, US$29.97 billion and US$18.67 billion, respectively (Yu, 2024).

In addition, Southeast Asia is central to the Green Silk Road's implementation, both as a geographic conduit of the Maritime Silk Road and as a region with rising aspirations for sustainable industrialization and energy transition. The Association of Southeast Asian Nations (ASEAN), through its frameworks such as the ASEAN

Plan of Action for Energy Cooperation and the ASEAN Smart Cities Network, offers a comparatively structured institutional landscape for regional cooperation on sustainability. China's green engagement in the region taps into this framework by positioning itself as a provider of low-carbon infrastructure, renewable technologies, and capacity-building partnerships.

Recent data underscores Southeast Asia's growing centrality to China's green industrial outreach. In 2023, the region accounted for over 44 percent of global GDP in purchasing power parity, up from 36 percent in 2010 (Yang, 2024). Chinese green investments, particularly in solar photovoltaic manufacturing and electric vehicle (EV) supply chains, have surged. Yuhan Yang (2024) reports that China's "new three" industries — solar cells, EVs, and lithium batteries — generated $147 billion in export value in 2023. Firms such as Trina Solar, BYD, CATL, and JinkoSolar are now key players in Southeast Asian economies, driving local employment, green skills development, and regional integration into global clean-tech value chains.

Of course, various sources have addressed the issue of the relationship between China's Belt and Road Initiative and Southeast Asia, the relationship between regionalism and the Global South, and the relationship between China and the Global South, such as Shintaro Hamanaka (2021) article's titled "Inter-regionalism in the Global South: comparison with extra-, cross-, trans-, and pan-regionalism", the chapter of the book entitled "African and Latin American Regionalism; Perspectives for interregionalism and South-South Cooperation" by Gladys Lechini and Carla Morasso (2021); The book *China's Rise in the Global South; The Middle East, Africa, and Beijing's Alternative World Order* by Dawn C. Murphy (2022); the article titled "To Build A "Harmonious World": China's Soft Power Wielding in the Global South", by Sheng Ding (2008); the report titled *China as a development actor in Southeast Asia* by Renwick, N. (2016) but none of them have addressed the four-faceted relationship between the Global South, China, the Belt and Road Initiative in Southeast Asia, and regionalism, and this article is innovative in this regard.

Therefore, the question that arises is what are the most important measures taken by China in the form of the Belt and Road Initiative (the Belt and Road Initiative and the Digital Silk Road) in the Southeast Asia Region? Which countries in the region are the most important countries of the Belt and Road Initiative, which countries are the most important countries of the Digital Silk Road and Green Silk Road, and what measures has China taken in these countries? This article uses a qualitative research method based on a comparative approach.

To examine the subject, the present article consists of four topics. In the first topic, while examining the background of the research, a theoretical framework that organizes regional space based on the category of interregionalism and Global South is presented. In the second topic, the history, dimensions and goals of the Belt and Road Initiative in the Southeast Asian region are examined, and in the third topic, using a comparative approach, the measures taken by China in the form of the Belt and Road Initiative in three forms (the Belt and Road Initiative, the Digital Silk Road, the Green Belt and Road Initiative) in the Southeast Asian region are presented, and in the last topic, these measures are evaluated.

CONCEPTUAL FRAMEWORK

As a researcher who focuses on the topic of interregionalism, Hänggi categorizes interregionalism into different types. He Say "the expanding network of interregional relations appears in a wide array of manifestations. In order to categorize existing interregional arrangements, three different forms can be distinguished:

(a) relations between regional groupings;
(b) biregional and transregional arrangements;
(c) hybrids such as relations between regional groupings and single powers.

China's attention to the Southeast Asian region and the expansion of cooperation with ASEAN in bilateral and multilateral formats (ASEAN Plus 1, ASEAN Plus 3 and ASEAN Plus 6) can be considered as a type of interregionalism of the relationship of a single power with a region. Meanwhile, Southeast Asia is part of the Global South, which will be discussed in the following.

Global South

"The emergence of the term Global South in its historical context constitutes an interesting process, which illustrates how the term has been charged with various shades of meaning. Some of the contributions touch on the historical genesis of the term and narrate how they experienced this process. Thomas Hylland Eriksen and Jonathan Rigg, among others, reflect on the emergence of the notion, with particular regard to the historical trajectory of defining different (poor and rich) parts of the world. Rigg explains, for example, why he used the term Global South in the title of a book. He acknowledges that the term is not perfect, yet he con- siders it more favorable than its predecessors, "Third World" or "Developing World" (Wolvers et al, 2015)". The urge to come up with a new term highlight not only the uncomfortable reality of previous terms, but also the political connotations of the Global South concept. It is not just a term; it also has political weight, for better or for worse. Leigh Anne Duck, who reflects on the Global South as co-editor of the journal The Global South, highlights "the positive impact of the term. In comparison with "Third World" and "Developing World", she considers the term Global South to carry more weight in resisting hegemonic forces. She emphasizes in its near-decade of publication, then, this journal has studied the Global South through two spatial paradigms that, however seemingly contradictory, often prove mutually dependent in practice: one traces the geographic pathways and demarcations through which power has historically operated, with continuing and often devastating variations and effects, and one seeks to disrupt the spatial imaginaries that have both underpinned and emerged from those geopolitical relations". (Duck, 2015:1).

From the perspective of Alvaro Mendez, as co- founder of the London School of Economics and Political Science's Global South Unit, "the Global South has embarked on an unprecedented upward trajectory. Already, the output of the developing world's three leading economies (Brazil, China and India) is close to equaling the combined output of the longstanding industrial powers of the North – Canada, France, Germany, Italy, the United Kingdom and the United States. Even smaller countries like Bangladesh, Chile, Ghana, Mauritius, Rwanda and Tunisia are experiencing rapid economic development. According to the 2013 UNDP Human Development Report, it is estimated that 80% of the world's middle-class population will be living in developing countries by 2030. This surge of the emerging economies is now in process of reconfiguring the political and economic geometry of the international system. New modalities of engagement in international development, from the state-led capitalism of Asian economies to the world-bestriding operations of global market-savvy Southern multinationals, are replacing the once-dominant North-South aid and investment paradigm. The dynamic global actors driving this process are pressing for a greater voice in the international system, and introducing norms and practices that are reshaping – or that aim to reshape – both the formal and the informal institutions of global governance. The world is being flipped on its axis – a redress that promises huge opportunities for potential development, whilst also posing major challenges, and indeed dangers. With material progress comes huge responsibility for effective human and social development. At the heart of this ongoing global transformation is a phenomenon known as "South South cooperation". Once consigned to the margins, South-South cooperation is coming to occupy an important place in the changing theory and discourse of development. Originally bound up in the response of the developing countries to the destabilising politics of the Cold War, South-South cooperation gave voice to aspirations for a development path untainted by ideological conflict, and to an acknowledgement that relations between developing countries should be a crucial means of achieving these aspirations. Against the backdrop of continuing growth in Southern economies – in the teeth of the concurrent economic travails afflicting the donor countries of the North – South-South cooperation has finally come to the fore. It has been formally recognized by the OECD-DAC in late 2011, at the Busan High Level Summit on Aid Effectiveness, as a dynamic form of engagement contributing to a rapid transformation of the developing world. Its patterns are far from homogenous, and each emerging economy – be it a potentially great-power BRIC country [Brazil, Russia, India and China] or a smaller CIVETS country [Colombia, Indonesia, Vietnam, Egypt, Turkey, and South Africa] – functions in a variety of ways. (Mendez, 2015) Barbara Potthast, the speaker of *Voices from around the world Global South Studies Center*, highlights" how this in the case of Latin America may actually lead to a reconsidering of its relationships with other parts of the world".

However, Boike Rehbein states that "the end of Euro-American domination opens up a new assessment of epistemological issues since an exclusive focus on one's own traditions is no longer possible in a globalized and multicentric world. The alternative, relativism, is still no option when it is no longer possible to close the borders and retreat into oneself. Under these conditions, it becomes possible to revise an epistemology that is constructed around the alternative of universalism and relativism to a hermeneutic whose goal is not the understanding of one's tradition but that of radically different traditions, using the concept of a relational configuration that has to be developed in a dialectical way at its core" (Rehbein, 2018). He states that "those choosing this terminology (Global South) are mainly members of the upper classes in the Global South who profit from the political and economic reality, through expanding south-south relations, for example. Which term is used barely matters for the large majority of the so-called Global South's inhabitants?" (Wolvers et. al, 2015).

"The question remains as to the geographical boundaries of the region referred to as the Global South. It readily conjures the notion of a division between the northern and southern hemispheres of the globe. A country like Kenya would then belong to both categories. But, as Rigg also highlights, the term should not be taken too literally, with the equator dividing the world in two. Instead, it should be understood in the wider context of globalization – or global capitalism, in the case of Arif Dirlik's reflection. In most cases, it then becomes related to an economic division between rich(er) and poor(er) countries, with most people in the so-called Global South actually living in the northern hemisphere (for example, in India and China). "

Dirlik states that "the term "global South" - or at least the "South" component of it - goes back to the 1970s, and is entangled in its implications with other terms that post World War II modernization discourse and revolutionary movements generated to describe societies that seemed to face difficulties in achieving the economic and political goals of either capitalist or socialist modernity. It was largely equivalent to, but not identical with, the popular designation for such societies in the 1950s and 1960s ("Third World") to which it bore a contradictory relationship. It was popularized by the so-called Brandt Commission reports published in 1980 and 1983, both of which bore "North-South" in their titles. The reports advocated large infusions of capital from the North to the South to enable their modernization. (Dirlik, 2007:13).

What is evident is that it is difficult to escape the political use and consequences of the term. “Dirlik and Rehbein, for example, are very adamant about the close correlation the Global South has with geopolitics. As a result, it is not a static concept. With geopolitical shifts, the definition of the Global South may also change; not only with regard to the meaning of the term, but also, as Dirlik shows, about which countries are considered to be part of the Global South and which are not. This implies that there is not necessarily agreement about who is part of the Global South and who is not, or about whether it is actually useful to apply the term in the first place. Rodolfo Magallanes states that the term Global South is ahistoric and decontextualized. It omits a critical core of dynamic variables that characterize different kinds of countries, especially historical, economic, social, cultural, and political variables, among others. It is these factors that might explain the reality of these countries as a product of a societal process, and the type and origin of the differences among them.” (Magallanes, 2015). Magallanes is particularly critical of the idea of grouping together a large variety of countries and regions into one category. This, he argues, “tends to obscure specific (historical) relationships between different countries and/or regions, especially when it comes to unequal power balances. Or, as Eriksen argues, it may obscure wealth differences within countries – and, therefore, similarities between the wealthy in the Global South and Global North, as well as the dire situation the poor may face all around the world” (Wolvers et. al, 2015).

A study of the concept of the Global South showed that analysts and researchers have different views on this concept, and each analyzes and defines the Global South from a different perspective. The main components discussed in the definition of the Global South include geography, distribution of power, geopolitics, political goals, intellectual and theoretical discourses, and finally a combination of these components, which applies to China's efforts to lead the Global South in the form of interregional activities.

China and the Global South

Since the end of World War II, China, perceiving itself as both a developing country and major power, has maintained friendly relations with many developing countries while at times leveraging that position in its relations with other major powers. China and various Global South countries loosely share views on several points: (1) dissatisfaction with Western countries due to historical reasons, (2) aspirations for economic development, and (3) the need for reform in global governance.

Against this backdrop of shared interests, China has launched a variety of initiatives aimed at rallying the Global South.

Under the Xi Jinping administration, China has expanded its military engagement in the Global South, including establishing an overseas military base, increasing military exchanges, and offering military education to the military officers and soldiers of developing countries. Although China's growing military engagement raises contradictions with its long-held principle of non-interference in internal affairs of other countries, it may strengthen its "constructive interventions" in political and military-related matters to protect its overseas interests.(Masaaki et al., 2024:3).

In November 2012, Chinese President Xi Jinping announced the "Chinese Dream," which envisions a grand process of China's national rejuvenation as a global power (Hudda, 2015). Such statements by Chinese leaders are controversial and continue to fuel realist assumptions that China is seeking global dominance and changing the world order. Given the realist premise that states act only in their own interests and compete for power in a zero-sum game, China's continued pursuit of dominance over Taiwan and its alignment with repressive regimes such as North Korea confirm realist claims about China's rise, which may lead to a "conflict with the status quo" among the great powers.

In this regard, realist scholar John Mearsheimer suggests that if China continues to expand its military capabilities, it will become "an aggressive state determined to achieve regional hegemony" (Kirshner, 2010: 59). According to Mearsheimer, US policies to boost trade with China are "misguided and doomed to fail." The US strategy to contain China has been criticized by countries such as Australia and South Korea, which have embraced China as a strong ally and trading partner.

China has increasingly used its economic power to build partnerships on a global scale, outstripping Western investments. These partnerships have increased China's influence and popularity, particularly in South America and Africa. In Ecuador, for example, Chinese investments account for about a quarter of the country's economic output (Aisch, Keller and Lai, 2015). This pattern of Chinese global investments points to a realist state that is determined to achieve hegemonic dominance through economic integration and alliances with weaker states. While China claims that its rise is "peaceful and development-oriented" (Yang, 2013:36), Western powers such as the United States remain skeptical of China's rise and continue to monitor its actions. Evidence suggests that since the 1970s, Chinese policies have shown less revisionist tendencies. It has increasingly become a state that embraces defensive realism. One sign of this is that China has toned down its revolutionary rhetoric. It also does not support insurgencies in other countries. The second line of evidence is that since the late 1970s, China has increasingly pursued a cooperative security approach in its relations with its neighbors in the regional arena and even in its relations with other countries in the international arena. In general, China has tried to establish friendly relations with its neighbors. One of these signs is the improvement in relations with countries such as India, which is traditionally considered a serious rival to China. Their relations soured in 2017 when a standoff between Indian and Chinese forces occurred on the Doklam plateau. However, India-China relations improved with the informal summit of the two countries in China in April 2018. The two countries even held a joint military exercise in December 2018 called "Hand in Hand" to resolve border issues with many neighboring countries. The country has resolved border disputes with countries such as Myanmar, Nepal, and Pakistan, and more recently with Russia, which shares borders with Central Asian countries and Vietnam (Yasmin Jalil, 2019: 49).

In an address at a BRICS-related meeting in August 2023, Chinese President Xi Jinping positioned China as a member of the Global South and expressed the view that the collective rise of emerging and developing countries is fundamentally reshaping the world map. In recent years, the Xi administration has been increasingly criticizing the international order formed under Western leadership as unfair, and has proposed a variety of independent Chinese diplomatic initiatives aimed at "democratization of international relations." In challenging the existing international order, China has been actively issuing rallying cries to the so-called "Global South," comprising developing and emerging countries with a remarkably growing presence in international relations.

Although "Global South" lacks a precise definition, it is generally used as a broad concept to collectively refer to developing and emerging countries in regions such as Asia, the Middle East, Africa, and Latin America. During the Cold War, newly independent states that achieved decolonization pursued a "Non-Aligned Movement," refusing to align with either the Western or Eastern sides, and were collectively referred to as the "Third World." Additionally, the term "South" was used to signify developing countries in contrast to the "North" which centered on developed nations, conceptualizing levels of economic development. Following the end of the Cold War, due to widening economic disparities across borders alongside the globalization of market economies, including poverty within developed countries, the term "Global South" came into academic use in some contexts. The current concept of the Global South is subject to various interpretations regarding its implications, and some caution is apparent in its definition (Masaaki, 2024:18).

China, Global South and BRI in Southeast Asia

The notion of the Silk Road was conceptualized during the Han Dynasty, approximately two millennia ago (circa second century BCE), as a mechanism to foster trade and economic collaboration. The Silk Road enabled the interchange of commodities, intellectual concepts, and cultural practices between the East and the

West, establishing a connection between China, Central Asia, the Middle East, and Europe. The People's Republic of China (PRC) undertook initiatives to revitalize the Silk Road in 2013 under the leadership of President Xi Jinping, who introduced the designation "One Belt One Road" (OBOR). Subsequently, the One Belt, One Road (OBOR) initiative was rebranded as the Belt and Road Initiative (BRI). The primary objective of the BRI is to establish connections between Asia, Europe, and Africa through an integrated land and maritime network aimed at enhancing regional partnerships and integration, as well as stimulating economic and trade collaboration. The terms "belt" and "road" denote two separate constructs, with the "Belt," also referred to as "The Silk Road Economic Belt" (SREB), pertaining to the linkage of overland routes within the Silk Road cooperative framework, while the "Road," or "21st Century Maritime Silk Road," pertains to the connection facilitated by shipping lanes associated with the Belt and Road Initiative (BRI) (Xie 2019).

China has forged extensive state-to-state linkages with the Global South. A survey by the Lowry Institute shows that average annual visits to China and the US by world leaders changed dramatically in China's favor. During the Bush presidency (1989–1993), the average annual visit by world leaders to the US was 65.8, in contrast to five to China. In 2018, the number to China was 127 compared with only 22 to the US. Far more leaders of the South visited China than the US between 2010 and 2019: African leaders visited China 172 times (83 to the US), Asian leaders visited China 287 times (compared with 90 times to the US), and South American leaders visited China 30 times (compared with 25 times to the US). This concluded the Lowry report, 'is both a symptom of [China's] growing power and one of its causes'. In short, as the largest country in the Global South, over the past two decades, China has substantially expanded its economic imprint not only in the world but also with other developing countries, a major driving force behind China's multi-layered engagement since the BRI's launch in 2013 (Liu, 2022: 15).

In the year 2013, Xi Jinping inaugurated the Belt and Road Initiative (BRI), which has subsequently emerged as China's preeminent diplomatic and economic strategy for engaging with the international community, particularly with developing nations. As reported by the Refinitiv BRI Database, by the year 2019, a total of 2,631 projects were identified, collectively valued at approximately $3.7 trillion, and close to 2,600 enterprises were involved in this flagship initiative. Notably, over 55 percent of these enterprises are non-Chinese entities. Despite reports in June 2020 indicating that approximately 20 percent of BRI projects had been 'seriously affected' or 'somewhat affected' by the COVID-19 pandemic, around 40 percent experienced minimal adverse effects. The BRI continues to represent China's most significant foreign policy initiative (Liu, 2022b). Furthermore, it serves as a crucial platform for China's engagement with the Global South. Despite a plethora of academic inquiries regarding the BRI (e.g., Blanchard, 2021; Liow et al., 2021; Schneider, 2021), few analyses adopt a perspective that prioritizes the Global South. While there exists a complex amalgamation of motivations underpinning China's recent engagements with developing nations, including political (for instance, the promotion of the One-China policy), diplomatic, and commercial dimensions (Fuchs & Rudyak, 2019), the BRI renders the Global South increasingly pivotal within China's overarching international strategy.

China's post-2013 engagement with the Global South has manifested both continuity and transformation. In addition to honoring the esteemed Bandung legacy, it perpetuates the transition initiated in the 1980s, specifically from an ideological framework towards an economic paradigm. Three salient characteristics delineate China's contemporary approach: development serving as a conduit between the BRI and the Global South; the institutionalization of multilateral and bilateral frameworks aimed at enhancing South-South cooperation alongside China's leadership role; and the expansion and deepening of knowledge transfer with the Global South, wherein the 'China Solution' is posited as an alternative developmental model to that proffered by the Global North.

Southeast Asia is getting a central position on the map of the BRI. In October 2013, China's President Xi Jinping focused towards Indonesia for deeper maritime cooperation and announced the maritime prong of the BRI. Indonesia is one of the largest countries in Southeast Asia and China is continuing to make its BRI projects in the country. Southeast Asia is a region where China is much interested to cooperate in the “Belt” and sea “Road” of the extensive programme of BRI projects initiated with converge . The BRI project is recognised in mainland Southeast Asia which is one of the sixth economic zones of China's BRI. Maritime Southeast Asia has immense significance through sea lanes of communication, trade, and transportation of energy in the Indian and Pacific Oceans. This region is strategically important and constitutes too much support for international players to establish partnerships for trade and commerce in the maritime domain of Southeast Asia. Thus, this region is called China's “strategic throat” and is crucial to its rise as an international player. China has established significant trade partnerships with several Southeast Asian countries, including Cambodia, Malaysia, Myanmar, Singapore, Vietnam, and Thailand. These countries are ranked among China's top trading partners in the region, contributing to the overall economic ties between China and ASEAN. China is one of Cambodia's largest trading partners, with substantial investments in infrastructure, agriculture, and tourism. Trade with Myanmar has increased significantly, driven by Chinese investments in energy, mining, and infrastructure. The China-Myanmar Economic Corridor, part of the BRI, aims to enhance connectivity and economic integration between the two nations. China has been deepening its trade and commerce relationship with Southeast countries. China and Thailand enjoy a robust trade relationship, focusing on machinery, electronics, and agricultural products.

Initiatives like the China-Thailand Railway Project aim to improve infrastructure and connectivity, further enhancing economic cooperation (Bharti and Kumari, 2024).

Moreover, China is gaining ground in its technological presence in Southeast Asia. The region's geopolitical importance and potential for robust economic growth have motivated China to engage in the region as one of the first opportunities for BRI and DSR (Digital Silk Road). The Digital Silk Road was conceived in a white paper released by the State Council in March 2015 on the subject of "Internet +". The document mentioned the term 'Information Silk Road' and noted that, "We (China) should jointly advance the construction of cross-border optical cables and other communications trunk line networks, improve international communications connectivity, and create an Information Silk Road". Although digital infrastructure projects were already underway since the early 2010s, the white paper was the earliest articulation of the branding for the DSR. The emphasis on multi- dimensional connectivity was reiterated in a white paper on BRI released by the National Development and Reform Commission (NDRC) in 2015 that stated, "(BRI) aims to promote the connectivity of Asian, European and African continents and their adjacent seas, set up all-dimensional, multi-tiered and composite connectivity networks". Chapter 26 of the 13th Five Year Plan for Economic and Social Development in 2016 called for the implementation of Internet+ projects and the initiation of pilot projects to develop a modern internet industry system. At the National Congress of the China Association for Science (CAS) in 2016, China's President Xi Jinping stated the central objective of the DSR: for China to become the leading player in science and technology globally by 2030. The State Council followed up with the 13th Five Year Plan for National Informatisation, calling for the construction of an online silk road and planning a bundle of digital connectivity projects from Guangxi in southern China to ASEAN countries (Reddy, 2023).

Southeast Asia is a key region for China's digital infrastructure because of its geography. Thus far, China has established multiple mechanisms and institutions to facilitate regional DSR investments. Key mechanisms in this regard include the *ASEAN-China Initiative on Enhancing Cooperation on E-Commerce* (2023), *Action Plan on Implementing the ASEAN-China Partnership on Digital Economy Cooperation (2021-2025)* (2022), *China-ASEAN Digital Economy Partnership Initiative* (2020), *ASEAN-China Cyber Dialogue Mechanism* (2020 and 2022) and *ASEAN-China Smart City Cooperation Initiative* (2019). Besides, China is negotiating with ASEAN countries to upgrade the ASEAN-China Free Trade Agreement (ACFTA 3.0), which will focus on three emerging domains: digital economy, green economy, and supply chain industries As for institutions, a key example is the China-ASEAN Information Harbor (CAIH) established by China's Guangxi autonomous region in 2016 to transform Guangxi into a "digital hub" connecting China and ASEAN. More recently, multiple companies and NGOs from China and ASEAN jointly launched the ASEAN-oriented "Digital Silk Road" Think Tank Alliance in September 2022 to enhance ASEAN-China cooperation on digital transformation. In April 2023, the Malaysia-based venture capital firm Kairous Capital announced the launch of the Malaysian-China Digital Cooperation Council, which aims to "facilitate long-term cross-border collaboration between Malaysian and Chinese companies in the areas of technology and innovation." (Zheng, 2024)

The DSR connects BRI countries by supporting fiber-optic terrestrial and submarine cable networks, and Beijing has emphasized building these cables to South Asia, Southeast Asia, and the Pacific, often then connecting on to Africa. Chinese-built telecommunications infrastructure in Southeast Asia aims to extend submarine cables connecting the region with landing points on China's coastline that then connect to cables in the country's western region. China Unicom has built a submarine cable project that is now the shortest cable route between Asia and Europe. This route, Asia-Africa-Europe 1 (AAE-1), is a new 25,000-kilometer submarine cable running from Hong Kong to France, and also connects China with Southeast Asia, South Asia, parts of Africa, the Middle East, and Europe. Furthermore, Beijing is building terrestrial and submarine cables to expand fiber-optic links between China and many parts of Eurasia. In some cases, Beijing is creating redundant connections that make China's networks to other countries resilient. These redundant connections provide alternative options to Chinese service providers when cables have communication failures. Southeast Asia is not only geographically important to China. It also has high economic growth rates and is a significant potential market for Chinese firms in ICT and digital services. In terms of economic potential, the digitally enabled services trade in the Southeast Asian market almost doubled between 2011 to 2019. Chinese messaging apps, e-commerce platforms, and payment firms are all expanding rapidly in Southeast Asia, and also investing heavily in local Southeast Asian firms. Chinese investors including Alibaba, JD.com, and Didi Chuxing all have made major investments in Southeast Asian firms such as e- commerce platform companies Lazada and Tiki and the ride-hailing company Grab (Mochinaga, 2021).

Despite significant investment in Southeast Asia, the region's digital infrastructure remains relatively underdeveloped, particularly in lower income countries such as Cambodia, Laos, and Myanmar. Governments in the region prioritize their development and are interested in China's globally standardized and low-cost infrastructure; many Southeast Asian states do not have comprehensive privacy, cybersecurity, or data protection laws and policies, and thus are not particularly concerned that Chinese investment could compromise local data privacy and security.

An analysis of the International Institute of Strategic Studies (IISS)'s China Connects dataset shows that: 1) all Southeast Asian countries received China's DSR investments between 2017 and 2020) China's DSR investments in Southeast Asia are clustered in five areas: Telecoms, 5G, Data Centres, Fintech, and E-commerce;

and 3) Huawei, Alibaba, and ZTE are the major investors of China's DSR projects in the region. Chinese tech companies have also made decent progress in investing in 5G, fibre optic cables, and cross-border e-commerce in Southeast Asia between 2020 and 2023 (Zheng, 2024).

Notwithstanding the DSR investments' progress in Southeast Asia, China faces multiple challenges in pushing the DSR forward, including the growing tensions between the state and private tech companies domestically as well as intensifying US-China technological rivalry and risks of tech bifurcation. The DSR's future in Southeast Asia will be determined by China's ability to secure dominant positions in frontier technologies and in growing its share of the region's digital market.

In addition as the Belt and Road Initiative (BRI) enters its second decade, Beijing seems focused on filling in the fine details of the project's ambitious outline, first announced by President Xi Jinping in 2013. It appears that the next iteration of the BRI will shift away from grand mega-projects to prioritise 'small and beautiful' high-quality projects. The green economy seems to be a particular focus, with Foreign Minister Wang Yi noting during a press conference in early March that China will 'redouble efforts to build a green Silk Road'.

Indeed, 2023 marked the 'greenest' year for the BRI, with green-energy investments reaching US$9.5 billion. Investments in critical minerals and mining, green technology (such as electric vehicles and batteries) and green energy (production and transmission) are now key elements of China's strategic engagement framework for pursuing small, beautiful and green projects. China is likely seeking to lead in green industries where it has achieved dominance, such as critical minerals, solar cells, batteries and electric vehicles (EVs). Moreover, in light of increasing pressure from the United States and its allies and partners – which seek to limit China's market access to their domestic green industries – Beijing is ramping up green investments in Southeast Asia to redirect exports, nearshore supply chains and consolidate regional influence (Lu Tan, 2024).

The strategic pivot towards small, beautiful and green projects comes amid China's economic struggles following the pandemic years and sluggish growth. As manufacturing slows and the real-estate market moves from boom to bust, China is looking to green industries as an alternative growth driver. The green-energy sector, for instance, accounted for 40% of China's economic growth in 2023, with technologies such as EVs, lithium-ion batteries, and solar cells responsible for a 2% increase in overall export growth. Meanwhile, China's previous BRI mega-projects are increasingly unsustainable from a budgetary standpoint, both in the eyes of Beijing and host countries. One estimate suggests that 80% of China's overseas lending portfolio in developing countries is backing states in financial distress. With China now the world's largest debt collector, senior Chinese officials are talking about sustainable debt and the need to shift to smaller-scale and bankable projects, underscoring the CCP's focus on reducing the repayment risks associated with BRI projects..(Lu Tan, 2024).

More broadly, Beijing seems aware of the reputational risks of the BRI and has likely decided to engage in some course correction as it seeks global leadership on key green development areas. Chinese scholars argue that Beijing has taken note of the international perception of its BRI projects, including criticisms labelling the process as opaque, resulting in 'debt-trap diplomacy', and generating 'low-quality' projects. BRI 2.0 responds by downsizing projects – 2023 recorded the second-lowest average deal size in construction engagements since the BRI was announced – and anchoring on buzzwords like 'open', 'sustainable debt' and 'high-quality' in official narratives.

Given its dominance in green industries, being seen to be responsive to these criticisms could serve Beijing's efforts to become a global leader in green stewardship. China has a near-monopoly in critical-minerals processing and dominates green technology, such as solar panels (for which China holds an over 80% market share in manufacturing), EVs, lithium-ion batteries and even grid technologies. The 'China Standards 2035' strategy, announced in 2018, is an example of Beijing's efforts to steer global green-technology environmental standards. It seeks to enhance dialogues and partnerships with BRI countries with a view to achieving 85% alignment between domestic and international standards, particularly in emerging industries.(Lu Tan, 2024).

The Laos–China 500kV power trade deal, signed in 2023, will allow China to import surplus hydroelectricity from Laos, likely contributing to southern China's electric decarbonization. Meanwhile, with China seeking to ensure the supply of upstream resources and raw materials, Indonesia and the Philippines (producers of some 45% of the global nickel output) have enticed major entities like CATL, China's leading lithium-ion-battery manufacturer, to invest in EV-battery projects. Southeast Asia is also becoming a critical element in Beijing's geo-economic strategy in light of the growing great-power competition between China and the West. The US anti-dumping probe into Chinese solar panels, its Inflation Reduction Act's exclusion of 'foreign entities of concern' from incentives, and rising American tariffs on Chinese EVs complicate China's market prospects in the US and increasingly in Europe. Most recently, President Biden announced a new round of tariffs on green products, including batteries and critical minerals. Meanwhile, the EU plans to impose levies as high as 48% on Chinese EVs, with Canada potentially following suit. (Lu Tan, 2024).

Southeast Asia is central to the Green Silk Road's implementation, both as a geographic conduit of the Maritime Silk Road and as a region with rising aspirations for sustainable industrialization and energy transition. The Association of Southeast Asian Nations (ASEAN), through its frameworks such as the ASEAN

Plan of Action for Energy Cooperation and the ASEAN Smart Cities Network, offers a comparatively structured institutional landscape for regional cooperation on sustainability. China's green engagement in the region taps into this framework by positioning itself as a provider of low-carbon infrastructure, renewable technologies, and capacity-building partnerships.

Recent data underscores Southeast Asia's growing centrality to China's green industrial outreach. In 2023, the region accounted for over 44 percent of global GDP in purchasing power parity, up from 36 percent in 2010 (Yang, 2024). Chinese green investments, particularly in solar photovoltaic manufacturing and electric vehicle (EV) supply chains, have surged. Yuhan Yang (2024) reports that China's "new three" industries — solar cells, EVs, and lithium batteries — generated $147 billion in export value in 2023. Firms such as Trina Solar, BYD, CATL, and JinkoSolar are now key players in Southeast Asian economies, driving local employment, green skills development, and regional integration into global clean-tech value chains.

These developments are not merely economic but deeply strategic. They reinforce China's normative role in shaping green governance frameworks through technology transfer, financial incentives, and South-South cooperation mechanisms. As articulated in the *UN Environment Belt and Road Strategy* (2017), the GSR provides a mechanism for aligning infrastructure investment with the 2030 Agenda for Sustainable Development, especially in urban development, transportation, and sustainable energy sectors. The document also emphasizes that sustainable outcomes require integrating green safeguards from project inception — a principle increasingly embedded in China's green finance platforms such as the AIIB and the Silk Road Fund.

Institutionally, China's engagement with ASEAN adopts a mixed strategy. While bilateral investment and diplomacy remain dominant, regional mechanisms such as the China-ASEAN Environmental Cooperation Center and the annual China-ASEAN Environmental Cooperation Forum are growing in relevance. These platforms facilitate knowledge exchange, coordinate policy dialogues, and promote initiatives such as the Green Silk Road Envoys Program, which supports environmental governance capacity across Southeast Asian states.

Yet, challenges persist. Despite notable successes in Vietnam, Malaysia, and Thailand, green BRI projects in other ASEAN countries face implementation lags, regulatory uncertainty, and weak stakeholder engagement. As Du, Qin, and Huang (2022) note, the absorptive capacity of local institutions and the alignment between national and regional policies remain critical variables in ensuring project sustainability. Moreover, critics caution against "greenwashing" — where environmental branding obscures the ecological risks of large-scale infrastructure development (Tanaka, 2022).

Overall, China's Green Silk Road in Southeast Asia reflects a more institutionalized, regionally embedded model of environmental diplomacy, one that leverages both bilateral and multilateral tools to shape development trajectories in line with ecological and geopolitical objectives.

With green market access in the West shrinking, China may find major growth potential in Southeast Asia. In the first quarter of 2024, the region saw EV sales double compared to 2023, with Chinese brands holding over 70% of total EV sales. China's export of solar cells to the region also increased by roughly 12.5% annually from 2019–23. China is also aggressively expanding its EV production in Thailand. Additionally, Beijing views the region as a useful 'buffer zone' to nearshore its green-industry supply chains in order to circumvent high Western tariffs. For example, Vietnam and Malaysia, benefiting from a two-year US tariff exemption granted in 2022, have become the world's second- and third-largest photovoltaic manufacturers, respectively. (Lu Tan, 2024).

In fact, China's presence in Southeast Asia through the Belt and Road Initiative can be analyzed under two concepts: regionalism and the attempt to lead the Global South. A review of China's actions in Southeast Asia proves this.The relationship between China and Southeast Asia can be analyzed under both the concepts of the Global South and interregionalism (the type of relationship between a region and a great power).

On the one hand, China has tried to expand its presence and influence in other regions, including Southeast Asia, Southwest Asia, Central Asia and the Caucasus, South Asia, Europe and Africa, with its Belt and Road Initiative. Regions where the countries are mainly defined as developing countries or the Global South. China has tried to expand and strengthen its presence in each of these regions and countries, and this presence has been different depending on their needs. In some, by investing in the infrastructure sector, in some by providing health and medical assistance, in some by expanding industrial parks, in some by providing digital services and investing in this sector, and in some by expanding trade and investing in the economy.

Furthermore, with the implementation of a decade of the Belt and Road Initiative and the serious criticisms it has received, including environmental threats and debt traps, it has tried to compensate for those criticisms and seize more opportunities to continue the Belt and Road Initiative under the concept of interregionalism by pursuing new initiatives such as the Green Silk Road, the Digital Silk Road, and the Health Silk Road. This has been accompanied by significant successes in the global south, and in particular, most Southeast Asian countries.

China's global ambitions were first made apparent in the context of BRI. This finding should not be surprising. BRI is not merely an infrastructure-building plan but the backbone of the new world order that the Chinese leadership under Xi Jinping wants to see emerge (Rolland, 2024). The Green Silk Road (GSR) represents one of the most ambitious experiments in contemporary global governance: the projection of sustainability through infrastructure-led diplomacy, embedded in China's broader Belt and Road Initiative (BRI). In addition, as a branch of BRI, the Health Silk Road (HSR) provides an informative model of Beijing's strategic planning and its use of specific mechanisms to expand its global influence: from the creation of medical and health standards to the penetration of foreign markets, and from shaping international norms to influencing the future of health. Finally, the Digital Silk Road (DSR) is part of the Belt and Road Initiative (BRI) that finances and supports digital connectivity infrastructure to support China's technology companies, goods and services. The initiative includes the provision of hard infrastructure like cellular networks and soft infrastructure like applications and mobile payment platforms to facilitate China's trade with developing countries. The DSR is also a nexus between the state and tech companies to establish China as the primary supplier of technology goods. The initiative is backed by policy banks and receives political support from the government to penetrate and dominate emerging markets in Africa, Asia and Latin America. The objective is to deepen China's commercial and geo-economic interests, create favourable norms and standards governing technology, cultivate political leverage with foreign governments and sustain the development of China's domestic economy and military industrial complex (Reddy, 2023).

Figure 1. China's presence in Southeast Asia

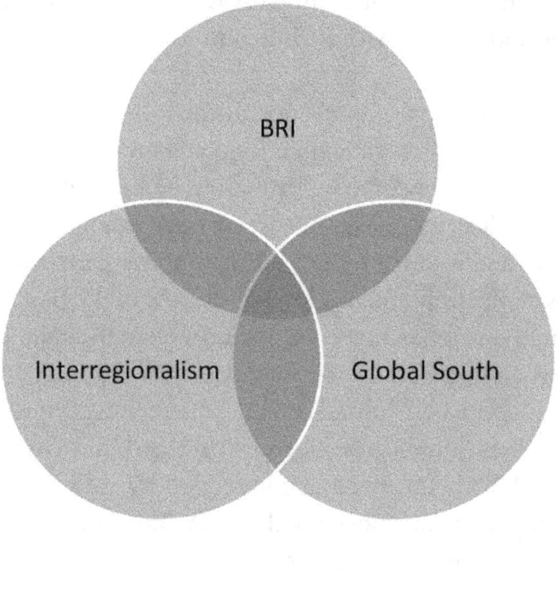

Source: Author

CONCLUSION

This chapter of the book attempted to address the relationship between China and the Global South from the perspective of its presence and position in the Southeast Asian region. For this reason, it was necessary to address the issue of China's rise from the perspective of the easternization of power in the international system. China's current rise can be considered and analyzed from two perspectives. One is from the perspective of the material components of power, which include economic, geopolitical, and geostrategic indicators, and the other is from the non-material and semantic perspective, through the presentation of non-Western and non-Chinese theories and approaches to international relations and regional studies. In this intellectual framework, one of the concepts that has attracted the attention of researchers in recent years is the concept of the Global South. Of course, this concept has a long history and its roots go back to the Bandung Conference in Indonesia, which led to the formation of the Non-Aligned Movement.

After that, China has always tried to act as a supporter of developing and underdeveloped countries. Of course, in the post-Cold War situation, this issue was pursued more seriously and had its own reasons. First, the structure of the international system had changed and more space had been provided for the emergence of other countries, including China. Second, the pragmatist perspective was pursued more intensively in China. Third, China tried to expand its sphere of influence among developing countries.

One of the regions that can be categorized under the Global South is the Southeast Asian region, and China has paid special attention to this region since the Cold War. It pursued its activities under the category of the Global South and bilaterally, multilaterally, and institutionally. After that, with the coming to power of Xi Jinping, this pragmatism intensified and the realization of the Chinese dream was put on the agenda. Then, the issue of the Belt and Road Initiative was put on the agenda as one of the tools to realize the Chinese dream, and one of the regions of China's attention for implementing the Belt and Road Initiative in the Global South development plan is the Southeast Asian region. From the very beginning of the Belt and Road Initiative in 2013, the countries of the Southeast Asian region announced their willingness to participate in the Belt and Road Initiative and joined this initiative. Of course, the Philippines and Thailand have taken a somewhat more cautious view of this initiative. This initiative, which was initially aimed at developing physical infrastructure and expanding economic and trade relations, has taken on other dimensions over time. Since 2017, the issue of the Digital Silk Road and the digitalization of the Belt and Road have been raised, and they have also received a lot of attention during the spread of the Corona pandemic. Then, after a decade of the Belt and Road Initiative, we are witnessing the introduction of the Green Silk

Road, which pays special attention to environmental aspects and welcomes projects that have less environmental pollution. In summary, it can be said that China is making extensive efforts to become a leader of the global south, both materially and intellectually, and one of its target regions is Southeast Asia.

REFERENCES

Aisch, G., ... (2015). "The World According to China". Nytimes.Com. Available at: http://www.nytimes.com/interactive/2015/07/24/business/international/ the-world-according-to-china-investment-maps.html. Accessed on: 10/1/2025.

Bharti, M. S., & Kumari, S. (2024). China's Belt and Road Initiative in Southeast Asia and its implications for ASEAN-China strategic partnership. *ARPE*, *3*(22), 22. Advance online publication. DOI: 10.1007/s44216-024-00042-4

Blanchard, J. M. (2021). Belt and Road Initiative (BRI) Blues: Powering BRI research back on track to avoid choppy seas. *Journal of Chinese Political Science*, *26*(1), 235–255. DOI: 10.1007/s11366-020-09717-0

Ding, S. (2008). To build a "harmonious world": China's soft power wielding in the global south. *Journal of Chinese Political Science*, *13*(2), 193–213. DOI: 10.1007/s11366-008-9023-9

Dirlik, A. (2007). Global South: Predicament and promise. *Global Society*, *1*(1), 12–23.

Du, X., Qin, Y., & Huang, C. M. (2022). Status and Prospect of Ecological Environment in the Belt and Road Initiative Regions. *International Journal of Environmental Research and Public Health*, *19*(24), 17091. DOI: 10.3390/ijerph192417091 PMID: 36554970

Duck, L. A. (2015). Preface: Remappings—Canada and the US South in a Global Age. *Global Society*, *9*(1), 1–4. DOI: 10.2979/globalsouth.9.1.01

Fuchs, A., & Rudyak, M. (2019). The motives of China's foreign aid. In Zeng, K. A. (Ed.), *Handbook on the international political economy of China* (pp. 392–410). Edward Elgar Publishing. DOI: 10.4337/9781786435064.00031

Hamanaka, S. (2021). Inter-regionalism in the Global South: Comparison with extra-, cross-, trans-, and pan-regionalism. *Cambridge Review of International Affairs*, *36*(5), 697–719. DOI: 10.1080/09557571.2021.1899135

Hänggi, H. (2000). "Inter-regionalism: empirical and theoretical perspectives". Paper presented for the workshop, Dollars, Democracy and Trade: External Influence on Economic Integration in the Americas", Los Angeles. http://www.cap.lmu.de/transatlantic/download/Haenggi.PDF

Hudda, N. (2015). "Interpreting the Rise of China: Realist and Liberalist Perspectives". Available at: https://www.e-ir.info/2015/04/03/interpreting-the-rise-of-china-realist-and-liberalist-perspectives/. [Accessed 1 January 2025].

Jalil, G. Y. (2019). China's Rise. *Strategic Studies*, *39*(1), 41–58.

Kirshner, J. (2010). 'The Tragedy of Offensive Realism: Classical Realism and The Rise of China'. *European Journal of International Relations*, *18*(1), 53–75. DOI: 10.1177/1354066110373949

Langenhove, L. V., & Costea, A. (2005). *Inter-regionalism and the Future of Multiregionalism*. UNU-CRIS Occasional Papers.

Lechini, G., & Morasso, C. (2021). African and Latin American regionalism: Perspectives for interregionalism and South-South cooperation. In: *Regionalism, Security and Development in Africa* (pp. 129-142). Routledge.

Liow, H. L., & Xue, G. (Eds.). (2021). Research handbook on the Belt and Road Initiative. Edward Elgar Publishing., Available from https://www.e-elgar.com/shop/gbp/research-handbook-on-the-belt-and-road-initiative-9781789908701.html, Retrieved November 23, 2021, from. DOI: 10.4337/9781789908718

Liu, H. (2022a). China engages the Global South: From Bandung to the Belt and Road Initiative. *Global Policy*, *13*(1), 11–22. DOI: 10.1111/1758-5899.13034

Liu, H. (2022b) The political economy of transnational governance: China and Southeast Asia in the 21st century. Routledge. Available from: https://www.routledge.com/The-Political-Economy-of-Transnational-Governance-in-Asia-China-and-Southeast/Liu/p/book/9780367608804 [Accessed 23 November 2021].

Magallanes, R. (2015) On the Global South. In: *Concepts of the Global South -Voices from around the world*. Available at: https://www.researchgate.net/publication/343141439. [Accessed 15 March 2025].

Masaaki, Y. (2024). China's Efforts to Rally the Global South. In: *The Rising Global South and China. NIDS China Security Report 2025*. The National Institute for Defense Studies. Available at: https://www.nids.mod.go.jp/english/. [Accessed: 15 March 2025].

Masaaki, Y., ... (2024). The Rising Global South and China. NIDS China Security Report 2025. The National Institute for Defense Studies. Available at: https://www.nids.mod.go.jp/english/. [Accessed: 15 March 2025].

Mendez, A. (2015). Discussions on the Global South. In:*Concepts of the Global South -Voices from around the world.* Available at: https://www.researchgate.net/publication/343141439. [Accessed 15 March 2025].

Mochinaga, D. (2021). The Digital Silk Road and China's Technology Influence in Southeast Asia. *Council for Foreign Relations.* Available from: https://www.cfr.org/blog/digital-silk-road-and-chinas-technology-influence-southeast-asia. [Accessed 16 April 2025].

Murphy, D. C. (2022). *China's rise in the Global South: The Middle East, Africa, and Beijing's alternative world order.* Stanford University Press.

Reddy, R. K. (2023). Beijing's Digital Footprint and its Political Implications. Available at: https://www.orcasia.org/digital-silk-road. [Accessed 9 May 2025].

Rehbein, B. (2018). Critical Theory After the Rise of the Global South. In Giri, A. (Ed.), *Social Theory and Asian Dialogues.*, DOI: 10.1007/978-981-10-7095-2_4

Renwick, N. (2016). *China as a development actor in Southeast Asia.* IDS Evidence Report 187, Brighton: IDS.

Rolland, N. (2024). The Health Silk Road: A Branch of China's Belt and Road Initiative. the national bureau of Asian research. NBR special report #113. Available at: https://www.nbr.org/wp-content/uploads/pdfs/publications/sr113_rolland_dec2024.pdf. [Accessed 5 May 2025].

Schneider, F. (Ed.). (2021) *Global perspectives on China's Belt and Road Initiative: Asserting agency through regional connectivity.* Amsterdam University Press. Available from: https://www.aup.nl/en/book/9789048553952/global-perspectives-on-china-s-belt-and-road-initiative [Accessed 23 November 2021].

Tan, L. S. (2024). China's evolving Belt and Road Initiative in Southeast Asia. Available from: https://www.iiss.org/online-analysis/online-analysis/2024/07/chinas-evolving-belt-and-road-initiative-in-southeast-asia/. [Accessed 16 April 2025].

Tanaka, M. (2022). Greening the Belt and Road Initiative in Central Asia: The Case of Uzbekistan's Renewable Energy Sector. .DOI: 10.5117/9789048557820/ICAS.2022.080

UN Environment Belt and Road Strategy. (2017). Retrieved April 24, 2025, from https://unemg.org/images/emgdocs/SOMMeetings/2018/EMGSOM24%20INF%20-%206.%20UN%20Environment_Belt%20and%20Road%20Strategy.pdf

Wolvers, A. (2015). Concepts of the Global South. University of Cologne., Available from https://gssc.uni-koeln.de/node/452, [Accessed 1 March 2025].

Yang, M. (2024). China and ASEAN Rising Together on the Green Front. Available at: https://asiasociety.org/australia/china-and-asean-rising-together-green-front. [Accessed 28 April 2025].

Yang, S.-Y. (2013). 'Power Transition, Balance of Power, And the Rise of China: A Theoretical Reflection About Rising Great Powers'. *China Review*, *13*(2), 35–66.

Yu, H. (2024). China-ASEAN Cooperation Under the BRI. In *Understanding China's Belt and Road Initiative. Asia in Transition* (Vol. 26). Springer., DOI: 10.1007/978-981-99-9633-9_3

Zheng, W. (2024). China's Digital Silk Road (DSR) in Southeast Asia: Progress and Challenges. Perspective, no.1. ISEAS – Yusof Ishak Institute. Available at: https://www.iseas.edu.sg/articles-commentaries/iseas-perspective/2024-1-chinas-digital-silk-road-dsr-in-southeast-asia-progress-and-challenges-by-wang-zheng/. [Accessed 2 May 2025].

Chapter 5
U.S. Strategies to Counterbalance China in the Indo-Pacific: US-China Great Competition

Alireza Samoudi
https://orcid.org/0009-0001-5089-7798
Research Institute for Security and Development Studies, Tehran, Iran

Mohammad Reza Majidi
University of Tehran, Iran

ABSTRACT

Over the past decade, there have been various discussions about the past, present, and future of China-US relations. Since 2017, when the US National Security Strategy labeled China a strategic competitor, this term has consistently been used to describe Washington's relationship with Beijing. Examining US National Security Strategy documents over the past two decades reveals a shift in perspective from viewing China as a responsible actor to a serious and challenging competitor. Regarding the US approach to China's neighborhood policy, the main goal of the US Indo-Pacific Strategy is to provide strategic alternatives to weaken China's growing influence in its surrounding environment. The US believes that Beijing is striving to establish regional hegemony in the Indo-Pacific, control Taiwan, and dominate disputed areas in the East and South China Seas. Therefore, in recent years, the United States has expanded and strengthened its network of allies and strategic partnerships in the region to counter China's growing influence in the Indo-Pacific.

DOI: 10.4018/979-8-3373-0938-5.ch005

INTRODUCTION

The relationship between China and the United States has always been positioned along a spectrum of cooperation and competition due to its significance and complexity. As a result, trends of cooperation and competition are concurrently observable in the relations between these two countries. However, over time, and considering the failure of the United States to change China's behavior in a way that aligns with its own interests, the perception of a threat from China has increased in the U.S. This has led Washington to focus more on the concept of competition. This development has progressed to the extent that Americans have introduced the concepts of "Strategic Competition" and "Great Power Competition" in numerous documents, even declaring the upcoming decade as one based on strategic competition. From Washington's perspective, Beijing seeks regional hegemony in the short term and global dominance in the long term—an ambition that could potentially threaten the position of the United States.

The strategic competition between the United States and China has taken on a more serious form since the second decade of the 21st century, with U.S. officials prioritizing the response to China's rise and influence in this new era. During Obama's presidency, the U.S. initiated a "Pivot to Asia" which designated East Asian countries and the Pacific region as focal points for U.S. economic, political, and military development. In this context, the U.S. has shifted its focus from military costs in Afghanistan to the alliances it leads in the Asia-Pacific, known as the San Francisco system, which secures U.S. political and military hegemony in the region. Washington has reduced its security commitments abroad in Europe and the Middle East, reallocating resources to increase military budgets and strengthen military pacts and alliances in the Asia-Pacific.

In the past decade, strategic documents from U.S. security and defense institutions, along with American think tanks, have increasingly focused on China's emergence and the perceived threat it poses to America. By the end of Obama's presidency, China had become the focal point of U.S. foreign policy, leading to a strategic shift from West Asia to East Asia. During Trump's administration, following Obama's trajectory, the U.S. concentrated its strategic focus on the Indo-Pacific, transforming regional relationships, which were primarily economic and commercial, into security and military concerns. In fact, after Donald Trump took office in 2017 and identified China as the main threat to U.S. foreign policy in the National Security Strategy document, the Indo-Pacific region entered a new wave of competition, alliances, and coalitions. During Biden's administration, alongside the intensification of competition between the United States and China, U.S. policies toward China in the Indo-Pacific region also became more robust. U.S. concerns about China's growing influence in the Indo-Pacific region are a recurring theme in its policy documents and actions. These concerns are evident in the U.S. Indo-Pacific strategy, the National Security Strategy, and even NATO's New Strategic Concept, as well as in its network of bilateral security arrangements with countries in the region.

The United States' strategic approach to competing with China in Asia seems focused on preserving the existing regional order, which has been in place for several decades. This objective is reflected in the phrase "free and open Indo-Pacific," a term also used by the Trump administration. On the contrary, China's strategy seeks to lessen its susceptibility to pressure from the United States and to counter what it sees as the threat posed by liberal ideologies. However, the United States remains uncertain whether China possesses the same far-reaching global aspirations as the Soviet Union to fundamentally reshape the world order. This article aims to highlight the concept of strategic competition while discussing the U.S. perception of China shifting from a partner to a strategic rival. It also examines the change in the U.S. viewpoint toward China in its strategic documents and reviews U.S. policies aimed at containing China in the Indo-Pacific region.

CONCEPTUAL FRAMEWORK: STRATEGIC COMPETITION BETWEEN CHINA AND THE UNITED STATES

Over the past two decades, numerous researchers have engaged in extensive discussions regarding the precise description of the bilateral relationship between these two countries and its implications for the global order. Some analyze this relationship through the lens of the Thucydides Trap and the inevitable conflict arising from the fear of domination by a new power, believing that the confrontation between the U.S. and China could lead to an international military crisis. Others, such as Joseph Nye, draw inspiration from hegemonic stability theory and examine the issue of the participation of a declining power and a rising power in maintaining global stability through the provision of public goods from the perspective of international economics. Additionally, some invoke Cold War literature and a hard strategy to elucidate Washington's approach towards its relations with China. Since 2017, when the U.S. National Security Strategy labeled China as a strategic competitor, this designation has frequently been used in discussing Washington and Beijing's relations. Historically, this concept was first introduced during the détente period of the 1970s. The term "strategic competition" was used to refer to the intense rivalry among powerful states across various military, economic, and cultural domains.

Despite the discussions about Sino-American relations in the late 1990s and early 2000s, officials from the Bush administration used the term strategic competition with China as a tool to distinguish themselves from the Clinton administration, to redefine U.S. foreign policy in the post-Cold War era, and to counter China's rise.

The tone of U.S. National Security Strategy documents has changed dramatically over the past two decades. In the 1990s, the tone regarding China was largely positive, in contrast to today. For example, A 1999 document characterizes China as a country striving for prosperity and adherence to international norms, viewing its integration into the international trading framework is clearly aligned with our national interests. (NSS, 1999, P. 37). Even during George W. Bush's presidency, the National Security Strategy of 2006 expressed appreciation for China's reform trajectory: "In one generation, China has transitioned from a state characterized by poverty and seclusion to one that is increasingly integrated into the global economic framework. Previously, China exhibited resistance to international institutions; however, it now holds a permanent seat on both the United Nations Security Council (UNSC) and the World Trade Organization (WTO). The leadership in China asserts that they have resolved to pursue a transformative trajectory of peaceful development. Should China adhere to this commitment, the United States would greet the rise of a China that embodies peace and prosperity, one that collaborates with us to tackle shared challenges and mutual interests. China possesses the potential to significantly enhance global prosperity and secure its own long-term economic stability by placing greater reliance on domestic demand rather than on global trade imbalances to stimulate its economic advancement (NSS, 2006, p. 41).

Likewise, the Obama administration's National Security Strategy welcomed the positive and constructive relationship with China. However, in the 2015 National Security document, the perspective on China turned more negative. Although it still welcomed China's growth, it remarked on the need for close monitoring of China's military modernization and expanding presence in Asia. By 2017, the tone of the U.S. National Security Strategy had fundamentally shifted. The document noted that for decades, U.S. policy was rooted in supporting and fostering China's growth and welcomed its integration into the post-World War II liberal international order. Since 2017, both the Trump and Biden administrations have utilized this concept as a means to achieve their objectives. Strategic competition in political discourse began in the late 1960s. However, before the détente period of the 1970s, neither scholars nor journalists referred to this rivalry as strategic competition. Overall, during the Cold War, strategic competition was contextualized through its association with concepts such as avoiding nuclear catastrophe, détente, and meaningful strategic arms reduction. In the late 1990s, the concept of strategic competition resurfaced during George Bush's electoral campaign against Al Gore, Bill Clinton's vice president. George W. Bush remarked that "the next president must realize that while agreements can be reached with China in certain areas, such as access to its market, it must still be viewed as a competitor—a strategic competitor—and one must be firm and resolute toward this country" (Baum, 2001, p. 192). Condoleezza Rice, who later became the U.S. Secretary of State, articulated a realistic policy towards China in a pre-election speech before the November 2000 elections, stating: "China represents a security problem and threatens Taiwan, and it resents our presence in East Asia. The art of politics is to have the ability to manage complex relations with China. The truth is that China is an important power in international politics, and we must engage with it. However, this engagement must be realistic" (Baum, 2001, p. 202).

During the Obama administration, the term strategic competition was used less frequently, with a greater emphasis on increasing cooperation with China. Even amidst the pivot to Asia, the White House stressed that it did not view China as a strategic competitor (Winkler, 2023, p. 347). However, the label of strategic competition experienced a powerful resurgence during the Trump administration. Particularly, the publication of the U.S. National Security Strategy during this period clearly illustrated the emergence of strategic competition between Beijing and Washington. This document emphasized that "the United States is currently engaged in strategic competition, as revisionist powers like Russia and China challenge the U.S. and seek to undermine its security and prosperity. These countries aim to shape a world that is contrary to American values and interests" (NSS, 2017, pp. 2- 25). The Trump administration viewed the label of strategic competition as a way to demonstrate its resolve against China and to move away from the era of engagement with China that began with the Clinton administration's National Security Strategy in 1994. The central message that the Trump administration wanted to communicate to other states was that the United States now sees itself in a new era of strategic competition, where it must utilize all available tools to protect its interests (Winkler, 2023, p. 349).

There are traditionally two main perspectives on China in the United States. The first viewpoint posits that with China's economic growth, this growth would spill over into political and human rights improvements. Proponents of this perspective often refer to Germany and Japan, which were once America's biggest adversaries but became allies through the application of liberal models. According to this view, China's economic liberalization would not pose a threat to the U.S., as it would foster positive changes in other areas as well. The second perspective is held by realists, led by figures such as John Mearsheimer, who argue that China's economic growth will lead to increased military power. Realists assert that China's economic power will eventually translate into military might, and the U.S. should not assist China in this regard (Mearsheimer, 2021). They contend that the growth of China aligns with a shift in the balance of power, warning that Washington should not facilitate a situation where China could replace the U.S. as the dominant power. According to realists, including Mearsheimer, liberal policies have inadvertently aided China's rise to a global standing equivalent to the U.S.; had such assistance not been offered, China's ascent would have been slower. Mearsheimer and others in the realist camp argue that had the U.S. considered balancing strategies during its unipolar moment, it should have worked to slow China's growth and maximize the power gap between Beijing and Washington. They view the engagement policy with China as one of the worst strategic blunders in history, suggesting there is no precedent for a great power actively bolstering the rise of a rival of comparable strength (Mearsheimer, 2021) For realists, the prospect of China's rise as an economic superpower is indeed a nightmare, signaling not only the end of unipolarity but also the inevitable emergence of a powerful military, as wealthy and populous nations typically convert economic power into military capabilities.

Although competition is possible in all areas, the most significant domains of strategic competition can be identified in the definition of concepts, governance models, economic and technological development, rules and regulations of the international order, and, in essence, the efforts to create a new order or reform the existing one. Overall, it can be said that after China's emergence as an economic power, the United States has increased its focus on the Indo-Pacific region and has incorporated various initiatives, mechanisms, and alliances including AUKUS, QUAD, PDI, IPEF, … into its agenda to counter China.

WASHINGTON'S SHIFTING PERCEPTION OF BEIJING IN US STRATEGY DOCUMENTS: FROM FRIEND TO COMPETITOR AND ADVERSARY

Since the establishment of formal relations between China and the United States in 1979, various events have occurred that contribute to the understanding of the context behind the emergence of strategic competition between the two nations. In the 1980s, despite ideological differences, the U.S. and China reached a model of strategic cooperation to counter Soviet influence. This collaboration not only transformed the global geopolitical landscape but also significantly altered the dynamics of the Cold War, leading to a weakening of the Soviet Union's international standing (Akrami & Mohammadi Ramezani, 2024). The reciprocal trade dependence and relative stability in the relationship between the two countries in the post-Cold War era, characterized by political, ideological, and military détente among major powers, began to weaken in the early 2010s. Of course, it should be noted that this shift in the U.S. perspective on China began several years ago. The initial point of this transformation can be seen in a change in the U.S. Department of Defense's perception of the potential threat posed by China. After the end of the Cold War, American policymakers did not have specific concerns regarding China. Nevertheless, there were signs that China could pose a danger to the U.S. With a population nearly five times larger than that of the United States and the initiation of economic reforms, China was seen as a potential challenge. Both Democratic and Republican governments in the U.S pursued a policy of engagement with China through liberal perspectives, aiming for China's advancement. Washington sought to increase investment in China and welcomed its entry into the global trading system. In fact, during the 1990s, influenced by liberal thought, there was a prevailing belief that engaging with China and integrating it into the global economy would result in China thriving and becoming a responsible global actor.

The shift in perspective towards China is also clearly reflected in the U.S. National Security Strategy documents and other strategic documents. However, various administrations in the U.S. welcomed engagement with China. For instance, the Clinton administration criticized George H.W. Bush during the 1992 election campaign for his soft stance and excessive attention to China, advocating for a tougher position toward Beijing. However, once in office, Clinton took a different path. In 1994, he stated: "The United States should increase its engagement with China; this will lead China to become a responsible power. Not only will it grow economically, but its political maturity will also increase, leading to greater respect for human rights. The best path for advancing freedom in China for the U.S. is through developing and expanding relations" (Clinton, 1994). This shift in strategy reflected a commitment to engaging with China not just for economic reasons but for fostering political and social changes as well. George W. Bush also made efforts to integrate China into the global economy, believing that trade with China would promote freedom within the country. Both Democrats and Republicans were encouraged to work together to normalize China as a trading partner (NYTimes, 2000). In his first year in office, Bush signed a statement granting China permanent normal trade relations and took final steps to facilitate China's accession to the World Trade Organization (WTO) during his administration.

In the 2006 Quadrennial Defense Review, the Pentagon warned that among the international challenges, the rise of major powers, including India, Russia, and China, could play a crucial role in the security environment of the international system in the 21st century. This report presented a positive assessment regarding India and Russia, but stated that among the major emerging powers, China has the greatest potential to compete militarily with the U.S. and possesses military technologies that could challenge America's traditional military advantages over time (QDRR, 2006, p. 29). Although the report identifies China as a potential threat, it also emphasizes that U.S. policy remains focused on encouraging China to play a constructive and peaceful role in the Asia-Pacific region and to act responsibly as a strategic partner in addressing common security challenges, including terrorism, the proliferation of weapons of mass destruction, and piracy (QDRR, 2006, p. 29).

During the Obama administration, there was still a sense of optimism regarding China. For example, in 2015, President Obama stated: "When I came into office, my goal was always to engage with China in a constructive way, managing differences and maximizing opportunities for cooperation. I have repeatedly said that I believe China's growth and the lifting of its people out of poverty are in America's interests; because a successful, stable, and peaceful China can be an effective partner for the U.S. on a range of international challenges" (Obama, 2015). In Obama's 2010 National Security Strategy, there was mention of comprehensive cooperation with China, and the U.S. aimed to have Beijing act as a responsible stakeholder: "We welcome a China that takes on a responsible leadership role in working with the United States and the international community to advance priorities like economic recovery, confronting climate change, and nonproliferation. Disagreements should not prevent cooperation on issues of mutual interest, because a pragmatic and effective relationship between the United States and China is essential to addressing the major challenges of the 21st century (NSS, 2010, p. 43). Even with the announcement of the "Pivot to Asia" strategy, there remained a positive outlook on China, with discussions suggesting that China's growth was beneficial for the U.S.

In the 2014 Quadrennial Defense Review, the Pentagon reiterated the concept of rebalancing in the Pacific region: "We shall persist in our contributions to the United States' strategic recalibration towards the Asia-Pacific region, endeavoring to uphold peace and stability within a region that is progressively becoming pivotal to U.S. political, economic, and security priorities" (QDR, 2014, p. VIII). This concept can be seen as a diplomatic interpretation of the strategy known as the "Pivot to Asia." Rebalancing indicated that the U.S. was not only strategically concerned about China's rise but was also seeking to mobilize military resources and diplomatic focus in East Asia to counter one of its major trading partners. Though the U.S. continued to avoid explicitly declaring a containment approach toward China until the end of the Obama administration, Washington's orientation toward Beijing had shifted. This shift became more pronounced during the Trump era. For instance, in President Trump's National Security Strategy (2017) it is said that "China and Russia contest the dominance, sway, and strategic interests of the United States, endeavoring to undermine American security and economic well-being. They are resolute in their objective to render their economies increasingly restrictive and inequitable, to enhance their military capabilities, and to manipulate information and data in order to suppress their populations and augment their geopolitical influence" (NSS, 2017, p. 2). "China and Russia aspire to construct a global order that is diametrically opposed to the values and interests espoused by the United States. China aims to supplant the United States in the Indo-Pacific region, broaden the scope of its state-driven economic paradigm, and reorganize the regional dynamics to its advantage" (NSS, 2017, p. 25). However, in the first term of the Trump presidency, the strategy of engagement that had characterized the previous four administrations was abandoned in favor of containment policy. Trump initiated a trade war with China in 2018, aiming to halt China's successes and targeting Chinese technology giant Huawei and other companies that were seen as threats to U.S. technological supremacy. The Trump administration also pursued closer ties with Taiwan and challenged China's claims in the South China Sea, marking a significant shift in U.S.-China relations toward a more confrontational stance.

The shift in the U.S. perspective under the Trump administration, "moving away from cooperation with China and acknowledging that China's integration into the international system has not led Beijing to embrace liberal policies to the degree desired by the U.S.", is clearly articulated in the 2017 National Security Strategy: "For decades, U.S. policy was rooted in the belief that support for China's rise and for its integration into the post-war international order would liberalize China. Contrary to our hopes, China expanded its power at the expense of the sovereignty of others. China gathers and exploits data on an unrivaled scale and spreads features of its authoritarian system, including corruption and the use of surveillance. It is building the most capable and well-funded military in the world, after our own. Its nuclear arsenal is growing and diversifying. Part of China's military modernization and economic expansion is due to its access to the U.S. innovation economy, including America's world-class universities" (NSS, 2017, p. 25). This document also explicitly mentions the great power competition between China and the United States: " in addition, after being dismissed as a phenomenon of an earlier century, great power competition returned. China and Russia began to reassert their influence regionally and globally. Today, they are fielding military capabilities designed to deny America access in times of crisis and to contest our ability to operate freely in critical commercial zones during peacetime. In short, they are contesting our geopolitical advantages and trying to change the international order in their favor" (NSS, 2017, p. 27).

In the Biden administration's 2022 National Security Strategy, China is identified as the sole competitor with the capacity to reshape the international order. It is depicted as an actor seeking to weaken U.S. alliances in the Indo-Pacific and worldwide, striving to expand its sphere of influence in the Indo-Pacific, and aspiring to global leadership. However, the document reiterates that despite competition between Washington and Beijing, the U.S. will cooperate with China in areas of shared interest: "The PRC is the only competitor with both the intent to reshape the international order and, increasingly, the economic, diplomatic, military, and technological power to do it. Beijing has ambitions to create an enhanced sphere of influence in the Indo-Pacific and to become the world's leading power. The PRC is also investing in a military that is rapidly modernizing, increasingly capable in the Indo-Pacific, and growing in strength and reach globally – all while seeking to erode U.S. alliances in the region and around the world. While we compete vigorously, we will always be willing to work with the PRC where our interests align" (NSS, 2022, p. 24- 25).

In the U.S. National Defense Strategy published in 2022, China is identified as the most serious challenge, seeking to change the regional order in the Indo-Pacific and attempting to destabilize conditions in the South China Sea and the East China Sea: "The most extensive and notable challenge to United States national security arises from the People's Republic of China's (PRC) coercive and progressively aggressive initiative to reshape the Indo-Pacific region and the global system to align with its own interests and authoritarian inclinations. The PRC endeavors to erode U.S. alliances and security partnerships within the Indo-Pacific region while capitalizing on its expanding capabilities, which encompass its economic sway and the increasing strength and military presence of the People's Liberation Army (PLA), to intimidate its neighboring states and jeopardize their interests. The PRC's progressively provocative rhetoric and coercive actions directed at Taiwan are destabilizing, pose a risk of miscalculation, and threaten the tranquility and stability of the Taiwan Strait. This behavior is indicative of a broader trend of destabilizing and coercive actions by the PRC that extends across the East China Sea, the South China Sea, and along the Line of Actual Control" (NDS, 2022, p. 4). An analysis of U.S. strategic documents shows that since the second decade of the 21st century, the positive perception of China has waned, and instead, China is viewed as a serious competitor and threat to America's dominant position in the international system.

THE IMPORTANCE OF THE INDO-PACIFIC REGION IN AMERICAN STRATEGIC DOCUMENTS

The strategic competition between China and the United States, along with China's presence in East Asia, has enhanced the role and significance of the continent in global affairs, making Asia a battleground for these two major powers. In fact, Asia is shaping the economic, political, and security order of the international system in the new millennium. Richard Haas and Charles Kupchan write in an article for Foreign Affairs, "The international system is at a historic turning point. As Asia continues its economic ascent, the era of Western dominance is coming to an end" (Hass & Kupchan, 2021). The Indo-Pacific region is stretching from American Pacific coastline to the Indian Ocean, is home to more than half of the world's people, nearly two-thirds of the world's economy, and seven of the world's largest militaries (Indo-Pacific Strategy, 2022: 4). Significant economic growth, the existence of various political systems, and short-, medium-, and long-term crises have made this region one of the primary areas where the United States seeks to expand its influence and, consequently, solidify its hegemony.

The U.S. has been working to prevent the rise of balancing competitors in this strategic region. The Indo-Pacific region, with its unique economic, political, and security characteristics, has become a battleground for the policies of major powers, especially the United States and China. The emergence of new developments in the international system, the rise of China, and the increasing influence and economic power of organizations like ASEAN have turned this region into a competition among great powers.

Since the presidency of George W. Bush, the U.S. strategy in the region has focused on increasing its military and economic presence to contain China while maintaining economic growth. While German geographer Karl Haushofer first used the term "Indo-Pacific" in the 1920s, referring to the geographical integration of the Pacific and Indian Oceans, the term's contemporary application can be traced back to a speech by Japanese Prime Minister Shinzo Abe in 2007. In that speech, Shinzo Abe discussed strategic partnerships in the broader Asia region and proposed a dialogue and cooperation framework involving Japan, the United States, Australia, and India. He envisioned a vast network encompassing the entire Pacific, the United States, Australia, and the Indian Ocean (Shinzo, 2007). The concept of the Indo-Pacific reflects strategic changes and the resurgence of great power competition at the international level, as well as the emergence of regional actors that will significantly influence global strategic developments.

Although the concept of the Indo-Pacific was somewhat forgotten for a time, it regained prominence with the return of Shinzo Abe and Trump's arrival at the White House in 2017. The notion of the Indo-Pacific acknowledges that the Indian and Pacific Oceans are the defining geopolitical arenas of the 21st century. This region is not only the site of the fastest economic growth and great power competition but is also teeming with terrestrial and maritime activities. As the strategic importance of the Indo-Pacific has grown, major powers are expanding their new policies to enhance their access to this vital region.

After the Cold War, the United States, declaring a new world order, continuously and significantly linked its security to that of Asia. By adopting a policy of maintaining the status quo, the U.S. aimed to prevent any country from gaining power that could alter the balance of power. In this context, Washington has pursued its strategy in Asia through continued presence in the region, based on economic relations and bilateral security ties. Given the importance of the Indo-Pacific, the attention of various U.S. presidents to this region has gradually increased. In fact, to sustain its desired hegemony in the Indo-Pacific region and to contain China's rising power, the U.S. has implemented a series of policies. The U.S. views China as an irresponsible stakeholder in the international system, unwilling to bear the costs associated with enjoying the existing order and stability derived from U.S. hegemony. Therefore, it must be contained (Jamshidi & Dehshiri, 2018, p. 208). By enhancing its military presence in East Asia, the United States aims to prevent the emergence of hegemonic forces and establish a form of deterrence in the region. Strengthening naval forces and balancing offshore power are among the measures taken by the U.S. to bolster its military capability in the Indo-Pacific. American leaders believe that global hegemony cannot continue without effective engagement in Asia. Accordingly, since the beginning of the second decade of the new millennium, all U.S. presidents have pursued an "Eastward tilt" policy to strategically compete with China through various means. In recent years, the U.S. has consistently sought to expand bilateral and multilateral security agreements with East Asian countries and its allies in the region. This section will discuss the policies of different U.S. administrations concerning the Indo-Pacific.

BUSH AND CLINTON ERA: COOPERATION AND A BIT OF COMPETITION

Bill Clinton, while supporting China's integration and alignment with the international order, also introduced the idea of a new Pacific community to alleviate security concerns by anchoring this region's security and to fueling its development (Clinton, 1993). In fact, Clinton's policy toward China in 1993 aimed to encourage Beijing to cooperate with the U.S.-led regional order in Asia and to create a framework for constructive engagement in the region (Derakhshandeh et al., 2022, p. 22). After Clinton took office, tensions emerged in U.S.-China relations, leading to a reevaluation of America's strategy in the Indo-Pacific. In 1995, the U.S. Department of Defense released a security strategy for the East Asia-Pacific region, emphasizing the central role of military power in maintaining America's presence in Asia (Manouchehri et al., 2023, p. 35).

During George W. Bush's presidency, the concept of a "responsible stakeholder" was first put forward by Robert Zoellick, then serving as Deputy Secretary of State, in September 2005. He emphasized the necessity of encouraging China to assume the role of a responsible stakeholder within the international system. In this capacity, China would transcend mere membership and collaborate with other nations to uphold the international framework that has contributed to its success (Zoellick, 2005). This concept proposed that the policy of engagement with Beijing, as a member of the international system, should progress further, transforming China from an emerging power outside the system into an emerging power within the international system. In this context, emphasis was placed on the necessity of encouraging China to play a constructive role in promoting peace in Asia and sharing responsibility for strengthening the international system.

Obama Administration: Pivot to Asia

During George W. Bush's presidency, the United States was unable to respond appropriately to China's rapid growth due to its focus on the Middle East and the wars in Afghanistan and Iraq. However, with Barack Obama taking office, the idea of a "Pivot to Asia" or rebalancing toward Asia emerged, which was first articulated by then-Secretary of State Hillary Clinton in her article titled "America's Pacific Century." While emphasizing that the administration under President Obama would endeavor to enhance relations with China, Clinton utilized an address preceding an Asia-Pacific summit (November 11, 2011) to dissuade Beijing and other entities from presuming that the United States is relinquishing its conventional function in the Pacific region: "The Asia-Pacific region is currently confronted with a multitude of challenges that necessitate the leadership of the United States, encompassing the safeguarding of navigational freedoms in the South China Sea, addressing the provocations and proliferation activities of North Korea, and fostering equitable and inclusive economic development. It is becoming increasingly evident that the Asia-Pacific will be the world's strategic and economic hub in the 21st century. One of the foremost objectives of U.S. policy over the coming decade is to ensure a significantly greater commitment to this region. Washington seeks to build, in this century, a network in the Asia-Pacific akin to the transatlantic network of institutions and alliances that the United States and its European partners established during the 20th century" (Reuters, 2011). In fact, the goal of this shift was to strengthen America's position through a multilateral approach that emphasized increased military presence, diplomatic engagement, and free trade negotiations.

Although the United States initially hoped that Obama's existing strategy of combining engagement and military deterrence in Asia would produce the desired outcomes, the primary purpose of the "pivot" was to reorient US strategic policy. This realignment aimed to account for both the shifting power dynamics and the evolving attitudes and intentions of the People's Republic of China's leadership (Bisley, 2023, p. 17). The strategy of shifting U.S. foreign policy from the Middle East to the Asia-Pacific region marked a turning point in Obama's approach towards China. From the beginning of his presidency, Obama aimed to redirect Washington's focus from the Middle East to the Asia-Pacific. In November 2011, during a speech to the Australian Parliament, he revealed this shift in U.S. attention from West Asia to the Asia-Pacific, emphasizing the region's importance as his priority. He said: " I wish to elucidate the overarching objective of my visit to this geographical area -- our initiatives aimed at promoting security, prosperity, and human dignity throughout the Asia Pacific. For the United States, this signifies a more comprehensive transformation. Following a decade marked by our engagement in two conflicts that exacted a significant toll, both in terms of human lives and economic resources, the United States is now redirecting its focus toward the immense possibilities inherent in the Asia Pacific region. The region is the fastest-growing in the world and houses over half of the global economy and has the potential to determine whether the coming century will be defined by cooperation or by conflict and competition. I have instructed his national security team to prioritize our mission and presence in the Pacific" (Obama, 2011).

In early 2012, the Obama administration announced plans to enhance the United States' role in the Asia-Pacific region. As a result, this region became a priority for U.S. foreign policy, planning, and economic strategies. As Obama stated in November 2011, the objective in the region was to ensure a greater and long-term role in shaping the future of Asia-Pacific. The approach and foreign policy of the United States during this period, as articulated by Tom Donilon, Obama's National Security Advisor, focused on advancing American interests by helping to shape norms and rules and ensuring that these norms and international laws are respected. This included ensuring that trade and freedom of navigation are not impeded, that emerging powers build trust with their neighbors, and that disputes are resolved peacefully without threats or coercion (Manouchehri et al., 2023, p. 36). From Beijing's viewpoint, the "pivot" strategy reinforced the belief among its policymakers that the United States was unwilling to acknowledge China's ascendant position. Some even interpreted it as evidence that the US aimed not only to preserve the existing global order but also to actively impede China's progress towards realizing its full potential (Bisley, 2023, p. 17)

The Trump Era: The Return of the Concept of Strategic Competition

Relations between China and the United States experienced significant deterioration during the tenure of the Trump administration. Under President Trump's leadership, Washington repudiated the longstanding policy of engagement that had been in place for four decades toward Beijing, designating China as a revisionist great power intent on disrupting both regional and global order. It involved implementing extensive tariffs on Chinese imports, intensifying scrutiny over Chinese investments and influence within the United States, and commencing a partial decoupling of the two largest economies in the world. Furthermore, the Trump administration introduced, for the first time, an Indo-Pacific strategy aimed at counterbalancing or even containing China's escalating influence within the region (Wei & Zhang, 2021, p. 159). It was during the Trump administration that the concept of strategic competition between Beijing and Washington became prominent, with China being recognized as a threat to the United States and greater attention given to the Indo-Pacific region.

The Trump Administration resurrected a concept first introduced under President George W. Bush to foster closer collaboration with Japan, Australia, and India through a Quadrilateral framework known as the "Quad." This partnership initially took shape in response to the devastating 2004 Indian Ocean earthquake and tsunami. The Quad has been described as "a loose geostrategic alignment of states concerned about China's potential challenge to their interests." Consequently, some observers regard it as a strategic counterweight to China's growing influence in the Indo-Pacific. The Quad first convened on the sidelines of the ASEAN Regional Forum in May 2007 (CRS, 2018, p. 13) and aimed to forge closer consultation and cooperation among democratic nations in the Asia-Pacific against a rising China. In addition to the security dialogue, the four countries also held their first- ever joint naval exercise, Malabar, which drew criticism and protests from China (Wei & Zhang, 2021, p. 168). Despite its initial failure and brief existence due to divergent security interests and unfavorable geopolitical circumstances, the group was revived ten years later. This revival was driven by a deteriorating security environment and a growing consensus among the four members regarding their shared interests (Bisley, 2023, p. 22). This coalition was formally re-established in November 2017 between the four countries in Manila, encompassing seven main topics: a rules-based order, freedom of navigation, respect for international laws, increased connectivity, maritime security, the North Korean threat, and the non-proliferation of nuclear weapons and terrorism (Keshvarian & Mirtorabi, 2022, p. 34).

Trump introduced the concept of a "Free and Open Indo-Pacific" in his speech at the APEC summit in November 2017 in Vietnam. Through various declarations and reports, the Trump administration articulated an objective to foster a "free and open Indo-Pacific" (FOIP) region, which aims to integrate U.S. strategies across East Asia and South Asia. Some analysts view this FOIP initiative as a continuation of the Obama Administration's policy of "strategic rebalancing" in the Asia-Pacific. (CRS, 2018, p. 3). The national security strategy and the national defense strategy of the Trump administration also presented the United States' ideas regarding the Indo-Pacific. Additionally, in 2017, the U.S. State Department released a program titled "Defining our relationship with India for the next century," which describes a rules-based international order that benefits both the U.S. and India against what is labeled as China's revisionist threats: "The assertive maneuvers executed by China in the South China Sea pose a direct challenge to the established international legal frameworks and norms that both the United States and India advocate. The United States seeks to foster constructive bilateral relations with China; however, we shall not retreat from addressing China's infringements upon the rules-based international order and instances in which China undermines the sovereignty of adjacent nations while disadvantaging the United States and its allies" (CSIS, 2017). In July 2018, Secretary of State Mike Pompeo articulated the aims of the Free and Open Indo-Pacific initiative, stating, "When we talk about a free Indo-Pacific, we mean that all nations can protect their sovereignty against coercion and aggression from other countries. 'Free' means good governance and ensuring that citizens can enjoy their freedoms and fundamental rights. When we say 'open,' we mean that all nations should have open access to the seas and airways. We want maritime disputes to be resolved peacefully" (Pompeo, 2018)

The 2017 National Security Strategy highlights that China's actions in the South China Sea violate the national sovereignty of its neighbors, and that China aims to displace the United States in the Indo-Pacific region. Furthermore, it notes that a geopolitical competition is emerging in this region between two visions of the world: one embracing repressive policies, and the other favoring open policies towards the Indo-Pacific. It also emphasizes strengthening U.S. partnerships and alliances in the region, and that the U.S. seeks to deepen its relationships with new partners: China's efforts to build and militarize outposts in the South China Sea endanger the free flow of trade, threaten the sovereignty of other nations, and undermine regional stability. China has mounted a rapid military modernization campaign designed to limit U.S. access to the region and provide China a freer hand there. China presents its ambitions as mutually beneficial, but Chinese dominance risks diminishing the sovereignty of many states in the Indo-Pacific. China seeks to displace the United States in the Indo-Pacific region, expand the reaches of its state-driven economic model, and reorder the region in its favor. A geopolitical competition between free and repressive visions of world order is taking place in the Indo-Pacific region. The U.S. interest in a free and open Indo-Pacific extends back to the earliest days of our republic. China presents its ambitions as mutually beneficial, but Chinese dominance risks diminishing the sovereignty of many states in the Indo-Pacific. States throughout the region are calling for sustained U.S. leadership in a collective response that upholds a regional order respectful of sovereignty and independence. The United States will redouble its commitment to established alliances and partnerships, while expanding and deepening relationships with new partners that share respect for sovereign-, fair and reciprocal trade, and the rule of law. We will reinforce our commitment to freedom of the seas and the peaceful resolution of territorial and maritime disputes in accordance with international law. We will work with allies and partners to achieve complete, verifiable, and irreversible denuclearization on the Korean Peninsula and preserve" (NSS, 2017, p. 25, 46-7).

In 2018, the U.S. National Defense Strategy was updated to emphasize great power competition—with a particular focus on China—as a top priority for the Pentagon. The strategy designates the Indo-Pacific region as the foremost theater of operations and identifies the resurgence of long-term strategic competition by revisionist powers as the principal threat to American prosperity and security. It further accuses China of "leveraging military modernization, influence operations, and predatory economics" to pressure neighboring countries into reshaping the Indo-Pacific region in its favor, while simultaneously aiming to displace the United States to secure future global preeminence (CRS, 2018, p.12).

Biden Era: Intensification of Strategic Competition

In his first major foreign policy address on February 4, 2021, President Biden identified China as America's most significant competitor. He asserted that the U.S. must counter rising authoritarianism, including the ambitions of China and Russia, and pledged to confront China's economic abuses and aggressive actions. Secretary of State Antony Blinken echoed this sentiment, identifying China as Washington's main rival. He argued that China is uniquely positioned, with its economic, diplomatic, military, and technological strength, to challenge the existing international order that reflects American values and interests (Wei & Zhang, 2021, p. 161).

During the Biden administration, the Indo-Pacific issue gained significant importance. For example, Lloyd Austin, the U.S. Secretary of Defense, in his speech at the Shangri-La Dialogue (June 2-4, 2023) titled "A Shared Vision for the Indo-Pacific," emphasized the "power of partnership" and noted that more countries in the Indo-Pacific have come together around a shared vision for the future: "We have found new friends, deepened longstanding alliances, and enhanced deterrence with the goal of preventing conflict. We are increasing planning and coordination with our friends from the East China Sea to the South China Sea and the Indian Ocean. We have loyal allies such as Australia, Japan, South Korea, the Philippines, and Thailand, and valuable partners like India, Indonesia, Vietnam, and Singapore. We have also increased defense cooperation with Japan, including enhancing the level of joint exercises such as "Keen Sword" and "Resolute Dragon", as well as with the Philippines, including designating new sites for force deployment. Since 2020, we have invested $1.2 billion in security cooperation with Australia and the UK to ensure that countries in the Indo-Pacific region can establish deterrence against coercive actions. Significant progress has also been made with Australia, India, and Japan under the Quad framework, with increased maritime cooperation and humanitarian assistance" (Austin, 2023).

With the arrival of Joe Biden on January 20, 2021, the focus on the Indo-Pacific region has increased, similar to the previous two administrations, as evidenced by U.S. political security documents. According to the "Indo-Pacific Strategy 2022" document, the Biden administration, like its predecessors, increased its attention to this region to counter its challenges. Additionally, the "Interim National Security Strategic Guidance" document identifies China as a competitor that threatens the free and stable international order across economic, military, diplomatic, and technological dimensions and has been assertive (INSSG, 2021, p. 8). The Annual Threat Assessment (2023) also identified China as the primary threat to the U.S. in the diplomatic, military, economic, and technological realms, emphasizing the need to counter its global influence:"China possesses the capacity to directly endeavor to reshape the rules-based international order across various domains and in diverse regions, functioning as a near-peer competitor that is progressively striving to modify global norms and potentially posing a threat to its neighboring countries. Beijing is increasingly amalgamating its expanding military capabilities with its economic, technological, and diplomatic clout to fortify the authority of the Chinese Communist Party, assert what it perceives as its sovereign territory and regional dominance, and pursue a broader global influence" (Annual Threat Assessment, 2023, p. 4- 6).

According to 2024 Worldwide Threat Assessment, China tries to challenge the United States: "In the forthcoming year, the People's Republic of China is anticipated to enhance its military capabilities, particularly in areas deemed paramount for military engagements against Taiwan and the United States, while simultaneously refining its competencies as a cohesive joint force. The Chinese government persistently seeks to develop its global capabilities to challenge the United States and its allies across various domains, including diplomatic, informational, military, and economic spheres. Chinese leadership is intent on equipping the nation for competition and potential confrontation with the United States and its allies both in East Asia and globally, while the People's Republic of China aims to erode popular and political support for U.S. military alliances and security partnerships on a worldwide scale" (Worldwide Threat Assessment, 2024, p. 1). According to the "Indo-Pacific Strategy 2022" document, the United States is determined to strengthen its long-term position and commitment to the Indo-Pacific region, focusing on every corner of Northeast Asia, Southeast Asia, South Asia, and Oceania. The document states that the U.S. must reinforce its position by collaborating closely with its closest allies and partners. The goal is to shape a strategic environment that balances competition with China and enhances U.S. interests, those of its allies and partners, as well as shared interests and values. Additionally, the U.S. seeks to establish a networked security architecture through a range of countries and regional organizations (Indo-Pacific Strategy, 2022, p. 5, 17). According to the Department of Defense's explanations regarding the "National Defense Strategy 2022," countering China and collaborating with allies and partners to create deterrence against China in the Indo-Pacific region are among the primary objectives of the United States (Keshvarian & Mirtorabi, 2022, p. 33).

Indeed, the Biden administration's policies have indicated that the U.S. is pivoting toward the Pacific and leading smaller, targeted alliances focused on American interests. At the summit of the leaders of the United States, the United Kingdom, Japan, and India- known as the Quad, held at the White House following the United Nations General Assembly in September 2021, the leaders issued a statement declaring that this summit provided an opportunity to refocus on the Indo-Pacific region and their shared vision for achieving their goals. Continuing the U.S. approach of multilateral security cooperation to counter China in the Indo-Pacific region, on September 16, 2021, the leaders of the United Kingdom, the United States, and Australia signed the AUKUS military defense pact. The alliance aims to bolster the mutual security interests of its three Indo-Pacific participants. It seeks to achieve this by enhancing both their individual and collective defense capabilities through the sharing of technology. This is most evident in the members' pledge to assist Australia in acquiring, deploying, and maintaining a fleet of at least eight nuclear-powered submarines (Bisley, 2023, p. 25). The signing of this pact resulted in a strong reaction from China, as well as a response from France due to the cancellation of a $40 billion defense contract with Australia, along with-reactions from the European Union. Under this pact, Australia will acquire U.S.-manufactured submarines equipped with nuclear propulsion, though not nuclear weapons, leveraging technology that was previously exclusive to the U.S. and the UK. In essence, the trilateral security agreement between Australia, the U.S., and the UK, known as AUKUS, focuses on enhancing Australia's military capabilities and is fundamentally aimed at balancing the influence of the People's Republic of China. It represents part of the U.S.'s multilateral security coalition-building in the Indo-Pacific region (Ghalkhanbaz et al., 2023, p. 40).

Therefore, the military bloc formed under the name AUKUS is a continuation of the U.S. policy regarding multilateral defense and security cooperation, centered around Australia and the UK in the Indo-Pacific region. Analyzing the pact reveals several fundamental issues that will significantly impact the future of East Asia and warrant attention: Australia will play a prominent role in the U.S. multilateral approach in East Asia now and in the future. The possibility of an arms race will likely increase in the region due to such agreements. The UK has joined the U.S. security network to counter China in the Indo-Pacific, thus complicating the American multilateral approach (Keshavarzian & Mirtorabi, 2022, p. 38). China has reacted strongly to the AUKUS pact, perceiving it as a catalyst for the emergence of a new Cold War in the world. The goal of this pact is to engage China within its own territorial boundaries to prevent its increasing economic, political, and military advances in various parts of the world, thereby ensuring that it does not threaten the United States' superpower status (Ghalkhanbaz et al., 2023, p. 41). In response to the question regarding the joint statement issued by the defense ministers of the

United States, Britain, and Australia on March 8, 2024, regarding the consideration of Japan joining AUKUS, the spokesperson for the Chinese Embassy in Britain stated " These nations, ignoring the widespread concerns of both regional countries and the international community regarding the risks of nuclear proliferation, are determined to push forward with their so-called trilateral security partnership and are even attempting to enlist additional countries. This will inevitably heighten the risk of nuclear proliferation, intensify the arms race in the Asia-Pacific, and threaten regional peace and stability. China expresses grave concern and strong opposition to this development. We urge the US, UK, and Australia to move away from a Cold War mindset, refrain from forming exclusive blocs, and stop inciting discord and confrontation in the Asia-Pacific region. Japan should take heed of historical lessons and exercise caution in its military security rhetoric and actions" (Embassy of PRC in the UK, 2024).

In May 2022, the United States, together with 13 partners, introduced the Indo-Pacific Economic Framework for Prosperity (IPEF), marking the Biden administration first major trade and economic initiative in the region. This framework is seen as a response to repeated calls from policymakers and stakeholders for a more vigorous U.S. economic and trade strategy in the Indo-Pacific—a strategy many felt had lagged behind its military engagement. This sentiment became particularly pronounced after the U.S. withdrew from the Trans-Pacific Partnership (TPP) in 2017 and did not join its successor, the Comprehensive and Progressive Agreement for Trans-Pacific Partnership (CPTPP). The IPEF coalition, representing 40% of global GDP, consists of countries that vary widely in size and stage of economic development. By 2023, Japan, South Korea, and India had become some of the United States' top 10 trading partners, while U.S.-Vietnam trade surged by more than 400% over the past decade. Overall, IPEF members accounted for nearly one-fifth of U.S. goods and services trade and, in 2022, comprised 11% of U.S. direct investment abroad and attracted 18% of foreign investment in the United States (CRS, 2024).

Figure 1. U.S. Trade with IPEF Partners, 2023

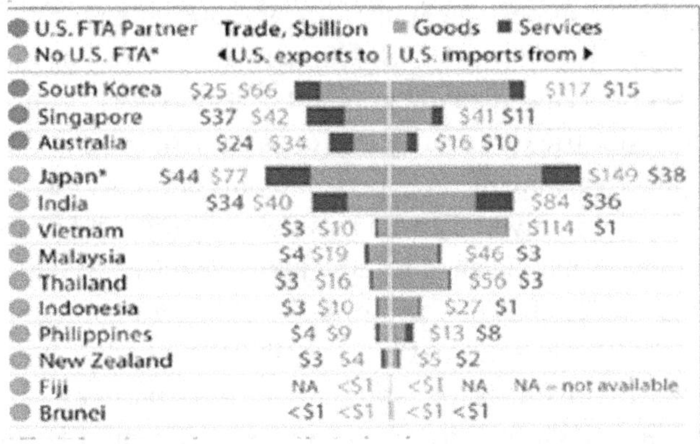

(CRS, 2024)

This framework aims to strengthen economic ties in the Indo-Pacific region, acknowledging the interconnected nature of economic and security concerns. In addition, the Pacific Deterrence Initiative (PDI), was devised in 2020 in response to perceived security threat from the People's Republic of China (PRC). Its name and framework were inspired by the European Deterrence Initiative (EDI), which was initiated in 2014 to address Russian aggression in Europe (CRS, 2024).

Proposed by the U.S. Indo-Pacific Command, the initiative encompasses a range of cooperative defense and preparedness activities. The Pacific Deterrence Initiative emphasizes the U.S.'s strategic focus, aiming to enhance deterrence, reassure allies and partners, and counter threats from adversaries in the region, particularly in response to China's increasing military capabilities (European Parliament, 2023: 9). From the U.S. perspective, the PDI sends a strong message to China, potential adversaries, and allied partners that Washington is deeply committed to defending its interests in the region (Keshvarian & Mirtorabi, 2022, p. 39). Furthermore, to counter China's influence, the U.S. has signed bilateral security agreements with several East Asian countries, including South Korea and Japan. These agreements aim to institutionalize and reinforce U.S. presence in East Asia, leveraging the capabilities of its allies in the region to balance and counteract Chinese influence. This approach reflects the broader U.S. strategy of building a robust security architecture in the Indo-Pacific as part of efforts to maintain regional stability and deter potential threats.

The United States believes that China, through assertive actions in the South China Sea and the East China Sea, aims to establish a maritime sphere of influence to expand its military power and counter Washington's capabilities. While Beijing firmly claims these areas as part of its territory, the U.S. does not make any territorial claims in these maritime regions. However, it considers the protection of these areas as part of its core policies in the region emphasizing stability, ensuring freedom of navigation, countering Chinese actions, and safeguarding U.S. security. Taiwan is also a contentious issue in U.S.-China relations. Beijing views the Taiwan issue as a domestic concern and an integral part of its territory. Conversely, the U.S. regards Taiwan as a significant security and economic partner in the region. While committing to support Taiwan, the U.S. perceives any actions threatening the peace, stability, security, or economy of Taiwan as a threat to regional peace. Washington also considers Taiwan as having an independent defensive legal status and views the provision of military assistance to Taiwan as essential for maintaining security and a symbol of balance of power against Beijing (Derakhshandeh et al., 2022, p. 21). John Mearsheimer, a realist theorist, states "regarding the outlook of U.S.-China rivalry, the United States is going to defend Taiwan, and it must. By limiting China's military activities in the first island chain that surrounds its mainland in Asia, China can be contained. Taiwan is part of the natural barrier surrounding the South China Sea, and for this reason, Washington will do everything in its power to ensure it does not fall under Beijing's influence" (Mgimo University, 2021).

In the Biden administration's National Security Strategy, emphasis is placed on the crucial role of the Indo-Pacific in the 21st century's global economy, emphasis is placed on the importance of the AUKUS security partnership and the continuation of cooperation with the Five Eyes alliance. The document underscores the significance of intelligence cooperation between the U.S. and its partners in the Indo-Pacific region in order to compete with America's rivals. It also stresses the need for free access to the South China Sea for all countries in the region. Furthermore, it mentions that the U.S. has maintained a defensive presence in the region for eight decades and reaffirms its strong commitment to treaties and alliances with regional countries. Finally, acknowledging that U.S. foreign policy has entered a new era, the strategy emphasizes the continuation of the U.S. presence in the Indo-Pacific: "Our AUKUS security partnership with Australia and the United Kingdom promotes stability in the Indo-Pacific while deepening defense and technology integration. We continue to deepen cooperation with the Five Eyes. The revitalized Quad, which brings the United States together with Japan, India, and Australia, addresses regional challenges and has demonstrated its ability to deliver for the Indo-Pacific, to deepening cybersecurity partnerships and promoting high standards for infrastructure and health security. Our intelligence relationships with our allies are a strategic asset that will increasingly factor in to our competition with our rivals, especially in technological competition. The United States will work with other regional states to keep the Indo-Pacific open and accessible and ensure that nations are free to make their own choices, consistent with obligations under international law. We support open societies through investments in democratic institutions, free press, and civil society and are cooperating with partners to counter information manipulation and corruption. And we will affirm freedom of the seas and build shared regional support for open access to the South China Sea—a throughway for nearly two-thirds of global maritime trade and a quarter of all global trade. For 75 years, the United States has maintained a strong and consistent defense presence and will continue to meaningfully contribute to the region's stability and peace. We reaffirm our ironclad commitments to our Indo-Pacific treaty allies—Australia, Japan, the Republic of Korea, the Philippines, and Thailand—and we will continue to modernize these alliances. We reaffirm our unwavering commitment to the defense of Japan under our mutual security treaty, which covers the Senkaku Islands. We have entered a consequential new period of American foreign policy that will demand more of the United States in the Indo-Pacific than has been asked of us since the Second World War. No region will be of more significance to the world and to everyday Americans than the Indo-Pacific. We are ambitious because we know that we and our allies and partners hold a common vision for its future" (NSS, 2022, p. 17, 37-8).

U.S. policymakers now view the Indo-Pacific as a networked region. While bilateral alliances remain central to its security strategy, the U.S. is increasingly focused on building networks of countries with shared interests and strategic partnerships among its allies. This includes trilateral agreements like AUKUS and smaller, flexible initiatives like the Quad. Two major trade agreements have boosted regional economic integration. The CPTPP represents a highly ambitious effort at trade liberalization with extensive tariff reductions and economic rules. The Regional Comprehensive Economic Partnership (RCEP), the world's largest trade deal, includes China. Notably, the United States is not a participant in either of these significant regional trade agreements. Beyond the primary networks, numerous other overlapping and parallel organizations operate in the Indo-Pacific. These include the Asia-Pacific Economic Cooperation forum, ASEAN, the ASEAN Regional Forum and the East Asia Summit; the Compacts of Free Association in the Pacific Islands and the Indian Ocean Rim Association; as well as Chinese-led multilateral efforts such as the Shanghai Cooperation Organization and the Asian Infrastructure Investment Bank (Bush et al., 2022, p. 3).

Figure 2. The US and China in a networked Indo-Pacific

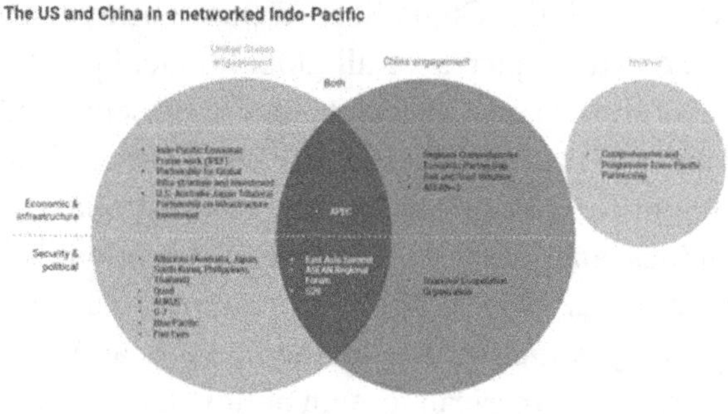

(Bush et al., 2022, p. 4)

CHINA'S REACTION TO U.S. POLICIES IN THE INDO-PACIFIC

China's perspective on the 'Indo-Pacific' has undergone significant evolution. While initially perceived by Chinese scholars as a politicized geopolitical construct aimed at containing China, Under Xi Jinping's leadership, Beijing has stepped up efforts to enhance its normative influence and discursive power—aiming to shape regional narratives, assert its centrality, and influence the regional order. In the context of the Indo-Pacific, China perceives minilateral arrangements such as the Quadrilateral Security Dialogue (Quad), the AUKUS security pact, and initiatives like the Indo-Pacific Strategy (IPS), the Indo-Pacific Economic Framework (IPEF), and the Pacific Deterrence Initiative as mechanisms for the United States to sustain its dominance and curb China's rise through a web of U.S.-led coalitions. In response, Beijing is actively working to undermine and delegitimize U.S. regional hegemony, while more prominently promoting alternative governance models that reflect China's own strengths and strategic preferences (Lokea & Guob, 2025, p.6).

In this context, Beijing has ramped up efforts to construct a "global network of partnerships," a concept initially introduced by Xi Jinping during the 2014 Central Conference on Foreign Affairs. China's coalition-building strategy extends beyond traditional partnership diplomacy; it is multilayered and interconnected, with various forms of relationships and institutional arrangements reinforcing each other. For example, the creation of a broad partnership network supports the development of multilateral cooperative platforms, which in turn help to deepen bilateral ties. Under Xi Jinping, these efforts have gained new momentum. Xi has stressed the importance of enhancing China's discourse power and expanding its "circle of friends who understand China" (Xinhua 2021). This expansion has taken on an increasingly global scope, with China attempting to integrate its "China + regional" formats within a broader framework of global initiatives. In just under two years, Xi has launched three such initiatives: the Global Development Initiative (GDI) in September 2021, the Global Security Initiative (GSI) in April 2022, and the Global Civilization Initiative (GCI) in March 2023. These are complemented by the BRICS expansion and the GDI's "Group of Friends. Following President Xi's announcement of the Global Development Initiative at the United Nations General Assembly, China established the Group of Friends of the Global Development Initiative. By December 2024, 82 countries had joined the Group of Friends, and 119 countries and international organizations had expressed their support for the Global Security Initiative. Moreover, the 78th session of the UN General Assembly unanimously adopted China's proposed resolution to establish an "International Day for Dialogue among Civilizations" (Yi, 2024).

At the 76th session of the United Nations General Assembly on September 21, 2022, amid the COVID-19 pandemic, Xi Jinping introduced the GDI with the aim of revitalizing the global economy. In his speech, Xi emphasized the need to align higher-level priorities with the current development needs outlined in the global policy agenda and called for greater equity in global development to accelerate the implementation of the UN's 2030 Agenda. Xi stated: "Countries must strengthen solidarity and promote win-win cooperation. In a world committed to peace and development, all civilizations and diverse paths to modernization must be respected. Democracy is not a privilege reserved for any one country, but a right for all nations. We must advance global governance and pursue true multilateralism. There is only one international system — that led by the United Nations — and only one international order — that based on international law. There is only one set of rules — the fundamental norms governing international relations, grounded in the purposes and principles of the UN Charter. The United Nations must fulfill its responsibilities in security, development, and human rights in a balanced manner and ensure the faithful implementation of all countries' commitments" (Xi, 2021). Wang Yi, then a senior adviser and former Chinese foreign minister, also emphasized during the 2021 Sustainable Development Forum that "the Global Development Initiative welcomes an inclusive and open spirit of partnership. It will create synergies with other initiatives, including the Belt and Road Initiative (BRI), the African Union's Agenda 2063, and the New Partnership for Africa's Development (NEPAD). The GDI will also leverage the strengths of multilateral cooperation mechanisms such as the United Nations, the G20, BRICS, and other regional and interregional platforms" (Yi, 2021).

Chinese President Xi Jinping also introduced the GSI at the Boao Forum in April 2022. This initiative was later elaborated in a concept paper published on February 21, 2023, which serves as a manifesto for an alternative international order envisioned by China — one that contrasts with the rules-based order led by the United States and its partners in Europe and the Indo-Pacific. In his speech introducing the GSI, Xi stated:

"We must embrace a philosophy of global governance based on extensive consultation, joint contribution, and shared benefits. This philosophy stands in opposition to unilateralism, practices of decoupling, disruption of supply chains, maximum pressure tactics, the excessive use of unilateral sanctions, unchecked assertion of power, and attempts to provoke confrontation along ideological lines — all of which are destined to fail" (Gewirtz, 2024). The initiative advocates for the concept of common, comprehensive, cooperative, and sustainable security — a vision that Chinese leaders have consistently promoted at various forums and events, including the Munich Security Conference. For example, at the 51st Munich Security Conference in 2015, Yang Jiechi, State Councilor of the People's Republic of China, stated: "The Chinese Dream is a dream of peace, development, and win-win cooperation. China advocates the creation of common, comprehensive, cooperative, and sustainable security. The world needs interactive security. A single strand cannot form a thread, and one tree does not make a forest. Likewise, no country can tackle the complex security challenges of today alone. Countries must work together to manage these challenges so that peace and security can be achieved through cooperation" (Yang, 2015).

The Global Civilization Initiative — the latest in China's suite of global development proposals — signals China's ambition not just to lead the execution of global governance but also to shape its conceptual framework. The GCI seeks to promote increased civilizational exchanges worldwide, an idea Xi Jinping first introduced during his speech at the "Conference on Dialogue of Asian Civilizations" on May 16, 2019. At the heart of all three major global initiatives — and China's broader proposals for reforming global governance — lies the concept of building "a community with a shared future for mankind," a vision Xi Jinping has frequently articulated since coming to power. Xi emphasizes that China should uphold the principle of independence, explore diverse paths to modernization, and allow each nation's people to decide for themselves what kind of modernization suits their country (Costigan, 2023). Ultimately, the Global Civilization Initiative aims to elevate China from merely a benevolent financial supporter to a key, influential actor shaping civilizational discourse. This plan seeks to create a shared understanding of civilization that simultaneously safeguards the sovereignty of states. China's 2023 document, "Proposal on Reform and Development of Global Governance," places particular emphasis on the Global Civilization Initiative (GCI). The document highlights China's core values: respect for the diversity of civilizations, sovereignty, and non-interference in the internal affairs of other countries. It explicitly states that there is no single, fixed model for human rights. While it refers to the "universality" of human rights, it stresses the need to balance universality with the specific national conditions of different countries. In one of its most radical statements, the document asserts that "the independent choice of all countries in pursuing their own paths to advance human rights must be respected. Human rights must not be politicized or used as a tool; double standards must be rejected, and human rights must not be used as a pretext for interfering in other countries' internal affairs or for imposing containment and suppression" (Chinese Ministry of Foreign Affairs, 2023).

China's coalition-building strategy draws heavily on its economic strength. These pragmatic, economically driven partnerships partly reflect the persistent mistrust China encounters on the global stage—particularly in security or ideology-based efforts, which are often more difficult to pursue and, in some cases, counterproductive. Nonetheless, there is a growing emphasis on alignment and solidarity with the Global South, as illustrated by Xi Jinping's notion of "natural alliance forces" presented at the 2018 Central Conference on Foreign Affairs. China's connectivity strategy aims to redefine new patterns of territorial organization across multiple spaces and scales. It has evolved into a fundamental element of Xi Jinping's foreign policy, representing a deliberate attempt to expand China's global influence and reshape international relations and dependencies. Leveraging its strengths in infrastructure, China uses connectivity as a tool to unite different countries and rally them around common development goals. In recent years, China has paid special attention to the Global South as part of its efforts to reform the international order and advance its initiatives. It should be noted that since the founding of the People's Republic of China, Beijing has shown particular interest in developing countries. At the Asia-Africa Summit held in Indonesia in April 2015, which marked the 60th anniversary of the Bandung Conference, Chinese President Xi Jinping emphasized the importance of promoting a fair and equitable international system and order. He also stressed that "China is committed to strengthening governance and cooperation with other countries based on the Five Principles of Peaceful Coexistence" (Fu, 2021: 25).

This approach to "building bridges" is prominently featured in key policy documents, such as the White Paper on the Belt and Road Initiative (BRI), which highlights the need to align regional development strategies and maximize each participant's potential and comparative advantages. Through advocating mutual benefits and fostering international cooperation under the BRI framework, China advances its broader ambition of creating a "Global Community of Shared Future" Since the launch of the BRI, Chinese leaders have consistently emphasized the crucial role of infrastructure in advancing regional development.

Xi Jinping has portrayed the BRI as providing the "wings" for regional progress, where "connectivity" acts as the lifeblood and infrastructure forms the critical "framework" or "skeleton" supporting growth (CCTV News 2023). An important milestone in China's ambitious (BRI) was the introduction of the China-Indochina Peninsula

Economic Corridor Initiative during the 9th Pan-Beibu Gulf Economic Cooperation Forum in 2016. This initiative laid the foundation for significant infrastructure projects like the China-Laos Railway and the Jakarta-Bandung High-Speed Railway, which have strengthened local economies and more closely integrated these nations into China's economic sphere. Similarly, the development of Gwadar Port in Pakistan and Kyaukpyu Port in Myanmar exemplifies China's strategy of building regional linkages and fostering mutual economic gains. Gwadar, a flagship project under the China–Pakistan Economic Corridor, not only stimulates Pakistan's economy but also enhances China's trade routes across Central Asia and decreases its dependence on the Malacca Strait — a vital global maritime chokepoint — thereby reinforcing China's strategic positioning control over critical trade routes and its influence in the region. Kyaukpyu Port project in Myanmar is anticipated to significantly revitalize the local economy by generating more than 100,000 new jobs annually. Once the industrial park and deep-sea port become fully operational, Myanmar's GDP could see an annual increase of around $10 billion (Lokea & Guob, 2025, pp.9-10).

BRI marks a new chapter in economic-security cooperation with its neighboring regions and served as a soft balancing strategy against the United States. Domestically, the BRI's economic approach aimed at building a strong state, developing inland regions, transferring surplus capital, and improving infrastructure. In this context, establishing corridors to develop China's interior and connect it with surrounding regions became a priority. The next step was to transfer surplus capital to peripheral regions to boost economic integration in Belt regions, primarily through a range of infrastructure projects—including the development of ports, airports, power transmission networks, economic corridors, railways, roads, pipelines, and energy development projects—seen as significant opportunities for the growth of countries along the BRI route and for enhancing Beijing's economic indicators (Xing, 2019: 37). Initially, the BRI, through its Digital Silk Road (Cyber Belt), emerged as a response to U.S. dominance in cyberspace architecture and network hegemony, motivating Beijing to establish a China-centric model of cyber governance. In this endeavor, telecom giants like Huawei and ZTE have focused on ICT infrastructure—such as fiber-optic cables, digital telecom networks, and smart city projects—in countries like Cambodia, the Philippines, Thailand, Vietnam, Malaysia, Singapore, and Indonesia (Gordon & Anderson, 2020: 19–22).

Another key strategic aspect is China's economic penetration, which has become the "center of gravity" in the competition for influence in Southeast Asia. In 2020, ASEAN replaced the European Union as China's largest trading partner—a mutual dependence expected to grow further following the signing of the Regional Comprehensive Economic Partnership (RCEP) in November 2020 (Kuik, 2021: 310). Energy is another major security component of the BRI. A notable example is the China-Bangladesh-Myanmar-India Economic Corridor. Another major security dimension of the BRI is the strengthening of maritime interests through the development of ports and strategic naval bases. Acknowledging the regional security environment (i.e., U.S. containment policies) and the expanded definition of national security beyond borders, China has redirected its military strategy toward offshore defense capabilities and modernizing its naval fleet. This strategic shift is encapsulated in the "Active Defense Military Doctrine" (Zhen & Paul, 2020: 7). Finally, an important security element of the initiative is the "Strategic Partnership Strategy"—a form of smart hedging where Beijing builds networks of regional alliances to deepen its geopolitical influence and shield itself from the negative impacts of U.S.-led regional coalitions.

Joseph Nye refers to the Belt and Road Initiative as Xi Jinping's "Marco Polo Strategy," arguing that "if China uses its surplus financial reserves to build infrastructure that helps poor countries and enhances international trade, it can provide global public goods" (Nye, 2023: 109, 110). The declared goal of the Belt and Road Initiative is primarily to assist countries in the Global South that have been unable to meet their infrastructure needs through other international financial providers. Chinese officials leverage this situation to promote the Belt and Road Initiative. The President of China views the initiative as a non-threatening and mutually beneficial path for all participating countries, providing opportunities for infrastructure development in developing nations while expanding trade opportunities for developed countries. The emphasis on the possibility of achieving win-win cooperation in the Belt and Road Initiative is one of the most important points stemming from the idea of the Chinese Dream. Xi Jinping, President of China, referred to the Belt and Road Initiative as the "Path of Peace" in 2017, suggesting that it can unite groups and nations under the banner of win-win cooperation. He also stated that "China seeks to establish win-win business partnerships with other countries involved in the Belt and Road Initiative to facilitate trade and investment with them and to create a network of free trade within the framework of this initiative" (Xi, 2017). In a white paper released by the Chinese government in 2023, it was noted that the Belt and Road Initiative injects positive energy into global peace and development. Chinese experts and scholars, while promoting the concept of peace alongside with development, point out that the Chinese model of rapid infrastructure-led development can be utilized to stabilize regions and environments prone to conflict.

In 2017, Xi Jinping referred to the BRI as a "road of peace," capable of bringing together groups and nations under the banner of win-win cooperation. Xi also noted that "China seeks to build win-win business partnerships with other countries participating in the Belt and Road Initiative, aiming to facilitate trade and investment and to create a free trade network within the framework of the Initiative" (Xi, 2017). In a white paper published by the Chinese government in 2023, it was stated that the Belt and Road injects positive energy into global peace and development.

Chinese experts and scholars, in promoting the notion of peace alongside development, argue that China's model of rapid, infrastructure-driven growth can be used to stabilize environments and regions vulnerable to conflict (Abb, 2024). China is clearly focused on boosting its regional influence and cementing its position as a key player in both regional and global development. In fact, BRI represents China's evolving foreign policy centered on connectivity, primarily driven by its expertise in infrastructure development. Through its connectivity strategy, China aspires to move beyond surface-level diplomatic ties, aiming instead to build more extensive and deeper networks that advance its geostrategic goals and highlight its commitment to regional cooperation. Since the launch of the Belt and Road Initiative in 2013, its primary goal has been to bridge the infrastructure gap across the Global South. In the contemporary geopolitical landscape, few initiatives are as ambitious and innovative as the Belt and Road Initiative, which has emerged from the visionary geopolitical strategies of China. It transcends conventional paradigms of economic development and infrastructure, presenting a narrative of ambition and innovation. The Belt and Road Initiative is not merely a conduit for China's economic development; it also serves as a bridge for cultural exchange and intercultural dialogue. As goods flow, ideas and traditions are also transferred, fostering a deeper sense of connection and a shared destiny. The Belt and Road Initiative places China at the core of the international system, allowing its physical, financial, cultural, and technological influence to extend into other regions. These geopolitical representations are part of China's peaceful rise, aiming to present its proposals for reconfiguring global geopolitical relations as non-threatening to other actors.

It can be said that China's initiatives — such as the Asian Infrastructure Investment Bank (AIIB), the Belt and Road Initiative (BRI), the Global Security Initiative (GSI), the Global Development Initiative (GDI), and the Global Civilization Initiative (GCI) — are part of its broader efforts to reform international politics and the global order. In these initiatives, the Global South has been a key focus. Despite its large economy, China continues to identify itself as the largest developing country, leveraging this status to gain support and foster unity among developing nations. At the World Political Parties Summit in July 2021, Chinese President Xi Jinping emphasized that "China's path to modernization has proven itself as a sustainable alternative to the existing system of party governance, and China is willing to share its experiences with other countries. Both history and practice have proven—and will continue to prove—that China's path is correct and sound" (SCMP, 2021). In terms of institution-building with the Global South, China has launched several platforms, including the Forum on China-Africa Cooperation (FOCAC), the China-Arab States Cooperation Forum (CASCF), the China-CELAC Forum (China and the Community of Latin American and Caribbean States), and the China-Caribbean Cooperation Forum. Each of these forums has ambassador-level representatives, regular meetings, and working groups to facilitate policy coordination between China and member states. Moreover, China established the South-South Cooperation Assistance Fund in 2015, and in June 2022, under the framework of the Global Development Initiative, launched another South-South Cooperation Fund. Beijing has also positioned itself as a key lender of last resort for developing countries. For instance, during 2020 and 2021, China conducted 128 lending operations across 22 countries, amounting to $240 billion. Between 2019 and the end of 2021, China provided a total of $104 billion in loans to various nations (Financial Times, 2023).

China's strategy of promoting connectivity through development infrastructure plays a crucial role in its efforts to build international coalitions. The primary objective is to reshape the regional economic landscape by establishing more efficient and strategically favorable trade routes that bypass traditional chokepoints. While these initiatives promote greater connectivity under the "bridging" model, they also create asymmetric dependencies that align participating countries with China's broader geostrategic and geoeconomic ambitions, resembling the transactional and binding dynamics discussed earlier (Lokea & Guob, 2025, p.10). Meanwhile, Association Strategy aims to foster a sense of shared identity and build ideational coalition support. This can be accomplished by highlighting common values and interests ("bonding") and/or by framing adversaries in a negative light ("othering") to undermine their legitimacy. In the realm of infrastructure development, although China frequently asserts that its development assistance is not directed against any third party (Xinhua 2024), it sometimes adopts an "othering" approach to discredit U.S. foreign aid. In contrast, China presents itself as a champion of recipient countries' interests, emphasizing shared development objectives. By promoting a vision where all nations benefit fairly from globalization and developmental inequalities are reduced, China seeks to offer an alternative narrative. This approach deliberately diverges from traditional Western models, aiming to reposition China as an advocate of equitable growth, distinct from the frequently criticized practices of Bretton Woods institutions toward the developing world.

China also frames the ongoing global "peace deficit" as a consequence of insufficient inclusivity. In its strategy of association, China also leverages the "bonding" approach by emphasizing friendship, shared experiences of colonial history, and South-South solidarity to build stronger symbolic and ideational influence within its coalitions. Xi Jinping (2014) states that "as a genuine friend of Pacific Island countries, China is committed to deepening mutually beneficial cooperation and offering greater support to accelerate their development, aiming for shared growth and prosperity. China and the Pacific Island nations have endured similar historical experiences, maintain deep-rooted friendships, and share a common vision for a better future." (Lokea & Guob, 2025, pp.11-12). China's efforts in coalition-building through development infrastructure go beyond constructing physical projects. By embedding principles of inclusivity and solidarity into its infrastructure initiatives, China is not only transforming the physical landscapes of its partner countries but also shaping their models of cooperation. It promotes a vision of a balanced, fair, and multipolar global order that emphasizes addressing the basic needs and development opportunities of the Global South. China's "bonding" and "othering" strategies work in tandem — strengthening its own coalition while simultaneously undermining the coalition-building efforts of the United States.

CONCLUSION

The relationships among great powers have evolved into the most significant global trend, marked by conflict and competition over the international order. Central to competition is the rivalry between the United States and China. As the dominant power in the post-Cold War era, the U.S. believes that if China, the most significant emerging power in the international system, is not contained, it will first dominate the Asia-Pacific region and subsequently challenge U.S. supremacy on a global scale. Consequently, containing China has become the foremost agenda of U.S. foreign policy, embraced by both Democratic and Republican administrations at both global and regional levels. In fact, the strategic competition between the U.S. and China has led to a shift in American strategy from West to East Asia. While this rivalry has resulted in a reduced U.S. presence in other regions, it has simultaneously sharpened Washington's focus on the Pacific. U.S. officials recognize that the coming century will be the "century of Asia," asserting that whoever governs the Indo-Pacific region will also govern Asia and ultimately the world. In response to China's growing influence, the U.S. has scaled back its commitments in various parts of the world to concentrate more on the Indo-Pacific region.

Buck-passing and containment are the policies of the United States in confronting China. The concept of burden-sharing regarding China encompasses two important points. As China's economic growth and its integration with the U.S. economy could bolster Beijing's power, Washington seeks to shift the responsibility for addressing this country onto other nations. This approach aims to reduce costs while maintaining an indirect presence in regional affairs, thereby placing less responsibility on itself. The U.S. military strategy toward China is anchored in three pillars: increasing military forces in the region, expanding power projection in East Asia, and enhancing the deterrent capabilities of U.S. allies and friends in the Asia-Pacific. The "Nodal Defense" approach reflects a complex multilateral strategy that the United States has developed in recent years to confront China. This strategy aims to establish both bilateral and multilateral security frameworks, creating an organized nodal defense network in the Indo-Pacific region. Strengthening bilateral security ties with longstanding allies such as Japan and Australia, forming the Quad alliance, and efforts to expand the Quad into a Quad Plus by including Indonesia or South Korea, as well as the AUKUS alliance, signify the establishment of intricate and interconnected defense and security mechanisms for the U.S. in the Indo-Pacific.

China has also adopted specific policies, including Connectivity and Association strategies, to build coalitions and to counter the United States' approaches in Indo-pacific. China's coalition-building efforts are not merely focused on extending its strategic influence but, more fundamentally, on legitimizing its position within an evolving regional and global order. By employing a connectivity strategy, China is leveraging its strengths in development infrastructure to pull regional states into its geoeconomic and geostrategic sphere. While fostering regional relationships and networks, it simultaneously creates layers of dependency that further consolidate its influence. Alongside this, China's association strategy emphasizes building affinity and solidarity, utilizing narratives of inclusiveness and shared development aspirations to strengthen its ideational and symbolic appeal. Currently, Beijing's approach to coalition-building is expansive, flexible, and multi-layered, reflecting its increasing sophistication in combining strategies of connectivity and association. In fact, through initiatives such as the Global Security Initiative, the Global Civilization Initiative, the Global Development Initiative, and the Belt and Road Initiative, China has not only sought to counter the threats and alliances led by the United States in the Indo-Pacific region, but has also aimed to implement its own agenda for managing global affairs, with a particular focus on the Global South.

One significant event in 2024 poised to have serious implications for global trends and the international system is Donald Trump's return. His stance against globalization—including opposition to free trade, support for protectionist economic policies, a transactional view of U.S. alliances, emphasis on the "America First" slogan, selective isolationism in foreign policy, and resistance to global concerns in areas like health and climate change—represents key elements of his approach to the world. It appears that great power competition will not only persist but likely intensify in the coming years. The U.S. will not abandon its strategy of containing China. The composition of Trump's second cabinet and his surrounding advisers indicate that U.S. focus on China is expected to increase. One of the main objectives of the Trump administration's efforts to end the Ukraine war may be to redirect more attention toward China. Indeed, it seems the Trump administration aims not only to separate Russia from China but also to concentrate more on China by reducing the need to focus on Russia.

REFERENCES

Abb, P. (2024). Is There a Chinese Developmental peace? Evidence from the Belt and Road Initiative's Impact on Conflict States. Retrieved November 12, 2024, from Journal of Contemporary China: https://www.tandfonline.com/doi/epdf/10.1080/10670564.2024.2378043?needAccess=true

Akrami, T., & Mohammadi Ramezani, M. (2024). Investigating the Strategic Competition between US and China; Case Study: The West Asia Region. *Scientific Journal Quarterly of Middle East Studies, 31* (1).

Annual Threat Assessment. (2023, February 6). *Office of the Director of National Intelligence*. Retrieved March 2, 2025, from https://www.odni.gov/files/ODNI/documents/assessments/ATA-2023-Unclassified-Report.pdf

Austin, L. (2023, June 2). *A Shared Vision for the Indo-Pacific: Remarks by Secretary of Defense at the Shangri-La Dialogue, US Department of Defense*. Retrieved February 12, 2025, from https://www.defense.gov/News/Speeches/Speech/Article/3415839/a-shared-vision-for-the-indo-pacific-remarks-by-secretary-of-defense-lloyd-j-au/

Baum, R. (2001). From Strategic Partners to Strategic Competitors: George W. Bush and the Politics of US China Policy. *Journal of East Asian Studies (Seoul), 1*(2), 191–220. DOI: 10.1017/S1598240800000497

Bisley, N. (2023, November). *Minilateralism and the Dynamics of Great Power Competition in Asia: AUKUS and Quad in the New Normal Great Power Competition: The U.S.-China-Russia Relationship and the Indo-Pacific Region*. Retrieved February 25, 2025, from The National Institute for Defense Studies, Japan: https://www.nids.mod.go.jp/event/proceedings/symposium/pdf/2022/e_all.pdf

Bush, R. C., Madan, T., Solis, M., Stormseth, J., & Yeo, A. (2022, November). *An American Strategy for the Indo-Pacific in an Age of US-China Competition: Enhancing Alliances, Economic Engagement, and Regional Stability*. Retrieved February 25, 2025, from Brookings: https://www.brookings.edu/articles/an-american-strategy-for-the-indo-pacific-in-an-age-of-us-china-competition/

CCTV News. (2023, October 19). *High Quality Joint Construction of the Belt and Road, Xi Jinping Promotes the Construction of This 'Three-Dimensional Network." CCTV News*. Retrieved April 12, 2025, from https://news.cctv.com/

Chee, M. T. (2024, November 7). *Why China is worried about a Second Trump Presidency – and how Beijing might React*. Retrieved February 10, 2025, from The Conversation: https://theconversation.com/why-china-is-worried-about-a-second-trump-presidency-and-how-beijing-might-react-243134

Chinese Ministry of Foreign Affairs. (2023, September 14). *Proposal of the People's Republic of China on the Reform and Development of Global Governance*. Retrieved September 22, 2024, from https://subsites.chinadaily.com.cn/Qiushi/2023-09/14/c_921174.htm

Clinton, B. (1993, July 7). *Building A New Pacific Community*. Retrieved March 1, 2025, from https://1997-2001.state.gov/regions/eap/930707.html

Clinton, B. (1994, May 26). *President Clinton Press Conference on Human Rights in China, 1994, USC US-China Institute*. Retrieved June 18, 2024, from https://china.usc.edu/president-clinton-press-conference-human-rights-china-1994

Congressional Research Service. (2018, October 3). *The Trump Administration 's "Free and Open Indo-Pacific": Issues for Congress*. Retrieved March 1, 2025, from https://crsreports.congress.gov/product/pdf/R/R45396

Congressional Research Service. (2024, July 22). *Indo-Pacific Economic Framework for Prosperity (IPEF)*. Retrieved March 1, 2025, from https://crsreports.congress.gov/product/pdf/IF/IF12373

Congressional Research Service. (2024, November 25). *The Pacific Deterrence Initiative*. Retrieved February 24, 2025, from https://crsreports.congress.gov/product/pdf/IF/IF12303

Costigan, J. M. (2023, December 7). *China's Vision for World Order*. Retrieved November 12, 2024, from China File: https://www.chinafile.com/reporting-opinion/viewpoint/chinas-vision-world-order

CSIS. (2017, October 18). *Defining Our Relationship with India for the Next Century: An Address by U.S. Secretary of State Rex Tillerson*. Retrieved February 12, 2025, from https://csis-website-prod.s3.amazonaws.com/s3fs-public/publication/171018_An_Address_by_U.S._Secretary_of_State_Rex_Tillerson.pdf

Derakhshandeh, M., & Shafiee, N. (2022). US Policy Towards China in the Framework of the Hedging (1990-2021). [{in Persian}]. *World Politics*, *11*(2), 7–38.

Embassy of PRC in the UK. (2024, April 4). *Embassy Spokesperson's response on relevant remarks in AUKUS Defense Ministers Joint Statement*. Retrieved February 24, 2025, from http://gb.china-embassy.gov.cn/eng/PressandMedia/Spokepersons/202404/t20240409_11278696.htm

European Parliament. (2023, July). *Geopolitics in the Indo-Pacific: Major Players' Strategic Perspectives*. Retrieved February 22, 2025, from https://www.europarl.europa.eu/thinktank/en/document/EPRS_BRI(2023)751398

Financial Times. (2023, March 28). *China Grants Billions in Bailouts as Belt and Road Initiative Falters*. Retrieved July 16, 2024, from https://www.ft.com/content/9b2cb53f-e6f0-479e-bb94-a2e0c8680e88

Fu, Y. (2021). *Seeing the World, Tehran, RISS {Translation in Persian*. RISS.

Gewirtz, P. (2024, July 22). *China, the United States and the Future of a Rule-0based International Order*. Retrieved June 22, 2024, from Brookings: https://www.brookings.edu/articles/china-the-united-states-and-the-future-of-a-rules-based-international-order/

Ghalkhanbaz, K., Yazdani, E., & Ebrahimi, S. (2023). U.S.-China Strategic Competition and its Impact on US Indo-Pacific Policy: Strategic Lessons for the Islamic Republic of Iran. *A Quarterly Journal of Foreign Relations, 15* (3), 28-56. {in Persian}

Gordon, D., Haoyu, T., & Tabatha, A. (2020, September). *Beyond the Myths – Towards a Realistic Assessment of China's Belt and Road Initiative: The Security Dimension,* Retrieved April 11, 2025, from The International Institute for Strategic Studies: https://ispmyanmarchinadesk.com/wp-content/uploads/2020/12/BRI-Report-Two-Beyond-the-Myths-Towards-a-Realistic-Assessment-of-Chinas-Belt-and-Road-Initiative.pdf

Hass, R. N., & Kupchan, C. (2021, March 23). *The New Concert of Powers, How to Prevent Catastrophe and Promote Stability in a Multipolar World*. Retrieved February 12, 2025, from https://www.foreignaffairs.com/articles/world/2021-03-23/new-concert-powers

Hawkins, A., & Davidson, H. (n.d.). *Tariffs, Tech and Taiwan: how China Hopes to Trump-proof its Economy*. Retrieved February 15, 2024, from The Guardian: https://www.theguardian.com/world/2024/nov/08/tariffs-tech-and-taiwan-how-china-hopes-to-trump-proof-its-economy

Indo-Pacific Strategy. (2022, September 24). *White House*, Retrieved March 17, 2024, from https://bidenwhitehouse.archives.gov/wp-content/uploads/2022/02/U.S.-Indo-Pacific-Strategy.pdf

Interim National Security Strategic Guidance. (2021, March 21). *White House*. Retrieved February 24, 2025, from https://bidenwhitehouse.archives.gov/wp-content/uploads/2021/03/NSC-1v2.pdf

Jamshidi, S., & Dehshiri, M. R. (2018). The US Strategy in the Indo-Pacific Region and its Impact on India-China Relations. *A Quarterly Journal of Foreign Relations, 10* (3), 203-229. {in Persian}

Kennedy, S. (2024, January 3). *U.S.-China Relations in 2024: Managing Competition without Conflict*. Retrieved September 16, 2024, from CSIS: https://www.csis.org/analysis/us-china-relations-2024-managing-competition-without-conflict

Kuik, C.-C. (2021). Getting Hedging right: a Small-state Perspective. *China International Strategy Review*, 300-315.

Lokea, B., & Guob, X. (2025). China's Coalition-building in the Indo-Pacific: Strategies of Connectivity and Association. *Australian Journal of International Affairs*, •••, 1–18. DOI: 10.1080/10357718.2025.2471351

Manouchehri, H., Moghtadae, A., & Esmaeili, B. (2023). The Competition between China and the United States in the Indo-Pacific and the Persian Gulf and its Security Implications for Iran. *The Islamic revolution, 17* (64), 27-48. {in Persian}

Mearsheimer, J. J. (2021, November/December). The Inevitable War, America, China, and the Tragedy of Great-Power Politics, Retrieved February 17, 2025, from *Foreign Affairs*. https://www.foreignaffairs.com/articles/china/2021-10-19/inevitable-rivalry-cold-war

Mgimo University. (2021, December 13). *John Mearsheimer on US-China Relations*. Retrieved February 13, 2025, from https://english.mgimo.ru/news/mearsheimer13-12-21

Minemura, K. (2024, August 17). *John Mearsheimer: Us-China Rift Runs Real Risk of Escalating in to a Nuclear War*. Retrieved February 17, 2025, from Asahi: https://www.asahi.com/ajw/articles/13629071

National Defense Strategy. (2022, October 27). *US Department of Defense*. Retrieved February 25, from https://media.defense.gov/2022/Oct/27/2003103845/-1/-1/1/2022-NATIONAL-DEFENSE-STRATEGY-NPR-MDR.pdf

National Security Strategy. (1999, December). *The White House*. Retrieved February 25, 2025, from https://clintonwhitehouse4.archives.gov/media/pdf/nssr-1299.pdf

National Security Strategy. (2006, March,). *The White House*. Retrieved February 25, 2025, from https://history.defense.gov/Portals/70/Documents/nss/nss2006.pdf

National Security Strategy. (2010, May). *The White House*. Retrieved February 25, 2025, from https://obamawhitehouse.archives.gov/sites/default/files/rss_viewer/national_security_strategy.pdf

National Security Strategy. (2017, December). *The White House*. Retrieved February 25, 2025, from https://trumpwhitehouse.archives.gov/wp-content/uploads/2017/12/NSS-Final-12-18-2017-0905.pdf

National Security Strategy. (2022, October). *The White House*. Retrieved February 25, 2025, from https://bidenwhitehouse.archives.gov/wp-content/uploads/2022/11/8-November-Combined-PDF-for-Upload.pdf

Nye, J. (2023). Xi Jinping's Marco Polo Strategy. In Nye, J. (Ed.), *Soft Power and Great Power Competition, China and Globalization* (pp. 109–111). Springer. DOI: 10.1007/978-981-99-0714-4_17

NYTimes. (2000, May 18). *In Bush's Words: 'Join Together in Making China a Normal Trading Partner'*. Retrieved July 1, 2024, from https://www.nytimes.com/2000/05/18/world/in-bush-s-words-join-together-in-making-china-a-normal-trading-partner.html

Obama, B. (2011, November 17). *Remarks By President Obama to the Australian Parliament*. Retrieved March 8, 20252025, from White House: https://obamawhitehouse.archives.gov/the-press-office/2011/11/17/remarks-president-obama-australian-parliament

Pierson, D. (2024, November 7). *China Braces for a New Phase of U.S. Rivalry With Trump's Return*. Retrieved February 12, 2025, from NYTimes: https://www.nytimes.com/2024/11/07/world/asia/china-trump-rivalry.html

Pompeo, M. (2018, July 30). *Secretary Pompeo Remarks on "America's Indo-Pacific Economic Vision*. Retrieved March 1, 2025, from U.S. Mission Korea: https://kr.usembassy.gov/073018-secretary-pompeo-remarks-on-americas-indo-pacific-economic-vision/

Quadrennial, D. R. R. (2006, February 6). *Department of Defense*. Retrieved January 25, 2025, from https://history.defense.gov/Portals/70/Documents/quadrennial/QDR2006.pdf?ver=2014-06-25-111017-150

Quadrennial Defense Review. (2014, March 4). *Department of Defense*. Retrieved January 25, 2025, from https://history.defense.gov/Portals/70/Documents/quadrennial/QDR2014.pdf?ver=tXH94SVvSQLVw-ENZ-a2pQ%3d%3d

Reuters. (2011, November 11). *Clinton Declares "America's Pacific century"*. Retrieved February 25, 2025, from https://www.reuters.com/article/world/us-politics/clinton-declares-americas-pacific-century-idUSTRE7AA2S2/

Shinzo, A. (2007, August 22). *"Confluence of the Two Seas", Speech by Prime Minister of Japan at the Parliament of the Republic of India*. Retrieved January 22, 2025, from https://www.mofa.go.jp/region/asia-paci/pmv0708/speech-2.html

South China Morning Post. (2021, July 7). *China Shows World an Alternative Path to Modern Future, Xi Jinping Says*. Retrieved April 2, 2025, from https://www.scmp.com/news/china/diplomacy/article/3140079/china-shows-world-alternative-path-modern-future-xi-jinping

Wei, Z., & Zhang, Y. (2021). The Biden Administration's Indo-Pacific Strategy and China-U.S. Strategic Competition. *China Quarterly of International Strategic Studies*, *7*(2), 157–178. DOI: 10.1142/S2377740021500068

Winkler, S. C. (2023). Strategic Competition and US-China Relations: A Conceptual Analysis. *the Chinese Journal of International Politics*, 333-356.

WorldwideThreat Assessment. (2024, April 5). *Defense Intelligence Agency*. Retrieved March 2, 2025, from https://www.congress.gov/118/meeting/house/117088/witnesses/HHRG-118-AS26-Wstate-KruseJ-20240411.pdf

Xi, J. (2017, May 14). *Work together to Build the Silk Road Economic Belt and the Twenty-first Century Maritime Silk Road, Speech at the Opening Ceremony of the BRI Forum for International Cooperation, 14,* Retrieved February 12, 2025, from http://2017.beltandroadforum.org/english/n100/2018

Xi, J. (2021, September 22). *Xi Jinping Attends the General Debate of the 76th Session of the United Nations General Assembly and Delivers an Important Speech*. Retrieved August 10, 2024, from https://www.mfa.gov.cn/eng/zy/jj/GDI_140002/xw/202109/t20210923_9580033.html

Xinhua. (2021, June 1). *"Xi Focus: Xi Stresses Improving China's International Communication Capacity"*. Retrieved April 11, 2025, from http://www.xinhuanet.com/english/2021-06/01/c_139983105.htm

Yang, J. (2015, February 7). *Statement by Yang Jiechi at the 51st Munich Security Conference*. Retrieved June 22, 2024, from China Daily: https://global.chinadaily.com.cn/china/2015-02/07/content_19517488.htm

Yi, W. (2021, September 27). *Building Consensus and Synergy for a Bright Future of Global Development -- Address by State Councilor Wang Yi At the Sustainable Development Forum 2021*. Retrieved September 11, 2024, from China Daily: https://subsites.chinadaily.com.cn/Qiushi/2021-09/27/c_664062.htm

Yi, W. (2024, December 11). *Riding the Trend of the Times with a Strong Sense of Responsiblity*. Retrieved December 22, 2024, from Ministry of Foreign Affairs of the People's Republic of China: https://www.mfa.gov.cn/eng/wjbzhd/202412/t20241218_11497818.html

Zoellick, R. (2005, September 21). *"Whither China? From Membership to Responsibility"*. Retrieved March 1, 2025, from https://www.ncuscr.org/wp-content/uploads/2020/04/migration_Zoellick_remarks_notes06_winter_spring.pdf

Chapter 6
China's Global South Strategy in the Mekong Region in Geopolitical Implications, Economic Prospects, and Challenge:
The Dragon's Reach Into Southern Arc

Tin Maung Htwe
https://orcid.org/0009-0002-3002-169X
Chiang Mai University, Thailand

ABSTRACT

This chapter argues that China's engagement in mainland Southeast Asia illustrates a new mode of hegemony: one that substitutes formal empire with economic corridors and strategic interdependence. China's rise as a global power is reshaping the political economy of the Global South, and the Mekong region now stands as a revealing case of this transformation. Through the Belt and Road Initiative (BRI) and Lancang-Mekong Cooperation (LMC), Beijing has fused infrastructure, influence, and ideology into a model of state-led development that promises modernization, but at the cost of sovereignty. In the absence of robust institutional buffers, Chinese investments have embedded asymmetric relationships that erode state autonomy and fragment regional coherence in Mekong Region.

DOI: 10.4018/979-8-3373-0938-5.ch006

1. INTRODUCTION

In the shadowed corridors of twenty-first-century geopolitics, few transformations have been as consequential as China's emergence as a global power (Curtis & Klaus, 2024). Now China become the world's second-largest economy (Moe et al., 2024). No longer a peripheral actor, China has reshaped the political and economic terrain of the Global South (Montano Ramirez & Petersen, 2025) through a web of calculated strategies, both overt and subtle (Xiaotong, 2025). Nowhere is this transformation more palpable than in the Mekong region. In this strategic crucible between South and Southeast Asia, China's ambitions find fertile ground, projected through grand infrastructure, economic corridors and the seduction of soft power (Carminati, 2024).

Mekong region is a landscape of rivers, jungles, and contested histories comprising Cambodia, Laos, Myanmar, Thailand and Vietnam. The Mekong offers Beijing more than just markets or minerals, it offers geographic leverage (Boer et al., 2015). With its labyrinthine riverways and fractured sovereignties, It is the connective tissue between China's heartland and the southern seas, a fulcrum for regional influence where development is often indistinguishable from domination (Rodríguez Álvarez, 2024). In this arena, two frameworks encapsulate Beijing's strategic drives. One is the Belt and Road Initiative (BRI) and other, the Lancang-Mekong Cooperation (LMC) (Siphana, 2018). Launched in 2013, BRI is not merely an economic program but a reimagining of Asia's very infrastructure map. Railways, special economic zones, and hydropower dams are the instruments of a vision that binds the region to China's logistical orbit (Lee, 2024). Meanwhile, the LMC, introduced in 2016, positions itself as a model of South-South cooperation. It ostensibly promotes shared development and water governance in Mekong region, even as it deepens bilateral asymmetries that favor Beijing (Gong & Li, 2024).

This narrative is not unilinear. For all the gleam of highways and high-speed rail, shadows gather beneath. China has bridged infrastructure gaps, expanded trade routes and bolstered energy grids across the Mekong region. The dividends of Chinese investment are real but so too are the costs (Ranjan & Changgang, 2021). Rising debt burdens, environmental degradation and anxieties over national sovereignty, the Mekong is thus not merely a theater of development. But a contested frontier where the promises of globalization meet the perils of dependency. Understanding this landscape demands more than technical assessments of dams and dollars. It calls for an excavation of the power structures and strategic intentions embedded within (Liu et al., 2025) region.

This study employs the lens of geopolitical economy to reveal the deeper undercurrents shaping China's posture in the Mekong. Unlike conventional paradigms that isolate state behavior within abstract notions of balance or rational interest (Sil

& Katzenstein, 2010), geopolitical economy locates China's engagement within the historical logic of global capitalism (Woodley, 2015). It scrutinizes the role of the state not just as a diplomatic actor but as an architect of production networks, resource control and internal stability (Norris, 2016). In this context, China's Mekong push is less a foreign policy maneuver than a structural necessity (Hensengerth, 2009). Johnson and Soukhaphon (2024) introduce the concept of hidden and visible power dynamics in the Mekong region that need to export surplus capital, secure energy flows and manage the contradictions of its own development trajectory.

By framing the Mekong as a geopolitical fault line, this approach reveals a terrain marked by overlapping sovereignties, ecological precarity and political ambivalence. Here, integration and autonomy, cooperation and resistance, are negotiated daily and often under the shadow of Chinese ambition (Gill, 2022). Rather than embracing the dualistic clichés of Beijing as either benefactor or hegemon, this analysis confronts the ambiguity of China's rise (Shih, 2024). It is a story not of clear answers, but of entangled futures that where power flows along the same riverbeds as commerce and contestation.

2. LITERATURE REVIEW

The Mekong region has emerged as a strategic frontier in China's twenty-first-century engagement with the Global South (Yen, 2024). It is in this liminal space between continental interiors and maritime spheres that Beijing's ambition finds its sharpest expression (Hiebert, 2020). China's presence here is not incidental. It is the product of a deliberate geopolitical vision, one that resurrects elements of classical theorists (Malcomson, 2016: Gray & Sloan, 2000) recast in the language of commerce and infrastructure (Calhoun et al., 2022: Adler, 2009). Through corridors of cement and steel, China seeks to consolidate its influence over a pivotal swath of mainland Southeast Asia (Anh, 2024), integrating it ever more tightly with its own southern provinces.

The Belt and Road Initiative (BRI) and Lancang-Mekong Cooperation (LMC) represent the physical and institutional scaffolding of this effort. Their railway lines, hydropower dams and special economic zones are not mere development projects. They are instruments of strategic depth (Kosaikanont, 2023: Busbarat, 2018). As Friedrich Ratzel's notion of Lebensraum echoes (Ratzel, 1898: Bluwstein et al., 2024) through the Mekong's economic geography, it becomes clear that China's ambitions are expansive, if not imperial (Lampton, Ho, & Kuik, 2020). Yet unlike past empires, its expansion is measured less in troops than in trade flows (Ratzel, 2017). Like Alfred Mahan (1890)'s connectivity-based power, the logic is maritime in mindset (Erickson, 2008), but terrestrial in execution. In the absence of a unified

ASEAN resistance, China thrives in fragmentation (Emmerson, 2020). Reminiscent of Saul B. Cohen (2003)'s "shatterbelt", bilateralism replaces regionalism, and asymmetry becomes a governing norm in Mekong Region (Liu, 2022).

Economically, China dangles the promise of modernization across the region (Zhang, 2022; Dongming & Guang, 2022; Harold, 2021). But behind the façade of uplift lie hierarchies that John Mearsheimer (2010:2015) cautions against that patterns of dominance of China repackaged as development. Kaplinsky (2005) notes that elite-driven rentierism can be a byproduct of integration into global value chains. However, when the terms of engagement are asymmetrical, this dynamic can entrench unequal power relations. Allowing domestic elites to capture rents while broader developmental benefits remain limited or bypass local populations entirely in South East Asia (Rodan, 2018). Even so, the Mekong states are not passive actors. They hedge. They navigate. They pivot between Chinese infrastructure and strategic cooperation with the United States, Japan, or India (Htwe, 2025). In navigating the strategic tensions of great power competition, Mekong states are adopting a form of balance-of-power realism reminiscent (Thompson, 1960) of classical realist thought of the geopolitical pragmatism (Bell, 2008). The real challenge, then, is not the scale of China's engagement but the disjuncture between rhetoric and footprint. Zbigniew Brzezinski's metaphor of the "Grand Chessboard" (Brzezinski, 2016) finds fresh relevance along the Mekong's muddy banks. Rivalries are mapped not through military alliances but through economic leverage (Mazarr et al., 2021). Yet, as Gearóid Ó Tuathail (1997)'scritical geopolitics view, these cartographies of power overlook the human terrains of the agency of local actors, the ecological consequences of development done in haste. Nature refuses to be managed like diplomacy. Environmental crises lay bare the fragility of transactional partnerships (Susskind & Ali, 2014).

China's ambitions collide most violently with the environment. The Mekong's hydropower surge reveals a civilizational wager. The complexities of water resource management is in the context of regional power structures and environmental sustainability. Energy security is over ecological resilience (Rodríguez Álvarez, 2024) . Its seasonal rhythms disrupted and biodiversity imperiled. mention that both BRI and LMC institutionalize an extractivist logic (Panke & Rüland, 2022). It is marginalizing ecological governance. In response, the Asian Development Bank promote "smart" hydropower as a climate solution, (Wright et al., 2017) but this faith in innovation often outpaces on-the-ground governance capacity (Nichols et al., 2024) . Between the immediacy of growth and the demands of long-term sustainability, What unfolds is a dialectic between developmental urgency and environmental justice (Crawford et al., 2023). Tuathail (2002) challenges traditional geopolitical perspectives by emphasizing the role of language and representation in shaping political understandings of space and power.

Sovereignty, too, is undergoing redefinition. Liu (2022) deconstructs the simplistic "debt trap" trope. He suggests that viewing the BRI through an infrastructural lens reveals the complex interplay between politics and technology in shaping regional dynamics and power structures. Dependency is not imposed but negotiated and co-produced by domestic elites and Chinese financiers (Hönke et al., 2024). In Beeson's (2019) broader geoeconomic framing, this pattern works to erode Western multilateral influence, a trend illustrated starkly in Chheang's (2021) study of Cambodia's strategic realignment. Still, there is pushback. Ki-Hyun Bae (2024) emphasizes ASEAN's enduring relevance. Smaller states leverage multilateralism as a hedge against Chinese dominance (Kim, 2023) and keep open a sliver of strategic autonomy amid deepening asymmetry (Ernst, 2025).

To grasp the ideological contours of China's regional strategy, one must turn to Radhika Desai's (2013) theory of Geopolitical Economy. Her work positions state-led capitalism as the countercurrent to Western neoliberal hegemony (Desai, 2013), with the BRI and LMC forming part of a global realignment (Oakes, 2021) . Wielding infrastructure as foreign policy, Beijing is not a mere market participant but a state-crafting force (Lu et al., 2024). It has identified the structural constraints to impose on peripheral states by the global economic system (Chase-Dunn, 1998) . Traditional system often treates these limitations as fixed outcomes of economic determinism. The concept of imperialism is within the context of global political economy (Callinicos, 2009). In contrast, a neo-institutionalist perspective provides that institutional development is not only possible (Scheuer & Scheuer, 2008) but essential for achieving greater autonomy and resilience within the global order (Crouch, 2005).

Yet Yusuf (2008) critique of developing economies trapped in unequal global value chains offers a sobering lens. Kaplinsky (2013)mentions that even amid rising trade volumes and digital modernization, structural dependencies persist. Boswell and Chase-Dunn (2000) inject a Gramscian skepticism in China development. They argue that China's rise represents not a rupture with the capitalist order but a recalibration. The language may be South-South solidarity, but the effect is familiar (Stephen, 2014). Elite partnerships, fragmented sovereignties, and a central power shape the periphery in its image (Adamson, 1983). Institutionally, ASEAN remains both shield and sieve (Acharya, 2021). Rodan (2022) diagnoses the bloc's structural deficiencies. Its failure to enforce normative cohesion or coordinate responses to external pressures (Kuik, 2021). Yet voices like Brown and Marsden (2023) and Martel (2022) defend ASEAN's consensual framework as a source of regional stability and holds the center even as external actors chip away at the periphery.

3. CHINA'S GEOPOLITICAL IMPLICATIONS IN MEKONG REGION

Launched in 2013 by President Xi Jinping, The BRI is more than a foreign policy. It is a transcontinental vision of connectivity and commerce. It is evoking the spirit of ancient Silk Roads while asserting modern Chinese power across land and sea (Akdağ, 2024). In mainland Southeast Asia, the BRI takes material form in a web of ambitious infrastructure projects that stitch China ever closer to its southern neighbors. Railways, highways, special economic zones, hydropower dams and logistics hubs now mark the landscape like signposts of a new regional order (Chuvilov, 2024). China's expansive investments across the Greater Mekong Sub-region (GMS) under the Belt and Road Initiative (BRI) have significantly reshaped regional geopolitics. While ostensibly economic in nature, these engagements carry deep political implications and challenge the sovereignty of host states (na Thalang & Eun, 2024). Prompting a recalibration of foreign policies among Southeast Asian nations, states in the GMS are navigating shifting strategic alignments. Chinese development aid often operates as a mechanism of political leverage (Li & Yang, 2024). One the other hand, Competing powers, particularly the United States, Japan, India and the Quadrilateral Security Dialogue (Quad), are responding to China's growing footprint in the region (Das, 2024).

China's development model challenges liberal norms by promoting state-led capitalism, opaque governance, and non-interference. This approach appeals to authoritarian and hybrid regimes across the Mekong. However, it also invites scrutiny. Informal political expectations, elite capture, and diminished civil society roles are recurring outcomes. ASEAN's inability to enforce collective norms exacerbates these challenges. True modernization requires institutional pluralism, transparency, and the empowerment of domestic actors—values at risk under China's dominant regional approach (Tang, 2021). China's development model poses a direct challenge to liberal norms by advancing a form of state-led capitalism characterized by centralized control, strategic opacity, and a doctrine of non-interference (Jones & Hameiri, 2021). This model has proven attractive to authoritarian and hybrid regimes across the Mekong region, where ruling elites often prioritize regime stability and economic growth over democratic accountability. Yet its appeal comes with consequences. Patterns of informal political expectations, elite capture, and the marginalization of civil society recur with alarming consistency.

ASEAN's institutional weakness and its principle of non-interference further exacerbate these dynamics, enabling the diffusion of a governance model that prioritizes state prerogatives over participatory norms (Halper, 2010). China's approach can be understood as an assertion of a counter-hegemonic order—an alternative modernity shaped not by liberal universalism, but by sovereign developmentalism. However, from a neo-institutionalist perspective, this model lacks the institutional pluralism and embedded transparency that underpin sustainable modernization (Jinhua, 2022).

Parallel to this outward-facing development strategy of BRI, Lancang-Mekong Cooperation is the more localized, yet no less strategic. Established in 2016, the LMC brings together China and the five lower Mekong countries (Myanmar, Laos, Thailand, Cambodia, and Vietnam), under the banner of shared river governance and socio-economic cooperation. It is a multilateral framework in name, but a bilateral instrument in function (Kun & Tian, 2022). The foreign policy responses of Mekong states toward China reveal a spectrum of strategic behavior. Ranging from bandwagoning and balancing to hedging, these alignments are not static. They evolve based on domestic political priorities, economic dependencies and perceptions of regional security (Ping, Hayes, & McCormick, 2025). Cambodia and Laos are frequently cited as prime examples of bandwagoning with China. Both governments have actively embraced Chinese capital and diplomatic support (Luo, 2025).

Lao's participation in the BRI has resulted in substantial infrastructure developments, such as the Laos-China Railway (Lertpusit, 2024). In Laos, the government's heavy reliance on Chinese loans for infrastructure development has raised concerns about debt diplomacy. Laos risks becoming economically beholden to China, compromising its ability to make independent policy decisions (Rosengren, 2024). Similarly, in Cambodia, Chinese-backed developments have allowed the long ruling party to consolidate power, marginalize opposition and suppress civil society without the pressure for democratic reforms typically associated with Western aids. However, these projects have led to increased debt exposure and a growing perception of strategic dependence, which some analysts interpret as a form of "quiet subordination. (Gu, 2024)" In Cambodia, the political elite has leaned heavily on Chinese investments to fuel economic growth while simultaneously consolidating authoritarian governance. Neil Loughlin (2024) examines the endurance of Cambodia's authoritarian regime over more than four decades. He delves into the formation and consolidation of the ruling coalition, emphasizing the roles of political elites, many with backgrounds in the state's coercive apparatu. State-dependent tycoons collectively dominate Cambodia's political and economic spheres (Ty, 2024). Through controversial projects like the Ream Naval Base, Cambodia's acquiescence to Chinese interests underscores its strategic alignment with Beijing (Yaacob, 2024).

Vietnam, in contrast, has adopted a balancing strategy. While economic relations with China are robust, Vietnam remains wary due to maritime disputes in the South China Sea and historical tensions. To offset Chinese influence, Vietnam has strengthened security ties with the United States and Japan, while also deepening engagement within ASEAN (Cuong et al., 2024). Its foreign policy is characterized by "strategic diversification," (Wu & Velasco, 2024) a blend of economic pragmatism and security-driven caution.

Thailand and Myanmar represent cases of hedging. Maintaining flexible foreign policy positions to preserve autonomy and maximize benefits from competing great powers, Thailand's policy of "bamboo diplomacy" allows it to sway with the prevailing geopolitical winds (Busbarat, 2024). Strong ties with both China and the United States, Thailand participates in BRI infrastructure development (Thongsawang, 2025). One the other hand, Myanmar's post-coup trajectory has made China a crucial diplomatic (Abb et al., 2024) and economic lifeline (Haque, 2024), yet concerns about overdependence and Chinese involvement in ethnic conflicts have led the junta to keep its options open, seeking support from Russia (Fumagalli, 2024). The Myitsone Dam project in Myanmar is a paradigmatic case of the sovereignty dilemma. Though officially suspended in 2011 due to public opposition, the dam continues to symbolize the disjuncture between elite decision-making and citizen interests toward China-backed megaprojects like the Letpadaung Copper Mine and Myitsone Dam in Myanmar (Egreteau, 2024). Its proposed resumption has generated anxiety among Myanmar's populace, who view it as evidence of China's undue influence over national resources and political decisions (Chan, 2024). These varied alignments underscore the complexity of regional geopolitics. While China has made significant inroads, it has not gone uncontested. Regional actors are actively recalibrating their foreign policies in response to China's rise.

China's development assistance and investments in Southeast Asia are often lauded for their speed, scale and lack of Western-style conditionality (Sobolik, 2024). However, the political implications of this aid are profound and alter governance dynamics and state sovereignty in recipient countries. Unlike traditional Western donors, China promotes a principle of non-interference and "win-win" cooperation that appeals to authoritarian and semi-authoritarian regimes (Ping et al., 2025). Yet, this approach often enables elite capture, fosters opaque negotiations and reduces accountability (Mierzejewski, 2024). In practice, China's economic assistance frequently comes with informal political expectations in terms of diplomatic alignment and compliance with Chinese strategic objectives (Wu & Kim, 2024). In this light, Chinese aid operates not merely as development assistance but as a strategic instrument of influence. Iti s reshaping governance norms and challenging traditional notions of national sovereignty by the people. China's growing clout in the GMS has spurred a countervailing response from other major powers. The United States led the Quad memebers have intensified engagement in Southeast Asia to offer viable alternatives to China's development and security paradigm.

4. INVESTMENT-DRIVEN MODERNIZATION AND STRATEGIC DEPENDENCY IN THE MEKONG

Infrastructure has emerged as a central pillar of China's regional integration strategy. Through the construction of railways, highways, bridges, ports and energy infrastructure, China aims to reduce logistical bottlenecks, facilitate cross-border mobility and integrate Mekong economies more tightly into regional and global supply chains. In many cases, these projects fill critical infrastructure gaps that have long hindered economic growth and trade expansion in the Mekong subregion (Gong, 2025). Infrastructures have improved connectivity, lowered transportation costs, shortened delivery times, and enabled the movement of goods and labor across previously inaccessible or inefficient routes. This is especially significant in landlocked and less-developed countries such as Laos and parts of northern Myanmar, where poor road and rail infrastructure has historically constrained economic development (Jeong, 2024). By linking these areas with regional markets of Mekong region including sourthen part of China, China's infrastructure investments aim to unlock new trade corridors and economic opportunities.

As part of the larger Kunming-Vientiane-Bangkok-Singapore rail corridor envisioned under the BRI, The China-Laos Railway exemplifies this approach. This project offers landlocked Laos a direct connection to Chinese markets, in the future, deeper integration into regional supply chains. It drastically reduces travel time among the capitals and is projected to increase trade volume and tourism. The railway has already begun transporting agricultural goods, consumer products and raw materials across borders. Similarly, road and port development projects in Cambodia and Myanmar are creating new logistical nodes that enhance regional integration (Xuan & Hai, 2023). The planned Kyaukphyu deep-sea port in Rakhine State in Myanmar will enable China to bypass the congested Strait of Malacca and establish an alternative trade route linking the Indian Ocean with Yunnan Province. Although still under construction, such projects signal the long-term strategic logic behind China's connectivity drive: to reroute and reconfigure the region's trade flows in ways that complement Chinese economic and geopolitical interests (Myoe, 2024).

Alongside physical infrastructure, Chinese investments in industry, energy and services are accelerating the modernization of Mekong economies. These investments are often packaged as part of broader economic cooperation agreements. Special economic zones (SEZs), industrial parks, energy plants and digital infrastructure development, Chinese capital contributes to job creation, technology transfer and diversification of economic activities. China's investments in the Mekong region have raised concerns over labor standards, environmental harm, and growing local dependency (Yu, 2024). The Sihanoukville Special Economic Zone (SSEZ) in Cambodia is a prominent example of this investment-led development. Developed jointly by Chinese and Cambodian firms, the SSEZ hosts over 170 enterprises. Primarily in garment manufacturing, electronics, and logistics, SSEZ has created tens of thousands of jobs and significantly increased Cambodia's export capacity. With modern infrastructure, preferential tax policies and access to Chinese financing, the SSEZ exemplifies that China uses economic zones to foster industrialization and integrate Mekong economies into Chinese-led production networks. However, heavy reliance on Chinese investment, coupled with opaque contract terms and lack of parliamentary oversight, has created an environment conducive to corruption and mismanagement. Institutional checks and balances are weak, with civil society and media facing growing restrictions (Erie et al., 2025; Gong, 2025).

The case of Laos is illustrative. With its ambition to become the "Battery of Southeast Asia," Laos has heavily invested in hydropower projects, most of which are funded and constructed by Chinese companies. The Vientiane Saysettha Development Zone, illustrate the combination of logistical connectivity (e.g., via the Laos-China Railway) and industrial clustering. As of 2024, external debt has reached nearly 90% of its GDP, with China accounting for over half of bilateral debt. In 2021, the government was forced to hand over a controlling stake in its national electricity grid to a Chinese company to avoid default, effectively ceding control over a strategic national asset. This scenario exemplifies concerns over "debt-trap diplomacy," whereby economic leverage translates into political influence and loss of sovereignty (Keothephar et al., 2024). The Laos-China Railway is perhaps the most transformative infrastructure project in the country's history. As part of the BRI's pan-Asian railway vision, it connects Vientiane to Kunming in China's Yunnan Province over a 414-kilometer route. This $6 billion project—equivalent to nearly one-third of Laos's GDP. Financed largely through loans from Chinese banks, ownership has shared between Chinese stakeholders and fewly the Lao government (Jumlongnark, 2024). the China-Laos Railway has not only improved logistics but also attracted ancillary investments in logistics parks, warehousing, real estate and tourism. As part of its broader industrialization strategy, the Lao government is positioning itself as a "land-linked" hub. Leveraging Chinese infrastructure to transition from a resource-based economy to a trade and services-oriented one. Chinese firms are increasingly involved in the construction of hydropower plants, telecom infrastructure and urban real estate sectors that are central to Laos's modernization ambitions (Eihmane, 2025). Despite concerns over debt sustainability and environmental impact, the railway is viewed by many Laotians as a symbol of progress. It has reduced travel time across the country and spurred the growth of logistics hubs and tourism businesses along its corridor. However, the benefits remain uneven, with critics warning of long-term financial burdens, limited local employment in construction phases, and potential marginalization of small businesses unable to compete with Chinese firms. In both countries, the limited capacity of regulatory bodies has led to poor project monitoring, substandard construction quality, and inflated costs.

In Cambodia and Laos, where institutional capacity remains uneven and fiscal space limited, China has emerged as the dominant external actor in the energy sectors, financing and constructing hydropower dams, coal-fired plants, and transmission networks at a scale unmatched by other partners. These projects have undeniably improved access to electricity for both industrial and household consumption, facilitating economic growth and regional integration. Yet the strategic implications of this development model are profound. In Laos, large segments of the national power grid are now operated or owned by Chinese state-owned enterprises. This case raises fundamental questions about national sovereignty and the direction of energy governance. What appears on the surface as an infrastructure-led solution to chronic energy deficits also reflects a deeper asymmetry in power and institutional influence. Local governments find themselves locked into long-term agreements that limit future policy flexibility and entrench external dependence and often lack the regulatory capacity or financial alternatives.

In Myanmar, the Kyaukphyu Deep-Sea Port and Special Economic Zone illustrate the paradox of infrastructural modernization under authoritarian governance. Chu, Jonathan and Lynn analyze that these enterprises navigate local regulatory frameworks, engage with community stakeholders, and implement corporate social responsibility (CSR) initiatives (Chu et al., 2025).. However, While ostensibly designed to integrate Myanmar into the regional economy via the Indian Ocean, the project primarily consolidates the power of entrenched military elites and Chinese state-owned enterprises (Myoe, 2024). The absence of institutional mechanisms for accountability or equitable benefit-sharing reflects a deeper pattern of extractive governance that privileges geopolitical utility over local development. By contrast, Thailand's China–Thailand high-speed railway marks a significant advance in regional connectivity and infrastructure. Bunnak et al.(2024) offer a governance analysis of the Sino-Thai railway project that challenges such as regulatory discrepancies, stakeholder coordination, and governance practices between China and Thailand. The authors emphasize the importance of effective governance mechanisms to ensure the project's success and its contribution to regional connectivity and economic development. Yet, the terms of engagement reveal a growing asymmetry. The limited transfer of technology and increasing debt obligations tether Thailand to a development model that aligns more closely with China's strategic objectives than with Thailand's long-term economic autonomy (He, 2024).

Here, modernization proceeds without the institutional maturation necessary to ensure sovereign control over national development. Despite being labeled a skeptic due to its limited participation in China's Belt and Road Initiative (BRI), Vietnam actively engages with China through trade, investment, energy sector projects, and economic corridor cooperation (Dang et al., 2024). This dual approach reflects Vietnam's strategy of balancing cooperation and resistance, influenced by factors such as elite legitimation and the availability of external alternatives. Epitomized by the Vinh Tan 1 coal power plant and cross-border industrial zones, Vietnam's embrace of Chinese-backed infrastructure has yielded short-term gains in energy and manufacturing capacity. (Abdullah et al., 2025). However, the high environmental cost and dependence on external capital and contractors underscore the vulnerabilities of a growth strategy rooted in external rents (Nguyen & Le, 2024). China's regional infrastructure investments function not merely as economic tools, but as instruments of influence that reshape the institutional trajectories and autonomy of Southeast Asian states.

China's Digital Silk Road exports surveillance technologies to countries like Cambodia and Laos (Zhou & Xue, 2020). Raising alarm about the erosion of digital sovereignty and the rise of authoritarian governance models, these technological investments are often embedded in broader infrastructure packages China's efforts to enhance digital connectivity through projects like cross-border optical cable networks and satellite information passageways and the DSR serves as a strategic tool for China to assert its influence in the global digital landscape (Baark, 2024). Chinese influence becomes increasingly entrenched in the political systems of recipient states, as authoritarian-leaning regimes adopt governance models and policy preferences reflective of Beijing's interests. Chinese tech giants—most notably Huawei, Alibaba, and ZTE—have made significant investments in the region's digital infrastructure, including 5G networks, data centers, and e-commerce platforms (Wang, 2024). Utilizing data on trade, investment, and tourism, ASEAN countries perceive both opportunities and challenges in their economic engagements with China (Tran et al., 2023).

Grassroots resistance to Chinese infrastructure in the Mekong is not a side story. It is the story unfolding beneath the fanfare of high-level deals. While state narratives celebrate connectivity and modernization, local communities tell of a different reality: land loss, cultural erasure, and the struggle to reclaim agency. In Myanmar, the Myitsone Dam project stirred a moral revolt. Backed by Chinese capital and poised to alter the sacred confluence of Irrawaddy river, it promised power but threatened to uproot thousands of Kachin lives. What began as a hydropower initiative became a national awakening. Civil society, monks, and villagers rallied not only to protect the river but to reassert ancestral belonging and sovereignty (Kiik, 2023). In Cambodia's Kratie province, Chinese-funded developments displaced Indigenous Chong communities. Evictions, lost graves, and militarized responses to protest marked a deeper struggle—where land became a bargaining chip in elite alliances (Mackenzie, Milne, van Kerkhoff, & Ray, 2023). Yet resistance endured through documentation, quiet defiance, and networks of solidarity. In Laos, the 2018 collapse of the Xe Pian-Xe Namnoy dam was a rupture both physical and political. Though the state was silent, affected communities spoke—in testimonies, in letters, in calls for accountability that crossed borders and awakened diaspora networks (Baird, 2021). These are not isolated events but expressions of a wider conflict. To the powerful, infrastructure means growth. To the people, it often means dispossession. The clash is not merely over territory, but over the definition of progress itself. And in this contested landscape, legitimacy is being redefined—from GDP metrics to community voices, from top-down planning to participatory stewardship. The resistance may not make headlines. It may be erased in official reports. But it lives on—in protest songs, in forest paths once marked by ancestors, and in the refusal to be silent. This is the Mekong's other history—still being written, from below.

5. THE MEMBERS OF QUAD'S ROLE IN SHAPING MEKONG FUTURES

The United States focuses on promoting transparency, environmental sustainability and human rights. The United States' engagement in the Mekong region through the Mekong-U.S. Partnership reflects a strategic emphasis on institutional integrity, transparency, and liberal democratic norms. Prioritizing soft infrastructure, U.S. aid supports environmental governance, civil society, human rights, and youth leadership through initiatives like the Mekong Water Data Initiative, YSEALI, and USAID health programs (Blinken, 2021). While modest in scale compared to China's infrastructural outreach, U.S. efforts seek to embed rule of law, pluralism, and accountable governance as foundations for regional stability. In the Mekong region, minilateralism has become a strategic tool through which the U.S. and China project competing visions of regional order amid their great power rivalry (Chowdhury, Tadjoeddin, & Vidyattama, 2025). The U.S. promotes flexible, value-driven groupings like the Mekong-U.S. Partnership to uphold transparency, environmental sustainability, and a rules-based order. In contrast, China advances initiatives like the Lancang-Mekong Cooperation, favoring sovereignty-first principles and infrastructural connectivity under its Belt and Road Initiative (Richey & Guseinova, 2024). US positions development not as coercion, but as a pathway to legitimate state-building. Aiming to strengthen democratic governance and resilience against authoritarian influence, U.S. programs often support civil society, media and grassroots environmental defenders (Htwe, 2025). However, U.S. efforts are frequently seen as reactive and insufficient in scale compared to China's massive infrastructure footprint.

Japan positions itself as a provider of quality infrastructure through initiatives like the Partnership for Quality Infrastructure and Mekong-Japan Cooperation Framewor. As a longstanding development partner in the region, Japan's engagement with the Mekong region reflects a deliberate strategy rooted in institutional development and liberal norms. Through frameworks like the Tokyo Strategy and the Japan-ASEAN Integration Fund, Japan has prioritized rule-based connectivity. Investing in corridors, infrastructure, and economic zones, Japan promotes integration rather than dependence. Its parallel focus on sustainable development, human security and institutional capacity-building speaks to a vision of modernization grounded not only in growth but in legitimacy (Ministry of Foreign Affairs of Japan, 2024). Despite these endeavors, Japan's historical actions during World War II continue to influence its relationships within the region. Japan balances its economic interests with the imperative of addressing historical grievances, offering insights into the complexities of its regional engagement (Chua, 2024). In contrast to China's state-centric model, Japan offers a path aligned with transparency, the rule of law and good governance. This approach reflects a deeper commitment to constructing resilient, autonomous states. While less coercive, this approach is critical to regional order and the consolidation of liberal democracy in Asia. China and Japan leverage high-speed rail investments as tools of economic and geopolitical influence. While Southeast Asian nations benefit from enhanced infrastructure and growth, they also face the strategic challenge of balancing between competing visions of regional order advanced by both powers (Wei & Tang, 2024).

India and Australia have deepened their engagement with the Mekong region through a shared emphasis on institutional development, capacity-building and regional autonomy. India's Mekong-Ganga Cooperation and initiatives under its Act East Policy include the construction of the India-Myanmar-Thailand Trilateral Highway and capacity-building in telemedicine, civil service training and digital connectivity programs in Cambodia and Laos (ASEAN-India Centre, 2023). These are embedded within a broader vision of South-South cooperation and mutual respect. Australia, meanwhile, is advancing the Mekong-Australia Partnership (MAP). At the ASEAN-Australia Special Summit in March 2024, the Australian Government announced a second phase of MAP, committing an additional $222.5 million over five years (2024–2029). This phase aims to build upon the initial successes and further deepen Australia's engagement in the region. Supporting projects on climate resilience, transboundary water governance, and counter-trafficking in persons, Austrial funds research institutions and civil society networks across the region (Department of Foreign Affairs and Trade, 2023). Together, these efforts reflect a strategic vision grounded in the cultivation of legitimate, rules-based political orders. It offers a decentralized, participatory alternative to centralized, extractive development models. Their engagement is not predicated on domination, but on the long-term stabilization of regional order through norm diffusion, institutional trust and capacity for self-rule.

Comprising the United States, India, Japan, and Australia, The Quad have emerged as a strategic grouping aimed at promoting a Free and Open Indo-Pacific. It offers joint initiatives in infrastructure, maritime security, cyber resilience and climate change In theory, the Quad provides an alternative framework to China's BRI. The strategic imperatives and geopolitical dynamics could drive the Quad towards a more formalized military alliance akin to the North Atlantic Treaty Organization against China's influence. (Bhaskar & Mishra, 2025). In practice, however, its on-the-ground influence remains nascent. Many Mekong states continue to see China as the more immediate and tangible partner (Yen, 2024). While competition among these powers provides GMS countries with strategic options, it also introduces the risk of geopolitical fragmentation. In Mekong region, development aid becomes a tool of rival influence rather than a vehicle for inclusive regional integration.

6. DISCUSSION

6.1. The Paradox of Integration: Dependency vs. Autonomy in in China-Mekong Economic Relations

Modernization becomes a double-edged swor. It builds physical infrastructure but deepens dependency on an external hegemon. Development without institutional accountability often leads not to liberal order but to elite entrenchment and external subordination. The Mekong case underscores the need for a rethinking of modernization beyond physical growth. Yet, the economic prospects generated by these initiatives come with contradictions. The promise of modernization is tempered by concerns about debt dependency, labor exploitation, environmental degradation and the erosion of sovereignty. As Mekong countries navigate their development pathways, they must grapple to leverage Chinese investment for inclusive and sustainable growth while maintaining agency in an increasingly asymmetric relationship.More broadly, China's energy engagement across the Mekong region reveals a pattern of short-term developmental gains coupled with long-term structural vulnerabilities. In the absence of robust governance mechanisms and diversified partnerships, infrastructure becomes not merely a response to material needs. But an instrument through which institutional autonomy is eroded. Development, in this context, is not ideologically neutral. It is embedded in strategic relations that shape the capacity of states to determine their own future (Duffield, 2007). Without institutional safeguards, the pursuit of energy access risks becoming a pathway to dependency in subordinating national interests to the imperatives of an emerging regional hegemon.

The incorporation of Mekong subregion countries into China's expanding economic orbit through the Belt and Road Initiative (BRI) and related cooperative mechanisms represents a paradigmatic instance of economic modernization entangled with geopolitical constraint. On the surface, the influx of Chinese capital has produced measurable developmental gains. Infrastructure has improved, trade volumes have increased, and foreign direct investment has surged. Yet these advances are not unambiguous. They unfold within a framework of asymmetric power relations that risk undermining the very institutional autonomy required for long-term governance and sovereignty.

The first dynamic at play is the structural imbalance between China and its Mekong counterparts. This asymmetry has allowed China to project influence far beyond the realm of commerce, penetrating into the domestic policy arenas of smaller states. Where institutional resilience is weak, such influence easily transforms into strategic dependency. Cambodia stands as a cautionary example: the intensification of Chinese investment has been accompanied by a growing alignment with Beijing's geopolitical positions, frequently at odds with ASEAN's multilateral ethos. Laos, similarly, finds itself enmeshed in unsustainable debt obligations stemming from Chinese-funded infrastructure projects.

Second, this condition of dependency does not occur passively. States within the Mekong subregion engage in a deliberate and ongoing calculus to balance developmental necessity against strategic autonomy. In institutional terms, this is a question of capacity: how can states build and preserve strong, coherent national institutions in the face of external economic inducements? Vietnam has responded by adopting a dual-track foreign policy. Deepening its economic ties with China, Vietnam simultaneously reinforces security and economic relations with the United States, Japan, and India. Thailand as well for its part, exemplifies a hedging strategy. Engaging in Chinese infrastructure initiatives, while maintaining defense and institutional links with the West. These responses suggest that the durability of sovereignty rests not merely on policy preference, but on the robustness of institutional pluralism and statecraft.

Third, the region suffers from a deficit of institutional coherence at the supranational level. Unlike the European Union, regulatory harmonization and legal enforceability create a buffer against unilateral domination (Egan, 2001), Mekong cooperation remains fragmented. China has leveraged this institutional weakness to negotiate bilateral agreements that bypass collective scrutiny. The Lancang-Mekong Cooperation (LMC) framework is structured around Chinese leadership and lacks the normative legitimacy and procedural rigor of ASEAN. The Mekong region's experience illustrates a central tension in modernization. Material gains without institutional strength lead to strategic dependency. Chinese-led development has improved infrastructure but eroded autonomy, embedding asymmetrical power structures.

True modernization requires more than economic growth. It demands resilient institutions, diversified partnerships and governance rooted in legitimacy (Root, 2013). Without this, development risks becoming a pathway not to sovereignty, but to subordination. Therefore, the sustainability of development in the Mekong will depend less on the volume of Chinese capital and more on the capacity of domestic institutions to govern it effectively. Without institutional depth, investment can become corrosive. Concentrating power, states will reduce transparency and undermining sovereignty of people (Lord, 2012). The challenge ahead lies in embedding economic globalization within rule-based governance systems that foster resilience, equity and political legitimacy. This is not merely an economic imperative but it is the central task of statecraft in the twenty-first century.

7. CONCLUSION

This paper has examined the complex duality at the heart of China-led regionalism in the Mekong subregion—an arena where infrastructural expansion and trade integration under the Belt and Road Initiative (BRI) are advancing alongside deepening structural dependencies, environmental vulnerabilities, and encroachments upon national sovereignty. The developmental benefits offered by Chinese investments—manifested most visibly in improved connectivity and economic growth—should not obscure the institutional deficits that accompany them: weakened regulatory oversight, marginalization of local actors, and the erosion of autonomous decision-making.

Mekong states exhibit divergent responses to these pressures. Vietnam and Thailand have pursued hedging strategies aimed at balancing China's economic largesse with other regional and global partnerships. In contrast, Cambodia and Laos have adopted a more acquiescent posture, increasingly embedded within China's sphere of influence. These variations are symptomatic of a broader institutional vacuum at the regional level. ASEAN's normative approach and lack of enforcement mechanisms have proven inadequate in mediating asymmetries of power and protecting the sovereignty of its weaker members.

In an emerging multipolar order, the central challenge facing Mekong states is not merely how to respond to China, but how to construct resilient institutions capable of mediating external influence while preserving domestic legitimacy. Sustainable development cannot rest on economic outcomes alone; it must be rooted in the strength of political institutions, the rule of law, and participatory governance.

Regionalism, therefore, must be reimagined—not as a vehicle for dependency, but as a framework for collective agency. The future of the Mekong lies in the ability of its states to assert their sovereignty through institutional diversification, strategic pluralism, and regional cooperation grounded in shared norms and accountability. This is not a purely technocratic endeavor; it is a fundamentally political project—one that requires the empowerment of domestic actors, the rebuilding of institutional legitimacy, and the cultivation of a regional identity capable of withstanding external asymmetries. Only then can the region chart a path that reconciles integration with autonomy, and development with sovereignty.

REFERENCES

Abb, P., Zin Khay, S. K., Overland, I., & Vakulchuk, R. (2024). Road through a broken place: The BRI in post-coup Myanmar. *The Pacific Review*, •••, 1–25. https://www.tandfonline.com/doi/abs/10.1080/09512748.2024.2420929. DOI: 10.1080/09512748.2024.2420929

Acharya, A. (2021). ASEAN and regional order: Revisiting security community in Southeast Asia. Routledge. https://www.taylorfrancis.com/books/mono/10.4324/9781003122333/asean-regional-order-amitav-acharya

Adamson, W. L. (1983). Hegemony and revolution: A study of Antonio Gramsci's political and cultural theory. Univ of California Press. https://monoskop.org/images/a/ac/Adamson_Walter_L_Hegemony_and_Revolution_A_Study_of_Antonio_Gramscis_Political_and_Cultural_Theory_1980.pdf

Akdağ, Z. (2024). China's Assertive Foreign Policy and Global Visions Under Xi Jinping. Akademik İncelemeler Dergisi, 19(1), 204-221. https://dergipark.org.tr/en/pub/akademikincelemeler/article/1423366

Anh, H. (2024). *Analyzing China's Influence by China's High-Speed Railway Diplomacy in Southeast Asia Countries*. Integrated Journal for Research in Arts and Humanities., DOI: 10.55544/ijrah.4.2.11

ASEAN-India Centre. (2023). Mekong-Ganga Policy Brief: July 2023. https://aseanindiacentre.org.in/sites/default/files/Publication/Mekong-Ganga-July-2023.pdf

Baark, E. (2024). China's Digital Silk Road: Innovation in a new geopolitical environment. *East Asian Policy*, *16*(1), 25–38. DOI: 10.1142/S1793930524000023

Bae, K. H. (2024). Enduring hypocrisy as ASEAN's organisational problem? *Journal of Current Southeast Asian Affairs*, *43*(1), 48–64. https://journals.sagepub.com/doi/abs/10.1177/18681034231215813. DOI: 10.1177/18681034231215813

Baird, I. G. (2021). Catastrophic and slow violence: Thinking about the impacts of the Xe Pian Xe Namnoy dam in southern Laos. *The Journal of Peasant Studies*, *48*(6), 1167–1186. https://www.tandfonline.com/doi/abs/10.1080/03066150.2020.1824181. DOI: 10.1080/03066150.2020.1824181

Beeson, M. (2019). Rethinking global governance. Bloomsbury Publishing. https://www.bloomsbury.com/us/rethinking-global-governance-9781137588609/

Bell, D. (Ed.). (2008). *Political thought and international relations: Variations on a realist theme*. Oxford University Press., https://global.oup.com/academic/product/political-thought-and-international-relations-9780199556274?cc=th&lang=

Berni, A. (2025). *The Complex Environments of Special Economic Zones: Challenges and Opportunities in Italy*. SpringerBriefs in Economics., DOI: 10.1007/978-3-031-83425-7

Bhaskar, P., & Mishra, S. (2025). Why the Quad Can Become an Asian NATO. *Journal of Territorial and Maritime Studies*, *12*(1), 113–126. https://search.proquest.com/openview/69d34df08393b7e704d7280894efbbd0/1?pq-origsite=gscholar&cbl=2069438

Blinken, A. J. (2021, August 5). The United States and the Friends of the Mekong: Proven partners for the Mekong region [Press statement]. U.S. Department of State. https://2021-2025.state.gov/the-united-states-and-the-friends-of-the-mekong-proven-partners-for-the-mekong-region/

Bluwstein, J., Cavanagh, C., & Fletcher, R. (2024). Securing conservation Lebensraum? The geo-, bio-, and ontopolitics of global conservation futures. *Geoforum*, *153*, 103752. DOI: 10.1016/j.geoforum.2023.103752

Boer, B., Hirsch, P., Johns, F., Saul, B., & Scurrah, N. (2015). The Mekong: A socio-legal approach to river basin development. Routledge. Pp.100-124 https://www.taylorfrancis.com/books/mono/10.4324/9781315765556/mekong-socio-legal-approach-river-basin-development-philip-hirsch-ben-boer-fleur-johns-ben-saul-natalia-scurrah

Boswell, T., & Chase-Dunn, C. K. (2000). The spiral of capitalism and socialism: Toward global democracy. Lynne Rienner Publishers. https://www.rienner.com/title/The_Spiral_of_Capitalism_and_Socialism_Toward_Global_Democracy

Brown, I., & Marsden, C. T. (2023). *Regulating code: Good governance and better regulation in the information age*. MIT press.

Brzezinski, Z. (2016). The grand chessboard: American primacy and its geostrategic imperatives. Basic books. https://www.cia.gov/library/abbottabad-compound/36/36669B7894E857AC4F3445EA646BFFE1_Zbigniew_Brzezinski_-_The_Grand_ChessBoard.doc.pdf

Bunnak, P., Song, N., Chen, X., & Thomson, R. (2024). A governance perspective on China's belt and road initiative: A case study of the Sino-Thai railway project. *Journal of Asian Public Policy*, •••, 1–20. https://www.tandfonline.com/doi/abs/10.1080/17516234.2024.2386719. DOI: 10.1080/17516234.2024.2386719

Busbarat, P. (2018). Grabbing the Forgotten: China's Leadership Consolidation in Mainland Southeast Asia through the Mekong-Lancang Cooperation. ISEAS-Yusof Ishak Institute. https://www.iseas.edu.sg/wp-content/uploads/pdfs/ISEAS_Perspective_2018_7@50.pdf

Busbarat, P. (2024). Bamboo Stuck in the Chinese Wind. *Contemporary Southeast Asia*, *46*(1), 125–146. https://www.jstor.org/stable/27301257. DOI: 10.1355/CS46-1f

Callinicos, A. (2009). Imperialism and global political economy. Polity. https://discovered.ed.ac.uk/discovery/fulldisplay?vid=44UOE_INST:44UOE_VU2&docid=alma9919181213502466&lang=en&context=L&adaptor=Local%20Search%20Engine

Carminati, D. (2024). The Soft (Power) Side of the Belt and Road Initiative: Connecting Southeast Asia. Hong Kong Review of Belt and Road Studies, (2), 18-32. https://oborjournal.org/index.php/journal/article/view/17

Chan, D. (2024). *Defying Beijing: Societal Resistance to the Belt and Road in Myanmar*. ANU Press., https://library.oapen.org/handle/20.500.12657/92202 DOI: 10.22459/DB.2024

Chase-Dunn, C. K. (1998). Global formation: Structures of the world-economy. Rowman & Littlefield. https://rowman.com/ISBN/9780847691029/Global-Formation-Structures-of-the-World-Economy

Chheang, V. (2021). Cambodia's Embrace of China's Belt and Road Initiative: Managing Asymmetries, Maximizing Authority. *Asian Perspective*, *45*(2), 375–396. https://muse.jhu.edu/pub/1/article/787857/summary. DOI: 10.1353/apr.2021.0005

Chu, T. W., Jonathan, S., & Lynn, K. (2025). Examining Chinese State-Owned Enterprise's Business Practices in the Kyaukphyu Special Economic Zone. In The Impact of China's Belt and Road Initiative in Southeast Asia: Evaluating Risks and Benefits (pp. 91-108). Singapore: Springer Nature Singapore. https://link.springer.com/chapter/10.1007/978-981-97-9511-6_5

Chua, K. I. U. C. (2024). Japan's Complicated Presence in Southeast Asia. *Current History (New York, N.Y.)*, *123*(854), 223–228. Advance online publication. DOI: 10.1525/curh.2024.123.854.223

Chuvilov, I. A. (2024). China's foreign policy under Xi Jinping: From the Belt and road initiative to a community with a shared future for mankind. Journal of the Belarusian State University. *International Relations*, (2), 9–13. https://journals.bsu.by/index.php/internationalRelations/article/view/6673

Cohen, S. B. (2003). *Geopolitics of the world system*. Rowman & Littlefield.

Crawford, N. J. W., Michael, K., & Mikulewicz, M. (Eds.). (2023). *Climate justice in the majority world: Vulnerability, resistance, and diverse knowledges*. Routledge., DOI: 10.4324/9781003214021

Crouch, C. (2005). Capitalist diversity and change: Recombinant governance and institutional entrepreneurs. OUP Oxford. https://academic.oup.com/book/6938

Cuong, N. M., Chelabi, K., Anjum, S., Sateeshchandra, N. G., Samoylenko, S., Silwizya, K., & Nghiem, T. (2024). US-China global competition and dilemma for Vietnam's strategic choices in the South China Sea conflict. *Heritage and Sustainable Development*, *6*(1), 349–364. DOI: 10.37868/hsd.v6i1.550

Curtis, S., & Klaus, I. (2024). *The Belt and Road City: Geopolitics, urbanization, and China's search for a new international order*. Yale University Press., https://yalebooks.yale.edu/book/9780300266900/the-belt-and-road-city/

Dang, Q., Rammal, H., Ghauri, P., Jasovska, P., & Velasquez, S. (2024). 'Caught in the middle': Effects on and reactions of Vietnamese timber exporters in the context of US-China economic sanctions. Journal of World Business. . Nguyen, V., & Le, H. (2024).DOI: 10.1016/j.jwb.2024.101583

Das, O. P. (2024). Navigating ASEAN Centrality amidst Internal Friction and Interplay of Strategic Frameworks between the US and China. *Journal of Defence Studies*, *18*(1), 43–66. https://www.idsa.in/wp-content/uploads/2024/05/18-1_Om-Prakash-Das.pdf

Department of Foreign Affairs and Trade. (2023). Mekong–Australia Partnership Factsheet. Australian Government. https://www.dfat.gov.au/sites/default/files/mekong-aust-partnership-factsheet.pdf

Desai, R. (2013). *Geopolitical economy: After US hegemony, globalization and empire (the future of world capitalism)*. Pluto Press., https://www.academia.edu/download/76455996/211319.pdf

Dongming, X., & Guang, T. (2022). Modernization, Innovation and Realization of the Chinese Dream: A Critical Review of Panmarketization Thinking Trend in China. *The Journal of Applied Business and Economics*, *24*(2), 9–23. https://articlegateway.com/index.php/JABE/article/view/5097

Duffield, M. (2007). Development, security and unending war: Governing the world of peoples. *Polity*.

Egan, M. (2001). *Constructing a European market: standards, regulation, and governance*. OUP Oxford. DOI: 10.1093/0199244057.001.0001

Egreteau, R. (2024). How Legislators Frame Contentious Megaprojects: Insights from Parliamentary Debates on Letpadaung Mines and Myitsone Dam in Myanmar. *Asian Studies Review*, *48*(2), 331–351. https://www.tandfonline.com/doi/abs/10.1080/10357823.2023.2212124. DOI: 10.1080/10357823.2023.2212124

Eihmane, H. (2025). Evaluating Modernization Through Hydropower: Social and Environmental Impacts of Nam Theun 2 and Nam Ou River Cascade in Laos. https://www.diva-portal.org/smash/record.jsf?pid=diva2:1930166

Emmerson, D. K. (Ed.). (2020). *The deer and the dragon: Southeast Asia and China in the 21st century*. Rowman & Littlefield., https://fsi9-prod.s3.us-west-1.amazonaws.com/s3fs-public/deer-and-dragon-fm-and-ch1.pdf?utm_source=chatgpt.com

Erickson, A. S. (2008). *Can China Become a Maritime Power. Asia Looks Seaward: Power and Maritime Strategy*. Praeger Security International.

Erie, M. S., Bodurtha, M., & Young, S. (2025). Legal Brokers of Chinese Investment in Cambodia: Compliance between Contract and Culture. Available at *SSRN*. https://papers.ssrn.com/sol3/papers.cfm?abstract_id=5181507 DOI: 10.1111/rego.70021

Ernst, M. (2025). China's Coercion of States in the Asia-Pacific Region: Balancing and Wedge Strategies in the Context of Sino-American Competition. Taylor & Francis. https://www.routledge.com/Chinas-Coercion-of-States-in-the-Asia-Pacific-Region-Balancing-and-Wedge-Strategies-in-the-Context-of-Sino-American-Competition/Ernst/p/book/9781032812335

Fumagalli, M. (2024). Myanmar 2023: New conflicts and coalitions reshape war narrative, challenging an embattled junta. Asia Maior. https://research-repository.st-andrews.ac.uk/handle/10023/30085

Gill, B. (2022). *Daring to struggle: China's global ambitions under Xi Jinping*. Oxford University Press., https://academic.oup.com/book/43062 DOI: 10.1093/oso/9780197545645.001.0001

Gong, X. (2025). Ponder the path of thy feet: How China's security–development nexus works in the Mekong region. European Journal of International Security, 1-19. https://www.cambridge.org/core/journals/european-journal-of-international-security/article/ponder-the-path-of-thy-feet-how-chinas-securitydevelopment-nexus-works-in-the-mekong-region/8278F8CC16039DEBAAAD86AA1329076B

Gong, X., & Li, M. (2024). Taking ideas and words seriously: Explaining the institutionalization of the Lancang-Mekong cooperation. *International Relations of the Asia-Pacific*, *24*(2), 253–287. https://academic.oup.com/irap/article/doi/10.1093/irap/lcad014/7304016. DOI: 10.1093/irap/lcad014

Gray, C. S., & Sloan, G. (2014). Geopolitics, geography and strategy. Routledge. https://www.taylorfrancis.com/books/edit/10.4324/9781315038339/geopolitics-geography-strategy-colin-gray-geoffrey-sloan

Gu, J. (2024). Building partnerships for sustainable development: Case study of Laos, the BRI, and the SDGs. *Asian Review of Political Economy*, *3*(1), 5. https://link.springer.com/article/10.1007/s44216-024-00025-5. DOI: 10.1007/s44216-024-00025-5

Halper, S. (2010). The Beijing consensus: how China's authoritarian model will dominate the twenty-first century (Vol. 16). ReadHowYouWant. com. Pp- 165-189

Haque, M. M. (2024). Protracted Conflict in Myanmar and the Role of International Actors. SINERGI. *Journal of Strategic Studies & International Affairs*, *4*(2), 117–126. https://spaj.ukm.my/sinergi/index.php/sei/article/view/109. DOI: 10.17576/sinergi.0402.2024.09

Harold, S. W. (2021). For China, the Cold War Never Ended. In Emergent Issues for US National Security (p. 19). https://nsiteam.com/social/wp-content/uploads/2021/09/2021Sept_SMA-Perspectives_USvChina-Competition-Paper-2.pdf#page=37

He, Z. (2024). How Can PPP-Financed Railway Infrastructure in Thailand Boost Logistics and Strengthen "the Belt and Road" Economic Integration? European Academic Journal-II CHINA, 1(1). https://eaj.ebujournals.lu/index.php/EAJ_II/article/view/117

Hensengerth, O. (2009). Regionalism in China–Vietnam relations: Institution-building in the Greater Mekong Subregion. Routledge. Pp. 21-86 https://www.taylorfrancis.com/books/mono/10.4324/9780203872383/regionalism-china-vietnam-relations-oliver-hensengerth

Hiebert, M. (2020). Under Beijing's Shadow: Southeast Asia's China Challenge. Rowman & Littlefield. https://macmillan.yale.edu/southeast-asia/under-beijings-shadow?utm

Ho, S. (2020). Infrastructure and Chinese power. *International Affairs*, *96*(6), 1461–1485. https://academic.oup.com/ia/article-abstract/96/6/1461/5930373. DOI: 10.1093/ia/iiaa171

Hönke, J., Cezne, E., & Yang, Y. (Eds.). (2024). *Africa's Global Infrastructures: South–South Transformations in Practice*. Hurst Publishers., https://www.hurstpublishers.com/book/africas-global-infrastructures/ DOI: 10.1093/oso/9780197775363.001.0001

Htwe, T. M. (2025). China's Strategic Influence and Rivalries in Southeast Asia: BRIC and China's Geopolitical Strategy. In Changing the Global Political Economy: BRICS Countries and Alternative Relations Strategies (pp. 119-146). IGI Global Scientific Publishing. https://www.igi-global.com/chapter/chinas-strategic-influence-and-rivalries-in-southeast-asia/365241

Jeong, J. (2024). Development Policies towards the Mekong River Basin Nations. International Aid and South Korea: Experience from Recipient to Donor, pp. 75-82 https://books.google.com/books?hl=en&lr=&id=nZI0EQAAQBAJ&oi=fnd&pg=PA82&dq=Infrastructure+has+emerged+as+a+central+pillar+of+China's+regional+integration+strategy+in+Mekong+region&ots=OcRRqFCNSE&sig=pUZ60ul9Vx__Ya9TOq9iN3GV_Pk

Jinhua, C. (2022). The state logic of modernizing the governance system. *Social Sciences in China*, *43*(1), 37–52. https://citeseerx.ist.psu.edu/document?repid=rep1&type=pdf&doi=8a1755ce0cf59bd4e19524c41ba5a402d3b47afc. DOI: 10.1080/02529203.2022.2051355

Johnson, A., & Soukhaphon, A. (2024). Introduction: In and out of plain sight: Interrogating power in the Mekong riverscape. *Pacific Affairs*, *97*(2), 4. Advance online publication. DOI: 10.5509/2024972-art4

Jones, L., & Hameiri, S. (2021). Fractured China. Cambridge University Press. pp-121-165 DOI: 10.1017/9781009047487

Jumlongnark, W. (2024). Unraveling the current economic downturn in Laos: A study of factors and implications. Journal of ASEAN PLUS+ Studies, 5(1). https://so06.tci-thaijo.org/index.php/aseanplus/article/view/269421

Kaplinsky, R. (2005). China, globalisation and neo-liberal dogma. Queen Elizabeth House, University of Oxford. https://content.csbs.utah.edu/~mli/Econ%205420-6420-Fall%202018/Kaplinsky-RKQEHChinaGlobalisation_NeoLiberalDogma.pdf

Kaplinsky, R. (2013). Globalization, poverty and inequality: Between a rock and a hard place. John Wiley & Sons. https://www.wiley.com/en-us/Globalization%2C+Poverty+and+Inequality%3A+Between+a+Rock+and+a+Hard+Place-p-9780745635545

Keothephar, K., Nakhiengchanh, A., Keokinnaly, T., & Lathsaath, C. (2024). Dynamic relationship between external debt, inflation, and exchange rate in Lao PDR. *International Journal of Science and Business*, *33*(1), 123–138. DOI: 10.58970/IJSB.2319

Kiik, L. (2023). Inter-national conspiracy? Speculating on the Myitsone Dam controversy in China, Burma, Kachin, and a displaced village. *Geopolitics*, *28*(1), 72–98. https://www.tandfonline.com/doi/abs/10.1080/14650045.2020.1808886. DOI: 10.1080/14650045.2020.1808886

Kim, S. C. (2023). China and Its Small Neighbors: The Political Economy of Asymmetry, Vulnerability, and Hedging. State University of New York Press. https://sunypress.edu/Books/C/China-and-Its-Small-Neighbors2

Kosaikanont, R. (2023). China's GDI, BRI, and LMC: Reshaping. The Impact of China's Belt and Road Initiative in Southeast Asia: Evaluating Risks and Benefits, 27. https://link.springer.com/chapter/10.1007/978-981-97-9511-6_2

Kuik, C. C. (2021). Asymmetry and authority: Theorizing Southeast Asian responses to China's belt and road initiative. *Asian Perspective*, *45*(2), 255–276. https://muse.jhu.edu/pub/1/article/787852/summary. DOI: 10.1353/apr.2021.0000

Kun, Z., & Tian, Z. (2022). Lancang-Mekong Cooperation: New Forms of Innovation in the Sub-Regional Order. China Int'l Stud., 97, 152. https://heinonline.org/hol-cgi-bin/get_pdf.cgi?handle=hein.journals/chintersd97&section=10

Lampton, D. M., Ho, S., & Kuik, C. C. (2020). *Rivers of iron: Railroads and Chinese power in Southeast Asia*. University of California Press.

Lee, K. C. (2024). *Researching the Belt and Road Initiative: A cross-civilizational and interdisciplinary approach*. Springer Nature., DOI: 10.1007/978-981-96-3388-3

Lertpusit, S. (2024). Evaluating the Benefits of the Current BRI Infrastructure Projects to Thailand: The Case of Cross-border Trade and the Laos–China Railway. East Asian Policy, 16(01). https://www.worldscientific.com/doi/abs/10.1142/S1793930524000047

Li, M., & Yang, B. (2024). Collective local liberalism: Orchestrated local governments and the expansion of the BRI. *Asian Journal of Political Science*, *32*(3), 353–379. DOI: 10.1080/02185377.2024.2417998

Liu, C., Li, Y., He, D., Deng, B., Zhang, E., Wei, S., & Duan, X. (2025). Dynamic monitoring of eco-environmental quality in the Greater Mekong Subregion: Evolutionary characteristics and country differences. *Environmental Impact Assessment Review*, *110*, 107700. Advance online publication. DOI: 10.1016/j.eiar.2024.107700

Liu, H. (2022). *The political economy of transnational governance: China and Southeast Asia in the 21st century*. Taylor & Francis.

Liu, P. (2022). *The Specter of Materialism: Queer Theory and Marxism in the Age of the Beijing Consensus*. Duke University Press. DOI: 10.2307/j.ctv31xf5qx

Lord, K. M. (2012). *The perils and promise of global transparency: Why the information revolution may not lead to security, democracy, or peace*. State University of New York Press.

Loughlin, N. (2024). The Politics of Coercion: State and Regime Making in Cambodia. Cornell University Press. https://www.cornellpress.cornell.edu/book/9781501776588/the-politics-of-coercion/

Lu, Y., Springer, C., & Steffen, B. (2024). Cofinancing and infrastructure project outcomes in Chinese lending and overseas development finance. *World Development*, *175*, 106473. DOI: 10.1016/j.worlddev.2023.106473

Luo, J. J. (2025). Cambodia's foreign policy (re) alignments amid great power geopolitical competition. *The Pacific Review*, *38*(1), 60–89. https://www.tandfonline.com/doi/abs/10.1080/09512748.2024.2322041. DOI: 10.1080/09512748.2024.2322041

Mackenzie, E., Milne, S., Van Kerkhoff, L., & Ray, B. (2023). Development or dispossession? Exploring the consequences of a major Chinese investment in rural Cambodia. *The Journal of Peasant Studies*, *50*(4), 1478–1500. https://www.tandfonline.com/doi/abs/10.1080/03066150.2022.2026929. DOI: 10.1080/03066150.2022.2026929

Mahan, A. T. (1890). The influence of sea power upon history, 1660–1783. Little, Brown and Company. https://history.state.gov/milestones/1866-1898/mahan?utm_source=chatgpt.com

Malcomson, S. (2016). Splinternet: How geopolitics and commerce are fragmenting the World Wide Web. OR books. https://www.jstor.org/stable/j.ctt20bbwp4

Malcomson, S. (2016). Splinternet: How geopolitics and commerce are fragmenting the World Wide Web. OR Books. https://www.jstor.org/stable/j.ctt20bbwp4

Martel, S. (2022). *Enacting the security community: ASEAN's never-ending story*. Stanford University Press.

Mazarr, M. J., Charap, S., Casey, A., Chindea, I. A., Curriden, C., Demus, A., . . . Wyne, A. (2021). Stabilizing Great-Power Rivalries. RAND Corporation. https://www.rand.org/content/dam/rand/pubs/research_reports/RRA400/RRA456-1/RAND_RRA456-1.pdf

Mearsheimer, J. J. (2010). The gathering storm: China's challenge to US power in Asia. The Chinese Journal of International Politics, 3(4), 381–396. https://doi.org/OpenURL+3DeepDyve+3Oxford Academic+3DOI: 10.1093/cjip/poq016EBSCO

Mearsheimer, J. J. (2015). Why we will soon miss the Cold War. In Betts, R. K. (Ed.), *Conflict after the Cold War: Arguments on causes of war and peace* (pp. 28–44). Routledge., DOI: 10.4324/9781315664484-

Mierzejewski, D. (2024). Deepening informal-consultative governance in China's relationship with ASEAN members during COVID-19. *Asian Affairs*, *55*(1), 3–33. https://www.tandfonline.com/doi/abs/10.1080/03068374.2024.2323995. DOI: 10.1080/03068374.2024.2323995

Ministry of Foreign Affairs of Japan. (2024). Mekong-Japan Cooperation Strategy 2024. https://www.mofa.go.jp/files/100703926.pdf

Moe, D. N., Kyaw, P. T., Win, S. S., & Pa, A. P. (2024). China economic development: How did China become the world's second-largest economy? *SSRN*. DOI: 10.2139/ssrn.5082439

Montano Ramirez, A., & Petersen, A. M. (2025). Transformation of global science core-periphery structure towards a multi-polar horizon: The rise of China and the global south from 1980-2020. *Globalizations*. Advance online publication. DOI: 10.1080/14747731.2024.2374432

Myoe, M. A. (2024). Chinese Seaports in Myanmar: Understanding Success and Stagnation. In Chinese Overseas Ports in Southeast and South Asia (pp. 70-89). Routledge. https://www.taylorfrancis.com/chapters/edit/10.4324/9781003495567-4/chinese-seaports-myanmar-maung-aung-myoe

Myoe, M. A. (2024). Chinese Seaports in Myanmar: Understanding Success and Stagnation. In Chinese Overseas Ports in Southeast and South Asia (pp. 70-89). Routledge. https://www.taylorfrancis.com/chapters/edit/10.4324/9781003495567-4/chinese-seaports-myanmar-maung-aung-myoe

na Thalang. C., & Eun, Y. S. (Eds.). (2024). Global International Relations in Southeast Asia. Taylor & Francis. https://www.taylorfrancis.com/books/edit/10.4324/9781003431169/global-international-relations-southeast-asia-chanintira-na-thalang-yong-soo-eun

Nguyen, V. C. T., & Le, H. Q. (2024, July 17). The impact of ICT infrastructure, technological innovation, renewable energy consumption and financial development on carbon dioxide emission in emerging economies: New evidence from Vietnam. *Management of Environmental Quality*, *35*(6), 1233–1253. Advance online publication. DOI: 10.1108/MEQ-09-2023-0325

Nichols, M. D., McKibben, B., Jacobson, M. Z., Howarth, R., Lee, A., Fedoruk, L., & Begum, L. (2024). Proven Climate Solutions: Leading Voices on How to Accelerate Change. Rowman & Littlefield. https://rowman.com/ISBN/9781538186534/Proven-Climate-Solutions-Leading-Voices-on-How-to-Accelerate-Change

Norris, W. J. (2016). *Chinese economic statecraft: Commercial actors, grand strategy, and state control.* Cornell University Press., https://www.cornellpress.cornell.edu/book/9781501725913/chinese-economic-statecraft/

Oakes, T. (2021). The Belt and Road as method: Geopolitics, technopolitics and power through an infrastructure lens. *Asia Pacific Viewpoint, 62*(3), 281–285. DOI: 10.1111/apv.12319

Panke, D., & Rüland, J. (2022). Why Asian states cooperate in regional arrangements: Asian regionalism in comparative perspective. *International Relations, 36*(3), 428–453. DOI: 10.1177/00471178211028970

Ping, J., Hayes, A., & McCormick, B. (Eds.). (2025). *Chinese International Relations Theory: As Emerging from Practice and Policy.* Taylor & Francis., https://www.taylorfrancis.com/books/edit/10.4324/9780429197697/chinese-international-relations-theory-jonathan-ping-anna-hayes-brett-mccormick DOI: 10.4324/9780429197697

Ping, J., Hayes, A., & McCormick, B. (Eds.). (2025). *Chinese International Relations Theory: As Emerging from Practice and Policy.* Taylor & Francis., DOI: 10.4324/9780429197697

Ranjan, R., & Changgang, G. (Eds.). (2021). *China and South Asia: Changing regional dynamics, development and power play.* Routledge India., DOI: 10.4324/9780367855413

Ratzel, F. (1898). The history of mankind (Vol. 3). Macmillan and Company, Limited. https://archive.org/details/in.ernet.dli.2015.22818

Ratzel, F. (2017). The laws of the spatial growth of states. In *The structure of political geography* (pp. 17–28). Routledge., DOI: 10.4324/9781315135267-4

Richey, M., & Guseinova, O. (2024). Disputed geometries of great power politics: US–China perspectives on minilateralism. *Australian Journal of International Affairs, 78*(6), 828–847. https://www.tandfonline.com/doi/abs/10.1080/10357718.2024.2412143. DOI: 10.1080/10357718.2024.2412143

Rodan, G. (2018). Participation without democracy: Containing conflict in Southeast Asia. Cornell University Press. https://www.cornellpress.cornell.edu/book/9781501720116/participation-without-democracy/?utm_source=chatgpt.com

Rodan, G. (2022). *Civil society in Southeast Asia: power struggles and political regimes*. Cambridge University Press., https://www.cambridge.org/core/elements/civil-society-in-southeast-asia/8513087DDFD7E72A018A4BF29F193E91 DOI: 10.1017/9781108757423

Rodríguez Álvarez, L. (2024). Chinese securitization of the main water sources in South and Southeast Asia: Brahmaputra and Mekong comparation. https://dspace.cuni.cz/handle/20.500.11956/194913

Rodríguez Álvarez, L. (2024). Chinese securitization of the main water sources in South and Southeast Asia: Brahmaputra and Mekong comparation [Master's thesis, Charles University]. Charles University Digital Repository. https://dspace.cuni.cz/handle/20.500.11956/194913

Root, H. L. (2013). *Dynamics among nations: The evolution of legitimacy and development in modern states*. MIT Press. DOI: 10.7551/mitpress/9534.001.0001

Rosengren, R. (2024). In the Shadow of China: A qualitative analysis of China's Belt and Road Initiative in Laos through a neo-colonial lens. https://www.diva-portal.org/smash/record.jsf?pid=diva2:1866783

Scheuer, S., & Scheuer, J. D. (Eds.). (2008). The anatomy of change: A neo-institutionalist perspective. Copenhagen Business School Press DK. https://forskning.ruc.dk/en/publications/the-anatomy-of-change-a-neo-institutionalist-perspective

Shih, C. Y. (2024). *Relations and Roles in China's Internationalism: Rediscovering Confucianism in a Pluriversal World*. State University of New York Press., https://www.jstor.org/stable/jj.18252766

Sil, R., & Katzenstein, P. J. (2010). *Beyond paradigms: Analytic eclecticism in the study of world politics*. Macmillan International Higher Education., DOI: 10.1007/978-1-137-01359-0

Siphana, S. (2018). Mekong Cooperation & BRI. Horizons: Journal of International Relations and Sustainable Development, (10), 86-95. https://www.jstor.org/stable/48573479

Sobolik, M. S. (2024). Countering China's Great Game: A Strategy for American Dominance. Naval Institute Press. https://link.springer.com/content/pdf/10.1007/978-3-031-63738-4.pdf

Stephen, M. D. (2014). Rising powers, global capitalism and liberal global governance: A historical materialist account of the BRICs challenge. *European Journal of International Relations*, *20*(4), 912–938. https://journals.sagepub.com/doi/abs/10.1177/1354066114523655. DOI: 10.1177/1354066114523655

Strange, A. (2023). *Chinese global infrastructure*. Cambridge University Press., https://www.cambridge.org/core/elements/chinese-global-infrastructure/35932BF8AEADDEFF1E96B19B13300FAE DOI: 10.1017/9781009090902

Susskind, L. E., & Ali, S. H. (2014). *Environmental diplomacy: Negotiating more effective global agreements*. Oxford University Press., https://academic.oup.com/book/12340 DOI: 10.1093/acprof:oso/9780199397976.001.0001

Tang, S. Y. (2021). Rethinking local and regional governance in China: An institutional design and development perspective. Urban Governance, 1(1), 51-58. https://www.sciencedirect.com/science/article/pii/S2664328621000073

Thompson, K. W. (1960). *Political realism and the crisis of world politics: An American approach to foreign policy*. Princeton University Press., https://www.jstor.org/stable/j.ctt183pt03 DOI: 10.1515/9781400878543

Thongsawang, S. (2025). Sociospatial relations through development projects: The alignment of Thailand's EEC and China's BRI. *Asian Geographer*, *42*(1), 23–38. https://www.tandfonline.com/doi/abs/10.1080/10225706.2024.2308901. DOI: 10.1080/10225706.2024.2308901

Tran, X. H., Le, H. K., & Phan, T. H. Y. (2023). Strategic hedging in Southeast Asia: ASEAN member states' policy responses to China's growing economic influence. Contemporary Chinese Political Economy and Strategic Relations: An International Journal, 9(2–3), 404–438. https://icaps.nsysu.edu.tw/static/file/131/1131/img/CCPS-9(2-3)-Hiep.pdf

Tuathail, G. Ó. (1997). *Critical Geopolitics* (1st ed.). Routledge., DOI: 10.4324/9780203973059

Tuathail, G. Ó. (2002). Postmodern Geopolitics?: The modern geopolitical imagination and beyond. In Rethinking geopolitics(pp. 28-50). Routledge.

Ty, P. (2024). Harmony and Turmoil: Comparative Study of Political Stability in Cambodia and Uganda (Master's thesis, Northern Illinois University). https://search.proquest.com/openview/782d70e68860c5e274d662085d3dec9c/1?pq-origsite=gscholar&cbl=18750&diss=y

Wang, Z. (2024). China's Digital Silk Road (DSR) in Southeast Asia: Progress and challenges. ISEAS Perspective, 2024(1). https://www.iseas.edu.sg/articles-commentaries/iseas-perspective/2024-1-chinas-digital-silk-road-dsr-in-southeast-asia-progress-and-challenges-by-wang-zheng/

Wei, D., & Tang, Z. (2024). *The Dual Impact of Japan's Infrastructure Diplomacy in Southeast Asia*. International Journal of Global Economics and Management., DOI: 10.62051/IJGEM.v3n1.49

Woodley, D. (2015). *Globalization and capitalist geopolitics: Sovereignty and state power in a multipolar world*. Routledge., DOI: 10.4324/9781315798165

Wright, H., Holmes, I., & Littlecott, C. (2017). Greening the Asian Development Bank: Aligning with Global Climate Goals. E3G. https://www.e3g.org/publications/greening-the-asian-development-bank-aligning-with-global-climate-goals/

Wu, X., & Kim, D. (2024). China's perception of minilateralism and Chinese-style multilateralism. *Australian Journal of International Affairs*, *78*(6), 869–888. https://www.tandfonline.com/doi/abs/10.1080/10357718.2024.2409969. DOI: 10.1080/10357718.2024.2409969

Wu, X., & Velasco, J. C. (2024). Navigating the Indo-Pacific: Vietnam's Hedging Strategies Amid the Geopolitical Rivalry Between China and the United States. *Asian Perspective*, *48*(1), 95–118. https://muse.jhu.edu/pub/1/article/919883/summary. DOI: 10.1353/apr.2024.a919883

Xiaotong, Z. (2025). *China's Modern Economic Statecraft: A Wealth-Power Dialectic*. Taylor & Francis., https://library.oapen.org/handle/20.500.12657/94009

Xuan, T., & Hai, P. T. (2023). Strategic hedging in Southeast Asia: ASEAN member states' policy responses to China's growing economic influence. Contemporary Chinese Political Economy and Strategic Relations: An International Journal, 9(2–3), 404–438. https://icaps.nsysu.edu.tw/static/file/131/1131/img/CCPS-9(2-3)-Hiep.pdf

Yaacob, R. (2024). Partnership of convenience: Ream Naval Base and the Cambodia–China convergence. https://www.lowyinstitute.org/sites/default/files/2024-12/YAACOB-Partnership-of-convenience.pdf

Yen, P. (2024). *The Strategic Adjustments of the United States and China in Southeast Asia: A Case Study of the Mekong Subregion*. International Journal of Religion., DOI: 10.61707/scfwgv24

Yu, H. (2024). *Understanding China's Belt and Road Initiative*. Springer Nature., https://library.oapen.org/handle/20.500.12657/88395 DOI: 10.1007/978-981-99-9633-9

Yusuf, S. (2008). Development economics through the decades: A critical look at thirty years of the world development report. World Bank Publications. https://documents.worldbank.org/en/publication/documents-reports/documentdetail/373331468159311438/development-economics-through-the-decades-a-critical-look-at-30-years-of-the-world-development-report

Zhang, C. Y. (2022). *Dreadful Desires: The Uses of Love in Neoliberal China*. Duke University Press., https://www.dukeupress.edu/dreadful-desires

Zhou, T., & Xue, Q. (2020). The Digital Silk Road and Southeast Asian countries. In A. Mulakala (Ed.), The Fourth Industrial Revolution and the Future of Work: Implications for Asian Development Cooperation (pp. 132–163). KDI School of Public Policy and Management; The Asia Foundation. https://asiafoundation.org/wp-content/uploads/2021/02/Korea-The-Fourth-Industrial-Revolution-and-the-Future-of-Work_EN.pdf#page=133

KEY TERMS AND DEFINITIONS

Asymmetric Interdependence: A condition in international relations where two states are interdependent, but one has significantly more power and leverage, shaping the rules of engagement.

Authoritarian Regionalism: A form of regional integration that aligns with or reinforces authoritarian governance, prioritizing state control and stability over democratic norms and participatory governance.

Bilateralism vs. Multilateralism: Bilateralism refers to state-to-state agreements (often used by China to exert targeted influence), while multilateralism involves broader regional or global cooperation frameworks like ASEAN or the UN.

Connectivity Diplomacy: The use of transnational infrastructure and digital connectivity projects as instruments of foreign policy to expand a country's sphere of influence and soft power.

Debt Diplomacy: The use of loans and infrastructure financing by a state (notably China) to gain political leverage over borrowing countries, sometimes leading to long-term dependency.

Digital Sovereignty: The ability of a state to exercise control over its digital infrastructure, including data storage, cybersecurity, and online communications, independent of foreign influence.

Elite Capture: A form of institutional manipulation where policy decisions and benefits are disproportionately influenced or controlled by political and economic elites, often at the expense of the broader public.

Extractivism: A development model reliant on the intensive extraction of natural resources, often driven by foreign capital, and associated with environmental degradation and social displacement.

Geopolitical Economy: A theoretical framework focusing on how states, rather than markets alone, shape global economic development through geopolitical interests, structural power, and state-led capitalism.

Greenwashing Diplomacy: Strategic use of environmental rhetoric by states or corporations to obscure the ecological harms of infrastructure or development projects under the banner of sustainability.

Hydropolitics: The politics surrounding water resources, especially transboundary rivers like the Mekong, where upstream control (e.g., China's dam-building) affects downstream countries' sovereignty, ecology, and security.

Infrastructure-as-Geopolitics: The strategic use of physical infrastructure (railways, ports, dams) by states to extend geopolitical influence, establish economic dependencies, and control regional flows of goods, energy, and capital.

Institutional Pluralism: The existence and interaction of multiple institutional actors—civil society, judiciary, legislature—ensuring checks and balances and preventing monopoly of power.

Institutional Voids: Gaps in governance structures, laws, or regulatory capacity within recipient countries, which allow external actors to exploit weak institutional environments for strategic or economic gains.

Neo-Colonial Development: A critique of foreign investments (especially from former colonial powers or rising powers like China) that replicate extractive, hierarchical, and dependency-inducing dynamics under the guise of development.

Sovereign Developmentalism: A development model emphasizing the role of a strong, interventionist state in guiding economic growth and infrastructure, often rejecting liberal-market prescriptions and emphasizing national autonomy.

Strategic Hedging: A foreign policy strategy employed by small or middle powers to balance between competing great powers by diversifying alliances without choosing sides definitively.

Chapter 7
The Role of BRI in China's Policy Toward Central Asia

Enayatollah Yazdani
https://orcid.org/0000-0003-0462-6185
Sun Yat-sen University, China

Ji Zeng
Sun Yat-sen University, China

ABSTRACT

One of China's main foreign policy destinations is Central Asia, which is in the hinterland of Eurasia. The Belt and Road Initiative (BRI) has become the most significant tool for developing ties between China and the five Central Asian republics. The BRI's launch signaled the beginning of a new phase in China's foreign policy toward Central Asia and a new round of cooperation between China and the Central Asian republics. Since the BRI's implementation in 2013, China's foreign policy has made Central Asia a priority. The initiative's execution has boosted China's economic interests and influence in the Central Asian countries. Beijing's foreign policy encompasses its bilateral and multilateral interactions with the prominent Central Asian republics in the age of the multipolar world order, in which China is one of the major powers playing a prominent role. This chapter explores how China's BRI has changed China's influence and exchange connections with Central Asian nations, as well as how the BRI has operated in each of the region's countries

DOI: 10.4018/979-8-3373-0938-5.ch007

INTRODUCTION

A previously unheard-of level of global activism, concretized in several regional and transcontinental projects, the most extensive of which is the Belt and Road Initiative (BRI), proposed in 2013, has accompanied China's rise to great power status in the new multipolar world order 2.0. The BRI, China's standout foreign policy initiative for the Twenty-First Century, is quickly spreading around the world, particularly, the Global South.

The Silk Road Economic Belt (SREB), or "belt," of overland economic corridors across Eurasia, is intended to link China to Central Asia and Europe. The 21st Century Maritime Silk Road, or "road," is a network of shipping lanes intended to link China to the Middle East, Southeast Asia, and some regions of Africa and Latin America through the South China Sea and the Indian Ocean. More than 140 nations are included in BRI, accounting for 63% of the world's population and nearly 40% of global output. Indeed, the Belt and Road Initiative is China's leading foreign policy and economic strategy in Eurasia and beyond. It is a massive transcontinental infrastructure, trade, and connectivity project spanning Europe, Africa, Latin America, and Asia. This project aims to boost mutual development and prosperity for both China and the recipient countries. BRI has enormous potential for recipient countries' development and stability.

The fall of the Soviet Union in late 1991 signalled the start of a new era in relations between China and the Central Asian republics of Kazakhstan, Kyrgyzstan, Tajikistan, Turkmenistan, and Uzbekistan, as well as the opening of the curtain on contemporary Chinese diplomacy in Central Asia. Since the announcement of the BRI, it has become the primary driving force behind China's foreign policy in Central Asia, as well as the primary tool for focusing on the region's countries. The BRI plays a central role in China's policy toward Central Asia, serving as a strategic framework to deepen economic, political, and security ties with the region. Central Asia is central to the Silk Road Economic Belt, with two of Eurasia's three economic corridors (the "Northern Corridor" and the "Central Corridor") passing through the region. This reflects both the spirit of today and the spirit of the ancient Silk Road. Central Asia is strategically important and a priority area for constructing the Silk Road Economic Belt. Central Asia is an important part of China's peripheral diplomacy because of its global role in the multipolar world order 2.0, the core area of the Shanghai Cooperation Organization (SCO), and the gateway to China's Western opening. Long before the Belt and Road Initiative was proposed, China and Central Asian countries had conducted extensive research into the formation of a community of common destiny.

The main question in this chapter is: How does China pursue its foreign policy in Central Asian countries through BRI? In answering this question, the chapter intends to discuss how the Chinese Belt and Road Initiative has reconfigured China's exchange relations and influences on Central Asian countries, as well as how the BRI has worked in each country in the region. Furthermore, the chapter discusses the related challenges and risks that China faces. The chapter employs a realistic approach to studying China's foreign policy in Central Asian countries through the BRI. This approach allows for the study of the political and economic dynamics of the BRI, as well as China's and the region's interests.

China's policy toward Central Asia

In the new multipolar world order 2.0 China has attempted to promote and improve an all-around, multi-level, and three-dimensional diplomatic layout by actively developing global partnerships, coordinating relations between great powers, promoting coordination and cooperation among major countries, and deepening ties with neighboring regions and countries by the concept of affinity, sincerity, and inclusiveness, as well as the diplomatic policy of treating neighbors as good neighbors. By adhering to the correct concept of righteousness and interests and the concept of true affinity, Beijing has attempted to build a community with a shared future among neighboring countries and strengthen solidarity and cooperation with developing countries (Chi, 2025).

The Belt and Road Initiative is a grand strategy and network to increase China's engagement and integration with the global economy (PARK, 2021). It aims to build commercial and trade corridors as well as infrastructure networks connecting Asia to Europe, Africa, and Latin America beyond the ancient Silk Road trade routes (Herd, 2019). China adheres to the fundamental national policy of opening up to the outside world, pursues a mutually beneficial and win-win opening strategy, promotes BRI joint construction, global development initiatives, and the establishment of a global development community in a multipolar world order 2.0, supports the multilateral trading system, encourages the development of an open world economy, and promotes economic globalization in a more open, inclusive, and inclusive manner.

After the Soviet Union's breakdown, the Central Asian region became a stage for the "modern great game" between and among various global and regional powers, with major roles played by Russia, the United States, China, the European Union, India, Iran, and Turkey (Sahakyan, 2021). A new phase in China's foreign policy towards Central Asia was marked by the launch of the BRI, which sparked a new round of cooperation between China and the Central Asian nations. Huge investments in the region's infrastructure, communications, and technology have shown Beijing's influence, and the Chinese Belt and Road Initiative has given the country's cooperation with Central Asian nations new life (Behera, 2021). Indeed, the importance of Central Asia for Chinese diplomacy has increased with the launch of the BRI, particularly the SREB project.

China's foreign policy prioritizes Central Asia as part of the BRI. China's economic interests and influence in the Central Asian republics have increased as a result of the initiative's implementation. In the era of the multipolar world order 2.0, in which China as one of the major powers, is playing a central role, Beijing's international policy includes its bilateral and multilateral relations with the Central Asian states.

The COVID-19 era marked a new stage in the BRI's growth in the Central Asian republics, one that saw the revival of the Health Silk Road (HSR). Beijing aimed to use the Health Silk Road to modify the BRI in response to the COVID-19 pandemic and bolster China's position in the area (Zhou, 2021). China used the BRI transportation networks—railroads, ports, airports, and logistics hubs—during the pandemic to deliver medical aid, health care, and vaccines to the Central Asian nations. China has increased joint production and transfer of vaccine technologies and medications for COVID-19, as well as providing medical assistance, vaccines, and anti-epidemic medications to the nations of Central Asia. Analysts theorize that China has implemented this policy primarily for two reasons: first, it has used medical tools and vaccines to bolster its soft power diplomacy in the region, and second, it has opened up new markets for its medical products by taking this action (Sahakyan, *op. cit.*).

Additionally, China proposed the creation of a China-Central Asia (C+C5) cooperation mechanism at the regional and multilateral levels. With the backing of the Central Asian governments, China has established the C+C5 as a new framework for multilateral cooperation with all five of the Central Asian nations that are not members of the Shanghai Cooperation Organization. A strategic tool in the reciprocal promotion of post-pandemic economic recovery and regional stability, the C+C5 "plays a crucial role in cultivating multilateral relations between all parties involved" (China Briefing Team, 2024).

China-Kazakhstan relations through BRI

Kazakhstan, which is located in the center of Eurasia, connecting the eastern, western, northern, and southern crossroads of Eurasia and shares a 1,108-mile border with China and, has played a significant role in China's Central Asian policy since independence (Neafie, 2022). Since the two countries' formal diplomatic relations were established in 1992, their relationship has taken an extraordinary turn, achieving new heights and producing novel outcomes. Bilateral cooperation in the fields of politics, economy, culture, and other areas has also grown and solidified, to the mutual benefit of both nations.

The economic structures of China and Kazakhstan are highly complementary, and there are clear benefits to working together in the areas of trade, commerce, and especially energy (see Figure 1). Kazakhstan, due to its geographic location, is also "a key western neighbor for China, and China is an immediate factor in Kazakhstan's security and well-being" (Schulz, 2022 a). Two years after the two states' official relations were established, the border dispute between them was settled (*Ibid.*). Additionally, the two governments have kept up their cooperation on a range of projects, including promoting a regional economic development vision through the Belt and Road Initiative, enhancing regional connectivity, and strengthening regional security through the Shanghai Cooperation Organization. China's initial foray into the oil industry of Central Asia is Kazakhstan.

Figure 1. China and Kazakhstan bilateral trade 2001-2021

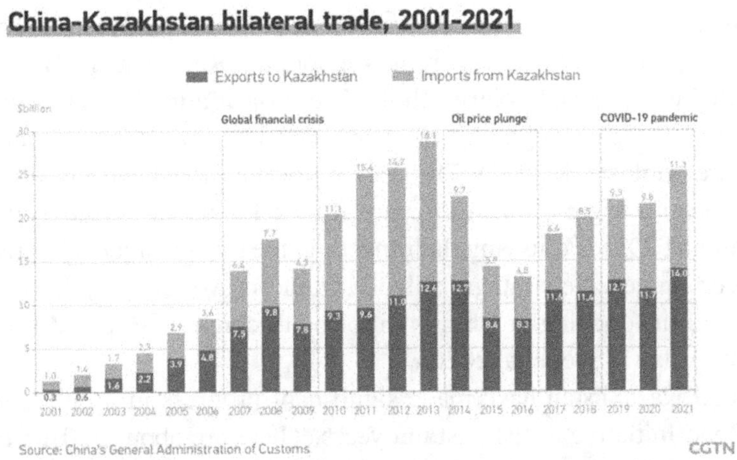

Sources: (China's General Administration of Customs, Ministry of Commerce, 2022)

Kazakhstan is the birthplace of the grand Chinese Belt and Road Initiative, which was first proposed by Chinese President Xi Jinping in a speech at Nazarbayev University in September 2013 during his visit to the country. Kazakhstan was one of the first countries to engage in BRI cooperation with Beijing, and it is a key partner for China. The BRI concept is based on China and Kazakhstan's existing good-neighborly, friendly, and cooperative relations. At the same time, the two sides' collaboration on the joint construction of the BRI has elevated bilateral relations to a new historical level. In terms of the Chinese Digital Silk Road (DSR), one of the two main Central Asian partner countries is Kazakhstan (the second one is Uzbekistan). In the framework of the DSR, China is carrying out several joint projects in Kazakhstan in various areas of the IT sector.

As a major transit country for at least two of the six economic corridors, Kazakhstan plays an important role in achieving many of the BRI's geopolitical goals (Ivleva, 2021). China and Kazakhstan have worked well together in oil and gas, among other fields, as part of the BRI. The two countries collaborated to build China's first cross-border oil pipeline, the China-Kazakhstan crude oil pipeline, as well as the three lines of the China-Central Asia natural gas pipeline, A, B, and C, which all pass through Kazakhstan.

Since Kazakhstan gained its independence, Beijing and Astana have developed a relationship based on friendship and good neighborliness. The two countries' interactions on the political, economic, and interpersonal levels are strategic and operative. In the context of the Belt and Road Initiative, China and Kazakhstan's relations continue to gradually deepen and develop. The two nations' overall cooperation spans a wide range of areas, including infrastructure for transportation and logistics, industry, agriculture, finance, new technologies, electronics, and tourism, as well as Kazakhstan's rapidly growing sectors of innovation, health care, and education.

China has publicly stated its strong support for Kazakhstan's BRI-compliant "Bright Path" plan(Kazakh: Nurly Zhol). The project aimed to take advantage of Kazakhstan's strategic geography by increasing investment in its transportation infrastructure (Goldstein, 2022). The docking of the SREB and the "Bright Path" made significant progress during former Kazak President Nazarbayev's visit to China in August 2015. Following their meeting, the two presidents jointly declared that their comprehensive strategic alliance would move forward, "confirming the consistency of the docking of China's Silk Road Economic Belt and Kazakhstan's "Bright Path" plan" (Svetlana, 2020).

China and Kazakhstan have made significant progress in jointly building the Belt and Road Initiative in the past ten years. There are about 51 BRI projects in progress in Kazakhstan, totaling $ 27 billion. China is among the top five largest foreign investors in Kazakhstan. The approximately 700 joint Kazakhstani-Chinese enterprises comprise 4.7 percent of total investment in Kazakhstan (CDR, 2021, Shayakhmetova, 2021). Beijing and Astana have worked together to build projects like the China-Kazakhstan Lianyungang Logistics Cooperation Base and the Khorgos International Border Cooperation Center, which enable the three-dimensional docking of railways, highways, shipping lanes, oil pipelines, and communication networks. Indeed, Kazakhstan has become an important transit country for China-Europe trains, and the China-Kazakhstan Lianyungang logistics cooperation base has become a substantial hub for Kazakhstan's export commodities to the Asia-Pacific region. Kazakh scholars believe that the BRI has laid the groundwork for both governments to work together to solve problems (Hassan Khan, 2022).

In collaboration with BRI and SRH, China also provided the Kazak government with masks, shields, other medical supplies, and facilities during the pandemic. Later, Beijing sent vaccines to Kazakhstan (Meirkhanova, 2021).

Uzbekistan's position in China's foreign policy: the role of BRI

Uzbekistan is a big country, the geopolitical center of Central Asia, and the most populated republic in the region. Internationally, foreign policy opening and dynamism have become an important part of Uzbekistan's diplomacy and "the most public element of the country's new strategy" (Qoraboyev, 2018). Due to its geopolitical position, the size of its population, its natural resources, and developments in its role in the international arena, Uzbekistan is playing a critical role in China's Central Asia policy. Uzbekistan "is a key player for Beijing, not only in terms of bilateral relations but also because of its regional importance, which fits with overall China's Central Asia strategy" (Sharifli. 2022). China established official relations with Uzbekistan in 1992, during the past 30 years the relations between China and Uzbekistan are developed considerably through different initiatives and policies such as the promotion of friendship and cooperation in 2000, the 2005 partnership treaty, the 2012 joint statement, the 2013 agreement, the BRI 2015 and the Comprehensive Strategic Partnership in June 2016. In particular, in light of the Russia-Ukraine war and tense relations between Russia and Kazakhstan, Uzbekistan's strategic importance for China's regional policy is growing. The relative stability of Uzbekistan, as well as its stable relations with regional and international powers, provide Beijing with an opportunity to diversify its relations with Central Asia and follow a more balanced approach to the region's states *(Ibid.)*.

More notably, Uzbekistan has a sizable potential for transportation. The economy of the country is significantly impacted by its infrastructure and transportation. To "strengthen its geopolitical and geoeconomic position through the Eurasian rail trade," Tashkent has pursued practical transport diplomacy. According to The Jamestown Foundation (2022), the Uzbek government's primary diplomatic objective is "to transform the country from a landlocked to a land-linked country with the rest of Eurasia." In fact, according to Loctier (2020), Uzbekistan is quickly developing "its transportation infrastructure to achieve its goal of becoming a transportation and logistics hub for Central Asia."

China's trade relations with Uzbekistan have also grown and deepened in this context as a result of Uzbekistan's support for and participation in Beijing's Belt and Road development initiative. The BRI has consistently improved and strengthened China's and Uzbekistan's economic and commercial ties (see Figure 2). (Qoraboyev, *op. cit.*).

Figure 2. China's trade with Uzbekistan (Million USD)

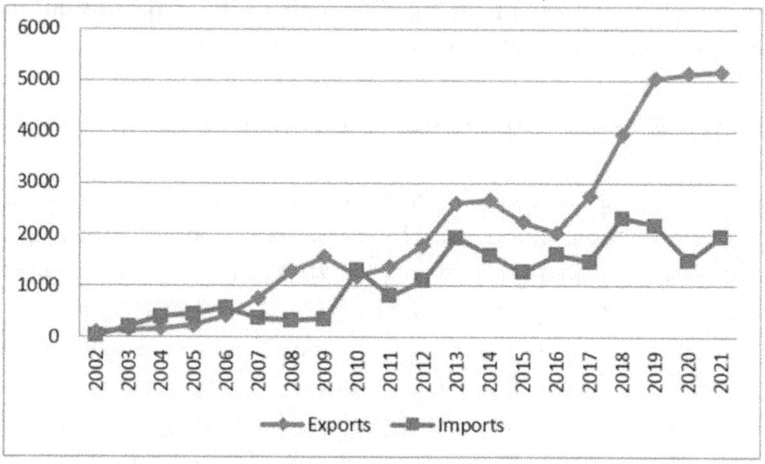

Source: (Khitakhunov, 2022).

Tashkent's transportation diplomacy specifically has two major, significant ramifications for BRI. First, new trade routes via Uzbek territory offer new options for the China-EU railroad commerce and trade and assist China's companies in reducing their reliance on Russian and Kazakh territory. Second, Tashkent's approach to Afghanistan is comparable to that of Beijing, which seeks to improve ties between China and Afghanistan through regional players and incorporate Afghanistan into the economies of the Central Asian region(Sharifli, *op. cit.).* As a result, China has been implementing the BRI to increase its trade connections, prosperity, new opportunities for stability and growth, investment, technology, and new markets, exports, industries, industrial promotion, green and digital economy, alleviate electricity shortages, and increase interactions with Uzbekistan.

The Belt and Road Project offers Tashkent a strong chance to create a link to the Persian Gulf region and beyond, which will provide Uzbekistan with an opportunity to increase its trading routes. Indeed, developing exports to more markets across the globe is a very alluring motivation for the Uzbek government (Devonshire-Ellis, 2021). In this regard, the building of the China-Kyrgyzstan-Uzbekistan (CKU) railway as part of the BRI project will increase the economic and business opportunities for both China and Uzbekistan (and Kyrgyzstan) and shorten access to the markets of the Persian Gulf, the Caucasus, Turkey, the Middle East, and Southern Europe (Niva Yau, 2024). In addition, two of the BRI routes in the China-Central Asia-West Asia BRI Corridor pass through Uzbekistan, linking the country to China and Iran more quickly than the Soviet-era alternatives. Kazakhstan, Turkmenistan (Tashkent, Samarkand, Navi), and Uzbekistan (Tashkent, Samarkand, Navi) Corridors are Routes 3 and 4, respectively, while Kyrgyzstan, Turkmenistan (Andijan, Pap,

Tashkent, Samarkand, Navi), and Turkmenistan-Iran Corridor is Route 4. Moreover, Uzbekistan is traversed by all four of the "China-Central Asia" gas pipeline corridors (Ramezani Bonesh, *op. cit.*).

One of Uzbekistan's top trading partners is China. 17–20% of the nation's overall commerce was with China in 2021 when the volume of trade between the two countries reached $7.4 billion. China is Uzbekistan's second-largest export market after Russia. Its exports to China from January through July 2022 totaled $1.5 billion. Between January and July 2021 and January to July 2022, China's trade with Uzbekistan surged by 32.5% (Sharifli, op. cit.). In the past three decades, the volume of trade between Beijing and Tashkent has multiplied 140 times. According to Ramezani Bonesh (2023a), bilateral trade climbed by 20% to around $9 billion in 2022.

In the framework of BRI Chinese businesses are engaged in a number of factory projects, special economic zones, free trade zones, industrial parks (SEZs), building materials, chemical and chemical industry companies, agriculture and logistics, textiles, and mining, particularly in the cement sector in Uzbekistan. Furthermore, China has taken on cooperation between the BRI and the development strategy of "New Uzbekistan" for 2022-2026" (Ramezani Bonesh, *op. cit.*). China also provided medical supplies, equipment, and vaccines to Uzbekistan during the pandemic outbreak as part of the BRI and SRH networks.

China policy toward Turkmenistan and BRI

As one of the major Central Asian courtiers after the fall of the Soviet Union, China resumed relations with Turkmenistan. The expansion of China-Turkmenistan relations has accelerated since the two countries first established diplomatic ties three decades ago. China was the first country to establish diplomatic relations with Turkmenistan, the first country to support Turkmenistan's policy of perpetual neutrality, the first country that Turkmenistan identified as a strategic partner through political documents, and the first nation that Turkmenistan traded the most natural gas with (Peng, 2024). President Xi commented on the significance of Beijing's ties with Ashgabat in the following manner: "Development of China- Turkmenistan relations has not only brought tangible benefits to the two countries and two nations but has also made important contributions to maintaining regional peace and stability" (Xinhua, 2022). Through its two railroads connections to Iran and the Caspian Sea port of Turkmenbashi, Turkmenistan also acts as a bridge in the China-Central Asia-West Asia Economic Corridor (CCAWAEC), which links China and Central Asia to the South Caucasus, the Middle East, and Europe. (Sahakyan, 2022).

Turkmenistan has the fourth-largest proven natural gas reserves in the world (9.4% of global capacity) (Pirani, 2019). As a result, Beijing has made a significant effort to enhance its energy relations with Turkmenistan. China has increased its natural gas cooperation with Turkmenistan and emerged as one of the country's major importers. According to President Xi Jinping, who visited Turkmenistan's president Serdar Berdimuhamedov in Beijing on January 6, 2023: "Natural gas cooperation is the cornerstone of China-Turkmenistan relations, and greater cooperation in this area serves the strategic and long-term interests of both countries" (Han and Qi, 2024). As a result, Turkmenistan is likely to play an important role in China's efforts to ensure energy security (Han and Qi, 2024). Due to Chinese BRI support, the two countries have constructed three gas pipelines as part of the China-Central Asia Gas Pipeline project. The project provides natural gas to over 500 million people in 27 provincial-level regions and the Hong Kong Special Administrative Region (Wei, 2023). The China-Turkmenistan BRI project is mainly built around gas cooperation, and spending in key areas like the chemical industry, transportation, and communication will increase and deepen (Ramezani Bonesh, 2023b). Under a 30-year agreement, the Turkmenistan and China gas pipeline, which consists of four lines, exports 30 billion cubic meters of natural gas to China each year starting in 2009 (Aminjonov and Dovgalyun, 2024). These pipelines originate at the Turkmenistan-Uzbekistan border, travel through Uzbekistan and Kazakhstan, and then converge at Khorgos, Xinjiang, with China's West-to-East gas pipeline, which ultimately connects as far east as Shanghai.

Turkmenistan prioritizes China in its foreign economic policy and views it as its most significant partner (for instance, see Figure 3). The Turkmen government has backed "the principle of one China, and Beijing's interests in Taiwan and Xinjiang" based on a neutral foreign policy (Ramezani Bonesh, *op.cit.*). As a result, the Turkmen government welcomed its association with the Chinese BRI. Of course, the Turkmen government had planned a small number of strategic energy infrastructure projects and routes before the BRI's implementation. However, the scope, funding, and participation of these projects were constrained at the time. Since their inclusion in the Chinese BRI scheme, these projects have been able to progress toward their goal of becoming intercontinental corridors with access to significant transportation networks and energy security. (Hassan Khan, 2023). According to the China Briefing Team (2024) these initiatives "include (but are not limited to) the Turkmenistan-China Gas Pipeline, the International North-South Transportation Corridor, the Lapis Lazuli International Transit Corridor, and the Turkmenistan-Afghanistan-Pakistan-India Gas Pipeline."

Table 1. China- Turkmenistan Bilateral Trade 2017-2021 (US$ Billion)

Year	Trade in total	China exports to Turkmenistan	China imports from Turkmenistan
2017	6.94	0.37	6.57
2018	8.44	0.32	8.12
2019	9.12	0.43	8.69
2020	6.52	0.44	6.07
2021	7.35	0.51	6.84

Source: (China Briefing Team, *op. cit.*)

More significantly, Turkmenistan's National Plan for Socio-Economic Development for 2022-2052, Turkmen Socio-Economic Development Plan for 2022-2028, National Economic Diversification Strategy, and Turkmenistan's Foreign Trade Strategy 2021-2030 are all in sync with China's Belt and Road Initiative, enhancing the country's international economic ties, particularly with the Chinese government, and, as a result, luring investment capital to the country (Ramezani Bonesh, *op. cit.*) Turkmenistan also serves as a route for China to access the Caspian Sea, which is on the country's western border, as well as important exports and imports and markets in South Asia, the Middle East, Eastern Europe, and elsewhere. The expansion of Turkmenistan's transit trade volume with Azerbaijan and INSTC routes to Iran and beyond will create more opportunities for Turkmenistan under the BRI, along with the expansion of the China-Kyrgyzstan-Turkmenistan-Iran railway transport volume, the China-Kyrgyzstan-Uzbekistan, and the China-Kazakhstan-Turkmenistan-Iran railway corridors (*Ibid.*).

China and Turkmenistan signed a joint declaration on the establishment of a strategic partnership in September 2013 as part of the BRI project and other bilateral relations between Beijing and Ashgabat. Since then, the two countries' cooperation has advanced to new heights. Additionally, Beijing and Ashgabat announced "the elevation of bilateral ties to a comprehensive strategic partnership, with both sides pledging to boost all-around cooperation, support each other on issues related to their core interests and build a community with a shared future" in January of this year (2023) (Wei, 2023). Serdar Berdimuhamedov, the president of Turkmenistan, and President Xi Jinping witnessed the signing of several cooperation agreements during their meeting in many different fields, including natural gas, Belt and Road joint development, green development, the digital economy, and health (*Ibid.*).

Turkmenistan also received medical assistance from China during the COVID-19 outbreak as part of the BRI and HSR. Additionally, the Turkmen government imported vaccines from China to combat the Coronavirus (Sahakyan, 2021).

China's relations with Kyrgyzstan via the BRI

Located also in the center of Eurasia, Kyrgyzstan is a small and landlocked country in Central Asia. For about ten years following its declaration of independence in 1991, Kyrgyzstan maintained a certain distance from world geopolitics as a liberally democratizing, then authoritarian regime with a very small economic base. Following the terrorist attacks of September 11, 2001, in America, when the attention and resources of the international coalition were focused on the Taliban regime in Afghanistan under the banner of "the war on terror," Kyrgyzstan and the entire Central Asian region came to the attention of world politics particularly after the establishment of US base (Manas) in the country (Djuraev, 2015).

China is neighboring Kyrgyzstan, and their relationship dates back many years. Since January 1992, when the Chinese and Kyrgyz governments established diplomatic ties, bilateral relations have progressed without incident, and a long-standing border dispute has been fully resolved. During the 1990s, economic cooperation between Kyrgyzstan and China was minimal, but it increased after the 1999 border demarcation treaty and the 2001 founding of the Shanghai Cooperation Organization(see, for instance, Figure 4)(Bamezani Bonesh, 2023c).

Figure 3. China and Kyrgyzstan bilateral trade 2000-2019 (Millions USD)

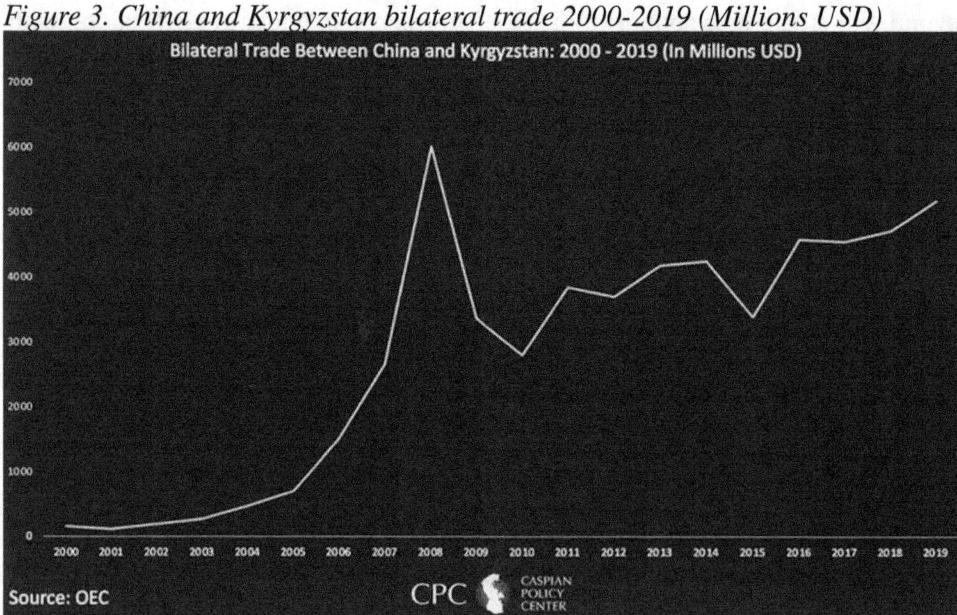

Sources: (Schulz, 2022b).

The Joint Declaration on the Establishment of Strategic Partnership between China and Kyrgyzstan, which was signed in September 2002 by the two heads of state, marked the strategic upgrading of bilateral relations and the beginning of a new phase in their development. The Joint Declaration of China-Kyrgyzstan on Further Deepening the Strategic Partnership, which was also jointly released in May 2013, was the result of ongoing development in the strategic partnership between the two countries. The Treaty of Good-Neighborliness, Friendship, and Cooperation between Beijing and Bishkek was signed in June 2022, and since then, cooperation in many areas has steadily increased.

Kyrgyzstan has worked hard to encourage the Belt and Road Initiative's implementation in the country. The level of cooperation between the two states has steadily increased, and under the auspices of the BRI, the two governments have undertaken several significant livelihood projects, such as the modernization of the southern power grid, the construction of the Osh hospital, and the reconstruction of the Bishkek municipal road network, all of which have had a significant impact on the local economy and social development and have raised the standard of living in Kyrgyzstan. (Mogilevskii, 2019).

Beijing and Bishkek are likely to work even more closely together as a result of the Chinese BRI and its networks, HRS, and DSR. Kyrgyz President Zhenbekov stated that "Kyrgyzstan's national development strategy is in line with the Belt and Road Initiative and that Kyrgyzstan is willing to establish institutional arrangements with China to promote docking and cooperation" during his meeting with President Xi Jinping in June 2019 (Xinhua, 2019).

China also gave the Kyrgyz government medical supplies and vaccines as part of the general cooperation between the two governments, as well as through the BRI networks and implementation of HSR during the pandemic. The relevant departments of China, Kyrgyzstan, and Uzbekistan signed a Memorandum of Understanding on Cooperation in the China-Kyrgyzstan-Uzbekistan (CKU) Railway Construction Project (Inner Section of Kyrgyzstan) as part of the Chinese BRI in September 2022. The survey of the CKU Railway's main plan, as well as the surveying and mapping along the line, were finished in October 2022, and other work, like geological exploration, was progressing steadily in accordance with the established work plan. In this regard, Kyrgyz President Sadr Zhaparov stated that Central Asia would have development opportunities and become a transcontinental transportation hub connecting the east, west, south, and north as a result of the BRI's joint construction. He continued, "Promoting the implementation of the China-Kyrgyzstan-Uzbekistan railway construction project will become an important measure to fully release the potential of regional transit transportation under the framework of cooperation in jointly building the "Belt and Road"" (Global Times, 2022). It is expected the CKU railroad construction will start this year (2023). The new route will cut the travel time from China to Europe and the Middle East even more once the CKU railway is finished. The CKU route will connect China, Kyrgyzstan, and Uzbekistan to Central and Eastern Europe as well as the Middle East via Iran and Turkey. It will become the southern portion of the China-Europe freight rail.

Indeed, the BRI implementation has grown to be the most significant framework for actual cooperation between China and Kyrgyzstan. In terms of regional and international Chinese policy, BRI-related interaction with Kyrgyzstan is crucial for linking China to South Asia, the Middle East, and Europe. The amount of trade between China and EU countries keeps growing. By making Central Asia one of the safest and shortest routes for road-rail travel to Europe and the Middle East, the distance between China, Europe, and the Middle East will be significantly cut (Bamezani Bonesh, *op. cit.)*. In Kyrgyzstan, 21 BRI projects totaling $2.11 billion have been completed or are in the planning stages since the country joined the initiative in 2013. The $5.59 billion in foreign direct investment that Kyrgyzstan had attracted by the end of 2019 was also almost entirely contributed by China (Schulz, *op. cit.)*.

Chinese BRI and Beijing's relations with Tajikistan

The eastern Central Asian Republic of Tajikistan was one of the most challenging during the Soviet era. Tajikistan's fragile economy was made worse by a five-year civil war that began after the country gained independence in 1991. Eighty-three percent of Tajikistan's citizens were considered to be poor in 1999 (Falkingham, 2000). The National Development Strategy to 2030, adopted by Tajikistan in 2016, outlines four strategic development goals to be accomplished by 2030, including ensuring energy security and improving energy efficiency; resolving the country's traffic problems and maximizing its potential for transit transportation; and ensuring food security and increasing the number of productive jobs (National Development Strategy, 2016).

In 1992, China and Tajikistan formally opened diplomatic ties. By developing cooperation in bilateral and multilateral frameworks like the Shanghai Cooperation Organization, the two states gradually expanded their economic cooperation after resolving their border dispute in 2011 (handing over 1158 square kilometres of land to China) (Ramezani Bonesh, *op. cit.*). As a long-standing friendly neighbour of Tajikistan, China has placed a high value on its relations with the country and has consistently pledged to support Dushanbe's efforts to achieve stability and growth. The least-developed republic to emerge from the Soviet Union is Tajikistan. Dushanbe has consequently grown extremely reliant on China as a source of capital and economic growth since it has the lowest per capita income among the states to emerge from the fall of the Soviet Union. China is a significant economic partner of

Tajikistan; at present, China accounts for more than 47% of all foreign investment in the country (see, for instance, Figure 5) (China Briefing Team, 2021).

Figure 4. China-Tajikistan Bilateral Trade 2000-2019 ((Million USD)

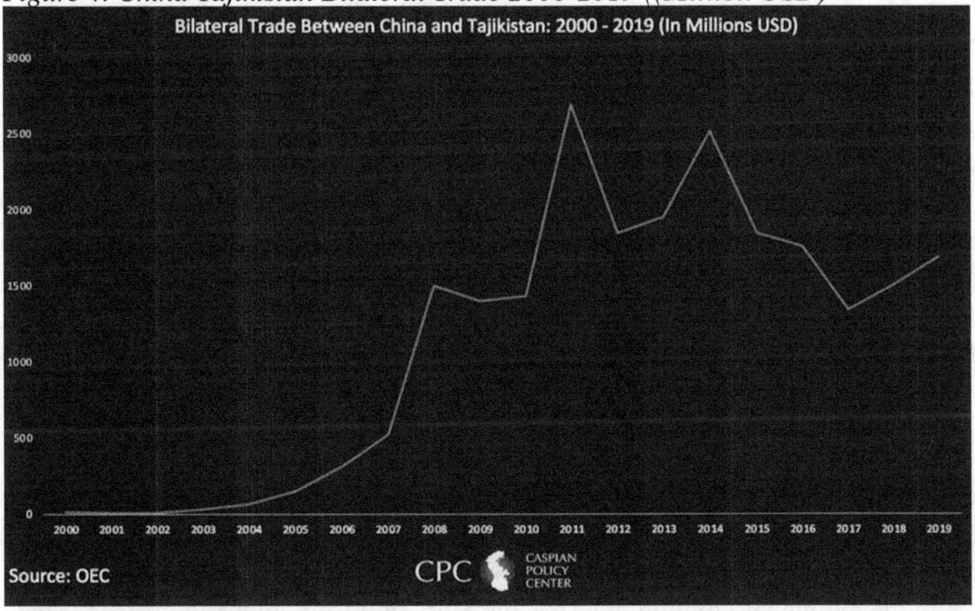

Source: (Schulz, 2022c).

One of the first republics to publicly declare support for the Belt and Road Initiative was Tajikistan, a significant country along the initiative. Tajikistan signed a memorandum of understanding on the Silk Road Economic Belt in Dushanbe in September 2014. Officials from Tajikistan have repeatedly stated that Dushanbe fully supports the building of the SREB and sees the country's participation in it as a significant opportunity to resolve transportation issues, guarantee food security, and achieve energy independence. Tajikistan's president Emomali Rahmon commented on the significance of the BRI for Tajikistan, stating: "I believe that the Belt and Road Initiative is like a bridge that connects our two countries in many ways and would facilitate the implementation of a series of strategic tasks for Tajikistan, including the development of Tajikistan's transit transport potential. Additionally, Tajikistan, a landlocked nation without access to the sea, will benefit from the Belt and Road Initiative by expanding its access to global markets" (Huaxia, 2019).

Numerous significant projects worth $320 million have been carried out in Tajikistan since the BRI was implemented, with a focus on mining, electric power, transportation and communication infrastructure, agricultural production, and other areas. This is highly consistent with the country's national strategy of "achieving energy independence, eliminating transportation difficulties, and ensuring food security." Simultaneously, the Tajik government has concurrently racked up a sizable amount of foreign debt (Schulz, *op. cit.*). Currently, China owes nearly half of the nation's $3.2 billion in foreign debt (China Briefing Team, op. *cit.*).

In the ten years since the Belt and Road Initiative was proposed, China and Tajikistan have comprehensively advanced their pragmatism in various fields, as mentioned, and a series of cooperation achievements have greatly changed Tajikistan's national face. Chinese firms have not only helped Tajikistan achieve basic energy and transportation independence, but they have also assisted Dushanbe in achieving basic industrialization, transforming Tajikistan from an importer to an exporter in the sector. Moreover, Tajikistan's infrastructure construction is accelerating as a result of the BRI. In the field of electricity, the Dushanbe No. 2 thermal power station was completed in 2016, with a total installed capacity of 400 MW and an annual power generation capacity of 22.70 billion kWh (Aminjonov and Kholmatov, 2022).

In the field of transportation infrastructure, a Chinese company completed the "Wahdat-Yawan" railway project in August 2016, which connects Tajikistan's central railway with the southern railway, which is of critical strategic importance. The completion of BRI transportation projects will boost the Tajik government's total exports, reduce border delays, and have a growing impact on its GDP, competitiveness, and transfer in the larger economy (Ramezani Bonesh, 2023d).

In the mining and mining industry, the Sino-Tajikistan joint venture Zeravshan Gold Company has grown to become Tajikistan's largest gold mining and processing enterprise, with an annual output of more than 3 tons of gold, accounting for two-thirds of Tajikistan's annual gold production (Aminjonov and Kholmatov, *op. cit.*).

Agriculture is a developing sector of Tajikistan's economy. Tajikistan's national development strategy for the period up to 2030 aims to improve food security. This has become more accessible as BRI projects have been completed and cash flow-generating trade results have been realized (Ramezani Bonesh, *op. cit.*). In the field of agricultural product processing, China's Xinjiang company's construction of the "China-Thailand New Silk Road Tajikistan Agricultural Textile Industrial Park" project in Tajikistan Khatlon region is proceeding smoothly; the first phase of the project has been completed and put into production; the products are exported to Egypt, Turkey, and other countries (Liang and Liena, 2017).

China and Tajikistan have a broad and multifaceted partnership. Not only the two countries have extensive economic, trade, and engineering cooperation, but they also have people-to-people exchange programs. To cultivate Chinese talents and promote people-to-people exchanges, China has established a Confucius Institute at Tajikistan's National University in Dushanbe. Tajik students are also sent to China as part of the BRI people-to-people program to learn the Chinese language and culture. Moreover, the Chinese government actively supported and helped Tajikistan in its fight against the pandemic within the context of the people-to-people concept and under the auspices of the BRI and SRH. Beijing sent Tajikistan numerous consignments of medical supplies, including vaccines, protective clothing, masks, and test reagents.

Tajikistan is also an important security focal point for China's counter-extremism and separatist strategy in Central Asia. As members of the SCO, both countries work together to combat terrorism, separatism, and religious extremism (Rehorst and Kuijl, 2021). Not only is it critical to remove the "three evils," as they are referred to in SCO doctrine, to alleviate China's concerns about Tajikistan becoming a hotbed for the Turkistan Islamic Movement, but ongoing hostilities between Dushanbe and the Taliban could jeopardize Tajikistan's participation in the BRI. Projects stalled due to extremist groups may discourage Chinese investment and other forms of economic engagement in Tajikistan (Schulz, *op. cit.*). Suppression of religious extremists and separatist movements will ensure that Chinese investment projects are carried out.

DISCUSSION AND CONCLUSION

Although the BRI has yielded some positive results for China and Central Asian countries, it also faces some challenges and risks, such as some Central Asian countries' strategic reservations about the BRI, the various regional cooperation strategies proposed by major world powers (. Russia: Eurasian Economic Union, America: US' New Silk Road) and international organizations, and the deterioration of the situation of non-traditional security threats. Furthermore, the presence of the "three forces", terrorism, extremism, and separatism, in the region could jeopardize the implementation of BRI projects in those countries, particularly in Uzbekistan, Kyrgyzstan, and Tajikistan (Schmidt, 2020).

The resurgence of the Taliban in Afghanistan is another obstacle to China's BRI implementation. This threatens Central Asian stability and poses a new challenge to the BRI, making it more crucial for the region's nations to use this initiative to advance their own national interests. (Sahakyan, 2022).

Furthermore, large-scale investment in Kazakhstan, as well as the power imbalance between Kazakhstan and China, has sparked outrage in Kazakh society. In Uzbekistan, on_ the one hand, religious groups such as Hizb ut-Tahrir and the Islamic Movement of Uzbekistan (IMU), as well as the Islamic State in Khorasan, have a more negative attitude toward China. Investors in Uzbekistan, on the other hand, may face confusing regulations, misinterpretation of regulatory laws, reduced benefits, restrictions on law enforcement, policy uncertainty, a large government presence in the economy, and arbitrary interpretation by different regions in Uzbekistan. The strict neutrality policy and Ashgabat's extremely political, self-maintained isolation, the dominance of government institutions over the economy, logistical risks, and infrastructure limitations are the challenges facing the BRI in Turkmenistan (Ramezani Bonesh, 2023b).

To sum up, Central Asia, which is located in Eurasia's hinterland, is one of China's primary foreign policy destinations. As an influential actor in the new multipolar world order 2.0, China's approach to Central Asia has become more than just a push for increased global status, but also about consolidating deeper economic ties to facilitate the escalation of China's economic expansion. In this regard, the Belt and Road Initiative has emerged as the most important means of furthering relations between China and the five Central Asian republics. China is attempting to expand its influence in Central Asia through the BRI, which provides opportunities for China to play a more influential role in greater Eurasia. Central Asia is critical to the success of the Chinese BRI in promoting integration between China and Europe due to its central, geopolitical, and strategic location.

The BRI is the cornerstone of China's policy toward Central Asia, combining infrastructure, energy, trade, and diplomacy into a comprehensive strategy. For China, Central Asia is both a gateway to the West and a frontline region for ensuring regional stability. While opportunities abound, balancing influence with sensitivity to local concerns and geopolitical tensions will shape the long-term success of China's BRI ambitions in the region. The implementation of the BRI in Central Asian countries has secured China's and the republics' interests and benefits; however, the BRI faces some challenges and risks for both China and the region's countries.

REFERENCES

Aminjonov, F., and Dovgalyun O., (2024). Central Asia–China Gas Pipeline (Line A, Line B, and Line C)

Aminjonov, R., and Kholmatov, M., (2022). The BRI in Central Asia: A View from Tajikistan.

Behera, A. (2021). China's Belt and Road Projects in Central Asia. *FIIB Business Review*. [e-journal] 14 October. Available at: <https://journals.sagepub.com/doi/abs/10.1177/23197145211042431?journalCode=fiba> [Accessed 17 February 2025].

Chi, Z. C. (2025). Central Asia in China's Strategic Mirror: Power, Perception and Policy. In: Zhang, C., Dadabayeva, G. (eds) The Implications of Ethnic Politics in Post-Socialist States for China. Palgrave Macmillan, Singapore. DOI: 10.1007/978-981-97-9458-4_1

China Briefing. [online] 3 September. Available at: <https://www.china-briefing.com/news/china-tajikistan-bilateral-investment-and-trade-ties/> [Accessed 23 February 2025].

China Briefing. [online] 6 January. Available at: <https://www.china-briefing.com/news/china-turkmenistan-bilateral-trade-investment-and-future-prospects/> [Accessed 10 October 2024].

China Briefing Team. (2021). China-Tajikistan: Bilateral Investment and Trade Ties.

China Briefing Team. (2024). China–Turkmenistan: Bilateral Trade, Investment, and Future Prospects.

China's General Administration of Customs. (2022). Ministry of Commerce. [online]. Available at: <2019http://english.customs.gov.cn/> [Accessed 28 February 2023].

Devonshire-Ellis, C. (2021). *An Economic Role Model For Central Asia's Belt and Road Initiative*.

Djuraev, E. (2015). The EEU and foreign policy of Kyrgyzstan. Central Asian Bureau for Analytical Reporting. [online] 30 June. Available at: <https://cabar.asia/en/emil-juraev-the-eeu-and-foreign-policy-of-kyrgyzstan-2> [Accessed 20 November 2024].

Falkingham, J. (2000). A Profile of Poverty in Tajikistan. RePEc. [online] January. Available at: https://www.researchgate.net/publication/4929025_A_Profile_of_Poverty_in_Tjikistan [Accessed 4 February 2025].

Global Times. (2022). Construction of China-Kyrgyzstan-Uzbekistan Railway will start soon. Global Times. [online] 7 June. Available at: <https://www.globaltimes.cn/page/202206/1267513.shtml> [Accessed 27 December 2024].

Goldstein, E. (2022). China's Kazakhstan Gambit. Harvard International Review. [online] 1 August. Available at: <https://hir.harvard.edu/chinas-kazakhstan-gambit/ > [Accessed 13 April 2024].

Han, Z., & Qi, W. (2024). China, Turkmenistan elevate ties to comprehensive strategic partnership. Global Times.[online] 6 January. Available at: <https://www.globaltimes.cn/page/202301/1283356.shtml> [Accessed 25 January 2025].

Hassan Khan, M. U. (2022). Kazakhstan-linchpin of China's Belt and Road Initiative. AZRTAG. [online] 13 January. Available at: <https://azertag.az/en/xeber/Kazakhstan_linchpin_of_Chinas_Belt_and_Road_Initiative-1974232> > [Accessed 28 December 2024].

Hassan Khan, M. U. (2023). BRI and Turkmenistan: A Way of Progress and Prosperity | Dr Mehmood Ul Hassan Khan, Pakistan Observer. [online] 11 January. Available at: <https://pakobserver.net/bri-and-turkmenistan-a-way-of-progress-and-prosperity-dr-mehmood-ul-hassan-khan/> [Accessed 14 November 2024]. C. B. eds., China's Global Influence: Perspectives and Recommendations. Honolulu: The Daniel K. Inouye Asia-Pacific Center for Security Studies, pp. 84-97.

Huang, Y. (2022). The Health Silk Road: How China Adapts the Belt and Road Initiative to the COVID-19 Pandemic. [AJPH]. *American Journal of Public Health, 112*(4), 567–569. DOI: 10.2105/AJPH.2021.306647 PMID: 35319947

Ivleva, D. (2021). The Belt and Road Initiative in Kazakhstan: Does the geopolitics of China's outward investments put the brakes on decarburization? Berlin: Adelphi. [online]3 February. Available at: ≤https://adelphi.de/en/publications/the-belt-and-road-initiative-in-kazakhstan≥ [Accessed 19 December 2024].

Khitakhunov, A. (2022). Economic Cooperation between Uzbekistan and China. Eurasian Research Institute. [online]. Available at: <https://www.eurasian-research.org/publication/economic-cooperation-between-uzbekistan-and-china/> [Accessed 6 November 2024].

Loctier, D. (2020). Uzbekistan's rise as the transport and logistics hub of Central Asia. Euronews. [online] 12 November. Available at: <https://www.euronews.com/next/2020/11/12/uzbekistan-s-rise-as-the-transport-and-logistics-hub-of-central-asia> [Accessed 15 September 2024].

Meirkhanova, A. (2021). Beijing's "Health Silk Road" abandons Central Asia. Eurasiannet. [online] 30 March. Available at: <https://eurasianet.org/perspectives-beijings-health-silk-road-abandons-central-asia> [Accessed 26 October 2024].

Mogilevskii, R. (2019). Kyrgyzstan and the Belt and Road Initiative. Working Paper, No. 50. [online] Available at: <https://ucentralasia.org/media/mxkawtsu/uca-ippa-wp50-eng.pdf> [Accessed 9 March 2025].

National Development Strategy. (2016). Tajikistan Government. [online] Available at: < https://nafaka.tj/images/zakoni/new/strategiya_2030_en.pdf> [Accessed 29 January 2025].

Neafie, J. (2022). Producing the Eurasian Land-Bridge: a case study of the geoeconomic contestation in Kazakhstan. International Politics. [online] 8 March. Available at: ≤https://link.springer.com/article/10.1057/s41311-022-00386-9#article-info> [Accessed 6 November 2024].

Niva Yau, T. Y. (2024). China Is Finally Making Progress on the China-Kyrgyzstan-Uzbekistan railway. Central Asia Papers. [online] 23 March. Available at: < https://www.fpri.org/article/2023/03/china-is-finally-making-progress-on-the-china-kyrgyzstan-uzbekistan-railway/> [Accessed 7 February 2025].

PARK. A., (2021). China's Belt and Road Initiative Confronts Deglobalization. South China Morning Post. [online] 15 July. Available at: <https://www.scmp.com/presented/business/topics/international-trade/article/3140259/chinas-belt-and-road-initiative> [Accessed 14 February 2025].

Peng, N. (2024). Berdimuhamedov's China Visit Pushes Forward China-Central Asia Relations. The Diplomat. [online] 10 January. Available at: <https://thediplomat.com/2023/01/berdimuhamedovs-china-visit-pushes-forward-china-central-asia-relations> [Accessed 11 March 2025].

Qoraboyev, I. (2018). The Belt and Road Initiative and Uzbekistan's New Strategy of Development: Sustainability of mutual relevance and positive dynamics. Uzbek Journal of Legal Studies. [e-journal] 2.pp.1-15. Available at: <https://www.researchgate.net/publication/324560481_The_Belt_and_Road_Initiative_and_Uzbekistan's_New_Strategy_of_Development_Sustainability_of_mutual_relevance_and_positive_dynamics> [Accessed 3 November 2024].

Ramezani Bonesh, F. (2023a). Uzbekistan's Opportunities and Challenges from China's Belt & Road Initiative. Silk Road Briefing. [online] 20 March. Available at: <https://www.silkroadbriefing.com/news/2023/03/20/uzbekistans-opportunities-and-challenges-from-chinas-belt-road-initiative/> [Accessed 2 January 2025].

Ramezani Bonesh, F. (2023b). Turkmenistan's Opportunities and Challenges from China's Belt & Road Initiative. Silk Road Briefing. [online] 28 March. Available at: < https://www.silkroadbriefing.com/news/2023/03/27/turkmenistans-opportunities-and-challenges-from-chinas-belt-road-initiative/> [Accessed 4 January 2025].

Ramezani Bonesh, F. (2023c). Kyrgyzstan's Opportunities and Challenges from China's Belt & Road Initiative. Silk Road Briefing.[online] 14 March. Available at: <https://www.silkroadbriefing.com/news/2023/03/14/kyrgyzstans-opportunities-and-challenges-from-chinas-belt-road-initiative/> [Accessed 1 March 2025].

Ramezani Bonesh, F. (2023d). Tajikistan's Opportunities And Development Progress Within The Belt & Road Initiative. Silk Road Briefing. [online] 28 February. Available at: <https://www.silkroadbriefing.com/news/2023/02/28/tajikistans-opportunities-and-development-progress-within-the-belt-road-initiative/> [Accessed 25 March 2023].

Rehorst, B., & Kuijl, W. (2021). Tajikistan's Catch-22: Foreign Investment and Sovereignty Risks. The Diplomat [online] 24 March. Available at <https://thediplomat.com/2021/03/tajikistans-catch-22-foreign-investment-and-sovereignty-risks/>.[Accessed 16 January 2025].

Saad Zaidi, S. M., & Saud, A. (2021). Ascent of the dragon: China's growing role in global affairs. *Asian Journal of Political Science*, *29*(2), 151–168. DOI: 10.1080/02185377.2021.1915171

Sahakyan, M. (2021). The New Great Power Competition in Central Asia: Opportunities and Challenges for the Gulf. AGDA Working Paper. Anwar Gargash Diplomatic Academy. [online] May. Available at: <file:///C:/Users/123/Downloads/agda-working-paper-apr-2021-dr-mher-sahakyan%2021.57.52%20(21).pdf> [Accessed 1 February 2025].

Sahakyan, M. (2022). 'China's Belt and Road Initiative and Central Asia', in Arase D. M., and Pedro Miguel Amakasu Raposo de Medeiros Carvalho, eds. The Belt and Road Initiative in Asia, Africa, and Europe. New York: Routledge, pp.90-106. DOI: 10.4324/9781003156246-8

Schmidt, M. (2020). Reconfigurations in Central Asia: Challenges, Opportunities and Risks of China's Belt and Road Initiative. In H. Pechlaner, G. Erschbamer, H. Thees, & M. Gruber (Eds.), China and the New Silk Road. Springer. [online], Retrieved March 1, 2025, from, DOI: 10.1007/978-3-030-43399-4_7

Schulz, D. (2022a). China-Kazakhstan Bilateral Relations. Caspian Policy Center. [online] 17 February. Available at: <https://www.caspianpolicy.org/research/security-and-politics-program-spp/china-kazakhstan-bilateral-relations#_edn1> [Accessed 17 November 2022].

Schulz, D. (2022b). China-Kyrgyzstan Relations. Caspian Policy Center. [online] 25 February. Available at: <https://www.caspianpolicy.org/research/security-and-politics-program-spp/china-kyrgyzstan-relation> [Accessed 5 December 2024].

Schulz, D. (2022c). hina-Tajikistan Bilateral Relations. Caspian Policy Center. [online] 4 March. Available at: https://www.caspianpolicy.org/research/security-and-politics-program-spp/china-tajikistan-bilateral-relations> [Accessed 8 December 2024].

Sharifli, Y. (2022). Growing Importance of Uzbekistan for China. Geopolitical Monitor. [online] 4 October. Available at: <https://www.geopoliticalmonitor.com/growing-importance-of-uzbekistan-for-china/ >[Accessed 12 January 2025].

Shayakhmetova, Z. (2021). Positive Dynamics Observed in Trade Between Kazakhstan and China., Astana Times. [online] Available at: < https://astanatimes.com/2021/04/positive-dynamics-observed-in-trade-between-kazakhstan-and-china/> [Accessed 19 November 2024].

Silk Road Briefing. [online] 2 July. Available at: <https://www.silkroadbriefing.com/news/2021/07/02/uzbekistan-an-economic-role-model-for-central-asias-belt-road-initiative/> [Accessed 21 December 2024].

Svetlana, G. (2020). China –Kazakhstan Economic Cooperation and Belt and Road Construction. *Scientific Review (Singapore)*, *30*(3), 42–49.

The Jamestown Foundation. (2022). Uzbekistan Looks To Position Itself As A Key Transport Hub In Central Asia. Oil Price. [online] 27 October. Available at: <https://oilprice.com/Geopolitics/International/Uzbekistan-Looks-To-Position-Itself-As-A-Key-Transport-Hub-In-Central-Asia.html> [Accessed 18 December 2022].

Wei, X. (2023). China, Turkmenistan upgrade ties. China Daily. [online] 7 January. Available at: <http://www.chinadaily.com.cn/a/202301/07/WS63b8a721a31057c47eba8315.html> [Accessed 8 January 2025].

Zhou, A. (2021). Health Silk Road' Gives the BRI a Rebranding. The China Guys. [online] 25 March. Available at: <https://thechinaguys.com/health-silk-road-gives-the-bri-a-rebranding/> [Accessed 20 December 2024].

Chapter 8
BRICS:
The Archetype of 21st Century International Cooperation Alternative or Challenge?

Figen Aydın
https://orcid.org/0000-0003-1777-278X
İstanbul Yeni Yüzyıl Üniversitesi, Turkey

ABSTRACT

In this context, the aim of the study is to examine the role of the rising and expanding BRICS in shaping global financial norms and governance. The question "Does BRICS offer an alternative or a challenge to the leadership of Western institutions in the global financial system?" is the starting point of the study. It is aimed to understand the potential of the coordination provided by the members with their differences to act as a destabilizing force against the political and economic structure of the West. First, the BRICS establishment will be examined within the framework of its purpose and challenges. The second heading will reveal the economic and political capacity of BRICS. China's influence factor on BRICS will be explained under this heading. The last heading will discuss whether BRICS, through China, offers an alternative or a challenge to Western financial institutions and governance, in short, to the status quo. It will be understood that BRICS undoubtedly offers an alternative in the medium term; on this basis, it aims to challenge in the long term.

DOI: 10.4018/979-8-3373-0938-5.ch008

INTRODUCTION

BRICS is a formation that refers to the economic cooperation established by Brazil, Russia, India, China and South Africa. Brazil, Russia, India and China held their first official summit in 2009. South Africa joined the union in 2010. Its members are quite different from each other in terms of regime, ideology, economy, foreign policy, religion and language. For this reason, BRICS is the archetype of 21st century international cooperation.

There are several effective reasons for the establishment of BRICS. The primary catalyst was the 2008 financial crisis. The 2008 crisis showed that the US could not manage the global financial system. It revealed the inadequacy of international financial institutions, the hegemony of the dollar and the imbalance of the global order. Thus, the 2008 financial crisis took its place among the primary catalysts of BRICS. In this direction, institutions that could correspond to organizations such as the World Bank and the International Monetary Fund were established. It was envisaged that the New Development Bank and the Contingent Reserve Arrangement (CRA) institutions could reduce reliance on inefficient financial institutions and increase global southern cooperation.

Another catalyst in the establishment of BRICS is the assessment that current international economic cooperation is dominated by Western countries. The desire of BRICS countries to channel their own economic power more into the system on a global scale has been effective. Thus, BRICS continues to expand as a strategic international economic organization representing the dominant economies of the global southern countries. Indeed, while the first catalyst in the establishment of BRICS was an external factor, the second catalyst was determined as an internal factor in line with the economic goals of the members.

Another "implicit factor" that was effective in the establishment of BRICS is China's perspective on the global liberal order and its idea of global leadership. China, which wants to change the current status quo and financial order, presents a challenge or an alternative to Western states and their systems through economic organizations. In this direction, China also gives a political role to the economic organizations it has been effective in establishing. As a rising power, China demonstrates its stance against global US leadership by trying to implement a revision within the global system. It aims to change the global financial system by increasing its political power through the economic and political partnerships it establishes.

BRICS was established around several main objectives. It aims to coordinate the economic and diplomatic policies of its members, to establish new financial institutions and to reduce dependence on dollarization. It has determined multipolarity by reducing dependence on Western financial systems. Thus, it is aimed to create a potential geopolitical balance for the global south countries. BRICS, which has become the economic and political representative of the global south bloc, thus emphasizes some thematic areas. It aims to increase the representation of its members in global organizations, to coordinate global economic policies, to reduce dependence on the US dollar and to create an alternative financial system.

BRICS has strengthened its cooperation with the establishment of the New Development Bank. It has provided financing for energy supply projects, infrastructure investments, and the Belt and Road Project. Unlike Western development banks, it does not impose its financial management and provides loans in local currency. It is anticipated that financial dependence on the US dollar may decrease and the renminbi may become international.

The largest economies of the global south were present at the 16th BRICS Summit on October 22-24, 2024, with the theme of development tendency and joint effort. BRICS was expanded with the participation of Saudi Arabia, Egypt, the United Arab Emirates, Iran and Ethiopia. Today, BRICS represents approximately half of the world's population and more than a quarter of the global economy.

BRICS, especially at its last summit, focused on the Middle East - global south countries. It is understood that the BRICS expansion aims to establish geopolitical balance and strengthen energy security. BRICS is now more important for energy markets. Because the exporting countries that provide global oil supply and the largest energy importing and energy consuming countries have come together.

There are two evaluations for BRICS targets. The first is that it offers an alternative to Western institutions in the global south block. It is thought to be an alternative international cooperation for countries that cannot find a place in Western institutions and adopt multilateralism. It is accepted that institutions such as the New Development Bank and the Conditional Reserve Arrangement offer only a simple alternative to the global financial system. The second idea is that BRICS poses a global challenge to Western institutions. It is thought that BRICS challenges the Western liberal world order. It is evaluated that it aims for global cooperation by replacing the Western financial system. It is stated that it represents a geostrategic challenge and a global transformative threat to the global order established by the norms of Western countries. Because it is foreseen that institutions such as the New Development Bank and the Conditional Reserve Arrangement actually pose a challenge to the global financial system established by the major industrial countries after World War II.

In addition to all these, there are also views that assess that BRICS has difficulties and therefore cannot offer long-term cooperation. BRICS is an archetype of 21st century international cooperation due to the differences and disagreements among its members. It is assessed that these differences and disagreements are not suitable for offering an alternative or challenging the global financial system. It is thought that insurmountable and historical difficulties among the members will undermine the potential of BRICS.

It is predicted that BRICS members will not allow their different economic visions to be combined on a common ground over time. However, it is stated that the historical disagreements and regional competition between the members will put BRICS in a difficult position. The border disputes between China and India and their competition for the leadership of the global south are controversial. It is thought that the increase in sanctions and diplomatic pressure due to Russia's invasion of Ukraine in 2022 will cause cracks within BRICS over time. It is evaluated that the economic fluctuations and political instabilities experienced by the members threaten the future of BRICS. In addition to the internal problems experienced by South Africa and Brazil, the high level of corruption is at a level that will affect the dynamism of BRICS. Particularly, the differences due to the regimes and historical tensions between the Middle Eastern countries show that it cannot be channeled to BRICS. The tensions and competition between Iran, Saudi Arabia and Egypt have been going on for many years and constitute a fault line for BRICS.

In this context, the aim of the study is to examine the role of the rising and expanding BRICS in shaping global financial norms and governance. The question "Does BRICS offer an alternative or a challenge to the leadership of Western institutions in the global financial system?" is the starting point of the study. It is aimed to understand the potential of the coordination provided by the members with their differences to act as a destabilizing force against the political and economic structure of the West. Thus, the geopolitical and geoeconomic profile offered by BRICS can be drawn. In addition, the role assumed by the Chinese state within BRICS will be explained. It will be determined what China's goal is on the global Western system through BRICS.

First, the BRICS establishment will be examined within the framework of its purpose and challenges. The need for BRICS and the reasons that led to its emergence will be stated. Historical disagreements and certain competitive dynamics among the members will be expressed. The second heading will reveal the economic and political capacity of BRICS. Thus, the characteristics of BRICS will be understood and the existence of coordination among its members will be determined. China's influence factor on BRICS will be explained under this heading. The last heading will discuss whether BRICS, through China, offers an alternative or a challenge to Western financial institutions and governance, in short, to the status quo. It will be understood that BRICS undoubtedly offers an alternative in the medium term; on this basis, it aims to challenge in the long term.

1.BRICS IN THE CONTEXT OF ITS ESTABLISHMENT PURPOSE AND FRAMEWORK

With the beginning of the new century, the global political system, on the one hand, exhibited an entropy in the context of randomness and disorder; on the other hand, it began to carry the economic and security threats brought by globalization. The fact that the existence of the unipolar system was not accepted by the developing economies and that multilateralism was given importance became more apparent with the economic crises. All these accelerated the paradigm shift in the global political system.

In a report published in 2001, Goldman Sachs[1] stated that emerging economies such as China, Russia, India, South Africa and Brazil would dominate investments and global economic growth in the coming decades. The financial crisis in 2008 proved the report's prediction (Green, 2016, pp. 13). In fact, following the crisis, China, Russia, India and Brazil came together to consider establishing coordination on an intergovernmental economic organization. Following the first evaluation in 2008, the first meeting was held in Yekaterinburg, Russia in 2009. The declaration stated that the aim was to "promote dialogue and cooperation between our countries in a gradual, proactive, pragmatic, open and transparent manner". It was stated that not only the cooperation of developing economies was targeted, but also that a harmonious world with common prosperity would be built (History of BRICS, 2020). The following year, with the inclusion of South Africa in the intergovernmental cooperation, the initials of the English equivalents of the country names were brought together and the name of the cooperation emerged as BRICS. The declarations stated the concerns of the participating countries regarding the global political system, their financial difficulties and their commitments to each other (Mare et al., 2024).

It is understood that the BRICS organization, which includes the countries of the global south, establishes a geopolitical balance against the G7 platform, which represents developed economies. In addition, it has created a potential unity against the financial system dominated by Western countries. It is accepted that BRICS, which is formed by countries with common political and economic goals, is largely informal due to the fact that its statute is not definitive, it does not have a secretariat and it does not have a common fund. The bloc, which brings together non-Western economies, offers an alternative to the blocs dominated by the West, including the G7, the World Bank, and the UN Security Council (Ferragamo, 2024).

The expansion of BRICS, which is sustained through the acceptance of multilateralism, sovereign equality, inclusiveness and strategic cooperation, has offered an alternative cooperation focused on economy to the unipolar political system. Because the cooperation covering developing economies challenges the global unipolar system with its focuses on financial unity, infrastructure development, peace and security

(Mare et al., 2024). BRICS presents itself as a group of nations. It states that they are the future of financial power, that they create new values and cooperation and that they are a potential alternative. The founding values of BRICS were expressed at the 2023 Summit. Accordingly, BRICS is defined as having adopted multilateralism aimed at restructuring the global political and economic architecture in a fair and balanced manner (Cochrane & Zaidan, 2024, pp. 4).

The group highlights several thematic areas: multilateralism and representation, economic coordination, de-dollarization and alternative financial system (Ferragamo, 2024). Assessing the need to renew the financial architecture, BRICS focuses on certain principles.

-Equal decision-making and implementation processes in global financial institutions;
-A solid legal basis exists globally;
-Compatibility of international standard-setting bodies;
-Strengthening risk management (Joint Statement of the BRIC, 2009).

The common themes of BRICS can be expressed under five headings. Practical cooperation among partner countries will lead to concrete results globally. Secondly, international financial institutions are not transparent for developing economies. International financial institutions should be inclusive for all economies and have a high level of representativeness. Developing and poor economies are particularly sensitive to global threats and challenges. Global institutions' measures against global threats are not sufficient, so reorganization should be made. Fourthly, the basis of BRICS cooperation is the acceptance of cultural diversity. This acceptance can be achieved through unions and forums. Finally, BRICS is subject to the principles of openness, solidarity and mutual assistance (Mare et al., 2024).

BRICS countries constitute 46% of the world population (approximately 3.21 billion people) as of 2023. Having a large population accounts for 29% of the world's GDP, which corresponds to almost 1/3. Having a large market share, BRICS has 25% of exports and 43% of oil production (Teke, 2024). Thus, developing economies become the main driving factor of the global economy. Having abundant natural resources and hosting the world's most populous countries enables BRICS to increase its influence.

The BRICS founding countries are members of globally influential political and policy organizations. Their influential presence in international organizations such as the UN, Group of 77[2], G20, and Non-Aligned Movement has brought them to the forefront of regional cooperation. China and Russia are members of the Shanghai Cooperation Organization and the Asia-Pacific Economic Cooperation.

China and Russia are members of the Shanghai Cooperation Organization as well as the Asia-Pacific Economic Cooperation. Russia is a founding member of the Commonwealth of Independent States, the Eurasian Economic Union, and the Collective Security Treaty Organization. India is an influential member of the South Asian Association for Regional Cooperation. South Africa is a member of the Southern African Development Community and the African Union. Brazil is a member of MERCOSUR, the Union of South American Nations, and the Community of Latin American and Caribbean States (History of BRICS, 2020).

The common paradigm among BRICS members is that the countries are almost hegemonic countries of their own continents. The members, who have become leaders of their own continents and regions, reveal a collective power when they come together. Thus, they ensure that the global south countries, which include more developing economies, increase their influence in the international system. BRICS, which produces an alternative to the Western Bretton Woods[3] institutions in this way, is critical of sovereignty based on a single pole (Mare et al., 2024).

The countries that make up the BRICS have unique histories that have influenced their current economic existence. Today, China is the world's second largest economy and the export leader. The country, which is described as the world's factory, ranks second after India in terms of population (Teke, 2024). China, which opened up to the world in 1978, developed its industry with the transition to a market economy. The economic rise it followed deeply affected global trade. Its strong industry and share in exports facilitated its emergence as an economic giant. However, a possible slowdown in the economy is seen as an economic disaster for China (BRICS'20 Russia'24, 2024, pp. 11-18).

Russia, which has the 5th largest economy in the world, is an agricultural giant and one of the important countries of the global economy with its natural resources (Teke, 2024). After the collapse of the Soviet Union, it experienced a transition from a centralized economic structure to an economy dominated by privatization. The country, which is rich in hydrocarbon resources, has followed liberalization in the economy. In addition, its oil and natural gas have made Russia a major economy (BRICS'20 Russia'24, 2024, pp. 11-18).

India, which has the largest population in the world, is the leader in information resources and also represents the world's 3rd largest economy (Teke, 2024). India, which has switched to a mixed economy model after the colonial period, aims to grow its industry. The country, which wants to overcome external dependency in the economy, has managed to grow in the information technology and service sectors with liberalization. However, in India, where poverty is still high, issues such as lack of infrastructure and legal issues pose problems (BRICS'20 Russia'24, 2024, pp. 11-18).

Brazil, which has the 8th largest economy, is an important market for agricultural exports (Teke, 2024). The country, which is an important partner of South American countries, has a difficult economic history. Having oil reserves and agricultural lands that are important for the region has been a primary factor in the growth of the Brazilian economy. However, the country has problems such as corruption, political instability, and income inequality (BRICS'20 Russia'24, 2024, pp. 11-18).

South Africa, which has important natural resources, primarily diamonds, is determined as the 23rd economy in the world (Teke, 2024). Even the abundance of natural resources has not allowed the country to eliminate the effects of its apartheid past. The country, which is rising in the service and manufacturing sectors, especially in mining, has high unemployment rates. The existence of social inequality reveals the need for comprehensive reform in development and economic growth (BRICS'20 Russia'24, 2024, pp. 11-18).

It is understood that BRICS countries have little in common in economic and political terms. In addition, countries that agree on comprehensive and global financial issues have very different political and economic backgrounds. BRICS members, who agree on global development issues, maintain their economies around opposing ideologies. However, the fact that they have joint decisions on global financial issues has enabled the countries to maintain BRICS as an intergovernmental institution (Mare et al., 2024). However, it is understood that BRICS countries follow a covert competition on global and regional issues.

In addition, it has been determined that there is competition between the BRICS countries on regional and continental issues. The effects of the Ukraine war between China and Russia; China and India, Iran and their regional partners; Russia and South Africa occur as regional and continental difficulties between the BRICS members. The political disagreements between Russia and China in the 20th century have deeply affected the relations of the two countries in the 21st century. Deepening political, economic and security cooperation does not change the history of the relations between the two countries. The communication of the countries that are considered not to be natural allies in the Asian continent mostly coincides at the point of limiting the influence of the West. The desire of Russia and China to challenge the unipolar system established by the West (Fong & Maizland, 2024) is shaped through the BRICS. However, since the autocratic governments of the Asian continent show their desire to be the rulers of the continent, it is accepted that there is a covert competition between them. The desire to expand their influence in the Asian continent is valid for China and Russia. While opposing the unipolar system of the West directs China and Russia to act together; The desire to dominate the Asian continent triggers a covert competition between the two countries.

The rivalry and regional tensions brought about by political history remain valid between China and India. The ongoing border disputes between the two countries affect the economic and political structure of the global south. The ongoing competition in the geopolitical and geoeconomic leadership of the global south determines the future of relations between the countries (Ferragamo, 2024). BRICS membership is important for India to reflect its regional leadership and multipolar foreign policy vision. On the one hand, BRICS does not want to damage its relations with the US, but wants to deepen its regional relations. For this reason, its position within BRICS is seen to be changeable in terms of the US / West's evaluation of cooperation. For this reason, India sees BRICS as a strategic tool that will not change its foreign policy stance in the long term but offers a broad perspective to its foreign policy (Panda, 2024).

The war that Russia launched against Ukraine in 2022 seems likely to deepen the cracks within BRICS. The sanctions and trade freeze attempts against Russia, which is the largest and one of the founding members of the group, have made member countries nervous. The diplomatic condemnations against Russia are considered to have shaken the international image of BRICS. The order issued by the International Criminal Court against Russian leader Putin for committing war crimes has complicated the internal relations of BRICS (Ferragamo, 2024). South Africa's call on Russia to withdraw its military presence in Ukraine and its expression of respect for sovereignty has suggested that there are cracks among the founding members and that there are real disagreements among BRICS members (van der Westhuizen, 2024, pp. 20-21).

The state capacity fluctuations experienced by South Africa and Brazil, the increase in corruption and the weakening of infrastructure seem likely to spread to the BRICS from its two important founding members. The inclusion of countries such as Saudi Arabia and Iran, which are autocracies and democracies in the Middle East, seems likely to deepen the competition within the BRICS (Ferragamo, 2024). Iran's presence challenges the unipolar system of the West but does not provide consensus on Islam (Green, 2016, pp. 16). In general, the increase in uncertainties in Asia and the global south, which constitute the most complex continent and region in the world, the development of defense technologies, the emergence of hybrid wars, and the existence of challenging dynamics are determined as natural reasons for deepening cooperation. Countries that face existential threats from each other try to expand their relations and deepen competition through natural allies.

2. BRICS ECONOMIC-POLITICAL CAPACITY AND CHINESE INFLUENCE

Building on the fact that global financial and governance institutions are dominated by Western and unipolar powers, BRICS focuses on ensuring the coordination of member countries and creating new non-Western financial institutions. In addition, BRICS aims to establish an international financial circulation network through the countries of the global south, hoping to reduce dependence on the US dollar.

BRICS, which has been publishing the intergovernmental declaration every year since 2009, focused on the financial crisis that primarily affected the global south countries, beyond creating a global impact at its first summit. The fact that the global south countries were affected first and the BRICS countries focused on increasing the financial resilience of the global south countries suggested that they had developed a challenge to the global financial system (Mare et al., 2024).

The annual statements create a different image structurally. However, each statement focuses on developing economies and refers to the failure to obtain the desired share from the global financial system. This situation clarifies that BRICS aims to eliminate the inequalities created by developed economies. Sharing a common pattern, BRICS countries have declared that they offer a better model for the global financial system. It envisages developing countries to act together with five governments within BRICS, thus becoming a strategic organization (Mare et al., 2024).

Until 2016, BRICS countries prioritized global issues. They displayed a common stance on issues that could be considered regional, in response to issues in Syria, Libya, Afghanistan, and Iran's nuclear programs. They also touched on the reforms carried out by the IMF and the World Bank. They stated that resources should be used adequately and balancedly and measures should be taken against global financial crises. They evaluated expanding the Credit Facility in Local Currency by establishing the "Interbank Cooperation Mechanism". They also reached a common decision on financial issues by establishing the "Exchange Alliance" (History of BRICS, 2020).

The 6th Summit held in 2014 was more important than all other summits. It was decided to establish the $200 billion "New Development Bank (NBD)" and "Conditional Reserve Arrangement". Decisions were made to initiate economic cooperation such as the "Economic Partnership Strategy" and "Trade, Economic and Investment Cooperation" (History of BRICS, 2020). Launched in 2016, the NBD supported projects that would focus on infrastructure investments and development. Unlike the World Bank, the loans it provided aim to provide flexible, equal and easy loans. More than $32 billion were approved for 96 projects (Ferragamo, 2024).

For the 2024 meeting, BRICS has set out the compass of its future. New members were included in the 16th Summit held in Kazan, Russia. The summit, which was held with the theme of "Strengthening Multilateralism for Equitable Global Development and Security", included new members from the Middle East: the United Arab Emirates, Iran, Egypt and Ethiopia (Ministry of Foreign Affairs, 2024). The BRICS group last added members 13 years ago. Therefore, the 2024 summit was the first meeting of the expanded BRICS. The BRICS bloc has thus become more heterogeneous (Baskaran & Cahill, 2023, pp. 1). Russia's hosting of the 2024 summit has shown that BRICS members have an inconsistent approach to global and regional issues in response to the occupation of Ukraine that has been ongoing for almost 3 years (Mare et al., 2024).

The expansion of the mechanism has led to the countries within BRICS now having more population, the growth of developing economies and the increase in countries with natural resources. Thus, BRICS has begun to express more multilateralism in global governance. At the summit, the idea of having the BRICS spirit and expanding the strategic partnership brought by BRICS came to the fore. In addition, three main driving forces were targeted: economy and trade; intercultural interaction, politics and security (Ministry of Foreign Affairs, 2024).

The expanded BRICS has brought together major oil producers and energy consuming countries in the same bloc. Thus, BRICS has advanced to the top ranks in terms of the share of natural resources and energy in global trade. With the addition of new members to BRICS, the bloc has 72% of rare earth elements, 75% of the world's manganese, 28% of the chemical elements, and 10% of the world's copper excluding Iran. The bloc has been included in the same group as Argentina, the world's third largest lithium reserve holder. Thus, China, Brazil and Argentina, three of the world's five largest lithium producers, are now in BRICS (Baskaran & Cahill, 2023, pp. 2-3). With the addition of the United Arab Emirates, Iran and Saudi Arabia, the three largest countries in global oil supply have taken their place in BRICS. This will strengthen BRICS's presence in global energy markets on the one hand, while on the other hand, it will enable the bypassing of Western sanctions imposed on oil producers (Baskaran & Cahill, 2023, pp. 3). In addition, the coming together of countries from different regions and with different administrations will further complicate the complex structure of BRICS. Therefore, it seems likely that different evaluations, divisions and new challenges will be experienced within the bloc (Ministry of External Affairs, 2024).

Steps aimed at increasing the integration of BRICS countries and the global economy are strengthening stability and simplifying financial transactions. One way to do this is to use the Chinese renminbi in exchange for the US dollar. BRICS governments, especially the Chinese renminbi, plan to use only their own currencies in global trade. In this way, the superiority of the US dollar in global trade is attempted to be broken (Ferragamo, 2024).

Countries that prioritize using their own national currencies to break the dominance of the US dollar will have to focus on a single currency over time. It will be replaced with a single currency to strengthen economic stability, prevent exchange rate fluctuations and facilitate trade channels. The change that needs to be made to break the influence of the US dollar seems beneficial in theory. However, in practice, especially in a period of economic conflicts, the creation of a new financial system will be tested with many difficulties. From this perspective, even if the transition to a single currency will encourage integration among the BRICS, it is seen as an extremely ambitious goal (Mare et al., 2024).

However, the possible transition of BRICS countries to a single currency will not only have economic but also geopolitical consequences. As targeted, the possibility of breaking the dominance of the US dollar will change the distribution of global financial power across continents. As such, it is of critical importance as it will change the stability points of financial centers, the possibility of changing the balance of power in national currencies, and the flow of global trade (Nach & Ncwadi, 2024, pp. 5-8). The weakening of the influence of the US dollar and the euro will increase the integration within BRICS and increase the influence of BRICS countries on the global economy. The emergence of an integrated economic area can ensure the consolidation of markets. With the expansion of the area of movement of capital, the common currency will create a strong global south economy (Curtis, 2024, pp. 12-14).

In addition, there are reasons that limit the effect of the US dollar among BRICS, that is, de-dollarization. The most important reason is that some countries within BRICS have deeper relations with the US. Therefore, even if unofficial de-dollarization is targeted, official de-dollarization does not seem possible in the near future. In addition, the fact that some BRICS countries are more dependent on the US dollar for global trade than others clearly shows that it is not easy to break the effect in the near future. Indeed, even if every BRICS country wants to reduce dependence on the US dollar, it does not seem possible for them to keep this among their primary goals. Because the presence of US dollars in the reserves of BRICS countries (Liu & Papa, 2022 pp. 5) weakens the countries economically by weakening the strength of the US dollar. Therefore, in order for BRICS countries to switch to a common currency, they must first reduce the US dollar in their reserves.

China stands out as the most influential country in BRICS. Its effectiveness within BRICS and the influence policies it pursues through BRICS present China as an influential actor in the global system. China began its participation in global-regional organizations and formations in the years it began to open up to the world economically. Increasing its participation as of the new century, China evaluates the BRICS bloc as a means of expanding its soft power and influence. Paying attention to the local dynamics of global southern countries, China prefers to persuade countries rather than forcing them to form any formation. By expanding its network of relations, it strives to be a country that respects the traditions of local actors and responds to their needs. Trying to show that it is the most influential actor in BRICS, China states that it is a partner of global southern countries (Garlick & Qin, 2023, pp. 38-39).

By presenting its normative diplomacy on global south countries within a general framework, it aims to expand its influence and multipolarity. By expanding globalization channels, it tries to integrate global south countries into the global system; thus, it reveals multipolarity. It expands its network of relations with regional partnerships and increases its regional influence in the global south. It provides the infrastructure investments that global south countries need, offers loans to countries, and deepens trade. BRICS, which offers a broad framework of all China's activities on global south countries, provides China with the opportunity to increase its political influence (Soong, 2021).

In addition to the goals pursued by China through BIRCS, its economic power provides China with privilege within BRICS. China, which can more easily fulfill its export and import needs thanks to the BRICS bloc, stands out within BRICS. For example, China has managed to become the largest importer of goods among BRICS countries over the years. The value of the goods imported by China has increased over the years. This has made China's presence within BRICS even more important (O'Neill, 2024).

China has managed to become the dominant country in trade within BRICS. It has strengthened its position among the countries by undertaking more than half of the intra-BRICS trade on its own. Between 2019 and 2021, it had an average share of more than 50% in exports among BRICS countries. This showed that China is the largest supplier within BRICS. Brazil is the second largest exporter within BRICS with a share of 20%. Russia is the third with a share of 17%, India is the fourth with an 8% share, and South Africa is the fifth intra-BRICS exporter with a share of 3% (Agarwal & Kumar, 2023, pp. 7).

Among the founding members, Russia is the only country that has eliminated poverty. However, China's annual growth rates have increased or remained stable, indicating that poverty can be eliminated. It is unlikely that the other founding partners will be able to achieve growth rates that can eliminate poverty. China, which opened up to the world with very high poverty rates, has increased its effectiveness within the BRICS and in the global economy by achieving growth rates every year. BRICS, which increased its share in the world GDP as a bloc, managed to reach 25.6% in 2021. However, China was the country that made the greatest contribution to this increase. Because Russia could not increase its share. The shares of South

Africa and Brazil decreased. Only the shares of India and China increased. China was the one that managed to increase its share the most between the two countries, from 5.7% to 18.2%. In addition, South Africa and Russia recorded a decrease in per capita national income after the pandemic. China, on the other hand, was able to achieve an increase in per capita national income compared to its growth rates (Agarwal & Kumar, 2023).

The country that has managed to continue its growth in the BRICS bloc is China. Moreover, its growth is much faster than other BRICS members (O'Neill, 2025). The majority of BRICS countries are considered middle-income countries in terms of income according to the World Bank criteria. Their share compared to other middle-income countries has decreased from almost 83% to 67%. However, China and India have managed to increase their income share despite the decrease in the income of the bloc as a whole. India has increased by 11%. China has increased its share by a tremendous 87%. The decrease in the share of the other three countries reduces the overall BRICS average (Agarwal & Kumar, 2023, pp. 3).

3. DO BRICS OFFER AN ALTERNATIVE OR A CHALLENGE TO WESTERN INSTITUTIONS AND GOVERNANCE?

There are two important ideas for the emergence and development of the BRICS bloc. The first idea is that BRICS brings an alternative to the Western global system. The second important idea is that BRICS was created to present a challenge to the Western global system. If we first evaluate the idea that it is an alternative; it is evaluated that BRICS was created as an intergovernmental formation that wanted to gather the global southern countries that could not integrate into the Western global systems within a bloc.

BRICS members, who have very different political and social dynamics, hold annual intergovernmental meetings to set a vision for the global political system. After nearly 16 years since its establishment, eliminating the fragile structures of the global south countries against financial crises is still seen as the most fundamental goal. Concerns about development problems require members to create new areas of cooperation as well as institutions that cannot be integrated within the global system. The commonality of goals and concerns suggested the collective structuring of BRICS and its offering of an alternative to the global system (Mare et al., 2024).

According to the declarations, BRICS provides ideas by producing alternatives to the global economic and political system. It develops new visions, but it is stated that it does not present this as a challenge to the global system dominated by the West. Because what brings the BRICS countries together is not the idea of transforming the global political and economic system dominated by the West. The real purpose that brings the BRIC members together is the desire to offer an alternative to countries that cannot find a place for themselves in the global political and economic system dominated by the West. Concerns about future economic-based issues are among the reasons for the development of BRICS. For this reason, despite all its different dynamics, BRICS meetings are held and alternatives are created on the basic dynamics. In addition, new memberships are made in order to increase the items offered as alternatives, and thus geopolitical partnerships are tested in a sense.

BRICS is seen as having a narrative that challenges the Western system. However, BRICS claims the opposite with its new memberships. Accordingly, countries such as Egypt, the United Arab Emirates, and Saudi Arabia, which are new members of BRICS, continue to cooperate closely with Western countries and institutions. BRICS states that its new members are in agreement in line with their preferences and that BRICS is compatible with being an alternative and emerging as an option (Boillot, 2024).

BRICS, which has brought out its soft power, wants to increase its national interests without being a coercive power in line with its principles. It is aimed for the development of its members without coercion against dominant economic and political powers. Thus, when its evolution and growth strategies are evaluated, the bloc focuses on developing economies. The fact that developing economies are located in the global south has resulted in BRICS having a paradigm that appeals to the global south. The dominance of the bloc members focuses on the areas where the Western states that dominate the global system fall short and their deficiencies. When evaluated, the emergence of BRICS is the thought of whether the Western system can cover all actors and whether a multilateral system is possible (Mare et al., 2024).

In addition, the mixed reactions of BRICS members to global events suggest that they can only be an alternative to the integrity of the Western system. The fact that BRICS does not have a multilateral integrity of action declares that the bloc cannot go beyond being an alternative (Vayez, 2023). BRICS, which has not yet managed to become a structured organization, is evaluated to remain simply as an alternative since it cannot be a single voice of the global southern countries (Boillot, 2024). The limited influence of its members on the global political system also reveals that BRICS will remain an alternative (Vayez, 2023). Another point is that the bloc, where China has an effective power, will not expand within the framework of Chinese norms. It is stated that the countries will not accept the norms of the dominant country China; therefore, it will not be able to offer integrity against Western countries in the global system. It is determined that BRICS, which does not have an agreed integrity of norms, is and will remain an alternative (Garlick & Qin, 2023, pp. 44).

Indeed, according to ideas that evaluate BRICS as an alternative, BRICS includes countries with deep differences within themselves. As an intergovernmental group, BRICS creates a common alternative to the political and economic system of Western countries. The bloc, which emerged from global concerns, brings countries together, but different dynamics cannot pose a challenge to the Western system as a whole. BRICS, which is based on developing economies, focuses on the global south countries geopolitically. This situation cannot pose a natural challenge to the formation of Western countries.

Another idea in the founding purpose of BRICS is that it has a vision of challenging the global system. According to this idea, BRICS has tried to transform the global system since its establishment. It has focused on restructuring international laws and norms. It has taken advanced steps in global issues such as security, peacebuilding processes, human rights, especially in the economic field and development. This has enabled BRICS to influence normative systems on a large scale (Mare et al., 2024).

There are several fundamental reasons why BRICS is considered to challenge the global Western economic and political system. First of all, economically, BRICS aims to change the direction of the global economy by focusing on developing economies, to direct trade flows to global southern countries, and thus to ensure that the global money supply is focused on global southern countries. This will cause the global economic system to transform.

BRICS aims to reshape the status quo in order to weaken the influence of the US dollar. For nearly 20 years, the founding members of BRICS have tried to reform the global financial system in their own favor. To this end, they have taken steps to break the dominance of the US dollar in global trade and diversify their currencies. The bloc members, who have expanded their areas of cooperation, aim to have an economic will and unite against dollarization. China, one of the founding members of BRICS that initiated the de-dollarization process, emerged as the first country that wanted to bypass the dollar's pressure on global finance. Criticizing the hegemonic weight of the dollar, China argued that the renminbi should have a place in the global financial system. China's desire for the renminbi to gain weight has been one of the reasons for the weakening of its relations with the US over time. China's exposure to sanctions and its strategic competition with the US have shown China that it needs to create more areas of cooperation (Liu & Papa, 2022).

While China is trying to bypass the US dollar dominance with BRICS, it is also trying to minimize the strategic effects it receives from the US. Therefore, the biggest advocate of de-dollarization policies is China within BRICS. In addition, the loans provided by the NDB allow BRICS members to borrow less from Western and US banks. In addition, countries providing loans in their own currencies prioritize overcoming their dependence on the hegemony of the dollar (Liu & Papa, 2022). Stating that the NDB will expand its institutional infrastructure, the bloc underlined that it will accelerate the flow of investment to the global south with investment funds. In addition to emphasizing that the bank will be a multilateral development bank, it was stated that it will not discriminate, will be fair, will prioritize local currencies, will increase innovation and will increase cooperation on dynamics (Kazan Declaration, 2024, pp. 17).

BRICS, which stated that it appreciated the increase in the number of members of the NDB, stated that the bank should have a high credit rating. The bloc, which is expanding institutionally, declared that the increase should be geographically balanced (XIII BRICS Summit, 2021). Stating that BRICS plays a critical role in improving the global financial system, the members state that the economic system that the bloc will offer will meet the needs of all countries (Kazan Declaration, 2024). BRICS has come to represent a financial wave that challenges the dominance of the West and the US in the global financial system. BRICS takes steps that prioritize the interests of its countries and meet their needs. This situation necessitates the reform of the governance structure of the global financial system (Vayez, 2023).

BRICS has managed to integrate more into the global financial system over the years and has demanded reforms. The investment paths it has followed have made BRICS a priority in the global south. Addressing the global economic system, BRICS is moving towards becoming a comprehensive financial power by bringing together the economic powers and developing economies of the global south. Therefore, BRICS aims to break the hegemony of the US dollar by increasing domestic trade, establishing banks, providing loans in national currencies and overcoming dependence on the US dollar. This situation proves that BRICS poses a challenge within the global financial system.

The idea that BRICS poses a challenge to the global system is also thought to be due to the fact that the global structure is not ignored. BRICS is trying to find solutions to international issues and trying to express that it has a say in the global system.

BRICS, which has developed a strategy for combating terrorism, demonstrates that it is acting to find a solution to a global problem. The bloc, which has prepared the Counter-Terrorism Action Plan, has directed its national security advisors to this end. They state that they have taken the initiative to determine a common stance and prepare an action plan for combating terrorism and to establish coordination. The joint action plan covers a wide range of issues, such as sharing intelligence information, preventing terrorized individuals from crossing borders, and preventing radical actions. BRICS has stated that it envisages cooperation with other global and multilateral counter-terrorism mechanisms, primarily the UN, in combating terrorism. However, the fact that BRICS has activated the counter-terrorism action plan within the framework of its members actually shows that global mechanisms are being left out. This situation underlines that BRICS has challenged the current global mechanisms by establishing a mechanism on terrorism and security issues (XIII BRICS Summit, 2021).

BRICS assesses that the UN does not have a comprehensive representation capability. According to BRICS, the UN cannot adequately represent developing economies. Therefore, the UN, including the UNSC, needs a comprehensive reform. Increasing the representation of developing countries in the UN will make the institution more efficient and effective. In this case, solutions to global problems can be found more easily. The bloc states that increasing the status of the BRICS founding members, especially China, at the UN is a prerequisite for finding joint solutions to global problems. The declaration on Strengthening and Reorganizing the Multilateral System shows that BRICS members want multilateral global systems, not Western global systems. It has been emphasized that global southern countries, especially Africa, should be included in decision-making processes on international issues. It was hoped that global institutions that are sensitive to international law will be established and that global organizations will be democratic, reliable and fair (XIII BRICS Summit, 2021).

BRICS' assessment that the scope of the UN is insufficient and its statement that its base should be expanded implicitly expresses that the bloc presents a global challenge. Because it is clear that the representation capacity of the BRICS founding members in the UN will not be increased. In this case, BRICS will express the dysfunctionality of the UN more and will create global institutions that will pacify the UN. Even if the emergence of multilateral global institutions does not seem possible in the near future, BRICS members will become more uncomfortable with the current situation and the dysfunctionality of the UN will be expressed more. In addition, signing a declaration on multilateral institutions portrays that BRICS is not satisfied with the functioning of the current global system and wants to change it.

On the other hand, the members, who accepted the commitment to the UN conditions with the declaration they published in 2021, underline that the UN is the cornerstone of the international system. The declaration, which refers to the central role of the organization, states that it is essential to build a common future. The same declaration states that the UN does not have a multilateral structure, but its conditions are absolutely binding for the international arena. Indeed, BRICS members complain about the lack of inclusiveness of the UN in the global system and accept that the ability of developing countries to represent should be increased. They aim for a democratic, fair, inclusive and solution-producing UN (XIII BRICS Summit, 2021).

Another piece of data supporting the BRICS' challenge to the global system is that it wants to increase its ability to find solutions to international problems. The bloc, which has declared that it has concerns about globalized or regional problems, states that it wants to play a role in peacebuilding processes. It is emphasized that priority should be given to mechanisms that can produce peaceful solutions to problems, and that domestic problems should not be interfered with. It is emphasized that diplomacy should be prioritized in global problems and that the use of force is unacceptable. It is frequently expressed that comprehensive solutions should be found for the regional problems experienced and created by Afghanistan, Palestine, Central Africa, Syria, Yemen and Iran (XIII BRICS Summit, 2021).

In addition, it is understood that the country that leads the BRICS bloc's challenge to the global system is founding member China. Priorities such as the demand for Afghanistan to be demilitarized, the condition of not interfering in the internal affairs of countries, and the establishment of the NDB in Shanghai, China, are in line with Chinese interests.

It is a fact that other members of BRICS do not criticize the global political system as much as China. They remain in the background and implicitly criticize the Western global system. China strongly criticizes the global economic and political orientation on every possible platform, emphasizes that Western dominance must be transformed into multilateralism, and states that it is imperative to establish a comprehensive platform that responds to the needs of every country. China criticizes more when global southern countries express their dissatisfaction with the Western global system. This situation brings global southern countries closer to China and its policies. It is thought that China's approach to the multilateralism of the global system attracts global southern countries (Soong, 2024, pp. 8).

China advocates multilateralism and mutual benefit, uses bilateral and multilateral diplomacy channels, and develops regional and global cooperation. It strengthens its connections with global south countries by supporting developing economies. It uses its economic power to increase its connections with Asia, the global south, and Eurasia more broadly. By increasing people-to-people contacts, it actually introduces, spreads, and imposes its own norms (Garlick & Qin, 2023).

By leading BRICS and NDB, it produces alternatives to the UN, the World Bank and the IMF. Leading institutions that will challenge Western global institutions reveals that China offers a model for the global system. Proposing new institutions for the international order and advocating multilateralism express China's global challenge. In fact, China states that it does not have a challenge and does not aim to change the global order. However, the initiatives carried out and the collaborations established are understood as being suitable for changing the global order (Soong, 2024, pp. 10).

China, which has revealed its desire to challenge with the institutions it has established, is laying the foundations of a global system that will grow by bringing together the countries of the global south. China, which aims to establish a global system that will be independent of the Western global system, aims to encompass the entire system economically and politically. It aims to surpass the US and evaluates eliminating the dominance of the West (Schirm, 2023, pp. 17). China's idea of embracing multilateralism represents a challenge to the existing global hegemony of the US and the West. China is establishing institutions with a global scope to accelerate multilateralism. Multilateralism will destroy the global dominance of the US and the West and enable China to be a leader in the global order together with the countries of the global south (Garlick & Qin, 2023, pp. 53).

CONCLUSION AND EVALUATION

BRICS was established as an intergovernmental organization under the leadership of China with significant contributions from Russia. The 2008 financial crisis was the trigger for its establishment. The bloc established between China, Russia, Brazil and India became BRICS with the participation of South Africa. BRICS, which provides geopolitical balance against the developed economies of the world, includes the countries of the global south. It is understood that the countries of the global south do not have the share they should have from the global financial system. The countries of the global south that come together within BRICS aim to get the share they should have from the global financial system. None of the issues of state administration, political unity, commonality of nation and language, cultural and social similarity apply to BRICS members. For this reason, BRICS is seen as the archetype of international cooperation.

In addition, BRICS members aim to increase cooperation. They assess that the global financial system is not transparent for developing economies. Therefore, they aim for the global financial system to be complementary for each country's economy. They declare that developing economies with fragile structures should be supported by the global financial system. Moreover, they emphasize that global institutions are not sufficient for global challenges and that a new regulation is appropriate.

BRICS, which constitutes approximately half of the world's population, has a high share in the global economy. Countries with natural resources account for a significant share in global trade. The establishment of the NDB has given rise to the idea that it is an alternative to the World Bank. Unlike the World Bank, the loans it provides and the funds it provides have begun to show the global financial system that the World Bank is not sufficient. The establishment of the NDB and the provision of loans to countries reveal the financial reality for the BRICS. By encouraging economic growth, it will integrate developing country economies with the global system.

In addition, BRICS, which wants to start the de-dollarization process, aims to eliminate the dependence on the US dollar in the global financial system. This step, which does not seem possible in the medium term, aims to replace the US dollar with the renminbi in the long term. China wants to overcome the hegemonic presence of the US in the global system with its dominant stance in BRICS. China, which wants its own currency to be preferred in international trade over the US dollar, is implementing BRICS as a tool of challenge to make changes in the global system.

The common currency creates advantages and disadvantages for BRICS. It is likely that the value of the US dollar will fall and the dependencies of the countries will decrease. It is certain that there will be an increase in trade within BRICS. The common currency will enable BRICS to play a more effective role in the global system. However, using the common currency requires the implementation of many mechanisms. It is necessary to have strong budgets and to prevent possible losses from harming the country's economies. BRICS, which mostly has developing economies, consists of countries that will be harmed if the transition to the common currency is accelerated. For this reason, it is considered essential to extend the process over a long term and to establish monitoring mechanisms. Although it is certain that the global influence of BRICS will increase, the common currency is an initiative that will be accepted by each country considering geopolitical realities.

BRICS, which expanded at the 2024 meeting, included the largest countries of the global south in BRICS. The new members, the majority of which are Middle Eastern countries, are countries that stand out in global natural resource reserves. For this reason, BRICS now has a much more important share in the world's natural resource reserves. The addition of new members has brought together countries that export natural resources and countries that import them within the same bloc. The new members' discomfort with the global system dominated by the US and their desire to abandon their dependence on the US dollar strengthens the structure of BRICS. This situation strengthens the thesis that BRICS presents a challenge rather than an alternative to the global system. The expansion of BRICS by adding members after many years strengthens the thesis that the bloc wants to realize a multipolar system. Because BRICS's wide range of members and its spread to a wider geography are seen as a challenging move that will reorganize the global order.

The creation of BRICS is seen as a possible start of a recovery phase for the global financial system. It is understood that it is an element that will provide stability for the countries that have suffered losses in the global financial system. The increase in market shares will be possible through economic cooperation. The facilitation of trade within the bloc and the expansion of connectivity will be achieved through the joint action of developing economies.

BRICS was developed as a bloc that expressed dissatisfaction with Western institutions of global politics in partnership with the global south countries. It is supported by countries that aim for multipolarity rather than unipolarity in a competitive global system. Countries that want the world political order to change do not want the US to be the hegemonic country of the global system.

The existence of insurmountable differences within the bloc predicts that BRICS can only remain as an alternative for the global system. Because the creation of a common currency is a very energy-intensive and long-term endeavor. The NDB, on the other hand, cannot surpass the existence of the World Bank today.

The expansion of the membership also expands the influence of BRICS. Bringing together countries that are dissatisfied with the global order established by the West shows that they will have the power to undermine the global order in time. When all the data is brought together, it is concluded that BRICS is an alternative for the global system today. However, when the purposes of BRICS' establishment, the structures it has established and the goals it continues to pursue are evaluated, it is revealed that it can challenge the Western system in time. Furthermore, the fact that member countries, especially China, express their dissatisfaction with the Western and US global system at every opportunity and take steps to change this order shows that the global system will be forced to change. The change of the global order, which will be carried out by using soft or hard power, is accelerated by the patient behavior of the countries and their preparations for tomorrow. BRICS constitutes the basis of the institutions established to challenge the global system and Western institutions.

REFERENCES

Agarwal, M., & Kumar, S. (2023). BRICS Countries' Increasing Role in the world economy, Including Institutional Innovation. *BRICS Journal of Economics.*, *4*(2), 173–191. DOI: 10.3897/brics-econ.4.e99451

Baskaran, G., & Cahill, B. (2023, 25 August). *Six New BRICS: Implications for Energy Trade.* CSIS Center for Strategic and International Studies. https://www.csis.org/analysis/six-new-brics-implications-energy-trade

Boillot, J. J. (2024, 6 June). BRICS+: Towards a New International Order? *International and Strategic Affairs (IRIS).*https://www.iris-france.org/en/186913-brics-towards-a-new-international-order/

BRICS'20 Russia'24. (2024). BRICS Joint Statistical Publication 2024. https://brics-russia2024.ru/

Cochrane, L., & Zaidan, E. (2024). Shifting global dynamics: An empirical analysis of BRICS + expansion and its economic, trade, and military implications in the context of the G7. *Cogent Social Sciences*, *10*(1), 2333422. Advance online publication. DOI: 10.1080/23311886.2024.2333422

Curtis, J. (2024, 11 November). *The BRICS Group: Overview and Recent Expansion.* House of Commons Library. Number 10136.

Ferragamo, M. (2024, 12 December). *What Is the BRICS Group and Why Is It Expanding?* Council on Foreign Relations. https://www.cfr.org/backgrounder/what-brics-group-and-why-it-expanding

Fong, C., & Maizland, L. (2024, 20 March). *China and Russia: Exploring Ties Between Two Authoritarian Powers.* Council on Foreign Relations. https://www.cfr.org/backgrounder/china-russia-relationship-xi-putin-taiwan-ukraine

Garlick, J., & Qin, F. (2023). China's 'do-as-I-do' paradigm: Practice-based normative diplomacy in the global South. *The Pacific Review*, *37*(5), 985–1015. DOI: 10.1080/09512748.2023.2290619

Green, M. J. (2016). *Is The Foundation of The U.S. -led Order Crumbling?* Global Forecast. https://csis-website-prod.s3.amazonaws.com/s3fs-public/publication/161215_GF2017_chapter2_green_foundation_crumbling.pdf

History of BRICS. (2020). BRICS. https://infobrics.org/page/history-of-brics/

Joint Statement of the BRIC Countries' Leaders. (2009, 16 June). BRICS. https://infobrics.org/document/3/

Kazan Declaration. (2024, 23 October). *XVI BRICS Summit.*https://cdn.brics-russia2024.ru/upload/docs/Kazan_Declaration_FINAL.pdf?1729693488349783

Liu, Z. Z., & Papa, M. (2022). Can BRICS De-dollarize the Global Financial System? Bruno S. Sergi (Ed.), *Elements in the Economics of Emerging Markets*. (pp. 1-94) Cambridge University Press. DOI:DOI: 10.1017/9781009029544

Mare, A., Ndzendze, B., & Prempeh, S. (2024, 28 October). *BRICS Thought Series*. APRI – Africa Policy Research Institute. https://afrpol.org/brcs-thought-seres

Ministry of External Affairs Goverment of India. (2024, 10 June). *Joint Statement of the BRICS Ministers of Foreign Affairs/International Relations.*https://www.mea.gov.in/bilateral-documents.htm?dtl/37860/joint+statement+of+the+brics+ministers+of+foreign+affairsinternational+relations

Ministry of Foreign Affairs The People's Republic of China. (2024, 23 October). *Xi Jinping Attends the 16th BRICS Summit and Makes an Important Statement*. https://www.mfa.gov.cn/eng/xw/zyxw/202410/t20241025_11516006.html

Nach, M., & Ncwadi, R. (2024). BRICS economic integration: Prospects and challenges. *The South African Journal of International Affairs*, *31*(2), 151–166. DOI: 10.1080/10220461.2024.2380676

O'Neill, A. (2024, 27 October). Import of goods into the BRICS countries from 2000 to 2023. *Statista.*https://www.statista.com/statistics/254307/import-of-the-bric-countries/#statisticContainer

O'Neill, A. (2025, 13 February). Gross domestic product (GDP) of the BRICS countries from 2000 to 2029. *Statista.*https://www.statista.com/statistics/254281/gdp-of-the-bric-countries/

Panda, J. (2024, 17 October). *India's BRICS Balancing Act*. United States Institute of Peace. https://www.usip.org/publications/2024/10/indias-brics-balancing-act

Schirm, S. A. (2023). Alternative World Orders? Russia's Ukraine War and the Domestic Politics of the BRICS. *The International Spectator*, *58*(3), 55–73. DOI: 10.1080/03932729.2023.2236937

Soong, J. J. (2021). The Political Economy of China's Rising Role in Regional International Organizations: Are There Strategies and Policies of the Chinese Way Considered and Applied? *Chinese Economy*, *55*(4), 243–254. DOI: 10.1080/10971475.2021.1972550

Soong, J. J. (2024). Opportunities and Challenges of China's Economic and Political Development Under the Third Term of Xi Leadership: Ascent of China's Dream? *Chinese Economy*, *58*(1), 1–16. DOI: 10.1080/10971475.2024.2373637

Teke, M. A. (2024, 23 Ekim). *16. BRICS Zirvesi (22-24 Ekim 2024)*. SETA. https://www.setav.org/5-soru/16-brics-zirvesi-22-24-ekim-2024

van der Westhuizen, J. (2024). Ukraine, the 2023 BRICS Summit and South Africa's non-alignment crisis. *Contemporary Security Policy*, *45*(4), 612–626. DOI: 10.1080/13523260.2024.2384007

Vayez, A. (2023, 23 August). Evolving Multilateralism: BRICS, the EU and Responses to the Russia-Ukraine Conflict. *Africa Policy Research Institute (APRI)*. DOI: https://doi.org/DOI: 10.59184/sa.028

XIII BRICS Summit- New Delhi Declaration. (2021, 9 October). https://infobrics.org/document/98/

Chapter 9
China and India in Africa:
Cooperation and Competition in Global South Health Strategies

Maziar Mozaffari Falarti
https://orcid.org/0000-0001-5305-8589
University of Tehran, Iran

Behzad Abdollahpour
https://orcid.org/0000-0002-8004-1878
Istanbul University, Turkey

ABSTRACT

This chapter examines the health strategies of China and India in Africa, using the geo-health strategy framework to integrate health diplomacy with geopolitical and economic objectives. It analyzes how China's Health Silk Road and India's Maitri Initiative leverage health interventions to expand influence in the Global South. China's state-led approach prioritizes medical infrastructure, vaccine diplomacy, and Traditional Chinese Medicine (TCM), while India's market-driven model focuses on affordable pharmaceuticals, digital health, and medical tourism. Despite promoting South-South cooperation, both nations intertwine humanitarian efforts with economic gains and strategic competition. The chapter argues that health diplomacy serves not only humanitarian goals but also functions as a geopolitical tool for reshaping power dynamics and challenging Western dominance in African healthcare sectors.

DOI: 10.4018/979-8-3373-0938-5.ch009

INTRODUCTION

China and India have significantly expanded their health strategies across Africa, intertwining health diplomacy with broader geopolitical and economic objectives. While previous analyses predominantly rely on soft power and health diplomacy frameworks (Nye, 2004; Fauci, 2007), these perspectives fail to comprehensively capture the strategic and economic underpinnings of their engagements. This study proposes the concept of "geo-health strategy" as a more holistic framework to explain how health initiatives serve as geopolitical tools to achieve broader strategic goals. Geo-health strategy integrates global health diplomacy with power dynamics, economic interests, and regional influence, revealing that health interventions are not solely humanitarian but can also reinforce geopolitical competition, economic advantage, and strategic balancing. In recent decades, the international relations landscape has undergone transformative changes, particularly regarding the roles of emerging powers like China and India in executing health diplomacy in Africa. The increasing prominence of health diplomacy within broader foreign policy agendas reflects the evolving dynamics of global governance, where health is no longer viewed merely as a humanitarian issue but as a strategic component of international relations (Adams et al., 2008; Mol et al., 2021). Both China and India have positioned themselves as critical players in addressing pressing health challenges on the continent while simultaneously competing for influence. As two of the most influential actors in the Global South, both nations have sought to expand their presence on the continent through health diplomacy, employing various approaches to improve public health infrastructure, provide medical assistance, and enhance pharmaceutical accessibility. These initiatives are not only driven by humanitarian concerns but also by broader strategic imperatives that seek to reshape power dynamics in Africa. While these efforts have contributed to addressing Africa's pressing health challenges, they have also fueled a competitive dynamic between China and India as they vie for geopolitical leverage (Cabana, 2014).

The rivalry between China and India in Africa's health sector is rooted in their broader foreign policy strategies that emphasize South-South cooperation (Grovogu, 2011). However, the motivations and mechanisms underlying their health diplomacy strategies differ significantly. China's Health Silk Road (HSR) initiative, a component of the Belt and Road Initiative (BRI), reflects a top-down, state-driven approach that integrates medical infrastructure development, pharmaceutical investments, vaccine diplomacy, and the promotion of Traditional Chinese Medicine (TCM) (Chan, 2024; Rolland, 2024). India, by contrast, adopts a more decentralized, market-oriented approach, leveraging its robust pharmaceutical industry, medical tourism, and digital health platforms such as the Maitri Initiative (MEA, 2020; PWC, 2020). This divergence highlights how both countries employ different models of health diplomacy to project influence, cultivate goodwill, and strengthen economic ties with African nations.

Despite the growing importance of health diplomacy, there exists a notable academic gap regarding the comparative analysis of health strategies deployed by China and India, particularly in the African context. While extensive literature discusses the broader geopolitical relations between these two countries, much less attention has been given to their specific health initiatives and the nuanced interplay of cooperation and competition within this domain. This chapter seeks to fill this gap by introducing the geo-health strategy framework, which allows for a more comprehensive understanding of how health diplomacy is intertwined with economic and strategic objectives. The geo-health strategy concept builds on existing scholarship by moving beyond the soft power paradigm and incorporating elements of geopolitical competition, economic interdependence, and strategic balancing (SWP, 2023).

The findings of this chapter hold significant scholarly importance, as they will not only enhance our understanding of Sino-Indian health diplomacy but also contribute to broader discussions on global health governance, South-South cooperation, and the shifting dynamics of global influence. By interrogating the health initiatives carried out by both nations, this chapter reveals how their respective approaches reflect larger foreign policy objectives, economic interests, and strategic aspirations. Additionally, it highlights how these health diplomacy efforts influence local health systems, foster economic dependency, and align with global health priorities, particularly in a post-pandemic context (Zhang, 2023). The geo-health strategy framework provides a critical lens through which to examine the intersection of health and geopolitics, offering new insights into the role of emerging powers in reshaping global health governance.

Moreover, the geo-health strategy framework underscores the dual nature of health interventions as both humanitarian and strategic tools. By integrating health diplomacy with broader geopolitical considerations, this framework challenges conventional understandings of health assistance as purely altruistic. Instead, it posits that health initiatives are often embedded within broader strategies aimed at securing economic gains, strengthening regional influence, and challenging the dominance of Western-led global health governance (Chipaike et al., 2023). This perspective is particularly relevant in the context of China and India's engagements in Africa, where health diplomacy serves as a mechanism for consolidating influence in a region that holds significant geopolitical and economic importance.

Ultimately, this chapter positions itself within the larger narrative of the book, which investigates the evolving dynamics of international health diplomacy and emerging powers. By situating the comparative analysis of China and India within these broader themes, we underscore the significance of geo-health strategy as an essential component of global engagement and a mechanism for achieving not only health equity but also geopolitical influence. This study not only seeks to contribute to academic scholarship but also aims to offer insights that may inform policymakers navigating the complexities of health diplomacy in an increasingly interconnected and competitive world.

LITERATURE REVIEW

Globalization and the rise of numerous global health issues have increased the significance of global health diplomacy. As a result, many countries, including China and India, have turned to health diplomacy to ensure their national and geopolitical interests. The centrality of health in geopolitics was highlighted in the Oslo Ministerial Declaration of 2007, which described global health as one of the most overlooked issues in foreign policy. Therefore, the signatories emphasized the need to consider a stronger and strategic role in international affairs (WHO, 2008). There are different ways to interpret the concept of global health diplomacy. Some scholars define it as a multi-level and multi- actor negotiation process that shapes the global policy environment for health (Kickbusch et al., 2007). Similarly, A. S. Fauci (2007) underlines it humanitarian aspect and depicting health diplomacy as an attempt to "winning the hearts and minds of people in poor countries by exporting medical care, expertise and personnel to help those who need it most." Similarly, some other scholars conceptualize it as a political shift aimed at enhancing health outcomes globally through international relations, especially in resource-limited areas. Their perspectives emphasize the necessity of cooperation among nations to tackle complex health issues (Adams et al., 2008). With that said, Mol et al (2021), identify four factors leading to the rise of global health diplomacy: strengthening health protection and public health; developing relations between nations and encouraging collaboration among various stakeholders to improve health; and (c) achieving equitable outcomes that align with poverty reduction and fairness. Therefore, health diplomacy in the works discussed above has been considered as a means of enhancing national reputation, establishing bilateral and multilateral alliances and suggesting moral leadership. Much of the literature in this regard also draws on Joseph Nye's concept of soft power, which put emphasis on the ability of states to "achieve goals through attraction rather than coercion" (Nye, 2004, p. x).With that said, soft power is closely linked with culture, political values, and ideology and health diplomacy. For instance, Mol and his colleagues argue that health diplomacy not only provides reciprocal benefits but also unifies the societies, offering a cooperative platform for countries to leverage their soft power in promoting multidimensional interests. International response to H5N1 (2007), H191 (2009), Ebola (2014), and the recent

COVID-19 pandemic have been some prime examples of successful global health diplomacy (Mol et al, 2021).

Complementing with soft power frameworks, global health diplomacy, focuses on how states and non-state actors use foreign policy tools to negotiate over global health objectives. In this regard, K. Lee and R. Smith (2011), D. Fidler (2005) and H. Feldbaum et al. (2010), have investigated the convergence of health and foreign policy, noting that health interventions increasingly fulfill two purposes: they meet humanitarian needs and advancing national interests. However, this literature often overlooks the perspectives and roles of emerging powers due to its frequent focuses on Western actors and international organizations such as the World Health Organization (WHO). Moreover, less focus is placed on the ways that health diplomacy appears in regions such as Africa, where local health systems are shaped by historical injustices, competing development paradigms and postcolonial dynamics.

This gap has been narrowed partially by the literature on South-South cooperation (SSC), which emphasized participation methods based on solidarity. Some scholars including S. Chaturvedi (2016), P. Riggirozzi and N. Yeates (2015), and E. Mawdsley (2012) focus on this issue and argue that how countries such as China and India establish their development ties with Africa through discourses of mutual benefit, shared historical struggle, and horizontal collaboration. However, even South-South cooperation literature still relies on idealistic cooperation, often overlooking strategic motivations and power imbalances within these relations. Furthermore, African perspectives- especially main African organizations such as African Union or the WHO Africa office- have been frequently marginalized, making it difficult to understand how recipient countries view and navigate health partnership. Considering this point, the chapter introduces the concept of geo-health strategy – a framework that encapsulates the way in which health interventions are used as instruments of cooperative diplomacy or soft power, as well as tools of geopolitical competition, economic leverage, and strategic realignment—this chapter expands upon and critiques these literatures. Unlike the existing approaches which consider health diplomacy as essentially cooperative or benevolent, the geo-health strategy framework highlights strategic considerations behind state-led health engagements especially in regions affected by conflict, such as certain parts of Africa. By combining aspects of competitiveness, economic interests, and regional influence, it enables more comprehensive analysis of China and India's health strategies. By doing so, this study fills the gap in literature including the need for a theoretical framework that address the marginalization of African actors, the absence of a structured comparative framework for Global South actors and links health to broader issues of international power dynamic. More details regarding this theoretical framework will be discussed in theoretical section.

China's Health Silk Road

China's Health Silk Road (HSR) initiative is one of the important pillars of Chinese foreign policy strategy that enables Beijing to expand its global health influence through expanding medical diplomacy, aid and technological infrastructure in developing countries. In fact medical aid has always played significant role in Chinese foreign policy and the roots of it traced back to 1960s when China provided medical assistance to developing countries especially in Africa (Chan, 2024). Later on, Chinese commitment to establish a healthy global community was depicted in a document published by the State Council in March 2015, in which five main axes of cooperation within BRI- "policy coordination, facilities connectivity, unimpeded trade, financial integration, and people-to-people bond"- were discussed (The State Council, 2015). The health sector was explicitly underlined as a key area for fostering deeper people-to-people connections between China and the rest of the world. The document clearly expressed China's intention to expand international cooperation "on epidemic information sharing, the exchange of prevention and treatment technologies and the training of medical professionals," which could enhance the "capability to jointly address public health emergencies" (The State Council, 2015). The document further mentioned that China seeks to provide the countries with "medical assistance and emergency medical aid", and "carry out practical cooperation in maternal and child health, disability rehabilitation, and major infectious diseases, including AIDS, tuberculosis, and malaria... [China] will also expand cooperation on traditional medicine" (The State Council, 2015). In October 2015, China's National Health Commission released a three-year plan drawing a roadmap for promoting health cooperation along the BRI (NHC, 2015). In fact, the plan sought to create a health cooperation network among the member countries of BRI by implementing relevant projects, which would both enhance China's soft power and its influence in global health governance (Rolland, 2024). As one of the least known component of China's broad Belt and Road Initiative (BRI), HSR pursues dual goals: domestically serves as a driving force to enhance the welfare and health of Chinese people and internationally it aims to improve the lives of people abroad especially those in the Global South (Chan, 2024).

Initially the term the Health Silk Road was introduced to international audiences in June 2016 when Xi Jinping had a speech at the Legislative Chamber of the Uzbek Supreme Assembly in Tashkent in which he highlighted the significance of building a "green, healthy, intelligent and peaceful Silk Road". He also asked for increasing cooperation in prevention of infectious disease, information sharing, traditional medicine and medical aids (Xinhua, 2016). In January 2017, during Xi's visit to the WHO headquarters in Geneva, China and WHO signed a memorandum of understanding on BRI health cooperation, which was referred by Chinese state media as a formal "pact" that solidified the foundation of the Health Silk Road (Baijie, 2017). A few months later, China sought to raise the international profile of HSR by holding various formal and international conferences and forums such as the first Belt and Road Forum in May 2017and the Belt and Road High-Level Meeting for Health Cooperation Conference in August 2017. About 300 important participants including representatives from international organizations such as WHO, the Gavi global vaccine alliance, the Global Fund and UNAIDS, senior health officials from 30 countries. Alongside these international representatives, Chinese officials and experts from health, industry and technological areas also attended the meeting. Medical cooperation, vaccines, scientific and technological innovation, maternal and child health, sustainable development in global health were among the main topics and issues of the meeting (The State Council, 2017).The Belt and Road Forum for Health Cooperation organized by Chinese helped to attract global attention towards the concept of the HSR. During the Conference, Tedros Adhanom Ghebreyesus, Director-General of the World Health Organization (WHO), gave a speech, entitled "Towards a Health Silk Road," in which he highlighted China's Health Silk Road as a means to strengthen and revive "ancient links between cultures and people, with health at its core." He further argues that the initiative encompasses "the fundamentals to achieve universal health coverage: infrastructure, access to medicines, human resources, and a platform to share experience and promote best practices" (WHO, 2017). At the end of the conference,key priorities for the HSR were outlined as follows: increasing medical aid in BRI countries, establishing health policy research centers and health industry alliance focusing on sustainable development, increasing cooperation in monitoring, prevention and responses of infectious diseases, increasing cooperation in training health professionals, boosting cooperation in medical R&D and the use of traditional medicine and finally supporting the role of WHO in global health governance and its reform process (NHC, 2017).

The proposal of the HSR evolved into a comprehensive multilateral initiative that sought to foster global health cooperation, integrating the policy measures that had previously been part of various international and domestic health strategies. Since its inception, China has focused on institutionalizing health cooperation within the HSR framework by organizing and supporting various regional health forums including the Silk Road Health Forum, China-ASEAN Health Forum, the China-Arab States Health Forum, and China-Central and Eastern European Countries Health Ministers Forum (Cao, 2020). All of these efforts were a part of China's health diplomacy before the emergence of COVID-19. The Covid-19 outbreak provided China with an opportunity to further advance international health cooperation under the banner of its grand BRI initiative. Again HSR gain global attention, especially in Western media when Xi Jinping referred to it during his phone call with Italy's Prime

Minister Giuseppe Conte in March 2020, in which Xi offered to send masks and medical supplies as Italy faced with a serious rise in COVID-19 cases (Kuo, 2020).

During the peak of the pandemic, China actively sought to promote the HSR as an essential component of its vision "community of shared future for mankind," which later evolved into the concept of "community of common health for mankind" (Rolland, 2024, p.6). In this regard, during his speech at the 73rd World Health Assembly in May 2020, Xi mentioned about the responsibility of China to ensure "not just the life and health of its own citizens, but also global public health" (SCIO, 2020). China's commitment to global health and building a global community of health for all was also emphasized in its June 2020 white paper entitled "Fighting Covid-19: China in Action" (SCIO, 2020a), and " the 14th Five-Year Plan for National Economic and Social Development and Long-Range Objectives for 2035" (The State Council, 2020).

China's Health Strategy in Africa

The long history of Chinese engagement in Africa traced back to the Bandung Conference of 1955 which was a turning point in south-south relations and create and opportunity for both Asian and African countries to foster anti-colonial solidarity and mutual economic cooperation between Asian and African states (Traoré, 2021). Therefore, the event laid ideological groundwork for two sides to establish long-term relations in the future. It was during 1960s that China's health strategy in Africa gained importance when Premier Zhou Enlai announced China's Eight Principles for Economic Aid and Technical Assistance at congress in Somalia which highlighted mutual benefit and unconditional assistance, helping the recipient countries to achieve self-reliance development. It also emphasized on prioritizing cost-effective projects with quick results and providing the local personnel with necessary skills and (China Daily, 2010). Some crucial factors such as American imperialism, the Soviet Union revisionism and China's exclusion from institutions like WHO and UN also motivated Chinese to increase their foothold in various regions such as Africa and Asia (Mangani et al., 2024). In this vein, in 1964 Zhou Enlai mentioned, "Our assistance to Asian and African countries is keenly important for our competition with the imperialists and revisionists for the middle strip. This is a critical link" (Wang & Sun, 2014, p.4).

In fact, the initial backbone of China's health strategy is shaped by the China-Africa Health Cooperation (CAHC) which is a broad framework constitutes a range of initiatives in public health systems and capacity building programs. Although the roots of CAHC traced back to 1963 when China sent some medical groups for the purpose of establishing diplomatic relations with African countries (Huang, 2014), currently it has been guided by the Forum on China-Africa Cooperation (FOCAC) which was launched in 2000. Through FOCAC initiatives, China has established various cooperation programs to enhance healthcare system in Africa, including African Human Resources Development Fund in 2000, the First China-Africa Forum on Traditional Medicine in 2002, and the $5 billion China-Africa Development Fund in 2006. In 2013, in order to commemorate the 50th anniversary of its first medical team sent to Algeria in 1963, China launched the First Ministerial Forum on China-Africa Health Development (Zhou & Ma, 2022). All of these initiatives suggest China's commitment to improve healthcare systems and capacity building in African countries.

Later on China evolved the CAHC into the China's Public Health Engagement (CPHE), which is more comprehensive and broad version of it highlighting global health governance, public health infrastructure, and epidemic response. While CAHC merely serves as a tool of diplomatic and medical aid, CPHE increase China's role in global health security. Furthermore, CPHE focuses on China-led multilateral initiatives usually involves various international actors and organizations and serves as "a part of China's global diplomatic strategy towards both Global South and Global North countries (Gao & Xu, 2023). Below the main components of China's health strategy in Africa will be discussed.

Medical Assistance and Infrastructure

Sending medical team abroad has been the first step of Chinese health strategy towards African continent. In 1963 at the request of Algeria to enhance its fractured medical system, China sent a team of 13 medical experts, supplies and equipment to help Algerians to develop an efficient health care system (Youde, 2010).Between 1963 and 1978, China's health aid strategy was characterized by a strong emphasis on preventive primary healthcare rather than emergency care, alongside efforts to strengthen local health infrastructure. Furthermore, Chinese medical teams—commonly referred to as 'barefoot doctors'—played a significant role in enhancing China's image across the African continent. These teams operated in impoverished and underdeveloped communities in countries such as Tanganyika, Zanzibar, Algeria, Mali, Guinea, Congo-Brazzaville, and Somalia, providing essential healthcare services while symbolizing China's commitment to South-South solidarity and developmental assistance. Meanwhile, Chinese government also actively supported aid projects to build various hospitals in African countries (Killeen et al., 2018).

In October 2000, Sino-African cooperation in the field of health experienced another important change. China within the framework of the China–Africa Cooperation Forum (CACF) pledged to increase its aid to Africa in key sectors like health, allocate $37 million for malaria treatment, including funding for anti-malarial drugs and construct at least 30 hospitals across the continent (Mangani et al., 2024). In the early 2000s, China began to launch a program to combat malaria in Africa in which some Chinese pharmaceutical companies supply anti-malarial drugs to African countries. Meanwhile, the Chinese government designated the Jiangsu Centre for Verminosis Control and Prevention as a global hub for malaria-related human resource development. The center has run various programs in training around 170 medical officials from 43 African countries, arranged, and implemented two anti-malaria programs in Cameroon, Kenya, and Madagascar (Anshan, 2022).In 2014, immediately after the Ebola crisis broke out in Western countries of Africa, China sent some groups of medical teams to three West African countries in which there were many Ebola cases and invested about US$102 million (Huang, 2017). After the Ebola Epidemic, as important elements of China-Africa cooperation, public health programs and medical teams are included in the Beijing Action Plan (2019–2021) the Forum on China-Africa Cooperation (FOCAC) (China International Development Cooperation Agency, 2018). Between 2010 and 2012, China completed the construction of China-Zimbabwe Friendship Hospital in Mahusekwa, and between 2013 and 2016, it modernized the General Hospital of Gagnoa in the Ivory Coast, the Tanzanian Abdulla Mzee Hospital and other facilities (Killeen et al., 2018).

With the emergence of COVID-19 emergence, Chinese health initiatives gave global attentions specifically in African countries. Considering as the first country in the world to hold an anti-epidemic summit with Africa in June 2020, China arranged the "Extraordinary China-Africa Summit on Solidarity against COVID". In the summit, China pledged to share its experiences with African countries and emphasize its commitment to help by providing medical aid and infrastructure, facilitating African hospitals and sending medical teams of experts to this continent (Zhang, 2023).At the opening ceremony of the Eighth FOCAC Ministerial Conference in 2021, Xi announced that China and Africa would jointly fight COVID-19 and Beijing would ensure the accessibility and affordability of vaccines, medical infrastructures and health experts in Africa (Zhou & Ma, 2022). In addition to Chinese government, Chinese Private Own Enterprises (POEs) also provided a large number of medical aid and donations to African countries during the recent pandemic. For instance, on March 22, 2020, the Jack Ma Foundation and Alibaba Foundation senta total of 5.4 million masks, 54 thousand protective clothing, 5.4 thousand face shields, and 1.08 million testing kits to African countries (Habibi & Zhu, 2021). On April 6, 2020, the two foundations sent their second medical cargo to all 54 African countries which included "500 ventilators, 200,000 suits and face shields, 2,000 thermometers, a million swabs and extraction kits, and 500,000 gloves" (Xinhua, 2020).

Overall, China's medical assistance and infrastructure development in Africa embody its comprehensive approach to health strategy through its commitments to develop Africa's health system, support-training programs to train local medical experts and modernizing medical infrastructure. China's unprecedented medical assistance during the pandemic especially towards African countries was dubbed 'mask diplomacy' by scholars which sought to enhance China's global image, expand its political and alliance and boost its influence in multinational institutions. Additionally, mask diplomacy enabled Beijing to position itself as a responsible and pragmatic global leader contrasted with Western inaction during the Pandemic (Wong, 2020; ERI, 2020). However, China avoids using mask diplomacy for its medical aid for African regions, since the term describes Chinese humanitarian aid as opportunistic (Habibi & Zhu, 2021).

Pharmaceutical and Vaccine Diplomacy

Pharmaceutical and Vaccine Diplomacy in Africa has emerged as an important aspect of Chinese policies to address critical health issues in global south countries including African countries. The high cost of medicine in Africa which is due to its heavy reliance on imported drugs, encouraged Chinese pharmaceutical companies to expand their footprint in the African countries. Between 2019 and 2021, China exported a large variety of pharmaceutical products with total value of US$ 791.907, US$ 884, 406, and US$ 2,884,777 in 2019, 2020 and 2021 respectively. In addition to this increase in pharmaceutical exports in general, Chinese exports of products aimed at fighting with the recent pandemic saw a notable increase with their total value reaching US$ 601.670 in 2020 and increasing to US$ 4.436.004(Júnior& Dugo, 2023).

In the Forum on China-Africa Cooperation Beijing Action Plan (2025-2027) on September 2024, China announced that it sought to increase its investments in Africa's pharmaceutical sector, and help to enhance "pharmaceutical production and the medical equipment industry in Africa including access to active pharmaceutical ingredients (API) through co-investment by Chinese and African private sectors". Therefore, Africa's medical sovereignty would be ensured by reducing its reliance on imported medicines and medical equipment. China will continue to encourage and support Chinese private enterprises in investing in Africa's pharmaceutical industry (MFA, 2024). The same year, Shanghai Fosun Pharmaceutical began to construct a plant in Côte d'Ivoire to produce antibiotics and anti-malarial drugs expected to produce 5 billion tablets annually and created 1,000 jobs once operational. Similarly, Jijia International Medical Technology collaborated with Zambia to establish an oral cholera vaccine facility, making Zambia the first African country to produce this vaccine (Xinhua, 2024a).

Closely aligned with China's health strategy in Africa, China's vaccine diplomacy increased its footprint in Africa through helping African instates to sustain their vaccination campaigns during the pandemic era, which further bolstered its relations with its African partners and simultaneously sent this message to its rivals that Africa fell within its sphere of influence (Chipaike et al., 2023).China's commitment to help its African partners combat with combat the pandemic reached its peak with the massive donation of vaccines to this continent. In 2020, Egypt has received 100,000 doses of COVID-19 vaccines produced by Chinese Sinopharm Group (Nyabiage, 2020). In addition, during the 8th FOCAC ministerial conference, China pledged to provide African countries with "one billion doses of vaccines" which would include"600 million doses as donation and 400 million doses to be provided through... joint production by Chinese companies and relevant African countries" (FOCAC, 2021).

China's pharmaceutical and vaccine diplomacy in Africa exemplify a multifaceted strategy that combines geopolitical ambitions with humanitarian aid, which would not only reinforced Beijing's diplomatic relations with its African partners but also pave the way for economic and political cooperation. In this vein, some scholars believe that China's medical aid and vaccines donations to Africa serve as a diplomatic weapon sought to open "new markets, as the action of a responsible power as well as an act of moral service to humanity in the context of a global crisis" (Chipaike et al., 2023, p. 11).

Tradition Chinese Medicine (TCM) Promotion

TCM is another important component of China's health strategy to build diplomatic relations with African countries and develop their healthcare system. According to WHO, the majority of Africans rely on traditional medicine for their primary healthcare (WHO, 2025). With that said, it is not surprising that the ancient Chinese medicine is gaining popularity among African people (Environmental Investigation Agency, 2021). Under Xi's leadership, the Chinese government has strongly emphasized the importance of TCM both domestically and internationally, while implementing more than 30 policy measures since the 18th Party Congress in 2012 (Rolland, 2024). The first White Paper on TCM released by the State Council on December 12, 2016, depicting it "equal status" with Western medicine "in terms of ideological understanding, legal status, academic development, and practical application" (The State Council, 2016). The document concludes with an emphasis on the introduction of TCM to the world in order to "explore a new model of healthcare to improve the well-being of all people of the world, and make a full contribution to global progress and a brighter future for mankind" (The State Council, 2016). Similarly, the Chinese government purposed "TCM Belt and Road Development Plan (2016-2020)" to promote the international use of TCM, with African countries as a major focus. A typical example was the China-Mauritius Chinese Medicine Center, which began operations at the end of 2019, becoming the first platform in Africa that focus on promoting the TCM (Habibi & Zhu, 2021). The center was established through collaborative efforts between the Yueyang Chinese and Western Medicine Hospital-affiliated with the Shanghai University of TCM- and the Mauritius City Medical Group. Providing TCM assistance to African countries, China seeks to make TCM better known and enhance the acceptance of TCM, while also facilitating the sales and outbound investment of Chinese pharmaceutical firms in this field (Habibi & Zhu, 2021).

China's promotion of TCM also suggests a sense of nationalistic pride, one that differentiates itself from the dominance of Western medicine. Official plans to promote TCM highlight its role in shaping China's global image, depicting it as a symbol of the nation's remarkable "contributions to human health." Related with China's national objective, TCM is depicted as a "beautiful business card for China on the international stage," a "carrier to spread Chinese traditional culture," and an "international language to tell Chinese stories" in the related Chinese documents (Rolland, 2024, p. 17). If the rationale of China's grand strategy can be understood as an effort to create a Sino-centric subsystem that excludes Western powers and focuses on the emerging and developing world, then Beijing's insistence on promoting a non-Western medical tradition makes sense. Countries of the global South may also be sensitive to the appeal of practicing traditional medicine (Rolland, 2020).

In sum, the expansion of TCM in Africa has constituted a key aspect of Sino-African relations, driven by China's broad geopolitical and national strategies including BRI. The outbreak of COVID-19 accelerated this momentum, as Beijing promoted TCM as an effective healthcare solution and increase its presence in the continent (Environmental Investigation Agency, 2021).

Telemedicine and Digital Health

The last component of Chinese health strategy is telemedicine and digital health. Telemedicine- also known as telehealth, digital health or e-health - is the use of technology and healthcare system remotely which transformed the healthcare systems and services such as " internet hospitals, online sales of drugs, artificial intelligence (AI)-based medical devices, big data, and medical robots, among other inventions and innovations" (Chen, 2024, p.16). During the pandemic, China has supplied African countries and many other countries with digital information technologies to improve their healthcare systems. Among these technologies are "the applications of big data, cloud computing, and advanced digital telecommunication technologies for containing the pandemic". Tele-medicine, for instance, has been widely used during the recent pandemic due to travel restrictions, social distancing, and physician shortages all over the world. Hence, China resorted to tele-medicine to address these challenges in Africa and help them to solve the problems (Habibi & Zhu, 2021, p. 12). According to a report released by Zhejiang Normal University, China's telemedicine assistance in Africa began in 2017, and in early 2019, a remote consultation platform at Maputo Central Hospital in Mozambique was established by China Huaxi Hospital, affiliated with Sichuan University (Zhejiang Normal University, 2020).

Chinese POEs also played a significant role in providing tele-medicine services to Africa during the pandemic. Shortly after the outbreak of the COVID-19, the Jack Ma Foundation and Alibaba Group established a major telemedicine platform called Global MediXchange for Combating COVID-19 (GMCC), to provide healthcare providers and doctors in the world with Chinese medical expertise. The platform is closely related with Alibaba's healthcare division, Ali Health, as well as its cloud computing and artificial intelligence provide, Alibaba Cloud (Habibi & Zhu, 2021). On April 15, 2020, Ali Health, in cooperation with the Sir Run-Run Shaw Hospital (SRRSH), affiliated with Zhejiang University School of Medicine, held a video conference with over 40 directors of 40 Rwandan hospital directors and Rwanda's Minister of Health, Daniel Ngamije. The discussion held through GMCC, focused on anti-pandemic strategies. Furthermore, in this video conference China's medical experts "shared their experience and knowledge about containing COVID-19, in various fields such as hospital management, emergency treatment, COVID-19 testing, quarantine measures, and training of medical personnel" (Habibi & Zhu, 2021, p. 13). By the end of April 2020, the Jack Ma Foundation and Ali Health had arranged six training sessions on GMCC for African medical teams and experts to enhance their preparedness for the pandemic treatment and containment (Forbes, 2020).

China's Health Strategy in the Cases of Ethiopia, Kenya and Nigeria

This section examines the cases of Ethiopia, Kenya, and Nigeria to elucidate China's broader health strategy in Africa, with specific attention to its implementation in these three countries. By highlighting China's multifaceted engagements—ranging from infrastructure development and medical assistance to capacity building, pharmaceutical manufacturing cooperation, Traditional Chinese Medicine (TCM), and digital health promotion—this analysis underscores key dimensions of China's global health diplomacy in the African context. Furthermore, such an examination offers valuable insights into the potential impact of these cooperative efforts on the resilience and sustainability of healthcare systems in the recipient states. The discussion below provides a detailed account of China's health-related initiatives in each country and reflects on the broader implications of these strategic engagements.

Ethiopia

The roots of collaboration between Ethiopia and China in healthcare sector traced back 1974, and since then China has sent medical experts to Ethiopia and help it to enhance its healthcare system. During the recent pandemic, China was the first nation sends several medical teams, supplies and equipment to help Ethiopian people (Fana Broadcasting Corporate, 2024). In September 2017, the Addis Ababa Silk Road General Hospital- the first privately funded Chinese hospital in East Africa-was established in Ethiopia under the Belt and Road healthcare infrastructure project financed by the Chinese private enterprise Seychelles Afei Holding Co., Ltd. (Xinhua, 2017). A landmark project which symbolized Sino-African friendship was the construction of a new headquarters for the Africa Centre for Disease Control and Prevention(Africa CDC) in Addis Ababa agreed upon at the FOCAC summit held in Beijing in 2018 and was fully funded by China (Global Times, 2023). The first phase of it was completed in January 2023 and constituted various biological and modern medical facilities which would help African countries, especially Ethiopia to better monitor and manage outbreaks (Global Times, 2023).In addition to government collaborations, Chinese Private Own Enterprises (POEs) have also been playing a critical role in enhancing healthcare system, particularly through sharing knowledge and facilitating technology transfer. In the context of HSR China expand health infrastructure in African countries to increase the presence of pharmaceutical firms in this continents, which sought to produce "low-priced and efficient drugs" (Mangani et al., 2024, p.498). In 2018, Chinese company SanSheng Pharmaceutical, which is known for producing and supplying antibiotics in Africa, Fosun Pharma, based in Shanghai, and POE Neusoft Medical Systems Company were established their branches in Ethiopia to develop its healthcare system, manufacturing medical products and reduce Ethiopian's reliance on imported drugs (Mangani et al., 2024; Xinhua, 2024). Align with China's health diplomacy, by 2022, as one of its important partners in Africa; China donated 10 million vaccine doses to Ethiopia, which played crucial role in Ethiopia's efforts to combat with the COVID-19 (The State Council, 2022). More broadly, through its vaccine diplomacy, Beijing not only strengthened its cooperation with Ethiopia in public health but also indicated its commitment to global health by practical and tangible actions.

The emergence of COVID-19 accelerated the widespread usage of telemedicine and digital health, enabling the physicians to provide health services more efficiently. In this regard, China has been actively involved in enhancing the medical technology and quality of healthcare system in Ethiopia (yidaiyilu, 2023). As for Traditional Chinese Medicine (TCM), which has gained popularity among African countries due to its effectiveness and affordability, China and Ethiopia signed several agreements to expand their cooperation in TCM since it can play an important role in pandemic preparedness and response and received widely by local Africans (consider as an alternative medical option that could be combined with African herbal medicine). Although there are some challenges, such as lack of objectives standards for evaluating and monitoring the quality and quantity of active ingredient content (Liu & Zhang, 2024).

Kenya

Like its other African partners, during the recent pandemic, China began to support Kenya in public health section. In 2020, through the Organization of African First Ladies for Development, China provides Kenya with medical aid and equipment. The donation was offered on behalf of China's First Lady, Peng Liyuan, to support Kenya's Beyond Zero Initiative, which sought to improve "maternal and child health in Kenya", and "reduce new HIV infections among children" (FOCAC,2020). The Chinese embassy highlighted the long-standing partnership between the two countries and emphasized China's commitment in supporting Kenyan people during the COVID-19 crisis and enhancing their healthcare system (FOCAC, 2020). Aligned with its medical aid and infrastructure development, between 2020 and 2021, China allocated $1 million for newborn and Child health projects, implemented by UNICEF and sought to provide medical services, equipment and medicine for 3 million people at less developed regions of Kenya. Cooperating with UNICEF under South-South Cooperation in enhancing healthcare systems, China positioned itself as an important factor in reducing maternal and child mortality rates as well as malaria in African regions particularly in Kenya (Xinhua, 2022).Many Chinese pharmaceutical companies are actively operating in the country, and China has launched several anti-malaria training programs and workshops, particularly in regions where malaria remains prevalent. For instance, in 2021, 6.7 million malaria cases and 4,000 deaths were reported in Kenya, but the fatalities among severely ill children reduced significantly due to malaria injection drugs provided and distributed by Chinese pharmaceutical companies (Xinhua, 2023). In 2022, China pledged to donate about 10 million doses of vaccine to this country which according to Chinese authorities was a part of Beijing's plan of providing one billion doses of vaccines to the African continent (Ayega, 2022).

During the pandemic, China helped Kenya to launch Africa's first telemedicine technology center at Kenyatta National Hospital (KNH) for COVID-19 detection. The hospital equipped with modern medical technology using AI, big data, and connectivity to provide effective health services to the people. Nicholas Gumbo, the Chairman of KNH highlighted Kenya's commitment to fighting the pandemic and expressed gratitude for China's government for their supports and cooperation in developing medical infrastructure of Kenya (China daily, 2020). Moreover, China, through Huawei, has played significant role in developing telemedicine in Kenya by enhancing fiber optic network and national data center in Kenya to secure video health consultations. Huawei introduced the IdeaHub, which is a smart touch-screen device with built-in videoconferencing, helping doctors to talk and see patients remotely, share medical documents, and provide specialist care to various regions across the country. It has enhanced healthcare accessibility, and medical training for local professionals, and led to the expansion of telemedicine services across Kenya (Huawei, 2025).

China and Kenya are also increasing their cooperation in Traditional Chinese Medicine (TCM), a prime example of this was the agreement signed by Shandong University of Traditional Chinese Medicine and Kenyatta University in 2023 to create China-Kenya Traditional Chinese Medicine Center which would focus on joint research, sharing knowledge and expertise integrating herbal medicine into Kenya's healthcare system and herbal medicine development under China's Belt and Road Initiative (Gao, 2023).

Nigeria

As the most populous country in Africa, Nigeria faces serious challenges in public health and medical infrastructure. Therefore, health sector has been one of the major issues in the agreements between the two countries. At 2006 China-Africa Cooperation Forum (FOCAC) held in Beijing, China announced to increase its co-operation with African countries, including Nigeria to provide timely assistant in the prevention of and treatment of Ebola, malaria, HIV/AIDS and other infectious diseases (FOCAC, 2006).China has played a significant role in improving Nigeria's healthcare system and infrastructure through significant aid and investment. In July 2012, the two countries deepened their cooperation in maternal and child health programs, such as the prevention of mother-to-child transmission of HIV/AIDS and immunization (People's Daily, 2013). In 2013, China funded and constructed the China-Nigeria Friendship Hospital with an investment of over $12 million. In addition, China held provide short-term training for doctors, nurses, and hospital managers, reflecting its broader commitment to strengthening Nigeria's healthcare sector (People's Daily, 2013). During the pandemic, China also helped Nigeria to construct the country's largest makeshift hospital located in Abuja in 2020, which further suggested China's commitment to support Nigeria's healthcare infrastructure during the crisis (Global Times, 2020), and in 2021, China donated 470,000 doses of COVID-19to Nigeria to fight against the virus (CGTN, 2021). Although China has committed to expand telemedicine and digital health in African countries, the direct examples of China's telemedicine projects in Nigeria are so scarce and considering

China's involvement in this field across most African countries, it is likely that the two nations will expand their cooperation in this field in the future.

As a part of China's health strategy, TCM has become an important aspect of China-Nigeria medical cooperation. Nigeria's agreement with Shijiazhuang Yiling Pharmaceutical Co., Ltd. enables the sale and hospital use of four registered TCM products. This partnership highlights China's role and commitment in Nigeria's healthcare sector and promotes TCM as a complementary treatment (Xinhua, 2023a).

India's Maitri Initiative

The *Vaccine Maitri* initiative or *Maitri initiative* (Vaccine Friendship) emerged as part of India's commitment to global solidarity in tackling the COVID-19 crisis. Its foundation was laid in September 2020, when India's Prime Minister Narendra Modi, in his virtual address to the UN General Assembly, emphasized that India's vaccine production and distribution capacity would serve humanity. Officially launched in January 2021, the initiative primarily prioritized India's neighboring nations include Bangladesh, Nepal, Maldives, Sri Lanka, Bhutan, Myanmar before extending to Mauritius, Seychelles, and other countries (Consulate General of India, 2021). Inspired by ancient Indian philosophy of 'Vasudhaiva Kutumbakam' (the world is one family), this humanitarian initiative seek to further highlight India's spirit of responsibility and compassion, its commitment to provide affordable vaccines, and ensure global immunization specifically during the recent pandemic crisis (MEA, 2020). Under this initiative, India distributed millions of vaccines to low- and middle-income countries, advocated against vaccine nationalism, and asked for international cooperation to ensure global access to vaccine (MP-IDSA, 2021). The Maitri Initiative also facilitated the global distribution of Made-in-India COVID-19 vaccines, providing it either free of cost or at an affordable prices. The key vaccines under this initiative include the Oxford-AstraZeneca vaccine produced by the Serum Institute of India and Covaxin, developed by Bharat Biotech, and Covishield (MP-IDSA, 2021). In fact, through Vaccine Maitri, India positioned itself as the "Pharmacy of the World" and supplied vaccines and essential medical aid to less developed countries, and thereby enhancing its soft power image in its health diplomacy. With that said, the initiative was received warmly by global leaders especially the US (Ramachandran, 2021). Moreover, India's Vaccine Maitri initiative has made significant contributions globally, with over 65 million doses sent to more than 70 countries during the pandemic. It enhanced India's diplomatic standing, receiving recognition from the WTO, and support of various countries- 79 Members from African-Caribbean-Pacific Group (ACP) and the 15 Members from Caribbean Community (CARICOM) for facilitating vaccine supply for the countries in need. Additionally, India donated 200,000 doses to UN peacekeeping forces which suggested its commitment to global health (Verma, 2021).

Through Vaccine Maitri, India also sought to counter China's vaccine diplomacy in South Asian and African region in which the two nations compete for dominance (Ramachandran, 2021). However, the temporary suspension of the Vaccine Maitri initiative during the second pandemic wave in the first half of 2021, left India's neighbors' in South Asia and Africa without vaccine supplies which provide an opportunity for China to increase its increase in these regions (Banerji, 2021; Koller et al,. 2021).

Overall, India's Vaccine Maitri initiative served as a humanitarian effort, providing affordable vaccines to less developed countries while reinforcing its soft power and diplomatic ties. It also could also serve as a geopolitical strategy to counter China's vaccine diplomacy, accelerated the momentum of economic and pharmaceutical leadership, showcasing its capability as the "Pharmacy of the World."

India's Health Strategy in Africa

India and Africa have deep historical, cultural and economic relations shaped by centuries of exchange and interaction. Today nearly three million people of Indian descent live in African countries contributing to the deep connection between Indian and African nations. After China, India has been Africa's second-largest trading partner and maintains strong relations with Southern and East Africa, where large Indian communities have families on both continents (Volodin, 2023). India's health engagement with African people dates back to the late 19th century when Indian doctors brought by the British to provide healthcare services to Indian labors working on Uganda Railway. Later on, as the British administration in Kenya solidified, Indian doctors played significant role in enhancing public health and epidemic control in Kenya (Greenwood & Topiwala, 2015). Having such historical footprint in Africa during the colonial period, India solidifies its relations with Africa states in health sector by adopting a multifaceted health strategy based on improving medical infrastructure, medical tourism, capacity building, and access to affordable medicine (Export-Import Bank of India, 2021). The two nations further deepen their collaboration during the third India-Africa Forum Summit (IAFS) in 2015, where both regions committed to sharing expertise and knowledge about enhancing public healthcare, and tackling diseases such as Malaria, HIV, Polio, Ebola and TB (MEA, 2015). Furthermore, In the Summit India committed $100 million to the India-Africa Development Fund and $10 million to the India-Africa Health Fund (Export-Import Bank of India, 2021). To further reinforce this cooperation, in his July 2018 address to the Ugandan Parliament, Modi mentioned ten guiding principles for India-Africa engagement. One of the important principles he referred to was leveraging India's digital expertise to improve Africa's healthcare and education systems. This health diplomacy fits with Africa's Agenda 2063 and the Sustainable Development Goals, making it a backbone of India-Africa relations that requires continued strengthening (Export-Import Bank of India, 2021).Besides The India-Africa Forum Summit (IAFS) which has played a key role in expanding cooperation between the two nations in various fields including health sector, India Africa Health Sciences Meet (IAHSM) which is a collaborative platform between India and African countries for strengthening capabilities and knowledge sharing in health sector (Bajpai & Wadhwa, 2021). The first India-Africa Health Sciences Meet (IAHSM) was held in New Delhi in September 2016 by the Indian Council of Medical Research (ICMR), in collaboration with the Ministry of External Affairs, other key Indian ministries, and African regional scientific and research organizations. During the event, the two sides agreed to strengthen their cooperation in biomedical research, as well as the development of indigenous and affordable medicine and vaccine (PWC, 2020). The same year, in order to further strengthen health relations between the two nations, Council of Medical Research (ICMR) established the India-Africa Health Sciences Collaborative Platform (IAHSP). The initiative was formalized through a Memorandum of Understanding between the Indian Council of Medical Research (ICMR) and the African Union, signed on March 27, 2019 which emphasized cooperation in improving joint research and development (R&D), capacity building, healthcare services, pharmaceutical trade and manufacturing of drugs (MEA, 2019). To gain a clear understanding of India's health strategy in Africa, its main components will be discussed below.

Medical Assistance and Infrastructure

HIV/AIDS has been considered as a serious public health challenge and a prevalent cause of premature death in many African countries. Hence, India has prioritized these issues in its health diplomacy towards Africa. For instance, in response to crises like AIDS and malaria in some African countries including Sierra Leone, Liberia, and Guinea, India provided financial aid, including contributions to the UN Secretary-General's Ebola Response Multi-Partner Trust Fund (Mol et al., 2022). In addition, India has provided medicines and medical equipment to enhance Africa's healthcare systems. In 2016, it pledged one ton of medicines over three years to support Namibia's health initiatives under the "Harambee Prosperity Plan" (Mol et al., 2022).Similar to China, much of India's development assistance in health has focused on modernizing and improving healthcare infrastructure in African countries. It has constructed various hospitals, clinics and medical schools in the continent and has utilized its expertise in information and communications technology to link hospitals and universities in West Africa with their Indian counterparts through the

Pan-African e-Network, facilitating knowledge sharing and best practices exchange (Huang, 2013).At the52nd African Development Bank (AfDB) Annual Meetings in India in 2017, Ministers from Burundi, Egypt, Mozambique, Tanzania, and the Seychelles sought stronger partnerships with India to improve and modernize their healthcare systems and medical infrastructure. India signed agreements with these countries to support them in the abovementioned fields particularly in drug administration, diagnostics, surgeries, and hospital management and put emphasis on addressing major health challenges such as cancer through South-South cooperation (African Development Bank Group, 2017). A prime example of India's role in constructing hospitals in Africa is the Indo-Guinea Friendship Hospital, a 300-bed facility in Conakry constructed with a $10 million investment (Embassy of India in Abidjan, 2019). Some Indian hospitals such as Dr. Agarwal's Eye Hospitals are present in some African countries-Nigeria, Uganda, Kenya, Zambia, Madagascar, Ghana, Tanzania, Rwanda Mozambique -and provide them essential health services (Export-Import Bank of India, 2021).

During the COVID-19 pandemic, India provided medical aid to some African countries such Mauritius, Madagascar, Comoros, and Seychelles under the SAGAR initiative. It sent essential medicines, medical teams, and protective equipment through its Navy (MEA, 2020a).The Indian medical teams associated with military, visited local hospitals in these countries, and provide the locals with required techniques and knowledge of fighting with COVID-19 (Mol et al., 2022). Unlike China, which resorted to conventional channels to send medical teams and equipment, India send them through its military (Júnior & Dugo, 2023). Furthermore, Indian private hospitals have also played significant role in improving African healthcare system. For instance, since 2003, Indian Appollo hospitals have provided Ghana and Nigeria with consulting services, medical facilities and aid. In addition, medical doctors from more than 20 African countries have been trained at Appollo hospitals (Mol et al., 2022).

Pharmaceutical and Vaccine Diplomacy

Considering as the "Pharmacy of the World" due to its key role in the global pharmaceutical industry, particularly in supplying affordable vaccines and medicines, India supplies more than 50% of global demand for various vaccines, 40% of generic demand in the US and 25% of all medicine in the UK. In addition, India's domestic pharmaceutical industry "includes a network of 3000 plus drug companies and more that 10000 manufacturing units" (Department of Pharmaceutical, 2023).As strong generic pharmaceutical industry, India has gained the trust of the Africans through supplying affordable medicines conforming to the standard qualities of global markets (Dhar, 2021). For instance with the outbreak of HIV/AIDS in 1990s, when major pharmaceutical companies had demanded very high prices for antiretroviral medicines, Indian pharmaceutical companies provided them to African nations at significantly lower and more affordable prices (Dhar & Gopakumar, 2020). Several major Indian pharmaceutical companies, such Cipla Ltd., Ranbaxy Laboratories, Dr. Reddy's Laboratories, Glenmark Pharmaceuticals, IPCA Laboratories, Parenteral Drugs, Emcure Pharmaceutical Ltd., Aurobindo Pharma Ltd., J B Chemicals, Cadila Healthcare, Lupin Ltd., and Intas Pharmaceutical Ltd., have established subsidiaries in Africa and enhanced their image in African markets bysupplying affordable generic medicines (Volodin, 2023). In addition, these Indian companies play significant role in Africa's healthcare sector by locally producing medicines and medical devices, creating jobs, and enhancing capacity (Volodin, 2023). With that said Africa's vast and profitable pharmaceutical markets offer both India and China with opportunities to expand their presence in the region. While India remains a major pharmaceutical exporter with its leading generic drug industry and the highest number of FDA-approved facilities, China is also actively engaged in this sector. However, realizing the challenges of competing in such regulated markets, China seeks to focus on establishing local production facilities to strengthen its position in Africa's healthcare sector (Volodin, 2023). Like China, COVID-19 gave India and opportunity to deepen its ties with Africans and win the heart of African people. Under its "Vaccine Maitri" program, India donated millions of doses of the COVID-19 vaccine to African countries, and Seychelles was the first African country to receive the Indian made vaccines. In fact, India donated more than 25 million doses of vaccines produced in India to 41 African nations, including about 1 million as a donation to 16 countries and over 16 million through the COVAX to 33 countries (Choudhary, 2021).With the outbreak of the pandemic, India's overall pharmaceutical exports to the African countries saw steady growth, reaching US$ 3,178,823 in 2019, US$ 3,529,692 in 2020, and US$ 3,907,093 in 2021. As for the value of its pandemic-related items, it stood at US$ 747,868 in 2020 and increased to US$ 926,624 in 2021 (Júnior & Dugo, 2023).

In sum, India's pharmaceutical and vaccine diplomacy play a crucial role in its health strategy in Africa, where it provides affordable medicines and vaccines. Leveraging its strong generic pharmaceutical industry and initiatives such as "Vaccine Maitri," India has not only increased its presence in Africa but also reinforced its commitment to international health efforts, supporting countries with limited access to essential healthcare.

Medical Tourism

Medical tourism has been one of the important components of India's health strategy in Africa. According to the Ministry of Tourism (2023), a significant number of visitors from around the world traveled to India for medical purposes, including 22.7% from West Asia, 21.2% from Africa, and 19.8% from South Asia. Despite the challenges caused by the COVID-19 pandemic, India's medical tourism market suggested resilience, reaching an estimated value of USD 7.69 billion in 2024. The future forecast indicates significant growth ahead, with the expectation to rise to USD 14.31 billion by 2029 (Times of India, 2024). With its state-of-the-art medical facilities, high quality and affordable medical services, India has emerged as an important destination for medical tourism, particularly among African nations (PWC, 2020). Encouraged by the growing number of patients, the Indian government has facilitated the visa process for several African countries and established the "National Medical & Wellness Tourism Promotion Board". The board consists of representatives from various government agencies, tourism industry and hospital chains addressing challenges in the health and tourism sectors while serving as a bridge between different health systems and supporting Indian private companies seeking investment in health infrastructure (Vaidyanathan, 2019).In 2021, Indian authorities introduced a special *Ayush visa* for those seeking traditional treatments like Ayurveda. Similarly, in 2022, Indian government launched "Heal in India" campaign to attract more international patients and boost medical tourism (Times of India, 2024). In May 2022, the Indian Embassy in Angola organized an event entitled "India – the Medical Tourism Destination for Angolans" to promote medical tourism between the two nations, foster joint initiatives in healthcare section and raise awareness among Angolans about the existence of modern medical facilities in India for those in need (Parkar, 2022).

By investing in Africa's healthcare infrastructure and telemedicine services, India is expanding its medical tourism in this continent. It also trains African doctors, facilitate knowledge exchange with local medical team and cooperate with India's major hospitals such as Narayana, Medanta, Apollo, and Fortis. Such partnership led to modernize medical facilities in countries like Nigeria, Uganda, Kenya, and South Africa (African Business, 2022).

In sum, India's medical tourism in Africa follows a two-pronged approach. On one hand, it facilitates the travel of Africa patients to India, which benefits its own healthcare sector economically and diplomatically. On the other hand, it invests in Africa's health infrastructure by establishing and modernizing hospitals, training experts and expanding pharmaceutical exports which increase its footprint in African regions.

Telemedicine and Digital Health

Digitalization of healthcare services is an important part of India's health strategy in Africa constituting tele-health, electronic medical records (EMRs), mobile health, and E-learning (Export-Import Bank of India, 2021). In this vein, the Pan-African e-Network was established in 2009 to share India's expertise in telemedicine and tele-education in healthcare sector with African countries. It connected remote hospitals in 53 African countries to 12 Indian hospitals and thereby exchanging special knowledge and consultation from prominent Indian specialists and doctors (Seth, 2019).Later on, the Pan Africa e-Network Project was upgraded in 2019, and known as the e-VidyaBharti (tele-education) and e-Arogya Bharti (tele-medicine) Project (e-VBAB). Under this initiative, medical teams at local healthcare centers can consult Indian specialists online, upload patients' medical records and information and get expert advice (Export-Import Bank of India, 2021). As part of India's health diplomacy in Africa, India and African Union (AU) signed the India-Africa Framework for Strategic Cooperation during Third India-Africa Forum Summit (IAFS) in 2015, emphasizing health as a pillar of their cooperation. The agreement promoted joint educational programs, recommending policies and digital health which includes tele-medicine and e-health applications (MEA, 2015).

During the recent pandemic, India provided African countries with telemedicine supports through some medical institutes including All India Institute of Medical Sciences (AIIMS), Raipur and engaged the local African institutions to train medical teams to combat and control COVID-19. Moreover, India under Indian Technical and Economic Cooperation (ITEC) program organized an online course entitled "COVID-19 pandemic: prevention and management guidelines for healthcare professionals" for healthcare workers of the African countries (Mol et al., 2022). In addition, in order to help Africans to map COVID-19 in rural areas, India offered them technical assistance by sharing ArogyaSetu and the E-Gram Swaraj apps with them (Mol et al., 2022).While the ArogyaSetu app, helped African health institutions to map and identify areas with at high risk of COVID-19 spread, and also uses GPS to determine whether a user had been in contact with an infected person, the E-Gram Swaraj app serves as an information portal for COVID-19, offering updates on health institutions' activities regarding COVID-19 (Júnior & Dugo, 2023).

In another example, Airtel Africa, a subsidiary of Bharti Airtel providing telecommunication services in 14 African countries, signed an agreement with Apollo Hospitals in 2016 to launch "Ask Apollo" which was a patient-centered online and mobile service. This platform provided remote access to healthcare and allowed patients to talk with Apollo doctors through video conferencing, voice calls, or email (Rathee, 2016).

India's Health Strategy in the Cases of Ethiopia, Kenya and Nigeria

In this part, we will focus on the cases of Ethiopia, Kenya and Nigeria to elucidate more on India's health strategy in Africa regions and the perceptions of Africans towards this strategy which seeks to focus on medical assistance, modernizing medical infrastructure, vaccine diplomacy, medical tourism, and digital health. The strategy gives priority to affordable medicines, and vaccines while attracting African patients for treatment and digital health and thereby strengthening India-Africa ties. Below more details will be given regarding these issues.

Ethiopia

India and Ethiopia have cultivated deep health cooperation up until now exemplified in 2019 by the establishment of "India-Ethiopia Centre for Innovation, Technology Transfer and Commercialization". The center focused on Healthcare as one of the key areas for development, utilizing Technologies and innovations (The Embassy of India in Addis Ababa, 2019). During the pandemic, India provides Ethiopia essential medical aid to combat with COVID-19 including 100,000 HCQ tablets and other antibiotics in August 2020. In addition to providing medical assistance, India helped Ethiopians to train professional medical teams, modernize their hospitals, and expand their telemedicine services (The Embassy of India in Addis Ababa, 2020). In line with its Vaccine diplomacy, as of June 2023, India donated 42 million COVID-19 vaccines to Ethiopia which were mostly facilitated by COVAX (MEA, 2023). Furthermore, currently India and Ethiopia have collaborated on the development of vaccine production and achieving vaccine self-sufficiency in Africa. In this regard, the Indian biotech company Tech Invention signed an agreement with Ethiopia's Ministry of Health which aligned with the African Union's Agenda 2063 and the Partnership for African Vaccine Manufacturing (PAVM). The initiative mainly focus on advancing healthcare resilience, producing vaccine and pandemic preparedness in Africa in general and Ethiopia as a key player in particular (ehealth, 2025). India also offers training opportunities for Ethiopian students at Indian universities and encourages its health sector companies to invest in Ethiopia's health sector which would contribute to the manufacturing of medical equipment, and pharmaceuticals that would be to the benefit of both Indians and Ethiopians (Fana Broadcasting Corporate, 2024a).

As for their cooperation in digital health sector, as part of the pilot study, in July 2007, Ethiopia Black Lion and Nkempte hospitals cooperated with the Care Hospital (Hyderabad) under Pan Africa e-Network Project and get connected with Indian medical institutions to improve its healthcare system and share medical expertise with Indians (Mol et al., 2022).

An finally, regarding India's medical tourism, Ethiopian look at India as a top destination for medical tourists, due to its affordable and high-quality healthcare services especially in cancer, organ transplants and cardiac issues. In this regard, the Apollo Hospitals Information Centre in Ethiopia plays a key role in offering such services and helping Ethiopian patients with technical and other issues related their medical journey including visa and accommodation (Appollo Information Center, 2024).

Kenya

Kenya hosts a large Indian community, estimated at 80,000 to 100,000people, making it the largest Indian community in Africa after South Africa (Eickhoff, 2022*)*, which draw the two nations together and motivate them to deepen their co-operation in various fields especially in healthcare sector. In 2002, under the Focus Africa initiative, India prioritized exporting essential medicines and pharmaceutical products to several African countries, including Kenya (Saint-Mézard & Nicolas, 2022). Similarly, at the India-Africa Forum Summit in New Delhi on October 28, 2015, India and Kenya agreed to work together to improve Kenya's healthcare sector, supporting Indian hospital investments, and strengthening capacity- building in health services (The East African, 2015). In 2016, in order to improve the public healthcare system, India provided Kenya approximately 30 ambulances, tele-cobalt cancer therapy machines, essential Alkaptonuria (AKU) medicines, and financial support to develop a 100-bed cancer hospital (MEA, 2016). Similarly, in 2017Medanta Africare, a joint venture between Kenyan investors and India's Delhi-based RJ Group, constructed a 200-bed tertiary-care facility in Nairobi, with an investment of $18 million (Nyambura-Mwaura & Gebre, 2016).

During the recent pandemic, India donated essential medicines valued USD 1.54 million to Kenya, demonstrating its support during the COVID-19 crisis and reaffirming its commitment as a reliable partner in healthcare. India also conducted online e-ITEC courses on COVID-19 management for Kenyan healthcare medical teams and developed various telemedicine initiatives to connect hospitals in Kenya and India (MEA, 2020b).As part of the Vaccine Maitri initiative, in March 2021, Kenya received 1.12 million doses of Covishield including 1.02 million through the COVAX alliance and 100,000 as a donation (MEA, 2020b).India played a key role in introducing telemedicine to Kenya through Chandigarh-based Doctor Z India Healthcare, which sought to launch a telemedicine project in Kenya in March 2011to improve healthcare accessibility in Kenya (Business Standard, 2011). Align with developing digital health, the two countries signed an agreement in 2023 to deepen their cooperation in digital field including healthcare sector. The agreement paved the way for sharing expertise, focusing on health, education and digital governance. The two sides also discussed the ways for Kenya to use digitalization and technology in telemedicine and tele-health initiatives (Njoya, 2023).

As for medical tourism, Kenya and India have developed strong medical tourism cooperation, with a significant number of Kenyans traveled to India for healthcare. This trend has been driven by Kenya's geographical proximity to India, modern medical facilities and affordable treatment in India (HBG Medical Assistance, 2025).

Nigeria

Like other African nations, India has deep relations with Nigeria in various areas including healthcare sector. In 2024, an Indian private company, Padiyath Healthcare committed to invest $100 million to improve medical infrastructure of Nigeria. The company constructed two modern hospitals in Abuja: Padiyath Mayfields Hospitals, a 300-bed facility in Suncity Estates, and Padiyath Cancare Hospitals, a 200-bed cancer center. The hospitals would offer advanced medical technologies, and specialized treatment equipment (Greenbarge Reporters, 2024). In order to combat with COVID-19 crisis, India donated essential medicine to Nigeria in 2020 (Lamai, 2020), and on March 2, 2021, Nigeria received 3.94 million doses of the AstraZeneca/Oxford vaccine, manufactured by the Serum Institute of India (SII) by COVAX. Later on, on March 26, 2021, it received 100000 doses of made in India Covishield vaccines (Punch, 2021). Nigeria is very eager to establish itself as a vaccine and pharmaceutical producer and looks to India for cooperation in developing local manufacturing. Realizing Nigeria's vast potential, India also sees an opportunity to increase cooperation in medicine production (Lamai, 2020).During India-Nigeria Pharmaceutical Business Meet in 2021, the two sides agreed to expand cooperation in providing and manufacturing affordable and reliable vaccines and medicines. They also committed to facilitating investment by Indian pharmaceutical companies, which had already invested in local manufacturing in Nigeria (High Commission of India in Abuja, 2021).As for their cooperation in digital health sector, Nigeria is one of the key African countries that has cooperated with India through Pan Africa e-Network Project in healthcare sector (MEA, 2013). On May 16, 2024 the Indian government as part of its efforts to enhance healthcare collaboration Nigeria under the HEAL-Thy Samvad initiative gather experts, policymakers, and representatives from both India and Nigeria to discuss technological advancement, digital health and capacity building that could serve as a model for other countries in the Global South (BioVoice News, 2024).

Regarding medical tourism, like other African countries, Nigerian patients 'consider India as a leading destination for medical tourism due to its cheaper treatments compared to Western countries. India's advanced healthcare infrastructure, particularly its expertise in kidney transplants, further enhance its image. Moreover, the availability of human organs, easy visa access, and short waiting times make India an attractive choice for Nigerian patients leading to financial outflows from Nigeria to India (Joseph et al., 2022).

Comparing Chinese and Indian Health Strategies in Africa

As two rising global powers, China and India have increased their footprints in African regions through their health strategies. While both give priority to health diplomacy and development cooperation, their strategies are shaped by their unique political, economic and cultural perspectives. Investigating their similarities and differences, we could gain understanding of their broader geopolitical goals and increasing influence in the Global South. Table 1 will better explain the nuance differences in their strategies. China's Belt and Road Initiative (BRI) in general and its Health Silk Road (HSR) in particular shaped its health strategy in Africa. Initially introduced in 2016, HSR seeks to facilitate health cooperation by integrating health assistance, infrastructure development, vaccine diplomacy, and traditional Chinese medicine (TCM) promotion. The recent COVID-19 pandemic provided an excellent opportunity for China to leverage HSR and position itself as a global health leader under the concept of a "community of common health for mankind."

China's medical assistance in Africa includes sending medical teams, enhancing public health infrastructure, and building hospitals. Typical examples include the China-Zimbabwe Friendship Hospital and the Africa Centre for Disease Control (CDC) headquarters in Ethiopia. Chinese pharmaceutical companies such as Fosun Pharma have also invested in pharmaceutical production, while private sectors like Jack Ma Foundation have played significant roles in facilitating delivering medical aid. During the COVID-19 pandemic, China supplied more than 1 billion vaccine doses to Africa, seeking to fill the gaps left by Western countries and India's temporary suspension of distributing vaccine during its second wave ofCOVID-19. China's capacity to quickly produce and distribute vaccines, among African countries such as in Ethiopia, Kenya, and Nigeria, bolsters its image as a reliable partner. Traditional Chinese Medicine (TCM) serves as another key component of China's health strategy, positioned as an alternative to Western medicine and integrated into its medical aid efforts. TCM not only serves healthcare needs but also reinforce China's cultural diplomacy and national identity. Finally, Telemedicine and digital health plat a key role in China's health Strategy. Platforms such as the Global MediXchange for Combating COVID-19 (GMCC), supported by Alibaba and the Jack Ma Foundation, facilitated remote consultations and capacity building during the COVID-19 crisis. Huawei's development of Kenya's telemedicine system was a prime example of combining technology with health diplomacy.

As for India's health strategy in Africa, its health strategy in Africa is heavily influenced with its strong pharmaceutical industry and historical ties. As the Pharmacy of the World, it has played crucial roles in supplying developing nations with affordable vaccines and medicines. This commitment is corroborated by its Vaccine Maitri (Vaccine Friendship) initiative, launched in 2021. Under this initiative, India supplied over 25 million vaccine doses to 41 African countries including Ethiopia, Kenya, and Nigeria. However, during the second wave of COVID-19 in India, vaccine exports were temporarily suspended, allowing China expand its presence in these regions. Another aspect of Indian health strategy is medical infrastructure development. India has financed and built hospitals, including the Indo-Guinea Friendship Hospital. Indian healthcare providers like Apollo and Medanta have also increased their presence in countries such as Kenya and Nigeria, offering specialized medical care and training for local professionals. Medical tourism, a key aspect of India's strategy, sets it apart from China's approach in Africa. Every year, many African patients, especially from Nigeria and Kenya, visit India for its affordable and qualified medical treatments. Programs such as the "Heal in India" campaign and easy visa access make India a popular healthcare destination for Africans. And the last component of India's strategy is Telemedicine. In this regard, India's Pan-African e-Network Project and e-VBAB (e-VidyaBharati and e-Arogya Bharati Network Project) have played significant role in promoting digital health in African regions.

After analyzing the strategies of both countries, five key aspects of difference emerge. The first aspect is their different approaches in policies. Both China and India participate in South-South cooperation in health, but their strategies differ. China's strategy is more integrated into its broader geopolitical vision, whereas India takes a more decentralized approach, emphasizing capacity building, affordable healthcare, and medical tourism. The second aspect is about the role of Public and Private sectors in their strategies. China's strategy is state-led, with government monitor medical assistance, infrastructure development, and vaccine diplomacy. However, private sectors like Alibaba and Fosun Pharma are playing increasingly active role. In contrast, India's approach is more market-driven, leveraging its strong pharmaceutical industry and private hospitals. The third aspect is vaccine diplomacy. China is very effective in vaccine distribution, leveraging state resources to deliver large quantities quickly. On the other hand, India's strength lies in vaccine production capacity and affordability. However, its export suspension in 2021 harmed its reputation, allowing China to step in and fill the gap. The fourth is Cultural and Nationalism aspects. China actively integrates TCM as part of its cultural diplomacy, depicting it as a source of national pride and a distinct alternative to western medicine. Similarly, India draws on its cultural heritage through concepts like "Vasudhaiva Kutumbakam" (the world is one family) in its Vaccine Maitri initiative, highlighting humanitarian solidarity. Finally the last aspect is reception and perception. African governments generally have favorable views of both China and India. China's swift response during the pandemic crisis was well-received, though some Africans consider Chinese aid as politically driven. India's affordable medicines and vaccine Maitri initiative earned goodwill, especially before the export suspension. In addition, India benefits from positive Western perceptions, whereas China faces criticism over debt diplomacy and alleged exploitation.

The convergent and divergent points of the cooperation realized by both countries in Africa have been analyzed below in Table 1:

Table 1. Convergent and Divergent Points in Chinese and Indian Health Strategies in Africa

Aspect	Convergent Points	Divergent Points
Health Diplomacy	Both prioritize South-South cooperation and use health as a soft power tool	China integrates health into BRI; India focuses on affordable care and medical tourism
Vaccine Strategy	Both engaged in large-scale vaccine distribution in Africa	China emphasized rapid delivery and state-led diplomacy; India focused on affordable production via private sector
Medical Infrastructure	Both built hospitals and funded health facilities in Africa	China focuses on public infrastructure; India includes private hospital partnerships
Cultural Influence	Both link health efforts to cultural diplomacy	China promotes Traditional Chinese Medicine (TCM); India promotes humanistic ideas like 'Vasudhaiva Kutumbakam'.
Digital Health/ Telemedicine	Both utilize digital platforms for remote healthcare and training	China emphasizes tech giants like Huawei and Alibaba; India uses government-led platforms like e-VBAB
Public-Private Roles	Private actors present in both strategies	China is state-dominated with selective private support; India relies heavily on private sector and PPPs
Reception in Africa	Both generally well received by African nations	China sometimes criticized for political motives; India viewed more favorably in the West

Source: The authors.

As for the effectiveness of Chinese and Indian health strategies in Africa, by 2014 China helped African countries to construct 30 hospitals and 30 malaria prevention and control centers, invested 123.9 million USD in medical supplies, equipment and anti-malaria drugs and trained more than 3000 healthcare workers from various

African nations (The State Council, 2014). China has been very successful in eradicating malaria in Africa, supporting various health facilities dedicating to malaria and providing related therapies which are now the WHO standard for malaria treatment. In addition, China also distributed special mosquito nets, which helped prevent about 68% of malaria cases in Africa between 2000 and 2015 (Dolan et al., 2023). Up until now, China has been actively involved in supporting African countries to fight with malaria, HIV/AIDS, tuberculosis, through projects aligned with the African Union's health goals (The Africa-China Centre, 2023). As mentioned above, China has also been very successful and active in infrastructure development, and capacity building. Its vaccine diplomacy has also received warmly by African countries. However, there is a climate of distrust between some African medical practitioners towards Chinese medical personnel the quality of Chinese medical products and vaccines (Itugbu, 2021). In addition, China's health diplomacy is sometimes considered as strategic blend of political and economic interests in which health aid serves as a vehicle for advancing geopolitical interests which complicates the evaluation of its effectiveness (Itugbu, 2021).

Similarly, as discussed above, like China, India is also active in supporting African nations to enhance their healthcare systems India's health strategy in Africa has been multifaceted involving technology-driven projects, collaborative platforms capacity building and pharmaceutical focus which deepens their collaborations in health, infrastructure and technological areas. Telemedicine and tele-education projects for instance, link Indian medical experts with African medical practitioners. India's public health achievement in controlling malaria- such as 69% decline between 2017 and 2023- suggests its valuable expertise that could be shared with African nations. In addition, its focus on affordable and accessible medical services closely aligns with health priorities of Africans (Ministry of Health & Family Welfare, 2024).

African countries have also faced significant deficits in health infrastructure, workforce, and financing, which could negatively impact India's health strategy in this continent. The African Development Bank's 2022-2030 Strategy for Quality Health Infrastructure released in 2022, also highlighted some challenges such as access barriers and shortages that Indian initiatives alone cannot fully address (African Development Bank Group, 2022).

Overall, China and India have adopted distinct but complementary health strategies in Africa. While China emphasizes infrastructure, disease control, and training, India focuses on technology, affordable medicine, and capacity building, offering relevant expertise. However, its impact is limited by structural gaps in Africa's health systems.

African Perspectives on Sino-Indian Health Engagements

Active engagement in global health is vital for African nations, which has serious problems in having access to essential health determinants and experience some of the highest disease burdens in the world, contributing to significant economic impacts on both national economies and individual household (African Union, 2010). In fact, African perspective of global health engagements especially in diplomatic areas focus on development, justice and unity the roots of which dated back to their history of colonization and liberation (Loewenson et al., 2014). African nations consider health as a right associated with sovereignty and equity not merely as aid. While sill aid plays a significant role, there are increasing tendencies among African leaders to expand regional cooperation and south-south alliance to improve healthcare systems and address deeper causes of poor health including inequalities of global policies (Loewenson et al., 2014). In this context, as discussed above, both China and India have been pivotal partners in Africa's healthcare system but their approaches and the perceptions of Africans towards them differ. A prime example of China's deep engagement in Africa's healthcare system was building of Africa Centers for Disease Control and Prevention (Africa CDC) headquarters in Addis Ababa, Ethiopia. The African Union Commission Chairperson, Moussa Faki Mahamat who left the office recently, noted that this initiative is part of a broader "New Health Order for Africa, "seeking to improve public health infrastructure and achieve self-sufficiency in health systems (African Union, 2023). Notwithstanding these efforts, some Africans voiced their concerns of the hospitals built by Chinese. They believed that most of these hospitals follow a standard design that often does not meet local requirements, resulting in limited use and difficulties in daily operations. Furthermore, they noted that Chinese aid project is fragmented and could not be integrated into national health strategies and of insufficient support for maintenance and sustainability after project completion (Zhou, 2015). Some African scholars also question whether China's aid is motivated by genuine goodwill or by strategic goals such as securing resources and influence. Nonetheless, many welcome China's "no strings attached" approach and respect for sovereignty, especially compared to Western aid conditions (Lin et al., 2016).

Accordingly, the Pan-African e-Network, founded in 2009, paved the way for further collaborations between Indian and African nations in education, technology and health systems. However, African health system faced serious challenges such as high disease burdens, workforce shortages, and limited resources. As a result, some African stakeholders worried about the coordination and alignment of Indian health initiatives with local health priorities in Africa (Azevedo, 2017). Some African observers also emphasize the significance of taking more active role in planning and implementing health projects- something that Indian initiatives have frequently failed to do. They argue that without local ownership, such efforts risk fading once Indian support or funding stops (PWC, 2020). Therefore, while both China and India are considered as important partners, Africans increasingly questioning the motives, effectiveness, local ownership and sustainability of their Chinese and Indian engagement in general.

THEORETICAL FRAMEWORK

The previous studies on China and India's engagement in Africa have focused on soft power and health diplomacy to analyze their health strategies and foreign policy agendas. However, using these frameworks, might not fully explain economic, geopolitical and strategic drives of China and India. In other words, when we look at their health strategies from these theoretical frameworks, some fundamental questions still arise that remain unanswered: Why the issue of health is so important in Sino-African and Indo-African relations? How the issue of health could affect security and stability in African regions? Why there is cooperation and competition in China and India's health strategies towards Africa?

In order to address these gaps in the existing literature, the authors of this study propose the concept of a "geo-health strategy" as a more effective analytical framework for examining Chinese and Indian health engagements with countries of the Global South, and particularly within the African continent. Notably, the term "geo-health strategy" remains underexplored in political science and strategic studies discourse, yet it holds significant potential for capturing the intersection of health diplomacy, geopolitical interests, and international development agendas. However, some scholars introduced the term geo-health as a new field of science that combines environmental, earth and health sciences to address contemporary issues such as the intersection between environmental issues, and social justice and how they could affect the marginalized communities (Hoffman-Hall et al., 2022). In an analysis released by German Institute for International and Security Affairs (SWP), discusses how the US under the Biden administration, China and Germany integrate global health into their national security and geopolitical strategies. The Biden administration has considered global health as a key component of its foreign policy in expanding its influence in Africa. Meanwhile, China through its Global Security Initiative uses health diplomacy to strengthen its ties with the Global South and Germany emphasizes on multilateral cooperation and supply chain security to reduce reliance on China (SWP, 2023). With that said, the authors believe that the term geo-health strategy could be used to better explain the use of health initiatives as a geopolitical tool to achieve broader strategic, economic and foreign policy objectives, as it enables us to integrate global health diplomacy with power dynamics, economic interests and global and regional influence. Therefore, health interventions are not always purely humanitarian but could serve as mechanisms for increasing geopolitical influence, ensuring economic interests and shaping regional and international alliances.

Overall, the framework highlights that in health strategies, health could also be used as a geopolitical tool, economic advantageous could play key role, strategic competition is always present, health could act as a balancing tool. When we apply this framework on our study we realize that both China and India use health initiatives not merely for humanitarian reasons but to improve their global standing and ensure long-standing influence in African regions. Both nations increase their investments in Africa's pharmaceutical industries, medical infrastructure and digital health to expand their own markets and increase economic interdependence with Africa. Their health initiatives also suggest geopolitical competition, in a way that while China's Health Silk Road is linked to the Belt and Road Initiative, India's Maitri Initiative supports its broader South-South Cooperation strategy. Through vaccine diplomacy, telemedicine, and hospital investments, China and India aim to not only challenge Western influence and position themselves as leaders of the Global South, but also seek to balance each other's increasing presence in Africa. While soft power captures the cultural and normative influence of health diplomacy, it falls short of explaining the deeper strategic and geopolitical dimensions that have become evident in the health engagements of emerging powers like China and India. This is where the concept of geo-health strategy diverges. Geo-health goes beyond mere attraction or influence—it integrates health initiatives with broader geopolitical and economic objectives. Unlike soft power, which primarily aims at winning hearts and minds, geo-health is designed to create lasting dependencies, secure economic footholds, and reshape regional power dynamics. Furthermore, geo-health strategies are embedded within foreign policy objectives to achieve broader economic and political goals. For instance, China's Health Silk Road is not merely a public health intervention; it is a mechanism to extend China's Belt and Road Initiative (BRI) into Africa, fostering economic dependencies and infrastructural ties that serve Chinese economic interests. Similarly, India's Vaccine Maitri extends its pharmaceutical markets and South-South cooperation narratives, securing influence while simultaneously expanding its global market share in generics and vaccines.

The application of geo-health involves the construction of medical infrastructure, the deployment of medical teams, and strategic health aid that aligns with the donor country's political and economic interests. For instance, in Ethiopia, China's funding of the Africa Centers for Disease Control and Prevention headquarters not only addresses health needs but also solidifies Chinese influence over African health governance. Similarly, India's Pan-African e-Network, which provides telemedicine services, not only enhances healthcare access but also strengthens digital and infrastructural ties to Indian technology markets. By differentiating geo-health from traditional soft power, the analysis recognizes health diplomacy as a strategic tool in the global competition for influence in the Global South. China and India's health engagements in Africa, thus, are not merely acts of goodwill but are instrumental in restructuring regional power dynamics and economic dependencies under the guise of humanitarian aid. Furthermore, this section positions geo-health as a transformative approach where health is not just a domain of cooperation but a calculated entry point for economic entrenchment and geopolitical alignment, redefining the terms of health sovereignty in recipient nations.

As with any strategic framework rooted in power dynamics, the geo-health strategy also raises critical questions regarding its potential risks and unintended consequences, particularly in the context of the Global South. Although the concept of geo-health strategy provides us with a useful framework for examining how emerging powers extend their influence through health initiatives, it is necessary to analyze the potential risks inherent within these strategies. The risks include fostering new forms of dependency, undermining national sovereignty and overlooking local health priorities, particularly in the regions where health systems are already vulnerable.

China's vast infrastructure projects and digital health platforms, such as telemedicine initiatives driven by Huawei and Alibaba, may improve technical capacity but also pose the risk of creating technological dependencies for African countries which restrict their policy independence. The reliance on Chinese –owned systems and technology could raise concerns about who controls the data and how it is used, especially when local governments don't have clear and proper rules of data governance.

Similarly, India's dominance in producing generic medicines helps African nations to have access to cheaper drugs. However, this could also unintentionally slow down the growth of local drug industries. While these strategies are presented as part of South-South cooperation, in reality it often suggests an imbalance in decision-making authority, with Africans often acting as passive recipients rather than equal partners in health governance.

In addition, both China and India often pursue projects that align with their strategic or economic interests, and sometimes ignore the local needs at African regions. For instance, during the COVID-19 pandemic, vaccine diplomacy was frequently driven by geopolitical motives rather than the epidemiological insights from African public health institutions. Therefore, there is a risk that donors' desire for recognition and influence might take priority over building long-term local health systems and meeting the real needs of communities. Addressing these criticisms enhances the geo-health strategy framework by recognizing that geopolitical goals can coexist with humanitarian narratives, and that health diplomacy, even when advantageous, is never free from ideological bias. A truly transformative health partnership requires mechanisms that give recipient countries the power to set their own priorities, control how technology is used, and ensures sustainability even after donor support ends. This implies that future implementations of geo-health strategy must more thoroughly address issues of power, agency, and structural inequality in global health.

CONCLUSION

The comparative analysis of China and India's health strategies in Africa reveals a complex interplay of cooperation, competition, and strategic alignment within the broader landscape of South-South cooperation. While both countries frame their health diplomacy within the rhetoric of solidarity and humanitarian assistance, their engagements are increasingly driven by geopolitical ambitions, economic interests, and the pursuit of influence in the Global South. This study, by integrating the newly proposed concept of geo-health strategy, offers a more comprehensive theoretical framework that transcends the conventional lenses of soft power and health diplomacy, thereby addressing the underlying strategic, economic, and geopolitical dynamics shaping Sino-Indian health interventions in Africa. The geo-health strategy framework underscores that health diplomacy operates not only as a tool for fostering goodwill but also as a strategic instrument for advancing broader geopolitical objectives. Both China and India leverage health initiatives to secure economic opportunities, expand their spheres of influence, and reshape regional power dynamics. The Health Silk Road (HSR) and the Maitri Initiative indeed represent competing visions of South-South cooperation. This is since health diplomacy has become a vehicle for asserting leadership in the Global South. The integration of vaccine diplomacy, telemedicine, traditional medicine, and pharmaceutical investments into their respective health strategies further illustrates how health interventions are embedded within wider economic and geopolitical calculations.

Moreover, the study highlights that geo-health strategies serve as balancing mechanisms in the strategic rivalry between China and India. While China's state-led, infrastructure-driven approach aligns with its Belt and Road Initiative (BRI), India's market-oriented model capitalizes on its strong pharmaceutical industry and historical ties with African countries. This divergence reflects broader differences in their foreign policy philosophies and economic priorities. The temporary suspension of India's Vaccine Maitri initiative during the COVID-19 pandemic created an opportunity for China to expand its vaccine diplomacy, illustrating how health crises can exacerbate strategic competition. However, the geo-health strategy framework also emphasizes that competition is not the sole defining feature of Sino-Indian health diplomacy in Africa. Instances of cooperation, such as knowledge-sharing platforms and joint pandemic preparedness efforts, demonstrate the potential for collaborative approaches to global health challenges. These cooperative efforts, if expanded, could contribute to more resilient health systems in African countries and foster greater South-South solidarity.

Despite these developments, significant gaps remain in the academic literature regarding the long-term implications of geo-health strategies on local health systems, economic sovereignty, and governance structures in African countries. Future research should explore how African countries navigate the dual pressures of geopolitical competition and their own health priorities, as well as how local actors shape the outcomes of external health interventions. Additionally, more attention should be given to the intersection of geo-health strategies with environmental sustainability, digital health governance, and the role of emerging technologies in reshaping global health diplomacy. By proposing the concept of geo-health strategy, this study not only contributes to the theoretical understanding of health diplomacy but also highlights the increasing significance of health as a geopolitical tool in the 21st century. The rising prominence of the Global South in shaping global health governance challenges the traditional dominance of Western-led models, opening new avenues for more equitable and multipolar health partnerships. As health diplomacy continues to evolve, the geo-health strategy framework provides a valuable lens for analyzing the intersections between health, geopolitics, and economic development in an increasingly interconnected world.

REFERENCES

Adams, V., Novotny, T. E., & Leslie, H. (2008). Global health diplomacy. *Medical Anthropology, 27*(4), 315–323. DOI: 10.1080/01459740802427067 PMID: 18958783

African Business. (2022, March 21). Medical tourism to India from Africa: Complete medical solution at an affordable cost. *African Business*.https://medigence.com/blog/medical-tourism-to-india-from-africa/

African Development Bank Group. (2017, May 30). African ministers seek greater partnership with India to enhance cancer diagnosis, check high disease burden. *African Development Bank Group*.https://www.afdb.org/fr/news-and-events/african-ministers-seek-greater-partnership-with-india-to-enhance-cancer-diagnosis-check-high-disease-burden-17063

African Development Bank Group. (2022, February). Strategy for quality health infrastructure in Africa 2022–2030. *African Development Bank Group*. https://www.afdb.org/sites/default/files/documents/publications/strategy_for_quality_health_infrastructure_in_africa_2022-2030.pdf

African Union. (2010, May 15). *Five-year review of the Abuja Call for accelerated action towards universal access to HIV/AIDS, tuberculosis, and malaria services by 2010*. https://au.int/en/documents/20100515/five-year-review-abuja-call-accelerated-action-towards-universal-access-hivaids

African Union. (2023, January 12). *China Foreign Affairs Minister H.E. Mr. Qin Gang visits the AU and takes part in the inauguration of the new headquarters of the Africa Center for Disease Control and Prevention (Africa CDC)*. https://au.int/en/pressreleases/20230112/inauguration-new-headquarters-africa-cdc

Appollo Information Center. (2024, April 6). India's top medical treatment destination for Ethiopians. *Appollo Information Center*.https://www.apolloinformationcentre.com/india-top-medical-treatment-destination-for-ethiopians/

Ayega, D. (2022). China pledges 10 million COVID-19 vaccine doses to Kenya during FM Wang Yi's visit. *Capital News*.https://www.capitalfm.co.ke/news/2022/01/china-pledges-10-million-covid-19-vaccine-doses-during-fm-wang-yis-visit/

Azevedo, M. J. (2017). The state of health system(s) in Africa: Challenges and opportunities. In Azevedo, M. J. (Ed.), *Historical perspectives on the state of health and health systems in Africa* (Vol. II, pp. 1–73). Springer., DOI: 10.1007/978-3-319-32564-4_1

Baijie, A. (2017, January 19). WHO, China sign pact establishing 'Health Silk Road.' *China Daily.*https://www.chinadaily.com.cn/business/2017wef/2017-01/19/content_27993857.htm

Bajpai, N., & Wadhwa, M. (2021, June). *India's experience with ICT in the health sector: Lessons for sub-Saharan Africa.* Center for Sustainable Development. https://csd.columbia.edu/sites/default/files/content/docs/ICT%20India/Papers/ICT_India_Working_Paper_51.pdf

Banerji, A. (2021, June 25). India's flawed vaccine diplomacy. *Stimson Center.* https://www.stimson.org/2021/indias-flawed-vaccine-diplomacy/

BioVoice News. (2024, May 24). India-Nigeria forge stronger ties to reach the 'last mile' in healthcare. *BioVoice News.*https://biovoicenews.com/india-nigeria-forge-stronger-ties-to-reach-the-last-mile-in-healthcare/?utm_source=chatgpt.com

Business Standard. (2011, March 4). Chandigarh firm to start telemedicine project in Kenya. *Business Standard.*https://www.business-standard.com/article/companies/chandigarh-firm-to-start-telemedicine-project-in-kenya-111030400083_1.html

Cabana, S. L. (2014). *Chronology and history of South-South cooperation.* Secretaria-Geral Ibero-Americana. https://segib.org/wp-content/uploads/Chrono-South-South2014.pdf

Cao, J. (2020). Toward a Health Silk Road: China's proposal for global health cooperation. *China Quarterly of International Strategic Studies*, *6*(1), 19–35. DOI: 10.1142/S2377740020500013

CGTN. (2021, July 25). China donates 470,000 COVID-19 vaccine doses to Nigeria. *CGTN News.*https://newsaf.cgtn.com/news/2021-07-25/China-donates-470-000-COVID-19-vaccine-doses-to-Nigeria-12apCplEW8U/index.html

Chan, G. (2024). *China's Health Silk Road: Vaccine diplomacy and health governance.* Edward Elgar Publishing. DOI: 10.4337/9781035320202

Chaturvedi, S. (2016). *The logic of sharing: Indian approach to South-South cooperation.* Cambridge University Press.

China Daily. (2010, August 10). Zhou Enlai announces eight principles of foreign aid. *China Daily.*https://www.chinadaily.com.cn/china/2010-08/13/content_11149131.htm

China Daily. (2020, March 22). Kenya launches telemedicine technology for detection of coronavirus. *China Daily.*https://www.chinadaily.com.cn/a/202003/22/WS5e774d33a3101282172810a5.html

China International Development Cooperation Agency. (2018). *Forum on China-Africa Cooperation - Beijing Action Plan (2019-2021)*.http://www.cidca.gov.cn/2018-09/07/c_129949203.htm

Chipaike, R., Nunoo, I., & Chingono, N. (2023). Chinese COVID diplomacy in Africa: Interrogating Zimbabwe's experience. *Cogent Social Sciences*, *9*(2), 1–13. DOI: 10.1080/23311886.2023.2275442

Choudhary, D. R. (2021). India announces vaccine support to Africa to fight Omicron. *The Economic Times*.https://economictimes.indiatimes.com/news/india/india-announces-vaccine-support-to-africa-to-fight-omicron/articleshow/87989068.cms

Consulate General of India. (2021, March 17). Statement by External Affairs Minister in Rajya Sabha and Lok Sabha on the Vaccine Maitri Initiative. https://www.cgisaopaulo.gov.in/pdf/Statement%20by%20External%20Affairs%20Minister%20in%20Rajya%20Sabha%20and%20Lok%20Sabha%20on%20Vaccine%20Maitri_17.3.2021.pdf

Department of Pharmaceuticals. (2023, August). Study on CRO sector in India conducted by Department of Pharmaceuticals, Ministry of Chemicals & Fertilizers, Government of India. https://pharma-dept.gov.in/sites/default/files/CRO%20Market%20Report_High%20Resolution.pdf

Dhar, B. (2021, April 8). India's vaccine diplomacy. *Global Policy*.https://www.globalpolicyjournal.com/blog/08/04/2021/indias-vaccine-diplomacy

Dhar, B., & Gopakumar, K. M. (2020). Towards more affordable medicine: A proposal to waive certain obligations from the Agreement on TRIPS. *Asia-Pacific Research and Training Network on Trade Working Paper*.https://www.econstor.eu/bitstream/10419/226692/1/1740924681.pdf

Dolan, C. B., Malik, A. A., Zhang, S., Mao, W., McDade, K. K., Svoboda, E., & Odhiambo, J. N. (2023). Chinese health funding in Africa: The untold story. *PLOS Global Public Health*, *3*(6), e0001637. Advance online publication. DOI: 10.1371/journal.pgph.0001637 PMID: 37379293

eHealth. (2025, January 7). TechInvention joins hands with Ethiopia to boost vaccine manufacturing and pandemic preparedness. *eHealth*.https://ehealth.eletsonline.com/2025/01/techinvention-joins-hands-with-ethiopia-to-boost-vaccine-manufacturing-and-pandemic-preparedness/

Eickhoff, K. (2022, March 10). Multipolarity in East Africa: India's role in Kenya. *Stiftung Wissenschaft und Politik*.https://www.swp-berlin.org/publikation/multipolarity-in-the-horn-of-africa-indias-role-in-kenya

Embassy of India in Abidjan. (2019, July 2). India-Guinea relations. https://www.eoiabidjan.gov.in/page/india-guinea-relations/

Embassy of India in Addis Ababa. (2019, March 4). India Ethiopia innovation technology transfer & commercialization program. *Embassy of India in Addis Ababa.* https://eoiaddisababa.gov.in/nnovation-technology-2019/?utm_source=chatgpt.com

Embassy of India in Addis Ababa. (2020, August 21). Gifting of medical aid package to Ethiopia. *Embassy of India in Addis Ababa.*https://eoiaddisababa.gov.in/wp-content/uploads/2020/08/press-release-handover-medicines-21-August-2020.pdf

Environmental Investigation Agency. (2021, November). *Lethal remedy: How the promotion of some traditional Chinese medicine in Africa poses a major threat to endangered wildlife.*https://eia-international.org/wp-content/uploads/2021-Lethal-Remedy-SINGLE-PAGES.pdf

ERI. (2020). *Overview of China's "Mask Diplomacy."*https://www.eurasian-research.org/publication/overview-of-chinas-mask-diplomacy/

Export-Import Bank of India. (2021). *India-Africa healthcare: Prospects and opportunities.*https://www.imcnet.org/storage/content_gallery/India-Exim-Bank-Working-Paper-102-India-Africa-Healthcare_Prospects-and-Opportunities.pdf

Fana Broadcasting Corporate. (2024, September 22). Chinese medical center pledges support to Ethiopia's efforts to become regional medical tourism hub. *Fana Broadcasting Corporate.*https://www.fanabc.com/english/chinese-medical-center-pledges-support-to-ethiopias-efforts-to-become-regional-medical-tourism-hub/

Fana Broadcasting Corporate. (2024a, August 24). India pledges commitment to health sector collaboration with Ethiopia. *Fana Broadcasting Corporate.*https://www.fanabc.com/english/india-pledges-commitment-to-health-sector-collaboration-with-ethiopia/

Fauci, A. S. (2007). The expanding global health agenda: A welcome development. *Nature Medicine, 13*(10), 1169–1171. https://www.nature.com/articles/nm1646. DOI: 10.1038/nm1646 PMID: 17917667

Feldbaum, H., Lee, K., & Michaud, J. (2010). Global health and foreign policy. *Epidemiologic Reviews, 32*(1), 82–92. DOI: 10.1093/epirev/mxq006 PMID: 20423936

Fidler, D. (2005). *Health and foreign policy: A conceptual overview.* Nuffield Trust.

FOCAC. (2006, November 16). *Forum on China-Africa Cooperation (FOCAC) Beijing Action Plan.*http://www.focac.org/eng/zywx_1/zywj/200611/t20061116_7933564.htm

FOCAC. (2020, July 24). Chinese embassy hands over medical supplies to Kenya to combat COVID-19. *Forum on China-Africa Cooperation.*http://www.focac.org/eng/zfgx_4/jmhz/202007/t20200724_8087763.htm

FOCAC. (2021, December 2). *Full text: Keynote speech by Chinese President Xi Jinping at opening ceremony of 8th FOCAC ministerial conference.*http://www.focac.org/focacdakar/eng/zxyw_1/202112/t20211202_10461076.htm

Forbes. (2020). Ma Yun shares Chinese experience with Africa. *Forbes China.* https://www.forbeschina.com/business/48625

Gao, J. (2023, October 27). Traditional Chinese medicine school inks deal with Kenyan institution to promote herbal medicine. *Belt and Road Portal.*https://eng.yidaiyilu.gov.cn/p/0DTHFR7N.html

Gao, L., & Xu, J. (2023, August 31). Public health engagement: New opportunities and challenges in 60 years of China's health aid to Africa. *BMJ Global Health,*https://gh.bmj.com/content/8/8/e012302

Global Times. (2020, May 13). China-assisted makeshift hospital handed over to Nigeria. *Global Times.*https://www.globaltimes.cn/content/1188189.shtml

Global Times. (2023, January 11). Phase-1 of Africa CDC center project completed thanks to deepened BRI cooperation. *Global Times.*https://www.globaltimes.cn/page/202301/1283618.shtml

Greenbarge Reporters. (2024, November 24). Indian investor commits $100 million to boost Nigeria health care sector. *Greenbarge Reporters.*https://greenbreporters.com/news/health/india-investor-commits-100-million-to-boost-nigeria-health-care-sector.html

Greenwood, A., & Topiwala, H. (2015). *Indian doctors in Kenya, 1895–1940: The forgotten history.* Palgrave Macmillan. DOI: 10.1057/9781137440532

Grovogu, S. (2011). A revolution nonetheless: The Global South in international relations. *Global Society, 5*(1), 175–190. DOI: 10.2979/globalsouth.5.1.175

Habibi, N., & Zhu, H. Y. (2021, February 16). The Health Silk Road as a new direction in China's Belt and Road strategy in Africa. *Global Development and Sustainability (GDS).*https://heller.brandeis.edu/gds/pdfs/working-papers/china-africa-2021.pdf

HBG Medical Assistance. (2025). What drives Kenyan patients to choose India's healthcare expertise: A bridge of healing across continents. *HBG Medical Assistance.* https://hbgmedicalassistance.com/kenyan-patients-indian-healthcare/

High Commission of India in Abuja. (2021, February 15). India-Nigeria pharmaceutical business meet. *Government of India.*https://hciabuja.gov.in/public_files/assets/pdf/PRESS_RELEASE_%27INDIA-NIGERIA_PHARMACEUTICAL_BUSINESS_MEET%27.pdf?utm_source=chatgpt.com

Hoffman-Hall, A., Gorris, M. E., Anenberg, S., Bredder, A. E., Dhaliwal, J. K., Diaz, M. A., Fortner, S. K., McAdoo, B. G., Reano, D., Rehr, R. C., Roop, H. A., & Zaitchik, B. F. (2022). A GeoHealth call to action: Moving beyond identifying environmental injustices to co-creating solutions. *GeoHealth*, *6*(11), 1–13. DOI: 10.1029/2022GH000706 PMID: 36348989

Huang, Y. (2013). *Enter the dragon and the elephant: China's and India's participation in global health governance.* Council on Foreign Relations. https://www.cfr.org/report/enter-dragon-and-elephant

Huang, Y. (2014). Domestic politics and China's health aid to Africa. *China. International Journal (Toronto, Ont.)*, *12*(3), 176–198.

Huang, Y. (2017). China's response to the 2014 Ebola outbreak in West Africa. *Global Challenges (Hoboken, NJ)*, *1*(2), 1–7. DOI: 10.1002/gch2.201600001 PMID: 31565261

Huawei. (2025). Connectivity delivers telemedicine to remote Kenya. *Huawei Media Center.*https://www.huawei.com/en/media-center/transform/06/connectivity-delivers-telemedicine-to-remote-kenya

Itugbu, S. (2021, December 10). *The politics of China's vaccine diplomacy in Africa.* Australian Institute of International Affairs. https://www.internationalaffairs.org.au/australianoutlook/the-politics-of-chinas-vaccine-diplomacy-in-africa/

Joseph, O., Ntombana, L., & Sibanda, F. (2022). Factors influencing outbound medical tourism: India as the preferred destination for Nigerians. *African Journal of Hospitality, Tourism and Leisure*, *11*(1), 310–327. DOI: 10.46222/ajhtl.19770720.227

Junior, L., & Dugo, R. (2023). China and India's health diplomacy in Africa during the COVID-19 pandemic. *Revista Chilena de Derecho y Ciencia Política*, *15*(1), 1–33. DOI: 10.7770/rchdcp-v15n1-art207

Kickbusch, I., Silberschmidt, G., & Buss, P. (2007). Global health diplomacy: The need for new perspectives, strategic approaches and skills in global health. *Bulletin of the World Health Organization*, *85*(3), 230–232. DOI: 10.2471/BLT.06.039222 PMID: 17486216

Killeen, O. J., Davis, A., Tucker, J. D., & Mason, B. (2018). Chinese global health diplomacy in Africa: Opportunities and challenges. Global Health Governance: The Scholarly Journal for the New Health Security Paradigm, 12(2), 4-29. https://pmc.ncbi.nlm.nih.gov/articles/PMC6447313/

Koller, C. N., Schwerzmann, C. J., Lang, A. S. A., Alexiou, E., & Krishnakumar, J. (2021). Addressing different needs: The challenges faced by India as the largest vaccine manufacturer while conducting the world's biggest COVID-19 vaccination campaign. *Epidemiologia*, *2*(3), 454–470. DOI: 10.3390/epidemiologia2030032 PMID: 36417236

Kuo, L. (2020, March 19). China sends doctors and masks overseas as domestic coronavirus infections drop. The Guardian. https://www.theguardian.com/world/2020/mar/19/china-positions-itself-as-a-leader-in-tackling-the-coronavirus

Lamai, S. (2020, July 17). India donates essential medicines to combat COVID-19 as Nigeria seeks collaboration to produce vaccines especially against pandemic. Federal Ministry of Information and National Orientation. https://fmino.gov.ng/india-donates-essential-medicines-to-combat-covid-19-as-nigeria-seeks-collaboration-to-produce-vaccines-especially-against-pandemic/

Lee, K., & Smith, R. (2011). What is 'global health diplomacy'? A conceptual review. *Global Health Governance*, *5*(1).

Li, A. (2022). *China and Africa in global context: Encounters, policy, cooperation and migration*. Routledge.

Lin, S., Gao, L., Reyes, M., Cheng, F., Kaufman, J., & El-Sadr, W. M. (2016). China's health assistance to Africa: Opportunism or altruism? *Globalization and Health*, *12*(1), 83. DOI: 10.1186/s12992-016-0217-1 PMID: 27912773

Liu, W., & Zhang, X. (2024). Public perception of traditional Chinese medicine in Africa and the impact of COVID-19: Based on a study of Africans. In Muchie, M., Baskaran, A., & Tang, M. (Eds.), *China-Africa science, technology and innovation collaboration* (pp. 505–519). Springer. DOI: 10.1007/978-981-97-4576-0_27

Loewenson, R., Modisenyane, M., & Pearcey, M. (2014). African perspectives in global health diplomacy. *Journal of Health Diplomacy*, 1–19.

Mangani, D. Y., Mutambara, M. V., & Shambare, R. (2024). A critical evaluation of health diplomacy as an altruistic underpinning of China–Africa relations. In Muchie, M., Baskaran, A., & Tang, M. (Eds.), *China-Africa science, technology and innovation collaboration* (pp. 489–503). Springer. DOI: 10.1007/978-981-97-4576-0_26

Manohar Parrikar Institute for Defence Studies and Analyses [MP-IDSA]. (2021). India's Vaccine Maitri with Africa. https://www.idsa.in/publisher/comments/indias-vaccine-maitri-with-africa/

Mawdsley, E. (2012). The changing geographies of foreign aid and development cooperation: Contributions from gift theory. *Transactions of the Institute of British Geographers*, *37*(2), 256–272. DOI: 10.1111/j.1475-5661.2011.00467.x

MEA. (2013, January). Pan African e-Network Project (PAENP). https://www.mea.gov.in/Portal/ForeignRelation/Pan_African_e_docx_for_xp.pdf

MEA. (2015, October 29). *Third India-Africa Forum Summit: India-Africa framework for strategic cooperation*. https://www.mea.gov.in/uploads/publicationdocs/25981_framework.pdf

MEA. (2016, July 11). Joint communique between India and Kenya during the visit of Prime Minister to Kenya. https://www.mea.gov.in/outoging-visit-detail.htm?27011/Joint+Communique+

MEA. (2019). MoU on India-Africa health sciences cooperation between the Indian Council of Medical Research and African Union. https://www.mea.gov.in/press-releases.htm?dtl%2F31184%2FMoU+on+IndiaAfrica+Health+Sciences+Cooperation+between+the+Indian+Council+of+Medical+Research+and+African+Union=&utm_source=chatgpt.com

MEA. (2020a, June 4). Prime Minister addresses the virtual Global Vaccine Summit 2020. https://www.mea.gov.in/press-releases.htm?dtl/32733/Prime_Minister_Addresses_the_virtual_Global_Vaccine_Summit_2020

MEA. (2020b, May 13). India donates essential medicines worth USD 1.54 million to the Government of Kenya. High Commission of India, Nairobi. https://hcinairobi.gov.in/eoinrb_listview/NzUx

MEA. (2020c, May 10). Mission Sagar: India's helping hand across the Indian Ocean. https://www.mea.gov.in/press-releases.htm?dtl/32678/Mission_Sagar_Indias_helping_hand_across_

MFA. (2024, September). Forum on China-Africa Cooperation Beijing Action Plan (2025-2027). https://www.mfa.gov.cn/eng/xw/zyxw/202409/t20240905_11485719.html

Ministry of Health & Family Welfare. (2024, December 16). Press Information Bureau. https://static.pib.gov.in/WriteReadData/specificdocs/documents/2024/dec/doc20241228477601.pdf

Mol, R., Singh, B., Chattu, V. K., Kaur, J., & Singh, B. (2022). India's health diplomacy as a soft power tool towards Africa: Humanitarian and geopolitical analysis. *Journal of Asian and African Studies*, *57*(6), 1109–1125. DOI: 10.1177/00219096211039539

Mondal, J. (2024). India's vaccine diplomacy and global health governance: A soft power approach in the context of public policy and religious values. *Religion and Policy Journal*, *2*(1), 20–32. DOI: 10.15575/rpj.v2i1.927

NHC. (2015, October 23). Notice of the General Office of the National Health and Family Planning Commission on issuing the three-year implementation plan of the National Health and Family Planning Commission on promoting health exchange and cooperation along the Belt and Road (2015-2017). http://www.nhc.gov.cn/wjw/ghjh/201510/ce634f7fed834992849e9611099bd7cc.shtml

NHC. (2017, August 18). Beijing communiqué of the Belt and Road health cooperation & health Silk Road. https://en.nhc.gov.cn/2017-08/18/c_72257.htm

Njoya, S. (2023, December 6). Kenyan President William Ruto strengthens digital ties with India on three-day visit. We Are Tech Africa. https://www.wearetech.africa/en/fils-uk/news/tech/kenyan-president-william-ruto-strengthens-digital-ties-with-india-on-three-day-visit

Nyabiage, J. (2020, December 26). Coronavirus: China plans cold-chain bridge to ship and distribute vaccines to African nations. *South China Morning Post.*https://www.scmp.com/news/china/diplomacy/article/3115356/coronavirus-china-plans-cold-chain-bridge-ship-and-distribute

Nyambura-Mwaura, H., & Gebre, S. (2016, November 25). Africans seeking healthcare in India draw hospitals to Kenya. *Mint.*https://www.livemint.com/Science/SHLb4drLlm1sqdNPrdGeBJ/Africans-seeking-healthcare-in-India-draw-hospitals-to-Keny.html

Nye, J. S. (2004). *Soft power: The means to success in world politics*. Public Affairs.

Parkar, P. (2022). Report on the 'India–the medical tourism destination for Angolans.' *The Embassy of India in Angola.*https://indembangola.gov.in/pdf/MedicalTourism_English_N.pdf

People's Daily. (2013). China-assisted hospital commissioned in Nigeria. http://en.people.cn/90777/8112725.html

Punch. (2021, April 5). India donates 100,000 doses of COVID-19 vaccines to Nigeria. *Punch.*https://punchng.com/india-donates-100000-doses-of-covid-19-vaccines-to-nigeria/

PWC. (2020). *Unlocking the potential of India-Africa collaboration for healthcare innovation*. https://nathealthindia.org/wp-content/uploads/2022/12/White-Paper_-Unlocking-the-potential-of-India-Africa-collaboration-for-healthcare-innovation.pdf

Ramachandran, S. (2021, January 26). India's vaccine diplomacy: A potent card? *The Diplomat*. https://thediplomat.com/2021/01/indias-vaccine-diplomacy-a-potent-card/

Rathee, K. (2016, July 12). Airtel, Apollo Hospitals partner for healthcare services in Africa. *Busine**ss Standard*.https://www.business-standard.com/article/companies/airtel-apollo-hospitals-partner-for-healthcare-services-in-africa-116071200437_1.html

Riggirozzi, P., & Yeates, N. (2015). Locating regional health policy: Institutions, politics, and practices. *Global Social Policy*, *15*(3), 212–228. DOI: 10.1177/1468018115599819 PMID: 26635495

Rolland, N. (2020, January). China's vision for a new world order (Special Report No. 83). *National Bureau of Asian Research*. https://www.nbr.org/wp-content/uploads/pdfs/publications/sr83_chinasvision_jan2020.pdf

Rolland, N. (2024, December 4). *The Health Silk Road: A branch of China's Belt and Road Initiative*. National Bureau of Asian Research. https://www.nbr.org/publication/the-health-silk-road-a-branch-of-chinas-belt-and-road-initiative/

Saint-Mézard, I., & Nicolas, F. (2022). India–East Africa: A not so healthy relationship? Ifri. https://www.policycenter.ma/sites/default/files/2022-03/Saint%20Mezard_Nicolas_India_East_Africa_2022.pdf

SCIO. (2020, May 19). Full text: Speech by President Xi Jinping at opening of 73rd World Health Assembly. http://english.scio.gov.cn/topnews/2020-05/19/content_76061159.htm

SCIO. (2020a, June 7). Full text: Fighting COVID-19: China in action. http://english.scio.gov.cn/whitepapers/2020-06/07/content_76135269.htm

Seth, M. (2019, November 16). India-Africa cooperation in the healthcare sector. *Diplomatist*.https://diplomatist.com/2019/11/16/india-africa-cooperation-in-the-healthcare-sector/

SWP. (2023, December 27). *Global health governance and geopolitics*. https://www.swp-berlin.org/publications/products/comments/2023C57_GlobalHealthGovernance.pdf

The Africa-China Centre. (2023, July 13). Tracking China's contributions to Africa's public health systems. https://africachinacentre.org/tracking-chinas-contributions-to-africas-public-health-systems/

The East African. (2015, October 29). India to help boost Kenya healthcare. *The East African.*https://www.theeastafrican.co.ke/tea/news/east-africa/india-to-help-boost-kenya-healthcare-1342132

The State Council. (2014).*China's foreign aid.* http://english.gov.cn/archive/white_paper/2014/08/23/content_281474982986592.htm

The State Council. (2015, March 30). *Full text: Action plan on the Belt and Road Initiative.* https://english.www.gov.cn/archive/publications/2015/03/30/content_281475080249035.htm

The State Council. (2016, December 6). Full text: Traditional Chinese medicine in China. https://english.www.gov.cn/archive/white_paper/2016/12/06/content_281475509333700.htm

The State Council. (2017, August 14). Weishengjishengwei jiu "Yidai Yilu" ji "Jiankang sichou zhilu" gaoji bie yantaohui xiangguan quingkuang juxing meiti chuifenghui [The Health and Family Planning Commission held a media briefing on the high-level seminars on "BRI" and the "Health Silk Road"]. *National Health Commission (PRC).* http://www.gov.cn/xinwen/2017-08/14/content_5217682.htm#allContent

The State Council. (2020, March 11). Zhongguo Zhongyang guanyu zhiding guomin jingji he shehui fazhan di shisige wunian guihua he erlingsanwu nian yuanjing mubiao de jianyi [Proposal of the CCP Central Committee on formulating the 14th Five-Year Plan for national economic and social development and long-range objectives for 2035]. *State Council Information Office (PRC).* https://www.gov.cn/zhengce/2020-11/03/content_5556991.htm

The State Council. (2022, June 28). China hands over additional 10m COVID-19 vaccine doses to Ethiopia. https://english.www.gov.cn/news/internationalexchanges/202206/28/content_WS62ba5760c6d02e533532cd6e.html

Times of India. (2024, July 14). Medical tourism: How India is leading the game. *Times of India.*https://timesofindia.indiatimes.com/life-style/health-fitness/health-news/medical-tourism-how-india-is-leading-the-game/articleshow/111728382.cms

Traoré, S. E. (2021). The strategy of China in Sino-African relations. *Open Journal of Political Science*, *11*(4), 614–629. DOI: 10.4236/ojps.2021.114039

Vaidyanathan, V. (2019). Indian health diplomacy in East Africa: Exploring the potential in pharmaceutical manufacturing. *The South African Journal of International Affairs*, *26*(1), 113–135. DOI: 10.1080/10220461.2019.1582088

Verma, A. (2021, April 29). Vaccine Maitri. Diplomatist. https://diplomatist.com/2021/04/29/vaccine-maitri/

Volodin, A. G. (2023). India-Africa: Development cooperation in healthcare. In Vasiliev, A. M. (Eds.), *Africa and the formation of the new system of international relations—Vol. II: Beyond summit diplomacy: Cooperation with Africa in the post-pandemic world*. Springer., DOI: 10.1007/978-3-031-34041-3_17

Wang, X., & Sun, T. (2014). China's engagement in global health governance: A critical analysis of China's assistance to the health sector of Africa. *Journal of Global Health*, *4*(1), 1–4. https://pmc.ncbi.nlm.nih.gov/articles/PMC4073246/. DOI: 10.7189/jogh.04.010301 PMID: 24976956

WHO. (2008). Letter dated 4 December 2008 from the Permanent Representative of Brazil to the United Nations addressed to the Secretary-General. https://digitallibrary.un.org/record/644505?ln=en&v=pdf#files

WHO. (2017, August 18). Towards a health Silk Road. https://www.who.int/director-general/speeches/detail/towards-a-health-silk-road

WHO. (2025). Traditional medicine. https://www.afro.who.int/health-topics/traditional-medicine

Wong, B. (2020, March 25). China's mask diplomacy. *The Diplomat*. https://thediplomat.com/2020/03/chinas-mask-diplomacy/

Xinhua. (2016, June 22). Xi calls for building "green, healthy, intelligent and peaceful" Silk Road. *People's Daily Online*. http://en.people.cn/n3/2016/0623/c90883-9076046.html

Xinhua. (2017, September 14). "Silk Road" hospital breaks ground in Ethiopian capital. *Xinhua News Agency*. http://www.xinhuanet.com//english/2017-09/14/c_136609571.htm

Xinhua. (2020, April 8). Jack Ma Foundation, Alibaba Foundation make second round of COVID-19 donations to Africa. *Xinhua News Agency*. http://www.xinhuanet.com/english/2020-04/08/c_138958284.htm

Xinhua. (2022, July 3). China-funded health project completed in Kenya. https://english.news.cn/20220703/751b259406c54d708066421fc7ac6825/c.html

Xinhua. (2023, October 17). Feature: Chinese-made drug transforms malaria treatment in Kenya. https://english.news.cn/africa/20231017/422f54ac017445a4a95807056253bc25/c.html

Xinhua. (2023a, July 1). China Focus: Chinese herbal medicine finds common ground in Africa. *Xinhua News Agency*. https://english.news.cn/20230701/8d09514dd5a94d4eab56e05dbbe5b3d0/c.html

Xinhua. (2024, October 25). China Focus: Chinese pharmaceutical companies make inroads into Africa amid growing health cooperation. *Belt and Road Portal*. https://eng.yidaiyilu.gov.cn/p/07J7DO43.html

Xinhua. (2024a, December 18). Zoom Africa: "Made in Africa, Used for Africa" leads China-Africa medicine cooperation. *Xinhua News Agency*. https://english.news.cn/20241218/41c160b396db46d6a54b0dd1ed0b770c/c.html

yidaiyilu. (2023, November 13). Feature: Chinese-invested hospital helps advance healthcare in Ethiopia. https://eng.yidaiyilu.gov.cn/p/0CN5D7TR.html

Youde, J. (2010). China's health diplomacy in Africa. China. *China*, *8*(1), 151–163. DOI: 10.1142/S0219747210000099

Zhang, H. (2023). Health Silk Road: The Chinese way to global health governance. *Governance and Politics*, *2*(1), 69–83. DOI: 10.24833/2782-7062-2023-2-1-69-83

Zhejiang Normal University. (2020, September 10). Smart healthcare changes Africa. https://www.cn-healthcare.com/article/20200910/content-542133.html (In Chinese).

Zhou, J. (2015, July 2). *China's health engagement in Africa—Soft power, public goods or investment opportunities?* Paper presented at the 3rd Annual Conference of the China International Development Research Network, Beijing, China.

Zhou, T., & Ma, T. (2022). Enhancing China–Africa health cooperation for a healthier and safer world: A multilateral perspective. *China Quarterly of International Strategic Studies*, *8*(1), 39–59. DOI: 10.1142/S2377740022500014

Chapter 10
Beyond the Belt and Road:
Evaluating China's Vision for Global South Partnerships

Arti Yadav

https://orcid.org/0000-0002-9392-3888

Ramanujan College, University of Delhi, India

Badar Alam Iqbal

Tshwane University of Technology, South Africa

ABSTRACT

The present study focuses on how China's Global South strategy impacts its globalization perspective, emphasizing this engagement's geopolitical, economic, and cultural dimensions. The research will explore how China attempts to reshape global governance structures and create a multipolar world order by focusing on initiatives such as the Belt and Road Initiative, the Global Security Initiative, and the Global Civilization Initiative. By analyzing these multifaceted approaches, the research seeks to understand China's role in reshaping global economic and political landscapes. This study adopted a mixed-methods approach. Qualitative data was gathered by analyzing Chinese government policy documents, academic literature, and media reports, while quantitative data on trade volumes and foreign direct investments (FDI) complemented the assessment. It aimed to build an understanding of China's Global South strategy in terms of how China's initiatives influence global trade patterns, investment flows, and economic alliances, affecting the broader international economic system.

DOI: 10.4018/979-8-3373-0938-5.ch010

INTRODUCTION

The People's Republic of China is the fourth largest country globally, covering an area of 9,596,961 km^2, and the second most populous, with around 1.4 billion residents. China's ongoing current account surpluses have resulted in foreign exchange reserves exceeding USD 3 trillion, the highest in the world (IMF, 2024). Since the government implemented open and reform economic policies in the 1970s and 1980s, China has experienced extraordinary economic growth, with per capita output soaring by approximately 3,000% in recent decades. This remarkable expansion has led many analysts to describe China's economic performance as a "wonder." However, in recent years, the pace of growth has begun to slow, with the International Monetary Fund (IMF) projecting a further deceleration to 3.3% by 2029 (Feingold, 2024). Figure 1 shows the GDP growth rate of China vs World economy, showing a significant rising trend. Last year, China's economy expanded by 5%, aligning with the target primarily driven by robust exports and a focused stimulus initiative that largely compensated for sluggish domestic demand (Leahy, 2025).

Figure 1. GDP Growth Rate (%) World vs China

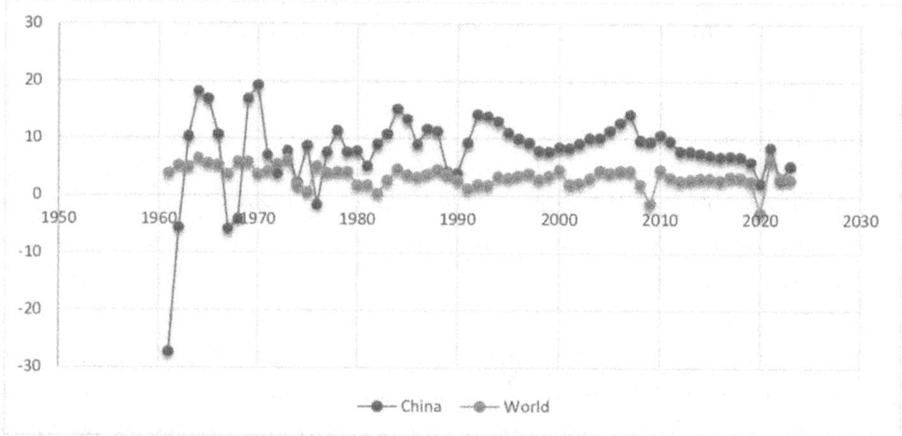

Source: World Bank Database (2025)

Source: World Bank Database (2025)

Still classified as a developing country, China is experiencing faster growth than developed economies. Its compound annual growth rate of 13.1 percent from 2000 to 2022 is significantly higher than that of the United States (4.2 percent), the European Union (3.85 percent), and Germany (3.41 percent). Over the past two decades, exports of goods and services have played a crucial role in this growth, stimulating domestic consumption and capital investments. As a result, China has become the leading economy in the absolute volume of exported goods and services, surpassing both the United States and Germany (Brühl, 2025).

Figure 2. FDI (Inward) in Selected Asian Countries (SA, in % of GDP)

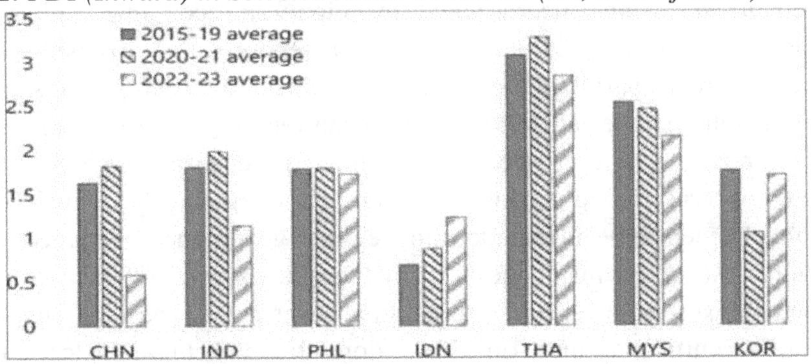

Source: SAFE; National Bureau of Statistics of China; Haver Analytics; and IMF staff calculations

Source: SAFE; National Bureau of Statistics of China; Haver Analytics; and IMF staff calculations

The One Belt and One Road Initiative or the New Silk Road also known as China's Belt and Road Initiative (BRI), has emerged as one of the major infrastructure plans ever developed by a country. This ambitious endeavour encompasses a wide array of financial investment and physical development projects, together with the satellite networks and construction of railways (Feingold, 2023). The BRI is established with two main components including the Silk Road Economic Belt and the 21st Century Maritime Silk Road. The Belt initiative focuses on evolving and expanding land routes that enable the movement of people and commerce across Central Asia, Asia, the Middle East and Europe. In contrast, the Maritime Silk Road objects to enhance sea routes throughout Africa, the Middle East, South Asia and East Asia (Komakech, and Ombati, 2023). Five key priorities central to the BRI are facility connectivity, policy coordination, financial integration, unhindered trade, and fostering people-to-people bonds. The Communist Party of China in 2017 formally integrated the progression of the BRI into its composition (Feingold, 2023). Furthermore, in recent years, China has intensified its outreach to the Global South, encompassing developing nations in Africa, Latin America, Asia, and Oceania. Substantial investments in infrastructure, trade partnerships, and diplomatic initiatives characterize this engagement. China's approach contrasts traditional Western models by emphasizing state-led development, non-interference in domestic affairs, and mutual benefit. China's rise as a global superpower has been underpinned by its strategic engagement with the Global South, a diverse group of developing countries representing over 120 nations across Asia, Africa, Latin America, and Oceania (Divya, 2024; Liu, 2022).

Despite its ambitious initiatives, China's Global South strategy faces several challenges. For example, Chinese loans have led to unsustainable debt levels in some partner countries, raising concerns about sovereignty and economic stability. As the Belt Road Initiative turns old, Beijing is looking to reboot it amid criticism of the debt load it often burdens partner countries (Xinyue, 2024). Further, public skepticism and fears of cultural imperialism persist in various regions, potentially undermining China's soft power aspirations. China's expanding influence has reached a point that has raised concerns among traditional powers in the region. They have noted that China's involvement appears to undermine regional governance (Wencheng, 2024). In addition, China's slowing economic growth and demographic shifts may impact its capacity to sustain extensive international investments and aid. The strategy seeks to rely significantly more on China's domestic market than its long-standing export-driven approach (Duarte, Gupta, and Delvaje, 2024).

Therefore, in light of the above discussion, the present study aims to understand China's Global South strategy in terms of how its initiatives influence global trade patterns, investment flows, and economic alliances, affecting the broader international economic system. China's efforts to reshape globalization challenge existing power structures and may lead to a more multipolar world order. The study holds significant policy implications for China and the Global South. For China, the research will signify the need to align its domestic policies with its international horizon, addressing inconsistencies undermining its soft power. The study in further sections will highlight the importance of strategic engagement with China for Global South nations, ensuring that partnerships align with national development goals and avoid excessive dependency. Ultimately, the findings will contribute to the broader discourse on globalization, multipolarity, and sustainable development, offering valuable insights for academics, policymakers, and international organizations.

LITERATURE REVIEW

Delgi Esposti (2025) discusses the Western narrative regarding the People's Republic of China's (PRC) presence in Africa and the broader Global South is primarily framed as neocolonialism and imperialism. Although key assertions—such as portraying the PRC as a purely predatory actor, its support for authoritarian regimes, and the concept of debt-trap diplomacy—have been largely discredited by academic studies, this perspective continues to prevail in Western media and policy discussions. The author focuses on how this discourse is not just the inaccuracies of these claims but the inconsistent standards applied to the PRC compared to the West, as well as the ideological biases evident in both liberal and conservative Western sources. This contrasts sharply with the more favorable, or at least nuanced, perceptions of Beijing found within the Global South.

Liu and Li (2025) assessed the rise of China's foreign aid over the past two decades, which has ignited significant debate and criticism regarding its methods and impact. This highlights that behavior is shaped by knowledge, capability, and institutional frameworks, influenced by prevailing values and environmental changes. This paper aims to contextualize these debates, examining the evolution of China's foreign aid policy and identifying its challenges. The findings of the study reveal that China's aid strategy is dynamic and motivated by more than just diplomatic or economic goals; it reflects the country's growing economic power and changing domestic and geopolitical priorities. This strategy has evolved through four phases: from genuine to mutual benefits for recipients, from project-specific initiatives to broader supply chain collaborations, from a focus on infrastructure to prioritizing value and impact, and from state-driven to market-driven dynamics. Despite its contributions to global development, challenges such as governance and transparency remain, necessitating ongoing adaptation in the learning process.

Chao (2024) This article examines how the dominant narrative from the West frequently meets competition in the strategies that India and China employ towards the Global South. While India and China have not aligned their policies, some similarities emerge in their responses to the Russia-Ukraine war. However, their approaches to the Israel-Palestine conflict diverge, even as both nations strive to elevate the collective voices of the Global South. Despite these efforts, the intricate relationships within the Global South hinder deeper cooperation, contributing to the group's ongoing underperformance against expectations.

Duarte, Gupta, and Delvaje (2024) This article employs role theory to examine the evolving nature of China's soft power and multilateralism, focusing on its self-perception and international expectations of its new role. In this context, Beijing's initiatives in the Global South and its win-win rhetoric under the Belt and Road Initiative (BRI) have been strategically paired with a robust application of soft power to cultivate support and enhance positive perceptions. Accordingly, China aims to achieve two main objectives: first, to curb the global rise of anti-Chinese sentiment, and second, to reshape international institutions to better reflect its interests and reaffirm its status as a prominent global actor. Through this lens the findings of the study suggested that the role theory highlights a gradual transformation in China's role conception, aligning more closely with international expectations as it seeks to be seen as a champion of a more sustainable world.

Yeung and Huber (2024) explored the impact of Chinese Belt and Road investments on the economic complexity of host countries, a topic that has not been previously discussed in the literature. Using a sequential generalized method of moments model selection approach, the research focuses on countries with economic complexities lower than China's. The findings reveal significant positive effects of Chinese investments on the economic complexities of these host nations, indicating that such investments have helped enhance their production capabilities. The authors suggest that this is particularly encouraging for countries in the Global South, urging them to strengthen their engagement with the Belt and Road initiative.

Komakech and Ombati (2023) aims to deepen our understanding of the Belt and Road Initiative (BRI) by analyzing its conceptual framework, comparing Africa-China relations before and after the BRI, and evaluating the associated benefits and challenges related to the "Five Connectivities." It focuses on five strategically selected African countries—Uganda, Kenya, Egypt, Djibouti, and Mozambique—using literature reviews and case studies, primarily drawing data from the Policies, Projects, Initiatives, and Strategies (PPIS). These countries were selected due to their long-standing relationships with China and their strategic significance. The findings reveal that the BRI lacks a clear definition, complicating the distinction between BRI projects and other economic or diplomatic initiatives. The study also identifies four main differences in Africa-China relations before and after the BRI. While the BRI has positively influenced all five connectivity pillars, it has also brought significant challenges, including issues like procurement corruption, low stakeholder engagement, high compensation costs, labor violations, increasing debts, and environmental risks.

Rudyak (2023) assessed the Belt and Road Initiative (BRI) of China that has generated significant debate since its inception in 2013. Although Beijing promotes it as a win-win opportunity, concerns have arisen regarding the potential risks for participating countries, especially those in the Global South. China's narrative seems to reflect an effort to enhance its communication strategy and assert its influence in international discourse, while its fundamental understanding of development remains unchanged. Developing countries are crucial to China's quest for global prominence. Firstly, China supports these nations, advocating for "diverse paths to modernization" and "true multilateralism." Secondly, it aims to redefine what it means to be a major power by prioritizing development and security over liberal democratic principles.

Liu (2022) explored China's engagement with the Global South in terms of the transnational transfer of knowledge and policy. It suggests that China's involvement in the Bandung Conference was crucial in establishing historical legitimacy for its leadership position in the Global South and presenting itself as an alternative model of modernity. Over the past decade, the significance of the Global South has grown for China, driven not only by geopolitical interests but also by expanding economic relationships with developing nations. These economic ties create a framework that facilitates transnational knowledge transfer, further emphasizing development through a push for institutionalization. The author concluded that China's involvement with the Global South, particularly within the Belt and Road Initiative context, reflects the intricate dynamics of the domestic political economy and evolving global geopolitics, many of which are beyond China's control. Consequently, adopting a stakeholder-centric approach would prove advantageous for all parties involved.

Liu, Xu, and Lim (2022) investigates whether China's growing economic influence serves as an opportunity or a challenge for regional economic integration, using longitudinal and cross-country data from Central, South, and Southeast Asia. The findings suggest that Chinese foreign direct investment generally supports deeper regional integration within these areas. However, increased trade with China may actually hinder such integration. Additionally, a country's level of regional economic integration is shaped by internal factors like infrastructure and information connectivity, GDP per capita, population size, trade openness, and the quality of governance.

Tudoroiu (2022) establishes a comprehensive framework to evaluate China's varied impact on the Global South by analyzing China's expanding impact in the developing world as an expression of normative power, where specific norms are used to define "what is normal" in ways that align with Beijing's views and interests. Though, this dynamic is not one-sided or free from opposition. Political elites frequently adjust their perspectives and their states' policies to align with Chinese local, regional, and global interests, a process driven by effective Chinese international socialization methods that involve normative persuasion and role-playing. At the same time, numerous socio-economic groups in the target nations resist Beijing's initiatives when they conflict with their own independently established interests and are not incorporated into this socialization process. Furthermore, these countries' cognitive and institutional structural factors can significantly shape the acceptance or rejection of Chinese actions, alongside the influence of local agency. The study's findings emphasize that the future of the intricate relationship between China and the countries of the Global South remains open-ended, with local players capable of exerting substantial influence over its development.

The Belt and Road Initiative: A Strategic Imperative

China's growing effect in the Global South, particularly through initiatives like the BRI, has been a focal point of international relations in recent years. The BRI, launched in 2013 by President Xi Jinping, aims to revitalize the ancient Silk Road trade routes and enhance global connectivity. Since its inception in 2013, total engagement in the BRI has amounted to USD 1.175 trillion, which includes approximately USD 704 billion in construction contracts and USD 470 billion in non-financial investments (Runde, Hardman, and Bonin, 2024). While the BRI has drawn considerable attention for its economic and infrastructural impact, China's broader vision for partnerships with the Global South extends far beyond this initiative. China's foreign policy seeks to foster deeper ties with developing countries, particularly in Africa, Asia, and Latin America. However, as the scope of these partnerships broadens, several questions arise about the underlying motives, benefits, and risks associated with China's vision for the Global South (Wang, 2025).

At its core, the BRI is a vast infrastructure and investment project designed to strengthen economic bonds between China and countries in the Global South. It involves a combination of infrastructure development (such as ports, roads, railways, and energy projects), trade partnerships, and financial investments in exchange for enhanced political and economic influence (Tsuji, 2025). Through this initiative, China has aimed to establish itself as a dominant force in the developing world, positioning itself as a global leader in development and a counterweight to Western-led financial institutions like the International Monetary Fund (IMF) and the World Bank (Lin, 2023). The BRI's impact on countries in the Global South has been significant. Many nations that have historically faced challenges in attracting investment have benefited from China's financial resources and technological expertise. For example, African countries like Kenya and Ethiopia have received substantial infrastructure investments under the BRI framework, which has facilitated improved connectivity and trade. Similarly, countries in South Asia, such as Pakistan, have gained access to much-needed infrastructure development and financial support, strengthening their economic ties with China (Hwang, 2024).

However, despite the apparent benefits, the BRI has also faced substantial criticism. One of the most glaring concerns is the growing debt burden in many recipient countries. Critics argue that the BRI's funding model often leaves developing countries heavily indebted to China, leading to concerns about "debt-trap diplomacy" (Omprasad, 2024). In some cases, countries struggling to repay loans have been forced to cede control of critical infrastructure to Chinese companies. Sri Lanka's Hambantota Port, for example, was leased to China for 99 years after the country struggled to repay loans, raising alarms about China's long-term strategic interests in the region (Siddiqui, 2025).

Following China's announcement of the Global Development Initiative (GDI) in September 2021, questions arose about the relevance of the Belt and Road Initiative (BRI), especially since it received minimal attention at the 20th CCP Party Congress. The GDI appeared to be designed to address the BRI's shortcomings by emphasizing developing countries and the Sustainable Development Goals (SDGs), as well as utilizing multilateral platforms like the United Nations. However, despite its reduced visibility, the BRI has certainly not disappeared (Center For International Knowledge On Development, 2023).

Beyond Infrastructure, China's Multifaceted Approach: Vision for Global South Partnerships

While the BRI is the most well-known aspect of China's engagement with the Global South, it represents only one part of a broader strategy. Beyond infrastructure, China has adopted a multifaceted approach to strengthen its partnerships with the Global South. This includes increased foreign direct investment (FDI), trade agreements, diplomatic initiatives, and cultural exchanges. China's FDI in the Global South has surged in recent years, with Chinese companies increasingly investing in sectors such as agriculture, manufacturing, and natural resources (CIMB Asian Research Institute, 2018; Posta, 2023). These investments are often framed as part of China's "South-South Cooperation," which emphasizes solidarity and mutual benefit.

At the G20 Summit in Rio de Janeiro, Brazil, in November 2024, Chinese President Xi Jinping announced eight initiatives aimed at enhancing global development. These initiatives include promoting high-quality cooperation under the Belt and Road Initiative, implementing the Global Development Initiative, supporting African development, and advocating for "practical cooperation for the benefit of the Global South" (Reuters, 2024). China's Global South strategy and the Western-led initiatives like the G7's Partnership for Global Infrastructure and Investment (PGII) reflect two distinct models of global engagement, each rooted in differing political ideologies, priorities, and historical contexts. China's approach, largely embodied in its Belt and Road Initiative (BRI), focuses on infrastructure development, economic cooperation, and mutual benefit under the principle of non-interference in domestic affairs. Through the BRI, China has financed and constructed roads, railways, ports, and power plants across Asia, Africa, and Latin America, positioning itself as a key development partner to many Global South nations. Its emphasis on quick funding and large-scale projects has appealed to countries with urgent development needs and limited access to Western financing.

In contrast, the PGII, launched by the G7 in response to the growing influence of China's BRI, presents an alternative rooted in democratic values, sustainability, and transparency. The PGII aims to mobilize $600 billion by 2027 to support global infrastructure, particularly in climate resilience, health systems, digital connectivity, and gender equality (Simonov, 2025). It prioritizes high-quality, rules-based investment, emphasizing strong governance, environmental and social safeguards, and respect for labor rights. The Western strategy often ties development aid and investment to political and institutional reforms, a practice that China typically avoids in its Global South partnerships.

While both strategies seek to expand influence and address infrastructure gaps in developing regions, their methods and motivations differ significantly. China positions its efforts as part of a broader vision of South-South cooperation, appealing to a shared history of colonialism and underdevelopment, and offering development models that challenge Western dominance (Grey and Gills, 2016). Meanwhile, the G7's PGII attempts to counterbalance China's rising clout by reinforcing a liberal international order and promoting infrastructure that aligns with global standards and norms.In essence, China's Global South strategy is pragmatic and state-led, often prioritizing bilateral ties and rapid execution, while Western initiatives like the PGII adopt a multilateral, value-driven approach aimed at long-term institutional change (Engel, 2019). The competition between these models is not just about infrastructure, but about shaping the future of global development norms and influence in the Global South. China also intends to strengthen collaboration with other developing nations on issues such as repatriating fugitives, asset recovery, preventing safe havens, and building anti-corruption capacities. Furthermore, at the APEC CEO Summit, Xi reaffirmed China's dedication to assisting Global South countries through multilateral platforms and seeking solutions for global prosperity (Xinhua, 2024).

In China's foreign policy the Global South plays a significant role. Beijing aims to increase its influence in this region to challenge the U.S.-led rules-based order and reshape the international security landscape while fostering conditions favorable to its economic growth. China seeks to accomplish this by showcasing its remarkable economic development as a model for other nations and by providing an alternative approach to Western involvement in the Global South (Liu, 2022). These initiatives encompass the Belt and Road Initiative (BRI), which has seen over $1 trillion committed to infrastructure investments across more than 140 countries and territories. Recently, China introduced three additional initiatives: the Global Development Initiative (GDI) in 2021, the Global Security Initiative (GSI) in 2022, and the Global Civilization Initiative (GCI) in 2023. These initiatives aim to promote fundamental principles such as mutual respect, peaceful coexistence, and win-win cooperation (Bang, 2024).

China is progressively enhancing its security cooperation with the Global South. In September 2024, it facilitated settlement talks among various Palestinian factions in Beijing following the recent escalation in the Palestinian- Israeli conflict. Additionally, China and African nations agreed to work together on the Global Security Initiative (GSI), enhancing collaboration in areas such as counter-terrorism, climate change, disaster prevention and mitigation, and public health (Xinyue, 2024). This focus on the Global South is strategic; as Western antagonism grows, China presents itself as a kindred nation with shared experiences of poverty and discrimination. It aims to establish itself as a de facto leader of the Global South, promoting its distinct model of modernization in contrast to the Western approach. Although there's debate about whether China fits within the Global South, its influence in these countries is expanding. The narrative it promotes emphasizes "fairness and justice" and "win-win cooperation," positioning itself as a counterweight to the US-led rules-based order (Zhou, 2024).

However, questions have been raised about whether these investments genuinely align with the interests of local communities or whether they primarily serve China's economic and geopolitical objectives. For example, Chinese mining and agricultural ventures in Africa have sometimes led to concerns about environmental degradation, labor exploitation, and the displacement of local populations (Garcia, Thompson, and Brito, 2024). China's trade relationships with the Global South have also deepened, with China emerging as a significant trading partner for many developing countries. The creation of free trade agreements (FTAs) and the expansion of trade networks through the BRI have helped foster economic growth in several regions (Burguete, 2023).

However, these trade agreements are often criticized for being asymmetrical, with China benefiting disproportionately from the exchange (Baier, Yotov, and Zylkin, 2019). The reliance on raw material exports from the Global South and the importation of Chinese-manufactured goods create an imbalanced economic relationship that reinforces dependency rather than fostering long-term economic independence for developing nations. In addition to economic engagement, China has increasingly used soft power as a tool of diplomacy. Promoting Chinese culture through Confucius Institutes, educational exchanges, and media partnerships is designed to enhance China's image and expand its influence. While these cultural initiatives are framed to build mutual understanding, they also serve China's strategic interests by shaping public opinion and fostering goodwill among Global South populations (Kilolo, 2020; Gong, 2024).

The Digital Silk Road: China's Expanding Technological Footprint in the Global South

China's Digital Silk Road (DSR), initiated in 2015 as part of the broader Belt and Road Initiative (BRI), objectives to improve global digital infrastructure through satellite services investments, ecommerce and telecommunications. This ambitious endeavour seeks to position China as a global digital economy's central hub, offering opportunities and challenges for participating nations (Patil and Gupta, 2024). The DSR has facilitated significant advancements in digital connectivity across Asia, Africa, and Latin America. Chinese tech giants like Huawei and ZTE have been instrumental in deploying 5G networks, providing faster and more affordable internet access to regions previously lacking robust digital infrastructure (Hussain et.al., 2023). This enhanced connectivity has spurred economic growth, enabled digital inclusion, and fostered innovation in various sectors. Additionally, establishing data centers and cloud computing facilities by companies such as Alibaba Cloud and Tencent Cloud has supported local businesses in their digital transformation efforts, offering scalable and cost-effective solutions (Heeks et al., 2024).

Despite these benefits, the DSR raises several concerns, particularly regarding cybersecurity and data sovereignty. Integrating Chinese technology into critical digital infrastructure has led to apprehensions about potential surveillance and espionage. For instance, security researchers have identified vulnerabilities in Chinese-manufactured devices, such as backdoors in robotics systems, which could be exploited for unauthorized surveillance (Yun, 2025). Moreover, the U.S. government has expressed worries about China's use of artificial intelligence to repress populations and spread misinformation, potentially undermining the security of other nations (Reuters, 2024). Furthermore, China's approach to data governance, which includes stringent data localization laws and extensive surveillance practices, has raised alarms about the potential exportation of these models to DSR partner countries. The Council on Foreign Relations highlights that China's efforts to globalize its authoritarian cyber controls could lead to increased censorship and surveillance in participating nations. Additionally, there are concerns about the potential for China to exert pressure on other states through control over digital infrastructure, as noted by reports on the BRI's Digital Silk Road (Wang, Zang and Lei, 2024; Zang, 2024).

While the DSR offers substantial opportunities for enhancing digital infrastructure and economic development, participating countries must carefully assess the associated risks. Implementing robust regulatory frameworks, ensuring transparency in technology agreements, and diversifying digital partnerships can help mitigate potential vulnerabilities (Ghimire et al., 2024). As the DSR expands, balancing leveraging its benefits and safeguarding national interests remains a critical challenge for the global community.

China's Global South Outreach: Insights from Recipient Nations

Recipient countries in the Global South exhibit a spectrum of perspectives on China's Belt and Road Initiative (BRI), reflecting a balance between the allure of rapid infrastructure development and concerns over economic sovereignty and transparency (Liu, 2022). In nations like Kenya, the BRI has facilitated significant projects such as the Mombasa-Nairobi Standard Gauge Railway, enhancing trade connectivity and creating employment opportunities. However, apprehensions persist regarding escalating debt levels and the dominance of Chinese firms in these ventures, which may limit local economic benefits (Rwangoga, 2022).

Similarly, Cambodia has experienced substantial infrastructure growth through Chinese investments, including major expressways and deep-water ports. While these developments have bolstered economic ties, they have also led to a significant trade imbalance, with Cambodia importing more from China than it exports (Heng and Po, 2017; IDI, 2020; Chandara, 2024). In Pakistan, the China-Pakistan Economic Corridor (CPEC) has introduced extensive infrastructure projects aimed at economic revitalization. CPEC is not only enhancing transportation infrastructure but also spearheading economic modernization across various sectors. A significant part of this transformation includes over $1 billion in increased agricultural trade, advancements in digital connectivity, and strengthened energy cooperation. Despite these advancements, concerns about heavy indebtedness to China and the potential for economic over-reliance have been raised (Shahid, 2025). Conversely, countries like Angola have leveraged Chinese partnerships for post-war reconstruction, exchanging natural resources for infrastructure development. This collaboration has yielded tangible benefits, including improved public utilities and transportation networks (Leandro, Li, and Costa, 2024; Yoshikawa, 2025). In South Africa, Chinese investments have targeted key sectors such as energy, with substantial loans provided to state-owned enterprises. While these funds have supported economic initiatives, debates continue over the implications of such debt on national autonomy and financial stability (Nkala, 2024).

For many countries in the Global South, the success of Belt and Road Initiative (BRI) projects is closely tied to the strength of their institutional frameworks. When supported by strong governance and transparent procurement systems, Chinese investments under the BRI can generate substantial benefits—enhancing local participation and promoting inclusive economic development. However, in the absence of robust institutions, challenges such as limited transparency and reduced community engagement may arise. While the BRI offers valuable opportunities for advancing infrastructure and connectivity, it is essential for Global South nations to approach these partnerships strategically, ensuring that economic gains are aligned with principles of fiscal prudence, transparency, and the protection of national sovereignty."

Challenges and Criticisms of Global South Vision

Despite China's strategic benefits, its expanding footprint in the Global South is not without significant challenges and criticisms. The debt burden imposed by BRI projects is a central concern. While these loans have spurred infrastructural development, they have also led to unsustainable debt levels in some countries, creating significant political and economic instability. The lack of transparency in some agreements, along with the absence of rigorous oversight, has fueled concerns about the long-term viability of these projects (Zhang, Jiang, and Hou, 2024). Critics often describe China's approach to the Global South as a form of neocolonialism. By offering loans and investments tied to Chinese companies, equipment, and expertise, China's relationships with developing nations can create dependencies that are difficult to escape. These dependencies could undermine the sovereignty of nations and limit their ability to pursue independent economic and political strategies. The term "debt-trap diplomacy" has been used to describe a situation in which countries become subjugated to China's influence due to their inability to repay loans (Garlick, and Qin, 2023; Rudyak, 2023). In addition to that China's growing influence in the Global South has also raised geopolitical concerns, particularly among Western powers. The United States and the European Union have voiced concerns about China's increasing control over key infrastructure projects, such as ports and transportation networks, which could have strategic military implications (Runde and Hardman, 2024). The growing presence of China in sensitive regions, such as the Indian Ocean and Africa, has led to tensions with countries like India and the United States, who view China's rise as a challenge to their influence (Butt, and Siddiqui, 2021). Further, in many cases, Chinese investments in the Global South have led to significant environmental and social consequences. Infrastructure projects, such as dams, roads, and railways, have disrupted ecosystems, displaced communities, and contributed to environmental degradation. Moreover, Chinese companies operating in the Global South have often been criticized for poor labor practices, including low wages, poor working conditions, and the use of imported labor instead of hiring locally (Siciliano et al., 2019; Zhu et.al, 2024).

DISCUSSION AND CONCLUSION: THE FUTURE OF CHINA'S GLOBAL SOUTH PARTNERSHIPS

Looking forward, China's vision for partnerships with the Global South is likely to evolve as it seeks to address some of the criticisms it has faced. The key to ensuring the long-term success of these partnerships lies in balancing economic development with sustainability, transparency, and equity. Firstly, China must prioritize debt sustainability and ensure that the projects it finances do not place excessive burdens on recipient countries. This could involve restructuring existing debt, offering more favorable loan terms, or promoting greater transparency in loan agreements. Additionally, China could focus on fostering more diversified economic relationships that go beyond raw material extraction and infrastructure development, ensuring that local industries and businesses in the Global South are given a chance to grow and prosper. Secondly, China could place greater emphasis on corporate social responsibility and environmental sustainability in its overseas investments. This would help address some of the social and environmental concerns raised by critics of Chinese projects in the Global South. Finally, China's global strategy will require careful navigation of the geopolitical tensions that its growing influence in the Global South has sparked. By working more closely with international organizations, ensuring that local needs are met, and fostering multilateral cooperation, China could mitigate some of the concerns about its long-term strategic intentions.

China's vision for partnerships with the Global South, mainly through initiatives like the BRI, is a bold and multifaceted strategy aimed at reshaping global trade, infrastructure, and political influence. While the initiative has brought significant economic benefits to many countries, it is also fraught with challenges related to debt sustainability, environmental impacts, and geopolitical tensions. As China continues to expand its influence in the developing world, it will need to address these issues to ensure that its vision is both beneficial and sustainable for all parties involved. Only through greater transparency, mutual respect, and equitable development can China's partnerships with the Global South achieve long-term success.

REFERENCES

Baier, S. L., Yotov, Y. V., & Zylkin, T. (2019). On the widely differing effects of free trade agreements: Lessons from twenty years of trade integration. *Journal of International Economics*, *116*, 206–226. DOI: 10.1016/j.jinteco.2018.11.002

Bang, C. Y. (2024). Can China's Global South Strategy Achieve Its Objectives in Central Asia? The Diplomat. Retrieved from https://thediplomat.com/2024/10/can-chinas-global-south-strategy-achieve-its-objectives-in-central-asia/

Brühl, V. (2025). The economic rise of China – an analysis of China's growth drivers. *International Economics and Economic Policy*, *22*(1), 16. DOI: 10.1007/s10368-024-00640-w

Burguete, V. (2023). China and the Global South: trade, investment and rescue loans. CIDOB Barcelona Centre for International Affairs. Retrieved from https://www.cidob.org/en/publications/china-and-global-south-trade-investment-and-rescue-loans

Butt, K. M., & Siddiqui, S. J. (2021). Growing Chinese Presence in the Indian Ocean: Prospects and Challenges. *Strategic Studies, 41*(2), 64–81. Retrieved from https://www.jstor.org/stable/48732275

Center For International Knowledge On Development. (2023). Progress Report on the Global Development Initiative 2023. Retrieved from https://www.mfa.gov.cn/eng/zy/jj/GDI_140002/wj/202406/P020240606606196155121.pdf

Chandara, S. (2024). Reimagining alliances: Cambodia's strategic position between China and US. The Phnom Penh Post. Retrieved from https://www.phnompenhpost.com/opinion/reimagining-alliances-cambodia-s-strategic-position-between-china-and-us

Chao, X. (2024). "All Roads Lead to South": India and China in Global South Narratives and Practices. *Strategic Analysis*, *48*(4), 346–358. DOI: 10.1080/09700161.2024.2404593

CIMB Asian Research Institute. (2018). China's Belt and Road Initiative (BRI) and Southeast Asia. Retrieved from https://www.lse.ac.uk/ideas/Assets/Documents/reports/LSE-IDEAS-China-SEA-BRI.pdf

Degli Esposti, N. (2025). Assessing Western Discourse on 'Chinese Neocolonialism' in the Global South. *The International Spectator*, •••, 1–17. DOI: 10.1080/03932729.2025.2454308

Della Posta, P. (2023). The Belt and Road Initiative: Inclusive Globalization and Poverty Reduction. Global Journal of Emerging Market Economies, 15(2), 273-288. (Original work published 2023)DOI: 10.1177/09749101231167448

Divya, A. (2024). China's G20 Agenda and Its Effect on Multilateralism: The Emerging Global South. The Diplomat. Retrieved from https://thediplomat.com/2024/12/chinas-g20-agenda-and-its-effect-on-multilateralism-the-emerging-global-south/

Duarte, P. A. B., Gupta, A., & Delvaje, B. C. (2024). Multilateralism and Soft Power Made-in-China: (re)Adjusting Role Conception to Meet International Expectations. *East Asia (Piscataway, N.J.)*, *41*(4), 325–345. DOI: 10.1007/s12140-024-09424-0

Engel, S. (2019). South–South Cooperation in Southeast Asia: From Bandung and Solidarity to Norms and Rivalry. *Journal of Current Southeast Asian Affairs*, *38*(2), 218–242. DOI: 10.1177/1868103419840456

Feingold, S. (2023). China's Belt and Road Initiative turns 10. Here's what to know. World Economic Forum. Retrieved from https://www.weforum.org/stories/2023/11/china-belt-road-initiative-trade-bri-silk-road/

Feingold, S. (2024). Where is China's economy headed? World Economic Forum. Retrieved from https://www.weforum.org/stories/2024/06/china-economic-outlook-growth-trade/

Garcia, A., Thompson, L., & Brito, C. (2024). South-South Investments: Driver for Alternative Globalization? Examining China-Led Special Economic Zones in Brazil and South Africa. *Critical Sociology*, *0*(0), 08969205241252445. Advance online publication. DOI: 10.1177/08969205241252445

Garlick, J., & Qin, F. (2023). China's 'do-as-I-do' paradigm: Practice-based normative diplomacy in the global South. *The Pacific Review*, *37*(5), 985–1015. DOI: 10.1080/09512748.2023.2290619

Ghimire, A., Ali, S., Long, X., Chen, L., & Sun, J. (2024). Effect of Digital Silk Road and innovation heterogeneity on digital economy growth across 29 countries: New evidence from PSM-DID. *Technological Forecasting and Social Change*, *198*, 122987. DOI: 10.1016/j.techfore.2023.122987

Gong, X. (2024). The Challenges Behind China's Global South Policies. Carnegie China. Retrieved from https://carnegieendowment.org/posts/2024/12/the-challenges-behind-chinas-global-south-policies?lang=en

Gray, K., & Gills, B. K. (2016). South–South cooperation and the rise of the Global South. *Third World Quarterly*, *37*(4), 557–574. DOI: 10.1080/01436597.2015.1128817

Heeks, R., Ospina, A. V., Foster, C., Gao, P., Han, X., Jepson, N., Schindler, S., & Zhou, Q. (2024). China's digital expansion in the Global South: Systematic literature review and future research agenda. *The Information Society*, *40*(2), 69–95. DOI: 10.1080/01972243.2024.2315875

Heng, K., & Po, S. (2017). Cambodia and China"s Belt and Road Initiative: Opportunities, challenges and future directions. UC Occasional Paper Series, 1(2), 1-18. Retrieved from https://www.uc.edu.kh/userfiles/image/2017/1_Cambodia_and_China_ Belt_and_Road.pdf

Hu, X. (2024). China's Global South Strategy: Twice the Efforts for Half the Result? RSiS, No. 108. Nanyang Technological University. Retrieved from https://rsis.edu.sg/rsis-publication/idss/ip24108-chinas-global-south-strategy-twice-the-efforts-for-half-the-result/

Hussain, F., Imran, A., Hussain, Z., & Khan, M. I. (2023). Infrastructure Development for the Digital Silk Road (DSR) and its Implications for China Under the Belt and Road Initiative, *Asia-Pacific Social. Scientific Review (Singapore)*, *23*(4), •••. https://www.dlsu.edu.ph/wp-content/uploads/pdf/research/journals/apssr/2023-december-vol23-4/rb1.pdf

Hwang, K., & Lee, J. (2024). Impact of the Belt and Road Initiative on Global Trade and Economic Growth Amid China's Slowing Growth. *China Report (New Delhi, India)*, *60*(3), 266–286. DOI: 10.1177/00094455241288083

IDI(Inclusive Development International). (2020). Reassessing China's Investment Footprint in Cambodia. Retrieved from https://www.inclusivedevelopment.net/wp-content/uploads/2020/08/2020_IDI_Briefing-on-Chinas-Footprint-in-Cambodia-Update.pdf

IMF. (2024). *International reserves and foreign currency liquidity*. IRFCL.

International Monetary Fund (IMF). (2024). Asia and Pacific Dept. China's Foreign Direct Investment: Inward and Outward. *IMF Staff Country Reports*, *276*, A004. DOI: 10.5089/9798400285998.002.A004

Kilolo, J.-M. M. (2020). Country asymmetry, trade agreements, and transfers. *Economics and Politics*, *33*(1), 37–51. DOI: 10.1111/ecpo.12156

Komakech, R. A., & Ombati, T. O. (2023). Belt and Road Initiative in Developing Countries: Lessons from Five Selected Countries in Africa. *Sustainability (Basel)*, *15*(16), 12334. DOI: 10.3390/su151612334

Leahy, J. (2025). China's economy grew 5% in 2024. Financial Times. Retrieved from https://www.ft.com/content/45c3f4ee-2825-45f3-aa4f-1d3615d06e3e

Leandro, F. J. B. S., Li, Y., & Costa, C. M. (2024). Forty Years of China-Angola Relations: Rethinking the Strategic Partnership. In Li, Y., Leandro, F. J. B. S., Tavares da Silva, J., & Rodrigues, C. (Eds.), *The Palgrave Handbook on China-Europe-Africa Relations*., DOI: 10.1007/978-981-97-5640-7_23

Lin, D. (2023). The Belt and Road Initiative and China's Pursuit of Agenda-Setting Power. *Orbis*, *67*(4), 496–523. DOI: 10.1016/j.orbis.2023.08.003

Liu, B., & Li, X. (2025). China's Aid in Global South Development Cooperation: A Study of Its Evolution. *Forum for Development Studies*, *52*(2), 1–25. DOI: 10.1080/08039410.2025.2460553

Liu, H. (2022). China engages the Global South: From Bandung to the Belt and Road Initiative. Global Policy. Wiley: Online Library. Retrieved from https://onlinelibrary.wiley.com/doi/10.1111/1758-5899.13034

Nkala, S. (2024). An Analysis of China's Investments in South Africa's Mining Sector. In Mazwi, F., Mudimu, G. T., & Helliker, K. (Eds.), *Chinese Investment in Africa. Economic Geography*. Springer., DOI: 10.1007/978-3-031-52815-6_8

Omprasad, G. (2024). Understanding China's Grand Strategy through the Belt and Road Initiative. *International Studies*, *61*(2), 170–184. DOI: 10.1177/00208817241247665

Patil, S., & Gupta, P. (2024). The Digital Silk Road in the Indo-Pacific: Mapping China's Vision for Global Tech Expansion. Observer Research Foundation. Retrieved from https://www.orfonline.org/public/uploads/posts/pdf/20240103105252.pdf

Reuters.(2024). Chinese President Xi arrives in Brazil for G20 summit talks with Lula. Retrieved from https://www.reuters.com/world/chinese-president-xi-arrives-brazil-g20-summit-talks-with-lula-2024-11-18/Retrieved from https://www.reuters.com/world/chinese-president-xi-arrives-brazil-g20-summit-talks-with-lula-2024-11-18/

Reuters.(2024). US concerned about China's use of AI, says it could make countries vulnerable to coercion. Retrieved from https://www.reuters.com/technology/artificial-intelligence/us-concerned-about-chinas-use-ai-says-it-could-make-countries-vulnerable-2024-10-24/

Rudyak, M. (2023). China and the Global South: Many Initiatives, One Narrative. *IAI Papers*. Retrieved from https://www.iai.it/sites/default/files/iaip2320.pdf

Runde, D. F., & Hardman, A. (2024). Great Power Competition in the Multilateral System. CSIS. Retrieved from https://www.csis.org/analysis/great-power-competition-multilateral-system

Runde, D. F., Hardman, A., & Bonin, C. (2024). Responding to China's Growing Influence in Ports of the Global South. CSIS. Retrieved from https://www.csis.org/analysis/ responding-chinas-growing-influence-ports-global-south

Rwangoga, D. A. (2022). China's Belt and Road Initiative: A Curse or Blessing for African Countries. Intergovernmental Research and Policy Journal. Retrieved from https://irpj.euclid.int/articles/chinas-belt-and-road-initiative-a-curse-or-blessing-for-african-countries/

Shahid, M. (2025). CPEC Driving Pakistan Toward Regional Prosperity And Economic Growth – OpEd. eurasiareview. Retrieved from https://www.eurasiareview.com/ 11042025-cpec-driving-pakistan-toward-regional-prosperity-and-economic-growth-oped/

Siciliano, G., Bene, D. D., Scheidel, A., Liu, J., & Urban, F. (2019). Environmental justice and Chinese dam-building in the global South. *Current Opinion in Environmental Sustainability*, *37*, 20–27. DOI: 10.1016/j.cosust.2019.04.003

Siddiqui, H. (2025). Debt Diplomacy or Dangerous Geo-Economic Strategy? Understanding the Complex Reality of China's BRI. Financial Express. Retrieved from https://www.financialexpress.com/world-news/debt-diplomacy-or-dangerous-geo-economic-strategy-understanding-the-complex-reality-of-chinas-bri/3714197/

Simonov, M. (2025). The Belt and Road Initiative and Partnership for Global Infrastructure and Investment: Comparison and current status. *Asia and the Global Economy*, *5*(1), 100106. DOI: 10.1016/j.aglobe.2025.100106

Tsuji, C. (2025). Belt and Road Initiative. Brittanica. Retrieved from https://www.britannica. com/topic/Belt-and-Road-Initiative

Tudoroiu, T. (2022). Normative Power China, Subnational Agency, and Structural Factors in the Global South. In Tudoroiu, T., & Kuteleva, A. (Eds.), *China in the Global South*. Springer., DOI: 10.1007/978-981-19-1344-0_12

Wang, C. N. (2025). China Belt and Road Initiative (BRI) Investment Report 2024. Green Finance and Development Centre. Retrieved from https://greenfdc.org/china-belt-and-road-initiative-bri-investment-report-2024/

Wang, R., Zhang, C., & Lei, Y. (2024). Justifying a Privacy Guardian in Discourse and Behaviour: The People's Republic of China's Strategic Framing in Data Governance. *The International Spectator*, *59*(2), 58–76. DOI: 10.1080/03932729.2024.2315064

Wencheng, G. (2024). Xinhua Commentary: What drives the growth of China's soft power. Retrieved from http://www.china.org.cn/world/Off_the_Wire/2024-03/14/content_117061870.htm

World Bank Database. (2025). Retrieved from https://databank.worldbank.org/reports. aspx?source=2&series=NY.GDP.MKTP.KD.ZG&country=#

Xinhua. (2024). Xi calls for building just world of common development, outlines China's actions for global development. Retrieved from https://english. www.gov.cn/news/202411/19/content_WS673bba1ec6d0868f4e8ed25d.html

Xinyue, H. (2024). IP24108 | China's Global South Strategy: Twice the Efforts for Half the Result? RSIS Publications. Retrieved from https://rsis.edu.sg/rsis-publication/idss/ip24108-chinas-global-south-strategy-twice-the-efforts-for-half-the-result/

Yeung, H., & Huber, J. (2024). Has China's belt and road initiative positively impacted the economic complexity of host countries? Empirical evidence. *Structural Change and Economic Dynamics*, *69*(June), 246–258. https://www.sciencedirect.com/science/article/abs/pii/S0954349X23001868. DOI: 10.1016/j.strueco.2023.12.012

Yoshikawa, S. (2025). China And Angola: From The Pioneering 'Angolan Model' To A 'New' Relationship – Analysis. eurasiareview. Retrieved from https://www.eurasiareview.com/01032025-china-and-angola-from-the-pioneering-angolan-model-to-a-new-relationship-analysis/

Yun, H. (2024). China's Data Sovereignty and Security: Implications for Global Digital Borders and Governance. *Chinese Political Science Review*. Advance online publication. DOI: 10.1007/s41111-024-00269-9

Zhang, C. (2024). China's privacy protection strategy and its geopolitical implications. *ARPE*, *3*(1), 6. DOI: 10.1007/s44216-024-00028-2

Zhang, H., Jiang, Y., & Hou, C. (2024). How Does the "Belt and Road" Initiative Affect Debt Sustainability? *Sustainability (Basel)*, *16*(23), 10512. DOI: 10.3390/su162310512

Zhou, G. (2024). Rise of Global South and changes in contemporary international order. *China Int Strategy Rev.*, *6*(1), 58–77. DOI: 10.1007/s42533-024-00160-x

Zhu, A. L., Weins, N., Lu, J., Harlan, T., Qian, J., & Seleguim, F. B. (2024). China's nature-based solutions in the Global South: Evidence from Asia, Africa, and Latin America. *Global Environmental Change*, *86*, 102842. DOI: 10.1016/j.gloenvcha.2024.102842

Chapter 11
China and the Persian Gulf:
A New Era of Strategic Cooperation

Alireza Samoudi
https://orcid.org/0009-0001-5089-7798
Research Institute for Security and Development Studies, Tehran, Iran

ABSTRACT

In recent years, China has managed to establish itself as an important and influential player in the Persian Gulf. Despite the dominant role and actorness of the United States in the Persian Gulf over the past few decades, Beijing has succeeded in enhancing its relations with Persian Gulf countries within the framework of strategic hedging. China's desire to expand cooperation with Persian Gulf nations and strengthen its presence in the region has been met with a positive response from these countries. The Persian Gulf states, in turn, are keen to balance and diversify their foreign policies by strengthening their ties with China. This article, utilizing the concept of strategic hedging, examines the growing strategic cooperation between China and Persian Gulf countries in the economic, technological, and security domains. It also highlights that the United States, in an effort to maintain its position in the Persian Gulf, is attempting to prevent the expansion of these countries' cooperation with China, particularly in the fields of technology and armaments.

DOI: 10.4018/979-8-3373-0938-5.ch011

INTRODUCTION

The rise of China stands as the most transformative development in 21st-century international politics and economics. In recent years, Beijing has intensified its pursuit of sustainable energy resources to support its booming economy. The Persian Gulf, a strategically vital region for energy supplies, has become a key focus for China, an emerging political and economic power. Once guided by revolutionary ideology in its approach to the Persian Gulf, China has shifted to a pragmatic stance, prioritizing energy security in its relations with the Persian Gulf countries. The Belt and Road Initiative (BRI) has further deepened ties, particularly with the UAE and Saudi Arabia, expanding cooperation beyond energy trade into sectors like defense and security.

China's rapid growth has heightened its reliance on foreign markets and energy resources, with the Persian Gulf emerging as a critical hub for both. Oil and energy resources have significantly strengthened the relationship between China and the Arab Persian Gulf states, leading to increased trade and economic exchange between the two parties. This dynamic has not only strengthened political ties but also elevated Beijing's role in the development strategies of Persian Gulf nations. Driven by growing energy demands, China positions itself as an active player in the global energy sector, pursuing mutual interests and benefits. It has consistently signaled its willingness to enhance dialogue and cooperation with other nations to ensure energy stability and security worldwide. Today, Beijing is the largest trading partner of Persian Gulf countries, wielding significant influence in energy, trade, and investment. Over the past six decades, China's diplomacy in the region has evolved from an ideological framework to a pragmatic one, transitioning from a focus on balancing power to achieving strategic equilibrium. This article explores the Persian Gulf's importance in China's foreign policy, Beijing's strategic hedging approach, the drivers behind its growing ties with Persian Gulf countries, and the U.S. perspective on this expanding relationship.

The Importance of the Persian Gulf for China

During the Cold War, China interpreted global events through an ideological lens. In the post-Cold War era, however, national interests and pragmatism have defined its foreign policy. China's remarkable economic growth has fueled a surging demand for fossil fuels like oil and gas, making the Persian Gulf a cornerstone of its energy strategy. Since losing energy self-sufficiency in the early 1990s, China has relied on oil imports and sought to secure a stable supply by forging closer ties with key Persian Gulf players such as Saudi Arabia, Qatar, the UAE, and Iran. The region's geographic and geopolitical significance—highlighted by the Strait of

Hormuz, a vital link between three continents—has long made it a focal point for major powers vying for influence.

For China, the Persian Gulf is a critical source of raw materials and minerals to sustain its expanding economy. Its foreign policy, now predominantly economic, prioritizes broadening relations with countries based on trade and commercial interests. The demand for natural resources and markets shapes Beijing's global strategy. However, China's growing presence in the Persian Gulf is perceived as a challenge to U.S. interests, where Washington has long seen itself as the dominant actor and is reluctant to accommodate China's expanding role. Amid rising energy needs, Beijing positions itself as a cooperative partner in the energy sector, emphasizing mutual benefits and expressing readiness to collaborate with others to promote global energy stability. This "oil diplomacy," reminiscent of Japan's energy policies in the 1970s and 1980s, involves diversifying supply sources, deepening ties with producing nations, encouraging Chinese oil firms to invest abroad, and forming strategic alliances to enhance energy security worldwide (Farokhparsa et al., 2024, p. 247).

Since Xi Jinping assumed leadership in 2012-2013, the Persian Gulf has become integral to the Belt and Road Initiative. Under the BRI's Silk Road Economic Belt and Twenty-First Century Maritime Silk Road, China has adopted a "1+2+3" cooperation model with Persian Gulf countries: energy as the core, infrastructure and trade/investment as the two wings, and breakthroughs in nuclear energy, space technology, and renewables as the three focus areas (Akbarzadeh & Saba, 2025, p. 4). Beyond Iran, Iraq, and Yemen, The Persian Gulf nations bolster China's energy security, expand its market access, and enhance its soft power in the modern era. Beijing adheres to its "Four No Foreign Policy"—no alliances, no interference in domestic affairs, no proxy forces, and no filling of political vacuums left by others (Sun, 2022, p. 33). Chinese leaders promote a narrative of "equality among nations regardless of size" and respect for sovereignty, encouraging Persian Gulf leaders to view ties with Beijing as a chance to enrich their strategic partnerships (Bazoobandi, 2024, p. 128). A key factor in China's rising influence has been the Persian Gulf countries' concerns over waning U.S. commitment to the region. Vulnerable to instability, these states are diversifying their transregional partnerships, with China emerging as a second-tier power that strengthens economic and diplomatic ties without upending the regional status quo.

Conceptual Framework: Strategic Hedging

Strategic hedging originated in economic discussions from the 1940s as a way to minimize investment risks, but it rose to prominence in international relations after the Cold War, particularly in Asia due to its unique regional dynamics. In this field, hedging describes how major powers adapt their behavior and indirectly address security threats and competition for influence. Medeiros, a key figure in shaping this concept, views strategic hedging as a blend of "realist-style balancing" for security purposes alongside efforts to promote cooperation and integration in other areas. Meanwhile, Tessman and Wolfe define hedging as a tactic employed by weaker states against stronger ones, using soft balancing approaches to position themselves for a potential decline in the dominant power's strength, before shifting to conventional balancing methods (Houghton, 2024, p. 10).

The notion of strategic hedging has been extended to various dimensions of Chinese foreign policy, such as regional security in the Asia-Pacific (Medeiros, 2005), China's energy security (Tessman & Wolfe, 2011), and a broader interpretation of China's national security (Wolfe, 2013). In academic discussions, strategic hedging—initially a concept from corporate finance tied to risk management (e.g., Mello & Parsons, 1999)—is frequently associated with realist balance of power theory. Kuik stands out as a key contributor to this framework, portraying strategic hedging as a strategy shaped by a mix of international, regional, and domestic factors, designed to optimize a state's benefits while reducing potential threats. This approach enables nations to mitigate risks through diverse political and economic measures, especially in scenarios involving security dilemmas, allowing them to protect their interests and security while seeking mutual gains (Derakhshandeh & Shafiee, 2022, p. 13). Tessman and Wolfe, however, apply the term more narrowly, defining it "as a structural explanation of competitive actions by second-tier states in a unipolar system," framing it "as a genuine structural evolution of traditional balance of power theory that also integrates valuable perspectives from advocates of the soft balancing approach" (Garlick & Havlova, 2020, p. 84).

To maximize its interests and leverage the advantages of a target country, a hedging state employs economic cooperation tactics in a relatively peaceful yet uncertain environment. Simultaneously, to ensure its survival and security amid perceived threats, it uses soft balancing strategies against the source of those threats. In essence, the hedging state adopts a dual approach: enhancing its benefits and power while mitigating long-term risks (Derakhshandeh & Shafiee, 2022, p. 13). For over four decades, China has pursued strategic hedging in the Persian Gulf, aiming to be a friend to all and an enemy to none. This policy allows Beijing to operate under the U.S. security umbrella while advancing its interests through trade and investment. As a second-tier power, China seeks to expand its regional influence without upending the existing order. Its strategic hedging in the Persian Gulf operates on two levels. At the structural and systemic level, China, as a tier-two state, manages the dominance of a leading global power—reducing the risk of direct conflict while steadily increasing its own power and influence. This systemic perspective is key to understanding China's approach to competitors and conflicts in the region. At the regional level, China maintains relations with all major Persian Gulf states, avoiding entanglement in local disputes or efforts to alter the status quo by favoring one side. Strategic hedging does not imply that China aims to displace the region's dominant actor. While several Persian Gulf states offer similar advantages—such as diverse investment opportunities and abundant energy resources—a rising power like China must cultivate ties with multiple states to maximize its influence and economic potential.

China's Economic Relations with the Persian Gulf States

In recent years, relations between China and the Persian Gulf States have increased significantly, and Beijing has become the main trading partner of most countries in the region, thus increasing Beijing's political influence in the West Asian region. To bolster its approach, China has forged bilateral strategic partnership agreements with most Middle Eastern nations. This form of diplomacy is a cornerstone of China's foreign policy, aimed at crafting a supportive global framework and ensuring a favorable setting for its ascent. These partnerships are structured hierarchically, reflecting the significance China places on each relationship, and are categorized from highest to lowest as "comprehensive strategic," "strategic," "comprehensive cooperative," "cooperative," and "friendly cooperative" partnerships. A "comprehensive strategic partnership" entails extensive collaboration and development in regional and global matters, while a "strategic partnership" emphasizes closer coordination on such issues, including military affairs. China has secured "comprehensive strategic partnerships" with Saudi Arabia (KSA), the UAE, Iran, and Bahrain, and "strategic partnerships" with Qatar, Oman, Iraq, and Kuwait, all of which involve deep cooperation and alignment on regional and international issues, including military dimensions. Beyond bilateral ties, China has enhanced its regional presence through multilateral platforms, which facilitate coordination with Middle Eastern countries. Key examples include the China–Arab States Cooperation Forum (CASCF), the China–PGCC Strategic Dialogue, and summits like the China–Saudi Arabia Summit, the China–Arab States Summit, and the China–PGCC Summit (Akbarzadeh & Saba, 2025, p. 5).

Table 1. Chinese Partnership Diplomacy in the Persian Gulf

State	Partnership Level	Year Signed
Saudi Arabia	Comprehensive Strategic Partnership	2016
Iran	Comprehensive Strategic Partnership	2016
UAE	Comprehensive Strategic Partnership	2018
Qatar	Strategic Partnership	2014

continued on following page

Table 1. Continued

State	Partnership Level	Year Signed
Iraq	Strategic Partnership	2015
Oman	Strategic Partnership	2018
Kuwait	Strategic Partnership	2018
Bahrain	N/A	N/A

(Houghton, 2024, p. 189)

Several factors come into play when pursuing partnership diplomacy, including the capabilities of the partner state—such as its economic power, regional clout, and political stability—and its readiness to engage in deeper cooperation, which can be gauged by existing economic ties or political goodwill. The absence of a partnership agreement between China and a given state suggests a current lack of interest from one or both parties. The table outlines the types of partnership diplomacy China has established in the Persian Gulf, along with the years of the most recent agreements for each case.

China is also generally seeking to strengthen its relations with Arab countries especially Saudi Arabia and UAE. Among the most significant recent diplomatic exchanges are Saudi Crown Prince Mohammed bin Salman's trip to China in February 2019 and President Xi Jinping's visit to Saudi Arabia in December 2022, which have laid the groundwork for enhanced political, economic, and strategic ties. In September 2024, Chinese Premier Li Qiang's visit to Saudi Arabia to co-chair the fourth meeting of the High-Level Chinese-Saudi Joint Committee underscored the importance China places on its relationship with Saudi Arabia within its broader foreign policy and engagement with the MENA region. During Xi's 2022 visit, both nations committed to deepening cooperation in fields like the digital economy, artificial intelligence, and mining. Additionally, in December 2024, the Saudi-Chinese Business Council Forum in Beijing brought together 25 Saudi and 30 Chinese investors, resulting in 24 agreements signed in sectors such as healthcare, biotechnology, and beyond (Quamar, 2025). Although the bilateral relationship primarily centers on energy and oil, China and Saudi Arabia established a comprehensive strategic partnership in 2016. This partnership seeks to deepen cooperation through agreements spanning multiple sectors, including politics, economics, trade, culture, humanitarian efforts, military, security, and energy. It also involves collaboration in regional and international forums to strengthen coordination between the two nations at the highest levels (Adrianov, 2024).

Before Jinping's visit to Saudi Arabia, Beijing and Doha signed a $60 billion contract and a 27-year agreement to supply four million tons of LNG per year. China also reached a 25-year agreement with Iran in March 2021 and has signed strategic partnerships with twelve Arab countries in the Middle East and North Africa. In fact, China seeks to create a positive balance in its interaction with countries in the region and is inclined to mediate in security in Iraq, Libya, Sudan, Yemen, and Palestine. The country has also used its veto power against Western resolutions on Syria. Also, in early 2022, Syria joined 19 other Arab countries in the Belt and Road Initiative. Iraq also became the most important investment destination of the Belt and Road Initiative in 2021 with $10.5 billion (Samoudi, 2023, p. 143). China's engagement with the Middle East and the Persian Gulf region is primarily centered around the Belt and Road Initiative (BRI), which was launched in 2013. At the China-PGCC Forum for Industries and Investment in Xiamen on May 23, 2024, President Xi Jinping emphasized that strengthening industrial and investment ties between China and the Persian Gulf nations would enhance the synergy between the Belt and Road Initiative and the developmental goals, visions, and strategies of Persian Gulf countries (Layla, 2024). China's emphasis on economic cooperation and development in its approach to the Persian Gulf is evident in two key governmental documents: the 2015 *Vision and Actions on Jointly Building Silk Road Economic Belt and 21st Century Maritime Silk Road* and the 2016 *Arab Policy Paper*. The *Arab Policy Paper* highlights five priority areas for cooperation with Arab states: energy, technology, aerospace, finance, and culture (Bulard, 2025).

These documents outline partnerships with Persian Gulf states in agriculture, trade, investment, energy, and infrastructure. The *Vision and Actions* paper identifies five key collaboration goals—facility connectivity, people-to-people ties, political coordination, unimpeded trade, and financial integration—aimed at fostering relationships among Belt and Road Initiative (BRI) participants. This focus underscores China's development-oriented approach rather than geopolitical ambitions. Similarly, the *Arab Policy Paper* articulates China's vision for aligned development strategies with Arab states to enhance national and regional production, deepen cooperation in energy, trade, investment, and infrastructure, and advance new energy, nuclear power, and satellite technology (Al Shidhani & Baig, 2024, p. 6). In his June 2014 address at the 6th Ministerial Conference of the China-Arab States Cooperation Forum (CASCF), President Xi Jinping described regional countries as "natural cooperative partners in jointly building the BRI." Since then, Chinese businesses, banks, and financial institutions have actively promoted the BRI in the Persian Gulf (Zulfikar Rakhmat, 2019, p. 6).

The BRI's goals are communicated in ways that resonate with Persian Gulf societies, most notably through the "Chinese Dream," a central legitimizing concept tied to the initiative. Xi has framed it as a universal aspiration, stating, "Everyone has their own ideals and aspirations, and each person has their own dream," emphasizing that the Chinese Dream is "the people's dream," reliant on public support and aimed at benefiting them (Zulfikar Rakhmat, 2019, p. 7). This framing aligns

Chinese interests with those of the Persian Gulf states, suggesting a shared pursuit of prosperity. Wang Jinglie, a member of the executive committee of the Chinese Society for Middle East Studies, reinforced this by expressing hope that "when we achieve the 'Chinese Dream,' the Arab countries will not only share in our happiness but also realize their own 'Arab Dream'" (Zulfikar Rakhmat, 2019, p. 8). The term "Arab Dream" seeks to equate China's ambitions with the national aspirations of Persian Gulf states, fostering a sense of mutual benefit. Over the past decade, China has sourced roughly half its oil from the region.

There is significant cooperation in the energy sector between China and the Persian Gulf states, as China has become the world's largest energy consumer. Currently, the Persian Gulf Arab states are the top exporters of oil to China, especially as the United States has reduced its oil imports. Consequently, China has become the primary market for oil exports from these countries, surpassing both the U.S. and Japan. Additionally, the Persian Gulf states view China as a vast market not just for oil, but also for petrochemical products and metallurgical industries. These countries believe that these sectors can play a crucial role in strengthening their economies and diversifying their income sources (Abdallh Bany Kasem, 2024: 1669). This long-term strategy focuses on resource diversification and leveraging mutual cooperation between China and the Persian Gulf states across various sectors, which enhances trade and deepens economic partnerships between them. In 2022, Persian Gulf Cooperation Council countries exported over 210 million tons of crude oil to China—double the amount from 2014—with Saudi Arabia alone supplying approximately 88 million tons. For the past two decades, China has been the leading buyer of hydrocarbons from the Persian Gulf, accounting for about a quarter of the region's exports, a position it is likely to maintain for decades to come. In 2023, the Persian Gulf nations shipped 4.06 million barrels per day (bpd) of crude oil to China, making up 36% of China's total crude oil imports, as reported by UN Comtrade. When factoring in imports from Iraq and Iran, the broader Persian Gulf region provided over half of China's crude oil requirements (Amighini, 2024). According to Chinese customs statistics, the country is the world's largest oil importer, importing 11 million barrels per day in 2023 (a 10% increase compared to 2022) (EIA, 2024).

Figure 1. China's Crude Oil Imports from 2011 to 2023

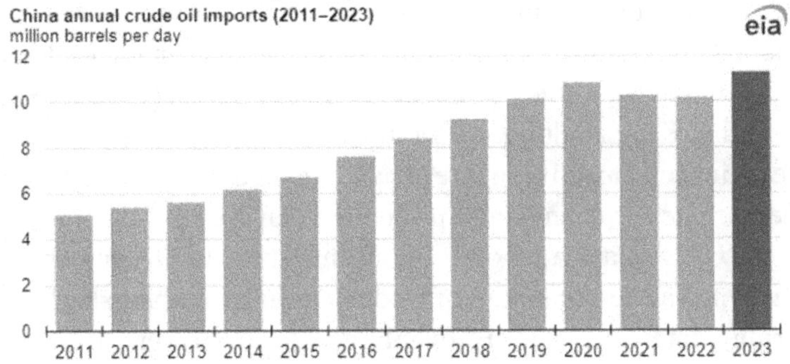

(EIA, 2024)

Under the Belt and Road Initiative, Chinese investment in Arab countries has been on an upward trend, covering various areas such as oil and gas, renewable energy, digital connectivity, ports and logistics. At the same time, negotiations between China and the Persian Gulf Cooperation Council for a free trade agreement, which has been underway since 2024, have gained momentum.

Table 2. BRI Projects (Digital and Physical) in the Persian Gulf States

State	No of Projects (not including cancelled)
UAE	>60
Saudi Arabia	>20
Iran	>20
Bahrain	>10
Oman	>10
Kuwait	>10
Iraq	>5
Qatar	>5

(Houghton, 2024, p. 210)

The shared interests of China, the UAE, and Saudi Arabia have led to the launch of numerous joint maritime projects in recent years. For example, in 2016, Abu Dhabi Ports signed a 35-year concession agreement with China Ocean Shipping Company (COSCO) to operate and develop the Khalifa Port, aimed at boosting trade revenues through China's BRI. Saudi Arabia has also been proactive in its maritime engagement with China. As part of its vision to become a global trade and logistics hub, Riyadh has signed multiple agreements with Chinese firms focused on port and infrastructure development. Noteworthy examples include a 2017 contract awarded to China Harbour Engineering Company for building a commercial port in Jazan Economic City, COSCO's acquisition of a 20% stake in the Red Sea Gateway Terminal in 2021, and the launch of the Persian Gulf-China weekly shipping route in 2022 connecting King Abdulaziz Port in Dammam to China's Ningbo (Urhova, 2023). Chinese financial institutions are expanding their presence in the Persian Gulf to streamline currency exchange and promote Yuan-based financing. The United Arab Emirates (UAE) plays a pivotal role in this shift. In December 2015, China and the UAE signed a Memorandum of Understanding to establish a Chinese Yuan (CNY) clearing center in the UAE, enabling local borrowers to access Chinese loans directly. The People's Bank of China and the Central Bank of the UAE also renewed an agreement to lower currency swap costs by bypassing the U.S. dollar for local currency transactions, initially for a three-year term. Such arrangements could position the UAE as a regional hub for Yuan financial flows as the currency's use grows. Additionally, numerous banks and financial institutions are establishing regional offices in China to support this trend (Al Shidhani & Baig, 2024, p. 10). In 2020, Bona, a monetary settlement system, linked with China's UnionPay, facilitating transfers in local currencies (Alhasan, 2024). In 2022, the UAE joined the Ambridge digital currency project, which explores cross-border transaction solutions using central bank digital currencies. In March 2023, the UAE completed its first liquefied natural gas (LNG) sale to China in renminbi. A few months later, Saudi Arabia and China signed their inaugural three-year currency swap agreement, valued at $7 billion. According to the Bank of China, Saudi oil exports to China are now increasingly settled in renminbi (Lons, 2024, p. 8). Despite these advances, the renminbi faces significant hurdles in challenging the U.S. dollar's dominance.

A Memorandum of Understanding between the Dubai Financial Market (DFM) and the Shenzhen Stock Exchange (SZSE) outlines efforts to explore the potential for new cross-market financing models, as well as enhanced collaboration on indexes, exchange-traded funds (ETFs), and fixed-income products. Furthermore, the SZSE and DFM have agreed to conduct joint research, collaborate on marketing initiatives and knowledge exchange, and establish regular senior-level meetings to strengthen financial connections (Amighini, 2024).

A key development in the evolving relationship between China and the Persian Gulf states is the growing acceptance of the Chinese renminbi in the region. Recent reports have highlighted China's push to globalize the Yuan through measures like currency swaps, increased use of electronic currency, cross-border transactions, and digitized currency, with Persian Gulf countries playing a leading role in these initiatives. On November 28, 2023, the People's Bank of China and the Central Bank of the United Arab Emirates extended their currency swap agreement, valued at US$4.89 billion, for an additional five years. These efforts to internationalize the Yuan are proving advantageous for the Persian Gulf states, potentially reducing transaction costs, mitigating risks, and encouraging other Middle Eastern countries to engage in similar trade practices with China. Over time, this could lead to a gradual shift from the US dollar to the Chinese Yuan in the oil trade, possibly setting the stage for a groundbreaking change: Saudi Arabia, a major oil supplier to China, might consider adopting the Yuan for oil transactions in the future to reduce its dependence on the dollar. Ultimately, these agreements could strengthen bilateral relations and support a transition from the petrodollar to the "petroyuan" (Amighini, 2024).

China's Cooperation with Persian Gulf Countries in the Field of Technology

China's economic cooperation with Saudi Arabia and the UAE is not limited to infrastructure projects and energy trade. China made significant progress in emerging technologies, with companies like Huawei and Alibaba being instrumental in developing the 5G network in Saudi Arabia and the UAE, as well as in areas such as cloud computing, cybersecurity, and smart city solutions. Saudi Arabia and the United Arab Emirates, two of the United States' key partners in the Persian Gulf, have dedicated substantial resources to economic and technological transformation. These countries have leveraged their financial power and geostrategic flexibility to pursue this goal by maintaining security ties with Washington while simultaneously expanding economic and technological relations with Beijing and other parts of Asia. Both American and Chinese firms have made notable advances in attracting investment and delivering cutting-edge technologies to regional actors in the Persian Gulf. One prominent area of AI innovation where Chinese companies have gained recognition is in electric and autonomous vehicles. For example, Pony.ai and WeRide have established a significant presence in the autonomous driving sector in the United Arab Emirates (Belbagi, 2024).

Two major initiatives in the Persian Gulf—G42 in the United Arab Emirates and King Abdullah University of Science and Technology (KAUST) in Saudi Arabia—stand out as particularly significant. These projects reflect the Persian Gulf states' commitment to advancing technology and innovation, while also embodying their broader strategies to enhance national capacities in the face of global competition. Such investments may help Persian Gulf countries position themselves at the forefront of technological transformation and achieve greater progress in this domain. In April 2024, G42 signed an agreement with Microsoft leading to a $1.5 billion investment. As part of the deal, the Emirati company committed to phasing out Chinese hardware and reducing collaboration with Chinese institutions. This agreement has been described as the "culmination of a comprehensive strategic partnership" at the government-to-government level (Ali, 2024a). In its early years, G42 had collaborated with Microsoft, OpenAI, as well as various Chinese tech firms. However, the recent agreements illustrate a shift in the UAE's approach—one that favors deeper engagement with Western powers and a strategic distancing from Chinese technology providers. Another significant development—widely interpreted as a sign of mounting pressure from Washington—is King Abdullah University of Science and Technology (KAUST)'s recent distancing from Chinese firms. Renowned for its work in fields such as telecommunications, semiconductors, energy, environmental engineering, artificial intelligence, materials design, and computer science, KAUST had previously signed multiple agreements with academic institutions in Shenzhen. In fact, it hosts the highest number of research collaborations and joint projects with China among Saudi institutions. In 2023, KAUST released an Arabic large language model called AceGPT, designed to enhance generative AI systems. The model was developed in cooperation with the Big Data Research Institute at a Chinese university in Shenzhen (Ali, 2024a). Perhaps most notably, KAUST has developed some of the region's most advanced supercomputers, which rely on thousands of high-performance chips produced by NVIDIA, the leading U.S. manufacturer of AI processors. In September 2023, Huawei launched a new "cloud zone" in Riyadh, which aims to support government services and AI applications. This was announced at the Huawei Cloud Summit in Saudi Arabia in 2023 (Swinhoe, 2023). Chinese professors also head major AI research institutions in Saudi Arabia and the UAE, and Chinese faculty members work at King Abdullah University of Science and Technology and Mohammed bin Zayed University of Artificial Intelligence.

However, as China's presence expanded, the U.S. exerted pressure on regional countries to limit cooperation with China. In fact, China's most remarkable advancements in the Persian Gulf are evident in telecommunications, e-commerce, and artificial intelligence (AI). As early as 2019, Huawei introduced its 5G network across all Persian Gulf states, collaborating with local firms. Despite being shunned by Western nations, particularly the US, which imposed a ban on it, Huawei has been instrumental in driving the region's digital evolution, contributing to areas like "smart cities," data centers, biogenetics, facial recognition, and public surveillance. In September 2024, the UAE launched the Arab world's first AI network. Meanwhile, by late January 2025, Saudi Arabia opened a digital cloud data storage facility constructed by China's Tencent group (Bulard, 2025). Under US pressure, companies such as G42 of the Emirates and Saudi Alat have shown signs of exiting the Chinese AI market, and Washington has imposed restrictions on the sale of Nvidia semiconductors to Persian Gulf states, believing that these semiconductors will eventually end up in China. The US has also forced Prosperity7, an investment fund backed by Aramco, to sell its stake in the startup Rain AI (Alhasan, 2024). In response to this U.S. pressure, King Abdullah University of Science and Technology publicly declared its intention to divest from Chinese technologies. The CEO of Saudi Alat mentioned that the company would cut ties with Chinese technology if demanded by the U.S. In April 2024, the UAE's G42 entered into an agreement with Microsoft, planning to phase out Chinese hardware and reduce connections with Chinese entities (Ali, 2024). Due to the tight partnership between G42, a major Emirati tech firm, and Chinese tech companies, the U.S. has limited G42's access to Nvidia and AMD graphics cards from the U.S., which are essential for handling the vast data sets needed for AI development (Adrianov, 2024). U.S. export control regulations—designed to curb China's technological advancement—may also restrict access for Saudi Arabia and the UAE, potentially delaying their progress in developing artificial intelligence. This could influence strategic decisions in Abu Dhabi and Riyadh regarding technological cooperation and raise concerns about the broader implications of such policies for technology development across the region.

Military and Defense Ties

As China's defense sector and international ambitions have expanded, it has worked to broaden its arms exports and security alliances. The 2016 "Arab Policy Paper," marking China's inaugural white paper on the region, highlighted "cooperation on weapons, equipment, and various specialized technologies" and the "development of national defense and military forces of Arab States" as central priorities. Since that time, Beijing has ramped up its shipments of ships, aircraft, and sophisticated missile systems to the area. From 2013 to 2023, Chinese military exports to the Middle East jumped by 80 percent (Tirziu, 2024).

Since the mid-2000s, the UAE and Saudi Arabia have signed numerous defense industry agreements with Asian countries, including China, India, Indonesia, and Malaysia. In 2017, Riyadh signed a deal with Beijing to set up a drone manufacturing plant in Saudi Arabia. In 2020, the Emirates Golden Group International and the China North Industries Group Company launched a joint project to develop and research in the field of drones. In recent times, Saudi Arabia has acquired combat drones from China and engaged in joint naval drills with the country. During the 2024 World Defense Show in Riyadh, China showcased its prominence by establishing the largest pavilion, and a J-10, one of its newest fighter jets, took part in the airshow. Additionally, reports suggest China has supported Saudi Arabia in domestically producing ballistic missiles and drones. While China's portion of Saudi Arabia's total arms market is still smaller than it was ten years ago, its progress is significant. For instance, between 2016 and 2020, Chinese arms deliveries to Saudi Arabia soared by almost 400 percent compared to the 2011-2015 period (Ali, 2024b).

From 2019 to 2024, China ranked as the world's fourth-largest arms exporter. In both 2020 and 2021, its military exports to Saudi Arabia reached a value of US$80 million. Between the periods of 2011-15 and 2016-20, China's arms shipments to

Saudi Arabia skyrocketed by 400 percent. In 2017, Saudi Arabia acquired China's Wing Loong II drones, and by March 2022, the two nations agreed to a joint venture for local design and production of these drones. This deal was formalized between Saudi Advanced Communications and Electronics Systems (SACES) and China Electronics Technology Group Corporation (CETC). In June 2024, Saudi Defence Minister Khalid bin Salman, the younger sibling of Mohammed bin Salman, traveled to China to discuss enhancing military and defense cooperation (Quamar, 2025). Arms transactions have paved the way for collaborative military exercises and partnerships in security and law enforcement. For example, China and Saudi Arabia conducted their inaugural joint naval drill in the Red Sea in 2019, followed by the Blue Sword-2023 operation in Guangdong province in October 2023.

In August 2023, Beijing and the UAE held their first joint air force exercise, widely seen as a signal to the U.S. This action conveyed a dual message: from Beijing, that Washington isn't the only security player in the Persian Gulf, and from Abu Dhabi, that it has alternatives. Recently, the two nations committed to upgrading and expanding their military and security frameworks, including law enforcement. China has set up at least two overseas police stations in the UAE—one in Dubai and another at an undisclosed site—reportedly managed by the Nantong and Wenzhou public security departments from Jiangsu and Zhejiang provinces, respectively, working alongside UAE authorities. In February, Beijing and the UAE initiated a strategic police dialogue to enhance cooperation on cross-border crime, cybercrime, and policing, emphasizing Chinese training for Emirati security personnel. Qatar's security forces have also benefited from similar training (Tirziu, 2024). At the International Defense Exhibition in Abu Dhabi in 2023, Beijing was present with several companies. Also, at the Unmanned Systems Conference in Abu Dhabi in 2024, China was the second largest participant (after the UAE and ahead of the United States) in terms of exhibition space for its companies. More than 50 Chinese companies were present at this exhibition. At the Saudi World Defense Exhibition in 2024, China also had a stronger presence compared to other countries. During Mohammed bin Zayed's visit to China in June 2024, Abu Dhabi and Beijing emphasized the exchange of their experiences in the field of defense and security (Ardemagni, 2024). The People's Republic of China's military established its first military base in Djibouti in 2017 and has since increased its joint exercises in the region. Qatar also uses Chinese short-range ballistic missiles among its weapons. China set up a naval base in Djibouti in 2016 primarily to safeguard its economic and energy interests, aiming to secure trade routes from Asia to Europe via the Bab el-Mandeb Strait (Adrianov, 2024).

Despite all these interpretations, the large gap in the Persian Gulf countries' arms imports from Western countries and China shows that the countries in the region are well aware that diversifying their arms purchase basket can hinder their defense convergence with the United States and, as a result, weaken their ability to confront threats. Saudi Arabia and the UAE aim to approach Chinese companies active in the defense industry to promote the national defense industry and localize weapons production with the aim of strengthening the non-oil sector and strengthening their software.

Reasons for the Persian Gulf Countries' Turn to China

Several strategic factors have deepened ties between the six Persian Gulf countries and China. Historically, the region depended on the United States and Europe for security and economic partnerships. However, shifting trade patterns and perceptions of waning U.S. commitment have prompted Persian Gulf states to seek new allies. The U.S. shale boom has reduced its reliance on Middle Eastern oil, positioning it as a competitor in global energy markets. The U.S.'s perceived inaction during the Arab Spring in 2011—failing to support allies like Egypt as governments fell and groups like the Muslim Brotherhood rose—eroded trust among nations such as Saudi Arabia, the UAE, and Qatar. Further doubts arose from the U.S. pivot to Asia and inconsistent policies across administrations from Barack Obama to Joe Biden, raising questions about the reliability of American security guarantees. This uncertainty has driven the Persian Gulf Countries to diversify its diplomatic and economic partnerships, with China emerging as a key player. China's appeal lies in its economic might and growing political influence, enabling the Persian Gulf states to better navigate global relations (Ulrichsen et al., 2024). The U.S.'s limited support—evident in its chaotic Afghanistan withdrawal and muted response to drone and missile attacks on Saudi Arabia and Abu Dhabi—has reinforced perceptions of it as an unreliable partner (Karimifard, 2024, p. 146).

Amid this insecurity, Persian Gulf states see multipolarity as offering greater flexibility. China's vision of a multipolar world aligns with their worldview, allowing Saudi Arabia and the UAE to assert themselves as regional powers and key players in a shifting global order. In 2023, they joined the Shanghai Cooperation Organization (SCO) as dialogue partners and were invited to BRICS—platforms that, while nascent, signal Riyadh and Abu Dhabi's ambition to become middle powers bridging the West and the Global South. China, in turn, views these nations not just as hydrocarbon suppliers but as pathways to secure its broader international interests and prestige. China's mediation in the Iran-Saudi Arabia reconciliation marks a diplomatic triumph, advancing its Global Security, Development, and Civilization Initiatives. The Persian Gulf states increasingly align with China over the West on issues like internet regulation and climate change (Lons, 2024, p. 16). Additionally, energy ties with the Persian Gulf bolster Beijing's push to internationalize the renminbi, potentially challenging the dollar's dominance.

Persian Gulf States' Investment in China

Investment from Persian Gulf states in China has surged in recent years, driven by mutual economic interests and strategic alignment. This growth reflects deliberate planning, particularly by Saudi Arabia, which sees China and Asia as integral to its long-term vision. China promotes the Belt and Road Initiative (BRI) as complementary to Persian Gulf states' development goals. During King Salman's 2019 visit to China, Xi Jinping linked the BRI's Silk Road revival to Saudi Vision 2030 (Zulfikar Rakhmat, 2019, p. 9). Similarly, in 2015, Xi told Crown Prince Mohammed bin Zayed Al-Nahyan that BRI cooperation would deliver "mutual benefits, win-win outcomes, and common development" (Zulfikar Rakhmat, 2019, p. 9), framing the initiative as a shared regional gain. Persian Gulf economies have steadily pivoted eastward, boosting trade with the Asia-Pacific. By 2030, this trade is projected to rise 60% to $578 billion (Samoudi, 2023, p. 140). Speculation persists that Riyadh may accept yuan for oil sales. In 2023, Persian Gulf investments and acquisitions in China soared 1,000% to $5.3 billion, largely due to petrochemical projects. At the 10th Arab-China Business Conference in Riyadh (June 2023), China expressed ambitions to attract $1–2 trillion from sovereign wealth funds by 2030. Persian Gulf sovereign wealth fund assets in China grew from $100 million in 2022 to over $2.3 billion in 2023. The number of Persian Gulf institutions seeking qualified foreign institutional investment certificates rose from three to nine between 2021 and 2022. While the Saudi Public Investment Fund entered China's stock market in 2016 via SoftBank, direct capital flows intensified recently. In February 2022, it opened a Hong Kong office, signaling deeper ties with Beijing (Ali, 2024).

In the first nine months of 2024, entities like the Abu Dhabi Investment Authority, the Saudi Arabian Public Investment Fund, and the Qatar Investment Authority supported transactions amounting to $55 billion, as reported by consultancy Global SWF. A Bloomberg report indicates that Middle Eastern firms have secured a record-breaking $9 billion in deals in China this year, with additional agreements anticipated over the next three months (Fernandez, 2024). In August 2024, Saudi Arabia's Public Investment Fund (PIF) entered into a memorandum of understanding (MoU) with six Chinese financial entities—the Agricultural Bank of China, Bank of China, China Construction Bank, China Export and Credit Insurance Corp., Export-Import Bank of China, and the Industrial and Commercial Bank of China—for investments totaling US$50 billion. PIF already has significant investments in China, particularly in the energy and petrochemical industries. In July 2024, Saudi Aramco purchased a US$3.4-billion stake in China's Rongsheng Petrochemical Co. Ltd. Chinese investments in Saudi Arabia have also grown, with nearly 750 Chinese firms operating in the Saudi market across sectors like construction, energy, and petrochemicals, according to Chinese sources. In September 2024, Aramco signed a five-year cooperation framework with China National Building Material Group Co. to collaborate on advanced materials and industrial development (Quamar, 2025).

Saudi Aramco has continued its robust investment drive in China, unveiling several investment plans. The company's ambitions extend beyond the energy and petrochemical industries. In 2024, it entered into a five-year cooperation framework agreement with China National Building Material Group Co., focusing on joint efforts in advanced materials and industrial development. In addition to Saudi Aramco, other Saudi entities such as the Public Investment Fund, SABIC, and private-sector firms have also poured significant capital into China (Wu, 2024). In recent years, Saudi companies have sharply increased their investments in China, signaling strong faith in the Chinese economy despite growing uncertainties in global markets and economic conditions.

In order to realize the vision of cooperation between China and the countries participating in the Belt and Road Initiative, the Asian Infrastructure Investment Bank was established in 2013. The initial capital of this bank was $50 billion, which has increased to more than $100 billion in recent years. Membership and investment in this bank was open to all governments, and by early 2016, six countries from the Persian Gulf had joined it (Vafamand & Arghavani, 2024, p. 285). Investment by the Persian Gulf countries and China should not be seen as a strategic shift away from other regions, but rather as an attempt to enhance the Persian Gulf's focus on Asia. The rationale behind these investments is not simply to capitalize on the growth potential of Asian markets, especially China, but to strengthen mutually beneficial relationships. This approach allows Persian Gulf investors to seize new opportunities in rapidly developing industries and foster economic growth and innovation on both sides. Persian Gulf investment and stock market presence have increased in both volume and diversity, and the convergence and alignment of the Persian Gulf's technological sectors with China is taking place. It should be noted that these trends do not indicate a change in China-Persian Gulf countries relations, but rather reflect a global shift towards Asia as a major economic hub. The level of Persian Gulf investment in China reflects a natural progression towards deepening economic ties with the region, which is increasingly influential in the global economy. Overall, Persian Gulf investment in China reflects a pragmatic approach to exploiting growth opportunities in Asia while maintaining a balanced global investment strategy that could pave the way for a bright future in global economic relations.

China's standing in Arab Public Opinion

It can be said that many Arabs see China as their friend. Chinese state television promotes and advertises economic relations with Arab countries while expressing its different political positions from the West. As long as Chinese media maintain this narrative, the country will be viewed positively in Arab countries. For example, CGTV broadcasts news, series, and other programs. This network is an instrument of China's soft power in the Arab world and has an audience of over 450 million. According to the Arab Barometer's survey, which spanned nine countries in the Middle East and North Africa (MENA) and included 23,000 interviews, China enjoys greater popularity than the US across the region, with Morocco standing out as the sole exception where the US is preferred overall. In a separate survey targeting Arab youth across more than 50 cities in the region, including the UAE—a significant economic partner of China—the overwhelming majority of respondents viewed China as a vital ally to their country (Kurma, 2023). A public opinion survey conducted in Dubai among Arab youth found that eight out of 10 participants viewed China as an ally, the highest proportion expressing this sentiment in four years. The results indicated that over 70 percent of those surveyed held a favorable view of China, compared to just 47 percent—less than half—who felt positively about the US. Furthermore, more than 70 percent of respondents were aware of the collaboration between China and Saudi Arabia in areas like infrastructure, trade, and energy, and over two-thirds reported personally experiencing the concrete benefits this partnership has brought to people's lives (Huang et al., 2023).

According to data published by Arab Barometer, the US's standing among ordinary Arab citizens has fallen sharply compared to 2022. Polls in late 2023 and early 2024 show that China's standing has grown in the face of America's decline. For example, in the Arab Barometer survey, when asked "Which international actors are committed to defending Palestinian rights?" the United States received the lowest percentage. Only eight percent of respondents in Kuwait, six percent in Morocco and Lebanon, five percent in Mauritania, and two percent in Jordan agreed with the statement that the United States defends Palestinian rights. Although China has not provided material support or taken a strong stance in Gaza, it has been the biggest beneficiary and winner of America's decline in credibility among Arabs. Although Arab support for China was declining in the 2021 Arab Barometer survey, this trend has reversed in the months since the Gaza crisis began in 2023. In all countries surveyed by the Arab Barometer since October 7, 2023, at least half of respondents said they viewed China favorably. In Jordan and Morocco, which are key U.S. allies, China's approval ratings have increased by at least 15%. Overall, the decline in U.S. approval ratings has been accompanied by a rise in favorable ratings of China in Arab countries (Robbins, et al., 2024). In another survey, respondents in both KSA (75 percent) and UAE (63 percent) hold positive or very positive views of China's overall role in the Middle East. Such favorable view of China is evident across the region (Akbarzadeh & Saba, 2025, p. 6).

Table 3. General Perception of China

Questions	Saudi Arabia			United Arab Emirates		
	Negative or very negative	Neutral	Positive or very positive	Negative or very negative	Neutral	Positive or very positive
How do you assess China's role in the Middle East?	22 (4 percent)	123 (21 percent)	449 (75 percent)	9 (3 percent)	85 (34 percent)	159 (63 percent)
What is your assessment of China's role as a reliable mediator in regional conflicts, such as the Israeli-Palestinian conflict or the Syrian civil war?	71 (12 percent)	232 (39 percent)	292 (49 percent)	41 (17 percent)	107 (42 percent)	105 (41 percent)
Do you trust China as a reliable partner for your country?	No	Neutral	Yes	No	Neutral	Yes
	69 (12 percent)	171 (29 percent)	354 (59 percent)	29 (11 percent)	67 (27 percent)	156 (62 percent)

(Akbarzadeh & Saba, 2025, p. 6)

In fact, China enjoys an overall positive image in KSA and the UAE, especially in relation to its economic model of development and as a trade partner. This suggests that Beijing's approach to soft power projection, with its heavy reliance on economic ties, has made a difference.

Table 4. China's Economic Appeal

Questions	Saudi Arabia					United Arab Emirates				
	China	United States	Japan	Russia	European Union	China	United States	Russia	Japan	European Union
Which of the following actor is the most influential foreign economic power in the Middle East?	312 (53 percent)	189 (32 percent)	36 (6 percent)	32 (5 percent)	26 (4 percent)	118 (47 percent)	85 (34 percent)	19 (7 percent)	13 (5 percent)	18 (7 percent)
With which of the following countries you would like your country to build stronger economic relations?	312 (53 percent)	55 (9 percent)	111 (19 percent)	67 (11 percent)	50 (8 percent)	109 (43 percent)	35 (14 percent)	33 (13 percent)	46 (18 percent)	30 (12 percent)

(Akbarzadeh & Saba, 2025, p. 7)

Arab countries view China positively. They see Beijing as a key ally for their policy. This should not come as a surprise; the Chinese have pointed out in various ways in their media that they have not been present militarily in the Arab world, unlike the United States. In addition to presenting a positive narrative of China's economic presence, CGTV has very critical content of the United States. Despite significant progress, it should also be noted that China- Persian Gulf relations are still in their early stages, and leaders of China and these countries tend to exaggerate the quality and depth of their interactions in order to use it both for domestic consumption and to strengthen their bargaining position with the West. China's relations with the Persian Gulf countries remain out of proportion to the deep military, economic, and political relations of the countries in the region with the West, especially the United States. Europe and the United States remain the most important investment destinations for the Persian Gulf countries. For example, European foreign direct investment in Saudi Arabia is ten times higher than that of China. Persian Gulf companies are also interested in partnering with Western companies in sensitive sectors. For example, the head of Saudi Arabia's Equipment Investment Company, which specializes in semiconductors and artificial intelligence, announced in May 2024 that the investment company would not cooperate with China if the United States requested it (Lons, 2024, p. 7).

America's View on the Development of China- Persian Gulf Relations

Since the end of the Cold War, the United States has been active as a dominant external actor in the Persian Gulf and has enjoyed unprecedented influence. In the 1990s and 2000s, the country carried out a series of military interventions with the aim of shaping the regional order and protecting its national interests. Barack Obama's entry into the White House in 2008 was a kind of new beginning for this country in the region, as Washington began to review its role in the Persian Gulf and turned its attention to the Asia-Pacific. For this reason, America's policies in the region have undergone changes. Meanwhile, China's expansion of relations with the Persian Gulf countries has caused increasing concern for the United States (Fardella & She, 2024, p.12). Over the past three decades, the strategic doctrines of all Arab Persian Gulf states have been shaped by the conviction that forming close and comprehensive ties with the United States is the most effective means of bolstering security and defense in the region. This conviction stems from the perception of the United States as the fundamental pillar of security and defense, which has resulted in a neglect of the development of independent regional security capabilities and the establishment of extensive security relations with other external parties beyond the US. It is evident that the American strategy in the Persian Gulf region is driven by interests and control, which has facilitated China's entry into the Persian Gulf arena. This Chinese presence is likely to impact the American role, particularly as China's relations with the Persian Gulf countries continue to evolve and deepen (Abdallh Bany Kasem, 2024, p. 1072).

The United States is concerned about regional countries' cooperation with China in the field of technology and has sent serious warnings to countries such as Saudi Arabia and the UAE not to cooperate with China on the development of artificial intelligence and the export of chips. Given the competition between great powers in the field of artificial intelligence, the US is forcing its allies to determine their own role and continue to cooperate with only one side of the competition. For example, the UAE-based company G42 was forced to stop cooperating with China in order to continue to have access to US-made chips. In fact, the US concerns were due to the Emirati company's connections with the Chinese company Huawei (Peel & Kerr, 2023). The war between Huawei and the US, within the framework of the great power competition between Washington and Beijing, first became public in 2018 when Meng Wanzhou, a senior Huawei official, was arrested on charges of collaborating with Iran. In another move, the Trump administration presented the "Clean Network Program" in August 2020. The program aimed to mobilize US allies against China and protect American assets. The Biden administration also issued the "Future of the Internet Declaration" in April 2022, which indicated Washington's dissatisfaction with China's increasing global role and influence in the technology sector of the Persian Gulf states. The US warned countries such as the UAE, Bahrain, Saudi Arabia, and Kuwait that were using Huawei technology in their 5G mobile infrastructure about using this equipment (Moreland, 2024, p. 158). The US efforts to dissuade the UAE and Saudi Arabia from using Huawei equipment show that Washington still has significant influence over its partners in the Persian Gulf.

China and the United States have different approaches to security governance in the Persian Gulf. There are three reasons for this difference in approach. First, the United States takes sides in the Persian Gulf conflicts. Washington has tried to form a coalition with its allies and create an Arab NATO. In contrast, China emphasizes principles such as non-alignment and non-intervention and seeks compatible and favorable partnerships with all interested parties. Second, there is a perception among Chinese officials that the United States is pursuing unilateralism, as demonstrated, for example, by its withdrawal from the JCPOA. Third, the United States mixes trade and economic issues with politics, while China opposes the politicization of economics and trade, which aims to separate trade and economic issues from political issues. The US sees the Persian Gulf as a battlefield, while China sees it as a market. Washington sees its adversaries in the Persian Gulf as problematic, while China sees all sides as actual or potential economic and political partners (Sun, 2022, p. 35). China's adherence to the zero-enemy policy, along with the trade-based international cooperation model in the Persian Gulf, has led Beijing to avoid a Cold War with the US.

It can be said that there is currently no strategic competition between Washington and Beijing in the Persian Gulf. The strategic competition between China and the US is almost exclusively in the Asia-Pacific region, and the Persian Gulf is currently of lesser importance than the Indo-Pacific. China does not have the ability or will to create a comprehensive economic bloc within the framework of the Belt and Road Initiative, and the Chinese themselves have stated that the Belt and Road Initiative and the Asian Infrastructure Investment Bank are complementary institutions to international economic institutions, not substitutes for them. Chinese President Xi Jinping has also stated that the country is not seeking a proxy, sphere of influence, or to fill a power vacuum (Sun, 2022: 36). China emphasizes that America's security partners in the Persian Gulf are simultaneously Beijing's economic and political partners, and these countries also prefer to establish a kind of balance in relations with great powers.

Despite the perception that the US will not pay much attention to the Persian Gulf due to its "Pivot to Asia policy", the country will continue to have a strong military presence in the region. From the presence of CENTCOM in Al Udeid in Qatar to the Fifth Fleet in Bahrain and the deployment of forces in Kuwait, Qatar, Oman, the UAE, Saudi Arabia and Iraq. Despite narratives about the US withdrawal from the region, the Persian Gulf remains of strategic importance for US macro policies. Washington's priority in the Indo-Pacific and its reorientation of its objectives in the Persian Gulf indicate that the United States is reconsidering its Middle East policy in light of China's growing presence in the region. The American policy toward the Persian Gulf states is often viewed as exploitative, with the United States aiming to leverage their oil resources. It is also evident that the U.S. seeks to exacerbate conflicts and disputes in the Persian Gulf region, as seen during the Arab Spring crises, where its involvement contributed to worsening these situations. Despite China's increased engagement with the Persian Gulf countries, the United States remains the guarantor of defense and security in the region and has shaped the security architecture in the Persian Gulf. Although there is much talk of China and the United States moving towards confrontation, China's economic interests, especially in the areas of energy security and access to markets in the Persian Gulf, have benefited from the US security umbrella in the region.

China's Challenges in the Persian Gulf

Despite China's growing presence in the Persian Gulf and its expanding ties with regional countries, it continues to face a range of challenges. A major power rivalry is unfolding in the Persian Gulf among China, the United States, Russia, and the European Union, with other regional and extra-regional actors also playing active roles. The previous section highlighted the presence of the United States as the most influential player in the Persian Gulf and its efforts to prevent China's rise in the region. This section will focus on the rivalries and tensions among regional countries, which could hinder the implementation of China's policies. In recent years, Saudi Crown Prince Mohammed bin Salman (MBS) and UAE President Sheikh Mohammed bin Zayed Al Nahyan have faced persistent challenges in reconciling their divergent views on key regional issues—particularly regarding the conflict in Yemen and disagreements over OPEC oil production quotas. Tensions between the two leaders reached a notable peak in a 2022 interview, during which MBS reportedly threatened economic sanctions and a potential blockade against the UAE, asserting that it would be "more severe than what I did with Qatar" (Doha News, 2023). Given their geostrategic significance, Saudi Arabia and the United Arab Emirates consider the advancement of maritime infrastructure and transportation systems essential components of their broader economic diversification strategies. While the UAE is already positioned as one of the world's top five maritime shipping hubs, Saudi Arabia's growing ambitions in this area directly challenge the UAE's established dominance. This emerging rivalry aligns with China's strategic interests, particularly its efforts to expand the Maritime Silk Road and secure access to key regional ports and waterways. Despite the UAE's considerable head start—serving as a primary transit point for Chinese exports to Europe, the Middle East, and Africa—Saudi Arabia holds a unique geostrategic advantage as the only country with direct access to both the Persian Gulf and the Red Sea. Nevertheless, tensions between Saudi Arabia and the United Arab Emirates are expected to intensify as both nations adopt increasingly pragmatic, assertive, and interest-driven foreign policy strategies (Urhova, 2023). Crown Prince Mohammed bin Salman and President Mohammed bin Zayed Al Nahyan are each determined to project their countries' economic and political influence, positioning themselves as proactive leaders in shaping the region's future. These parallel ambitions are likely to produce consequences that extend beyond bilateral competition, potentially undermining regional initiatives aimed at countering Iran, resolving the conflict in Yemen, and normalizing relations between Israel and the broader Islamic world.

In line with its commitment to the Five Principles of Peaceful Coexistence, China advocates for respect for sovereignty, territorial integrity, non-interference in internal affairs, and the peaceful and diplomatic resolution of conflicts and tensions. The consistent promotion of these principles at the domestic level has significantly constrained China's foreign policy options abroad. One of the key consequences of this stance is the transformation of China's mediatory diplomacy into a form of quasi-mediation, as well as its deliberate avoidance of any military alliances or formal security commitments. In practice, China's mediation policy has taken on the characteristics of quasi-mediation due to two key features. First, rather than aiming to resolve conflicts, it focuses on managing them in a way that excessively and self-servingly safeguards its own interests. Second, instead of setting the agenda, China tends to follow pre-established ones in order to avoid deep entanglement in crises. China's concern about the potential entanglement of its economic interests with regional conflicts has, in effect, functioned as a form of risk aversion—forming a substantial barrier to more decisive involvement in conflict resolution and management across the region (Dehghan & Arghavani, 2025, p. 200). The Persian Gulf region is characterized by significant ethnic and religious diversity, which has contributed to ongoing tensions and divisions among its countries. While the majority of the region's population is Arab, there are also sizable Kurdish and Persian communities, and both Sunni and Shi'a sects are present—often with a history of geopolitical rivalry. The presence of ethnic and linguistic groups that transcend national boundaries, such as the Kurds in Iraq, undermines national cohesion and deepens both internal and external political divides. The Persian Gulf states are inherently multi-ethnic and multi-identity societies, frequently facing challenges from within (Sazmand & Ramezani, 2021, p. 98).

The rivalry between Saudi Arabia and Iran in volatile regions such as Yemen, Iraq, and Syria contributes to regional instability, driven by factors like sectarian tensions, zero-sum calculations, and the lack of mutual interest recognition. This persistent instability in the Persian Gulf and its surrounding areas—key nodes for regional connectivity—poses a significant challenge to China's strategic ambitions (Sazmand & Ramezani, 2021, p. 97). Tehran is also dissatisfied with what it views as Riyadh's wariness of exploring common ground on how to settle various crises in the region. Events in Gaza are a case in point. While the two sides agree on the need to avert a broader conflagration, Riyadh has pursued its own agenda vis-à-vis the Gaza war in cooperation with other Arab states, mainly Egypt, the UAE, Qatar and Jordan (ICG, 2024, p. 10). Despite all the rhetoric about rapprochement, the two countries remain indirectly opposed to each other in Yemen and the current rapprochement between Iran and Saudi Arabia has several advantages from the latter's perspective (Knipp, 2024). There has also been little tangible progress in boosting political, social and cultural ties, including people-to-people and cultural exchanges – an area in which Iran had expected some advances.

In an effort to consolidate its cultural presence and influence in the region, China annually invests approximately $10 billion through a variety of cultural instruments. A portion of this expenditure is directed toward China's diverse cultural activities in the region. Despite notable achievements Beijing has made in recent years through these investments, significant obstacles continue to hinder the expansion—or even the maintenance—of its cultural influence in the region. Some of these challenges stem from the Chinese government's approach to deploying soft power resources, while others arise from historical contexts and fundamental clashes in cultural norms, religious practices, and broader worldviews prevalent among the region's populations. The political affinities between Persian Gulf regimes and the Chinese political system—coupled with Beijing's state-driven soft power strategy based on mechanisms of coercion and reward—have led regional elites and ruling authorities to be drawn to China's cultural appeal. This attraction is rooted in a shared perspective on political values, particularly the principle of non-interference in internal affairs, which resonates more with governing authorities than with their populations, who often demand greater political freedoms. However, the Chinese government's top-down application of soft power toward the broader public in the region has in many cases provoked negative sentiments among local populations and generated resistance rather than receptivity to Beijing's cultural influence (Dehghan & Arghavani, 2025, pp. 207- 208).Cultural unfamiliarity has also played a fundamental role in shaping this situation. While traditional Chinese culture is relatively well known in East and Southeast Asia, it remains largely unfamiliar to many countries in the Middle East. This unfamiliarity is further exacerbated by the absence of shared religious and spiritual worldviews. As a result, it is difficult for China and the predominantly Muslim societies of the region to foster any meaningful religious or cultural convergence between their peoples.

CONCLUSION

In the 21st century, as China aimed to assert itself as a global power amid rising Sino-U.S. tensions, Chinese academic circles began reevaluating the principle of non-alignment. This discourse gave rise to the Global Security Initiative (GSI), unveiled by Xi Jinping at the Boao Economic Forum in April 2022. The GSI outlines China's vision for international security, advocating a comprehensive framework that prioritizes national sovereignty. It critiques U.S. alliances, challenges American leadership, and positions the Chinese model as an alternative, influencing Beijing's security strategy toward the Persian Gulf states. From a military-security standpoint, China seeks to establish itself as a significant player in the region but not to displace U.S. influence or reshape the security landscape. Instead, it views Western efforts—particularly those of the United States—to maintain order as an opportunity to safeguard and advance its economic interests under an existing security umbrella. Beijing consistently avoids entanglement in regional conflicts and long-term commitments, opting for strategic hedging while fostering cooperative ties in the Persian Gulf. China's security approach diverges from the West's traditional reliance on military bases, arms sales, enemy suppression, and alliances. Instead, it promotes peace through economic development and expanded relations, reflecting a distinct model tailored to its priorities.

China's primary goal in building ties with Persian Gulf nations, particularly Iran and Saudi Arabia (though not limited to them), is to bolster its own national security rather than to diminish U.S. influence in the area. Reducing American dominance would actually harm China's interests rather than advance them. Beijing has no intention of disrupting the U.S.-led order in the Persian Gulf, since Washington's role in ensuring regional stability aligns with China's key objectives. Unlike the U.S. and Europe, China focuses on practical cooperation rather than ideological conformity, valuing stability and a hands-off approach to other countries' internal matters. Amid global "great chaos" (daluan ju) and rising anti-Western sentiment in the Middle East and North Africa, China positions itself as a more appealing major power option for MENA countries disillusioned with the Global West. The basis of China's presence in Persian Gulf security affairs is the principle of having relations with all parties and multilateralism in resolving conflicts in the region. Beijing believes that this approach can help elevate China's international discourse, thereby increasing its political influence and moral appeal, and thus ensuring that it can pursue a policy of zero hostility both among the Persian Gulf states and outside powers, while maximizing its commercial interests. China uses bilateral channels to advance strategic cooperation with the Persian Gulf countries. Beijing does this through regional governments and, of course, through multilateral mechanisms.

Leaders in the Persian Gulf, growing frustrated with U.S. actions—such as the 2003 Iraq invasion, backing of the 2011 Arab Spring, abrupt Afghanistan withdrawal, and retreat from Iran nuclear talks—have increasingly viewed China as a steadier ally. For these nations, ties with China have evolved from mere convenience to a deliberate strategy. China's readiness to engage with regional actors without pushing political or human rights agendas resonates with Middle Eastern leaders' priorities. This shift reflects a broader realignment in the region, with China emerging as a vital economic and development partner. The Persian Gulf countries have pursued a policy of non-alignment in their interactions with both the United States and China, particularly in the context of their ongoing geopolitical rivalry, given that one serves as their primary security guarantor while the other constitutes their principal economic partner. In addressing the imperative of balancing foreign relations and fostering the realization of developmental initiatives, the Persian Gulf states have adeptly navigated their requirements amidst a protracted trade conflict between the United States and China. The United States government has imposed restrictions on the exportation or sale of certain high-technology apparatus, such as sophisticated computer chips, to various Middle Eastern nations.

The Persian Gulf countries and China are natural partners, as the Persian Gulf states possess abundant energy resources like oil and natural gas, which are crucial for supporting Beijing's sustainable economic growth. Today, China is the largest trading partner for the Persian Gulf countries and their top oil customer. The Persian Gulf countries seek a dependable export market for the long term, while China's growing economic power and increasing energy demand—expected to rise in the coming years—combined with its investments and construction projects supporting the Belt and Road Initiative (BRI), will further strengthen China-Persian Gulf relationships. This interdependence will enhance energy security for China and foster a long-term, trustworthy partnership with the Persian Gulf countries. Even though the U.S. has hinted at potential repercussions for deepening ties between the Persian Gulf and China, Persian Gulf nations are likely to persist in strengthening their connections with Beijing. The expanding economic partnership between the two regions highlights a rising trend in global investment, where conventional Western-focused strategies are increasingly paired with collaborations between Asia and the Middle East.

REFERENCES

Abdallh Bany Kasem, S. (2024). Chinese-Gulf Relations and their Impact on the American Role. *Library Progress International*, *44*(3), 1666–1677.

Adrianov, A. (2024, May 21). *China in the Persian Gulf: Tried Its Best, You Know the Rest*. Retrieved March 25, 2025, from RIAC: https://russiancouncil.ru/en/analytics-and-comments/analytics/china-in-the-gulf-tried-its-best-you-know-the-rest/

Akbarzadeh, S., & Saba, A. (2025). China's Soft Power: Views from Saudi Arabia and the UAE. *Global Studies Quarterly*, 1-14.

Alhasan, H. (2024, June 25). *Contesting the West: China's Middle East Strategy*. Retrieved September 10, 2024, from IISS: https://www.iiss.org/online-analysis/online-analysis/2024/06/contesting-the-west-chinas-middle-east-strategy/.Ali, G. (2024, July 3). *(2024) China's Achilles' Heel in Relationship with Arab Gulf States*. Retrieved February 10, 2025, from China Focus: https://www.chinausfocus.com/foreign-policy/chinas-achilles-heel-in-relationship-with-arab-gulf-states

Ali, G. (2024a, May 8). *China-U.S. Tech Rivalry Enters into the Gulf States*. Retrieved February 2, 2025, from China Us Focus: https://www.chinausfocus.com/finance-economy/china-us-tech-rivalry-enters-into-the-gulf-states

Ali, G. (2024b, August 16). *Saudi Arabia Balances Defense Cooperation*. Retrieved March 12, 2025, from https://www.chinausfocus.com/peace-security/saudi-arabia-balances-defense-cooperation

Ali, L. (2024, June 18). *Persian Gulf Investments in China: A New Era of Strategic Partnerships*. Retrieved February 8, 2025, from ISPI: https://www.ispionline.it/en/publication/gulf-investments-in-china-a-new-era-of-strategic-partnerships-177971

Amighini, A. (2024, November 22). *Deepening Cooperation Between China and the Persian Gulf*. Retrieved January 20, 2025, from ISPI: https://www.ispionline.it/en/publication/deepening-cooperation-between-china-and-the-gulf-191672

Ardemagni, E. (2024, June 18). *In GCC-Asia Rising Ties, Defence Industries is the Key*. Retrieved August 12, 2024, from ISPI: https://www.ispionline.it/en/publication/in-gcc-asia-rising-ties-defence-industry-is-the-key-177951.AlShidhan, R., & Baig, S. (2024). Balancing Power and Prosperity: China's Geo-economic Engagement with the Persian Gulf, Cooperation Council. *Asian Review of Political Economy, 3* (20).

Bazoobandi, S. (2024). Iran's Strategies in Response to Changes in US-China Relations. *Middle East Policy*, *31*(1), 120–132. DOI: 10.1111/mepo.12727

Belbagi, Z. M. (2024, April 17). *Persian Gulf States Balance China, US Collaborations in AI Space*. Retrieved February 16, 2025, from Arab News: https://www.arabnews.com/node/2494616

Bulard, M. (2025, March 17). *Behind China's Breakthrough in the Middle-East*. Retrieved March 22, 2025, from https://orientxxi.info/magazine/behind-china-s-breakthrough-in-the-middle-east,8096

Dehghan, A., & Arghavanipirsalami, F. (2025). China and the New Middle East; Opportunities and Challenges for the New Regional Order. [{in Persian}]. *International Quarterly of Geopolitics*, *177*, 216.

Derakhshandeh, M., & Shafiee, N. (2022). US Policy Towards China in the Framework of the Hedging (1990-2021). [{in Persian}]. *World Politics*, *11*(2), 7–38.

Doha News. (2023, July 19). *Saudi Crown Prince Threatened UAE with 'Worse' Blockade than Qatar: Reports*. Retrieved May 1, 2025, from http:// https://dohanews.co/saudi-crown-prince-threatened-uae-with-worse-blockade-than-qatar-reports/

EIA. (2024, April 6). China Imported Record Amounts of Crude Oil in 2023. Retrieved September 20, 2024, from https://www.eia.gov/todayinenergy/detail.php?id=61843

Fardella, E., & She, G. (2024). The Role of the Gulf in the Longue Duree of China's Foreign Policy. *Middle East Policy*, *31*(1), 50–65. DOI: 10.1111/mepo.12734

Farokhparsa, Y., Razani, E., & Mirk, A. (2024). China's Foreign Policy towards the Persian Gulf region and its Effects on the Interests of the Islamic Republic of Iran (2015-2025). [{In Persian}]. *International Relations Researches*, *14*(1), 231–258.

Fernandez, E. (2024, September 30). *Arab Capital Inflows into China Break Investment Records*. Retrieved Febryary 22, 2025, from https://www.atalayar.com/en/articulo/economy-and-business/arab-capital-inflows-into-china-break-investment-records/20240930061000205628.html

Garlick, J., & Havlova, R. (2020). China's "Belt and Road" Economic Diplomacy in the Persian Gulf: Strategic Hedging amidst Saudi– Iranian Regional Rivalry. *Journal of Current Chinese Affairs*, *49*(1), 82–105. DOI: 10.1177/1868102619898706

Houghton, B. (2024). *Everyone's Friend, No-One's Foe: China's Persian Gulf Hedging Strategy Since1979*. Retrieved February 10, 2025, from Durham University: http://etheses.dur.ac.uk/15606/

Hu, W. (2024, November 26). *China-Saudi Arabia Investment Cooperation Strengthening amid Global Uncertainties*. Retrieved January 15, 2025, from Global Times: https://www.globaltimes.cn/page/202411/1323824.shtml

Huang, P., Wang, C., Ren, H., & Chen, Z. (2023, August 7). *Growing Fondness: Why are Arab Youth Increasingly Drawn to China?* Retrieved March 11, 2025, from Global Times: https://www.globaltimes.cn/page/202308/1295813.shtm

International Crisis Group. (2024, June 13). *Great Expectations: The Future of Iranian-Saudi Detente*. Retrieved May 1, 2025, from https://www.crisisgroup.org/middle-east-north-africa/gulf-and-arabian-peninsula/iran-saudi-arabia/b92-great-expectations-future

Karimifard, H. (2024). Explaining the Economic and Political Relations between America and China in the Middle East (2021-2023). *IIWFS*, *5*(4), 137–162.

Khurma, M. (2023, June 5). *China has a Growing Presence in Arab Hearts and Minds*. Retrieved March 25, 2025, from Wilson Center: https://www.wilsoncenter.org/article/china-has-growing-presence-arab-hearts-and-minds

Knipp, K. (2024, November 10). *Iran and Saudi Arabia Persue Cautious Rapproachment*. Retrieved April28 2025, from DW: https://www.dw.com/en/iran-and-saudi-arabia-pursue-cautious-rapprochement/a-70715889

Lons, C. (2024, May). *East Meets Middle: China's Blossoming Relationship with Saudi Arabia and the UAE*. Retrieved August 18, 2024, from ECFR: https://ecfr.eu/publication/east-meets-middle-chinas-blossoming-relationship-with-saudi-arabia-and-the-uae/

Moreland, R. (2024). Shifting Sands: US Gulf Policy Recalibrates as China's Regional Ambitions Grow. *Middle East Policy*, *31*(1), 149–161. DOI: 10.1111/mepo.12726

Peel, M., & Kerr, S. (2023, December 7). *UAE's Top AI Group Vows to Phaseout Chinese Hardware to Appease US*. Retrieved June 12, 2024, from Financial Times: https://www.ft.com/content/6710c259-0746-4e09-804f-8a48ecf50ba3

Quamar, M. (2025, January 16). *China and Saudi Arabia: A Deepening Strategic Partnership*. Retrieved February 13, 2025, from ORF: https://www.orfonline.org/research/china-and-saudi-arabia-a-deepening-strategic-partnership

Robbins, M., Jamal, A. A., & Tessler, M. (2024, July/August,). *America Is Losing the Arab World*. Retrieved 10 September, from Foreign Affairs: https://www.foreignaffairs.com/united-states/america-losing-arab-world?utm_source=twitter_posts&utm_medium=social&utm_campaign=tw_dai

Samoudi, A. (2023). China's Presence in the Persian Gulf: Reasons and Consequences . *Strategic Monthly National Security Watch, April-May 132&133*, 115-135. {In persian}

Sazmand, B., & Ramezani, A. (2021). The Importance and Challenges of the Persian Gulf for China's Belt and Road Initiative (BRI). *Journal of Iran and Central Eurasia Studies*, *4*(1), 75–108.

Sun, D. (2022). China's Zero- Enemy Policy in the Gulf, Dynamics and Tactics. In Fulton, J. (Ed.), *Sim, Asian Perceptions of Gulf Security*. Routledge. DOI: 10.4324/9781003227373-3

Swinhoe, D. (2023, September 4). *Huawei Launches Saudi Cloud Region in Riyadh*. Retrieved August 22, 2024, from Data Center Dynamics: https://www.datacenterdynamics.com/en/news/huawei-launches-saudi-cloud-region-in-riyadh/

Tirziu, A. G. (2024, July 4). *China's Strategic Evolution in the Middle East: From oil to Security*. Retrieved March 12, 2025, from https://www.gisreportsonline.com/r/china-middle-east-security/

Urhova, D. (2023, August 22). *China Catching the Wave of Intensifying Saudi-UAE Rivalry*. Retrieved May 1, 2025, from China Observer: https://chinaobservers.eu/china-catching-the-wave-of-intensifying-saudi-uae-rivalry/

Vafamand, Z., & Arghavani, P. (204). Regional Competitions and China's Economic Diplomcy in Persian Gulf Subsystem in 21st Century. *FASIW, 6* (2), 271-303. {In Persian}

Chapter 12
China's Concurrent Gradual Strategy of De-Dollarization and Internationalization of the Yuan

Ali Omidi
https://orcid.org/0000-0003-1882-0456
University of Isfahan, Iran

ABSTRACT

When the United States froze the reserves of the Russian Central Bank following Moscow's invasion of Ukraine in February 2022, it raised concerns in China. Previously, Washington had used the dollar as a weapon against countries such as Iran, Venezuela, and Cuba. This "weaponization" of the dollar and manipulation of it for domestic economic purposes by the US seems to have prompted China to reduce its vulnerability to it. There is ample data showing that China has taken several measures to mitigate the risks associated with the U.S. dollar. This chapter examines the various measures taken by China toward de-dollarization and internalization of the Yuan simultaneously and its prospects. The research is conducted in a descriptive-analytical manner, based on data from library and internet sources.

DOI: 10.4018/979-8-3373-0938-5.ch012

INTRODUCTION

One of the pillars of U.S. hegemony is the centrality of the dollar in the international monetary regime, which has reinforced the global position of the United States as the dominant currency in international transactions since World War II. Through the dollar, the U.S. not only benefits from free riding in the global economy and reduces its substantial trade imbalances but also wields it as an economic weapon against its adversaries.

Following the collapse of Bretton Woods in the 1970s and the subsequent decline of the U.S. economy, particularly with the introduction of the euro and the rise of China, the U.S. has faced challenges from currency rivals. Speculation has emerged regarding the weakening of the dollar's position and the strengthening of its competitors, leading to discussions about the emergence of a multipolar currency system. One of the most notable developments strengthening the feasibility of this transition is China's efforts to internationalize its currency.

Countries such as China, Brazil, Russia, Turkey, Iran, and India are rapidly expanding their gold reserves, which is driving up gold prices. China, once the largest holder of U.S. Treasuries, is now selling these bonds and actively de-dollarizing its economy. The BRICS group is working to reduce the dollar from its trade transactions. There are many indicators that the world's second-largest economy, China, is seeking to de-dollarize.

But what does "de-dollarize" mean? De-dollarization occurs when a country reduces or completely eliminates its dependence on the U.S. dollar in its financial transactions. This move aims to increase economic independence, especially when a country desires greater control over its financial policies. Consequently, the U.S.'s use of the dollar as a weapon against other nations such as Iran, Russia, Venezuela and so on has prompted many to turn to their national currencies or consider alternatives to the dollar in transactions. China seeks to diminish its dependence on the U.S. dollar, positioning itself as a rising geopolitical power deserving of financial independence from U.S. influence. Weakening the dollar's role as the world's dominant currency would represent a significant geopolitical victory for China, if successful. The BRICS effort to de-dollarize is expected to lead to a gradual, albeit slow, reduction in the dollar's role within the international monetary system.

This research explores the future of the U.S. dollar as the dominant global currency, with a focus on China's strategy to reduce its dependence on the dollar and to internationalize its own currency. The study employs a descriptive-analytical methodology, drawing on information and data from library and internet sources. This chapter first reviews the main research relevant to the topic and defines the specific contribution this paper makes. It then elaborates on the theoretical foundations regarding when and how a currency achieves hegemonic status, and why various countries have joined the de-dollarization movement. Subsequently, the chapter analyzes China's currency regime and the key components of its strategy to reduce reliance on the U.S. dollar. The final section addresses the limitations China faces in its efforts to internationalize its currency.

1. LITERATURE REVIEW

Numerous scientific studies have examined China's de-dollarization strategy and the internationalization of the yuan, with several works closely related to this research. For example, Zeidan (2024) explores the evolution of the Chinese yuan and the impact of the Belt and Road Initiative (BRI) on China's currency strategy. The study highlights how economic demands and capital outflow controls have shifted China's focus from pursuing full de-dollarization to developing cross-border, yuan-denominated trade settlements. It emphasizes that, while de-dollarization remains a goal, China's current strategy is more about managing risks—particularly in response to U.S. sanctions—than about completely abandoning the dollar. Similarly, Sutter and Nelson (2021) examine the sanctions imposed on China and Russia as key factors behind the reduced use of the dollar in both countries. They argue that, due to the high volume of China's dollar reserves and the limited international adoption of the Russian ruble, both countries remain significantly dependent on the dollar. Ryan (2024) contends that China has been leveraging its political and economic capital to form strategic alliances aimed, in part, at establishing a new currency regime. He argues that geopolitics, particularly the sanctions imposed by the G7 alliance, is a major driver of China's de-dollarization policy.

Gutierrez and Gouvea (2023) note that the current sanctions environment is prompting non-Western countries to move away from the dollar. They argue that since 2023, the global economy has become increasingly fragmented and that BRICS countries will play a significant role in shaping the future of globalization. Iselin (2024) discusses the broader implications of China's de-dollarization strategy within the context of the Global South, contending that the dominance of the U.S. dollar has perpetuated economic challenges for developing countries. The article argues that China's promotion of local currency settlements and the formation of financial alliances are crucial steps toward establishing a more equitable global economic order. The author advocates for a collaborative approach among developing nations to reduce the risks associated with dollar dependency.

Greene (2024) asserts that the primary motivation behind China's de-dollarization efforts lies in concerns over the vulnerability of its dollar-denominated assets, particularly in the wake of U.S. sanctions against Russia. Chinese economists, including former central bank officials, have urged a reduction in holdings of U.S.

government debt, fearing these assets could become "hostages" in the event of sanctions targeting China. Geddes and Grain (2025) also examine the broader impacts of China's de-dollarization strategy on the Global South, similarly emphasizing that dollar dominance has created persistent economic challenges for developing countries. Salehi et al (2024) have shown in their research that although China's de-dollarization policy poses a potential threat to dollar hegemony, it has so far failed to challenge US currency dominance, and the dollar-based order appears likely to continue for the foreseeable future. Karimi et al (2022) believe that the continuation of the US dollar's hegemony relies on the country's structural power in both economic and political spheres, and is based on factors such as the depth of the capital market, ease of access, security commitments, and international trust, which have synergistically provided the basis for the consolidation and continuation of the hegemony of this currency. Therefore, it is unlikely that the Chinese yuan will be able to compete with the US dollar in the short term.

Finally, Krauss (2023) analyzes the benefits, risks, and potential impacts of the yuan's internationalization, aimed at reducing China's dependence on the dollar and enhancing its economic and geopolitical influence. However, it is noted that while China's efforts in this area have intensified, the overall effectiveness of these policies has so far been limited.

Table 1. Summarizing the key points from the literature review

Author(s)	Year	Focus	Key Points
Zeidan	2024	Evolution of yuan; Belt and Road Initiative (BRI)	China has shifted from full de-dollarization to risk management and cross-border yuan trade settlements due to capital controls and U.S. sanctions.
Sutter & Nelson	2021	Sanctions on China and Russia	Despite attempts at de-dollarization, both China and Russia remain dependent on the dollar due to large reserves and limited alternatives like the ruble.
Ryan	2024	Geopolitical drivers and alliances	China uses its political/economic power to build alliances aiming at a new currency regime; G7 sanctions are key drivers of de-dollarization.
Gutierrez & Gouvea	2023	Sanctions and BRICS' role in globalization	The sanctions push non-Western countries away from the dollar; BRICS will be pivotal in reshaping global economic order.
Iselin	2024	Global South perspective	U.S. dollar dominance harms developing nations; China's push for local currency settlements and alliances can lead to a more equitable global economy.
Greene	2024	Vulnerability of China's dollar assets	Chinese economists are concerned U.S. sanctions could threaten dollar assets; urges reduction in U.S. debt holdings to avoid asset "hostage" scenarios.

continued on following page

Table 1. Continued

Author(s)	Year	Focus	Key Points
Geddes & Grain	2025	Global South impact of China's de-dollarization	Dollar dominance continues to challenge developing countries; echoes Iselin's call for a more balanced currency system.
Salehi et al	2024	China's de-dollarization strategy components	The dollar-based order appears likely to continue for the foreseeable future.
Karimi et al	2022	How a currency gets international status	The US dollar has enough political and economic components to keep its higher status.
Krauss	2023	Risks and benefits of yuan internationalization	Yuan internationalization is meant to reduce dollar dependence and boost China's influence, but its effectiveness remains limited so far.

Although there are thematic similarities between this research and some of the aforementioned studies, none have comprehensively analyzed China's strategy concerning both de-dollarization and the internationalization of the yuan. Each of the existing studies has focused on specific aspects or the primary motivations behind China's de-dollarization efforts. Therefore, given the significance of this issue, a thorough examination of this currency confrontation and its implications for the international political economy is essential—an undertaking that this research seeks to address.

2. CONCEPTUAL FRAMEWORK: THE DIALECTICS BETWEEN DOLLAR HEGEMONY AND DEDOLLARIZATION

A conceptual framework is a representation of a set of interrelated elements using constituent factors and a pattern of causal relationships between these factors. When a single theory is not sufficient to explain a problem, a conceptual model that is extracted from different theories can be used. After World War II, the U.S. dollar emerged as the world's leading currency, underpinned by the country's gold reserves. It became the cornerstone of the international monetary system and played a crucial role in facilitating international trade. With more than half of the world's gold reserves held in the United States and given its magnificent share of global economic cake (around 50%), global financial stability increasingly depended on U.S. decisions. The primary goal of the international monetary system is to maintain an orderly payment mechanism while facilitating trade through a common medium of exchange. To achieve this, the system must ensure the creation of adequate liquidity, establish an exchange rate regime between national currencies, and provide a regulatory framework to prevent excessive external financial imbalances.

To understand how a country's currency functions internationally—as a unit of exchange, a measure of value, and a store of value (the tripartite functions of money)—the interaction between political and economic power must be considered. The conversion of a national currency into an international currency primarily depends on the economic capabilities of the issuing country. Key economic factors influencing international currency competition are typically categorized into three areas: safety, ease of access, and market depth. Currency stability is essential for international use; instability increases the risks associated with holding the currency and reduces its attractiveness. The security of the exchange rate can be influenced by various factors, including the country's net debt position and the independence of its central bank. Ease of access is another important characteristic of an international currency. The presence of developed and open financial markets in the issuing country reduces currency exchange costs, making it more appealing for international use. A market capable of handling a large volume of orders with minimal slippage is referred to as a deep market. Deep markets lower transaction costs, attract more customers, and further reduce costs (McKinnon, R. I.,1993).

In addition to economic factors, political elements such as political and economic stability, financial transparency, and the ability to foster global political loyalty significantly contribute to a country's currency achieving international status (Helleiner, E., 2008). Financial transparency involves a healthy flow of information, minimizing fraud and errors, and ensuring timely access to complete financial data. Political stability refers to a calm and reliable political and social environment, characterized by consistent laws, management, and policies, and the absence of conditions such as war, rebellion, coups, chaos, or threats to the system. "Economic stability" implies the absence of excessive fluctuations in the macroeconomic environment and the presence of transparent, stable laws. Political and economic stability reduces uncertainty and enhances the predictability of a country's political and economic behavior. Since World War II, the U.S. dollar has largely embodied these characteristics, and any other currency aspiring to achieve international status must possess these attributes to some degree.

Dedollarization refers to the process by which countries and global markets gradually reduce their reliance on the U.S. dollar as the primary reserve currency and medium of exchange in international trade. This trend has accelerated in recent years due to various economic, geopolitical, and technological factors. Although the dollar remains the cornerstone of the global financial system, its dominance is increasingly being challenged. Geopolitical tensions, unilateral economic sanctions, and countries' desires for monetary independence are among the factors driving this shift. Dedollarization is not limited to U.S. competitors; varying degrees of dedollarization exist even among U.S. strategic allies. The three main reasons for dedollarization are: 1) Managing foreign exchange reserves and preserving asset value, 2) Economic governance, and 3) Geopolitical considerations (Tshikovhi, et al., 2025).

Just as individuals and entities in different markets design diverse capital portfolios, central banks around the world are increasingly seeking to diversify their foreign exchange reserves and precious metals. Traditionally, the U.S. dollar has constituted a significant portion of these reserves due to its stability and liquidity. However, holding a large amount of reserves in a single currency exposes countries to various currency risks. In contrast, diversifying reserves with other currencies, such as the euro, yen, or Chinese yuan, can mitigate this risk and potentially yield better returns. By diversifying their foreign exchange reserves and investing in alternative assets like gold, countries can reduce their economies' vulnerability to dollar fluctuations. This low-risk and gradual strategy does not fundamentally alter a country's economic structure but serves as an effective first step toward diminishing the dollar's dominance. According to the International Monetary Fund, the share of dollar reserves held by countries has decreased from 71% in 1999 to 59% in 2021, with this decline being offset by increases in gold, the euro, and the yuan. Global holdings of nontraditional reserve currencies have risen from US$30 billion in 1999 to US$1.2 trillion by 2021(Arslanalp, et al., 2022). Similarly, India's share of gold in the country's total forex reserves is as high as 11.7% of $677.8 billion in 2024(The New Indian Express, 2025). Or Russia has decreased the US dollar share of its foreign exchange reserves from about 40% in 2014 to below 15% in 2021(Laser et al, 2024).

Another motivation for dedollarization is the desire for more dynamic economic governance. Countries that rely on the U.S. dollar are significantly affected by the Federal Reserve's monetary policy decisions. When the Federal Reserve adjusts interest rates, it impacts global financial markets, and countries with substantial dollar-denominated assets or liabilities are more likely to experience financial and credit shocks. This dependence can lead to severe economic instability in countries where U.S. policies do not align with their economic conditions or governance styles. By reducing reliance on the dollar, countries can gain greater control over their monetary policy, achieve their own economic goals, and insulate themselves from external shocks. For example, Brazil has forged a new path to reduce its dependence on the dollar in intra-regional trade by signing bilateral trade agreements in local currencies with countries such as China and Argentina, and by launching the SML payment system (Reuters, 2024). Similarly, the United Arab Emirates is working to diversify its currency exchanges by developing bilateral payment mechanisms and establishing a regional currency settlement platform (India Briefing, 2023). These countries do not adopt a confrontational approach toward the United States; instead, they prioritize stability in policymaking. Their high dependence on the U.S. economy means they are continually affected by domestic economic issues in the U.S.

Perhaps the most significant reason for dedollarization is geopolitical factors. The dollar serves as a crucial lever of American superpower, effectively becoming the economic and political arm of Washington. After World War II, the United States established its currency as the world's primary reserve currency, compelling oil-rich countries to trade their oil in dollars. This leverage has allowed the U.S. to unilaterally impose sanctions on other countries as it sees fit. Countries such as Russia, Venezuela, Iran, and potentially China in the near future face heavy economic sanctions from the United States. These sanctions can severely impact the economies of targeted nations by limiting their access to international markets and financial systems. To mitigate such risks and diminish the leverage the U.S. holds over their economies, these countries are actively seeking alternatives to the dollar. By doing so, they aim to enhance economic flexibility and reduce their vulnerability to political and geopolitical pressures.

In the process of dedollarization, states use various strategies such as diversifying foreign assets, trading based on national currencies or currencies other than the dollar, lending and investing based on their national currencies, digitizing national currencies, and designing financial messaging systems other than SWIFT. China is also pursuing a de-dollarization strategy for those reasons and apply those strategies among others. Viewing its national currency as a potential competitor to the U.S. dollar, China is gradually and strategically working toward the internationalization of the yuan. In the following sections, we will explore more how China pursues this goal and the limitations it faces.

Table 2. Conceptual model of prerequisite for a currency hegemony and drivers to the de-dollarization campaign

Theme	Main Points
Functions of a strong International Currency	- Medium of exchange - Measure of value - Store of value
Fulfilling Key Economic Functions	- Safety: Stability and low risk - Access: Open and developed markets - Depth: High liquidity, low transaction costs
Key Political-economic prerequisite	- Political/economic stability - Financial transparency - Global political trust

continued on following page

Table 2. Continued

Theme	Main Points
Drivers of Dedollarization	- Reserve management: Diversify to reduce risk - Economic governance: Reduce Fed policy impact - Geopolitical: Avoid U.S. weaponising of its dollar
Strategy to Dedollarization	- Diversification of foreign assets - National Currency Swap Agreements - Lending and investing based on national currency - Digitizing a national currency and launching a parallel SWIFT system

3. CHINA'S CURRENCY REGIME AND MANAGING THE IMPOSSIBLE TRINITY

In the financial world, currencies are traded against each other, and the exchange rate of each currency compared to another changes based on supply and demand, monetary policies, and economic conditions. A currency regime, also known as an exchange rate system, is a set of rules and policies developed by a country's central bank to manage and determine its exchange rate against the currencies of other countries. Three types of currency regimes are commonly used to determine a country's currency: fixed rate (or pegged exchange rate), floating rate, and managed floating rate.

A *fixed exchange rate system*, also known as dollarization, is a currency system in which the value of a country's national currency is tied to a specific foreign currency. The goal of this system is to stabilize the exchange rate and prevent severe currency fluctuations, with the central bank actively intervening in the foreign exchange market to achieve these goals. This intervention requires high foreign exchange reserves to stabilize the market. Advantages of a fixed exchange rate system include reduced exchange rate fluctuations, increased investment security, and controlled inflation. However, the disadvantages include the need for substantial foreign exchange reserves and the potential for speculation during crises. For example, Saudi Arabia's currency system is a fixed exchange rate system, maintaining an exchange rate of about 3 riyals to the U.S. dollar for nearly 40 years.

A *floating exchange rate system* is one in which the exchange rate is determined by supply and demand in the international currency market, with no direct intervention by the central bank. Factors such as interest rates, inflation rates, and political and economic conditions significantly impact exchange rate fluctuations. Many advanced economies, including the United States, Switzerland, the United Kingdom, the Eurozone, and Australia, operate under a floating exchange rate system. The advantages of this system include high flexibility regarding economic conditions, reduced need for large foreign exchange reserves, and better overall management. However, countries with a floating exchange rate system are more vulnerable to short-term political and economic risks. For instance, after the 2008 financial crisis and the COVID-19 pandemic in 2020, developed economies faced significant challenges, including rising inflation and unemployment.

The *managed float system*, also known as a dirty float, is a modified model compared to the free float system. In this system, the exchange rate is mainly determined by supply and demand, and the central bank intervenes only during crises. Factors such as export volume, foreign investment, and interest rates play significant roles in this currency system. Countries such as India and Singapore utilize this system to determine exchange rates. While the currency value fluctuates in the market, the central bank intervenes as needed to control extreme fluctuations(Levy-Yeyati, & Sturzenegger,2005).

The Chinese yuan operates within a tightly managed system. China maintains strict capital controls, foreign investment quotas, and a complex system that regulates onshore trading. The Chinese central bank sets a daily reference rate and does not allow the yuan to fluctuate beyond a specified range. This means the Chinese government actively controls the value of the yuan and intervenes whenever necessary to adjust it (Hua, et al., 2022). Few countries exercise such tight control over their currencies, with China, Iran, Venezuela, and Egypt being notable examples. To manage the yuan's value, the Chinese central bank sets it against a basket of major global currencies, including the U.S. dollar, euro, and Japanese yen. However, the U.S. dollar remains the most significant currency in this basket, exerting a greater influence on the yuan's fluctuations than other currencies. In 2023, 48% of all Chinese international payments were made in U.S. dollars and it is estimated that around 50 percent of China's overall reserves are in dollars, while less than 20% of Chinese exports went to the U.S(Greene, 2024). This indicates that China remains more dependent on the dollar than it might appear, often using it for financial transactions with other countries. This reliance poses a challenge for a country like China, which seeks to assert itself on the global stage alongside the United States. For instance, if China were to engage in military action against Taiwan, the U.S. and its allies could easily freeze or seize China's dollar reserves. Given that most of the international financial system operates on the dollar, China faces a significant dilemma. Additionally, China relies on the SWIFT financial network for global transactions, which connects over 11,000 banks and financial institutions. However, the yuan accounts for only 4.61% of all SWIFT transactions, whereas the U.S. dollar constitutes 48% and the euro nearly 22%. This means that U.S.-dependent currencies account for about 70% of all global financial transactions, giving the United States and its allies greater control over access to SWIFT and the ability to restrict China's international transactions(Global Times, 2024).

This context explains why China is pursuing de-dollarization. To address its dependence on the dollar, China must find solutions while recognizing that its economy is built on exports. China imports raw materials, processes them, and then exports the final products for assembly or packaging in destination countries. Severing ties from global trade could jeopardize this economic model, prompting China to proceed cautiously and incrementally.

China faces a significant challenge related to a fundamental economic concept known as the impossible trinity. Every country in the global economy must choose two of the following three options, sacrificing one: 1) exchange rate stability, which links the value of the currency to that of a major power (like the U.S. dollar) to protect it from fluctuations; 2) independent monetary policy, allowing control over interest rates and money supply; and 3) free capital flow, enabling unrestricted movement of money across borders. The Mundell–Fleming trinity model illustrates that no economy can maintain all three simultaneously. Most large economies opt for an independent monetary policy and free capital flow, often necessitating a floating exchange rate. Countries like the U.S., Australia, the U.K., Japan, and South Korea follow this model. Conversely, closed economies like North Korea restrict capital flow, allowing for an independent monetary policy and dictated exchange rates without global financial integration.

Some economies, such as Hong Kong, the UAE, Panama, and Latvia, lack independent monetary policies and central banks but maintain fixed exchange rates with free capital flows, making them attractive to foreign investors. China, however, strives to navigate the impossible trinity. With an independent monetary policy and billions of dollars in daily capital flows, China connects freely to global financial networks while attempting to maintain the yuan's exchange rate within a specific range through strict controls. This balancing act poses significant risks.

China has sought to monitor capital flows rigorously. However, managing every transaction in an economy with a vast volume of daily interactions is practically impossible. In December 2024, the value of transactions in China's foreign exchange market amounted to around 3.7 trillion U.S. dollars monthly (Statista, 2025). Due to this high transaction volume, total control over exchanges remains elusive. To mitigate this, China has implemented a system of limiting capital flows, allowing money to enter or exit the country only when the amounts are approximately equal or within limits set by the central bank. If capital outflows exceed inflows, China restricts further outflows until sufficient funds have entered the country.

Currently, the Xi Jinping administration aims to balance all three vertices of the trinity through strict measures. However, ultimately, one must be sacrificed. If China restricts capital flow, it risks becoming akin to a large North Korea, counter to Xi Jinping's vision for China as a significant global power. One approach could involve opening a capital account while maintaining a fixed exchange rate. This would allow capital mobility but limit the ability to stimulate the economy with cheap financing. A scenario similar to Japan's 1990s market collapse is a potential concern for China, which seeks to avoid a similar fate. A complete opening of the capital account under such circumstances could trigger capital flight and severe instability(Lo, & Lo, 2015).

Abandoning the controlled exchange rate of the yuan and sharply devaluing it appears to be the only logical option for China. However, this process would need to be gradual; sudden liberalization could see the yuan-dollar exchange rate rise dramatically from 5 to 1 to as high as two-digit yuan per dollar. While devaluation may enhance the competitiveness of Chinese exports, it could also lead to domestic unrest, increased inflation, and reduced purchasing power for the Chinese populace. This would be a challenging position for a country that has always sought to project its economic strength.

Rather than abruptly freeing the exchange rate, China will likely adopt a managed policy to prevent sharp declines in the yuan's value while allowing for greater floating. This is a crucial first step toward de-dollarization, as achieving global trust in the yuan hinges on its freedom from tight government control. By floating the yuan and stabilizing the impossible trinity, China can focus on genuine de-dollarization. Over the past decade, China has made strides in this direction, exemplified by its cooperation with Russia to establish the BRICS economic group, which now includes several new members aimed at countering U.S. dollar hegemony.

4. MAIN INGREDIENTS OF CHINESE STRATEGY IN DEDOLLARISATION

The main elements of China grand strategy in dedollarisation and internationalization of the renminbi are selling US bonds and buying gold, mutual swap currency agreements, Yuan-based lending and investing, digitizing the Yuan and launching the Chinese national SWIFT.

4-1. Selling US Treasuries, Buying Gold, and Developing a National Bond Market

In recent years, China has shifted from being the largest buyer of U.S. Treasuries to becoming the largest seller, converting these bonds increasingly into gold. This strategic move indicates China's effort to reduce its dependence on the U.S. dollar. A significant change occurred in September 2023, when China's holdings of U.S.

Treasuries fell to their lowest level since May 2009, as reported by the U.S. Treasury Department in mid-November 2023. Specifically, China reduced its holdings of U.S. Treasuries by $27.3 billion, bringing the total down to $778.1 billion(Tavex Bullion, 2024).

This trend is part of a broader pattern where many countries are moving away from U.S. government bonds. However, despite this trend, Japan remains the largest U.S. creditor, followed by the United Kingdom. Both countries have also reduced their holdings, with reductions of $28.5 billion and $29.2 billion, respectively, as of September 2023.

Several factors may explain China's shift away from U.S. bonds. Here are three main reasons:

1. *Strengthening the Yuan*: By selling U.S. debt, China raises dollars, which can then be used to buy yuan. This strategy helps improve the yuan's exchange rate. Since the onset of the COVID-19 crisis, China's economy has faced challenges, including a downturn in the real estate market, a trade deficit exacerbated by the trade war with the United States, and sluggish economic growth. Given these challenges, China is likely aiming to prevent significant depreciation of the yuan against other currencies in the global financial system.
2. *Geopolitical Tensions:* The deterioration of U.S.-China relations has prompted China to reassess its stance on U.S. bonds. The United States has increasingly used the dollar as a tool in its geopolitical strategies, a situation that has worsened since Donald Trump took office in 2025. In this context, gold emerges as a viable alternative. Physical gold is one of the few assets that is sufficiently liquid to attract investments worth tens of billions of dollars.
3. *Declining Confidence in U.S. Sovereign Debt:* The U.S. financial situation has seen a significant decline, a sentiment echoed by various rating agencies. This lack of trust is partly why U.S. Treasury bond prices have fallen, forcing the U.S. to offer higher interest rates on its debt(Tavex Bullion, 2024).

Historically, China has been on a buying spree of U.S. bonds, peaking in May 2013, when it held nearly $1.3 trillion in U.S. government securities. This recent shift to selling U.S. bonds and hoarding gold marks a significant change in China's investment strategy. China's gold reserves have grown rapidly over the past few years, indicating preparations for a major economic shock. By the end of December 2024, China's official gold reserves China's official gold holdings stand at 2,280t, accounting for 5.5% of total foreign reserves, a record high(World Gold Council, 2025). However, many analysts believe the true figure for China's gold reserves is likely much higher.

China's gold purchases may signal a readiness to de-dollarize its economy. For a full transition away from the dollar, trust in local fiat currencies must be strengthened. Gold, with its long-standing reputation as a reliable store of value and a fundamental element of monetary systems, serves as an ideal medium for building trust between countries and ensuring currency stability. While China may be considering steps to back the yuan with gold, such a change is currently feasible only to a limited extent. Even significantly higher gold reserves than the official figures suggest would not be enough to cover all the yuan in circulation at the current exchange rate. This indicates that China's strategy may involve a gradual or piecemeal approach to adopting the gold standard. Bond issuances in China totaled 71 trillion yuan (about 10 trillion U.S. dollars) in 2023, up 14.8 percent year on year, according to data from the central bank.

China has established the world's second-largest bond market, following the United States, to support its investment projects and promote the international use of the yuan. In 2023, the issuance of treasury bonds reached 11 trillion yuan, while local government bonds totaled 9.3 trillion yuan, according to the People's Bank of China. Financial bonds were issued at 10.2 trillion yuan, and corporate credit bonds amounted to 14 trillion yuan that year. Additionally, credit-asset-backed securities issuance was 348.52 billion yuan, and interbank deposit certificates reached 25.8 trillion yuan. By the end of 2023, the total value of bonds held in custody was 157.9 trillion yuan, reflecting a year-on-year increase of 9.1 percent. As of 2024, outstanding bonds held by foreign institutional investors reached 3.72 trillion yuan, representing 2.4 percent of the total bonds under custody(The State Council, the People's Republic of China, 2024).

4-2. National Currency Swap Agreements and Petroyuan

Following the 1998 East Asian financial crisis, the countries of the region convened a meeting in Chiang Mai, Thailand, in 2000 to discuss future solutions. This meeting resulted in several important resolutions known as the "Chiang Mai Plan." The most significant resolution was the signing of bilateral monetary swap agreements among member countries to prevent the recurrence of financial crises. Consequently, the first bilateral monetary agreement was signed in 2001 between the central banks of China and Thailand, and by 2003, all ASEAN countries had signed such agreements in pairs. These agreements were subsequently extended in 2005 and 2008.

While the initial monetary agreements were primarily unilateral and based on the U.S. dollar (with the exception of the China-South Korea and China-Japan agreements, which were established in local currencies from the outset), the newer agreements utilize two national currencies instead of relying on one. This shift allows for the use of these currencies as reserve currencies during financial crises and for trade settlements under normal conditions. A review of international experiences indicates that the process of concluding monetary agreements has accelerated since 2008, particularly following the financial crisis in the West, largely due to Chinese initiatives. Since 2008, China concluded a total of 40 monetary agreements with various countries which 31 bilateral currency swap agreements are in force, with a total scale of about 4.16 trillion yuan (about 586 billion U.S. dollars)(The State Council, the People's Republic of China, 2024).

Various studies have highlighted the advantages of monetary pacts, including: 1) enhancing the value of the national currency, 2) creating relative stability and improving expectations, 3) positively impacting economic growth, and 4) helping to hedge risk. Conversely, disadvantages include: 1) dependence on trading partner countries, 2) imbalances in the trade balance, and 3) reductions in the central bank's foreign exchange assets. However, proponents argue that if a country can export effectively and use its official currency in monetary pacts rather than common currencies for international transactions, it enhances the status and value of its national currency globally(Ranaldo, 2023). China benefits this advantage and it bolsters its yuan. Additionally, 60% of China's total foreign trade volume is conducted with countries with which it has currency agreements. Among these is China's currency agreement with Japan, which, according to the Bank of Japan, is valid until October 25, 2021, allowing for the exchange of local currencies between the two central banks up to 200 billion yuan or 3.4 trillion yen (approximately $30 billion). It was subsequently renewed in October 2021 for an additional three-year term(al24news.com: 2025). China's experience demonstrates that if a country like China, with strong production and export capabilities, can extensively use its national currency—creating international demand for it—it can even serve as a store of value.

In a press conference following his return from Saudi Arabia in 2022, the Chinese President announced that, under agreements reached with Gulf Cooperation Council countries, over the next three to five years, more than 40% of international payments for oil and gas exports from these members would be made in yuan. In November 2023, Saudi Arabia and UAE renewed currency swap with China valued $13 billion for three years(East Asian Forum, 2024). This indicates that the emergence of the "petroyuan" is no longer an unattainable dream. As the world's largest oil importer, China has fundamentally altered dollar-based economic relations in this strategic region, and the Middle East is increasingly welcoming Chinese investments to diversify its economies.

A major component of China's defensive strategy against perceived Western containment is the establishment of a global commodity trading system based on the yuan. This strategy aims to improve the yuan's pricing power, reduce China's vulnerability in global resource trade, and strengthen its global financial position.

Major oil suppliers to China—including Russia, Angola, Venezuela, Iran, and Nigeria—now accept yuan for oil trade. The Shanghai International Energy Exchange launched yuan-denominated crude oil futures in 2018, with total trading volume reaching 44 trillion yuan (approximately $6.7 trillion) by April 2021, servicing clients from 23 countries and regions(Liu, 2022). Oil exporters have been able to convert yuan-denominated oil revenues into gold on the Shanghai and Hong Kong Gold Exchanges. This convertibility indicates that China, as the world's largest oil importer, possesses the complete domestic infrastructure to trade oil indirectly using gold. This marks the beginning of utilizing alternative currencies to price a major global commodity and aligns fully with Beijing's de-dollarization policy.

4-3. Yuan-based Lending and investing

China's lending to developing countries has intensified in recent years. However, the lack of regular reporting on Chinese loans has created a "hidden debt" problem, leaving debtor countries and international institutions with an incomplete picture of the total debt owed to China. According to available data, the Chinese government and its subsidiaries have provided approximately $1.5 trillion in direct loans and trade credits to more than 150 countries worldwide, primarily in yuan(Harvard Business Review, 2020). This has made China the world's largest official creditor, surpassing traditional lenders like the World Bank, the International Monetary Fund, and the Organization for Economic Cooperation and Development.

Despite the surge in lending to foreign countries, China does not publish any official data on the number and amount of loans it has granted. Information on these loans is often leaked from borrowing countries or informal sources. According to these reports, since 1949, China has issued nearly 3,000 loan packages to borrowing countries, with Djibouti, Tonga, the Maldives, the Republic of Congo, Kyrgyzstan, Cambodia, Niger, Laos, Zambia, Samoa, Vanuatu, and Mongolia being the top recipients. Studies indicate that the interest rates on loans from China are comparable to those in private capital markets, whereas other official institutions, such as the World Bank, typically offer loans at concessional, below-market rates with longer maturities. The debt levels of countries borrowing from China have been steadily increasing. Estimates show that the debt of the 50 primary countries borrowing from China has risen from 1% of their GDP to 15% since 2005, with dozens of these countries owing China at least 20% of their nominal GDP(Horn et al., 2023).

China has also involved 138 countries and 30 international organizations in the Belt and Road Initiative (BRI). Statistical data reveals that since 2013, China invested USD 1.175 trillion primarily in 149 countries(Green Finance and Development Center, 2024). A review of this data indicates that Beijing's investment in the

"New Silk Road" plan has increased in recent years, driven by loans to developing countries for infrastructure development.

To facilitate these projects, China has established financial institutions. For example, it launched the "Silk Road Fund" with a capital of $40 billion in 2014 and established the Asian Infrastructure Investment Bank with a base capital of $100 billion in partnership with other countries in 2015. Additionally, the Chinese government has allocated $82 billion to three banks in 2015 for investment in Silk Road projects, with most of the credits from these banks denominated in yuan (Callaghan,& Hubbard, 2016). This approach has paved the way for Chinese companies to implement infrastructure development projects in other countries, further enhancing reliance on the Chinese government and strengthening the Chinese national currency. This will aid in the gradual process of de-dollarization.

4-4. Digitizing the Yuan and Launching the Chinese National SWIFT

As of April 2021, the People's Bank of China has introduced the digital yuan, also known as the white yuan, e-RMB, or e-CNY, as legal tender to facilitate and accelerate money transfers. The digital yuan serves as a digital equivalent of the physical yuan, effectively acting as its digitized version. The primary goal of introducing this digital currency is to streamline money transfers and reduce reliance on physical cash (Wang, 2022).

A key feature of the digital yuan is that it generates no profit through investments. It retains a value equivalent to the physical yuan and is intended solely for money transfers and commerce. The People's Bank of China distributes the digital currency to banks and other financial institutions in a centralized manner, without utilizing the blockchain technology common in other cryptocurrencies. However, these institutions are permitted to use blockchain in the distribution of the currency. Thus, while the digital yuan is centrally managed—contrary to the decentralized nature of other cryptocurrencies—it mitigates the risk of misuse.

In the next phase, the digital yuan is expected to be used for paying salaries to ministries, institutions, and state-owned enterprises. Future plans may even include the potential for utilizing this digital currency for short-term accounts and investments. Estimates suggest that within a few years, the volume of China's digital currency could reach 1 trillion yuan (approximately $140 billion), representing more than one-eighth of China's total liquidity. In contrast, the total volume of the global cryptocurrency market, including Bitcoin, is around $200 billion(Wang, 2022).

The issuance of a digital currency will significantly enhance the Chinese government's ability to control the country's financial transactions. This will enable regulatory bodies to monitor the payment and financial systems comprehensively and provide the government with detailed reports on money and capital flows. Digital business activities and transactions will create a comprehensive database of liquidity information and credit structures across society, facilitating decision-making for regulatory institutions. Consequently, the Chinese central bank will have more information to maintain stability, regulate the business cycle, and reduce the risk of economic bubbles within the financial system. Increased transparency in financial transactions will help prevent money laundering, tax evasion, and other financial crimes, allowing the People's Bank of China to combat suspicious transactions, particularly those related to sensitive areas such as the Middle East.

Previously, China launched the "CNY Interbank Cross-Border Payment System" (CIPS) in 2015, and with the introduction of the digital yuan, this system will undergo updates. Prior to this, transparency and cross-border settlements were facilitated through CHIPS and SWIFT, both of which have posed challenges for China. CHIPS is an American company, and SWIFT, being integral to international banking, is influenced by U.S. interests; twelve of the twenty-five SWIFT heads are Americans or their allies, and transaction information is accessible to the United States. Hence, for the yuan's internationalization project, China requires its own global currency banking transparency system, making the digital yuan particularly important in this context. By employing this Chinese banking system, transaction data will be made available to the Central Bank of China, while Western institutions will be unable to track these transactions, thereby minimizing potential sanctions from China's trading partners.

The acceptance of the Chinese digital currency by multinational companies, including news reports that firms like McDonald's and Starbucks will accept it, lays the groundwork for a relative weakening of the dollar. Nevertheless, this initiative marks the beginning of a challenge to the dollar, which will unfold over the long term. According to World Bank statistics in 2018, about 1.7 billion people worldwide rely solely on cash due to the lack of bank accounts(World Bank,2018), while two-thirds of these individuals have mobile phones that can facilitate money transactions. This potential aligns with the digital payment systems developing in China. The platform for using digital currency is also integrated into the "Belt and Road" initiative, considering China's trade and projects in the countries along this route. The "Digital Belt and Road" initiative will continue to gain momentum.

As of February 2025, China's foreign exchange reserves totaled US$3.22 trillion(tradingeconomics, 2025), largely accumulated through trade between Chinese and American companies, as well as the conversion of dollars received by these companies into yuan. If foreign importers and exporters in China establish a common blockchain network for using the yuan, a new payment method could emerge that eliminates the need for dollars and the associated currency conversion costs.

Consequently, the Chinese digital currency is expected to promote much wider international use of the yuan.

If China's digital currency is institutionalized within the Belt and Road Initiative, it could encompass the economies of about half the world's population. Additionally, the potential for the Chinese government to confiscate individuals' digital assets exists. Therefore, the success of China's digital yuan initiative could have a detrimental impact on the United States and the Western capitalist system. In the absence of reciprocal actions from the U.S., the dollar's status as the primary international currency may weaken. While the digital yuan is still in its infancy, it represents a step forward in China's de-dollarization policy, enabling it to conduct transactions outside the purview of Western systems.

Table 3. China's Strategy components in dedollarization and internationalization of Yuan

Main Strategy	Key Elements	Details
1. Selling US Treasuries & Buying Gold	- Shift from US debt to gold - Building national bond market	- China cut US Treasury holdings to $778.1B (Sept 2023) - Gold reserves officially at 2,280 tons (likely underestimated) - Strengthening yuan, geopolitical tensions, and lack of confidence in US debt are main drivers - Chinese Bond market grew to ¥157.9 trillion by 2023
2. Currency Swap Agreements & Petroyuan	- Bilateral currency swaps - Oil payments in yuan	- 31 active swap agreements worth ¥4.16 trillion - 60% of China's trade is with countries in such agreements - Oil deals with Saudi Arabia, UAE, Russia, etc., increasingly in yuan - Shanghai Energy Exchange launched yuan oil futures in 2018
3. Yuan-based Lending & Investing	- Lending to developing nations - Belt and Road Initiative (BRI)	- ~$1.5 trillion in global loans, mostly in yuan - Involvement in 138 countries under BRI - Creation of AIIB and Silk Road Fund - Top loan recipients include Djibouti, Laos, Zambia, etc.
4. Digital Yuan & National SWIFT (CIPS)	- Launch of e-CNY - Creation of Chinese alternative to SWIFT	- Digital yuan centralized, not blockchain-based - Projected to reach ¥1 trillion circulation - CIPS supports cross-border yuan transactions - Aims to reduce dependence on CHIPS/SWIFT - Firms like McDonald's, Starbucks accept e-CNY - Integrated with Belt and Road's "Digital Silk Road"

5. LIMITATIONS IN INTERNATIONALIZATION OF YUAN

Although China is the world's largest trading nation, the second-largest economy, and a key trading partner for more than a dozen countries, it remains heavily dependent on the U.S. dollar within the international financial system. One of the primary challenges facing the yuan in competing with the dollar is the latter's entrenched dominance. Additionally, substantial internal barriers—particularly infrastructural and systemic issues—undermine international confidence in the yuan. Chief among these are China's managed exchange rate and a banking system that lacks resilience and transparency. The value of the yuan is largely determined and maintained by the Chinese government, and this level of control over the exchange rate continues to hinder its widespread international acceptance. Despite growing calls for reform, China has shown little willingness to significantly liberalize its exchange rate regime (Picardo, 2019). This issue explains why renminbi faces severe impediments to becoming an international reserve currency. Moreover, China's financial system lacks transparency and its capital market lacks enough depth and convertibility. It does not operate sufficiently according to clear market principles, which creates uncertainty among international economic actors (Laser et al, 2024).

A key factor influencing international confidence in a currency is the debt profile of the issuing country. Unlike the U.S., which maintains a persistent trade deficit, China's development model has consistently produced trade surpluses. According to the World Bank, China has maintained a positive current account balance since 2000 (World Bank, 2022). While this may signal economic strength, it also limits the global circulation of the yuan, restricting its liquidity and availability in international markets.

Perhaps the most significant concern among global economic actors is the political –economic uncertainty and the absence of robust democratic institutions in China. Especially, if we suppose the liberal democracy as the best model of governance as political scientists such as Francis Fukuyama maintain. This foggy environment elevates the perceived risks of economic engagement and undermines trust in China's financial governance. While state-controlled economies may appear stable in the short term due to centralized manipulation, they are ultimately perceived as unreliable safe havens. In such systems, the overlap between government and market functions increases the risk of political interference in economic operations, raising concerns about market stability in times of political unrest. Improving transparency and regulatory accountability in both government and markets would help foster greater international trust and economic participation. This, in turn, would strengthen the role of the national currency in global financial and monetary markets.

Geopolitical uncertainties—such as the Taiwan issue, disputes in the South China Sea, strained relations with Southeast Asian neighbors, trade war with the US and the Korean Peninsula crisis—further complicate global perceptions of China as a stable great power. These geopolitical tensions hinder broader acceptance of Chinese mechanisms in the international financial order, including the yuan's internationalization.

6. CONCLUSION

China, as the world's most significant emerging power, is the only country that can meaningfully challenge the Western-led international order dominated by the United States, leveraging its rapid growth and economic strength. Viewing the current system as unjust, China has expressed its commitment to an alternative framework that rejects unilateralism, foreign intervention, and power politics. The U.S.-China rivalry spans multiple dimensions, with one of the most critical being the challenge to the hegemony of the dollar. The dominance of the U.S. currency and Washington's control over interbank payment systems represent major vulnerabilities for China.

In response, China has adopted a policy of de-dollarization, aiming to reduce its dependence on the dollar and mitigate its exposure to Western pressure. Significant steps in this direction include strengthening non-dollar financial reserves (particularly gold), establishing currency swap agreements, engaging in large-scale lending and investment in yuan, promoting the internationalization of the renminbi, and launching its own interbank payment system. These efforts—along with bilateral and multilateral banking agreements, the development of the digital yuan, and the establishment of the Shanghai Energy Exchange—demonstrate China's determination to reduce its reliance on the dollar.

Despite these efforts, it is widely acknowledged that the dollar will remain the world's dominant currency for the foreseeable future. The U.S. economy accounts for approximately 25% of global GDP and benefits from a dynamic foundation rooted in innovation and entrepreneurship. U.S. financial markets are the deepest, most liquid, and most open globally. Moreover, the relative rule of law and high transparency standards provide strong investor protections for both domestic and international participants. The global dollar network further strengthens its role as a universal currency, with around 60% of global reserves held in dollars and three-quarters of safe-haven dollar assets owned by countries that maintain military ties with the United States. Other competitors remain secondary. The euro, for instance, has maintained a roughly 20% share of global reserves since its introduction, but its influence remains largely regional. The European economy lacks the dynamism of the U.S., and efforts to create a European Capital Markets Union have stalled.

Politically, the European Union also lacks strong incentives to internationalize its currency and compete seriously with the dollar.

The only serious contender is the Chinese yuan. China's economy is vast, and the country is actively developing an international payments infrastructure independent of the dollar. It is also at the forefront of central bank digital currency (CBDC) development, and more than a quarter of its trade is now settled in yuan. However, the yuan's role as a medium of exchange has not yet translated into it becoming a reliable store of value. The yuan is not easily convertible, China enforces strict capital controls, and its financial markets remain underdeveloped and heavily regulated by the government. As a result, the yuan currently accounts for only about 3% of global reserves (Siripurapu & Berman, 2022).

Political uncertainty surrounding China's future further complicates its challenge to dollar dominance. The lack of transparency stemming from state hegemony over domestic politics and economy raises concerns among international investors. Despite China's significant initiatives to counter dollar hegemony, the dollar's supremacy is likely to persist in the near term. Nonetheless, China's efforts represent a potential and meaningful long-term challenge to U.S. monetary dominance. Just as dollar hegemony was established through historical processes and global realignments, its gradual decline and the emergence of a multipolar currency system are conceivable. China, alongside key BRICS partners such as Russia and Iran, aspires to hasten this transition as swiftly as possible.

REFERENCES

al24news.com. (2025). China and Japan Renew Currency Swap Deal for Three Years. https://al24news.com/en/china-and-japan-renew-currency-swap-deal-for-three-years/#:~:text=The%20initial%20currency%20swap%20agreement,an%20additional%20three%2Dyear%20term

Arslanalp, S., Eichengreen, B., & Simpson-Bell, C. (2022). The stealth erosion of dollar dominance and the rise of nontraditional reserve currencies. *Journal of International Economics*, *138*, 103656. DOI: 10.1016/j.jinteco.2022.103656

Briefing, I. (2023). India, UAE Agreements on Currency Settlement, Payment Systems, and Key Sector Collaboration. https://www.india-briefing.com/news/india-uae-agreements-on-currency-settlement-payment-systems-and-key-sector-collaboration-28929.html/

Bullion, T. (2024). China Sells US Treasuries and Buys Gold. https://tavexbullion.co.uk/china-sells-us-treasuries-and-buys-gold/

Callaghan, M., & Hubbard, P. (2016). The Asian infrastructure investment bank: Multilateralism on the silk road. *China Economic Journal*, *9*(2), 116–139. DOI: 10.1080/17538963.2016.1162970

East Asian Forum. (2024). Chinese yuan gains currency in the Gulf states. https://eastasiaforum.org/2024/01/17/chinese-yuan-gains-currency-in-the-gulf-states/

Geddes, Thomas des Garets & Crain, Daniel (2025). Towards a New Economic Order: De-Dollarisation, China and the Global South. https://www.sinification.com/p/towards-a-new-economic-order-de-dollarisation

Global Times. (2024). Yuan's global payment ranking remains in fourth place for eighth consecutive month in June. https://www.globaltimes.cn/page/202407/1316298.shtml

Gouvea, R., & Gutierrez, M. (2023). "BRICS Plus": A new global economic paradigm in the making? *Modern Economy*, *14*(5), 539–550. DOI: 10.4236/me.2023.145029

Green Finance and Development Center. (2024). China Belt and Road Initiative (BRI) Investment Report 2024. https://greenfdc.org/china-belt-and-road-initiative-bri-investment-report-2024/#:~:text=Cumulatively%2C%20Chinese%20BRI%20engagement%20has,8%20billion

Greene, R. (2024). China's Dollar Dilemma. Carnegie Endowment. https://carnegieendowment.org/research/2024/10/chinas-dollar-dilemma?center=europe&lang=en

Harvard Business Review(2020). How Much Money Does the World Owe China? https://hbr.org/2020/02/how-much-money-does-the-world-owe-china

Helleiner, E. (2008). Political determinants of international currencies: What future for the US dollar? *Review of International Political Economy*, *15*(3), 354–378. DOI: 10.1080/09692290801928731

Horn, S., Parks, B. C., Reinhart, C. M., & Trebesch, C. (2023). *China as an international lender of last resort* (No. w31105). National Bureau of Economic Research.

Hua, X., Huang, W., & Jiang, Y. (2022). Controlled currency regime and pricing of exchange rate risk: Evidence from China. *Journal of Accounting, Auditing & Finance*, *37*(1), 39–76. DOI: 10.1177/0148558X18781144

Iselin, B. (2024). The Economic Leash: China's Financial Tethers and Global Power Plays. https://www.isdp.eu/wp-content/uploads/2024/11/ISDP-Special-Paper-Brian.pdf

Karimi, G., Zadeh, M. N., & Mirtorabi, S. S. (2022). The hegemonic position of the US Dollar and the prospect of its challenge by the Euro and the Yuan [in Persian Language]. *Quarterly Foreign Relations*, *13*(52), 715–753.

Krauss, S. (2023). The RMB Internationalization Strategy and the Role of the eCNY. Master's thesis. Department of International Politics. University of International Relations People's Republic of China.

Laser, F., Mihailov, A., & Weidner, J. (2024). Currency denomination of foreign exchange reserves: From taboo in the past towards disclosure and exciting research nowadays. https://cepr.org/voxeu/columns/currency-denomination-foreign-exchange-reserves-taboo-past-towards-disclosure-and

Levy-Yeyati, E., & Sturzenegger, F. (2005). Classifying exchange rate regimes: Deeds vs. words. *European Economic Review*, *49*(6), 1603–1635. DOI: 10.1016/j.euroecorev.2004.01.001

Liu, Z. Z. (2022). China Is Hardening Itself for Economic War. Foreign Policy. https://foreignpolicy.com/2022/06/16/china-economic-war-decoupling-united-statescontainment/#:~:text=The%20Shanghai%20International%20Energy%20Exchange,from%2023%20countries%20and%20regions

Lo, C., & Lo, C. (2015). The Impossible Trinity in China. *China's Impossible Trinity: The Structural Challenges to the "Chinese Dream"*, 1-15.

Maronoti, B. (2022). Revisiting the international role of the US dollar. *BIS Quarterly Review, 5.*

McKinnon, R. I. (1993). The rules of the game: International money in historical perspective. *Journal of Economic Literature, 31*(1), 1–44.

Nelson, R., & Sutter, K. (2021, July 23). De-Dollarization Efforts in China and Russia. Congressional Research Service.

https://crsreports.congress.gov/product/pdf/IF/IF11885

Picardo, Elvis(20219). Why China's Currency Tangos With The USD. https://www.investopedia.com/articles/forex/09/chinas-peg-to-the-dollar.asp

Ranaldo, A. (2023). Foreign exchange swaps and cross-currency swaps. In *Research Handbook of Financial Markets* (pp. 451–469). Edward Elgar Publishing. DOI: 10.4337/9781800375321.00030

Reuters(2025). Brazil nixes BRICS currency, eyes less reliance on 'mighty' dollar. https://www.reuters.com/markets/currencies/brazil-nixes-brics-currency-eyes-less-reliance-mighty-dollar-2025-02-13/

Ryan, J. M. (2024). Will Geopolitics Accelerate China's Drive Towards De-Dollarization? *The Economists' Voice, 21*(2), 297–309. DOI: 10.1515/ev-2024-0026

Salehi, S. H., Seyed, M. M. S., Golmohammadi, V., & Haji-Yousefi, A. (2024). China's de-dollarization policy and its impact on the hegemony of the US dollar [in Persian Language]. *Journal of Countries Studies, 2*(2), 189–220.

Siripurapu, A., & Berman, N. (2022). The contentious US-China trade relationship. *Council on Foreign Relations, 2.*

Statista(2023). monthly transaction value in foreign exchange market 2024. https://www.statista.com/statistics/1073120/china-monthly-transaction-value-in-foreign-exchange-market/

The New Indian Express. (2025). Reserve Bank of India is on a gold-buying spree. https://www.newindianexpress.com/business/2025/Apr/20/reserve-bank-of-india-is-on-a-gold-buying-spree

The State Council. the People's Republic of China(2024). China's central bank signs 40 currency swap agreements with foreign counterparts. https://english.www.gov.cn/news/202402/16/content_WS65cef3efc6d0868f4e8e40d3.html

The State Council. the People's Republic of China(2024). China's bond market issuances total 71 trillion yuan in 2023. https://english.www.gov.cn/archive/statistics/202401/29/content_WS65b7a326c6d0868f4e8e399e.html

Tradingeconomics.com. (2025). China Foreign Exchange Reserves. https://tradingeconomics.com/china/foreign-exchange-reserves

Tshikovhi, N., Netswera, F., & De Conti, B. (2025). De-dollarization, the New Development Bank, and BRICS Trade Currency Changing Multilateralism and Geopolitical Arrangements. In *The Multilateralism of the New Development Bank on the Sustainable Economic Growth in BRICS Nations and Beyond* (pp. 65–79). Emerald Publishing Limited. DOI: 10.1108/978-1-83662-292-520251007

Wang, H. (2022). China's Approach to Central Bank Digital Currency: Selectively Reshaping International Financial Order? *U. Pa. Asian L. Rev.*, *18*, 77.

World Bank. (2018). Financial Inclusion on the Rise, But Gaps Remain, Global Findex Database Shows. https://www.worldbank.org/en/news/press-release/2018/04/19/financial-inclusion-on-the-rise-but-gaps-remain-global-findex-database-shows

World Bank. (2022). Between Shocks and Stimulus. https://thedocs.worldbank.org/en/doc/9b7191d416b0dbfd7d36f1a935464ea0-0070012022/original/CEU-June-2022-EN.pdf

World Gold Council. (2025). China's gold market update: Seasonal strength in December. https://www.gold.org/goldhub/gold-focus/2025/01/chinas-gold-market-update-seasonal-strength-december

Zeidan, R. (2024). *De-dollarization, the Belt and Road Initiative, and the Future of the Chinese Yuan*. Georgetown Journail Of International Affairs.

Chapter 13
Building the Great Wall Abroad:
China's Security Engagement in Africa

Amrita Jash
https://orcid.org/0000-0002-7004-694X
Manipal Institute of Social Sciences Humanities and Arts, Manipal Academy of Higher Education, Manipal, India

V. Anand
https://orcid.org/0000-0002-0459-9159
Manipal Institute of Social Sciences Humanities and Arts, Manipal Academy of Higher Education, Manipal, India

ABSTRACT

While China's economic influence in Africa has been widely studied, its security-related activities have received less scrutiny. This chapter positions China's security initiatives as a critical but underexplored dimension of its African policy. This chapter explores China's growing security engagement in Africa, framing it as an extension of its domestic principles of stability and strategic defense, symbolized metaphorically by the "Great Wall." It investigates how China's security policies in Africa align with its broader geopolitical and economic objectives. Through an analysis of military cooperation, peacekeeping missions, arms trade, and the establishment of overseas military bases, the chapter evaluates the implications of China's security engagement for Africa's governance, development, and global security dynamics. In doing so, the metaphor of the "Great Wall" is employed to symbolize China's efforts to project stability, safeguard its interests, and expand its strategic influence beyond its borders.

DOI: 10.4018/979-8-3373-0938-5.ch013

INTRODUCTION

At the 9th Forum on China-Africa Cooperation (FOCAC), Chinese President Xi Jinping explicitly linked China-Africa security cooperation to the "Global Security Initiative"[1] (GSI), by affirming:

China is ready to help Africa improve its capacity in safeguarding peace and stability independently, prioritize Africa in implementing the Global Security Initiative (GSI), promote mutual reinforcement of high-quality development and greater security, and work together with Africa to uphold world peace and stability (The State Council, 2024).

Underscoring the commitment, Xi announced concrete steps under the "Partnership Action for Common Security", stating:

We [China] will give Africa RMB1 billion yuan of grants in military assistance, provide training for 6,000 military personnel and 1,000 police and law enforcement officers from Africa, and invite 500 young African military officers to visit China. The two sides will conduct joint military exercises, training and patrol, carry out an "action for a mine-free Africa," and jointly ensure the safety of personnel and projects (The State Council, 2024).

Complementing the GSI, Beijing's Global Development Initiative (GDI, launched in 2021) also plays a key role in shaping China-Africa cooperation. Closely aligned with the African Union's (AU) "Agenda 2063,"[2] the GDI reflects a shared development vision — Steve Lalande, AU's Director of Partnerships Management and Resource Mobilization noted: "Together [Africa and China] we can transform the ambitious goals of the GDI into concrete results that enhance the quality of life of all Africans and Chinese citizens alike, and also people of the world" (Forum on China-Africa Cooperation, 2024). Taken together, the GSI and GDI reflect a significant broadening of China's engagement in Africa, evolving from a largely economic focus to a more strategic, multidimensional partnership.

China's security interest in Africa has become increasingly prominent, reflecting its broader strategic and geopolitical objectives on the continent. This shift is evident in the "2021 Dakar China-Africa Action Plan" (2022–2024), adopted at the 8th FOCAC Summit. The plan expanded China-Africa cooperation to include military and police collaboration, counterterrorism, and law enforcement—marking a notable evolution in Beijing's Africa policy and introducing a formal 'security' dimension to its engagement. This development aligns with China's broader economic and infrastructure agenda in Africa, particularly through the Belt and Road Initiative (BRI), which has provided a further boost to China's security calculus in Africa. Since its launch in 2013, 53 African nations except Eswatini (formerly Swaziland), have joined the BRI, and by 2023, they had received US$21.7 billion in deals involving ports, railways, and renewable energy (Kluiver, 2024). Beyond infrastructure, the BRI has served as a platform for deepening security cooperation, including arms sales, counterterrorism efforts, peacekeeping missions, and military partnerships across the continent. Underscoring China's growing security presence across the continent, Chinese Ambassador to Somalia, Fei Shengchao, in his 2022 article "No One is Safe until Everyone is Safe—China's View on Global Security Governance," stated:

China believes that the more turbulent the international situation is, the more difficulties and challenges Africa faces, the more we must pay attention to the voices of African countries and increase our support and assistance to Africa. As a good brother of African nations, China will continue to stand with Africa, firmly support Africa in maintaining peace and security, firmly support Africa in achieving economic recovery, firmly support Africa in defending its legitimate rights and interests, and make due contribution to Africa's independence and sustainable development (Embassy of the People's Republic of China in the Federal Republic of Somalia, 2022).

This highlights Beijing's view of global and regional security as interconnected and underscores its intent to position itself not only as an economic partner but also as a security actor in Africa's evolving geopolitical landscape.

It is argued that China's increased security engagement with Africa stems in part from lessons drawn from the conflict in Sudan and the independence of oil-rich South Sudan in 2011. Since then, China's security involvement has steadily expanded, becoming a routine facet of FOCAC and China's activities in Africa (Freeman & Gill, 2024). To give an overview: since 2008, China has deepened its military and security cooperation with African nations by dispatching 44 escort task forces to the Gulf of Aden and Somali waters, conducting joint anti-piracy exercises with countries like Nigeria and Cameroon, and participating in peace conferences related to the Sahel, South Sudan, and the Horn of Africa. It has also played mediation roles in conflicts such as those in Darfur (2007), Zimbabwe, the DRC, Rwanda (2008), and South Sudan (2013); supported AU-led efforts in the Ethiopia-Tigray conflict (2020–2022); expanded its participation in UN peacekeeping missions; and established its first overseas military base in Djibouti (2017). Additionally, China has broadened its network of defense attachés, enhanced military ties through arms exports, training, education, and joint exercises, and engaged multilaterally through platforms such as FOCAC, the China-Africa Peace and Security Forum (CAPSF), and the China–Horn of Africa Peace, Governance, and Development Conference, among others (Jash, 2025).

Today, China's security engagement in Africa encompasses UN peacekeeping, multilateral initiatives, arms sales and military cooperation, response to non-traditional security threats, and conflict mediation. This expanded role demonstrates that China is not only working to safeguard its economic interests but is also challenging

Western dominance in African security affairs. In the words of Horace Campbell (2008, p. 91): "The emergence of China as a force in Africa complicated the tussle between the EU and the USA over the 'who controls Africa'."

As China's security posture evolves, it raises critical questions about its long-term strategic objectives, which this chapter describes as "building the Great Wall abroad"—a metaphor for China's efforts to protect its interests, extend its influence, and reshape global security governance. Given this context, the chapter examines China's evolving role as a security actor or guarantor in Africa through a three-fold lens: first, by assessing the key drivers behind China's broader engagement on the continent; second, by analyzing its security-related roles and involvement; and third, by evaluating the impact through observable trends and patterns in China's security engagement.

From Aid to Ambition: The Factors Behind China's African Engagement

China's engagement with Africa is not new. According to George T. Yu (1988), the 1955 Bandung Conference marked the beginning of Chinese appreciation for the Third World's role in combating adversaries (United States) and winning international recognition and support against the Republic of China (ROC, Taiwan) as well as marked the beginning of China's interest in and policy toward Africa (expanding its foreign policy beyond Asia and the Communist bloc into Africa) (p. 850). Primarily, three key factors shaped China's initial interests in Africa: First, a perception that the Third World offered China an arena in which to achieve its political/ideological objectives, as well-put in Lin Biao's famous statement of 1965, stating:

Since World War II, the proletarian revolutionary movement has for various reasons been temporarily held back in North America and West European capitalist countries, while the people's revolutionary movement in Asia, Africa and Latin America has been growing vigorously.... In the final analysis, the whole cause of world revolution hinges on the revolutionary struggles of the Asian, African and Latin American people who make up the overwhelming majority of the world's population. The socialist countries should regard it as their international duty to support the people's revolutionary struggles in Asia, Africa and Latin America (Yu, 1988, p. 850).

Here, it is important to note that the Chinese attitude to the Third World was not simply the product of revolutionary zeal; it was also the outcome of the Chinese (Mao Zedong's) assessment of the policies of the two powers (United States and Soviet Union) and therefore, if friendship, support, and influence could not be found within the two global alliance systems, they would have to be sought in the Third World (Camilleri, 1980, p. 19).

The second aspect was to gain international recognition and support as the sole legitimate government of China against the ROC- based on twin goals of gaining its seat in the United Nations (UN) and isolating Taiwan, its political opponent. As a result, Beijing viewed the African vote in the General Assembly as a determining factor in replacing Taiwan with China in the UN (African nations made up approximately 30 percent of the UN membership) (Yu, 1988, p. 851). Owing to these political objectives, Beijing entered Africa with massive financial and military aid, which yielded political payoffs: First, in 1971, the votes of African countries were instrumental in winning the People's Republic of China's (PRC) control of China's seat in the UN General Assembly and Security Council (Vines & Wallace, 2023), as also affirmed by Mao Zedong's words, "It's our African brothers who got the People's Republic of China back into the United Nations" (Li, 2017). And second, Beijing was able to isolate Taiwan, as it succeeded in persuading most African countries to switch their diplomatic recognition from Taipei to Beijing (Wang & Elliot, 2014, p. 1013). For instance, Egypt—one of the six African states at the Bandung Conference—was the first African country to recognize the PRC in 1956. Today, 53 out of 54 African countries, except Eswatini, recognize the PRC. Several countries have switched their recognition from the ROC to the PRC, as shown in Table 1. This diplomatic shift by African nations in support of the PRC's One China policy—leaving Taiwan with only one African ally as of 2024—is widely seen as a result of China's "chequebook diplomacy" (Bagwandeen, 2024, p. 7). Given that China has largely succeeded in curbing Taiwan's diplomatic presence in Africa, the One China policy, while still significant, no longer holds the same level of priority as it once did.

Table 1. African Countries that switched recognition from ROC to PRC

Country	Recognition of PRC	Recognition of ROC
Central African Republic	1964 *(switched back in 1998)*	Until 1998
Democratic Republic of Congo	1972	Until 1972
Senegal	1971 *(switched back in 2005)*	Until 1996
South Africa	1998	Until 1997
Liberia	1977 *(switched multiple times, with the latest in 2003)*	Until 2003
Malawi	2008	Until 2007

continued on following page

Table 1. Continued

Country	Recognition of PRC	Recognition of ROC
Gambia	1974 *(switched back in 2016)*	Until 2013
Democratic Republic of São Tomé and Príncipe	2016	Until 2016
Burkina Faso	2018	Until 2018

Source: Compiled by Authors

The third factor is the Sino-Soviet conflict, which fueled China's ambitions in Africa: China wanted to keep the Soviet Union out of Africa, politically and in other ways. For instance, China campaigned for African support to exclude Soviet Union's participation at the 1965 Afro-Asian conference, as well as supported groups of African liberation movements such as the Uniao Nacional Para a Independencia Total de Angola (UNITA) and Zimbabwe African National Union (ZANU), while opposing Soviet-backed groups such as the Movimento Popular de Libertacao de Angola (MPLA) and the Zimbabwe African People's Union (ZAPU) (Yu, 1988, p. 851). Due to this, throughout the 1960s and the 1970s, China provided support to liberation movements across Africa (Beri, 2007, p. 298). Besides, the Sino-Soviet split was well-noted, when on November 13, 1977, Somalia abrogated its Treaty of Friendship and Cooperation with the Soviet Union and expelled some 5 to 6 thousand Soviet advisors, which China's news agency "hailed" as a "just action against Soviet hegemonism" (Shelton, 1979, p. 78 and 80). Furthermore, on November 15, a delegation led by Chinese Vice Minister of the State Physical Cultural and Sports Commission, Yu Pu-hsueh, dedicated a new stadium in Mogadishu built with Chinese financial and technical assistance- a timely move by Beijing to proclaim friendship with the Somalis, following the latter's break from Moscow (Shelton, 1979, p. 80).

To say that the Sino-Soviet split heightened China's interests in Africa is also exemplified by Chinese Premier Zhou Enlai's visit to 10 African countries (Egypt, Algeria, Morocco, Tunisia, Ghana, Mali, Guinea, Sudan, Ethiopia and Somalia) from December 14, 1963 to February 4, 1964. This marked the first such visit by a Chinese state leader to Africa and the second such venture by China outside of Asia since it intervened in the Eastern European crisis of 1956- "presenting itself 'in person' internationally to Africa and the Third World" as well as "directly manifest[ing] its orientations and policy toward Africa" (Yu, 1988, pp.851-852). With these visits, China aimed to deepen China-Africa friendship, support Africa's national liberation movement, expand China's international influence, and break new ground in China's diplomatic work (Global Times, 2021). Since 1991, it has become a diplomatic tradition for the Chinese foreign minister to visit multiple

African countries at the start of each year to mark the beginning of China's Africa diplomatic calendar (Nantulya, 2025a)- demonstrating China's prioritization of relations with the African nations. Similarly, President Xi Jinping's first overseas trip in 2013, which included Africa (after Russia), further signaled the continent's strategic relevance, reinforced by the release of China's first official White Paper[3] on China-Africa relations that same year.

From Revolution to Relations: China's Post–Cold War Pivot to Africa

Apart from the three factors discussed above, China's presence in Africa has rapidly expanded as "an active donor, financier, contractor and builder, marketer, buyer, and investor" (Wang & Elliot, 2014, p. 1015). In the post–Cold War era, China's engagement with Africa has grown significantly in both scale and scope. As Mandira Bagwandeen (2024, p. 4) argues, unlike the United States, China has spent the past two decades actively cultivating its relationship with African nations to the point where it is widely regarded as the "development partner of choice"—surpassing all other countries in trade, investment, and development finance across the continent. For instance, by 1980, the Sino-Africa trade was only about US$1 billion and has grown rapidly over the years- reaching US$55 billion in 2006, to make China Africa's second largest trade partner by surpassing France (Wang & Elliot, 2014, pp. 1013-1014). The bilateral trade has surged from US$6.5 billion in 1999 to US$40 billion in 2005 (Beri, 2007, p. 298) to reach a record high of US$295.56 billion in 2024,[4] marking a 6.1 percent increase from 2023 (The Africa Report, 2025). About 16 percent of Africa's imports come from China, whilst about 20 percent of the region's exports are shipped to China (Winyi, 2024). Important to note that China has been Africa's biggest trading partner for 15 consecutive years, and the proportion of Sino-African trade in Africa's total foreign trade has been rising steadily. Additionally, Chinese investment in Africa has also boomed. Today, China is the largest provider of foreign direct investment (FDI) to Africa,[5] roughly double the level of American FDI. For example, in 2021, China committed US$10 billion in private FDI for 2022–2025 (Forum on China-Africa Cooperation, 2021), and in 2024, it pledged RMB 360 billion in financial support over the next three years, including at least RMB 70 billion in investments by Chinese companies (Ministry of Foreign Affairs, 2024). Besides, China is also by far the largest sovereign lender of development finance to African countries—of Africa's total external debt,[6] China's share grew from 1 percent in 2000 to 13 percent in 2022 (Moses, 2024). Between 2000 and 2023[7], Chinese lenders issued 1,306 loans totaling US$182.28 billion to 49 African countries and seven regional borrowers, with the majority of funding directed toward Africa's energy (US$62.72 billion), transportation (US$52.65 billion), information and communication technology (US$15.67 billion), and financial (US$11.98 billion) sectors (Engel et al., 2024, p. 1). However, it is important to note that Beijing's loan practices have been criticized for a lack of transparency and have earned China a reputation as a "shrewd negotiator" due to the imposition of stringent conditions that secure repayment priority over other creditors (Bagwandeen, 2024, p. 6).

China is active in just about every industry, with significant investments, mainly in construction, energy, and mining (see Tables 2 and 3). To note, in 2022, the gross annual revenues of Chinese companies' engineering and construction projects in Africa totaled US$38 billion—with Nigeria, Angola, Algeria, Egypt, and the Democratic Republic of Congo accounting for 41 percent of it (China Africa Research Initiative, n.d.). For instance, the Chinese companies have funded and constructed, expanded, or refurbished: a minimum of 24 presidential or prime ministerial residences or offices; at least 26 parliamentary buildings or offices; no fewer than 32 military or police facilities; at least 19 foreign affairs ministry offices; and a minimum of 14 critical intra-governmental telecommunications networks (Winyi, 2024). China also controls an estimated 8 percent of Africa's mining sector, which is much lower than the Western presence (Egyin, 2024) and is mainly concentrated in five countries: Guinea, Zambia, South Africa, Zimbabwe, and the Democratic Republic of Congo (Johnston, 2024). In addition, China is also a dominant player in the telecommunications, digital infrastructure, and cybersecurity sectors, with Huawei making up around 70 percent of 4G networks across the continent (Ehl, 2022) (see able 4).

Table 2. China's Investments in the Energy Sector in Africa (Select Countries)

Energy Type	Project	Country
Hydropower	Kariba South Bank Expansion Project	Zimbabwe
	Bui Dam	Ghana
	Grand Ethiopian Renaissance Dam (GERD)	Ethiopia
Solar Power	Garissa Solar Power Plant *(one of Africa's largest solar plants)*	Kenya
Wind Energy	De Aar Wind Farm **one of South Africa's largest wind energy projects supported by Chinese companies*	South Africa
Oil and Gas Exploration	Investments in oil fields	Angola
	Partnership in oil extraction and pipeline development	South Sudan
Natural Gas	Investments in liquefied natural gas	Mozambique
	Partnership in gas extraction and processing	Algeria

continued on following page

Table 2. Continued

Energy Type	Project	Country
Coal Power	Morupule B Power Station	Botswana
Geothermal Energy	Menengai Geothermal Plant	Kenya
Nuclear Energy	El Dabaa Nuclear Power Plant	Egypt

Source: (Jash, 2025, p. 20)

Table 3. China's Presence in the Mineral Sector in Africa (Select Countries)

Country	Mineral	Usage in Industry	Role Played by China
Angola	Diamonds	Jewellery, Electronics industry	China is a key buyer of Angolan diamonds
Democratic Republic of Congo	Cobalt	Batteries, mainly for electric vehicles	China is the largest importer and processor of cobalt from the Democratic Republic of Congo
Gabon	Manganese	Steel production, batteries and chemical applications	Gabon is the key supplier of manganese for China's steel industry
Guinea	Bauxite	Aluminium production for the aerospace, construction and packaging industry	China is the largest importer of bauxite from Guinea
Madagascar	Graphite	Steelmaking and anodes in lithium-ion batteries	China dominates graphite extraction and processing from Madagascar
Mozambique	Graphite	Batteries and industrial applications	China is increasing its investments in high-grade graphite in Mozambique
Namibia	Uranium	Nuclear energy production	China is a major investor in uranium mining projects in Namibia
South Africa	Platinum Group Metals (PGMs)	Electronics, catalytic converters and hydrogen fuel cells	China is a major partner in platinum and palladium mining in South Africa
Tanzania	Rare Earth Elements (REEs)	Electronics (used in various high-tech products like smartphones, and computers), magnets for wind turbines	China is a key player in rare earth exploration and extraction in Tanzania
Zambia	Copper	Electronics, Electrical wiring, construction	Chinese companies are among the largest players in Zambia's copper mining industry
Zimbabwe	Lithium	EV batteries, electronics, renewable energy storage	China is a key investor and miner in Zimbabwe's lithium sector

Source: (Jash, 2025, p. 21)

Table 4. Major Huawei Projects in Africa

Project	Country	Description
5G Deployment	South Africa	Launched Africa's first 5G network (2020)
Safe City Initiative	Kenya, Nigeria	AI-powered surveillance and security systems
Cloud Computing & Data Centers	Egypt, South Africa	Huawei Cloud is expanding its digital infrastructure
National Fiber Networks	Ethiopia, Zambia	Developing fiber-optic internet connectivity

Source: Compiled by the Authors

Besides, the BRI has provided a significant boost to China's investments in Africa. According to the *China Belt and Road Initiative Investment Report 2023*: investments in Africa grew by an impressive 114 percent, totalling US$21.7 billion—a surge driven by China's strategic investments, particularly in the port and shipping sectors, where construction contracts in Africa increased by 47 percent in 2023 alone (Jash, 2025, p. 22). As of now, Chinese firms are involved in 62 African port projects: 33 in West Africa, 17 in East Africa, 9 in North Africa, and 3 in Southern Africa (Nantulya, 2025a). The China Communications Construction Corporation (CCCC), a major player in the African port construction space, holds contracts for at least 38 ports (Container News, 2024). In reviewing the impact of BRI, Haban Sibiri argues that for Africa—now a significant participant in the BRI—the past decade has seen a surge in mega projects across vital sectors such as transportation, energy, telecommunications, and maritime infrastructure (as noted in Table 5); however, this progress has been accompanied by growing concerns over rising debt burdens and environmental impacts.

Table 5. China's BRI Investments in Africa (Select Countries)

Project	Countries	Description	Investment	Year
RAILWAYS				
Mombasa-Nairobi Standard Gauge Railway	Kenya	A 472 km railway connecting Mombasa to Nairobi, enhancing trade and transportation.	US$3.6 billion	2017
Addis Ababa-Djibouti Railway	Ethiopia, Djibouti	A 756-km railway linking Addis Ababa to Djibouti's port is crucial for Ethiopian trade.	US$4 billion	2016
Abuja-Kaduna Railway	Nigeria	186 km railway connecting Abuja to Kaduna, Nigeria's first modern rail line.	US$850 million	2016

continued on following page

Table 5. Continued

Project	Countries	Description	Investment	Year
Tanzania Standard Gauge Railway	Tanzania	1,219 km project connecting Dar es Salaam to inland regions and neighboring countries.	US$7.6 billion	2021
PORTS				
Lamu Port	Kenya	Part of the LAPSSET corridor, this deep-water port expands regional trade.	US$3.5 billion	2020
Doraleh Port	Djibouti	Multi-purpose port enhancing trade routes between Africa, the Middle East, and Asia.	US$590 million	2017
ENERGY PROJECTS				
Kafue Gorge Lower Hydroelectric Project	Zambia	750 MW hydropower project, increasing Zambia's energy capacity.	US$2 billion	2020
Benban Solar Power Plant	Egypt	Africa's largest solar park, with a capacity of 1.8 GW, contributing to renewable energy.	US$4 billion	2019

Source: Compiled by Authors

In addition to these, China's engagement with Africa is also motivated by its leadership in the developing world and its commitment to South-South cooperation, as former Chinese Premier Wen Jiabao had posited:

China is the largest developing country, and Africa the largest developing continent. China-Africa cooperation is part and parcel of South-South cooperation. It is an unshakable policy of the new Chinese Government to strengthen solidarity and cooperation with African countries and other developing nations. We are ready to work with African countries to further develop and strengthen our new-type partnership featuring long-term stability, equality and mutual benefit and all-round cooperation, so as to make it a paragon of South-South cooperation (Beri, 2007, p. 300).

Broadly, China's interests and strategy in Africa can be understood under five key objectives: First, gaining diplomatic support, particularly for its "One China" policy and foreign policy positions in multilateral forums like the UN. Second, accessing natural resources and securing markets for Chinese exports. Third, protecting its strategic interests amid political instability in parts of the continent. Fourth, promoting the "China model" of development—particularly appealing to non-democratic regimes in countries such as Zimbabwe, Sudan, South Sudan, Angola, and Rwanda—as an ideological counterweight to Western liberal democratic norms—finally consolidating its role as a leader among developing nations (Delage, 2022; Yun, 2024).

These strategic priorities raise an important question: why are many African countries increasingly aligning with China? A significant factor is Beijing's policy of "non-interference"—unlike the Unted States or international financial institutions such as the International Monetary Fund and the World Bank, China offers loans and investments with minimal political conditions. Unlike the West, it does not exert pressure on African governments regarding governance standards, democracy, human rights, or transparency—making it a more appealing partner for many regimes on the continent (Jash, 2025, p. 3). While some scholars argue that "why African countries are attracted to China goes beyond the Chinese Yuan"—wherein non-economic drivers such as Xi Jinping's personality, China's global outreach and the politics of megaprojects, among others, have enabled China to penetrate the continent with ease surpassing already established traditional actors like the United States, United Kingdom and France (Nyadera et al., 2020, p. 443).

Nevertheless, China's engagement in Africa—particularly through investment—has drawn considerable scrutiny. The existing literature on Sino-African relations stands polarized between those who see it as a catalyst for economic growth and those who caution against its political risks and long-term implications. For instance, given its loans are long-term rather than grants, China has been accused of creating a "debt trap" that China may use to gain strategic advantages on the continent; some argue that African countries that borrow from China may lose key assets if they are unable to pay back their loans; and while others contend that China is using its influence to promote its political ideas on the continent (Sanny & Selormey, 2021).

Challenging the "debt trap" narrative, Yunnan Chen (2020) argues that "China as a creditor, is one of far greater flexibility and leniency" in dealing with debt. For instance, in 2018, amid Ethiopia's foreign exchange shortages, Beijing allowed the deferral of interest payments on the Addis Ababa–Djibouti railway loan and extended the repayment period from 15 to 30 years, easing the country's financial burden. While Marcus Vinicius de Freitas (2023) refutes criticisms of China's role in Africa by arguing that, unlike Western powers, China does not export its governance model, build networks of dependent states for resources or military bases, but instead invests heavily in mutually beneficial partnerships without interfering in domestic politics and internal affairs. However, from an African perspective, the picture is more nuanced. According to Afrobarometer's 2019/2021 national surveys across 34 African countries:

Africans hold positive views of China's assistance and influence on the continent, though its perceived level of influence on African economies has waned over the past five years. Positive views of China's influence do not appear to affect Africans' attitudes toward democracy. China remains second to the United States as the preferred development model for Africans. And majorities of those who are aware of

Chinese loans and development assistance to their countries are concerned about being heavily indebted to China (Sanny & Selormey, 2021, p. 1).

Given China's expanded presence across Africa, it is imperative to assess the strategic motivations behind its security engagement and the various political, economic, and geopolitical drivers that are shaping Beijing's evolving approach to the continental engagement.

Security by Strategy: Drivers & Factors Behind China's African Engagement

Taking it further from economic, political and diplomatic engagements, there is an incremental increase in China's security engagement with African countries. For instance, China has expressed its willingness to "provide mediation efforts for the peaceful settlement of disputes based on the will of countries in this region" as well as to work with the Horn of Africa countries to turn the region into a "horn of peace, development, and prosperity" (Jash, 2025, p. 10). On a broader canvass, the "GSI Concept Paper" categorically outlines Beijing's interest towards playing a bigger role in Africa's peace and security, to:

Support the efforts of African countries, the AU and sub-regional organizations to resolve regional conflicts, fight terrorism and safeguard maritime security, call on the international community to provide financial and technical support to Africa led counter-terrorism operations, and support African countries in strengthening their ability to safeguard peace independently. (Ministry of Foreign Affairs, 2023).

In this context, it is essential to explore the motivations for China's security engagement with Africa. Understanding broadly the key drivers of the security dimension in China's approach towards Africa and specifically the fundamental factors which create insecurity for China in the continent can help better comprehend Beijing's rationale in this regard.

Drivers Behind a Security-Oriented Engagement

The key drivers behind China's such an engagement remains a topic of debate. According to Oita Etyang and Simon Oswan Panyako (2020), China's engagement in Africa's peace and security agenda is driven by four main interests: First, to protect its trade market and its investments, as most of China's investments are in conflict-prone regions of the continent. Second, by playing an active role in Africa's peace and security, China seeks to boost its image as a peacemaker and as a valuable and responsible actor in the global arena. Third is the domestic political imperative to protect its citizens abroad as, in Africa, Chinese nationals are engaged in various activities such as mining, construction projects, trade and others. Fourth, it also provides China with the opportunity to gain practical experience in dealing with emerging security threats and challenges in the global world (Etyang & Panyako, 2020, p. 340).

Broadly, China's security cooperation with Africa has been largely viewed as driven by narrow realist motivations (Lammich, 2025, p. 4), according to which Beijing's activities across the continent are purely guided by its interests and shaped by its capabilities. Africa accounts for only four percent of China's trade with the rest of the world, as well as just three percent of China's overseas investments (Cannon, 2024, p. 164). However, the second-largest continent in the world represents more than a quarter of the total UN General Assembly votes. It is also home to a substantial portion of the world's critical mineral reserves – almost half of the world's cobalt and manganese, which are extremely significant considering the global imperatives of energy transition (UNCTAD, 2024). Moreover, Africa figures heavily in China's blue-water naval ambitions – the continent is located along China's strategic maritime access route to the Euro-Atlantic. The emerging framework of China-Africa security cooperation also provides China with a template for its security cooperation with the rest of the Global South. Besides these factors, the revitalization of great power competition across the world in the past decade has permeated all facets of geopolitics – and China's security relations with Africa is certainly not an exception to this. All of the above aspects are very visibly linked to China's global ambitions.

On the other hand, some have argued that China's security engagement with Africa is rooted in a much wider perspective, driven by a 'development-security nexus' approach. According to this approach, China has identified lack of development as the root cause of conflict in Africa, and has been working towards addressing it (Benabdallah, 2016). In its 2021 White Paper on "China and Africa in the New Era: A Partnership of Equals," Beijing highlighted that "China has always championed the principle of African people solving African issues in their own ways, and advocated the need to address root causes as well as symptoms and seek cooperation for the benefit of all parties" (The State Council, 2021). This is seen as the reason why China has incorporated infrastructure and capacity building as part of its security engagement with Africa. Nevertheless, this approach does not appear to work in some cases – like that of Sudan and South Sudan – where deep-seated ethno-religious and socio-political divisions keep fueling conflicts despite the investments in development (Benabdallah, 2016).

Factors of China's Insecurity in Africa

Notwithstanding the perspectives, the actors themselves have their innate features which impart a security dimension to the China-Africa relations. In this context, the insecurity of Africa itself is a factor which drives China's security approach towards the continent. Africa has continued to remain insecure for decades and centuries because of colonial experiences, underdevelopment, misgovernance, societal cleavages, and major power interventions. The resulting perpetual and periodic conflict in the form of civil wars, international terrorism, and transnational crime not just hinders Africa's growth potential, but also imposes substantial security risks for commercial and developmental activities in the continent by foreign actors. These security threats directly and indirectly impact China's economic and political interests in Africa by disrupting supply chains and undermining political stability. For example, the civil war in Libya led to a US$20 billion loss for Chinese companies, which had high stakes in the country. China has also been facing terrorist threats on its personnel and interests in West Africa (Boko-Haram and Al Qaeda) and East Africa (Al-Shabab), as well as in Central Africa from militant groups (Lammich, 2025, pp. 5-6). The countries in Africa hosting Chinese investments also largely lack the necessary capacity to ensure their security, in which case China has to get involved by itself (Barton, 2018, p. 6). Additionally, security risks faced by Chinese migrants have remained high (Figure 1), and even increased in some countries, such as the Central African Republic, where nine Chinese gold miners were killed in March 2023, or in Sudan, where infighting among military factions convinced Beijing to evacuate its nationals from the country (Cabestan, 2023, p. 558). These inherent risks have necessitated the incorporation of a security angle in Beijing's engagement with the continent.

Figure 1. Attacks on Chinese Citizens in Africa (2012-2024)

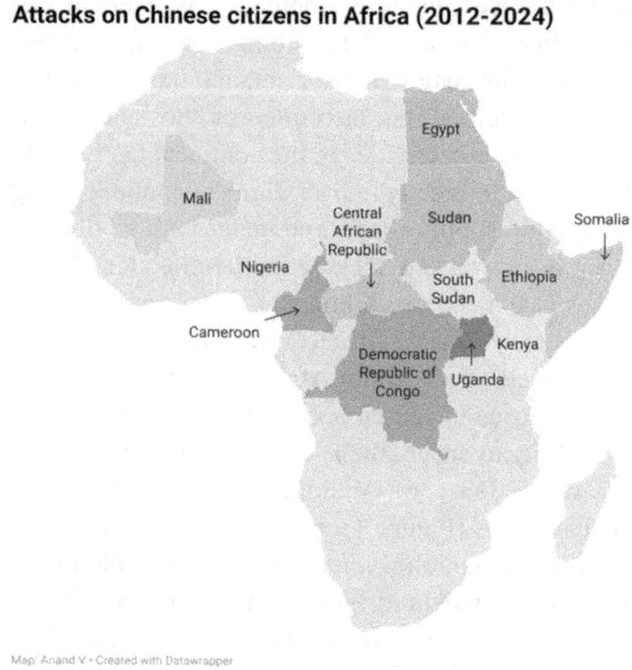

Source: Created by the authors using data from Barton (2018) and various other sources

China's approach to engagement with Africa has, in some cases, contributed to the deepening of security risks on the continent. Since becoming a net importer of oil in 1993, Beijing has increasingly invested in African energy resources to help meet its growing energy demands and sustain rapid industrial growth at home. With China starting to pursue a "Going out" strategy since 1999, its State-Owned Enterprises and later on its private firms started venturing into Africa in search of fresh pastures to facilitate their global growth (Grieger, 2019). China has been Africa's largest trading partner since 2009, as a result of the relative weakening of Western economies and their investment capacities due to the Global Financial Crisis (Kovrig, 2018). BRI significantly expanded the scale and scope of China's investments in Africa, heightening the exposure of its interests to security risks—arguably more so than those of other foreign powers. One of the reasons why China's investments in Africa are more susceptible to threats is due to the risk taken by China to invest in countries isolated by the West due to political reasons, such as the case of Sudan (Barton, 2018, p. 3). This has led to higher exposure for China to security threats in the continent. What adds to this is anti-China sentiments over Beijing's investments and business practices, referring to Chinese companies' unfair and unfavorable labor policies, lack of employment opportunities for locals, with few jobs going to African workers (Orfosu & Sarpong, 2021). Sergio Carciotto and Ringisai Chikohomero's (2022) study highlights numerous labor rights violations linked to Chinese companies in sectors such as mining, construction, fisheries, and manufacturing, including noncompliance with compensation, contracts, health and safety, and labour dispute handling—further exacerbated by non-standard employment relations that leave vulnerable workers, particularly women, exposed to abuse and exploitation. Moreover, China's practice of non-intervention sometimes witnesses setbacks, especially in cases where a longstanding regime in an African country gets challenged or deposed by protests, democratic elections or other means, leading to the opposition or the new government perceiving China as supporting the regime—thereby increasing security risks to China's interests in those countries (Walsh, 2019, pp. 3-4).

Thus, there are certain fundamental reasons behind China seeking to engage with Africa in the security domain. China's quest for securing its economic interests in the continent, cultivating a responsible power in the world, sustaining legitimacy at home, as well as gaining military experience, as well as protecting its citizens in Africa, plays an important role in driving such an engagement. China's motivations, though a matter of debate, are seen to be part of its realist global ambitions and, at the same time, seeking to address the root causes of the continent's security. The unique characteristics of Africa, as well as the ways in which China engages with the continent, are fundamental factors in shaping the insecurity in Africa that China seeks to deal with.

Securing Influence: Patterns of China's Engagement in Africa

China's security engagement with Africa spans all major regions of the continent and includes a growing range of sub-domains within security cooperation. Complementing this, China has been developing a policy and institutional framework aimed at sustaining, expanding, and deepening the security dimension of its relations with Africa.

China's security engagement in Africa is seen to be more concentrated in the Sahel region as well as the Horn of Africa – the security focus on the latter region is a result of maritime piracy and that of the former is due to terrorism (Devecioglu & Akçomak, 2024, pp. 17-12) Elsewhere, China's economic stakes and their security drives China's security engagement. In the security domain, there is a growing diversification of China's security activities in Africa into 'soft' and 'hard' areas. As far as the policy framework is concerned, the introduction of the GSI has led to speculations that China is going to bridge the gap between developmental and security cooperation with the Global South in general and Africa in particular. Whereas China has traditionally emphasized the developmental nature of its relations, the security ties could witness a catch-up (Lammich, 2025, pp. 3-9). This can be seen in China's approach towards other regions as well – for instance, China's growing security overtures in its relationship with the Pacific Island Countries of late have set alarm bells ringing in the Indo-Pacific. Although there is a broad acceptance of the GSI in China, there are criticisms against African countries blindly adopting China's multilateral security norms as they could go against African values and agency. (Nantulya, 2023) The following discussion on the structure and content of China's security ties with Africa reveal the expanding contours and emerging trends in the relations.

Policy and Institutional Frameworks

China has steadily deepened its engagement with Africa, particularly in the realm of security cooperation, through a combination of strategic policies and institutional mechanisms. There has been a progressive evolution of a security policy outlook in China's relations with Africa. China's Africa policy of 2006 provides the earliest framework for China's security engagement with the continent. China's signature BRI is also increasingly incorporating security dimensions – there is a growing need to protect China's trade and investments in Africa, and some of the BRI projects are directly or indirectly related to Africa's security interests. In the 2013 and 2015 Defence White Papers, China has explicitly articulated the need to deploy its military presence to protect its overseas interests (Grieger, 2019). Further, according to the 2021 White Paper, it is articulated that "Based on the principles of respecting the will of African countries, not interfering in African countries' internal affairs, and observing the basic norms governing international relations, China is actively exploring constructive participation in promoting and maintaining peace and security in Africa." (The State Council, 2021). The GSI, operating under the larger umbrella of his "Community of Common Destiny for Mankind"[8] concept, perhaps sets the most recent framework through which China's security engagement with Africa needs to be viewed. The GSI has been interpreted as expanding the scope of China's security engagement with the world, and it certainly does apply to Africa as well. China's recent documents outlining its plans for the continent – the 'China-Africa Cooperation Vision 2035' and the 'Outlook on Peace and Development in the Horn of Africa' seem to be based on the precepts of the GSI (Lammich, 2025, pp. 7-9). The implementation of these concepts provides a framework under which China's security ties with African countries could be shaped, unfolding the next stage of China's security engagement with Africa.

China's security engagement in Africa is primarily bilateral, however, it is increasingly seeking to leverage multilateral and regional level partnerships. The FOCAC, established in 2000, is a triennial ministerial forum between China and the 53 African nations which recognize it, providing an important multilateral platform for addressing shared concerns, including peace and security issues. Over time, FOCAC has institutionalized China's engagement not only with individual African states but also with the with the AU and various Regional Economic Communities across the continent. While FOCAC is often viewed as "China-centric," Cliff Mboya (2024) contends that the forum increasingly reflects Africa's agency to move away from "unbalanced, colonial-style economic relationships towards those formed by equals." This perspective is echoed by South African President Cyril Ramaphosa, who emphasized the pursuit of "shared prosperity while recognizing our [Africa and China] individual developmental aspirations", and ECOWAS President Bola Tinubu, who underscored that the foundation of China-Africa relations lies in "trust, mutual respect, and the pursuit of common goals," stressing the need to "maintain momentum, through peaceful dialogue and transparent business practices" (Mboya, 2024).

Resultantly, deliberations at the FOCAC summits have developed further nodes for expanding China's security cooperation with Africa at the multilateral level. One such effort has been the Initiative on 'China-Africa Cooperative Partnership for Peace and Security' (ICACPPS)[9], which was established in the 2012 FOCAC Summit. In the 2015 FOCAC summit, President Xi pledged US$100 million in military assistance to the AU for over four years to support the African Standby Force (ASF)[10] and its interim mechanism, the African Capacity for Immediate Response to Crises (ACIRC). Later, at the 2018 FOCAC Summit, China pledged an additional US$60 million for the same– nevertheless, the realization of these promises have remained unknown.

Subsequently, China initiated the 'China-Africa Peace and Security Initiative and the China–Africa Peace and Security Fund' in 2018 to support the 'African Peace and Security Architecture' (APSA)[11] and the ASF. Further that year, China hosted the 'China-Africa Defense and Security Forum' (CADSF), followed by rebranding its second iteration in 2019 as 'CAPSF' in response to the criticism that China was trying to use the platform to sell its military equipment to African countries (Lammich, 2025, pp. 14-17). With such a series of initiatives, China has attempted to deepen its multilateral engagement with Africa on security matters. At the same time, these institutional developments cannot be seen as just pushed ahead by China – they also reflect the agency of African countries, especially in a collective manner, in taking forward the security ties in a course which also benefits them. (Baxter & Yang, 2024) China, therefore, has developed a policy as well as an institutional framework for enhancing its security ties with Africa. They have evolved consistently, provide meaning and structure to the relationship, and can also provide a glimpse of its emerging trajectory.

UN Peacekeeping Activities

Among the permanent members of the UN Security Council, China has the largest number of peacekeepers in Africa (Bagwandeen, 2024; Barrios et al., 2025). Today, China provides about 10 percent of funding for the UN's peacekeeping missions globally (Benabdallah, 2016, p. 25), and it is also the second largest source of funding for UN peacekeeping operations in Africa (Lammich, 2025, p. 6). Among the five permanent UN Security Council Members, China has sent the largest number of UN peacekeeping troops to Africa. Since it first took part in UN peacekeeping operations in 1990, more than 80 percent of China's peacekeeping troops – about 30,000 personnel – have been sent by Beijing to the continent (The State Council, 2021). However, China has not always been forthcoming on the UN's peacekeeping agenda.

Before the 1980s, China used to keep vetoing from such initiatives in the UN Security Council because they violated the principle of non-interference. However, China has changed its attitude towards peacekeeping gradually and has today emerged as a leader in this field. China started funding peacekeeping operations since 1982, and by 1988, it joined the UN Special Committee on Peacekeeping Operations (Grieger, 2019). China has traditionally sent non-combat troops for its peacekeeping missions in Africa, which changed with the MINUSMA mission in Mali in 2013 (Kuo, 2015, p. 174). Today, as depicted in Figure 2, China's UN peacekeeping forces are active in Western Sahara, Mali, South Sudan, the Central African Republic, and the Democratic Republic of Congo. China is currently contributing 1793 troops for peacekeeping in Africa, out of which 95 percent are combat troops – the rest being police personnel, officers and experts. However, China ranks only eighth in the total number of troops deployed currently in Africa (UN Peacekeeping, 2025).

Figure 2. China's UN Peacekeeping Presence in Africa

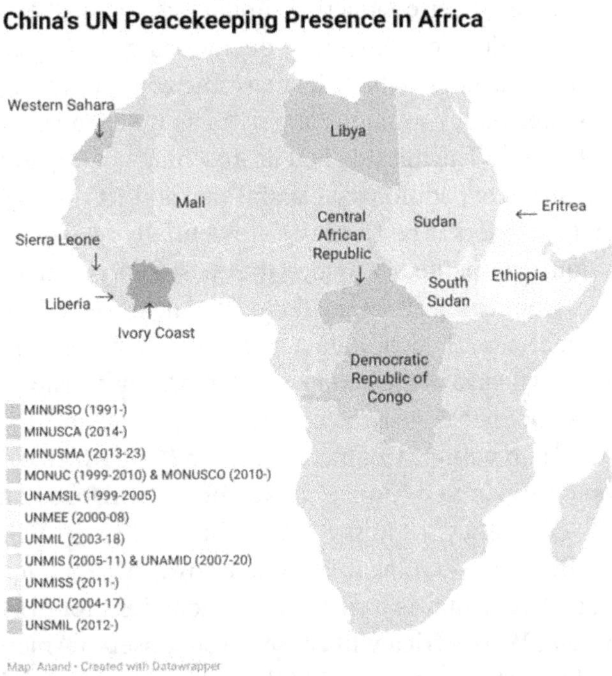

Source: Created by authors with data compiled from UN Peacekeeping (2025)

Apart from enhancing peace and stability in a continent where China has significant interests, China's peacekeeping operations provide it with various other advantages. It enhances China's image of being a responsible power in world affairs. It also bolsters China's efforts to project its rise in the international system as being peaceful. These operations enhance China's role within the UN system, strengthening its credentials as a global leader. Further, they also provide some experience to China's military personnel – China has not engaged of late in any wars in the past four decades, despite its rising military capabilities (Devecioglu & Akçomak, 2024, p. 19) China's peacekeeping operations also helps it undercut and counter the criticism that Beijing is interested only in exploiting African resources. China's deployment of its peacekeeping troops in countries without much of its economic stakes highlights this intent (Walsh, 2019, p. 4).

Deployment of Security Forces

China's significant deployment of its security forces outside the ambit of peacekeeping started in the wake of the piracy menace off the Horn of Africa. Since 2008, China has been conducting counter-piracy operations in the Gulf of Aden and has sent 43 counter-piracy escort task forces to the region to secure the maritime traffic. (Blasko, 2024) China has also been conducting similar missions in the Gulf of Guinea since 2014. The Gulf of Aden counter-piracy operations were China's first major multi-year deployment of its navy outside its maritime zones of control, and China has carried out its counter-piracy missions largely in an independent and unilateral mode (Grieger, 2019, p. 11). The mission had far-reaching consequences for China as it boosted the country's expeditionary capabilities and its ability to deploy its naval forces in what it considers to be "far seas" – essentially realizing its blue water ambitions. The mission also sparked in Beijing the quest for a permanent base in the horn of Africa. Apart from being strategically located near to the Bab-el-Mandab, the presence of the American, French, Italian and Japanese bases in Djibouti made China's opening of its own base in the country look more legitimate (Barton, 2018, p. 13-14) Djibouti may not necessarily be a one-off deployment.

In 2015, China came up with its Counter Terrorism Law, which enabled the deployment of the People's Liberation Amry troops in foreign soil for counter-terrorism operations, subject to consent by the host country (Grieger, 2019). China has likely considered Angola, Equatorial Guinea, Gabon, Kenya, Mozambique, Namibia, Nigeria, Seychelles, and Tanzania as possible future locations for PLA facilities. A possible Chinese base in West Africa will cause severe upset to American security interests in Africa, taking China closer towards breaching the Monroe Doctrine and risking direct conflict with the United States. In total, the PLA has conducted 55 port calls and 19 bilateral and multilateral military exercises in Africa since 2000 (Nantulya, 2025b). China has even conducted joint military exercises with Russia and South Africa in 2019 and 2023 (Barrios et al., 2025). Moreover, China has expanded the deployment of its defense attaches to cover at least half of the African capitals (Krukowska, 2024, p. 9).

The Chinese government highlights the need for such expansive deployments as the requirement to protect and safeguard Chinese citizens in Africa. Popular culture from China also mirrors Beijing's security outlook on Africa. For instance, a hugely popular Chinese feature film of 2017, "Wolf Warrior-2," set against the backdrop of conflict in a fictitious African country, showcases how the Chinese government could go to any extent to rescue its citizens from any part of the world (Kovrig, 2018). The tagline of the film's poster reads, "Whoever offends China will be punished, no matter how far away!" China's official foreign ministry website ran a story in 2022 titled "When You Are in Danger, Motherland Takes You Home", where it was noted "As many netizens said, the value of a Chinese passport lies not in the number of countries you can visit visa-free, but in the fact that the motherland will always take you home when you are in danger" (Ministry of Foreign Affairs, 2022).

This was demonstrated in Libya (2011) and Sudan (2023) in the case of Africa. When Libya descended into civil war in the wake of the Arab Spring, China evacuated 35,860 of its citizens, in addition to 2100 foreign nationals over 12 days through air and sea (Our China Story, 2025). When civil war erupted in Sudan, China rescued 940 of its citizens and 231 foreigners through its Navy (China Daily, 2023). In addition to its regular troops, China has also deployed private military contractors across Africa to protect its commercial interests (Barrios et al., 2025). Some of the major ones include Beijing De We Security Service, Huaxin Zhong An Security Group, Shandong Huawei Security Group, China Security Technology Group, China Overseas Security Group, Frontier Services Group, China Overseas Security Service, VSS Security Group and Zhongjun Junhong Security Service.

Figure 3. Chinese Private Military Contractors in Africa

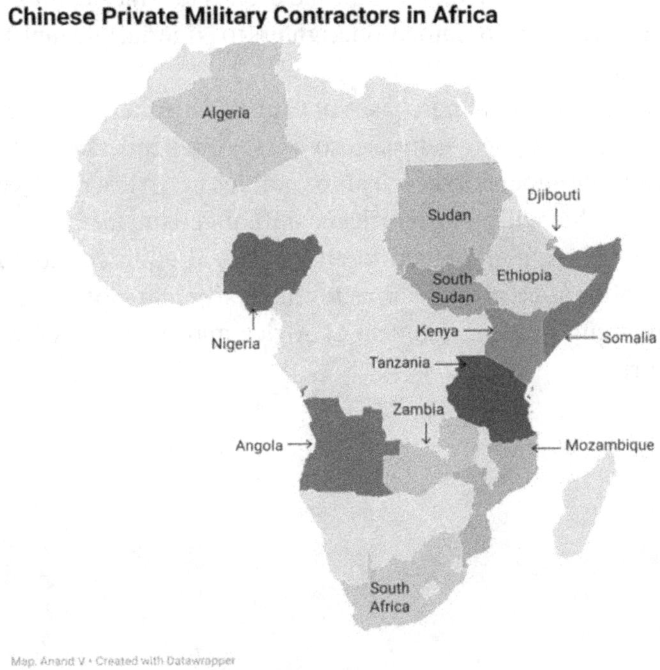

Source: Created by authors with data compiled from Sukhankin (2023)

As depicted in Figure 3, Chinese private contractors operate in Djibouti, Ethiopia, Kenya, Nigeria, Sudan, South Sudan, Tanzania, South Africa, Algeria, Angola, Mozambique, Somalia, Zambia, and work towards securing both continental and maritime assets of China in Africa. (Sukhankin, 2023) This indicates a widening of the range of security actors being deployed by China across the continent, imparting more flexibility in the country's protection of its interests.

Arms and Security Assistance

In addition to sending personnel, China is also exporting arms to Africa. China has been a net-exporter of arms for the past two decades. According to SIPRI, during 2019-23, China was the largest supplier of arms to African countries (Barrios et al., 2025). However, as of 2024, China is lagging behind Russia in arms supply to African countries – the former occupies only 18 percent of the African market compared to the latter, which occupies 21 percent. Nevertheless, as depicted in Figure 4, China has so far sold arms to 42 African countries, more than other major arms exporting states in the world (George et al., 2025). Six of them – Tanzania, Namibia, Zimbabwe, Zambia, Mozambique and Seychelles – are near-dedicated customers of China in this regard, with 90 percent of their arms supplies sourced from China. Additionally, China also has increased its supply of large equipment to more countries: frigates, artillery, mortars and drones to Algeria, trainer aircrafts to Angola, combat helicopters to Cameroon, fighters to Nigeria, and tanks and missiles to Sudan (Cabestan, 2023, p. 560).

Notably, African countries' purchases of Chinese arms are often linked to loans from China and access to their natural resources. A dependence on Chinese arms could lead to the development of security bloc politics in Africa, resulting in growing risks of instability. This will be a significant shift, given the fact that African countries traditionally have a non-aligned foreign policy (Lammich, 2025, pp. 11-13). Moreover, the proliferation of these arms to subversive and violent non-state actors within the weak regulatory environment of Africa may also further undermine the continent's security.

Figure 4. China's Arms Sales across Africa

Source: Created by authors with data compiled from George et al. (2025)

Apart from arms sales, China also provides extensive security assistance to African countries and has a long history of doing so. During the Maoist ideological fervor of the 1960s, China supplied revolutionary forces in Africa with military training and assistance. Further, after gaining independence, some of the African countries' newly established militaries were trained by China. Over a period of time, China appears to have spread its security assistance to African militaries "widely but thinly" (Carrozza & Marsh, 2022, pp. 6-13) China has sent trainers to most of the African countries and have also hosted several African troops for training (Barton, 2018, p. 10). Intelligence sharing and support in counter-terrorism as well as cybersecurity are important components of these training programmes (Devecioglu & Akçomak, 2024, p. 20). Several African nations have started incorporating Chinese surveillance technologies – such as facial recognition tools, widespread CCTV networks, and advanced data analytics systems – into their law enforcement and security infrastructure to bolster monitoring and public safety efforts. However, these dual-use technologies can pose a threat to the sovereignty of African states as well as infringe upon the rights of African citizens (Diallo & Descamps, 2024).

China's security ties in Africa are the strongest with Tanzania since the latter shares the longest history of sustained cooperation–including military cooperation, compared to any other African country; and it is therefore the recipient of the largest share of Chinese military assistance in Africa (Lammich, 2025, p. 9). For this reason, China had set up a military training school in Tanzania in 2018 (Barrios et al., 2025). China's security assistance is not just limited to the military, but also to the police forces. China has also been training African police forces for securing its investments in the continent, such as the elite Kenyan police division trained by the Chinese security forces to protect the Mombasa-Nairobi railway (Grieger, 2019, p. 9). Around 21 police academies in China have access to the International Law Enforcement Training Program of China's Ministry of Public Security. During the 2024 FOCAC Summit, China announced US$ 138 million towards security assistance in Africa and training for 6000 military personnel as well as 1000 law enforcement officials of the continent (Nouwens & Nouwens, 2024, pp. 14-15). This pledge aligns clearly with the direction of the GSI, which is increasingly dictating China's security engagement with Africa. Though this may boost the capacity of African security forces, it can also lead to dependence and the formation of bloc politics, as discussed in the case of Chinese arms exports.

CONCLUSION

Over the past two decades, China has firmly established the security pillar of its engagement with Africa. Its approach to building a security framework on the continent has evolved gradually, following the trajectory of its economic and political involvement. What motivates Beijing to assume a greater security role in Africa is a pragmatic calculation: it recognizes that trade and investments—particularly those tied to the BRI—are vulnerable to instability on the continent.

While China's security ties with Africa can be viewed from multiple perspectives, a clear coherence in its strategy is evident. Rather than cultivating a specific linchpin state as a strategic anchor, China has adopted a continent-wide approach, advancing its security agenda through both bilateral and multilateral channels. This strategy aligns with its GSI and Community of Common Destiny worldview, both of which are poised to play a central role in shaping the future trajectory of China-Africa security relations.

The expansion of China's security footprint in Africa is likely to have significant geopolitical implications, especially amid intensifying great power competition. In contrast to the current U.S.-led international order, China seeks to position itself as a champion of global peace and security by offering 'Chinese solutions' to global challenges, as illustrated by the GSI. Through active engagement, China aims not only to portray itself as a stabilizing force but also to build a new form of strategic influence in reshaping Africa's security landscape.

REFERENCES

Bagwandeen, M. (2024, February). Developing a common African approach to China in a divided world. [Institute for Security Studies. https://issafrica.org/research/africa-report/developing-a-common-african-approach-to-china-in-a-divided-world]. *Africa Report, 44.*

Barrios, R. (2025, January 31). *China and Sub-Saharan Africa.* Congressional Research Service. https://www.congress.gov/crs-product/IF12566

Barton, B. (2018). China's security policy in Africa: A new or false dawn for the evolution of the application of China's non-interference principle? *The South African Journal of International Affairs, 25*(3), 413–434. DOI: 10.1080/10220461.2018.1526707

Baxter, T., & Yang, Y. (2024, November 21). *African governments are shaping the future of the China-Africa relations.* The London School of Economics and Political Science. http://eprints.lse.ac.uk/126440/1/africaatlse_2024_11_21_african-governments-are-shaping-the-future-of-the-china-africa-relations.pdf

Benabdallah, L. (2016). China's Peace and Security Strategies in Africa: Building Capacity is Building Peace? *African Studies Quarterly, 16*(3–4), 17–34. https://doi.org/https://doi.org/10.32473/asq.16.3%20&%204

Blasko, D. J. (2024, August 13). *CMSI note #8: Recent Changes in the PLA Navy's Gulf of Aden Deployment Pattern.* US Naval War College. https://digital-commons.usnwc.edu/cgi/viewcontent.cgi?article=1007&context=cmsi-notes

Cabestan, J. P. (2023). The Belt and Road Initiative and China's Hegemony in Africa. *Orbis, 64*(4), 544–564. DOI: 10.1016/j.orbis.2023.08.005

Cambell, H. (2008). China in Africa: Challenging US global hegemony. *Third World Quarterly, 29*(1), 89–105. DOI: 10.1080/01436590701726517

Camilleri, J. (1980). *Chinese Foreign Policy: The Maoist Era and its Aftermath.* Martin Robertson.

Cannon, B. J. (2024). Maps, flags, and security in the Indo-Pacific: Reframing China's influence in Africa. *African Security, 17*(3–4), 148–176. DOI: 10.1080/19392206.2024.2415832

Carciotto, S., & Chikohomero, R. (2022, August 26). Chinese labour practices in six southern African countries. Monograph 207. Institute for Security Studies. https://issafrica.org/research/monographs/chinese-labour-practices-in-six-southern-african-countries

Carrozza, I., & Marsh, N. J. (2022). Great Power Competition and China's Security Assistance to Africa: Arms, Training, and Influence. *Journal of Global Security Studies*, *7*(4), ogac027. Advance online publication. DOI: 10.1093/jogss/ogac027

Chen, Y. (2020, July 20). *Chinese Debt and the Myth of the Debt-Trap in Africa*. ISPI. https://www.ispionline.it/en/publication/chinese-debt-and-myth-debt-trap-africa-27024

China Africa Research Initiative. (n.d.). *CARI Data Overview*. https://lucid-cari.squarespace.com/data-chinese-contracts-in-africa

Container News. (2024, September 12). *China's Expanding Presence in African Ports*. https://container-news.com/chinas-expanding-presence-in-african-ports/

Daily, C. (2023, June 8). *Sudan evacuation shows China fulfills its international obligation*. https://www.chinadaily.com.cn/a/202305/08/WS64583aa5a310b6054fad1896.html

de Freitas, M. V. (2023, August 2). *The Impact of Chinese Investments in Africa: Neocolonialism or Cooperation?* Policy Brief 30/23. Policy Center for the New South. https://www.policycenter.ma/publications/impact-chinese-investments-africa-neocolonialism-or-cooperation

de Kluiver, J. (2024, July 24). *Africa has much to gain from a contained BRI. Institute for Security Studies*. https://issafrica.org/iss-today/africa-has-much-to-gain-from-a-more-contained-bri

Delage, F. (2022). China in Africa: Objectives, Instruments and Strategic Implications. *Revista UNISCI, 60*, 21-48. https://www.unisci.es/china-en-africa-objetivos-instrumentos-e-implicaciones-estrategicas/

Devecioglu, K., & Akçomak, D. (2024). China's Africa policy during the Xi Jinping Era (2012-2022). *ChronAfrica, 1*(1), 11–22. DOI: 10.62841/ChronAfrica.2024.196

Diallo, F., & Descamps, M. (2024, October 21). *China's security engagement with Africa & the "Global South" Narrative*. European Hub for Contemporary China. https://eh4s.eu/publication/chinas-security-engagement-with-africa-the-global-south-narrative

Egyin, D. (2024, May 2). *Addressing China's Monopoly over Africa's Renewable Energy Minerals*. Wilson Center. https://www.wilsoncenter.org/blog-post/addressing-chinas-monopoly-over-africas-renewable-energy-minerals#:%7E:text=China%20(PRC)%20currently%20controls%20an,from%206.7%20percent%20in%202018

Ehl, D. (2022, February 8). Africa embraces Huawei tech despite security concerns. *Deutsche Welle*. https://www.dw.com/en/africa-embraces-huawei-technology-despite-security-concerns/a-60665700

Embassy of the People's Republic of China in the Federal Republic of Somalia. (2022, August 10). *Ambassador Fei Shengchao Publishes a Signed Article Titled "No One is Safe until Everyone is Safe—China's View on Global Security Governance"*. http://so.china-embassy.gov.cn/eng/zfgx_1/202208/t20220810_10740081.htm

Engel, L. (2024, August 21). *Relative Risk and the Rate of Return: Chinese Loans to Africa Database, 2000-2023*. GCI Policy Brief 023. Boston University Global Development Policy Center. https://www.bu.edu/gdp/files/2024/08/GCI-PB-23-CLA-2024-FIN.pdf

Etyang, O., & Panyako, S. O. (2020). China's Footprint in Africa's Peace and Security: The Contending Views. *The African Review: A Journal of African Politics. Development and International Affairs*, *47*(2), 336–356. DOI: 10.1163/1821889X-12340022

Forum on China-Africa Cooperation. (2021, December 2). *Full Text: Keynote speech by Chinese President Xi Jinping at Opening Ceremony of 8th FOCAC Ministerial Conference*. Forum on China-Africa Cooperation (FOCAC). http://www.focac.org/eng/gdtp/202112/t20211202_10461080.htm

Forum on China-Africa Cooperation. (2024, October 12). *Roundup: Experts, officials laud China's initiative as key driver of global development*. Xinhua. http://www.focac.org/eng/zfzs_1/202410/t20241012_11505909.htm

Freeman, C., & Gill, B. (2024, September 12). *China's Bid for a Bigger Security Role in Africa*. United States Institute of Peace. https://www.usip.org/publications/2024/09/chinas-bid-bigger-security-role-africa

George, M., Djokic, K., Hussain, Z., Wezeman, P. D., & Wezeman, S. T. (2025, March). *Trends in international arms transfers, 2024*. Stockholm International Peace Research Institute. https://www.sipri.org/sites/default/files/2025-03/fs_2503_at_2024_0.pdf

Global Times. (2021, June 18). *A Friend Doesn't Cancel a Visit — Premier Zhou Enlai's Visits to 10 African Countries*. https://www.globaltimes.cn/page/202106/1226506.shtml

Grieger, G. (2019, October 8). *China's growing role as a security actor in Africa*. European Parliamentary Research Service Briefing. https://www.europarl.europa.eu/RegData/etudes/BRIE/2019/642232/EPRS_BRI(2019)642232_EN.pdf

Jash, A. (2025, March 3). *Africa Pivots to China's Global Security Initiative.* ORF Issue Brief No. 784. Observer Research Foundation. https://www.orfonline.org/research/africa-pivots-to-china-s-global-security-initiative

Johnston, L. (2024, September 2). *China's interests in Africa are being shaped by the race for renewable energy* [Online forum post]. The Conversation. https://theconversation.com/chinas-interests-in-africa-are-being-shaped-by-the-race-for-renewable-energy-237679

Kovrig, M. (2018, October 24). *China expands its peace and security footprint in Africa.* International Crisis Group Commentary. https://www.crisisgroup.org/asia/north-east-asia/china/china-expands-its-peace-and-security-footprint-africa

Krukowska, M. M. (2024). China's security relations with Africa in the 21st Century. *Security and Defence Quarterly, 46*(2), 4–23. DOI: 10.35467/sdq/190066

Kuo, S. C. (2015). Chinese peace? An emergent norm in African Peace Operations. *China Quarterly of International Strategic Studies, 01*(01), 155–181. DOI: 10.1142/S2377740015500086

Lammich, G. (2025). China's evolving security engagement in Africa: Policies, strategies, and implications. *European Journal of International Security*, 1–18. DOI: 10.1017/eis.2025.3

Li, K. (2017, September 26). Opinion: China should speak for the developing world. *CGTN.* https://news.cgtn.com/news/784d444f77597a6333566d54/index.html

Mboya, C. (2024, November 4). *What happened in Beijing in September? An Analysis of FOCAC and the Geopolitics of Africa's Partnerships.* Africa Policy Research Institute. https://afripoli.org/what-happened-in-beijing-in-september-an-analysis-of-focac-and-the-geopolitics-of-africas-partnerships

Ministry of Foreign Affairs. (2022, August 26). *When you are in Danger, motherland takes you home.* Ministry of Foreign Affairs of the People's Republic of China. https://www.mfa.gov.cn/eng/zy/jj/zggcddwjw100ggs/xsd/202406/t20240606_11377983.html

Ministry of Foreign Affairs. (2023, February 21). *The Global Security Initiative Concept Paper.* Ministry of Foreign Affairs of the People's Republic of China. https://www.mfa.gov.cn/mfa_eng/xw/wjbxw/202405/t20240530_11343274.html

Ministry of Foreign Affairs. (2024, September 5). *Forum on China-Africa Cooperation Beijing Action Plan (2025-2027).* Ministry of Foreign Affairs of the People's Republic of China. https://www.mfa.gov.cn/eng/xw/zyxw/202409/t20240905_11485719.html

Moses, O. (2024, April 2). *10 Charts to Explain 22 Years of China-Africa Trade, Overseas Development Finance and Foreign Direct Investment.* Global Development Policy Center. https://www.bu.edu/gdp/2024/04/02/10-charts-to-explain-22-years-of-china-africa-trade-overseasdevelopment-finance-and-foreign-direct-investment/

Nantulya, P. (2023, April 17). Africa's role in China's multilateralism strategy. Africa Center. https://africacenter.org/spotlight/africa-china-multilateralism/

Nantulya, P. (2025a, January 7). *What to Expect from Africa-China Relations in 2025.* Africa Center for Strategic Studies. https://africacenter.org/spotlight/africa-china-relations-2025/

Nantulya, P. (2025b, March 10). *Mapping China's strategic port development in Africa.* Africa Center for Strategic Studies. https://africacenter.org/spotlight/china-port-development-africa/

Nouwens, M., & Nouwens, V. (2024, October 24). *The Global Security Initiative: China's International Policing Activities.* International Institute for Strategic Studies Research Papers. https://www.iiss.org/globalassets/media-library---content--migration/files/research-papers/2024/10/gsi/iiss_the-gloabl-security-initiative_24102024.pdf

Nyadera, I. N., Agwanda, B., & Kisaka, M. O. (2020). Beyond the Yuan: Rethinking China's Attractiveness to Africa. *China Report (New Delhi, India)*, *56*(4), 429–446. DOI: 10.1177/0009445520954793

Ofosu, G., & Sarpong, D. (2021). The evolving perspectives on the Chinese labour regime in Africa. *Economic and Industrial Democracy*, *43*(4), 1747–1766. DOI: 10.1177/0143831X211029382

Our China Story. (2025, February 21). *China's largest evacuation in its history.* https://www.ourchinastory.com/en/14119/China'-largest-evacuation-in-its-history

Peacekeeping, U. N. (2025). *Troop and police contributors.* United Nations Peacekeeping. https://peacekeeping.un.org/en/troop-and-police-contributors

Sanny, J. A.-N., & Selormey, E. (2021, November 21). *Africans welcome China's influence but maintain democratic aspirations.* Afrobarometer Dispatch No. 489. AFRO Barometer. https://www.afrobarometer.org/publication/ad489-africans-welcome-chinas-influence-maintain-democratic-aspirations/

Shelton, L. G. (1979). The Sino-Soviet Split: The Horn of Arica, November 1977 to February 1979. *Naval War College Review*, *32*(3), 78–87. https://www.jstor.org/stable/44641847

Sibiri, H. (2023, November 5). *A Decade of China's BRI: Assessing its Impact & Implications for Africa's Agenda 2063*. Africa-China Center for Policy & Advisory. https://africachinacentre.org/a-decade-of-chinas-bri-assessing-its-impact-implications-for-africas-agenda-2063/

Sukhankin, S. (2023, May 19). *Chinese PSCs in Sub-Saharan Africa: The Case of Anglophone Africa*. The Jamestown Foundation. https://jamestown.org/program/chinese-pscs-in-sub-saharan-africa-the-case-of-anglophone-africa/

The Africa Report. (2025, January 30). *Infographic: Who Are China's Top Trading Partners in Africa?* [Online forum post]. https://www.theafricareport.com/374995/infographics-who-are-chinas-top-trading-partners-in-africa/?redirect_to=https://www.theafricareport.com/374995/infographics-who-are-chinas-top-trading-partners-in-africa/#continue-reading

The State Council. (2021, November 26). *China and Africa in the New Era: A Partnership of Equals*. Ministry of Foreign Affairs of the People's Republic of China. https://www.mfa.gov.cn/eng/zy/gb/202405/t20240531_11367447.html

The State Council. (2024, September 5). *Full Text: Keynote Address by Chinese President Xi Jinping at Opening Ceremony of 2024 FOCAC Summit*. The State Council of the People's Republic of China. https://english.www.gov.cn/news/202409/05/content_WS66d964bdc6d0868f4e8eaa07.html

UNCTAD. (2024, June 5). *Critical minerals: Africa holds key to Sustainable Energy Future*. UN Trade and Development (UNCTAD). https://unctad.org/news/critical-minerals-africa-holds-key-sustainable-energy-future

Vines, A., & Wallace, J. (2023, January 18). *China-Africa Relations*. Chatham House. https://www.chathamhouse.org/2023/01/china-africa-relations

Walsh, B. (2019). China's pervasive yet forgotten regional security role in Africa. *Journal of Contemporary China*, *28*(120), 965–983. DOI: 10.1080/10670564.2019.1594107

Wang, F.-L., & Elliot, E. (2014). China in Africa: Presence, Perceptions and Prospects. *Journal of Contemporary China*, *23*(90), 1012–1032. DOI: 10.1080/10670564.2014.898888

Winyi, S. (2024, December 11). *Despite concerns, Chinese aid is supporting African development* [Online forum post]. Africa in LSE. https://blogs.lse.ac.uk/africaatlse/about/

Yu, G. T. (1988). Africa in Chinese Foreign Policy. *Asian Survey*, *28*(8), 849–862. DOI: 10.2307/2644590

Yun, S. (2024, April 14). Africa in China's Foreign Policy. Brookings. https://www.brookings.edu/articles/africa-in-chinas-foreign-policy/

Chapter 14
China and the Global South:
A Postcolonial Reading of the Northern-Led Global Order

Alireza Samiee Esfahani
https://orcid.org/0009-0001-4729-075X
University of Isfahan, Iran

Ali Alihosseini
University of Isfahan, Iran

ABSTRACT

The concept of "Global South" has recently emerged as a symbol of unity, and geopolitical reality among postcolonial and developing nations. Following decolonization, these countries have sought to reclaim political and economic agency through movements such as the Non-Aligned Movement (NAM) and G77, consistently advocating for a more just international order. From the perspective of postcolonial studies, this research seeks to answer the following central questions: (1) How has the Global South deconstructed the Western liberal order in international relations? (2) What are the tangible manifestations of "agency" within this emerging order of the Global South? The findings suggest that over the past few decades, the Global South, led by countries like China and other emerging economies, has critically challenged the epistemological and ontological foundations of the liberal world order, which is Western, imperialist, and hierarchical, and has promoted its agency through South-South cooperation to escape from its inferiority/marginalized position in the international system.

DOI: 10.4018/979-8-3373-0938-5.ch014

INTRODUCTION

The rise of the Global South as a geopolitical and geo-economic reality has led to significant systemic changes in the global order. The unipolar moment has run its course, and a multipolar world order is steadily emerging. While the geopolitical center of military power remains in the West, still primarily led by the United States, economic power and growth are gradually shifting eastward, thanks to the rise of actors such as China, India, and the Association of Southeast Asian Nations (ASEAN). This global divergence, in which geopolitical power is centered in the West while economic power is increasingly located in Asia, represents a unique feature of the current historical moment, unprecedented in the history of capitalism.

This shift in political and economic power has prompted geopolitical thinkers such as Parag Khanna and Kishore Mahbubani to speak of the arrival of an "Asian century." Others, like political scientist Oliver Stuenkel, have begun referring to a "post-Western world" (Heine, 2023). The transformation of international politics and the rise of new powers, especially within the Global South, are key characteristics of today's global order. Above actors, through the creation of alternatives such as the Non-Aligned Movement (NAM), BRICS, and the Group of 77 (G77) as a coalition of developing countries within the United Nations, have challenged the ontology of dominant Northern/Western discourses in shaping the international agenda. The critique of dominant discourses, particularly in the era of decolonization, has been prominently articulated through critical concepts emerging from the Global South, along with other alternative frameworks aimed at "reordering the global system" and enabling the "coexistence of multiple orders," with a particular emphasis on South–South cooperation. According to some analysts, the shared experiences and solidarities of the Global South have been most effectively embodied in a common foreign policy ideology. This ideology has been variously referred to as "anti-colonialism," "non-alignment," "positive neutrality," "Afro-Asianism," "Third-Worldism," "South–South solidarity," "structuralist perspectives," and a "multipolar development outlook" (Roberts and Parks, 2007; Solarz, 2012; Mielniczuk, 2013; Lüthi, 2016; Lewis and Stolte, 2019).

From a postcolonial standpoint, the Global South functions both as a discursive construct and as a geopolitical force of resistance. This part of the world, long considered a "secondary" and "passive" variable in global geopolitics, has now attained a degree of self-awareness and agency that actively challenges the Global North. The resistance and proactive initiatives of the Global South over the past few decades have already initiated, and will continue to initiate, profound transformations in the international order. Since World War II, the Global South has passed through three historical phases: (a) decolonization (1945–1989), (b) globalization (1990–2008), and (c) the emergence of developing economies as a group (since 2009). Initially, countries of the Global South acted as "rebels," then as "responsive participants," and now as "active agents" within the international system (Zhou, 2024, p. 58). Although the Global South is heterogeneous, most of its countries agree that the current global order, constructed by the West and still largely dominated by the United States, is neither peaceful nor just nor democratic. It often acts contrary to their economic and environmental interests.

Among the actors in this shifting landscape, China occupies a central and exceptional position in the geopolitics of the Global South, serving as a key engine driving this emerging order. Through its expansive economic and diplomatic engagement with the Global South, including regions in Southeast Asia, Africa, and Latin America, China has positioned itself as a credible rival to Western hegemony. In fact, Chinese President Xi Jinping has articulated his vision of a "community with a shared future for mankind" as a blueprint for reshaping the current global order (Honghua, 2024).

The liberal global order is essentially an exclusive Western/Northern "club," in which the Global South has historically been marginalized and relegated to a subordinate position. Thus, this study poses the following central question: From a postcolonial lens, how has the Global South, particularly actors like China, deconstructed the epistemological and ontological foundations of the Western liberal order in international relations? And what are the concrete expressions of their agency in building an alternative, rival order, of the order of the Global South? Since conventional theories of international relations have primarily focused on dominant powers, this study aims to examine the constructive power of Global South countries through the dialectic between the will to dominate (the North) and the will to resist (the South).

The findings of this research suggest that, in recent decades, the Global South, led by actors such as China and other emerging economies critically challenged the liberal and imperial global order. From a postcolonial and critical perspective, this order is characterized by a Western orientation, hierarchical and vertical relations, and a core-periphery structure. Through efforts to reform and transform both the structure and logic of the liberal global order, the Global South has contributed to the democratization of international relations and the construction of a new, independent collective identity for the South.

LITERATURE REVIEW

The "Global South" and its position within the "global order" have been central to heated debates among scholars and analysts in this field over the past few decades. Consequently, this topic has been examined from a variety of ideological and case study perspectives. Below are some of the most significant of these approaches.

Several analysts have discussed, through the lens of critical and postcolonial theories, how the discourse of the Global South has emerged and contrasts with the dominant discourse of the North. For example, Tripathi (2024), argues that the rise of emerging powers and new actors, particularly in the Global South (often considered marginalized in international politics), has challenged the cosmology of Northern/Western liberal discourses on agenda-setting by creating alternatives such as the Non-Aligned Movement, BRICS, and the G77, with a focus on South-South cooperation. Olasolo et al. (2021) critically examine how postcolonial and Global South theories perceive the role of international criminal law, exploring the process of case selection by the International Criminal Court and how this reflects the colonial interests of the Global North. Artner & Yin (2023) argue that the formation of the modern world order is a dialectical process between the will to dominate and the will to resist (embodied by the Global South). Patel (2023) suggests that, from the late 1980s, new approaches to global social theory emerged, including indigenism, orientalism, Eurocentrism, postcolonialism, decolonialism, and sociology. This study proposes that these trends should be collectively referred to as anti-colonial social theory, as they all examine the relationship between colonialism and knowledge production. Theres Klob (2017) asserts that the "Global South," when not simply defined geographically, holds significant potential to consolidate and empower diverse social actors who view themselves in subordinate positions within global power networks. The Global South is not an inherent entity but must be understood as something created, imagined, and continuously reshaped by the ever-changing dynamics of social actors and institutions. Tamang & Hazarika (2013), in their book International Relations, Perspectives for the Global South, provide critical insights into various discourses and aspects of international relations. The book offers a narrative that presents new ideas and approaches to better explain international relations and reform the current global order.

Another group of researchers examined the liberal international order from the standpoint of the Global South's emergence as a "challenging and stake-seeking actor" striving to change existing unjust relations and establish an alternative or rival order. For instance, Roy (2022) discusses the challenges posed by "new multilateralism" to the liberal international order and argues that "Southern multilateralism" is not a direct challenge to the liberal international order but rather an emerging order that both complements and competes with it. Forough et al. (2023) contend that the global order is transitioning from a unipolar world dominated by the West to a multipolar world, with Asia as the main center of gravity. According to Lees (2023), the voting patterns of Global South countries in the UN General Assembly reveal their dissatisfaction with the US-led liberal international order. Through a textual analysis of public debate speeches using multiple regression models, Lees concludes that this foreign policy ideology has a distinct intellectual history and conceptual morphology rooted in a shared experience of colonial domination and international peripherality. Benabdallah (2017), argues that perspectives from the Global South not only challenge the dominant theoretical perspectives that have perpetuated unjust relations between the Global North and South but also enhance the possibility of more equitable relations, reflecting the interests of all stakeholders and pressuring international institutions to adopt more representative power structures and decision-making processes. Zhou (2024) contends that the rise of the Global South, a significant factor in contemporary global politics, has initiated substantial changes in the international order. The author posits that through three stages of development, the Global South has altered power structures, modes of international interaction, and international laws, and understanding these changes, both vertically and horizontally, is crucial for grasping the major shifts in global politics today. According to Bull & Banik (2025), the term "Global South" has been revitalized in recent years, evolving from a synonym for the "Third World" to a geo-historical concept representing low and middle-income countries and emerging powers. The authors argue that the role of the Global South extends beyond critiquing the West and the liberal world order, offering insights into how the complexities of the Global South intersect with geopolitical shifts, challenging traditional norms, and providing new frameworks for global governance.

Finally, a further group of scholars has analyzed the rise and actions of these actors from the perspective of the "China-led Global South coalition." Gu (2025), in China and the Global South in a Contested Order, provides a systematic critique of China-Global South relations, analyzing the dynamics of change and China's core ideas on "real" multilateralism and international law. He also explores China-Global South development diplomacy, including cases such as the Belt and Road Initiative and China's development relations with Africa and Southeast Asia. Murphy (2022) notes that the world is currently undergoing a power transition between the United States and China, with China's rise representing a crucial economic, political, and military phenomenon of the 21st century. Through a detailed analysis of China's relations with the Middle East and Sub-Saharan Africa in the post-Cold War era, Murphy argues that although China does not seek to change territorial distributions in these regions, it is increasingly establishing spheres of influence, challenging the international system's rules by creating an alternative order to facilitate interactions. Thi Ha & Thi Phuong Thao (2024) write that the focus on the Global South has gained increasing prominence in Chinese foreign policy over the past decade amid China's growing alienation from the West. Global South countries have become vital economic partners and essential constituencies in China's efforts to build a more China-centered, less West-centric global system. Theodor & Kuteleva (2022), using a multidisciplinary approach and eleven case studies, examine the agency of often overlooked sub-actors in the Global South in their interactions with China. The contributors to this book aim to answer two critical questions: What is the real economic, political, and social impact of China's growing presence in the Global South? And, from a critical perspective, how do citizens of the Global South perceive and interpret China's rise? Together, these case studies provide a comprehensive view of the complex and sometimes problematic process of China's inclusion in the economic, social, and political realities of the Global South.

THEORETICAL FRAMEWORK

Postcolonial theory is a multifaceted approach that became part of the critical theory toolbox in the 1970s. Postcolonial studies examine the impacts of colonialism on both colonizers and the colonized, investigating the complex dynamics of power that emerge during and after the colonial experience. At its core, this theory seeks to challenge and deconstruct dominant narratives constructed by colonial powers and emphasizes the importance of understanding alternative perspectives and amplifying the voices of those historically marginalized (Ivison, 2025; Spivak, 1990, pp. 227–228).

The theoretical foundations of the postcolonial approach can be traced to Marxism, postmodernism, and the philosophical contributions of thinkers such as Nietzsche, Adorno, Foucault, Derrida, Deleuze, and Lacan, all of whom critically interrogated imperial ideologies and structures of power within academic discourse. Key concepts in this framework include: "Orientalism", "subalternity", "metropole", "representation", "hegemony", "domination", "subjectivity", "agency", "resistance", "otherness", "deconstruction", "mimicry", "hybridity", and "ambivalence". Orientalism refers to the West's construction of the East as the "Other," while subalternity highlights the experiences of those who have been excluded from mainstream narratives. Moreover, postcolonial theory explores notions of agency, hybridity, assimilation, and contests how colonized individuals and cultures respond to and resist colonial domination. The intellectual outputs of figures such as C.L.R. James, Aimé Césaire, Albert Memmi, Frantz Fanon, Edward Said, Homi K. Bhabha, Gayatri Chakravorty Spivak, as well as historians associated with the Subaltern Studies editorial collective, reflect the diversity and complexity of this critical legacy (Ivison, 2025).

Among these thinkers, Edward Said, Homi Bhabha, and Gayatri Chakravorty Spivak are often referred to as the postcolonial theoretical trinity, whose ideas have since become central to the practice of critical theory in North American and European academic settings. As this intellectual current gained legitimacy, it expanded globally as a critical academic method (Schwarz & Ray, 2005; Albrecht, 2020). According to these scholars, there is no singular or universal "Enlightenment," but rather multiple Enlightenments shaped by different historical and political contexts. Furthermore, the concepts and ideals often associated with "Enlightenment" are themselves plural, open to a range of interpretations and critiques (Ivison, 2025).

A significant branch of contemporary postcolonial studies has increasingly turned its attention to broad international issues. Scholars interested in this dimension of postcolonial theory often situate the literature within, or in opposition to, global phenomena such as capitalism and globalization. Among these thinkers are Arif Dirlik, Aijaz Ahmad, Ella Shohat, and Fredric Jameson. This group critiques both classical postcolonial theorists and the field itself, while emphasizing that although formal colonialism may have ended, it has been replaced by a more powerful and pervasive global system. This system, while subtler, continues to dominate the world with remarkable reach and intensity. Their arguments—particularly those of Jameson—are grounded in neo-Marxist thought, with one of the most prominent examples being his concept of late capitalism's cultural logic (Haji-Yousefi & Ghaebi, 2017, pp. 15–16).

Overall, postcolonial approaches to international relations reflect deep dissatisfaction with the mainstream discipline, which has traditionally focused on great power politics, state actors, and balance-of-power dynamics. Under such conditions, IR has evolved as a discourse of the "strong and wealthy," primarily reflecting a Western worldview while marginalizing the concerns of the poor and oppressed nations (Ghavam & Mohseni, 2016, p. 10). In this context, Achille Mbembe argues that colonialism was accompanied by a "discursive infrastructure" that projected the interests and values of the North while silencing or distorting those of the South (Mbembe et al., 2006, p. 123). From a postcolonial perspective, this Western-centric bias has produced a hegemonic epistemology, wherein dominant theories are developed in the North and disseminated through Northern academic and media institutions. According to this view, the entire history of modern knowledge production has been shaped by the experience of empire and the North–South divide.

The postcolonial approach often identifies the Western-centric features of mainstream International Relations (IR) and argues that the interpretations of this discipline are rooted in Western experiences and discursive practices. By centering the "Global South" and the "subaltern," this perspective reveals the complex power/knowledge nexus that continues to reproduce the contemporary world order (Linklater et al., 2016, p. 43). From this viewpoint, understanding contemporary

IR requires a detailed account of the multiple and diverse power relations that have historically and currently linked the North and South through both colonial and postcolonial dynamics.

Instead of focusing on state-centrism and elite-driven aspects of IR, postcolonialism emphasizes the roles and perspectives of the South and marginalized nations. Its critical agenda aims to demonstrate that the Global South is capable of offering alternative "truth regimes" to those dictated by the North. This epistemic project involves a dual process of deconstruction and reconstruction. While deconstruction focuses on exposing the gaps in dominant theories, more broadly, it also recognizes the fundamental reality that the North and South experience the international system in profoundly different ways (Smith and Tickner, 2020, p. 11). The postcolonial approach is equally concerned with reconstructing knowledge, which requires dismantling global structures of domination. For instance, Boaventura de Sousa Santos (2018) speaks of an "epistemological and non-geographical South" that encompasses all forms of knowledge born from struggles against capitalism, colonialism, and patriarchy (Thérien, 2024, p. 8).

In sum, postcolonial approaches place the "Third World" and the "subaltern" at the heart of their analysis and seek, through a deconstructive lens, to dismantle Western views toward these countries and societies. As such, they are deeply committed to exposing and transforming the complex and hegemonic power relations that sustain and reproduce the contemporary global order. Compared to mainstream IR theories, these approaches offer a more comprehensive and accurate understanding of global politics and the unequal position of countries in the North/South.

CONCEPT AND NATURE OF THE "GLOBAL SOUTH"

The "Global South" encompasses a vast region, including many countries and areas, such as powerful nations like China, India, and Brazil, as well as 46 of the world's least developed countries. Carl Oglesby, an American writer and New Left activist, seemingly coined the term "Global South" in 1969 at the height of the Vietnam War, referring to the dominance of the North over the South and the creation of an "intolerable" social order. (Heine, 2023). At that time, most Western analysts divided the world into three parts, as first depicted by French demographer Alfred Sauvy in 1952. The "Second World" was composed of the Soviet Union and its satellites in the Eastern Bloc, while the "Third World" included "developing" countries, often non-aligned, many of which had recently freed themselves from colonial powers. (Patrick & Huggins, 2023). Nearly a decade later, Willy Brandt, the Chancellor of Germany, in a famous report in 1980 entitled "North-South: A Program for Survival," which he chaired, referred to this concept. The suffix "global" was added in the 1990s, after the Cold War ended, likely as a byproduct of the growing popularity of another term, "globalization," which had become common at the time (Shidour, 2023).

A review of the literature on the Global South reveals at least three interpretations of the term "Global South" within scholarly discourse: (a) as a designation for economically poorer regions of the world that have been marginalized by colonialism and/or capitalism; (b) as a reference to emerging spaces of resistance against Northern dominance in multilateral settings, as well as broader forms of global hegemonic power; and (c) as a descriptor of various interregional alliances (Haug et al., 2021). While there is no clear agreement on which countries constitute the Global South, it can be affirmed that the term, as a critical concept, describes developing regions with shared economic, political, and social histories marked by colonialism and imperialism. It also encapsulates their subsequent organization into what is known as the "Third World," the Non-Aligned Movement, the Group of 77, and the decolonization of colonial peoples during the Cold War. The term "Global South" primarily refers to developing countries that were largely former colonies of Western powers. The geopolitical space of the Global South is one marked by widespread public criticism, dissatisfaction, and a desire to change the international order and its institutions. This order is primarily supported by the United States and its close allies in Europe and Asia, revealing their inability to meet the development needs of the Global South (Rofel & Rojas, 2023). From a postcolonial perspective, it can be argued that: "The North–South opposition is part of a lexical field that includes all sorts of contested dichotomies: developed–developing, rich–poor, core–periphery, First World–Third World, West–Rest, and civilized–uncivilized" (Farias 2019, pp. 668–687).

Post-Cold War, the rapid emergence of large developing countries like China, India, and Brazil marked the beginning of economic growth for the "Global South," becoming a key driver for South-South cooperation and developing countries. In 2009, the BRICS organization was established, with large developing countries such as Brazil, China, India, Russia, and South Africa taking on the historical mission of promoting South-South cooperation and reinvigorating the South-South development agenda. In 2009, the G20 summit became the main stage for leaders of the world's major economies to discuss pressing global issues. Emerging economies have become indispensable champions, with the position and role of large developing countries like China and India, in particular, becoming especially prominent (Honghua, 2024).

Today, the Global South is increasingly synonymous with the G77, a coalition of postcolonial and developing countries that came together in 1964 to collectively defend their economic interests and enhance their negotiating capacity at the United Nations. Today, the G77, which now consists of 134 countries, regularly identifies itself as the Global South, and the United Nations has established several bodies and initiatives, including the United Nations Office for South-South Cooperation, to address their needs and aspirations.

GLOBAL SOUTH AND THE CRITIQUE OF LIBERAL GLOBALIZATION DISCOURSE

Supporters of the liberal international order (LIO) argue that this order is characterized by an institutionalized commitment to democracy, human rights, regulated free markets, and "principled multilateralism" (Lake et al., 2021, p. 232). Therefore, they expect liberal states to align and vote together on resolutions related to various aspects of this order. According to scholars of the dominant mainstream theory, global North dominance remains unchallenged (Fischer, 2019), and the liberal international order (LIO), which underpins global governance, is sufficiently flexible to not only accommodate rising powers but also socialize them (Ikenberry, 2018). In contrast, countries outside this "club" have significant criticisms regarding both global U.S. leadership and the perceived unequal, exclusive, and disruptive characteristics of the liberal international order. Critical narratives, predominantly from the perspective of the Global South, believe that the recent global changes have given rise to hybrid, pluralistic, and mixed orders (Acharya, 2017; Mazarr, 2017; Taggart, 2020). For instance, Amitav Acharya argues that in a multipolar global order, no nation, idea, or institution is capable of setting rules and dominating global governance institutions and the global order in the way the United States has done in many periods following World War II. In this calculus, elements of the liberal international order will survive, and may even grow, but "they must accommodate new actors and approaches that do not bow to the dictates and preferences of the United States" (Acharya, 2017, p. 277).

Narratives of order and change are powerful tools that shape political agendas and enable local, national, and global actors to understand historical or contemporary orders or changes. Such narratives, which stem from the Global North, have dominated social science fields like International Relations (IR). For instance, the overarching narrative of "global order" in the form of the liberal peace discourse (emphasizing the role of open economies and the rule of law in promoting global justice), established by the West, led by the United States after World War II and remaining unchallenged for a period following the collapse of the Soviet Union, is now under pressure from internal contradictions as well as the alternative and inverted reading of this order by the Global South. "This hegemonic view sees the world hierarchically and envisions the formation of a global order based on Hobbesian state theory. It adheres to the assumption that the 'governance of international systems' is impossible without the presence of "empires, hegemonies, and great powers" (Gilpin, 1981).

From the perspective of postcolonial studies, knowledge based on the relationship between socially constructed rules is historically and culturally grounded "epistemology" (Foucault, 1970, pp. 285-287). In such contexts, the production of knowledge becomes a contested logic that is used by states and political parties to spread narratives that legitimize their political actions. In International Relations and social sciences more broadly, knowledge production is based on hierarchical perceptions of the world between the Global North and Global South (Tripathi, 2024).

Postcolonial thinkers believe that Western perceptions of the non-Western world are a product of the legacy of European colonialism and imperialism. Western-centric discourses constructed non-Western states and peoples as the "Other" or different from the West, often in a way that portrayed them as inferior. In doing so, they helped European powers to justify their dominance over other peoples by invoking civilization or progress. To better understand post-colonialism, we can consider discourses that present certain power relations as natural or even inevitable. For example, regarding "global inequality," postcolonial studies suggest that to better understand how global class relations emerged and were maintained, we must look at ideas about why these relations appear normal. This approach shows how depictions of global poverty are often accompanied by images and narratives of non-Western states and societies as backward, primitive, aggressive, childish, or feminine. Post-colonialism provides a more nuanced perspective on key concepts like power, state, and security, compared to mainstream International Relations (IR) theories, by analyzing how these concepts serve to reproduce the status quo. For instance, the concept of sovereignty, along with the boundaries of the modern state, was imposed on the colonized world by European powers. However, this is a concept that is often taken for granted by realist and liberal scholars. Post-colonialism also challenges the Marxist view that class struggle is the root of historical change – instead, it shows how race shapes history. Analyses that focus solely on class fail to recognize how identifying the "Third World" (a term used during the Cold War to describe countries that were neither aligned with the United States nor the Soviet Union) as "backward," "primitive," or "irrational" is tied to ongoing economic marginalization. Similarly, while mainstream IR theories view the international system as a kind of anarchy, postcolonial scholars see it as a hierarchy. Colonialism and imperialism strengthened the long process of Western domination over other parts of the world, and cultural, economic, and political dominance remains a defining feature of global politics (Nair, 2017, p. 3).

Furthermore, in contrast to liberals who emphasize human rights, democracy, and freedom as Europe's contribution to humanity, postcolonial theorists and leftist activists note that contemporary Europe is postcolonial in so far as it logically maintains colonial differences, distinguishing between Europeans and non-Europeans (or still migrants and citizens, majorities and Europeans) (Kerner, 2024).

Postcolonialism also reveals how Western views of Islam and its followers are a reflection of the West's insecurities. The rise of political Islam across the Muslim world, epitomized by the 1979 Islamic Revolution in Iran, not only faced neo-imperialist interventions but also highlighted the impacts of cultural and social changes, alongside an increasingly interconnected global economy. However, in the West, this revival was interpreted by policymakers and prominent academics as the herald of a "clash of civilizations" (Huntington, 1993) and, worse, as a direct threat to Western civilization (Nair, 2017, p. 2).

Another example of racism can be found in discourses surrounding "nuclear non-proliferation". In such discourses, it is often assumed that countries and their leaders in the Global South cannot be trusted with nuclear weapons. These dominant discourses portray these states as dangerous, unpredictable, irresponsible, and violators of basic human rights norms. A clear example is the portrayal of North Korea and Iran, two countries seeking nuclear weapons, as rogue states in U.S. foreign policy discourse. However, for decades, the West's disregard for human rights can be observed in the extraction of uranium, often carried out in lands inhabited by indigenous people across the world—including in the United States—leading to death, illness, and environmental degradation. More importantly, what often gets overlooked in nuclear discussions is the fact that the United States is the only power to have ever used nuclear weapons (apart from tests), when it dropped atomic bombs on the Japanese cities of Nagasaki and Hiroshima in 1945, with horrific and devastating human casualties.

Therefore, for postcolonial scholars such as Shampa Biswas (2014), the notion that some states can be trusted with nuclear weapons while others cannot, because they are seen as less developed, less mature in their approach to human life, or less rational, is a racialized discourse (Nair, 2017, pp. 2-3)

The idea of modernity and progress is deeply rooted in Eurocentric perspectives, which consider it a universal narrative and a singular path of development. Western views on how societies should be organized, including dominance over the environment, have become the gold standard for peace and progress. Development models, through globalization processes, emphasize the reliance on resource extraction and economic growth as crucial for modernization, progress, and ultimately peace (Kerner, 2024). However, while this Western/Eurocentric worldview perceives the world as secular, rational, and culturally superior, it is, in reality, a very specific worldview grounded in the "local culture" (which is now globalized) of the West. In this sense, the idea of development can be seen as a form of power that enables Western dominance in the global system and acts as a standard through which the Global South is measured.

Thus, from the perspective of postcolonial theorists, the realization of the dream of "peace and prosperity" through development and globalization processes is more often described as a "nightmare" for marginalized groups (Fitzgerald, 2019, pp. 1-7). The policy of enforced development through endless economic growth and resource extraction leads to increased inequalities and poverty, environmental destruction, climate change, and rising levels of conflict and insecurity in the Global South. From the viewpoint of governments in developing countries, the production of knowledge often fails to address development issues sufficiently and does not adequately account for the power asymmetry between the North and the South. Therefore, Southern governments emphasize "the need to create consensus and also to frame a development narrative on issues that affect global trade and the global economy" (Thérien, 2024, p. 3). It seems that this objective has largely been achieved through the accumulation of experiences in the development of emerging economies in East Asia, as well as in China, India, Brazil, and South Africa. As a result, some observers have already referred to the "Southernization of development" (Mawdsey, 2018, p. 175). This reflects the significance of the global development of ideas, models, practices, and procedures derived from the experiences of the Global South countries.

In the realm of development, hegemonic perspectives assume that only the dominance of a hegemonic power or a group of powers can form the optimal condition for ensuring and maintaining a stable and open global economy. Small and weak countries have little influence on global affairs. Instead, their development is primarily evaluated through two criteria: their level of integration into the neoliberal global economy and the similarity of their political system to the liberal democracies in the Global North. Such a hegemonic worldview of the global order believes that the decline of one hegemon leads to confrontations and conflicts, which always result in the rise of another hegemonic power. In this teleological fate, nationalism across the world always repeats the historical experience of Europe, leading to aggressive expansionism and the destruction of peoples and the world. A state either strives to become a regional or global hegemon and succeeds, or falls under the control of an emerging hegemon. (Keohane, 1980, 1984; Gilpin, 1975, 1981; Kindleberger, 1987). The prevalence of this hegemonic worldview aligns with the rise of the unipolar global order, largely under the hegemony of the United States. This is described as the "era of globalization." However, international institutions remain strategic tools of U.S. will. The U.S. government is undoubtedly the "systemic hegemon," exercising its power through military intervention, nuclear arsenals, massive conventional weaponry, dominance of the dollar in international finance, and selective deregulation of markets (Strange, 1982).

GLOBAL SOUTH, POLITICAL AGENCY, AND THE TRANSFORMATION OF GLOBAL GOVERNANCE

The global order is shifting from a unipolar world dominated by the West to a multipolar world with Asia emerging as the central pivot. While the leaders of the G7 countries chose to avoid any reference to the "Global South" in their final statement at the Hiroshima summit in 2023, the 134 members of the G77, who held their third summit in January 2024, continue to emphasize the importance of this term (Japan Times 2023; G77 2024a).

Today, the Global South is largely aware of its subordinate and submissive position within the liberal global order and seeks to utilize the collective self-awareness gained through colonial and post-colonial experiences, as well as the opportunities presented by the dynamics of the international system, to assert its political agency to change the hegemonic international order. Accordingly, the Global South has sought to challenge the hegemonic discourse of the North by engaging in bottom-up discourse-building and offering alternative narratives on lifestyles and development agendas. Through this process, it aims to break free from its marginalized and subordinate position and to lay the foundation for the creation of a new order from below. In the following discussion, we will examine the political agency of the Global South, focusing on three important issues: (a) China's Leadership, (b) South-South cooperation through the G77, BRICS, and (c) the Global South's efforts to reform the structure of the international system through "Southern multilateralism".

CHINA'S LEADERSHIP

China is the backbone of the "Global South," at the forefront of the will for resistance and rebellion from the Global South to reform and change the hegemonic order of the North. Many analysts view China's participation in "South-South Cooperation" as a clear manifestation of the emergence of the Global South. South-South Cooperation, based on the concept of "collective self-reliance," formulated in the 1970s, is increasingly expressed in a set of institutionalized practices. This cooperation is based on the idea that developing countries have different needs and interests compared to the countries of the North. The distinct nature of this cooperation is characterized by rejecting OECD norms related to the effectiveness of aid by emerging countries. As Waibisch explains, recent policy discussions on South-South cooperation have "revealed unresolved North-South differences over power, status, and responsibility in international development and broader international affairs" (Waibisch, 2022, p. 335). The prominence of the Global South in China's foreign policy over the past decade, especially amid China's increasing estrangement from the West, has grown significantly. The countries of the Global South have become vital economic partners and also essential areas and normative allies in China's efforts to create a global system more favorable to China and less centered on the West. (Table 1)

Table 1. China and Global South-Focused Mechanisms

Institutions	Membership	Year of Establishment
Group of Friends of the Global Development Initiative	Over 80 countries	2021
Belt and Road Initiative	151 countries	2013
Group of 77 and China	134 countries	1964
BRICS	9 members and over 40 countries are interested in joining	2009
Forum on China-Africa Cooperation (FOCAC)	53 African countries, the African Union, and China	2000
China-Community of Latin American and Caribbean States (CELAC) Forum	33 Latin American/Caribbean countries, China	2014
China-Arab States Cooperation Forum (CASCF)	22 Arab states, China	2004
Shanghai Cooperation Organization (SCO) – 10 member states, two Observers, and 14 Dialogue Partners	China, India, Kazakhstan, Kyrgyzstan, Russia, Tajikistan, Uzbekistan, Pakistan, Iran (joined 2023), Belarus (joined 2024)	200

Source: Thi Ha & Thi Phuong Thao, 2024

For a large segment of the Chinese elite, the approach of American neocolonialism and its European allies is in stark contrast to the West's discourse on universal values. In practice, China strives to distinguish itself from Western powers by following a foreign policy based on three fundamental principles: non-interference, mutual respect, and mutually beneficial cooperation (Sun, 2017). Based on the sacred principle of non-interference, Chinese diplomats are reluctant to play a key role in resolving conflicts. Traditionally, China's involvement in conflicts is limited to three forms of governance: (1) Political governance through participation in UN peacekeeping missions in Jerusalem, Lebanon, Western Sahara, and Sudan. (2) Conflict governance, indirectly through the UN Security Council, with its participation in resolutions favoring dialogue and peace in Yemen and Syria and combating the Islamic State. (3) Social governance through humanitarian aid to Iraqi, Palestinian, and Syrian refugees, among others (Sun, 2017. p. 360). The principle of non-interference, grounded in respect for sovereignty and non-intervention in internal affairs, is based on the idea that each country should chart its development path.

For Beijing, improving the living standards of people is crucial for achieving peace and stability. Therefore, issues related to the rule of law, democracy, or respect for human rights are not raised in discussions between the Chinese leadership and their Arab counterparts. Including them would be considered interference in domestic politics. However, the fact that the People's Republic of China supports a very strict and Westphalian interpretation of sovereignty and seeks to establish positive relations with all Middle Eastern and African governments, regardless of regime type, has resonated with many ruling elites in these regions and many other countries.

In various regions of the Global South, including the Middle East and Africa, China presents itself as a major power that defends national sovereignty, supports development and South-South cooperation, facilitates communication between countries, and advocates for multilateral institutions. China emphasizes that it plays a balanced role among countries in these regions and does not take sides in international or internal conflicts. Additionally, it stresses that, in contrast to Western countries, it lacks a colonial history. This narrative appears to resonate with many governments and elites in these regions. Public opinion surveys in many countries of these regions often show relatively positive views toward China.

China's approach can be described as "large-scale institutional balancing" through three main strategies: (1) utilizing extensive, multilateral organizations, particularly the UN and other groups that include Global South nations; (2) developing a China-centered model with a global reach (illustrated by the Belt and Road Initiative, which involves partnerships with over 150 countries for Chinese-financed infrastructure projects); and (3) establishing or expanding platforms such as BRICS, to unite developing nations in support of China's vision for global governance reform. In these methods, China's primary focus is on developing countries where it has growing economic and diplomatic influence. These countries share China's desire for a multipolar world and have grievances regarding the Western dominance in the international system established after World War II. (Thi Ha & Thi Phuong Thao, 2024. p. 3)

China's approach to managing its relationships with other developing countries has consistently been a fundamental strategic focus for Chinese leaders and a key priority of China's diplomatic strategy. The 20th National Congress report of the Communist Party of China emphasized that China should strengthen solidarity and cooperation with other developing countries by adhering to principles of sincerity, proximity, goodwill, and a just and beneficial approach, while supporting mutual interests. China is committed to increasing input resources for global development cooperation, working to bridge the North-South gap, and firmly assisting other developing countries in accelerating their development. Furthermore, China aims to enhance its influence within the BRICS, Shanghai Cooperation Organization, and other cooperation mechanisms, as well as to increase the representation and voice of emerging markets and developing countries in global affairs. (Honghua, 2024) On August 22, 2023, during the closing ceremony of the BRICS Business Forum, President Xi Jinping stated, "As a developing country and a member of the 'Global South,' we share a common destiny with other developing countries. We firmly protect their common interests and promote the enhancement of their representation and voice in the global market." (Honghua, 2024).

China's development model (the Beijing Consensus) contrasts with the neoliberal development model promoted by the International Monetary Fund and other Western-led institutions (the Washington Consensus). The Washington Consensus, which stresses liberalization and minimizing the role of the state in markets, has been condemned by many African leaders as neo-colonial and exploitative. In contrast, the Beijing Consensus, with its emphasis on non-intervention, offers an attractive alternative for some African countries. As a result, the appeal of China's modernization model has spread in the "Global South," laying a solid foundation for deepening cooperation between China and developing nations (Benabdallah et al., 2017).

THE G77

As previously discussed, in the realm of international relations, global development agendas, and multilateral negotiations, the Group of 77 (G77) has emerged as a prominent representative of the agency and voice of the Global South. Established in 1964 after the first session of the United Nations Conference on Trade and Development (UNCTAD), the G77 is the largest intergovernmental organization of developing countries. Its creation paved the way for subsequent branches within other UN specialized agencies. Closely linked with the Non-Aligned Movement, the G77 has evolved into one of the earliest diplomatic coalitions of Global South states, expanding its membership from the original 77 to 134 countries (Lees, 2023, p. 311). Representing predominantly post-colonial non-Western nations in Asia, Africa, the Middle East, and Latin America, the G77 encompasses over 80% of the world's population and two-thirds of UN member states. Often characterized as the "weapon of the weak," the group has sought to amplify the collective voice of the Global South in multilateral institutions since its inception (Adebajo, 2024).

The G77 consists of a diverse array of states united under the ideological framework of "South-South" cooperation. This shared foreign policy orientation has a distinct intellectual lineage rooted in the common experience of colonial subjugation and international marginalization. It emerged during decolonization and subsequent efforts by economically underdeveloped postcolonial states to assert and defend their sovereignty. Thus, the G77 serves as an institutional expression of the South-South ideology, one that originates in opposition to Western colonialism, emphasizes a specific interpretation of national sovereignty, critiques the inequities of the liberal international order, and fosters a degree of solidarity among its heterogeneous members (Lees, 2023, p. 311).

Although the G77 has retained its original name, it has significantly expanded since 1964, encompassing a wider range of actors, including Least Developed Countries (LDCs), oil-exporting nations, and emerging economies in Asia and the Pacific. According to its founding 1967 Charter, the group maintains a global presence and convenes annually at the United Nations headquarters in New York. The G77 asserts a shared geography and a historical narrative of collective struggle for liberation, sovereignty, and South-South solidarity against a Western-dominated global order. It champions a "fair and equitable multilateral trading system" and advocates for a New International Economic Order (NIEO) aimed at advancing the interests of developing countries, particularly through equal participation and self-determination.

The group emphasizes sovereignty, non-interference, and broader participation of developing nations in global governance via multilateral institutions. It contends that Bretton Woods's institutions, like the IMF and World Bank, favor wealthier states and that the global neoliberal order disproportionately benefits Western powers. Accordingly, its policy proposals call for a restructured global economic system that creates a more level playing field and advances the interests of underprivileged nations through fair and inclusive negotiation processes (Al Khazraji & Cubukcuoglu, 2023).

In the 1970s, the OPEC oil embargo, which nearly quadrupled oil prices, provided a powerful new tool for the Global South, galvanizing the G77 to call for a New International Economic Order. This ambitious vision sought to redistribute resources and technology from the Global North to the South, foster self-reliance through intra-regional trade, bolster infrastructure investment, and promote industrialization. However, the group's stance softened in the post–Cold War era, a pragmatic shift partly attributed to the "lost decades" of the 1980s and 1990s, during which many developing countries became heavily indebted and increasingly dependent on Western-dominated financial institutions. Since 2000, while the G77 has continued advocating institutional reform and remained steadfast in its support for Palestinian rights and the lifting of the U.S. embargo on Cuba, its summits have focused more broadly on themes such as security, justice, and democracy (Adebajo, 2024).

From its early years, the G77 has fostered a unique and enduring alliance with China. This relationship deepened during contentious North-South debates in the UN General Assembly, especially after the G77 played a pivotal role in expelling Taiwan from the UN in 1971 and facilitating the entry of the People's Republic of China. Although China is not a formal member of the G77, it remains the only permanent member of the Security Council regularly invited to its meetings (Adebajo,

2024). Despite its upper-middle-income status, China's voting patterns at the UN closely align with those of the G77 rather than with high-income countries (Thi Ha & Thi Phuong Thao, 2024).

Over the past few decades, China has actively leveraged the G77 as a platform to cultivate alternative global narratives and rally support for its flagship initiatives, including the Belt and Road Initiative (BRI), the Shanghai Cooperation Organization (SCO), and the BRICS consortium. These initiatives promote deeper solidarity among Eurasian, African, and Latin American nations in opposition to Western-driven neoliberal globalization, advocating instead for a more equitable, bottom-up form of distributive globalization (Al Khazraji & Cubukcuoglu, 2023). In June 2008, the G77 and China Summit adopted a development agenda for the Global South, calling for enhanced South–South cooperation, reform of the international economic system, and the amplification of developing countries' voices in global financial governance through renewed North–South cooperation.

At the G77 plus China Leaders' Summit held in Cuba in September 2023, under the theme "Current Development Challenges: The Role of Science, Technology and Innovation," sharp critiques were directed at Western-led trends such as trade liberalization, U.S. hegemony in global politics, and interference in the domestic affairs of developing nations. The summit encouraged the Global South to adopt a unified stance on pressing issues, including external debt, poverty eradication, equitable trade, multilateralism, and access to advanced technology. Through the G77, developing countries articulated coherent perspectives aimed at shaping the global agenda in alignment with the principles established in 1964. From Cuba's perspective, the summit served not only as a platform for advancing South–South cooperation, but also as a collective indictment of U.S. policies—particularly economic sanctions.

Arguably, the most constructive outcome of the summit was the opportunity it created for Global South nations to continue dialogue and coalesce around a shared agenda for expressing grievances in an inclusive setting. Presided over by China, the summit provided a venue for Southern leaders to reaffirm their commitment to collective autonomy, even as Washington remained wary of deepening ties between China and Cuba and is likely to push back against the summit's outcomes (Al Khazraji & Cubukcuoglu, 2023).

As a result, the G77 continues to realign the interests of the South while empowering member states to play a more active role in global negotiations on critical issues such as food and energy security, financial sovereignty, and alternatives to the U.S. dollar. In a world transitioning from multi-centricity to multi-polarity, Global South nations are demanding a stronger voice, a level playing field, and more just outcomes in efforts to reform or reconstitute the international economic system. The global order is increasingly being reshaped along the lines of rival economic blocs: the industrialized West spearheads the "rules-based liberal order" through the G7; rising powers from the South—such as India, Turkey, Saudi Arabia, Russia, and South Africa—are asserting influence within the G20; and the world's more marginalized nations in Africa, Asia, and Latin America are coalescing around China within the G77.

BRICS

BRICS represents the most prominent and strategic alliance of Global South countries in their pursuit to transcend colonial marginalization and subordination. In essence, it stands as a powerful initiative aimed at asserting influence and fostering deeper solidarity and cooperation across the Global South. From a purchasing power parity (PPP) perspective, the combined GDP of BRICS countries, led predominantly by the Global South, has surpassed that of the G77 nations, which traditionally represent the Global North. As illustrated in Figure 1, the share of BRICS countries in global GDP based on PPP has shown a steady upward trajectory since 2000, whereas the share of G77 countries has exhibited a consistent decline over the same period.

Figure 1. Share of World's GDP by PPP (BRICS vs. G77)

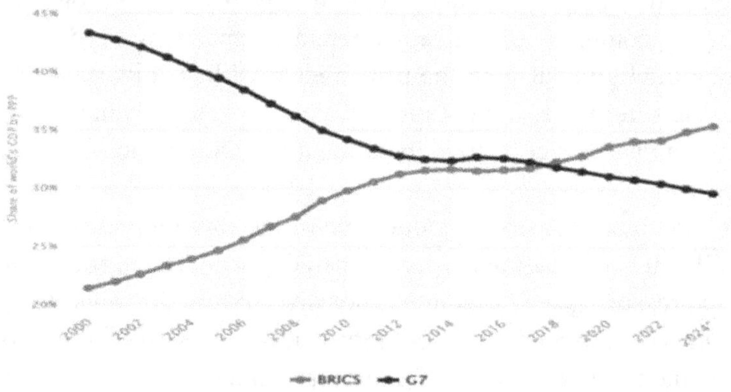

Statista. Country Report 2025 Source:

With the formation of BRICS as an alliance of major emerging economies in 2001, the notion of uncontested global ownership rooted in the American-led liberal order began to face significant challenges. BRICS, alongside the broader Global South and the vision of a new paradigm within the international system, often referred to as the post-polar order, represents a promising trajectory toward restructuring the current unjust global framework. Now expanding under the term "BRICS Plus," this coalition has grown beyond its original members—Russia, China, South Africa, Brazil, and India—to include a wider array of states such as Iran, the United Arab Emirates, Ethiopia, Egypt, and Turkey. Currently, over 40 countries have expressed interest in joining the group.

BRICS directly challenges the dominant Westphalian-based narrative of modern Western civilization, advocating instead for the equitable distribution of global privileges irrespective of geographic constraints. It seeks to establish unprecedented opportunities for international engagement across political, economic, military, and security spheres. Through its commitment to multilateralism, BRICS promotes alternative political and economic paradigms shaped by non-Western perspectives. In this context, the bloc's parallel institutional structures—such as the Contingent Reserve Arrangement and the New Development Bank, designed to rival the IMF and the World Bank—reflect its growing ambition. These developments further reinforce the likelihood of large-scale de-dollarization, a core initiative aligned with BRICS' broader objectives (Escriche & Burguete, 2023).

In contrast to the Bretton Woods system, whose socio-political foundations are rooted in principles such as democracy and human rights, the BRICS Plus framework promotes state sovereignty through models of governmental authoritarianism and calls for a more equitable global order. Fundamentally, BRICS Plus is born from fatigue and disillusionment with U.S. unilateralism, acting as a reaction to America's declining ability to maintain global stability. Through fostering political, economic, and security convergence—especially under the umbrella of the Shanghai Cooperation Organization (SCO), which has emerged as the second most important global security structure after NATO, BRICS Plus seeks to serve as a strategic counterweight. Its security vision, resembling a post-colonial doctrine, aims to fulfill a military role akin to that of NATO but grounded in anti-imperialist principles.

Economically, the BRICS coalition has the potential to promote a large-scale non-Western paradigm and evolve into a dominant force in global affairs. With a collective population exceeding 3.27 billion, over 41.13% of the world's population and accounting for nearly 25% of global GDP (France 24, August 22, 2023), BRICS members now contribute to more than 50% of global economic growth, with China alone responsible for over 30% of that growth (Global Times, 2024). According to the 2024 "United Nations Trade and Development Report", the average global GDP growth for developed countries in 2024 is 1.8 percent and its forecast for 2025 is 1.7 percent, while this figure for developing countries including the Group of 77, BRICS, etc., which are located in the Global South, is predicted to be 4.1 percent for 2024 and 4.2 percent for 2025. Meanwhile, the Asian continent has the highest annual GDP growth rate among other continents, with a rate of 4.0. Africa, as another region of the Global South, ranks second in the world with a rate of 3.0, and the Americas, Europe, and Oceania, which are considered among the developed countries of the world, are in the next ranks, respectively (see Table 2).

Table 2. World output growth 1991-2025, GDP growth rates (Annual percentage change)

Country groups	1991–1999[a]	2000–2009[a]	2010–2014[a]	2015–2019[a]	2019	2020	2021	2022	2023	2024[b]	2025[b]
World	**2.9**	**3.4**	**3.2**	**3.0**	**2.6**	**-3.0**	**6.3**	**3.1**	**2.7**	**2.7**	**2.7**
▸ Africa	**2.4**	**5.5**	**2.6**	**2.9**	**2.6**	**-2.4**	**4.6**	**3.4**	**3.0**	**3.0**	**3.2**
South Africa	2.7	4.0	2.5	1.0	0.3	-6.0	4.7	1.9	0.6	0.9	1.4
▸ North Africa (incl. South Sudan)	2.7	5.3	-1.9	3.8	2.3	-3.3	4.7	2.6	2.5	2.6	3.2
▸ Sub-Saharan Africa (excl. South Africa and South Sudan)	2.0	6.4	6.2	2.9	3.4	-1.0	4.4	4.3	3.8	3.8	3.6
▸ America	**3.4**	**2.5**	**2.4**	**1.9**	**1.8**	**-3.4**	**6.0**	**2.5**	**2.4**	**2.3**	**2.0**
▸ Latin America and the Caribbean	3.2	3.4	3.4	0.1	-0.6	-7.3	7.1	4.1	2.1	2.0	2.5
Mexico	3.0	1.9	3.2	2.0	-0.4	-8.4	6.0	3.7	3.2	2.0	1.5
▸ Central America (excl. Mexico) and Caribbean	2.8	4.4	3.6	3.0	2.2	-8.7	8.3	4.8	3.6	3.1	3.0
▸ South America	3.4	3.9	3.4	-0.9	-1.1	-6.7	7.3	4.1	1.5	1.8	2.8
Argentina	4.6	3.8	2.7	-0.3	-2.0	-9.9	10.4	5.0	-1.6	-3.5	4.8
Brazil	2.9	3.6	3.2	-0.4	1.2	-3.3	4.8	3.0	2.9	2.8	2.2
▸ Northern America	3.4	2.3	2.1	2.3	2.4	-2.4	5.8	2.1	2.4	2.4	1.8
Canada	2.8	2.3	2.6	2.0	1.9	-5.0	5.3	3.8	1.2	1.1	2.1
United States	3.5	2.3	2.1	2.4	2.5	-2.2	5.8	1.9	2.5	2.5	1.8
▸ Asia (excl. Cyprus)	**4.4**	**5.6**	**5.7**	**4.8**	**3.8**	**-0.9**	**6.7**	**3.6**	**4.2**	**4.0**	**4.0**
▸ Central Asia	-4.4	8.1	6.7	3.7	4.2	-1.2	5.4	4.1	5.6	3.6	3.5
▸ East Asia	4.4	5.6	5.8	4.8	4.0	0.4	6.9	2.5	4.2	3.9	3.7
China	11.0	10.6	8.6	6.8	6.0	2.2	8.4	3.0	5.2	4.9	4.6
Japan	1.2	0.9	1.4	0.9	-0.4	-4.2	2.7	1.2	1.8	0.9	1.0
Republic of Korea	6.8	4.9	3.7	3.1	2.3	-0.7	4.6	2.7	1.4	2.3	2.1
▸ South Asia	4.7	6.3	5.4	6.1	3.7	-3.8	8.1	5.7	6.1	5.7	5.5
India	5.9	7.2	6.6	7.0	4.6	-5.9	9.4	6.5	7.7	6.8	6.3
▸ South-East Asia	5.3	5.5	5.7	5.0	4.4	-3.8	3.6	5.6	3.9	4.5	4.4
Indonesia	4.8	5.2	5.8	5.1	5.0	-2.1	3.7	5.3	5.0	5.1	5.2
▸ Western Asia (excl. Cyprus)	4.3	5.1	5.4	2.9	1.6	-2.9	6.9	6.2	2.0	2.4	3.9
Saudi Arabia	2.2	4.3	5.7	2.2	1.1	-3.6	5.1	7.5	-0.8	1.7	4.7
Türkiye	3.9	5.0	7.6	4.3	0.9	1.7	11.8	5.3	4.5	3.5	3.8
▸ Europe (incl. Cyprus)	**1.4**	**2.2**	**1.2**	**2.1**	**1.8**	**-5.9**	**6.3**	**3.0**	**0.7**	**1.2**	**1.6**
Russian Federation	-5.9	6.2	3.1	1.2	2.2	-2.7	5.9	-1.2	3.6	3.5	1.5
United Kingdom	2.6	2.0	1.8	2.0	1.6	-10.4	8.7	4.3	0.1	0.9	1.4
▸ European Union	1.9	1.8	0.8	2.2	1.8	-5.6	6.1	3.5	0.5	1.0	1.6
▸ Euro area	1.9	1.6	0.6	2.0	1.6	-6.1	6.0	3.5	0.5	0.9	1.4
France	1.8	1.6	1.1	1.7	1.8	-7.5	6.4	2.6	1.1	1.0	1.3
Germany	1.6	1.0	2.0	1.8	1.1	-3.8	3.2	1.8	-0.2	0.2	1.2
Italy	1.4	0.7	-0.8	1.1	0.5	-9.0	8.3	4.0	0.9	0.9	1.0
▸ Oceania	**3.7**	**3.2**	**2.8**	**2.7**	**2.0**	**-2.1**	**5.4**	**3.7**	**1.9**	**1.4**	**2.1**
Australia	3.7	3.3	2.8	2.5	1.8	-2.1	5.5	3.9	2.0	1.4	2.1
▸ Developed countries	**2.3**	**2.2**	**1.7**	**2.1**	**1.9**	**-3.9**	**5.7**	**2.5**	**1.6**	**1.8**	**1.7**
▸ Developing countries	**4.9**	**6.4**	**5.8**	**4.4**	**3.6**	**-1.6**	**7.2**	**3.9**	**4.2**	**4.1**	**4.2**

Trade and Development Report. (2024)

Despite these impressive figures, BRICS still faces a long journey before it can credibly rival the existing U.S.-led international order. Numerous challenges have hindered deeper political and economic integration among BRICS members. Nonetheless, BRICS Plus has achieved notable successes: implementing China's Belt and Road Initiative, establishing the New Development Bank and the Contingent Reserve Arrangement, supporting India's and Brazil's bids for permanent seats on the UN Security Council, promoting Eastern-oriented policy shifts at the UN, attracting new membership applications, creating greater non-Western political space, forming independent international institutions, advancing a post-liberal global order, advocating for de-dollarization, proposing a common currency, and providing financial support to underdeveloped countries in the Global South.

In the political and diplomatic spheres as well, the "Greater BRICS" demonstrates a strong capacity for unity and serves as a leading representative of the Global South. At the 2024 G20 Summit, the primary focus on the concept of "global governance" underscored the growing significance of platforms for Global South participation in international affairs. Amid protracted tensions between Russia and Ukraine, escalating conflicts in the Middle East, and widespread geopolitical and geo-economic instability, the role of the Global South in the world economy has become increasingly prominent (Patrick, 2024). The Ukraine crisis has come to symbolize the political decline of the Global North and the political ascendance of the Global South. Most countries of the Global South did not align with NATO's stance on Ukraine, instead emphasizing strategic autonomy for emerging and developing nations at a time when the international order is confronting a critical crossroads. These countries prioritize post-COVID economic development and national revitalization over political confrontation and bloc alignments led by the U.S. and the West.

In the case of Ukraine, many Global South nations have adopted a strategy of neutrality and "strategic detachment" (Spektor, 2023, pp. 6–8), while in Gaza, they have positioned themselves as early advocates for a humanitarian ceasefire (Heine, 2023). The diplomatic rapprochement between Saudi Arabia and Iran, facilitated within the emerging economies' bloc, is widely regarded as a strategic diplomatic achievement led by China, allowing Beijing to expand its influence in the Middle East.

Some analysts note that BRICS includes members with divergent political systems and objectives, and remains largely reactive rather than proactive, falling short of achieving a coherent geopolitical convergence. According to these observers, BRICS members have different attitudes towards the "Global North", as recent discussions on BRICS expansion have shown, some (China, Russia, Iran) want to position BRICS as an anti-Western alliance and an incubator for a new multipolar world order, while others (South Africa, Brazil) are more concerned with strengthening their international autonomy and reforming the global system to better represent the Global South (Baumann, 2024, p. 42). Nonetheless, BRICS signals the formation of an alternative pole of power that aspires to parity with its Western counterpart, particularly the United States. In this sense, "BRICS+" or the "Greater BRICS" is increasingly seen as the vanguard of the Global South. Accordingly, the Global South may be referred to as the "BRICS+ South," emphasizing collective leadership in addressing the pressing challenges of the current world order (Global Times, 2024). From a postcolonial perspective, the emergence of this structure represents a symbolic call for liberation from neocolonial dominance. It seeks to resonate with the marginalized and subordinated populations of the Global South—those historically sidelined by global power structures—by advocating for justice and taking meaningful steps toward the establishment of fair and equitable economic systems.

REFORMING THE INTERNATIONAL SYSTEM

The Global South, led by leading countries in the region such as China, India, and Russia, has intensified its efforts to "reform the global governance system" towards what it calls "Southern multilateralism" or "Genuine Multilateralism." One of the alternative models increasingly advanced by Global South countries is "Southern multilateralism," a form of institutional arrangement initiated and led by developing nations themselves. These frameworks are not only conceptualized within the Global South but are also frequently funded by Southern actors, involving the mobilization of financial resources, technical expertise, and the exchange of ideas among member states. Historically, particularly in the post-decolonization period, Global South countries have collaborated within and beyond the United Nations to assert their collective perspectives. The Non-Aligned Movement (NAM), for instance, emerged in the 1960s with demands for global decolonization and respect for the principles of racial, national, and economic equality. In the 1970s, a coalition of seventy-seven countries worked collectively through the United Nations to promote what came to be known as the New International Economic Order (NIEO). However, as Roy (2022, pp. 2–16) notes, "Southern multilateralism" is a distinct evolution from earlier modes of South–South cooperation. It is not merely a continuation of past initiatives, but rather a transformative political strategy grounded in the shared postcolonial consciousness of Global South nations. This model aspires to challenge, reform, and—where possible—reconstruct the dominant international order. Rooted in a spirit of solidarity, Southern multilateralism seeks to articulate an alternative vision of global governance, one that is more equitable and reflective of the priorities and values of the formerly colonized and structurally marginalized majority of the world.

"At the global level, China, with the aim of strengthening the South through unity, has fostered a "Global South" consensus on major global issues such as changing the global order, reforming institutions created after World War II such as the United Nations and the Bretton Woods financial institutions, the Ukraine crisis, and climate change negotiations. It has actively responded to the reasonable demands of the Southern countries and is committed to increasing their representation and voice in global affairs.

One of the most important demands of some of these countries is to increase the number of permanent members of the United Nations Security Council with veto power. It should be noted that, beyond the countries of the Global South such as Brazil, India, Indonesia, and Nigeria, countries outside this category, such as Japan and Germany, are also demanding permanent seats on the Security Council. Meanwhile, "China, as the most influential country in the South, has steadily increased its influence by appointing Chinese nationals to leadership positions in UN agencies. The number of Chinese nationals working at the UN has almost doubled, from 794 in 2009 to 1,564 in 2022. Since 2019, China has surpassed Japan as the second-largest contributor to the UN's regular budget. China's assessed contribution to all UN agencies has tripled in the past decade, increasing from 4.8 percent of total government funding in 2013 to 14.9 percent in 2022. China has also strengthened South-South cooperation at the UN through initiatives such as providing additional funding to upgrade the South-South Cooperation Assistance Fund to the Global Development and South-South Cooperation Fund; establishing the China Global Development Initiative (GDI) Friends Group, with more than 80 participating countries; and expanding China's South-South Cooperation Network, with the participation of 50 technical committees. (Thi Ha & Thi Phuong Thao, 2024, p. 4)

Similarly, China has positioned itself as a prominent voice and leader of the Global South through its active engagement in the "G77 plus China" coalition, an alliance comprising 134 developing countries. This bloc advocates for reforming global governance and promotes state-centered norms and values that align with China's core interests, such as national sovereignty, non-interference in domestic affairs, and prioritizing national development over individual rights. The platform has proved instrumental for China in forging normative solidarity with many developing nations seeking greater representation and influence in the global governance system.

Despite being classified as an upper-middle-income country, China's voting patterns in the United Nations are more closely aligned with those of the G77 than with high-income states. Furthermore, China has successfully embedded its concept of a "Community of Shared Future for Mankind" into various G77 documents and United Nations General Assembly (UNGA) resolutions, demonstrating its effort to globalize this vision (Thi Ha & Thi Phuong Thao, 2024, p. 4).

One of the key challenges facing the Global South coalition is the issue of currency. The BRICS summit, which initially represented Brazil, Russia, India, China, and South Africa, has supported the idea of establishing a new currency mechanism for conducting international transactions, aimed at bypassing the dominance of the US dollar in the global monetary system. China has been advancing this idea since the early 2000s, with renewed vigor following the 2008 Wall Street financial crisis. Its most recent and enthusiastic supporter is Brazilian President Luiz Inácio Lula da Silva (Rampini, 2024). While the full realization of this initiative remains a long-term goal, several Global South countries, such as Argentina and Brazil, have already begun using China's yuan in bilateral trade.

In addition, efforts are underway to create alternatives to the Bretton Woods institutions through new initiatives such as the BRICS New Development Bank, headquartered in Shanghai and currently led by former Brazilian President Dilma Rousseff, as well as the China-led Asian Infrastructure Investment Bank (AIIB).

The Belt and Road Initiative (BRI) represents another postcolonial strategy aimed at strengthening the agency of the Global South and breaking free from dependency and subordination within the hegemonic international order. The third Belt and Road Forum, held in Beijing in October 2023, marking the tenth anniversary of the initiative launched by China, brought together 23 heads of state and delegations from over 130 countries. This event symbolized a shifting multipolar order driven by the Asian giant, reflecting its ongoing commitment to empowering the Global South and its ambition to challenge the liberal international order. Under the framework of South-South cooperation and in the context of intensifying geopolitical competition with the West, particularly the United States, China's relations with the Global South have expanded rapidly. This growth has been especially notable since the country shifted from its Maoist ideological orientation to a foreign policy centered on trade and investment. In this context, the Belt and Road Initiative has become one of the main tools of China's foreign policy under President Xi Jinping. It aims to connect China with the Global South and Europe through extensive infrastructure development. Over the past two decades, China has emerged as a key trade partner for more than 100 countries, a major development investor, and, in times of crisis, a viable alternative to the International Monetary Fund (IMF) and the Bretton Woods economic order (Escriche & Burguete, 2023, p. 5).

In essence, "Southern multilateralism," as a defining feature of the emerging multiplex world order, exemplifies what Acharya (2017, pp. 280) refers to as a "G-Plus world," a complex and pluralistic international environment comprising established and rising powers, global and regional institutions, sovereign states, social movements, multinational corporations, philanthropic foundations, and various forms of cross-sector partnerships. This model of multilateralism strengthens a decentralized global system in which liberal internationalism represents merely one of several coexisting normative frameworks. Within such a decentralized order, countries and societies in the Global South are afforded unprecedented agency and alternative pathways to pursue their development trajectories according to their own values and interests. Rather than being regarded with apprehension, this shift towards a more plural global governance architecture should be seen as an opportunity for inclusion and equity (Acharya, 2017, pp. 13).

CONCLUSION

The primary objective of this study was to explore how, from a postcolonial perspective, the "Global South" has deconstructed the epistemological and ontological foundations of the Western liberal order in international relations. It also sought to identify the concrete manifestations of agency within this emerging Southern order. As discussed, post-colonialism, at its core, aims to challenge and dismantle dominant narratives constructed by colonial powers, emphasizing the importance of recognizing alternative perspectives and amplifying the voices of historically marginalized communities. Compared to mainstream international relations theories, which largely serve to justify existing power relations, the postcolonial lens provides a more nuanced and critical framework for understanding the structures, dynamics, and functioning of the current global order. By employing the "Global South" as a critical concept, this study demonstrated how, for over half a century, countries historically categorized as the Third World, developing nations, and now the Global South, have contested the grand narrative of global liberal hegemony.

In the first part of the study, we outlined how intellectuals and civil society actors from the Global South have critically interrogated the epistemological and ontological underpinnings of Western discourse. They have deconstructed the logic of binary oppositions and the Foucauldian "regime of truth" that casts non-Western states as inferior "Others." In doing so, they have questioned the legitimacy of liberal global norms such as power, security, development, human rights, freedom, and democracy, revealing the hidden power structures embedded within them. The findings in the second part of the study highlighted how the Global South, drawing upon a shared postcolonial consciousness and the structural openings in the current international system, is asserting its political agency to transform the hegemonic global order. This agency manifests in three primary domains: China's leadership, South–South cooperation through platforms like G77, BRICS, and broader efforts to reform global governance institutions in the form of "Southern multilateralism".

Led by key regional powers such as China, India, Russia, and Iran, the Global South has intensified its efforts toward what it defines as "genuine multilateralism." At the global level, China has actively promoted unity and consensus within the Global South on critical issues such as reforming post–World War II institutions, including the United Nations and Bretton Woods financial structures, the Ukraine crisis, and climate negotiations. China has also responded to the legitimate demands of Southern countries and committed to enhancing their representation and voice in global affairs. In postcolonial terms, the Global South has, over the past five decades, constructed alternative narratives of development and modernity from below. By doing so, it has begun to dismantle the hegemonic discourse of the North, moving beyond its ambiguous marginality as a subordinate "Other," and laying the foundation for reforming the current international order, or potentially constructing a new one, rooted in justice, plurality, and equitable development.

REFERENCES

Acharya, A. (2017). After liberal hegemony: The advent of a multiplex world order. *Ethics & International Affairs*, *31*(3), 271–285. DOI: 10.1017/S089267941700020X

Adebajo, A. (2024). Is the G77 the future of multilateralism? *Project Syndicate*. https://www.project-syndicate.org/commentary/g77-in-the-age-of-trump-by-adekeye-adebajo-2024-11

Al Khazraji, R., & Cubukcuoglu, S. S. (2023). G77+China summit in Cuba and its global implications. *Trends Research*. Retrieved from https://trendsresearch.org/insight/g77china-summit-in-cuba-and-its-global-implications/?srsltid=AfmBOor_Ga0sfEHwTjm8KolUyQjphT-HeIeKZy0jSmMDX_6aquOMgE1U

Albrecht, M. (2020). Postcolonialism cross-examined. In *Multidirectional perspectives on imperial and colonial pasts and the neocolonial present* (pp. 117–133). Routledge., DOI: 10.4324/9780367222543

Artner, A., & Yin, Z. (2023). Towards a non-hegemonic world order – Emancipation and the political agency of the Global South in a changing world order. *Third World Quarterly*, *44*(10), 2193–2207. Advance online publication. DOI: 10.1080/01436597.2023.2251422

Baumann, M. O., Novoselova, A., Surasky, J., & Schönrock, P. (2024). The Group of 77 and global dialogue in the United Nations General Assembly. *IDOS Discussion Paper*. Retrieved from https://www.idos-research.de/discussion-paper/article/the-group-of-77-and-global-dialogue-in-the-united-nations-general-assembly/

Benabdallah, L., Murillo-Zamora, C., & Adetula, V. (2017). Global South perspectives on international relations theory. *E-International Relations*. https://www.e-ir.info/2017/11/19/global-south-perspectives-on-international-relations-theory/

Bull, B., & Dan, B. (2025). *The rebirth of the Global South: Geopolitics, imageries and developmental realities*. DOI: 10.1080/08039410.2025.2490696

Escriche, I. A., & Burguete, V. (2023). China and the Global South: Old friends, new dynamics. *CIDOB*. https://www.cidob.org/en/publications/china-and-global-south-old-friends-new-dynamics

Farias, D. B. L. (2019). Outlook for the 'developing country' category: A paradox of demise and continuity. *Third World Quarterly*, *40*(4), 668–687. DOI: 10.1080/01436597.2019.1573139

Fischer, A. M. (2019). Bringing development back into development studies. *Development and Change*, *50*(2), 426–444. DOI: 10.1111/dech.12490 PMID: 31007272

Fitzgerald, S. (2019, June 26). Do postcolonial approaches explain world politics better than other IR theories? *E-International Relations*. https://www.e-ir.info/2019/06/26/do-postcolonial-approaches-explain-world-politics-better-than-other-ir-theories/

Forough, M., Dahbi, K., Waterman, A., & Woertz, E. (2023). Narratives of global order and re-ordering from the Global South. *Global Society*, *16*(31), 292–325.

France 24. (2023, August 22). Size, population, GDP: The BRICS nations in numbers. *France 24*. https://www.france24.com/en/business/20230822-size-population-gdp-the-brics-nations-in-numbers

Gilpin, R. (1975). *U.S. power and the multinational corporation: The political economy of foreign direct investment*. Basic Books. DOI: 10.1007/978-1-349-01354-8

Gilpin, R. (1981). *War and change in world politics*. Cambridge University Press. DOI: 10.1017/CBO9780511664267

Gu, J. (2025). *China and the Global South in a contested world order: The changing dynamics of policy and practice in an era of polycrisis*. Palgrave Macmillan.

Haji Yosefi, A. M., & Ghaebi, R. (2018). The concept of "right to development" in international relations from the view of post-colonial theory. *World Politics*, *6*(4), 7–40.

Haug, S., Braveboy-Wagner, J., & Maihold, G. (2021). The 'Global South' in the study of world politics: Examining a meta category. *Third World Quarterly*, *42*(9), 1923–1944. DOI: 10.1080/01436597.2021.1948831

Heine, J. (2023, March 24). The Global South is on the rise – but what exactly is the Global South? *The Conversation*. https://theconversation.com/the-global-south-is-on-the-rise-but-what-exactly-is-the-global-south-207959

Heine, J. (2023, November 8). Reaction to Gaza siege exposed the rift between the West and the Global South. *The Conversation*. https://theconversation.com/international-reaction-to-gaza-siege-has-exposed-the-growing-rift-between-the-west-and-the-global-south-216938

Honghua, M. (2024, March 1). The rise of the "Global South" and the new picture of international game on China's strategic response. *International Cooperation Center*. https://en.icc.org.cn/thinktank_theories/theoretical_research/346.html

Ikenberry, G. J. (2018). The end of liberal international order? *International Affairs*, *94*(1), 7–23. DOI: 10.1093/ia/iix241

Ivison, D. (2025). Postcolonialism historical period. *Encyclopedia Britannica.* https://www.britannica.com/topic/postcolonialism

Keohane, R. O. (1980). The theory of hegemonic stability and changes in international economic regimes, 1967–1977. In Holsti, O. R., Siverson, R. M., & George, A. L. (Eds.), *Change in the international system* (pp. 131–162). Westview Press.

Keohane, R. O. (1984). *After hegemony: Cooperation and discord in the world political economy.* Princeton University Press.

Kerner, I. (2024). Considering the coloniality of the liberal script: Post- and decolonial perspectives. In Börzel, T. A. (Ed.), *The liberal script at the beginning of the 21st century: Conceptions, components, and tensions.* Oxford University Press., https://academic.oup.com/book/58951/chapter/493015592 DOI: 10.1093/oso/9780198924241.003.0003

Kindleberger, C. P. (1987). *The world in depression, 1929–1939.* Pelican Books.

Klob, S. T. (2017). The Global South as subversive practice: Challenges and potentials of a heuristic concept. *Global Society, 11*(2), 1–17.

Lake, D. A., Martin, L. L., & Risse, T. (2021). Challenges to the liberal order: Reflections on *International Organization. International Organization, 75*(2), 225–257. DOI: 10.1017/S0020818320000636

Lees, N. (2023). The endurance of the G77 in international relations: South–South ideology and voting at the United Nations, 1970–2015. *Japanese Journal of Political Science.* Retrieved from https://www.cambridge.org/core/journals/japanese-journal-of-political-science/article/endurance-of-the-g77-in-international-relations-southsouth-ideology-and-voting-at-the-united-nations-19702015/384214A0BA4D9A050DA653E507C1A13E

Lewis, S. L., & Stolte, C. (2019). Other Bandungs: Afro-Asian internationalisms in the early Cold War. *Journal of World History, 30*(1), 1–19.

Linklater, A. (2016). *Theories of international relations* (Talebi-Arani, R., & Moshirzadeh, H., Trans.). Mizan Pub.

Lüthi, L. M. (2016). The non-aligned movement and the Cold War, 1961–1973. *Journal of Cold War Studies, 18*(1), 98–147.

Mawdsley, E. (2018). The 'Southernisation' of development? *Asia Pacific Viewpoint, 59*(2), 173–185. DOI: 10.1111/apv.12192

Mazarr, M. J. (2017). The once and future order: What comes after hegemony? *Foreign Affairs, 96*(1).

Mbembe, A., Mongin, O., Lempereur, N., & Schlegel, J.-L. (2006). Qu'est-ce que la pensée post-coloniale? Entretien avec Achille Mbembe. *Esprit (Paris, France)*, *12*, 117–133. DOI: 10.3917/espri.0612.0117

Mielniczuk, F. (2013). BRICS in the contemporary world: Changing identities, converging interests. *Third World Quarterly*, *34*(6), 1075–1090.

Murphy, D. C. (2022). *China's rise in the Global South: The Middle East, Africa, and Beijing's alternative world order* (1st ed.). Stanford University Press.

Nair, S. (2017, December 8). Introducing postcolonialism in international relations theory. *E-International Relations*. https://www.e-ir.info/2017/12/08/postcolonialism-in-international-relations-theory/

Patel, S. (2023). Anti-colonial thought and global social theory. *Sociological Theory*, *8*, 1143776. Advance online publication. DOI: 10.3389/fsoc.2023.1143776 PMID: 37066066

Patrick, S., & Huggins, A. (2023, March 29). The term "Global South" is surging. It should be retired. The phrase lacks the depth and diversity of the world it purports to describe. *Foreign Affairs*. https://www.foreignaffairs.com/articles/2023

Rampini, F. (2024). Russia and China: Aligning with the Global South? *Aspenia Online*. https://aspeniaonline.it/russia-and-china-aligning-with-the-global-south/

Roberts, J. T., & Parks, B. C. (2007). *A climate of injustice: Global inequality, North-South politics, and climate policy*. MIT Press.

Report, S. C. (2025). Global North and Global South divide. *Statista*. https://www.statista.com/topics/13236/global-north-and-global-south-divide/#topicOverview

Roy, I. (2022). Southern multilateralism: Complementary competition vis-à-vis the liberal international order. *Global Perspectives*, *3*(1), 39589. Advance online publication. DOI: 10.1525/gp.2022.39589

Schwarz, H., & Ray, S. (2005). *A companion to postcolonial studies*. Blackwell., DOI: 10.1002/9780470997024

Shidore, S. (2023). The return of the Global South: Realism, not moralism, drives a new critique of Western power. *Foreign Affairs*. https://www.foreignaffairs.com/world/return-global-south-critique-western-power

Smith, K., & Tickner, A. B. (Eds.). (2020). *International relations from the Global South* (pp. 1–14). Routledge.

Solarz, M. W. (2012). 'Third world': The 60th anniversary of a concept that changed history. *Third World Quarterly*, *33*(8), 1561–1573.

Spektor, M. (2023). In defense of the fence sitters. *Foreign Affairs*, *102*(3), 8–16.

Sun, D. (2017). China and the Middle East security governance in the new era. *Contemporary Arab Affairs*, *10*(3), 354–371. DOI: 10.1080/17550912.2017.1353791

Tamang, D., & Hazarika, O. (2023). International relations: Perspectives for the Global South. *India Quarterly. Journal of International Affairs*, *69*(2), 207–210.

Thérien, J.-P. (2024). The North–South distinction: From consensus to contestation. *Global Studies Quarterly*, *4*(4), ksae080. Advance online publication. DOI: 10.1093/isagsq/ksae080

Thi Ha, H., & Thi Phuong Thao, P. (2024). Re-ordering the world: China's Global South focus versus the ally-centric approach of the US. *Researchers at ISEAS – Yusof Ishak Institute*. https://www.iseas.edu.sg/articles-commentaries/iseas-perspective/2024-90-re-ordering-the-world-chinas-global-south-focus-versus-the-ally-centric-approach-of-the-us-by-hoang-thi-ha-and-pham-thi-phuong-thao/

Tripathi, S. (2024). (Post) colonial complexities and world (re)ordering: Contestations from/within the "margin(alized)". *Global Studies Quarterly, 4*(3).

Tudoroiu, T., & Kuteleva, A. (2022). *China in the Global South: Impact and perceptions* (1st ed.). Springer. DOI: 10.1007/978-981-19-1344-0

United Nations Conference on Trade and Development. (2024). *Trade and development report 2024*. Retrieved from https://unctad.org/publication/trade-and-development-report-2024

Waisbich, L. T. (2022). 'It takes two to tango': South–South cooperation measurement politics in a multiplex world. *Global Policy*, *13*(3), 334–345. DOI: 10.1111/1758-5899.13086

Zhou, G. (2024). Rise of Global South and changes in the contemporary international order. *China International Strategy Review*, *6*(1), 58–77. DOI: 10.1007/s42533-024-00160-x

KEY TERMS AND DEFINITIONS

Post-colonialism: Post-colonialism is a critical approach to theoretical approaches that seeks to dismantle dominant readings and narratives created by colonial powers and emphasizes the importance of understanding diverse perspectives and the voices of those who have been historically marginalized.

The Global South: The Global South is a collection of developing countries that have typically experienced colonial rule and have a low to medium average national income. Increasingly, the Global South became synonymous with the Group of 77, a collection of postcolonial and developing countries that united in 1964 to jointly advocate for their collective economic interests and to enhance their negotiating capacity at the UN. Today the members of the G77, now 134 countries strong, regularly refer to themselves as the Global South.

Northern-Led Global Order: A critical Concept that means reading the International Liberal Order (ILO) from the perspective of the subordinates. From this point of view, ILO is dominated by the advanced and powerful countries of the North (especially the United States and the EU), revealing the unequal relations between North and South.

Agency: the ability, willingness, and capability of an individual, group, or country to perform purposeful and intentional action; a type of independent action to defend one's identity and emancipate from the domination of others.

The Group of 77 (G77): The G77 is the second biggest international organization in the world that was set up on 15 June, 1964, at the first session of the UN Conference on Trade and Development (UNCTAD). The group is a coalition of developing countries, designed to promote its members' collective economic interests and create an enhanced joint negotiating capacity in the United Nations. The group consists of a diverse set of states with a common South-South ideology. There were 77 founding members of the organization headquartered in Geneva, but it has since expanded to 134 member countries.

BRICS: BRICS, founded on June 16, 2009, is an intergovernmental organization and a forum for cooperation among a group of leading emerging economies, comprising ten countries: Brazil, Russia, India, China, South Africa, Egypt, Ethiopia, Indonesia, Iran, and the United Arab Emirates. The acronym BRICS+ (in its expanded form, BRICS Plus) has been informally used to reflect new membership since 2024. China has the largest economy in the group, accounting for about 70% of the organization's total.

The Non-Aligned Movement (NAM): is a group of countries that was founded during the collapse of the colonial system, promoting a policy of neutrality towards the blocs led by the two superpowers – the USA and the Soviet Union –who were by then fully engaged in the Cold War. In April 1955, a conference of Asian and African countries was held in Bandung (Indonesia) to promote unity and independence for the Third World, decolonization, and an end to racial segregation. The initiators were Tito (Yugoslavia), Nasser (Egypt), Nehru (India), and Sukarno (Indonesia). Currently, 120 countries are members of this movement. NAM is currently considered one of the Global South organizations and represents the interests and aspirations of developing countries.

Chapter 15
China's "Grand Strategy" Interests in Africa

Nika Chitadze
https://orcid.org/0000-0003-2806-6426
International Black Sea University, Georgia

ABSTRACT

China, a newly empowered state that aspires to regional and ultimately global hegemony, is interested in strengthening the extremely backward and underdeveloped Africa. We believe that the reason for this policy can be traced back to China's "grand strategy." To confirm this, the study aims to examine China-Africa relations in the context of the "Grand Strategy", analyze the reasons for China's interest in this region, and investigate how the Asian giant uses "soft power" on the African continent to achieve its goals. To this end, the study formulates the following research question: What role does Africa play in implementing the goals of China's fourth "Grand Strategy"? As a result of the study, we will try to show that China's interest in African states is related to the implementation of the goals of China's "Grand Strategy" (the fourth – the rising phase) and serves to increase the latter's political, economic, institutional, and cultural influence.

INTRODUCTION

"China is a sleeping Goliath, and when it wakes up, the world will tremble" Napoleon Bonaparte.

Since 2003, the main driving force of Chinese policy, the so-called "Grand Strategy", has entered its fourth, renewal, resurgence phase, the goal of which is to establish China as a "world-class power". In turn, on the way to achieving this goal, China is interested in the African continent and is trying to bring it into its sphere

DOI: 10.4018/979-8-3373-0938-5.ch015

of influence. This strategy has been evident since the 2000s when China actively began to invest in Africa and increase its export-import and ideological, economic, and political influence (Nantulya et al, 2018). An important mechanism of China's "Grand Strategy" is the "Go Global" policy, which implies the spread of its influence on an international scale. In turn, the main tool of the fourth "grand strategy" is "soft power", with which it tries to increase political, economic, and ideological influence in different regions of the world.

The African continent is one of the first target regions of China's "grand strategy". Sino-African relations are one of the most important modern global events that deserve more interest at the international level. The urgency of the issue is determined by the unprecedented economic growth rates of China. Based on the BBC forecast, China's GDP will surpass that of the world's first economy, the United States, by 2028 (BBC, 2020). This fact alone is enough to understand how big a role China plays on the world stage. In turn, the interest in Africa in the "resurgence phase" of the "Grand Strategy" has a great impact on China's political influence and its positions in important international organizations (the UN) and the international system in general. The relevance of the topic is also confirmed by the fact that China's export value to Africa, as a result of the implementation of the goals of the "Grand Strategy", increased from US$5 billion to US$113 billion between 2000 and 2019 (Statista, 2019). These numbers directly indicate the intensity of Sino-African relations. Therefore, it is particularly interesting to explore - what role does Africa play in the implementation of China's fourth "Grand Strategy"? The study aims to examine Sino-African relations through the prism of China's fourth "grand strategy" and to reveal, on the one hand, what causes China's interest in the region and, on the other hand, what is manifested in its active involvement in the processes taking place on the African continent.

To this end, the study examines Sino-African relations in the context of the "grand strategy" and the theoretical framework of "soft power", the analysis of which well explains China's real motives and aspirations. On the other hand, given that China-Africa relations span a fairly long period, to make the study more specific, we took the first two decades of the twenty-first century for consideration, because we believe that it is during this period that the influences of China "grand strategy" and "soft power" on the African continent are most clearly manifested. Methodology The paper uses qualitative research methods, namely narrative literature review, through which the information surrounding the research topic is processed and analyzed in depth. In addition, the study uses documentary analysis, for which it applies the qualitative content analysis method and carries out textual analysis of primary and secondary sources, several documents, speeches of leaders, media, and statements and reports of governmental and non-governmental organizations.

Literature Review To critically analyze the literature surrounding the topic under discussion, the paper uses the narrative method of literature review and the progressive coherence technique of the process of constructing intertextual coherence, which implies the analysis of sources with a common consensus. Considering that the Georgian sources surrounding the topic provide rather scarce information, the study is mainly based on several works, studies, and statistics by foreign authors and organizations. China's growing interest in the African continent is a more or less studied topic in international relations. Many scientific works and studies have been written on this issue. In this regard, Lloyd Troll's book "China's Growing African Relations" stands out, where the author identifies three main interests of China in the African continent: economic, political, and security interests. In this regard, Troll pays special attention to China's interest in the rich resources of Africa (Troll, 2015). In turn, Yun Sun draws attention to other economic issues in addition to natural resources and notes that China's policy in Africa is very pragmatic. In particular, according to him, China's policy paves the way for Chinese companies, private owners, and investors to the African market, which is considered one of the best markets for investing (Sun, 2014). According to the widespread opinion, establishing political and economic influence in Africa helps China strengthen its position in the international system and increase its prestige. This narrative is shared by Thierry Paillot in an article published in "The Diplomat", in which he draws interesting conclusions. In particular, he notes that China is trying to develop a peculiar scenario of globalization, where it will emerge as a major political power, whose influence will be strengthened by the political networks of the "Silk Road" or "One Belt, One Road" (Pairault, 2021). As for security interests, the opinions of experts in the field on this issue still coincide - they believe that the scale of China's economic activity on the continent is so large that it is unacceptable to put them at risk. Accordingly, Chinese investments and the Chinese population in Africa need protection. This is one of the reasons why China is active in the region. However, the authors we have discussed concentrate on individual Chinese interests but do not offer a synthetic analysis of all the main motives. This creates the need for research to determine China's real goals. Accordingly, in this paper, we attempt to link China's interests in Africa to its "grand strategy," which will help us fill the gaps in the reviewed literature.

As for "grand strategy," the concept was coined in the early 20th century to explain German foreign policy. Since then, it has been used many times by various great powers. In the case of China, there is some disagreement about whether the latter has a "grand strategy" at all. In his work, "The Great Game: China's Grand Strategy to Replace the American Order," Rush Dosh distinguishes between two groups of opinions. He calls those who do not believe that China has already developed a "grand strategy" "skeptics." Moreover, some believe that it is even impossible to formulate a single coherent strategy, given China's multifaceted national interests. In the opposite "camp" are the so-called "advocates," who believe that China does have a "grand strategy" and that it aims to displace the United States on a regional and global level. Doshi's work offers a different approach to studying "grand strategy" and seeks to find evidence for the existence of this concept in influential Chinese texts, national security documents, and the behavior of the state itself. The work seeks to show that China's "grand strategy" consists of changing the hegemonic agenda established by the United States (Doshi, 2021). Although Doshi's work offers a thorough analysis of the concept of "grand strategy" in general, we believe that the work focuses too much attention on the rivalry with the United States for international hegemony. Consequently, the possible economic aspects of China's "grand strategy" are largely ignored.

The gap in this regard is somewhat filled by Daniel Araya's article "China's Grand Strategy" published in Forbes, which discusses the role of technology in the "grand strategy": "[China's] grand strategy is built on creating new markets for highly developed Chinese technologies." These markets include the continents of Latin America and Africa. The article specifically mentions the role of ports, highways, and gas pipelines in the implementation of Chinese ambitions. Araya calls Xi Jinping's "signature project" the "One Belt, One Road" initiative and believes that if the bets placed on developing countries prove successful, this will be a major geopolitical move for China (Araya, 2019). Focusing on the economic significance of China's "grand strategy" allows us to better understand this complex concept. Accordingly, Daniel Araya's article is a valuable addition to the research begun in this regard. However, we believe that when talking about China from any angle, it is necessary to take into account one very important feature - its size. This one of the largest states, both in terms of area and population, is always characterized by complexity and multi-layeredness. Accordingly, we believe that the concept of China's "grand strategy" also includes many interconnected aspects, the separate study of which is necessary for an in-depth study of the issue. We believe that there is a certain "gap" in the diverse literature written on this topic in terms of analyzing China-Africa relations directly through China's "grand strategy". Accordingly, with this paper, we would like to contribute to studying the issue from a different perspective.

STRENGTHENING THE GEOPOLITICAL AND ECONOMIC POSITIONS OF CHINA IN THE WORLD

The rise of the People's Republic of China (PRC, China) will undoubtedly be one of the great dramas of the 21st century. China's extraordinary economic growth and proactive diplomacy are already transforming many parts of the world, and Chinese power and influence will grow even greater in the years ahead.

Some experts believe that As China's power grows. The United States of America weakens, what is likely to happen is that the world will enter a new stage—perhaps less dramatic than the one following World War II, but new—in which the architecture of international order will once again be open to formation and reshaping. Other powers, of course, will also seek to influence and shape these founding rules and institutions. Meanwhile, the United States and China, with their unique power, are in a position to lead the struggle over the principles and logic of organizing world order in the 21st century.

For many years, Western governments assumed that China would easily join and support the existing international system, its architecture, institutions, values, and the norms that underpin them (Kudayarov, 2022). Beijing had no reason to seek to revise or transform a system from which it benefited, especially after joining the World Trade Organization (WTO) in 2001. However, since President Xi Jinping came to power, China has sought not only to occupy a central position on the world stage commensurate with its economic and military power but also to reshape elements of the existing system to better suit its views and interests (Kudayarov, 2022). Chinese officials and analysts increasingly argue that America has lost its status as a major global power, or at least that Washington is unable to cope with this status. Where China's "hedging" against the systemic leader is heading now is less clear, but Beijing is behaving as if it is developing strategies to outflank the United States. Official statements from high-level Chinese government officials provide some important clues; for more, see R. Doshi's "The Long Game: China's Grand Strategy to Displace American Order."

This work represents one of the most significant attempts to understand China's emergence as a global power. Written by Rush Doshi, a former Brookings Institution fellow and former National Security Council official in the Biden administration, the book draws on rigorous social science research and a variety of sources, ranking them by authority, and has a clear narrative structure. The book is divided into thirteen chapters, which together form three main parts. The book's structure allows us to chart the development of the People's Republic of China's foreign policy positioning, thereby providing insight into the evolution and continuity of Chinese leaders' perceptions of international politics over more than forty years of history. Doshi argues that since the end of the Cold War, China has been pursuing a "grand" long-term strategy aimed at reshaping the U.S.-imposed order, first at the regional level, and, as it succeeds, at the global level. Intentions are notoriously difficult to assess, so to shed light on them, Doshi looks for evidence of grand strategy in authoritative texts, national security institutions, and state behavior. The author emphasizes primary Chinese sources, supplementing them with detailed case studies, each of which tests hypotheses and considers alternative explanations for China's actions.

Doshi argues that Chinese behavior is determined by two variables:

The power gap between the rising power and the established hegemon, and the threat the rising power perceives from the hegemon. They intersect to determine the rising power's strategy. Given this, the grand strategies of rising powers typically, though not exclusively, evolve "in a sequence from accommodation, blunting, augmenting, and then dominating." And China's behavior fits this pattern precisely. The blunting phase occurred when China moved from viewing America as a potential ally during the Cold War, especially after Richard Nixon's diplomacy, to perceiving it first as an existential threat and then as a competitor that could be outmaneuvered. Chinese leaders were deeply impressed by three events that fundamentally changed the perception of the United States as a threat: the United States' criticism of and attempts to intervene in the aftermath of Tiananmen Square (1989); the ease with which the United States defeated Iraq during the Gulf War (1990–91); and the collapse of the Soviet Union (1991) (Kudayarov, 2022). Beijing concluded that the United States was no longer quasi-ally confronting the Soviet Union. With the threat from Moscow gone, America once again became China's main enemy. China's preeminent leader of the time, Deng Xiaoping, noted shortly before the collapse of the USSR: "The issue now is not whether the banner of the Soviet Union will fall… but whether the banner of China will fall." This new threat perception, Doshi writes, became "the crucible in which a new Chinese grand strategy would be forged (Doshi, 2021)."

In 1993, General Secretary Jiang Zemin addressed the First Ambassadors' Conference, one of China's major foreign policy meetings, and declared that "from now on and for a relatively long period, the United States will be our main diplomatic adversary" (Kudayarov, 2022). However, Jiang Zemin did not advocate challenging America at the time. Instead, he called for a foreign policy known today as "hiding and biding its time" (Tao Guang Yang Hui). China abandoned any illusions about the possibility of cooperating with Washington and began to deploy a strategy aimed at continuing beneficial trade, scientific, and technological relations and at weakening the hegemonic influence of the United States without revealing its intentions as a rising power. In military terms, this meant investing in weapons that would limit the United States' ability to sustain its presence in the Pacific. Concrete expressions of this approach included building submarines, sea mines, and anti-ship missiles, rather than investing in overtly offensive weapons such as aircraft carriers. Moreover, Doshi finds authoritative Chinese texts confirming the striking similarities between

China's force structure and that of now-defeated Iraq and calling for investment in "shashoujian" (assassin's mace) capabilities. This involves developing the concept of deterring an adversary (usually with a suite of weapons) by making it more difficult for an adversary to deploy or move forces into a defended area (Anti-Access/Area-Denial Capabilities - A2/AD) than an attacking force. Politically, this involved a strategy of joining major U.S.-dominated international organizations, such as APEC (Asia-Pacific Economic Cooperation), to change the way they function and win the support of Washington's allies in Asia. Finally, economically, the strategy was to secure access to the U.S. market and to guarantee its companies' investment in China, primarily through WTO membership. While U.S. leaders saw WTO membership as a way to make China a more liberal trading power, their Chinese counterparts saw it as a way to escape American control. This policy produced an economic boom the likes of which the world had rarely seen. The next turning point, Doshi writes, came in 2008 with the onset of the global financial crisis. China saw this as an opportunity not only to continue to weaken American power but also to begin to build a Chinese sphere of influence in Asia. The financial crisis had fundamentally changed Beijing's view of American power; China now saw America as significantly weakened because its economic model had failed.

Doshi calls attention to Chairman Hu Jintao's speech at the 11th China Ambassadors' Conference in 2009. In his address, Hu Jintao replaced China's policy of "hiding and biding his time" with a strategy of "actively pursuing something," signifying the start of the "build-up" phase. "This seemingly trivial semantic shift," Doshi writes, "had enormous significance" (Doshi, 2021). Beijing is no longer interested in merely weakening American power. Over the next eight years, China—first under Hu Jintao and then under his successor, Xi Jinping—moved from undermining US influence in Asia to directly challenging it.

China has become much more assertive, and confident in its ability to build an alternative world order to Washington and to create the conditions for a "community of shared destiny" in Asia based on an alliance between Asian states under China's leadership.

Militarily, this has meant a shift in focus from countering the US military to strengthening its offensive capabilities. It has invested more in military affairs and the conduct and development of explicitly offensive strategies: building aircraft carriers, amphibious ships (to invade Taiwan), military bases abroad, and intervening militarily in other countries to secure their political and economic interests.

Politically, the new strategy has been to establish a regional order in Asia so that China can become a regional leader, a provider of international public goods, create new international norms consistent with its interests, and isolate the US and its main ally in Asia, Japan. In its version of the Monroe Doctrine, China began to present its interests as those of all Asian countries and peoples and to achieve these by creating new international organizations, such as the Asian Infrastructure Investment Bank (AIIB) (Doshi, 2021). Finally, from an economic point of view, the strategy consisted of pursuing a series of ambitious projects aimed at integrating many countries into their development model, to build an economic interdependence that would be in line with Beijing's interests and those of other countries, and to reduce the influence of the US dollar as a dominant currency. Concrete examples of this economic strategy to date include the Belt and Road Initiative (BRI), based on major investment projects in Asia, Africa, and Europe, and the creation of a multilateral and less dollar-centric financial environment, such as by promoting the yuan, creating alternative rating agencies, or attempting to replace the SWIFT international financial communications network. Since Xi Jinping's election to a second term as General Secretary of the Communist Party of China (CPC) in 2017, China has been determined to aggressively expand its global presence (Doshi, 2021).

Like other changes in China's grand strategy, this shift toward greater global ambitions was driven by what Beijing saw as the irreversible decay and decline of the West. In 2016, a year before Xi's speech at the CPC Congress, the United Kingdom voted to leave the European Union, and Donald

Trump was elected President of the United States. From the perspective of China, which is highly sensitive to shifts in perceptions of American power, these two events were globally significant. The world's most powerful democracies were emerging from the international order they had helped create, creating what China's leadership and foreign policy elite called a "period of historic opportunity" to expand the country's strategic focus from Asia to Africa and other parts of the world and its system of management.

In the run-up to these events, senior Chinese officials have spoken more boldly about China's ambitions and the onset of "great changes unseen in a century." This phrase, a favorite of Xi Jinping, signifies the Chinese leadership's assessment that the very polarity of the international system has changed forever: China has been reborn, and the decline of the West seems inevitable.

Xi has therefore become the first CPC chairman to never use and to abandon the term "hide and bide his time" (tao guang yang hui).

Given this, China's heightened interest in shaping the global political order and building a "community of common destiny for mankind" is manifested in a wide range of efforts. Doshi argues that these efforts are generally helping China build the foundations of its order and are being implemented through a variety of means: reforming the UN system; ensuring China's representation in global regional organizations; forming new coalitions; and exporting certain governance methods. In all areas, Beijing has made significant strides, bringing the country's leadership closer to where it wants to be. For example, according to Doshi's analysis, Chinese government documents record that "the global community of common destiny and the BRI initiative … have been included in many UN resolutions and … have received wide recognition and warm response from the international community." To gain influence at the UN, Beijing has taken advantage of U.S. neglect and has worked hard to place its citizens in the top leadership positions of four of the UN's fifteen specialized agencies, including the United Nations Industrial Development Organization (UNIDO), the International Civil Aviation Organization (ICAO), the International Telecommunication Union (ITU), and the Food and Agriculture Organization of the United Nations (FAO). This is more than any other country. Moreover, China previously chaired the WHO and Interpol, currently leads the UN Department of Economic and Social Affairs (DESA), and narrowly missed out on becoming the leader of the World Intellectual Property Organization (WIPO) in 2020 (Doshi, 2021).

In addition to its participation in the UN system and regional leadership in Asia, Doshi says China has also established relationships with virtually every region in the world. The most significant of these include the Forum on China-Africa Cooperation (FOCAC), the China-Arab States Cooperation Forum (CACF), the Forum on China-Central and Eastern European Cooperation (CEEC, or "17+1"), and China and the Community of Latin American States (China – CELAC). These fora cover 125 countries and shape China's relations with regions on a bilateral basis rather than facilitating multilateral engagement among multiple stakeholders (Doshi, 2021).

Economically, according to Doshi, Beijing relies on technology as a central part of its ambitions to displace the American order.

A key component of China's "great changes unseen in a century" is the belief that the world is experiencing a new wave of technological innovation, sometimes called the "fourth industrial revolution," that allows China to overtake the West.

This term, originally coined at the World Economic Forum in 2015, has now been adopted by Beijing and generally refers to a wide range of technologies: artificial intelligence (AI), quantum computing, biotechnology, and even digital currencies. Beijing believes that the intersection of technology with supply chains, trade patterns, financial power, and information flows has the potential to reorder the traditional economic instruments that have been central to Chinese grand strategy for the past century. For this reason, economic instruments, and technology in particular, are increasingly at the center of the U.S.-China standoff over global order. Finally, in the military sphere, China has increasingly shifted toward "offshore" power projection, namely, maintaining bases around the world to protect its economic interests abroad and ensure the security of its natural resources. The ultimate goal, according to Doshi, is for Beijing to "create a zone of super-high influence" in its region and "partial hegemony" in developing countries linked to its Belt and Road Initiative, which could eventually extend to developed countries (Doshi, 2021).

Overall, Doshi lays out his vision of what a Chinese order might look like if China achieves its goal of "national rejuvenation" by the centennial of the founding of the Republic in 2049. At the regional level, China already accounts for more than half of Asia's GDP and half of Asia's military spending, which unbalances the region and leads to the formation of a Chinese sphere of influence. A fully realized Chinese order could eventually include the withdrawal of U.S. troops from Japan and Korea, the end of U.S. regional alliances, the virtual removal of U.S. naval forces from the Western Pacific, support/endorsement of China's regional neighbors, unification with Taiwan, and the resolution of territorial disputes in the East and South China Seas (Doshi, 2021).

A Chinese order would likely be more coercive and less consensual than the current one, would be primarily beneficial to, and would be seen as legitimate mainly by, the few it directly rewards. China would implement this order in ways that would be detrimental to liberal values, and Chinese-style authoritarianism would spread more widely throughout the region. Order abroad often reflects order at home, and the Chinese order would be distinctly illiberal compared to the U.S. order.

According to Doshi, part of the strategy for achieving such a global order is already evident in Xi's speeches. Politically, Beijing will project leadership over global governance and international institutions, fracture Western alliances, and promote autocratic norms at the expense of liberal ones. Economically, it will weaken the financial advantages that underpin U.S. hegemony and secure its dominance in the strategically important sectors of the "fourth industrial revolution," from artificial intelligence to quantum computing, transforming the United States into "a deindustrialized English-speaking version of a Latin American republic, specializing in commodities, real estate, tourism, and perhaps transnational tax evasion." Militarily, the People's Liberation Army (PLA) will have world-class forces with bases around the world, capable of defending China's interests in most regions and even in new areas such as space and the deep sea.

In summing up his research, Doshi argues that however real this structural shift in the balance of power may be, the United States can still compete effectively. While the presence of nuclear weapons makes a direct war between China and the United States suicidal, it creates a strategic chessboard for the "long game"(Doshi, 2021).

Hence, after devoting twelve chapters of his work to explaining Chinese grand strategy and its driving forces, Doshi begins his normative chapter on U.S. grand strategic adaptation. In this section, the author calls for the effective use of U.S. Resources and argues that this will be important in the long run, since China is a much more economically powerful competitor than any other hegemonic power the United States has faced. Doshi calls for an end to ineffective approaches such as containment and regime subversion, as well as "grand bargaining" with a rival.

Instead, the author argues for accepting China's rise as a fact, in the face of which it is wiser to develop a strategy similar to that pursued by Beijing after the end of the Cold War, that is, a strategy aimed at weakening China's power by avoiding confrontations and limiting its efforts to become a globally dominant power. In such an asymmetric competition, America can emulate China's historical strategy of "blunting and building up," optimizing the use of resources, and putting "the adversary at a cost-benefit disadvantage, thereby making it more difficult to invest in military coercion and power projection." If China is using the A2/AD (Anti-Access/ Area-Denial Capabilities) package, it should apply them. If China has thwarted U.S. institution-building efforts in Asia by joining them and slowing them down from within, the U.S. should do the same with China-led initiatives.

In terms of building a sphere of influence, the U.S. must build on its strengths, build momentum in its alliances, and build international institutions with like-minded partners. It is especially important, Doshi argues, for the U.S. to commit to building genuine democracy at home by finding "positive ways to restore the solidarity and civic identity that makes democracy work." Citing historian Julle Lepore, Doshi calls for "efforts to emphasize a shared liberal nationalism... a 'new Americanism' that has been part of U.S. civic culture and can be again." Doshi argues that the China threat must be the catalyst for this goal.

The overall message of the book, then, that China began competing with the United States decades before the global community realized that we were in a state of great power rivalry, is well-founded. China is an ambitious power, and what Beijing wants does not coincide with the interests of the United States and its allies. Doshi provides a solid interpretive framework for understanding China's foreign policy aspirations and provides recommendations for how the United States can avoid its "unacceptable" rise.

Echoing Samuel Huntington's famous argument in the late 1980s, Doshi proposes to restore the spirit of "self-renewal" that has characterized America at many points in its history. To curb the decline, the most sensible thing to do is to reform the country internally and make it more competitive internationally, returning to investing in those sectors that used to be its strengths: education, technology, and industry. This approach allows, on the one hand, to avoid the radicalism of those who see confrontation as the only way out, and on the other, to avoid the illusions of those who underestimated China, believing that it would agree to integrate into the system of Western norms and values (Doshi, 2021).

One possible criticism of the book, however, is that it shows signs of bias on the part of its author. Throughout the book, the author argues that Beijing is only "blunting," building its world and doing so aggressively.

In contrast, Xi has transformed China's foreign policy, though not in the way that is commonly understood in the West. Despite frequent comparisons with Mao Zedong, he is not a revolutionary seeking to overthrow the global order and impose a Chinese brave new world in its place. He is a revisionist in the sense that he seeks to maximize China's influence and status. But, like his predecessors Hu Jintao, Jiang Zemin, and Deng Xiaoping, he seeks to do so within the existing international system.

In this regard, Xi's OBOR initiative is not a harbinger of an alternative world order. Its agenda is more prosaic: to improve China's access to natural resources; to open new markets for its goods and services; to extend Beijing's economic influence across Eurasia; and to ensure a friendly and secure neighborhood. However, Beijing has not achieved even these more limited goals through OBOR. 3 Likewise, China's actions in the Western Pacific are not aimed at advancing Sino-centric hegemony but reflect long-standing goals: to project power; to gain control over resources; to have a decisive voice in regional security; to reduce or contain American influence; and to assert authority over Taiwan. This approach is hardly comforting to the United States, but it is neither new nor radical. 4 It is therefore worth examining the significance of the fact that China has not been a revolutionary power seeking to undermine every aspect of the existing system. This raises further questions about the conditions under which China might seek to "blunt" or "build," and how Beijing achieves these goals. For example, why not build an institution separate from the UN, opting instead to assert greater control from within? Accordingly, the argument that China is already expanding seems also questionable. Doshi notes that China's commitment to "hiding capabilities and biding its time" was based on its then-current assessment of U.S. power and that Deng Xiaoping, Jiang Zemin, and Hu Jintao had all pointed out that as the assessment of U.S. power changed, so would China's strategy (Doshi, 2021). However, this does not necessarily mean that the strategy would change to "building" its world order. China appears to have sought to build power to create strategic space for itself—the right to decide how it wanted to use its power.

CHINA'S SOFT POWER

Chinese scholars and academics were referring to soft power from the 1990s, but an important shift that turned China's attention to introducing soft power in their diplomacy was in 2007 when Hu Jintao at the 17th National Congress of Communist Party devoted his speech to the importance of power and promoted the idea to "enhance culture as part of the soft power of...country to better guarantee the people's basic cultural rights and interests" (Zandzava, 2021). As Nye put it, this address became a turning point because when the idea was promoted by "the boss" and set as the priority of the country, China increased its investments in soft power, realizing that by mixing soft power with economic and military power would be more beneficial for increasing country's influence globally (Zandzava, 2021). Reliance on soft power has been further accelerated under Xi Jinping, in 2014 announced to "increase China's soft power, give a good Chinese narrative, and better communicate China's messages to the world". Several new concepts, part of which has already been discussed in the second chapter of the paper, such as "the Chinese dream", "the Silk Road Economic Belt", and "new type of major-country relations", followed Xi's announcement (Gagnidze, 2021).

China tries to increase its attractiveness with various tools. The economic power of China still plays the biggest role in this process. ADB (Asia Development Bank) and the new development Bank with BRICS, Silk Road Fund, investments in the Maritime Silk Road – on which China spent about 156 Billion dollars and the BRI project ($770 Billion by 2020), are considered a part of China's soft power strategy, to promote China's integration throughout different regions and to spread a positive image of the country (CFR, 2018). Another China's soft power tool is its foreign aid programs to developing countries. China's unique style of Aid projects is even considered more effective, compared to the largest donor programs, such as the US or the EU. Chinese aid is oriented on "south-south" partnership, with less "moralizing tone" and respect for the countries' sovereignty, being mainly bilateral, including a wide range of sectors - commerce, agriculture, public health, international affairs, and defense. And against raised concerns internationally that Chinese aid represented a kind of "colonialist" intention to only exploit the resources, China seems not to have a certain categorization, its aid being equally allocated in resource-rich or poor underdeveloped countries (Zandzava, 2021)

Education is another field by which China spreads its soft power. Offering a wide range of educational exchange programs, China became the 4th most popular study destination in 2019 (Institute of International Education, 2020). China offers scholarships not only to Chinese students but to foreign students studying in China as well. More than 490 thousand students studied in China in 2019. But Chinese universities still lack authority and quality, as only two universities of China – Beijing University(29th) and Tsinghua University(35th), are included in the top 50 universities globally (Zandzava, 2021). The reasons for this are problems in educational institutions such as restrictions on free thought and inquiry, plagiarism and intellectual property theft, study methods oriented on memorization over the development of independent thinking, and censorship of the writings over the issues undermining the party's authority in China (Gagnidze, 2021).

More than 500 of China's Confucious institutes around the world are one more instrument of China's educational soft power. These institutes, which seem to be analogous to Germany's Goethe Institute or the UK's British Council, offer Chinese language courses and different classes aimed at increasing awareness of China's culture. However, these institutes have been highly criticized in the last decade, because of the lack of academic freedom and China's attempts to control information, damaging its international image – e.g. demanding to delete pages from conference reports that mentioned Taiwan (Zandzava, 2021).

International Media is a tool for controlling the narrative on China. One of the most influential among Chinese media is considered Xinhua News Agency which has about 170 foreign bureaus, mainly writes descriptive news, spreads communist party propaganda, and works on the crafting of China's international image. China Daily and Global Times also publish English publications available worldwide. China Global Television Network broadcasts channels in six languages around the world, while China International Radio broadcasts programs in 38 languages. Information is strictly controlled and Chinese state organs are even warning foreign journalists not to publish information that might anger China, or not issuing visas to Western journalists who are on the blacklist because of their "unfriendly" approach towards China (Zandzava, 2021).

Government-affiliated exchanges also have their share in generating China's soft power. The annual conference called "The Party and the World Dialogue" gathers foreign politicians and intellectuals from around the world in China, through financially fully covered tours. This helps China to build relations with existing or upcoming politicians globally. Foreign policy think tanks, such as the China Institutes of Contemporary International Relations and the Shanghai Institutes for International Studies, also take the function of serving states' soft power strategy (Zandzava, 2021). China also employed so-called "host diplomacy", which implied hosting important international events in different fields, hosting the 2008 Olympics, 2009 Shanghai Expo, 2014 APEC Summit, and 2016 G20 Summit (Zandzava, 2021).

China's soft power tools also include unofficial channels, such as art, literature, film, music, scholars, and sports figures. China has several so-called "cultural ambassadors" from these fields, e.g. pianist Lang Lang, actor Jackie Chan, and ballet dancer Tan Yuanyuan. This kind of "cultural ambassadors" are appreciated at home as well, being awarded with special honor, more recently as it was in the case of Florence Fang, philanthropist, and entrepreneur living in the US, for "her efforts to nurture better communication between China and the United States" (Zandzava, 2021). Chinese writers are also becoming popular, such as Mo Yan, the Nobel Prize winner in Literature in 2012. Chinese athletes also have been awarded Olympic medals in various events. Pandas are also considered as one of the cultural symbols, being sent to zoos all over the world, as a part of "panda diplomacy" (Zandzava, 2021). China's recent actions in the coping with global pandemic can also be considered as an additional opportunity for China to enhance its image. So-called "mask diplomacy" is one example, when China offered aid to the countries damaged by the pandemic, sending millions of masks and other important medical supplies, like sanitizers around the world (Gagnidze,2021). "Vaccine diplomacy" became another opportunity, when Xi Jinping declared that it would become universally available (in contrast with the US desire to purchase a vaccine from Germany to be used firstly by Americans) and has already distributed vaccine in more than 60 countries (mainly developing countries) around the world (Gagnidze, 2021).

EFFECTIVENESS OF CHINA'S SOFT POWER AND CHALLENGES

In general, it is hard to assess the effectiveness of soft power, because of its nature. Because e.g. BRI project might help China to exert its influence by offering benefits and bringing economic prosperity to the countries, but the reality showed that this might not be enough and some of the countries have become concerned with this increasing influence looking for other alternatives to decrease dependence on China (Zandzava, 2021).

One of the components by which experts try to measure the effectiveness of a country's soft power is public opinion polls conducted in different countries trying to collect data about the favorability of the country. According to Pew Research public opinion polls, on the question, of whether one holds a favorable or unfavorable view of China, most of the respondents who answered that they hold favorable views were from Africa, often ranging above 75%. The majority of the population from Latin America also views China favorably, but the results are less than in Africa. Russia and Pakistan are the ones who view China positively as well. But what concerns Western countries and countries from neighborhoods like Japan, it seems that China's soft power has achieved the least results here, and since 2011 trend is that China's favorability in these countries continues to decline (Zandzava, 2021).

The challenges to China's soft power campaign and its efforts to create the image of a responsible power are coming from what constructivists might call a contradiction between the image or an identity portrayed by the state and its actions. Authoritarianism, increased assertiveness and claims in territorial disputes, censorship of free thought among academics or in media, nationalism, and human rights abuses are part of the problems that go in contradiction with the international image of China that it desires others to accept (Zandzava, 2021). So, in this sense, China's reliance on soft power strategies can also be viewed as its attempt to distract attention from the problems in the country, which are not acceptable for many democratized countries in the international system.

Before the turn of the millennium, China maintained reactive diplomacy and a strategy of “keeping a low” profile, adopted by Deng Xiaoping, which allowed the country to distance itself from the protests in socialist countries against the system and post-Cold War conflicts. The policy of keeping a low profile helped China to concentrate on domestic modernization and economic development and keep the country out of the problems not being the direct concern of China’s national interest. The policy was still maintained under the leadership of Jiang Zemin, but in 1996, changes began, and already by the turn of the century, China’s diplomacy was altered to a proactive multilateral and omnidirectional strategy.

There were several external and internal factors behind the transformation of China’s diplomacy. The external factors included the post-cold War international order with Western influence, promotion of liberal rule and values, and increased economic dependence and cooperation among the states, which was further accelerated by the process of globalization, which made diplomatic agendas more diverse, including more players in the process, and also brought challenges such as pandemics, terrorism, trafficking, that required cooperation and mutual response by the states. As for the internal driving force, the ideas derived from the Marxist ideology of emphasizing economic development as a source of social stability can be outlined. The Chinese government had to serve the aim of economic development and to respond to the increased domestic demands for resources, which at the same time, would promote the regime's legitimacy. Coupled with external factors, the CCP analyzed the benefits of economic globalization and involvement in multilateral institutions and realized the cost of isolation.

China has been promoting proactive multilateral diplomacy since the 2000s and the starting point was China’s accession to WTO, which promoted China’s integration into the global economy. By 2020, China had already become a member of more than 130 intergovernmental organizations and signed around 400 multilateral agreements. However, the transformation of China’s diplomacy was not an instant outcome, it has been gradually developing under the leadership of Hu Jintao and Xi Jinping. Hu Jintao introduced the idea of building a “harmonious world” with durable peace and security referring to the need for cooperation and mutual effort on the international level for the achievement of this goal. He also emphasized the idea of China’s peaceful development, against raised international concerns and “China threat” rhetoric. Under his leadership China also started to construct an omnidirectional diplomatic structure, building a system of diplomatic networks connecting China to Asia, Africa, Europe, and North, and Latin America, and various multilateral organizations, forums, and conferences were set up. But Hu was challenged by increased nationalism at home, because of Which he had to officially continue supporting the policy of keeping a low profile. Under Xi Jinping's leadership, China’s contemporary diplomacy has become even more proactive, continuing to emphasize peaceful development, introducing a "new type of major-power relations", and demanding reciprocity from international society. His most ambitious BRI project and various financial funds created in support of this project, demonstrate the degree of multilateralism under Xi Jinping, which was even more valued under the current conditions of a global pandemic.

China has been able to construct an omnidirectional diplomatic structure with four main directions, including relations with major powers, relations with neighboring countries, relations with developing countries, and multilateral relations. Relations with major powers mainly serve China's economic interests, as those countries are considered major trade partners and sources of capital. Good relations with immediate surrounding countries are essential for creating a stable external environment for China's development, decreasing the US influence in the region, and demonstrating its aspirations for regional power status. Relations with developing countries help China to show its dual character of both developed and developing countries.

Special attention has to be paid to the China-US relations, as relations between the world's two biggest powers and the largest economies. China-US relations have dual characteristics, countries both cooperate and compete, and the degree of these relations varies under different administrations. Despite Trump's anti-Chinese rhetoric, the declaration of China as one of the main threats to the US national security, and Biden's continuation of sanctioning Chinese companies in the US, the country realizes the importance and benefit derived from cooperation with such a powerful country, like China.

Alongside with above-mentioned developments, China has been actively promoting its positive international image, against the increased concerns about rising China. China started to craft a new image and identity of a peaceful country, China as a peace-builder and safeguard of global peace and security, China as a responsible stakeholder, and China's actions aimed at "socializing" states to its new identity.

China's efforts for building its international image, include its active participation in peacekeeping operations as well. China also realizes the importance of soft power and started to invest more promotion of its soft power strategies, which include economic diplomacy, educational exchanges and institutions, international media, governmental exchanges, and unofficial sources, such as art, literature, movies, sport, scholars, "panda diplomacy", and more recent "mask diplomacy" and "vaccine diplomacy" associated with pandemic and China's efforts to exert influence.

China's soft power has been more effective in the African and Latin American regions when its attractiveness declines in Western countries. China fails to meet its internationally promoted image by its actions. Its soft power strategy also can be viewed as an attempt to distract attention from Authoritarianism, increased assertiveness and claims in territorial disputes, censorship of free thought among academics or in media, nationalism, and human rights abuses are part of the problems that go in contradiction with the international image of China that it desires others to accept.

CHINA'S "GRAND STRATEGY" IN AFRICA

"Grand strategy" is a well-known term in political science, popularized by the eminent American professor John Lewis Geddes. Geddes is the author of several books on the topic, the most famous of which is his work "On Grand Strategy". In this book, Geddes defines "grand strategy" as "the combination of potentially unlimited aspirations with limited capabilities". The idea of a grand strategy primarily involves connecting existing expectations with real capabilities (CaspianReport, 2018). In turn, Peter Layton defines "grand strategy" as the formation of forms of power aimed at deliberately changing the existing relationship between two or more political entities (Layton, 2018). The presence of a "grand strategy" is not a characteristic feature of all influential and powerful states in the international system. However, China, as one of the main players in the international system and a potential world power whose goals go far beyond regional hegemony, has its own unique "grand strategy" that changes periodically. Since 1949, China has had four "grand strategies":

- I "Grand Strategy" - Revolution (1949 - 1977);
- II "Grand Strategy" - Restoration (1978 - 1989);
- III "Grand Strategy" - the creation of a comprehensive military force (1990 - 2003);
- IV "Grand Strategy" - Rejuvenation - a term that can be translated as "rejuvenation", revival, strengthening (2004 - present) (Scobbel et al 2020)

I "Grand Strategy" - Revolution (1949 - 1977); • II "Grand Strategy" - Restoration (1978 - 1989); • III "Grand Strategy" - the creation of a comprehensive military force (1990 - 2003); • IV "Grand Strategy" - Rejuvenation - a term that can be translated as "rejuvenation", revival, strengthening (2004 - present) (Scobbel et al 2020) All four "grand strategies" are united by 3 core interests: security, sovereignty, and development. China's renewed desire to satisfy these interests is particularly evident in the era of the fourth "Grand Strategy", which began under Hu Jintao in 2003 and reached its peak under Xi Jinping. Notably, the latter, upon coming to power in 2012, set himself very bold and ambitious goals for China's future. Throughout his career, he repeatedly refers to the term "Chinese Dream". This includes the following: "building a prosperous, strong, democratic, civilized, harmonious socialist modernized country". To achieve this goal, China prioritizes economic development, ensuring social stability, effective functioning of the political control mechanism, maximizing national security and defense, and developing science and technology. It is believed that China's means of achieving these goals and its Grand Strategy IV as a whole is the use of hard and soft power at the expense of stability, control, reputation, and firm policies (Scobbel et al 2020).

"Soft Power"

The main goal of China's fourth "grand strategy" is to spread soft power globally. In 2014, Xi Jinping made the following important statement in his speech at the 18th National Congress of the Communist Party of China: "We must enhance China's soft power..." (Biswas and Tortajada, 2018). Given that China's contemporary policies are characterized by the use of soft power rather than hard power, it is interesting to know what this term means. One of the most prominent neoliberal scholars in the field of international relations, Joseph Nye, in his 1990 book The Responsibility to Lead, offers definitions of soft, hard, and "smart" power, or a combination of hard and soft power. In NYI International Dzandzava/Gagnidze/Student Journal in Social Sciences/April 2021 20 systemic power is defined as the ability of actors to influence other actors to achieve personal (national) goals and pursue interests through coercion or taxation, or seduction or persuasion. On the other hand, soft power is the ability to achieve a desired outcome through persuasion rather than coercion. (Ney, 2017). States that properly use the levers of their national power can influence the actions of other political actors. Some states use soft power to exert such influence. A state's soft power largely depends on its global image and international prestige. In the case of China, the ruling power has developed so-called "soft power strategies" that cover the realm of public diplomacy and are aimed at creating and promoting a positive international image of China (China Power Team, 2016). In this latest phase of China-Africa relations, China is particularly relying on soft power aspects to achieve its desired outcomes both on the African continent and in the international arena. The existing literature on the topic offers many different answers to the question: what role does Africa play in the implementation of China's fourth "grand strategy"? However, we have selected some of the most important ones. The soft power mechanisms of China's "grand strategy" in Africa are manifested in the acquisition of 4 types of influence. These are political, economic, ideological, and military. (Rønning 2014).

Africa - a treasure trove of natural resources

One of the main goals of China's fourth "grand strategy" is to implement the "going global" policy, which involves establishing closer economic ties with the outside world. One of the reasons for this is the needs of China's steadily growing economy. As of 2021, the country with the second-largest economy in the world is in dire need of new markets and additional resources. This applies to minerals, energy, and other resources, especially oil. As of 2016, China consumed 13.2% of the world's oil reserves, ranking second in the world after the United States (Worldometer, 2016). In terms of production, as of 2018, the country ranked seventh (The World Factbook, 2021). It is therefore obvious that oil is one of China's top priorities. Likewise, with economic growth, the demand for other minerals has also increased. China is the world's largest producer and consumer of minerals such as aluminum, iron ore, lead, and zinc (Alden, K. and Christina, A., 2009). China has chosen Africa as one of the first targets of its "going global" policy. Everyone knows that Africa is a source of very rare minerals and other natural resources. It is noteworthy that Africa holds 30% of the world's mineral reserves, including 8% of natural gas and 12% of oil. On the other hand, Libya and Nigeria hold the tenth and eleventh-largest oil reserves in the world (USA Today, 2019). Other African countries also have resources that China is particularly interested in: Zambia (iron ore and copper), Gabon (manganese), Zimbabwe (platinum), and Angola (diamonds, copper, and iron ore). These are crucial for the development and growth of China's economy. It is widely believed that the famous Belt and Road Initiative partly serves this purpose – diversifying China's access to these resources (Nantoulya, 2018). The African continent accounts for 30% of China's oil imports. African countries occupy a fairly significant place in the list of oil suppliers to China: Angola - 7.9%, Congo - 1.7% and Gabon - 1.2% (The World Factbook, 2021). Moreover, this number is expected to increase even more in the current decade. The Asian giant is particularly active in the oil-producing African states of Sudan, Angola, and Nigeria. In the case of Sudan, China does not have to compete with Western companies, as they are either suspicious of investing in the country or are restricted by sanctions. As for Angola and Nigeria, China is increasing its competitiveness through several diplomatic, financial, and defense practices that are often unknown to the general public (Cook, 2019).

Other Economic Aspects of the "Grand Strategy"

China's "soft power" in Africa is largely related to the economy. The "tools" of this power are trade, investment, low-interest or even interest-free loans, grants, and much more. Since the early 2000s, Beijing has spent millions of dollars to "make friends" in Africa – Chinese state-owned and private companies, with the support of the government, have invested huge amounts of money and investments in African countries, receiving various benefits in return. This is what China's "resource diplomacy" serves (Liang, 2012). China's interest in the African continent is also due to the economic potential of these countries themselves. Just a few decades ago, China was an underdeveloped, so-called "second-rate country". Today, Africa is in the same situation – although the continent has many natural resources, their extraction and use require appropriate infrastructure, and the latter – large financial investments. It can be said that using Africa's potential, which in the West may be considered a "risky investment", is a good chance for China to expand its sphere of influence and gain economic benefits. At one time, when China began to open up and reform its economy, it felt the importance of foreign direct investment. The African region today clearly shows similarities with China forty years ago and, more importantly, it also shows similar potential. One of the arguments explaining China's economic interest is based on the idea that lack of development promotes rapid growth. Over time, China's annual GDP growth has been slowly declining (World Bank, 2020) (Appendix No. 1). China is already among the industrialized countries. At the same time, Africa is the least developed region in the world. Now it has a chance to develop rapidly and even repeat the "Chinese miracle". In turn, investments in Africa expand the Chinese export market, which will contribute to the restructuring of the Chinese economy itself. This is especially true about the transition away from labor-intensive industries, since labor costs in China are steadily rising. China, the main supplier of cheap labor in the world, now needs it. As a result of rapid economic development, a large part of the country's population has moved into the middle class; The skills of the labor force have moved from the low to the middle level. As a result, the cost of labor in China has increased. Therefore, Chinese companies are already using Africa for these needs. As the youngest continent in the world, with almost 60% of the population under 25, Africa is a "resource" of young, cheap labor, most of whom are ready to do any job for a better future. As for the Asian giant itself, it is "aging" at a very fast pace - according to the latest data, the average age of Chinese residents is 38.4 years, and this figure is expected to reach 48 years by 2050 (Statista, 2019). A clear logical connection can be seen from these data - China, which has reached the highest stage of development, with an ever-increasing average age of the population and labor costs, is interested in the potential of Africa, which can offer low-skilled, but young and cheap labor. The economic aspects of China's "soft power" are also manifested through investments in Africa. During this time, Beijing has taken significant steps to expand trade and investment with African countries. In 2019, Chinese direct investment (FDI) in Africa reached $110 billion (Ze Yu, 2021).

These investments go into many different areas, most notably the multi-million dollar infrastructure projects that we will discuss below. However, the capital that China has invested in Africa is certainly not a gift. Even the aforementioned infrastructure projects are financed by the Export-Import Bank of China, which is state-owned. However, it is interesting that such large-scale Chinese-financed projects are often considered risky. For example, there is less chance of getting financing for such projects from Western governments or Western corporations. The Bank of China, influenced by the existing relationships between Beijing and African countries, provides them with low-interest or no-interest loans (Wendover Productions, 2018).

Also interesting is the FDI structure discussed above. At the closing ceremony of the 2018 Forum on China-Africa Cooperation (FOCAC) summit, China announced a new US$60 billion fund to support African development. China's infrastructure projects in Africa are quite ambitious. These include: railway systems (such as the 578-kilometer Mombasa-Nairobi railway line, which covers the distance in just 4 and a half hours); factories (Nigeria's state-owned oil refinery built with Chinese funding); hydropower (a 450-megawatt dam in Guinea and a hydroelectric power station in Angola), and even projects such as the new parliament in Zimbabwe, which the government built with a million-dollar donation from China (Tubei, 2018). Notably, some of these projects are part of China's well-known "Belt and Road" initiative. Another successful tool of China's soft power is the introduction of its economic development model into African states. "Neo-Confucian state capitalism" appeals to many members of the African elite. They even actively advocate this model in China (Harper, 2019).

China's Political and Military Interests in Africa

"China believes it cannot become a global power... unless it can charm." "Unless it has soft power." Joseph Nye

International relations scholar Ted Hall identifies the following types of power in the international arena: institutional, reputational, and representative power. Politically, China uses the institutional power mechanism of "grand strategy" in Africa, which involves the relative power and influence of actors within a particular organization, thereby influencing other actors and through them satisfying its own interests (Ronning 2014).

When talking about institutional power, we must mention the United Nations. In 1971, the United Nations General Assembly discussed one of the most important issues in China's modern history. In particular, a vote was held on which government should become a permanent member of the UN Security Council - the People's Republic of China or the Republic of China. The Assembly adopted a resolution recognizing the supremacy of the People's Republic of China and granting it the status of official representative. In this vote, several dozen African states voted against the People's Republic of China. It turns out that in the 1970s, China had virtually no influence on African countries, although the situation changed to the opposite a few decades later, in 2007, when the UN voted to ban North Korea. About human rights violations in Korea. This time, China, which acted as the main defender of Korea, received the support or abstention from the vote against 43 African states. Why are African votes in the UN so important for China? It is worth emphasizing that 54 African states represent 54 votes in the United Nations, which is a huge political force. (Wendover Productions 2018). Consider other cases: after the Tiananmen Square incident in 1989, only African states supported China in the UN (Martinez 2015). In 1996, a majority of them sided with China in a UN vote on China's human rights abuses, and in 2004, a similar US resolution on China's abuses was rejected by 27 states, half of which were again African countries (Martinez 2015, 42). Also of note was the 2020 Geneva vote on Hong Kong, where China was supported by 25 African states, which, as the BBC notes, was the largest group of countries from any continent in that vote (Olewe, 2021). China's military policy on the African continent is also noteworthy. Interestingly, since 2017, a military base with 400 personnel has been located in Djibouti, just 7 kilometers from US military units. French, Italian, Chinese, and American bases are converging on Djibouti, doubling the importance of this point. In addition, Djibouti is a so-called "sovereign territory" of China. A bridge to other, richer African states such as Ethiopia. Djibouti is perceived by China as a "Maritime Silk Road" and is a stable country: up to 70% of its external debt is owed to China. Accordingly, for the first time in modern history, China is placing a military base on the territory of a foreign country, thereby setting a new precedent - the growth of China's military influence around the world, especially in Africa (Chowdhury, 2021).

The role of culture in China's fourth "grand strategy," which encompasses political, economic, and military forces, has already been discussed above. As for ideology (here we can mean culture), China also actively uses "soft power" mechanisms to achieve its own goals. Moreover, one of the most important "tools" of China's "soft power" is undoubtedly culture and education. In 2007, at the 17th National Congress, then-President Hu Jintao of China said, "The 'great rejuvenation' of the Chinese nation will inevitably be accompanied by the flourishing of Chinese culture… We must make culture a part of our country's soft power… In the future, we will strengthen the process of cultural exchanges at the international level to deepen the influence of Chinese culture throughout the world." A good example of an attempt to fulfill this statement is the Mwalimu Nyerere Memorial Academy in Tanzania, which was built with full Chinese funding. In July 2018, the Chinese government invested $45 million in this project, which was intended to help nurture and train emerging leaders in the FLMSA countries. The Former Liberation Movements of Southern Africa (FLMSA) includes the governments of six southern African countries: South Africa, Zimbabwe, Tanzania, Mozambique, Namibia, and Angola. According to the author, this initiative and many other examples below demonstrate China's growing ability to achieve its strategic goals through collaboration and leverage (Nantulya, 2018). The academy, in conjunction with China's Confucius Institute project, offers students the opportunity to study and work in China through Chinese language courses and exchange programs. The Confucius Institute has also become a symbol of China's soft power. The institute is spread across the African continent and has about 50 branches there. In addition to the institute's projects, China's official language, Mandarin, is gaining ground in Africa, increasingly appearing in South African school curricula (Harper, 2019). As of 2015, China hosts up to 50,000 African students in exchange programs. According to the UNESCO Institute for Statistics, China surpassed the US and UK in this indicator back in 2014 (The Conversation, 2017).

CONCLUSION

As a relatively new and responsible power on the global political stage, the People's Republic of China is the focus of constant international attention. Rapid economic growth and unprecedented progress make it clear that the Asian giant has far-reaching plans to expand its influence. These plans are best expressed in China's "grand strategy", which is in its fourth phase of "rejuvenation". At this stage of implementing the goals of the fourth "grand strategy", China is increasingly less inclined to resort to hard and aggressive policies - this Asian giant prefers to act with "soft power", which is best demonstrated on the African continent. China's relations with African states are indeed an excellent example of "soft power" in action. In this article, we tried to analyze Sino-African relations in the context of China's "grand strategy", examining what drives the Asian giant's interest in the African continent and what "soft power" methods it uses to achieve its goals. To summarize, the answer to this question consists of several aspects: firstly, China is attracted to Africa by its vast but untapped resources - be it minerals and energy, or young and cheap labor; In addition, African states represent a platform for China to expand and restructure its ever-growing economy; Ultimately, the success of Sino-African relations represents an opportunity for China to expand its political influence, as well as a chance to enhance its prestige in the international arena. To achieve these goals, China actively uses soft power methods, which include: trade facilitation, investment promotion, low-interest/interest-free loans, infrastructure project financing, diplomatic and personal ties, promotion of Chinese culture, and much more. Ultimately, it all comes down to one thing - China's final, fourth grand strategy. To borrow the words of the country's current ruler, the latter refers to the "Chinese dream of national rejuvenation", in which, as it seems, the African continent with all its potential occupies a huge place.

REFERENCES

Alden, C., & Christina, A. (2009). *China and Africa's Natural Resources: The Challenges and Implications for Development and Governance*. South African Institute of International Affairs.

Araya, D. (2019, January 14). China's Grand Strategy. In The Forbes. Retrieved from https://www.forbes.com/sites/danielaraya/2019/01/14/chinas-grand-strategy/?sh=7586dc581f18

Biswas, A. K., & Tortajada, C. (2018, February 23). China's soft power is on the rise. In China Daily. Retrieved from https://www.chinadaily.com.cn/a/201802/23/WS5a8f59a9a3106e7dcc13d7b8.html

CaspianReport. (2018, August 1). Review: On Grand Strategy by John Lewis Gaddis. [Video]. Youtube. Retrieved: 28.07.2021, https://www.youtube.com/watch?v=OpGwi2Z_wL0

Chaudhury, D. R. (2021). Djibouti & Zambia: Victims of Chinese Grand Strategy in Africa. In The Economic Times. Retrieved July 31, 2021, from https://economictimes.indiatimes.com/news/international/world-news/djibouti-zambia-victims-ofchinese-grand-strategy-in-africa/articleshow/82032763.cms?from=mdr

China Power Team. (2016) "Is China's Soft Power Strategy Working?" China Power. 19.07.2021. https://chinapower.csis.org/is-chinas-soft-power-strategy-working

Chinese economy to overtake US 'by 2028' due to Covid. (2020). BBC News. July 31, 2021, https://www.bbc.com/news/world-asia-china-55454146

Cooke, J. (2019). "China's Soft Power in Africa". 21.07.2021 https://csis-websiteprod.s3.amazonaws.com/s3fspublic/legacy_files/files/media/csis/pubs/090310_chinesesoftpower__chap3.pdf

Doshi, R. (2021, August 2). The long game: China's grand strategy to displace American order. In Brookings. Retrieved from https://www.brookings.edu/essay/the-long-game-chinas-grand-strategy-todisplace-american-order/

Faria, J. (2021, March 22). Value of Chinese exports to Africa from 2000 to 2019. Statista. July 31, 2021. https://www.statista.com/statistics/1222683/value-of-chinese-exports-to-africa/

Harper, T. (2019). "Chinese Soft Power in Africa: Is It Soft Power". China-US Focus. 23.07.2021 https://www.chinausfocus.com/society-culture/chinese-cultural-soft-power-in-africa-is-it-really-softpower--

Kamal, R., & Haroon, O. (2019). “China in Africa”. 22.07.2021 https://www.researchgate.net/publication/333836728_China_in_Africa

Kudayarov, U. 2022. Grand Strategy of China. Retrieved from: https://www.vestnik.mgimo.ru/jour/article/view/3281/2488

Layton, P. (2018). Grand Strategy. July 28, 2021, https://www.researchgate.net/publication/326249412_Grand_Strategy

Liang, W. (2012). China's Soft Power in Africa: Is Economic Power Sufficient? Asian Perspective. July 29, 2021 https://www.jstor.org/stable/42704810

Martinez, R. (2015). Chinese Soft power, Africa, and the United Nations General Assembly. Las Vegas: University of Nevada. July 31, 2021. https://digitalscholarship.unlv.edu/cgi/viewcontent.cgi?article=3491&context=thesesdissertations

Nantulya, P. (2018). “Grand Strategy and China’s Soft Power in Africa”. Africa Center For Strategic Studies. 20.07.2021 https://africacenter.org/spotlight/grand-strategy-and-chinas-soft-power-push-inafrica/

Nye, J. (2017). “Soft power: the origins and political progress of a concept”. Palgrave Communications. 22.07.2021

Olewe, D. (2021). Why did African countries back China on human rights? In BBC News. July 31, 2021, https://www.bbc.com/news/world-africa-56717986

Pairault, T. (2021, August 11). China’s Presence in Africa Is at Heart Political. In The Diplomat. Retrieved from https://thediplomat.com/2021/08/chinas-presence-in-africa-is-at-heart-political/

Productions, W. (2018). “How Africa is Becoming China’s China”. [Video]. https://www.youtube.com/watch?v=zQV_DKQkT8o 21.06.2021

Ronning, H. (2014). How much “Soft Power” does China have in Africa? Beijing, China: Chr. Michelsen Institute. July 31, 2021, https://www.cmi.no/file/2916-.pdf

Scobbel, A. (2020). China's Grand Strategy: Trends, Trajectories and Long-Term Competition. Santa Monica, CA: Rand Corporation. July 31, 2021, https://www.rand.org/content/dam/rand/pubs/research_reports/RR2700/RR2798/RAND_RR2798.pdf

Statista (2019). “Median Age of the Population in China From 1950 to 2100”. 30.07.2021 https://www.statista.com/statistics/232265/mean-age-of-the-chinese-population/

Stebbins, S. (2019). "These 15 Countries, as Home to the Largest Reserves, Control the World's Oil". USA Today. 30.07.2021 https://www.usatoday.com/story/money/2019/05/22/largest-oil-reserves-inworld-15-countries-that-control-the-worlds-oil/39497945/

Sun, Y. (2014, February 7). China's Aid to Africa: Monster or Messiah? In Brookings. Retrieved from https://www.brookings.edu/opinions/chinas-aid-to-africa-monster-or-messiah/

The Conversation. (2017). "Why African Students Are Choosing China". U.S News and World Report. 19.07.2021 https://www.usnews.com/news/best-countries/articles/2017-06-29/china-second-mostpopular-country-for-african-students

The World Bank. (2019). Foreign direct investment, net inflows - Sub-Saharan Africa. July 31, 2021 https://data.worldbank.org/indicator/BX.KLT.DINV.CD.WD?end=2019&locations=ZG&start=2000 (Appendix #2)

The World Bank. (2020). "GDP Growth (Annual %) – China". 22.07.2021 https://data.worldbank.org/indicator/NY.GDP.MKTP.KD.ZG?locations=CN

The World Factbook. (2021) "China". 23.07.2021 https://www.cia.gov/the-worldfactbook/countries/china/#economy%20-

Thrall, L. (2015). *China's Expanding African Relations Implications for U.S. National Security*. RAND Corporation., Retrieved from https://www.rand.org/pubs/research_reports/RR905.html

Toft, P. (2005). John J. Mearsheimer: An offensive realist between geopolitics and power. Journal of International Relations and Development. July 31, 2021. https://www.researchgate.net/publication/263323588_John_J_Mearsheimer_An_offensive_realist_betw een_geopolitics_and_power?enrichId=rgreq-d9c4c57fdac970d-42f93072b15423ffbXXX&enrichSource=Y292ZXJQYWdlOz

Tubei, G. (2018). "10 Massive Projects the Chinese are Funding in Africa". Business Insider South Africa. 22.07.2021 https://www.businessinsider.co.za/here-are-150-million-rand-projects-in-africa-funded-bychina-2018-9

UN Environment Program. (2021)." Our Work in Africa". 27.07.2021 https://www.unep.org/regions/africa/our-work-africa

Worldometer (2016). "Oil Consumption by Country". 24.07.2021 https://www.worldometers.info/oil/oil-consumption-by-country/

Yu, Z. S. (2021). "Why Substantial Chinese FDI is Flowing into Africa". The London School of Economics and Political Science.

Zandzava, N., & Gagnidze, L. 2021. China's "Grand Strategy": Interests in Africa. Tbilisi State University. Retrieved from: https://sjss.tsu.ge/img/zandzava%20 gagnidze.pdf

Chapter 16
China's Global South Engagement:
Balancing Soft Power and Strategic Influence

Mohamad Mokdad
https://orcid.org/0009-0002-9188-5272
Zaragoza University, Lebanon

Mohamad Zreik
https://orcid.org/0000-0002-6812-6529
Sun Yat-sen University, China

ABSTRACT

China's engagement with the Global South has emerged as a cornerstone of its foreign policy, reflecting a nuanced interplay between soft power and strategic influence. Through initiatives like the Belt and Road Initiative (BRI), foreign direct investments, and cultural diplomacy, China has positioned itself as a pivotal partner for developing nations in Asia, Africa, and Latin America. This chapter critically examines how China balances its economic, political, and cultural tools to advance its interests while promoting a narrative of mutual benefit. By offering a balanced critique of China's approach, this chapter contributes to a deeper understanding of the multifaceted and evolving nature of its Global South strategy. It underscores the need for a more inclusive and equitable partnership that aligns with the sustainable development goals and addresses the diverse needs of the Global South.

DOI: 10.4018/979-8-3373-0938-5.ch016

INTRODUCTION

China's engagement with the Global South has emerged as one of the defining dynamics of international relations in the 21st century. By fostering extensive economic, cultural, and diplomatic partnerships, China has significantly bolstered its influence across Asia, Africa, and Latin America. Central to this strategy is the Belt and Road Initiative (BRI), a multi-trillion-dollar infrastructure development project aimed at enhancing global connectivity and trade (Blanchard, 2018). Through this initiative and other collaborative efforts, China has positioned itself as an alternative to traditional Western-dominated development frameworks, such as those of the International Monetary Fund (IMF) and the World Bank (Cai, 2017). This strategic pivot has not only reshaped the economic landscapes of participating countries but has also introduced new dimensions to global power structures.

The appeal of China's engagement lies in its distinctive approach, emphasizing principles of mutual benefit, non-interference in domestic affairs, and respect for national sovereignty (Shambaugh, 2015). This contrasts sharply with the conditional aid and development programs often associated with Western institutions, which are frequently criticized for imposing structural adjustments that undermine local autonomy. By presenting itself as a partner rather than a patron, China has cultivated a narrative of solidarity with the Global South, drawing on historical ties and shared experiences of colonialism and underdevelopment (Chen et al., 2019). Despite its emphasis on soft power, China's engagement with the Global South is not devoid of strategic considerations. Its investments in critical infrastructure, natural resources, and emerging markets are designed to secure long-term economic and geopolitical advantages (Jones & Zeng, 2019). For instance, the development of ports and logistics hubs under the BRI serves both commercial and strategic purposes, facilitating trade while expanding China's maritime reach. Similarly, partnerships in energy and technology sectors provide China with access to vital resources and emerging technologies, ensuring its competitiveness in the global economy (Zhang, 2018).

The duality of China's approach combining soft power initiatives with strategic imperatives has sparked debates about its implications for the Global South. On one hand, Chinese investments have been lauded for addressing critical infrastructure gaps, creating jobs, and fostering economic growth in developing countries (Blanchard, 2018). On the other hand, concerns have been raised about the potential risks of dependency, debt sustainability, and environmental degradation (Cai, 2017). Critics argue that while China's projects promise long-term benefits, they often come with hidden costs, including loss of local control over key assets and increased vulnerability to external pressures (Shambaugh, 2015). The significance of China's engagement extends beyond its economic impact. By actively participating in regional and global governance, China is reshaping the norms and institutions that underpin the international order (Jones & Zeng, 2019). Its involvement in multilateral organizations, such as the Asian Infrastructure Investment Bank (AIIB), demonstrates a commitment to providing alternative platforms for cooperation and development. At the same time, China's assertive diplomacy and military presence in contested regions, such as the South China Sea, reflect a broader ambition to assert its influence on the global stage (Zhang, 2018).

This chapter aims to explore the multifaceted nature of China's engagement with the Global South, focusing on the interplay between its soft power initiatives and strategic ambitions. It seeks to address the following objectives:

1. To trace the historical evolution of China's engagement with the Global South, from its ideological alliances during the Cold War to its contemporary emphasis on economic and cultural partnerships.
2. To identify and examine the key mechanisms of China's engagement, including cultural diplomacy, infrastructure development, and trade agreements.
3. To assess the implications of China's approach for the Global South, highlighting both opportunities and challenges for developing nations.
4. To analyze the criticisms and challenges China faces in maintaining a balance between soft power and strategic influence, including geopolitical competition and domestic constraints.
5. To explore the future trajectory of China's Global South strategy, considering the evolving global landscape and the potential for more inclusive and equitable partnerships.

The methodology employed in this analysis integrates case studies, thematic analysis, and a review of scholarly literature. Case studies from Africa and Southeast Asia provide concrete examples of how China's strategies manifest in different regional contexts. For instance, the Standard Gauge Railway in Kenya and the economic zones in Cambodia illustrate the tangible outcomes and controversies surrounding Chinese investments (Blanchard, 2018; Chen et al., 2019). Thematic analysis identifies recurring patterns in China's engagement, such as its emphasis on infrastructure development and cultural diplomacy. This approach is complemented by a critical review of academic and policy literature, ensuring a balanced perspective that acknowledges both achievements and limitations. By examining these dimensions, the chapter contributes to a deeper understanding of the dynamics of China's engagement with the Global South. It argues that while China's approach offers valuable lessons for fostering international cooperation, it also underscores the complexities of balancing soft power with strategic influence in a rapidly changing global environment. Ultimately, the chapter calls for a more nuanced and inclusive framework for global engagement, one that aligns with the aspirations and needs of the Global South while addressing the challenges of sustainable development and equitable growth.

HISTORICAL CONTEXT OF CHINA'S ENGAGEMENT WITH THE GLOBAL SOUTH

China's engagement with the Global South has its roots in the mid-20th century, particularly during the Cold War, when it sought to position itself as a leader among developing nations. In the aftermath of its revolution in 1949, the People's Republic of China (PRC) emerged as a staunch advocate for anti-imperialism and decolonization, aligning itself with countries in Asia, Africa, and Latin America that were seeking independence from colonial rule. This solidarity was evident in China's active participation in the Non-Aligned Movement (NAM), a coalition of states that sought to remain independent from the polarizing influence of the United States and the Soviet Union (Chen, 2020). A key moment in China's early engagement with the Global South was its involvement in the Bandung Conference of 1955. Held in Indonesia, this landmark gathering brought together leaders from 29 Asian and African nations to promote economic and cultural cooperation, as well as to oppose colonialism and neocolonialism. Premier Zhou Enlai's participation in the conference underscored China's commitment to fostering solidarity with other developing countries. Zhou's emphasis on mutual respect for sovereignty, territorial integrity, and non-interference laid the foundation for what would become the Five Principles of Peaceful Coexistence, a cornerstone of China's foreign policy (Miller, 2019).

China's support for revolutionary movements further demonstrated its solidarity with the Global South during this period. By providing financial aid, military training, and ideological guidance to liberation movements in Africa and Latin America, China sought to strengthen its ideological influence and counter Western and Soviet narratives. However, its approach was not without challenges. The Sino-Soviet split in the 1960s created divisions within the communist bloc, complicating China's ability to present a unified front with the Global South (Zhang, 2018).

Post-Cold War Shift

The end of the Cold War marked a significant shift in China's approach to the Global South. As the bipolar world order dissolved, China reoriented its foreign policy to prioritize economic development and integration into the global economy.

The transformation of China's engagement with the Global South cannot be fully understood without considering the significant domestic political changes that began before the end of the Cold War. Starting in the late 1970s, under the leadership of Deng Xiaoping, China initiated a sweeping program of economic reform and opening up (gaige kaifang), marking a decisive shift away from Maoist ideological struggle toward economic modernization and international integration (Shirk, 2007). The "Four Modernizations" policy, which focused on agriculture, industry, national defense, and science and technology, became the cornerstone of China's domestic and foreign policy transformation. This internal reorientation prioritized economic growth, attracting foreign investment, and engaging in global trade, setting the stage for China's pivot toward pragmatic economic partnerships with the Global South.

These domestic reforms preceded the dissolution of the bipolar world order and were essential in redefining China's foreign policy priorities. When the Cold War ended in the late 1980s and early 1990s, China was already well-positioned to expand its influence through economic means rather than ideological solidarity. The global shift away from ideological confrontation provided additional momentum for China to deepen its engagement with the Global South, emphasizing development cooperation, trade, and infrastructure investment. China's approach evolved from revolutionary support to a pragmatic focus on mutual economic benefit, reflecting the interplay between domestic transformations and external geopolitical changes (Bräutigam, 2011; Shambaugh, 2015).

This transformation was driven by the reforms initiated under Deng Xiaoping in the late 1970s, which emphasized market liberalization and opening up to foreign investment (Shambaugh, 2015). These changes not only spurred rapid domestic economic growth but also reshaped China's relationships with developing countries. During the 1990s, China's focus shifted from ideological solidarity to pragmatic economic partnerships. Recognizing the potential of the Global South as both a source of raw materials and a market for its goods, China began to invest heavily in infrastructure projects, trade agreements, and development initiatives. The establishment of the Forum on China-Africa Cooperation (FOCAC) in 2000 exemplified this new approach, providing a platform for dialogue and collaboration between China and African nations. Through FOCAC, China has pledged billions of dollars in loans and aid, focusing on areas such as transportation, energy, and telecommunications (Carmody, 2019). China's entry into global markets also necessitated a shift in its diplomatic strategy. As a member of the World Trade Organization (WTO) since

2001, China has sought to integrate itself into the international economic system while maintaining its emphasis on South-South cooperation. This dual strategy has enabled China to position itself as a bridge between developed and developing nations, advocating for the interests of the Global South in multilateral forums (Blanchard, 2018). The transition from ideological ties to economic partnerships has not diminished China's commitment to fostering solidarity with the Global South. Instead, it has evolved to reflect the changing priorities of both China and its partners. For instance, the Belt and Road Initiative (BRI), launched in 2013, represents a continuation of China's efforts to promote connectivity and development across Asia, Africa, and Latin America. By investing in infrastructure projects such as railways, ports, and energy facilities, the BRI aims to enhance regional integration and create new opportunities for trade and investment. However, it has also faced criticism for contributing to debt dependency and environmental degradation (Cai, 2017).

Historical Context of China's Engagement with the Global South

China's relationship with the Global South has evolved over decades, marked by distinct phases of ideological solidarity, strategic alignment, and economic pragmatism. This historical trajectory has not only shaped China's foreign policy but also profoundly influenced the development paths of many nations in the Global South. Understanding these phases is key to contextualizing China's current role as a global power. In the aftermath of its revolution in 1949, the People's Republic of China (PRC) emerged as a vocal advocate for anti-imperialism and the decolonization of Asia, Africa, and Latin America. This period saw China positioning itself as a leader among newly independent nations, fostering solidarity against the backdrop of Cold War tensions. Beijing's approach was rooted in ideological alignment with countries seeking to escape colonial domination and establish independent governance (Chen, 2020). The Bandung Conference of 1955 stands out as a pivotal moment in China's early engagement with the Global South. Held in Indonesia, the conference brought together leaders from 29 Asian and African countries to promote solidarity, economic cooperation, and opposition to colonialism and neocolonialism. Premier Zhou Enlai represented China at the conference, emphasizing principles that would later become central to its foreign policy: mutual respect for sovereignty, non-aggression, non-interference in internal affairs, equality, and mutual benefit (Miller, 2019). These principles resonated with many Global South nations that were seeking a voice independent of the United States or the Soviet Union.

During the Cold War, China also provided ideological and material support to liberation movements and revolutionary groups across Africa and Latin America. Beijing supplied financial aid, military training, and ideological guidance, presenting itself as a champion of global proletarian revolution. This was particularly evident in countries like Algeria, Tanzania, and Zambia, where China contributed to infrastructure projects and the training of freedom fighters (Zhang, 2018). However, the Sino-Soviet split in the 1960s complicated China's ambitions, as it competed with the Soviet Union for influence over these movements. Despite its ideological commitments, China's engagement with the Global South during this era was not without challenges. Domestic upheavals, such as the Great Leap Forward and the Cultural Revolution, strained Beijing's ability to maintain consistent foreign policy initiatives. Additionally, its ideological rigidity sometimes clashed with the pragmatic concerns of partner nations, limiting the effectiveness of its solidarity campaigns (Shambaugh, 2015)

Post-Cold War Shift

The end of the Cold War marked a transformative period in China's approach to the Global South. As the bipolar world order dissolved, China shifted its foreign policy focus from ideological solidarity to economic pragmatism. This transition was driven by the domestic reforms initiated under Deng Xiaoping in the late 1970s, which emphasized market liberalization, economic modernization, and integration into the global economy (Cai, 2017). Economic liberalization provided the foundation for China's re-engagement with the Global South, now framed around mutual economic benefit rather than ideological alignment. During the 1990s, China began to identify the Global South as a critical source of raw materials and a burgeoning market for its exports. This pragmatic shift was reflected in the establishment of institutions like the Forum on China-Africa Cooperation (FOCAC) in 2000, which institutionalized Beijing's partnerships with African nations and facilitated extensive trade and investment initiatives (Carmody, 2019). China's entry into the World Trade Organization (WTO) in 2001 further accelerated its integration into the global economy. As a member of the WTO, China expanded its trade relationships with developing countries, offering them access to Chinese goods, services, and investment. This period also saw the rise of major infrastructure projects, supported by Chinese loans and executed by Chinese companies. These initiatives, such as the Standard Gauge Railway in Kenya and hydropower projects in Southeast Asia, symbolized Beijing's commitment to fostering development in the Global South (Blanchard, 2018). The transition from ideological ties to economic partnerships also reflected a broader shift in China's foreign policy narrative. While it continued to emphasize principles of non-interference and mutual respect, Beijing increasingly highlighted its role as a partner in development. This narrative was particularly evident in the Belt and Road Initiative (BRI), launched in 2013. Through the BRI, China sought to create new trade routes and economic corridors connecting Asia, Africa, and

Latin America. By investing in critical infrastructure, the BRI aimed to enhance regional connectivity, stimulate economic growth, and create mutually beneficial opportunities for participating countries (Zhang, 2018).

However, China's economic engagement has not been without criticism. Concerns about debt dependency have emerged in several countries, with critics accusing Beijing of engaging in "debt-trap diplomacy" to extract strategic concessions. Environmental and social sustainability issues have also been raised, particularly in relation to large-scale infrastructure projects that disrupt local ecosystems and communities (Cai, 2017). Despite these challenges, China has continued to deepen its ties with the Global South, leveraging its economic resources to strengthen its global influence.

Mechanisms of Soft Power

China's increasing global influence is underpinned by its adept use of soft power mechanisms, which play a vital role in shaping its relationships with the Global South. Through cultural diplomacy, educational initiatives, and development assistance, China seeks to foster goodwill, strengthen partnerships, and promote its image as a responsible global actor. This section examines these mechanisms in detail, highlighting their scope, impact, and implications for China's engagement with the Global South.

Cultural Diplomacy

Cultural diplomacy is one of the most visible manifestations of China's soft power strategy. By promoting its culture, values, and traditions, China aims to create a favorable image among foreign populations, fostering trust and cooperation. Confucius Institutes (CIs) have become a cornerstone of China's cultural diplomacy. Established under the auspices of the Chinese government, these institutions promote Chinese language and culture worldwide, particularly in countries across the Global South. By 2022, over 500 CIs had been established globally, with a significant number in Africa, Latin America, and Southeast Asia (Paradise, 2009). These institutes offer language classes, cultural programs, and exchange opportunities, which help bridge cultural gaps and foster mutual understanding. However, some critics argue that CIs are tools of propaganda, citing concerns about their influence on academic freedom and their promotion of a state-sanctioned version of Chinese culture (Leung & Du Cros, 2014). In addition to CIs, China has actively engaged in cultural exchanges, including arts performances, film festivals, and exhibitions. Events such as the annual China-Africa Cultural Cooperation Forum provide platforms for cultural interaction, strengthening people-to-people ties (Kurlantzick, 2007). Such initiatives not only promote Chinese culture but also emphasize shared values and histories, particularly in relation to anti-colonial struggles.

China's media presence in the Global South has grown substantially over the past two decades. State-run outlets such as China Global Television Network (CGTN) and Xinhua News Agency have expanded their operations, providing news and programming tailored to regional audiences (Nye, 2017). These media platforms promote Chinese perspectives on global issues, countering Western narratives and showcasing China's developmental achievements. Films, television dramas, and other cultural exports have also been employed to promote Chinese culture. For example, Chinese historical dramas and martial arts films have gained popularity in Africa and Latin America, helping to build a positive image of China (Thussu, 2016). This media strategy complements China's broader efforts to cultivate soft power by highlighting its cultural heritage and modern successes.

Educational Initiatives

Education is another critical avenue through which China exercises soft power. By providing scholarships, building academic partnerships, and offering training programs, China positions itself as a leader in knowledge sharing and capacity building. China has become a top destination for students from the Global South. Each year, thousands of students receive scholarships from the Chinese government to pursue higher education in Chinese universities. In 2021 alone, over 50,000 students from Africa were studying in China, making it one of the most popular destinations for African students (Li et al., 2020). These scholarships not only provide access to quality education but also expose students to Chinese language and culture, creating lasting connections. University partnerships have also flourished, with Chinese institutions collaborating with counterparts in the Global South on research, faculty exchanges, and joint programs. For instance, partnerships between Chinese and African universities have focused on agriculture, engineering, and public health, addressing critical developmental needs in the region (King, 2013). These collaborations reinforce China's image as a partner in development while fostering academic networks that extend its influence. China's training programs for government officials and professionals are another important component of its educational initiatives. These programs, often conducted in China, provide training in areas such as public administration, urban planning, and governance. For example, the China Executive Leadership Academy in Pudong (CELAP) regularly hosts workshops for officials from Africa and Asia, sharing China's development experiences and governance models (Bräutigam, 2011). These training programs serve multiple purposes. They equip participants with practical skills and knowledge, promote China's governance practices, and strengthen bilateral ties. Additionally, they help cultivate a network of alumni who are sympathetic to Chinese policies and perspectives, furthering Beijing's soft power goals (King, 2013).

Development Assistance

China's development assistance has emerged as a key mechanism for building influence and fostering goodwill in the Global South. By providing grants, technical cooperation, and humanitarian aid, China demonstrates its commitment to addressing global challenges. China's provision of grant aid and technical assistance is a central pillar of its development strategy. Unlike traditional Western donors, China emphasizes infrastructure development, funding projects such as roads, bridges, and energy facilities. These initiatives are often delivered as part of the Belt and Road Initiative (BRI), which aims to enhance connectivity and economic integration across the Global South (Zhang, 2018). For example, China has financed major infrastructure projects in Kenya, Ethiopia, and Cambodia, contributing to economic growth and improved living standards (Carmody, 2019). Technical cooperation programs, which involve the transfer of skills and technology, are another important component of China's development assistance. For instance, Chinese agricultural experts have worked with farmers in Africa to improve crop yields and food security, showcasing China's expertise in addressing pressing developmental challenges (Bräutigam, 2011).

China's public health diplomacy has gained prominence, particularly during global crises such as the COVID-19 pandemic. Beijing provided medical supplies, vaccines, and technical support to numerous countries in the Global South, reinforcing its image as a responsible global actor (Huang, 2020). The establishment of health facilities and medical training programs further underscores China's commitment to improving health outcomes in developing nations. Humanitarian efforts have also been a key aspect of China's soft power strategy. From disaster relief to poverty alleviation, China has provided assistance to countries facing crises. For example, following the 2010 earthquake in Haiti, China sent rescue teams and medical supplies, demonstrating solidarity with the affected population (Nye, 2017).

Economic Engagement

Economic engagement remains the cornerstone of China's strategic influence in the Global South, with the Belt and Road Initiative (BRI) at its center. The BRI is China's flagship economic initiative aimed at revitalizing ancient trade routes by creating modern infrastructure networks across Asia, Africa, and Latin America. With projects such as railways, ports, and energy facilities, the BRI underscores China's commitment to fostering connectivity and trade in the Global South. For instance, the construction of Kenya's Standard Gauge Railway and Sri Lanka's Hambantota Port illustrates China's willingness to invest heavily in infrastructure development (Hurley et al., 2018). These projects, however, have sparked significant debate. Supporters argue that they address critical infrastructure gaps, stimulate local economies, and create jobs. Critics, on the other hand, highlight issues such as debt dependency, where countries face difficulties in repaying Chinese loans, and concerns about the lack of transparency in project implementation (Brautigam, 2020). Despite these challenges, the BRI has undoubtedly positioned China as a key economic partner in the Global South. Beyond the BRI, China has signed numerous trade agreements to enhance its economic footprint. For example, free trade agreements with nations like Chile and ASEAN have bolstered bilateral trade volumes, offering preferential market access to Chinese goods and services (Ferdinand, 2016). Furthermore, China's investments in Special Economic Zones (SEZs) in Africa have created hubs for manufacturing and export, fostering industrialization in host countries. Infrastructure development remains a central component of China's economic engagement strategy. By financing and constructing roads, bridges, and energy plants, China facilitates trade and economic activity in the Global South. This aligns with its long-term goal of creating supply chains that integrate developing nations into the global economy, with China as a central player (Zeng, 2021).

Geopolitical Ambitions

China's strategic influence extends beyond economics, encompassing efforts to expand its role in global governance and foster military and security ties. China has made significant strides in reshaping global governance structures to reflect its interests and those of the Global South. Within the United Nations (UN), China has increased its financial contributions and leadership roles, advocating for reforms that enhance the representation of developing countries (Chen et al., 2021). For instance, China's emphasis on the concept of a "Community of Shared Future for Mankind" reflects its push for a more inclusive and equitable global order. Similarly, China's participation in the World Trade Organization (WTO) highlights its commitment to advancing trade liberalization while addressing the concerns of developing nations. By championing the rights of the Global South within these institutions, China aims to position itself as a voice for emerging economies, challenging the dominance of Western powers (Fung & Garcia-Herrero, 2019). China's military engagements in the Global South are another facet of its strategic influence. Through arms sales, joint military exercises, and security training programs, China has strengthened its defense ties with countries in Africa, Asia, and Latin America. For example, China has been a leading supplier of military equipment to nations like Pakistan and Nigeria, enhancing their defense capabilities while fostering dependence on Chinese technology (Wezeman et al., 2018). China's participation in peacekeeping missions under the UN further underscores its commitment to global security. As the largest contributor of troops among the permanent members of the UN Security Council, China's efforts in Africa and the Middle East reflect its ambition to be a stabilizing force in the Global South (Gill & Huang, 2020).

Resource Diplomacy

China's growing demand for natural resources and energy has driven its engagement with resource-rich countries in the Global South, highlighting the strategic importance of resource diplomacy. China's investments in the natural resource sectors of Africa and Latin America are critical to its resource security strategy. For instance, China has heavily invested in oil fields in Angola, copper mines in Zambia, and lithium projects in Bolivia, securing supplies essential for its industrial and technological growth (Zhang et al., 2021). These investments are often tied to infrastructure projects, creating synergies between resource extraction and development. China's energy diplomacy has also been significant, particularly in fostering partnerships in renewable energy. For example, Chinese companies have collaborated with African governments to develop solar and wind power projects, showcasing China's commitment to sustainable energy solutions while reducing its reliance on traditional fossil fuels (Xu et al., 2022). While resource diplomacy has created economic opportunities in the Global South, it has also raised concerns about its long-term impact on local communities and the environment. Critics argue that resource extraction often leads to environmental degradation, displacement of communities, and unequal distribution of benefits. To address these concerns, China has increasingly emphasized corporate social responsibility (CSR) in its overseas investments, encouraging Chinese firms to adopt sustainable practices and contribute to local development (Tan-Mullins et al., 2020).

Economic Opportunities

China's involvement in the Global South has brought tangible economic benefits, particularly in trade, infrastructure development, employment, technology transfer, and industrialization. China has become a vital trade partner for many Global South nations, with bilateral trade volumes increasing significantly over the past two decades. In Africa alone, China's trade exceeded $200 billion in 2022, making it the continent's largest trading partner (Brautigam & Tang, 2022). This robust trade growth provides access to Chinese markets for raw materials and agricultural products, boosting exports from developing nations. Infrastructure development is another key area of economic benefit. Under the Belt and Road Initiative (BRI), China has funded and constructed critical infrastructure projects, including railways, ports, and power plants, across Asia, Africa, and Latin America. For instance, the Addis Ababa-Djibouti Railway and the Mombasa-Nairobi Standard Gauge Railway have reduced transportation costs, facilitated trade, and created employment opportunities in Ethiopia and Kenya (Carmody & Owusu, 2021).

Additionally, Chinese investments have generated employment in host countries. Many infrastructure projects employ local workers, providing job opportunities in construction, logistics, and maintenance. However, concerns persist about the ratio of local versus Chinese labor in these projects, with some accusing China of favoring its workers over local hires (Lee, 2017). China's engagement has also facilitated technology transfer and industrialization in the Global South. Through joint ventures, Chinese firms share knowledge and expertise in sectors such as manufacturing, telecommunications, and renewable energy. For example, Huawei and ZTE have established technology hubs in Africa, providing training and building local capacity in the telecommunications sector (Chen, 2020). Industrialization has been further supported by the establishment of Special Economic Zones (SEZs) in countries like Ethiopia and Zambia. These zones, developed with Chinese assistance, have attracted foreign investment, boosted manufacturing output, and enhanced export capacities. In Ethiopia's Hawassa Industrial Park, Chinese firms have played a pivotal role in developing the textile industry, creating jobs and fostering skills development (Gebre-Egziabher, 2019).

Challenges and Criticisms

Despite these economic opportunities, China's engagement with the Global South faces significant criticism, particularly regarding debt dependency and sustainability concerns. One of the most contentious issues surrounding China's engagement is the accusation of "debt-trap diplomacy." Critics argue that China deliberately extends loans to countries with limited repayment capacity, gaining leverage over strategic assets when they default. Examples often cited include Sri Lanka's Hambantota Port, which was leased to a Chinese company after the government struggled to service its debt (Hurley et al., 2018). While China refutes these claims, emphasizing that its loans are aimed at fostering development, the high debt levels in some countries raise legitimate concerns. For instance, African nations collectively owe over $145 billion to China, prompting fears of financial instability and loss of sovereignty (Brautigam & Tang, 2022). To address these concerns, Beijing has initiated debt restructuring and forgiveness programs for some of its partners, but skepticism remains. Environmental and social sustainability issues also mar China's initiatives in the Global South. Large-scale infrastructure projects have been criticized for their environmental impact, including deforestation, water pollution, and disruption of ecosystems. For example, the construction of the Merowe Dam in Sudan, financed by Chinese loans, led to the displacement of thousands of people and significant ecological damage (Tilt, 2019). Socially, Chinese investments have been accused of neglecting local communities. Critics argue that some projects prioritize profits over social welfare, exacerbating inequalities and marginalizing vulnerable populations. To mitigate these issues, calls for greater transparency, community involvement, and adherence to international environmental and social standards have grown louder (Tan-Mullins et al., 2020).

Shifts in Power Dynamics

China's rise as a key partner for the Global South has profound implications for global power dynamics, challenging the dominance of traditional powers like the United States and the European Union.

China's growing influence in the Global South has created a new axis of power that competes with Western-led models of development and governance. By providing alternative financing through mechanisms like the Asian Infrastructure Investment Bank (AIIB) and the Silk Road Fund, China offers a counterbalance to institutions such as the World Bank and the International Monetary Fund (Ferdinand, 2016). This shift reduces the dependence of Global South nations on Western financial systems, allowing them to diversify their partnerships. Politically, China's rise challenges Western narratives of democracy and human rights by promoting a model of development that prioritizes economic growth and political stability. This approach resonates with many Global South governments, particularly those seeking alternatives to Western conditional aid (Kynge et al., 2021). Consequently, China's influence has grown in multilateral forums, where it advocates for reforms to increase the representation of developing nations. Security dynamics have also shifted, with China expanding its military footprint in the Global South. The establishment of a military base in Djibouti and increased arms sales to African nations underscore Beijing's ambition to project power and secure its interests in key regions (Gill & Huang, 2020). These developments have heightened geopolitical competition, particularly with the United States, which views China's growing influence as a strategic threat.

Case Studies

China's engagement with the Global South can be best understood through detailed case studies, highlighting the successes and challenges of its strategic involvement. Africa and Southeast Asia are two regions where China's influence is particularly pronounced, showcasing its approach to infrastructure development, economic partnerships, and geopolitical dynamics.

Africa

China's role in Africa underscores its focus on infrastructure, trade, and development. Two key partnerships, China-Kenya and China-Ethiopia, exemplify the scale and scope of this engagement. Kenya is a cornerstone of China's Belt and Road Initiative (BRI) in Africa. The flagship project of this partnership is the Standard Gauge Railway (SGR), linking Mombasa to Nairobi. The SGR, completed in 2017 at a cost of approximately $3.2 billion, was financed by Chinese loans and constructed by Chinese firms (Mwase & Yang, 2020). This project aimed to reduce transportation costs, enhance trade, and spur regional integration. While the SGR has improved freight and passenger transport, its economic impact has been mixed. Critics argue that the project has contributed to Kenya's rising debt levels, with repayment obligations straining the national budget. Moreover, the railway's operational revenues have struggled to cover its maintenance costs, raising concerns about its long-term sustainability (Bräutigam & Kidane, 2021). However, proponents highlight the potential for the SGR to stimulate economic growth by linking key economic hubs and facilitating trade within the East African Community. Ethiopia represents another significant case of Chinese involvement in Africa, with infrastructure development forming the backbone of the relationship. The Addis Ababa-Djibouti Railway, completed in 2016, is a landmark project that connects Ethiopia to the Port of Djibouti. Financed through Chinese loans and constructed by Chinese firms, the railway has reduced transportation time for goods, boosting Ethiopia's export competitiveness (Gebre-Egziabher, 2020).

Beyond infrastructure, China has been instrumental in developing Ethiopia's industrial sector. The Hawassa Industrial Park, a Chinese-backed initiative, has become a hub for textile manufacturing, creating thousands of jobs and fostering skills transfer (Tang, 2021). However, Ethiopia's dependency on Chinese financing has raised concerns about debt sustainability, with critics pointing to the risks of over-reliance on a single partner for development projects.

Southeast Asia

In Southeast Asia, China's engagement is shaped by a combination of economic cooperation and geopolitical tensions. The South China Sea disputes and the case of Cambodia illustrate the complexities of China's influence in the region. China's territorial claims in the South China Sea have been a source of tension with Southeast Asian nations, including the Philippines, Vietnam, and Malaysia. These disputes have escalated due to China's construction of artificial islands and militarization of the region, which have drawn international criticism and strained relations with neighboring countries (Hayton, 2020). Despite these tensions, economic cooperation between China and Southeast Asia remains robust. Through the BRI, China has invested heavily in infrastructure projects, such as ports and highways, across the region. For example, in Malaysia, the East Coast Rail Link (ECRL) is a key BRI project aimed at enhancing connectivity between the east and west coasts of the country. While the ECRL has faced delays and renegotiations, it underscores China's commitment to fostering economic ties with Southeast Asia (Lim, 2019). The Association of Southeast Asian Nations (ASEAN) has also benefited from its economic partnership with China, with bilateral trade surpassing $800 billion in 2022. ASEAN has become China's largest trading partner, reflecting the deep economic interdependence between the two regions (Chen et al., 2022). This dual dynamic of geopolitical rivalry and economic cooperation highlights the complexity of China's engagement in Southeast Asia. Cambodia exemplifies a case where China's influence has fostered both economic growth and political dependency. As one of China's closest allies in Southeast Asia, Cambodia has received significant Chinese investments in infrastructure, energy, and real estate. The construction of the Sihanoukville Special Economic Zone (SSEZ) is a prominent example, serving as a hub for manufacturing and export (Ear, 2021). However, Cambodia's reliance on Chinese investments has raised concerns about sovereignty and over-dependence. Critics argue that Chinese projects often prioritize Chinese interests, with limited benefits for local communities. For instance, the influx of Chinese businesses and workers in Sihanoukville has led to rising property prices and social tensions, marginalizing local residents (Tan, 2020). Politically, Cambodia's alignment with China has drawn scrutiny, particularly regarding its stance on the South China Sea disputes. Cambodia has repeatedly blocked ASEAN resolutions critical of China, reinforcing perceptions that its foreign policy is heavily influenced by Beijing. This dependency model illustrates the risks associated with over-reliance on a single partner for economic and political support.

Challenges for China

China's expanding role in the Global South has brought significant benefits to its global influence but also poses numerous challenges. These challenges arise from geopolitical competition, reputational risks, and domestic constraints, each of which threatens to undermine Beijing's ability to maintain and expand its strategic influence.

Geopolitical Competition

China's growing presence in the Global South has heightened tensions with other global powers, particularly the United States, and triggered competition with emerging regional players such as India and Japan. The United States perceives China's influence in the Global South as a strategic threat and has adopted various containment strategies to counter it. Through initiatives like the Blue Dot Network and the Indo-Pacific Economic Framework, Washington has sought to offer alternatives to China's Belt and Road Initiative (BRI), emphasizing transparency, sustainability, and high standards (Grossman, 2020). These measures aim to limit China's dominance in infrastructure financing and development, particularly in regions like Southeast Asia and Africa. Additionally, the US has leveraged its alliances to push back against China's influence. The Quadrilateral Security Dialogue (Quad), comprising the US, Japan, India, and Australia, has emerged as a platform to counter China's assertive policies in the Indo-Pacific. Although primarily focused on security, the Quad's initiatives, such as vaccine diplomacy and infrastructure funding, overlap with China's efforts in the Global South, intensifying the competition (Medeiros, 2021). Beyond the US, China faces competition from regional powers like India and Japan, which are also seeking to expand their influence in the Global South. India's development partnerships, particularly in Africa and the Indian Ocean region, rival China's investments. Programs such as the India-Africa Forum Summit and projects like the development of Chabahar Port in Iran are examples of India's attempts to counterbalance China's presence (Pant & Passi, 2018). Similarly, Japan's Free and Open Indo-Pacific (FOIP) strategy focuses on promoting connectivity and sustainable development. Japan has collaborated with nations in Southeast Asia and Africa, offering infrastructure investments that emphasize local ownership and environmental sustainability, in direct contrast to criticisms of China's BRI projects (Hosoya, 2020). This emerging competition complicates China's efforts to dominate the development landscape in the Global South.

Reputational Risks

China's engagement with the Global South has not been without criticism, leading to reputational challenges that threaten its soft power and strategic goals. Critics often accuse China of engaging in "debt-trap diplomacy," where developing nations are allegedly burdened with unsustainable loans, forcing them to make concessions on key assets. While China disputes these allegations, projects like Sri Lanka's Hambantota Port and Zambia's copper mines have fueled these perceptions, impacting China's image in the Global South (Bräutigam, 2020). Additionally, concerns about labor practices, environmental degradation, and the lack of transparency in Chinese projects further tarnish its reputation. For example, the influx of Chinese workers and businesses in African countries has led to accusations of exploitation and marginalization of local communities (Leung & Shi, 2021). Such criticisms undermine China's narrative of being a development partner focused on mutual benefit. China faces the challenge of aligning its strategic ambitions with the expectations of its partners in the Global South. Developing nations often expect China to deliver on its promises of infrastructure, technology transfer, and job creation without imposing undue costs or compromising their sovereignty. However, instances where China's projects have failed to meet these expectations have led to growing skepticism.

For example, delays in BRI projects due to financial or logistical challenges have eroded trust among partner nations. The high costs of some initiatives, coupled with limited local benefits, have led to questions about the fairness and equity of China's engagement (Hurley et al., 2018). Balancing its strategic goals while maintaining the trust of its partners is an ongoing challenge for Beijing.

Domestic Constraints

China's ability to sustain its influence in the Global South is also constrained by internal challenges, including economic pressures and political dynamics. China's slowing economic growth poses a significant challenge to its global ambitions. The COVID-19 pandemic and ongoing structural issues, such as rising debt and declining productivity, have strained Beijing's financial capacity to fund large-scale overseas projects (Chen et al., 2022). As China prioritizes domestic economic recovery, its ability to sustain investments in the Global South may diminish. Additionally, resource allocation is a growing concern. China's vast infrastructure commitments under the BRI require substantial financial and human resources. Balancing these external commitments with domestic needs, such as addressing income inequality and supporting social welfare programs, places considerable pressure on the Chinese government (He, 2020). China's foreign policy is increasingly shaped by domestic political considerations and public opinion. Nationalist sentiments within China often demand assertive foreign policies, particularly in response to perceived external challenges or criticisms. However, overly aggressive actions can alienate Global South partners, undermining China's soft power. Public skepticism about the benefits of overseas investments is also growing. Critics within China question whether the massive resources allocated to the BRI and other initiatives yield sufficient returns, particularly when domestic needs remain unmet. Managing these political and public pressures while pursuing its global ambitions is a delicate balancing act for Beijing (Wang, 2021).

CONCLUSION

China's engagement with the Global South reflects a complex interplay between soft power and strategic influence. By leveraging cultural diplomacy, educational initiatives, development assistance, and economic partnerships, China has cultivated goodwill while simultaneously advancing its geopolitical and economic interests. Soft power initiatives, such as Confucius Institutes and scholarships, have fostered people-to-people connections and enhanced China's global image (Kurlantzick, 2007). At the same time, strategic investments in infrastructure, trade, and resource diplomacy have allowed China to secure access to critical markets and materials, reinforcing its global influence (Carmody & Owusu, 2021). The impacts on the Global South are multifaceted. China's investments have addressed critical infrastructure gaps, boosted trade, and created employment opportunities, contributing to economic growth in partner nations (Bräutigam, 2020). However, these benefits are accompanied by challenges, including concerns over debt dependency, environmental sustainability, and potential erosion of local sovereignty. On the global stage, China's rise has disrupted traditional power dynamics, challenged the dominance of Western-led institutions and offered an alternative model of development cooperation (Ferdinand, 2016).

Future Outlook

Looking ahead, China's relationship with the Global South will likely continue to evolve, driven by mutual economic interests and the shifting dynamics of global geopolitics.

The future of China's engagement hinges on its ability to foster sustainable partnerships that address the aspirations and needs of the Global South. To achieve this, China must ensure that its investments are transparent, inclusive, and aligned with the developmental priorities of partner nations. For instance, greater emphasis on renewable energy projects and climate-resilient infrastructure could position China as a leader in sustainable development (Tan-Mullins et al., 2020). Additionally, China's efforts to integrate Global South nations into global value chains could create more equitable economic opportunities. By focusing on technology transfer and capacity building, China can help its partners move beyond resource dependence and foster industrialization. For example, expanding partnerships in sectors like renewable energy and digital technology could yield long-term benefits for both sides (Xu et al., 2022). China's engagement strategy must also become more inclusive, ensuring that the voices of local stakeholders are heard and their concerns addressed. Greater involvement of civil society organizations and local communities in the planning and implementation of projects can help mitigate negative social and environmental impacts. Moreover, fostering multilateral partnerships that involve regional organizations, such as the African Union and ASEAN, can enhance the legitimacy and effectiveness of China's initiatives (Gill & Huang, 2020). On the diplomatic front, China must balance its strategic ambitions with its soft power objectives. Avoiding aggressive postures in regions like the South China Sea and emphasizing cooperative frameworks for dispute resolution will be essential for maintaining trust and goodwill among its partners (Hayton, 2020).

Policy Recommendations

To ensure the long-term success and sustainability of its engagement with the Global South, specific policy measures are needed for China, Global South nations, and the international community.

For China

1. **Enhance Transparency and Accountability**: China should adopt international best practices for project implementation, ensuring that contracts, financing terms, and environmental assessments are made publicly available. This will address concerns about debt sustainability and foster greater trust among partner nations (Hurley et al., 2018).
2. **Promote Green Development**: Investing in renewable energy, sustainable agriculture, and eco-friendly technologies can help China position itself as a global leader in addressing climate change while meeting the developmental needs of the Global South.
3. **Strengthen Local Partnerships**: Prioritizing the employment of local workers and sourcing materials locally can enhance the socioeconomic impact of Chinese projects while mitigating criticism about labor practices and resource exploitation.

For Global South Nations

1. **Diversify Partnerships**: While China is an important partner, Global South nations should avoid over-reliance on a single country. Engaging with multiple stakeholders, including regional organizations and other global powers, can provide greater resilience and bargaining power (Pant & Passi, 2018).
2. **Enhance Negotiating Capacity**: Governments in the Global South should invest in building their technical and legal expertise to negotiate equitable terms in their agreements with China, ensuring that projects align with their developmental priorities.
3. **Foster Regional Collaboration**: By working together through regional initiatives, Global South nations can address shared challenges and leverage collective bargaining to negotiate better terms with external partners, including China.

For the International Community

1. **Offer Alternatives**: Western nations and multilateral institutions should provide competitive alternatives to Chinese investments, emphasizing high standards, transparency, and sustainability.
2. **Facilitate Multilateral Engagement**: International organizations should act as mediators and facilitators to ensure that projects involving China and Global South nations adhere to international norms and benefit all stakeholders.
3. **Promote Knowledge Sharing**: The international community should support research, capacity building, and technology transfer initiatives that empower Global South nations to address their developmental challenges independently.

REFERENCES

Blanchard, J.-M. F. (2018). Belt and Road Initiative (BRI) Blues: Powering BRI Research Back on Track to Avoid Choppy Seas. *Journal of Chinese Political Science*, *24*(2), 1–22.

Bräutigam, D. (2011). *The Dragon's Gift: The Real Story of China in Africa*. Oxford University Press.

Brautigam, D. (2020). *Will Africa Feed China?* Oxford University Press.

Bräutigam, D. (2020). The Chinese Debt Trap? Myth and Reality in Kenya's Standard Gauge Railway. *African Studies Review*, *64*(3), 541–567.

Bräutigam, D., & Kidane, W. (2021). The Chinese Debt Trap? Myth and Reality in Kenya's Standard Gauge Railway. *African Studies Review*, *64*(3), 541–567.

Brautigam, D., & Tang, X. (2022). Debunking the Myth of China's "Debt-Trap Diplomacy.". *Journal of International Development*, *34*(3), 312–328.

Cai, P. (2017). Understanding China's Belt and Road Initiative. *Lowy Institute*. Retrieved from https://www.lowyinstitute.org/publications/understanding-belt-and-road-initiative

Carmody, P. (2019). *Development Policy Review: China's Engagement in Africa*. Wiley Online Library.

Carmody, P., & Owusu, F. (2021). *Africa-China Engagement: The Belt and Road Initiative and Its Implications for Development*. Routledge.

Chen, W. (2020). Huawei and the Role of Technology Transfer in Africa. *Technology in Society*, *62*, 101271.

Chen, X.. (2021). China's Role in Global Governance: Rising Power, Responsibilities, and Reforms. *Global Policy*, *12*(1), 15–25.

Chen, X.. (2022). ASEAN-China Economic Relations: Trends and Prospects. *Journal of Contemporary Asia*, *52*(4), 567–590.

Chen, Y., Fan, Z., Zhang, J., & Mo, M. (2019). Does the Connectivity of the Belt and Road Initiative Contribute to the Economic Growth of the Belt and Road Countries? *Emerging Markets Finance & Trade*, *55*(14), 3227–3240. DOI: 10.1080/1540496X.2019.1643315

Ferdinand, P. (2016). Westward Ho the China Dream and 'One Belt, One Road': Chinese Foreign Policy Under Xi Jinping. *International Affairs*, *92*(4), 941–957. DOI: 10.1111/1468-2346.12660

Fung, K. C., & Garcia-Herrero, A. (2019). China's Trade and Investment in the Global South. *China Economic Review*, *54*, 134–152.

Gebre-Egziabher, T. (2019). Industrialization and Technology Transfer in Ethiopia. *African Development Review*, *31*(2), 179–194.

Gill, B., & Huang, C. (2020). China's Expanding Role in UN Peacekeeping: Implications and Challenges. *The China Quarterly*, *244*, 903–927.

Hayton, B. (2020). *The South China Sea: The Struggle for Power in Asia.* Yale University Press. DOI: 10.12987/9780300189544

Huang, Y. (2020). China's Health Diplomacy in Africa and COVID-19. *Lancet*, *396*(10261), 1454–1455.

Hurley, J.. (2018). *Examining the Debt Implications of the Belt and Road Initiative from a Policy Perspective*. Center for Global Development.

Jones, L., & Zeng, J. (2019). Understanding China's 'Belt and Road Initiative': Beyond 'Grand Strategy' to a State Transformation Analysis. *Third World Quarterly*, *40*(8), 1415–1439. DOI: 10.1080/01436597.2018.1559046

Kalanick, J. (2007). *Charm Offensive: How China's Soft Power Is Transforming the World.* Yale University Press.

King, K. (2013). China's Aid and Soft Power in Africa: The Case of Education and Training. *International Journal of Educational Development*, *33*(5), 645–653.

Kurlantzick, J. (2007). *Charm Offensive: How China's Soft Power Is Transforming the World.* Yale University Press.

Kynge, J.. (2021). China's Belt and Road Initiative and Global Governance. *Foreign Policy Analysis*, *17*(1), 45–63.

Lee, C. K. (2017). *The Specter of Global China: Politics, Labor, and Foreign Investment in Africa.* The University of Chicago Press. DOI: 10.7208/chicago/9780226340975.001.0001

Leung, C., & Du Cros, H. (2014). Confucius Institutes: Multiple Reactions and Interactions. *China. International Journal (Toronto, Ont.)*, *12*(1), 92–113.

Li, Z.. (2020). The Rise of China as a Destination for African Students. *Journal of Higher Education in Africa*, *18*(2), 123–139.

Mwase, N., & Yang, Y. (2020). Infrastructure Development in Africa: Lessons from China-Kenya Partnerships. *IMF Working Papers*.

Nye, J. S. (2017). Soft Power: The Origins and Political Progress of a Concept. *Palgrave Communications*, *3*(1), 17008. DOI: 10.1057/palcomms.2017.8

Pant, H. V., & Passi, R. (2018). India's Africa Policy: Balancing Geopolitical Ambitions and Development Needs. *Contemporary South Asia*, *26*(4), 365–379.

Shambaugh, D. (2015). China's Soft-Power Push: The Search for Respect. *Foreign Affairs*, *94*(4), 99–107.

Tan, C. (2020). Socioeconomic Impacts of Chinese Investments in Cambodia's Sihanoukville. *Journal of Southeast Asian Studies*, *51*(3), 345–366.

Tan-Mullins, M.. (2020). The Belt and Road Initiative: Environmental Impacts and Risks. *Environmental Policy and Governance*, *30*(5), 298–309.

Tang, X. (2021). China and Ethiopia's Industrialization: A Case of the Hawassa Industrial Park. *World Development*, *141*, 105392.

Thuds, D. K. (2016). China's Media and Soft Power in Africa: Promotion and Perceptions. *The International Communication Gazette*, *78*(7), 659–673.

Tilt, B. (2019). Dams, Displacement, and Development: Environmental and Social Consequences of Large Dams in China. *Environmental Policy and Governance*, *29*(5), 320–334.

Wiseman, P. D.. (2018). *Trends in International Arms Transfers*. Stockholm International Peace Research Institute.

Xu, C.. (2022). Renewable Energy Cooperation Between China and Africa. *Renewable & Sustainable Energy Reviews*, *158*, 112088.

Zeng, J. (2021). China's Global Economic Strategy and the Role of Special Economic Zones. *Journal of Asian Public Policy*, *14*(2), 207–222.

Zhang, D. (2018). The Concept of 'Community of Common Destiny' in China's Diplomacy: Meaning, Motives and Implications. *Asia & the Pacific Policy Studies*, *5*(2), 196–207. DOI: 10.1002/app5.231

About The Contributors

Enayatollah Yazdani is a Professor at the School of International Studies, Sun Yat-sen University, Zhuhai, China since 2019 , and previously taught at the Department of Political Science, University of Isfahan, Isfahan, Iran. He has also been a Visiting Professor and Visiting Scholar in America for Russian, East European and Central Asian Studies at the Jackson School of International Studies, University of Washington, Seattle, USA, 2012-2013; the Department of Central Eurasian Studies at Indiana University, Bloomington, USA; 2003; and for Russian, East European and Central Asian Studies at the Jackson School of International Studies, University of Washington, Seattle, USA, 2003. He received his PhD in International Relations from the Australian National University (ANU), Canberra, Australia, in 2005. He has supervised over 80 PhD and MA students. He has also published 9 books and book chapters, as well as over 150 papers in scholarly journals. He was the editor-in-chief of the Journal of Political and International Research Quarterly and is on the editorial boards of several other journals. He has delivered speeches at numerous international conferences in Iran, the United Kingdom, the United States, Russia, China, Germany, Australia, India, Turkey, Poland, Greece, Thailand, Kyrgyzstan, and other countries. His primary research interests encompass International Relations and Regional Studies, with a focus on the Middle East, Central Asia, Iran, China, and the United States.

***

Behzad Abdollahpour is a PhD candidate in Political Science and International Relations at Istanbul University. His research focuses on global health diplomacy, South-South cooperation, and the geopolitical dynamics of emerging powers in the Global South. His academic interests include China's Belt and Road Initiative, India's health diplomacy, and comparative studies on international development strategies. Abdollahpour has contributed to several publications analyzing the intersection of politics, and international relations, with a particular emphasis on West and East Asian context.

Ali Alihosseini is an Associated Professor of the Department of Political Sciences at the University of Isfahan. He is the author of a book and several published papers at national and international levels in refereed journals and conferences. His research interests include western, Islamic and Iranian political thought, political jurisprudence and methodology in humanities.

Meryem Nergis Ataçay received her PhD from Middle East Technical University and is a full-time instructor at Kastamonu University in Türkiye.

Figen Aydın received her master's degree from Gazi University Institute of Social Sciences and received her specialist degree. She completed her doctorate at National Defense University, Department of International Relations and Regional Studies in 2022. The author, who has articles in international and national refereed journals as well as book chapters, focuses on Asia, especially China and Central Asian states in regional studies. In addition, her main areas of study are economics-politics and foreign policy. Aydın is a faculty member at Istanbul Yeni Yüzyıl University, Department of Political Science and International Relations.

Nika Chitadze is a specialist in Global and Caucasus geopolitics, World Politics, Economics, World Geography, Democracy/Human Rights, Environmental Security, Combating Terrorism, Energy Security, and strategic affairs. He is currently (from October 2017) the Director of the Center for International Studies and Professor and Coordinator of the Bachelor and Master Programs at the Faculty of Humanities and Social Sciences (Direction: International Relations and Politics) at the International Black Sea University (IBSU). He is also President of the George C. Marshall Alumni Union, Georgia – International and Security Research Center. He is a member of Regional Stability in South Caucasus Study Group of the PfP Consortium since 2019. He has about 25 years of teaching experience at several Universities and Schools in Georgia and abroad and has taught more than 30 lecture courses in the fields of Political science, Human Geography, International relations, and Economics.

Tin Maung Htwe is a Research Fellow at Chiang Mai University and a lecturer at the Myanmar Institute of Theology. With a Master's in Development Studies and over a decade of experience in human rights and policy research, his work focuses on China's geoeconomic influence in Southeast Asia, labor dynamics, and post-coup Myanmar. His recent publications include China's Strategic Influence and Rivalries in Southeast Asia (IGI Global, 2025), Chinese Investment in Southeast Asia's

Post-Pandemic Recovery (OBOR Journal, 2024), Livelihood and Social Capital of Myanmar Migrants in Mae Sot Post-Coup (YCU Research Institute, 2025).

Badar Alam Iqbal; (Ph.D. & DBA; M. Com; DSW; B.A. [Hons] Economics. had been the DAAD, Fellow at German Institute of Economic Research; Berlin, Kiel Institute of World Economics; Kiel, South Asia Institute, University of Heidelberg; Germany; Ford Foundation, American Research Center USA; Fulbright Visiting Professor; USA; Institute of Developing Economies; Tokyo; Former Fulbright scholar-in-Residence (SIR) 2004-05 at School of Business; Claflin University; South Carolina, USA. In 2016-17, the Fulbright Commission Washington has again nominated for Scholar-in-residence (SIR) at School of Business; Kentucky State University; USA. Now Dr. Iqbal is Emeritus Professor; External-Relation- Chair of Research; at Federic Bastiat Institute for African Research; Ghana. Adjunct Professor; Faculty of Economics and Finance; Monarch University; Switzerland; Visiting Professor at University of Rennes1; France; University of South Africa; Pretoria; Former Extra Ordinary Professor, School of Economic Sciences; North-West University; South Africa; Visiting Professor of Research; Vaal University of Technology; South Africa; International Islamic University Malaysia. In 2021, 2022, the Vice Chancellors of the three leading South African Universities [University of South Africa; Tshwane University of Technology; and Walter Sisulu University] have appointed Prof. Badar Iqbal as an Extraordinary Professor at their respective universities.

Amrita Jash is an Assistant Professor at the Department of Geopolitics and International Relations, Manipal Institute of Social Sciences Humanities and Arts, Manipal Academy of Higher Education, Manipal, India. She holds a Ph.D. from Jawaharlal Nehru University. Before Manipal, she was a Research Fellow at the Centre for Land Warfare Studies, New Delhi, where she received a commendation by the Chief of the Army Staff, General Bipin Rawat. She was a Pavate Fellow at the University of Cambridge and an IAS Visiting Fellow at Loughborough University. She has authored Mao Zedong & China's Foreign Policy: The Man, the Mind and Vietnam (forthcoming, 2025), China's Japan Policy: Learning from the Past (2023) and The Concept of Active Defence in China's Military Strategy (2021). Her research interests include China's foreign policy, the People's Liberation Army, security and strategic issues related to India-China, China-Japan, and the Indo-Pacific.

Mohammad Reza Majidi has received his PhD from France in Political Science. He is faculty member of Department of Regional Studies at University of Tehran, Tehran, Iran. He has also served as Iran's representative at UNESCO in France for several years.

Mohamad Mokdad holds a double Ph.D. in International Relations and Geopolitics. He is an expert in strategic studies, specialized in the MENA region, professional with a rich academic background and diverse professional experience in international relations, strategic management, social policies, and humanitarian law. He is the CEO of Intelligentsia center for research and studies, at the same time he is an International Consultant at PGS University in France. Dr Mokdad has an impressive record of publications in major indexed journals, affirming his significant contributions to his field.

Maziar Mozaffari Falarti is an Assistant Professor in the Department of South, East Asian and Oceanian Studies at the Faculty of World Studies, University of Tehran. His research focuses on international relations, South-South cooperation, political systems and the geopolitical strategies of emerging powers in Asia and the Global South. His academic work spans global health diplomacy, maritime security, and regional integration, with a particular emphasis on South Asia, Southeast Asia and Africa. He has authored numerous publications exploring the intersections of politics, history, and international development. He can be contacted via mmfalarti@ ut.ac.ir

Ali Omidi is a professor of International Relations at the Dept of Political Science, University of Isfahan, Isfahan, Iran. He published dozens of articles, books, and analyses on Iranian foreign policy, International new trends relevant to International Political Economy, and IR. He was awarded a prestigious fellowship from SIPRI in Stockholm and UNITAR in the Hague. He took part in many international conferences and events. He teaches and does research on Middle East Politics, Iranian Foreign Policy, Comparative Foreign Policy, and International Political Economy. He has often been interviewed and inquired about Iranian foreign policy by local, national, and international media.

Alireza Samiee Esfahani, is a Ph.D. Graduated in Political Science from the University of Tehran, Iran. He is an Associate Professor at the Political Science Department, University of Isfahan, Iran. His specialized field of teaching and research is "Political Sociology of Iran and the Middle East", "Comparative Politics," and "Theory and Methodology in Political Science". Samiee Esfahani has published extensively in his specialized field. Some of his Noteworthy projects are; "A theoretical Introduction to the Concept, Nature and Performance of Populism" (2019), "Strong Society, Weak State; a Sociological Explanation of State-Society Relationship in Qajar Iran"(2008), " The global Economic Crisis and its Impact on Citizens' Political Trust in European Union countries "(2015) and "Turkey under

Erdoğan: Investigating the Relationship between Populism and Governance Quality Since 2013" (2025, under published).

Alireza Samoudi is a faculty member at the Institute for Security and Development Studies (ISDS) in Iran. He received his Ph.D. in Regional Studies from the University of Tehran. His research focuses on Chinese foreign policy, European Union Politics and Great Power Competition. He is the editor of the books Chinese Foreign Policy: Issues, Relations and Prospects (ISDS) and the Author of Chinese Desired Order, European Populism.

Bahareh Sazmand, is an Associate Professor at the Department of Regional Studies, Southeast Asia region, University of Tehran. She holds a Ph.D. in International Relations from the University of Tehran. Dr. Sazmand is a member of the National Elite Foundation and has authored 15 books, more than 60 scientific-research articles and over 70 conference papers at national and international levels. Her research focuses on the international relations and regional dynamics of Southeast Asia.

V. Anand is an Assistant Professor (Senior Scale) at the Department of Geopolitics and International Relations, Manipal Institute of Social Sciences Humanities and Arts, Manipal Academy of Higher Education, Manipal, India. He holds a Ph.D. in Geopolitics and International Relations from Manipal Academy of Higher Education. He is also Coordinator of the China Study Centre at the Department. Dr. Anand teaches subjects related to the theoretical and well as science and technology dimensions of geopolitics, among others, at the Masters level. His areas of research include China's strategic culture and capabilities; its approaches to various regions as well as the technological domains like outer space. Dr. Anand's doctoral thesis was on China's Strategic Culture, and involved field visit to China. He is also an alumni of the US Department of State's distinguished International Visitor Leadership Programme, wherein he visited the US for a month-long project related to the Indo-Pacific.

Arti Yadav is presently working as an Assistant Professor in the Department of Commerce, Ramanujan College, University of Delhi, India. Previously, she has worked as a Post Doctoral Research Fellow at the Indian Council of Social Science Research. She has also worked as an assistant professor at the Department of Commerce, Daulat Ram College, University of Delhi. She is a Ph.D. in Commerce from the Department of Commerce, Aligarh Muslim University, India, and holds her master's degree from the Delhi School of Economics, University of Delhi. She is also the managing editor of the journal RIJBR, India, and has worked as a guest editor for special issues in various International Journals. She has several research papers and chapters to her credit, published in well-known journals including Springer International Publishing, SAGE, France forum, IGI Global, and Emerald, most of which are Scopus, Web of Science, and ABDC-listed journals.

Ji Zeng has received his PhD in Literary Criticism and Translation Studies from Sun Yat-sen University (SYSU), Guangzhou, China, 2004-2009. He is an associate professor who has been teaching in School of International Studies at Sun Yat-sen University since 2010, acting as Chair of the Department of English and Deputy Director of the Center for Middle Eastern Studies. He has published widely on literature, translation studies and Middle Eastern history and culture, including four books and translated books and numerous articles.

Mohamad Zreik, a Postdoctoral Fellow at Sun Yat-sen University, is a recognized scholar in International Relations, specializing in China's Arab-region foreign policy. His recent work in soft power diplomacy compares China's methods in the Middle East and East Asia. His extensive knowledge spans Middle Eastern Studies, China-Arab relations, East Asian and Asian Affairs, Eurasian geopolitics, and Political Economy, providing him a unique viewpoint in his field. Dr. Zreik is a proud recipient of a PhD from Central China Normal University (Wuhan). He's written numerous acclaimed papers, many focusing on China's Belt and Road Initiative and its Arab-region impact. His groundbreaking research has established him as a leading expert in his field. Presently, he furthers his research on China's soft power diplomacy tactics at Sun Yat-sen University. His significant contributions make him a crucial figure in understanding contemporary international relations.

Index

C

D

E

F

G

H

I

L

M

www.ingramcontent.com/pod-product-compliance
Lightning Source LLC
LaVergne TN
LVHW080613300926
849162LV00005B/1138
* 9 7 9 8 3 3 7 3 0 9 3 8 5 *